JUDICIAL REVIEW OF ADMINISTRATIVE ACTION ACROSS THE COMMON LAW WORLD

Research on comparative administrative law, in contrast to comparative constitutional law, remains largely underdeveloped. This book plugs that gap. It considers how a wide range of common law systems have received and adapted English common law to the needs of their own socio-political context. Readers will be given complex insights into a wide range of common law systems of administrative law, which they may not otherwise have access to given how difficult it would be to research all of the systems covered in the volume single-handedly. The book covers Scotland, Ireland, the USA, Canada, Israel, South Africa, Kenya, Malaysia, Singapore, Hong Kong SAR, India, Bangladesh, Australia and New Zealand. Comparative public lawyers will have a much greater range of common law models of administrative law – either to pursue conversations about their own common law system or to sophisticate their comparison of their system (civil law or otherwise) with common law systems.

SWATI JHAVERI, B.A. (OXON), B.CL. (OXON), previously taught at the Faculty of Law of the Chinese University of Hong Kong and the National University of Singapore. Her areas of research include comparative constitutional and administrative law. She has published in these areas in *Public Law*, the *Singapore Journal of Legal Studies*, *Federal Law Review*, the *Tort Law Review*, and the *International Journal of Constitutional Law*. While at CUHK, she was awarded the Vice Chancellor's Exemplary Teaching Award. She was also awarded a competitive research grant from the General Research Fund of the Research Grants Council of Hong Kong to investigate the post-1997 impact of judicial review on legislative process and content. At NUS, she has been awarded the Faculty and University's Annual Teaching Excellence Awards for three consecutive years and was placed on the University Honour Roll for Sustained Excellence in Teaching in 2018. Swati obtained her Bachelor of Arts in Jurisprudence (First Class Honours) and Bachelor of Civil Law (Distinction) from the University of Oxford. She previously practiced law at Allen & Overy, specializing in international commercial arbitration. She is a solicitor of the Hong Kong SAR and England and Wales and is a member of the Chartered Institute of Arbitrators. She is currently pursuing a Doctorate in Law at the University of Oxford on the role of the Executive branch of the government in advancing constitutionalism.

MICHAEL RAMSDEN is an Associate Professor in the Faculty of Law at the Chinese University of Hong Kong, where he was previously Assistant Dean for Research and Executive Director of the Centre for Rights & Justice. He has published extensively in the fields of comparative public law and international institutional law in journals including the *International and Comparative Law Quarterly*, *International Journal of Constitutional Law*, *Human Rights Law Review*, *Public Law*, *Journal of International Criminal Justice* and *the Civil Justice Quarterly*. He was educated at Berkeley, Cambridge and King's College London. Professor Ramsden is also a Barrister of Lincoln's Inn and a Door Tenant at 25 Bedford Row, London.

Judicial Review of Administrative Action across the Common Law World

ORIGINS AND ADAPTATION

Edited by

SWATI JHAVERI

DPhil Candidate in law, University of Oxford

MICHAEL RAMSDEN

The Chinese University of Hong Kong

CAMBRIDGE
UNIVERSITY PRESS

CAMBRIDGE
UNIVERSITY PRESS

University Printing House, Cambridge CB2 8BS, United Kingdom

One Liberty Plaza, 20th Floor, New York, NY 10006, USA

477 Williamstown Road, Port Melbourne, VIC 3207, Australia

314–321, 3rd Floor, Plot 3, Splendor Forum, Jasola District Centre,
New Delhi – 110025, India
79 Anson Road, #06–04/06, Singapore 079906

Cambridge University Press is part of the University of Cambridge.

It furthers the University's mission by disseminating knowledge in the pursuit of education, learning, and research at the highest international levels of excellence.

www.cambridge.org
Information on this title: www.cambridge.org/9781108481571
DOI: 10.1017/9781108674355

First published 2021

A catalogue record for this publication is available from the British Library.

ISBN 978-1-108-48157-1 Hardback

Contents

Contributors

Farrah Ahmed is an associate professor at the Melbourne Law School. Before this, she was a lecturer in law at Queen's College, University of Oxford. Farrah graduated with an LL.B. from the University of Delhi, and a Bachelor of Civil Law and D.Phil. from the University of Oxford. Farrah's research spans public law, legal theory, and family law. Her recent work on constitutional statutes, religious freedom, the doctrine of legitimate expectations, the duty to give reasons, social rights adjudication, and religious tribunals has been published in the *Cambridge Law Journal*, the *Modern Law Review*, the *Oxford Journal of Legal Studies*, *Public Law*, and the *Child and Family Law Quarterly*. Her book, *Religious Freedom under the Personal Law System*, was published by Oxford University Press in 2016. Farrah is currently a Chief Investigator on an Australian Research Council Discovery grant studying religious dispute resolution processes, and is working on projects on public interest standing, secularism, constitutional conventions, constitutional principles, and arbitrariness in public law. Farrah has taught legal theory, legal methods, constitutional law, and administrative law. She has offered electives on human rights, legal responses to multiculturalism and religion, and legal practice in Asia. Farrah is a founding editor of the *Indian Law Review* and the *Admin Law Blog*. She also serves as Associate Director (India) of the Asian Law Centre at Melbourne Law School.

Migai Akech currently works as a Governance Expert at the African Union's African Peer Review Mechanism. Prior to that, he taught law at the University of Nairobi's School of Law for twenty-one years. He has published widely on legal and public policy issues, including *Administrative Law* (Strathmore University Press, 2016), "Constraining Government Power in Africa" (*Journal of Democracy*, 2011), and *Privatization and Democracy in East Africa: The Promise of Administrative Law* (East African Educational Publishers Limited, 2009). He has consulted for Kenyan, regional, and international organizations as an expert on policy development, policy analysis, rule of law, governance, devolution, anti-corruption, accountability, police reforms, justice sector reforms, prosecutorial reforms, legislative reforms, transitional justice, environmental crime, reform of criminal law and procedures, sentencing policy development, land policy development, curriculum development, monitoring human rights compliance, and mineral policies and regulatory frameworks.

Justice Daphne Barak-Erez is a Justice of the Supreme Court of Israel. Justice Barak-Erez was Dean of the Faculty of Law at Tel-Aviv University and the Stewart and Judy Colton Professor in Law and Security before her appointment to the court. She served as Director of the Minerva Center for Human Rights and Director of the Cegla Center for Interdisciplinary Research of Law. She holds a J.S.D., LL.M., and LL.B. from the Tel Aviv Faculty of Law. Justice Barak-Erez has been a visiting professor at various universities, including the University of Toronto, Columbia Law School, and Stanford Law School. She has chaired the Israeli Association of Public Law and was President of the Israeli Law and Society Association. She is the author and editor of several books and many articles published in Israel, England, Canada, and the United States.

Peter Cane is Senior Research Fellow at Christ's College, Cambridge; an Emeritus Distinguished Professor of the Australian National University; and a Corresponding Fellow of the British Academy. His publications include *Controlling Administrative Power: An Historical Comparison* (Cambridge University Press, 2016).

Margit Cohn, is the Henry J. and Fannie Harkavy Chair in Comparative Law at the Faculty of Law, Hebrew University of Jerusalem. Prior to her current appointment (2006), she was Lecturer in Law at the University of Leicester, UK, and a Legal Advisor at Israel's Central Bank. Professor Cohn's teaching and research interests span administrative law, comparative public law, constitutional theory, law and politics, law and society, and judicial review. She has visited and taught at University College London, Columbia Law School, Centre for Transnational Legal Studies London, Tulane University Law School, Georgetown University, and the University of Trento. She has published inter alia in the *Oxford Journal of Legal Studies*, the *American Journal of Comparative Law*, the *International and Comparative Law Quarterly, Public Law, Law and Policy*, and the *Canadian Journal of Law and Jurisprudence*. Her book on the executive branch is to be published by Oxford University Press (2021).

Paul Craig is Emeritus Professor of English Law, St John's College, Oxford. His principal research interests are constitutional law, administrative law, EU law, and comparative administrative law. He was the Alternative UK Member on the Venice Commission for Law and Democracy for ten years and is a fellow of the British Academy.

Paul Daly returned to Canada in 2019 to the University Research Chair in Administrative Law and Governance at the University of Ottawa. Professor Daly completed his law studies at University College Cork before attending the University of Pennsylvania Law School (LL.M.) as a Fulbright scholar and completing his doctorate at the University of Cambridge (Ph.D.) as a National University of Ireland Travelling Scholar and a Modern Law Review Scholar. At the University of Montreal (2012–2016), Professor Daly was successively Assistant Professor, Associate Dean, and Associate Professor, before moving to the University of Cambridge (2016–2019) as a Senior Lecturer in Public Law and the Derek Bowett Fellow in Law at Queens' College, Cambridge. At Cambridge, he was also (2017–2019) Deputy Director of Graduate Studies. In addition, he has held visiting positions at Harvard Law School (visiting researcher), the University of Ottawa (replacement professor), and Paris II Panthéon-Assas University (visiting professor). He is also a part-time member (Review Officer) of the Environmental Protection Tribunal of Canada.

Cynthia Farid is a lawyer with experience in legal practice as well as international development, with a particular focus on court reform. Having completed her bar in the United Kingdom and Bangladesh, she graduated with a master's degree (LL.M.) from Cornell University and S.J.D. from the University of Wisconsin Law School. Cynthia's research interests include legal history, constitutional and administrative law, and law and development.

Christopher Forsyth is the Emeritus Sir David Williams Professor of Public Law at the University of Cambridge, Honorary Professor of Law at the University of Stellenbosch, and Cheng Yu Tung Visiting Professor of Law at the University of Hong Kong. He is the author of about one hundred scholarly articles on a range of subjects but is known particularly for his work with the late Sir William Wade in writing the classic work *Administrative Law* (Oxford University Press, 11th ed., 2014), cited before and accepted as authoritative by courts across the common law world. Before retiring, Professor Forsyth sat as a Deputy High Court Judge in the Administrative Court and as a Recorder in the Crown Court.

Kris Gledhill is a professor in the Faculty of Business, Economics, and Law at the Auckland University of Technology (AUT). He was a barrister in London from 1989 to 2006, appearing in criminal and public law matters, including in various precedent-setting cases in the European Court of Human Rights, the House of Lords, and the Court of Appeal; he also sat as a Tribunal Judge on mental health cases. At the same time, he maintained an academic career, teaching part-time at various institutions, including University College Oxford, and publishing several articles and three books. He came to New Zealand in 2006 and moved into full-time academia in 2007. He joined AUT in March 2016, where he teaches criminal law, international human rights law, and clinical legal education, as well as criminal law electives and postgraduate courses. He is also the Director of the Postgraduate Programme and the Director of Clinical Legal Education at AUT. Kris has been trusted by various publishers to write or edit books in different areas of law, in addition to writing many book chapters and academic articles. His contribution to his main area of interest, mental health law, has been recognized by his appointment as Editor in Chief of the *International Journal of Mental Health and Capacity Law*. He is also the General Editor of the *New Zealand Criminal Law Review* and Series Editor of the *Legal Pedagogy Series for Routledge*.

Matthew Groves is the Alfred Deakin Professor of Law in the Law School of Deakin University, Australia. Matthew teaches and researches in the fields of administrative law, human rights, and military justice. Matthew is co-author of the leading Australian monograph and student text on administrative law: *Judicial Review of Administrative Action and Government Liability* (Thomson Reuters, 6th ed., 2017) and *Control of Government Action: Text, Cases and Commentary* (LexisNexis, 5th ed., 2019). Matthew is also General Editor of the *Australian Journal of Administrative Law*.

Cora Hoexter, B.A., LL.B. (Natal), M.A. (Oxon), Ph.D. (Witwatersrand), is a part-time Professor in the School of Law at the University of the Witwatersrand, Johannesburg. She has written extensively on administrative law. The third edition of her leading work, *Administrative Law in South Africa*, will be published by Juta & Co., Ltd., in 2021. Her publications in this area are frequently cited with approval by the superior courts of South Africa, as well as in other countries of the region. Cora has been a foreign contributor to *De Smith's Judicial Review* since 2007. She is on the advisory board of the Centre for Rights and Justice at the Chinese University of Hong Kong and on the editorial board of the Cambridge Studies in Constitutional Law book series. She was the inaugural President of the Administrative Justice Association of South Africa and is currently a Vice-President of the association.

Swati Jhaveri, B.A. (Oxon), B.CL. (Oxon), Swati previously taught at the Faculty of Law of the Chinese University of Hong Kong and the National University of Singapore. Her areas of research include comparative constitutional and administrative law. She has published in these areas in *Public Law*, the *Singapore Journal of Legal Studies*, *Federal Law Review*, the *Tort Law Review*, and the *International Journal of Constitutional Law*. While at CUHK, she was awarded the Vice Chancellor's Exemplary Teaching Award. She was also awarded a competitive research grant from the General Research Fund of the Research Grants Council of Hong Kong to investigate the post-1997 impact of judicial review on legislative process and content. At NUS, she has been awarded the Faculty and University's Annual Teaching Excellence Awards for three consecutive years and was placed on the University Honour Roll for Sustained Excellence in Teaching in 2018. Swati obtained her Bachelor of Arts in Jurisprudence (First Class Honours) and Bachelor of Civil Law (Distinction) from the University of Oxford. She previously practiced law at Allen & Overy, specializing in international commercial arbitration. She is a solicitor of the Hong Kong SAR and England and Wales and is a member of the Chartered Institute of Arbitrators. She is currently pursuing a Doctorate in Law at the University of Oxford on the role of the Executive branch of the government in advancing constitutionalism.

Michael Ramsden is an associate professor in the Faculty of Law at the Chinese University of Hong Kong, where he was previously Assistant Dean for Research and Executive Director of the Centre for Rights and Justice. He has published extensively in the fields of comparative public law and international institutional law. He was educated at Berkeley, Cambridge, and King's College London. Professor Ramsden is also a barrister of Lincoln's Inn and a Door Tenant at 25 Bedford Row, London.

Dian A. H. Shah, LL.B. (Hons.) (Warwick), LL.M., S.J.D. (Duke), is an assistant professor at the Faculty of Law, National University of Singapore. Her research interests span the fields of law and religion, comparative constitutional law, and human rights, and her work focuses on the interaction of law, religion, and politics in plural and divided societies. Dian is the author of *Constitutions, Religion and Politics in Asia: Indonesia, Malaysia and Sri Lanka* (Cambridge University Press, 2017) and the co-editor of *Law and Society in Malaysia: Pluralism, Religion and Ethnicity* (Routledge, 2018). She has also published in the *International Journal of Constitutional Law*, *Oxford Journal of Law and Religion*, and the *Indonesian Journal of International and Comparative Law*. She was the Editor of the As. J.C.L.'s *Special Issue on Religion and Constitutional Practices in Asia* (December 2018) a columnist for the *Blog of the International Journal of Constitutional Law* (2019).

Kevin Y. L. Tan, LL.B. (Hons.) (National University of Singapore), LL.M., J.S.D. (Yale), is an adjunct professor at the Faculty of Law, National University of Singapore, and visiting professor at the S. Rajaratnam School of International Studies, Nanyang Technological University, Singapore. Kevin specializes in the public law of Singapore and Malaysia, the Singapore Legal System, the legal history of Singapore, and international human rights. He has written and edited more than fifty books on the law, history, and politics of Singapore, including *Constitutional Law in Malaysia and Singapore* (LexisNexis, 2010, with Thio Li-ann; *Constitutionalism in Asia* (Hart Publishing, 2014); and *The Constitution of Singapore: A Contextual Analysis* (Hart Publishing, 2015).

Stephen Thomson is an associate professor at the School of Law, City University of Hong Kong. He is the author of *Administrative Law in Hong Kong* (Cambridge University Press, 2018) and *The Nobile Officium* (Avizandum, 2015). His work appears in journals such as the *Harvard Journal of Law and Technology*, *Melbourne University Law Review*, *Public Law*, *Civil Justice Quarterly*, and the *University of Pennsylvania Journal of International Law*. Dr. Thomson is a legal adviser to the Ombudsman of Hong Kong, a member of the Constitutional Affairs and Human Rights Committee of the Law Society of Hong Kong, and an examiner on the Law Society of Hong Kong's Overseas Lawyers Qualification Examination. He has advised the Scottish judiciary on the reform of civil procedure, and was recently a Herbert Smith Freehills Visitor at the Faculty of Law, University of Cambridge. He holds the degrees of LL.B. (Hons.) (First Class), LL.M. (Res.), Ph.D., and Dip.L.P. from the University of Edinburgh.

Greg Weeks is an associate professor and the Deputy Head of School in the Australian National University College of Law, where he teaches a range of courses. He has published widely on his research interests, which are primarily related to judicial review, state liability, and remedies against public authorities. He is the author of *Soft Law and Public Authorities: Remedies and Reform* (Hart Publishing, 2016) and a co-author of *Government Liability: Principles and Remedies* (LexisNexis, 2019) and *Judicial Review of Administrative Action and Government Liability* (Thomson Reuters, 6th ed., 2017), Australia's leading administrative law text. With Matthew Groves, he was the editor of two collections of essays: *Legitimate Expectations in the Common Law World* (Hart Publishing, 2016) and *Administrative Redress Inside and Outside the Courts: Essays in Honour of Robyn Creyke and John McMillan* (Federation Press, 2019). Greg is the General Editor of the Australian Journal of Administrative Law.

Hanna Wilberg, B.A., LL.B. (Hons.) (Otago), B.CL. M.Phil. (Oxon), is an associate professor at the University of Auckland. Her main research areas are administrative law and the tort liability of public authorities. Her publications include *The Scope and Intensity of Substantive Review: Traversing Michael Taggart's Rainbow* (Hart Publishing, 2015), edited by Wilberg and Elliott. She has written on topics including interpretive presumptions in statutory interpretation, the approach to statutory bills of rights in judicial review cases, provisions purporting to grant absolute discretion, mistake of fact as a ground of review, reasoning process grounds, deference on questions of law, various issues concerning the negligence liability of public authorities, the effect of the Treaty of Waitangi in New Zealand, and comparative administrative law.

Foreword

Comparative law is an exercise in finding similarity in difference and difference in similarity. This volume is an excellent example of both. Focusing on judicial review of administrative action, the book illustrates the complex legacy of the English common law as it spread and metastasized across the British colonies and their independent successor states. With the exception of Ireland, Israel, and the United States, the countries covered are all currently part of the Commonwealth. In all cases, the connection to the UK has both historical and present-day roots. Yet, in each country the heritage of the English common law, as filtered through history and current political and social conditions, is complex. A great merit of this volume is that it does not try to squeeze that diversity into a single narrative about legal influence. Such a reductive effort would have been particularly troublesome given the open-ended and shape-shifting nature of the common law itself even in England, its point of origin.

The volume's focus on judicial review of administrative action required the authors to look beyond the resolution of private disputes in common-law courts. For public law disputes, the judiciary cannot rely only on principles derived from the common law. It must apply and interpret statutes, constitutional texts, and treaties. Even though the UK continues to operate without a written constitution, most of the other countries discussed here have written constitutions or, at least, founding documents. Even the UK has moved toward the use of legal texts for foundational matters, most importantly the Human Rights Act. Furthermore, in some countries indigenous legal traditions remain important, sometimes reflected in a parallel system of dispute resolution.

These essays both recognize the continuing vitality of the common law and acknowledge the way that local traditions interact with each country's legal system as interpreted by its courts. Of course, cross-country differences lead one to ask if common threads remain on which to draw. The authors point to some such threads, but the question cannot be answered without the addition of countries whose colonial history differs from those studied. In particular, the nations of Latin America and Francophone Africa draw on the public law traditions of France, sometimes by way of Spain. Public law in other countries, such as Japan, embodies a strong German influence. Others, again mostly in Latin America, operate under constitutions derived from the US model. Today, the public law of most former parts of the British Empire diverges from the UK's Westminster model in fundamental ways. A central claim of this volume is the diverse experience and present day situation of these former parts of the Empire and others under British influence. This volume's fascinating overview will, I hope, inspire comparative law scholars to extend these comparisons to countries with diverse legal traditions that go cannot simply be characterized as "common" law or "civil" law, full stop. The contributions decisively refute overly simple claims for the countries in the common law family. I assume that similar patterns of diversity and overlap are also characteristic of the public law of nations influenced by continental European models.

The value of remaining within the common law framework allows the authors to focus on how legal borrowing from one source has produced different results. In the colonial context, a key tension is between British efforts both to control and to shape colonial governments as well as exporting the common law. The result, as outlined in several chapters, was to use English law in the service of an executive-led government dominated by the British Governor General. These authorities controlled the British colonies, with the franchise limited to white settlers, often a small minority of the population. As the chapter on Kenya makes especially clear, the legacy of strong executive dominance of the legislature and the judiciary then carried over into a strong presidential government after independence. Another aspect of the colonial legacy is the co-existence in some countries of dual systems of law, one based on indigenous practices and the other derived from British law. Conflicts between traditional law and English common law have been an ongoing feature of these jurisdictions, both as colonies and as independent states trying to balance competing traditions.

The development of judicial review in the settler colonies that gained independence from Britain in the eighteenth and nineteenth centuries does not present a uniform pattern. Some adopted constitutional structures close to the UK's parliamentary model, that is, Canada, Australia, and New Zealand. However, the legal systems in all three have had to accommodate the interests of indigenous populations that have had a history of exclusion dating to the colonial period, and in some, a history of slavery. Furthermore, the case of Canada is more complex because of French-influenced law in Quebec. The United States, in contrast, adopted a separation-of-powers presidential system, as outlined in the chapters by Paul Craig and Peter Cane. The US history of slavery and discrimination against minorities continue to influence state-society relations and the role of the courts. Under its presidential, separation-of-powers system, US administrative law relies heavily on statutes, especially the 1946 Administrative Procedure Act with its provisions for notice-and-comment rulemaking. Other countries with a common-law heritage have not copied its provisions for judicial review of rulemaking processes, but everywhere there is pressure for more public consultation on secondary norms and greater access to the courts for public-interest claims. In the US, the common law's reliance on case law has carried over to judicial opinions that interpret statutes. Judicial review of administrative action has led to common-law-like evolution over time. It is this developmental feature of common law adjudication, rather than its established doctrines, that have survived the shift to a quite different form of government.

Taken as a whole this volume is a valuable addition to comparative public law. It follows the thread of influence of the English common law across a wide range of disparate political, economic, and social situations and into geographical locations with widely varying histories. The result is a fine addition to comparative public law. It will enlighten readers about the fascinating ways in which legal borrowing occurs, about resistance from local inhabitants, both indigenous people and settlers, and it shows how similar legal doctrines can have dramatically different effects depending upon the soil in which they are planted.

Professor Susan Rose-Ackerman, Yale Law School

Acknowledgments

This book is a part of a research project funded by the Centre for Asian Legal Studies (CALS) at the National University of Singapore Faculty of Law. We are grateful to Dan W. Puchniak, Weitseng Chen, and CALS for supporting this project; Cambridge University Press for supporting the publication of this book; and the contributors for their excellent work. We would also like to thank our student research assistants – Benjamin Tan Zhi Xiong, Kaustab Narendran, Shawn Teo, Carol Yuen Ai Zhen, and Chee Jun An. Finally, we are thankful to the National University of Singapore Faculty of Law and the Chinese University of Hong Kong Faculty of Law for their continued support.

Table of Cases

AUSTRALIA

Annetts *v*. McCann (1990) 170 CLR 596
Attorney-General (NSW) *v*. Quin (1990) 170 CLR 1
Australian Broadcasting Tribunal *v*. Bond (1990) 170 CLR 321
Bodruddaza *v*. Minister for Immigration and Multicultural Affairs (2007) 228 CLR 651
Brandy *v*. Human Rights and Equal Opportunity Commission (1995) 183 CLR 245
Chan *v*. Minister for Immigration and Ethnic Affairs (1989) 169 CLR 379
Colonial Bank of Australasia *v*. Willan (1874) LR 5 PC 417
Craig *v*. South Australia (1990) 184 CLR 163
Cunliffe *v*. Commonwealth (1994) 182 CLR 272
D'Amore *v*. Independent Commission for Corruption (2013) 303 ALR 242
Director of Housing *v*. Sudi (2011) 33 VR 559
Drake *v*. Minister for Immigration and Ethnic Affairs (1979) 24 ALR 577
Electrolux Home Products Pty Ltd *v*. Australian Workers' Union (2004) 221 CLR 309
Farah Constructions Pty Ltd *v*. Say-Dee Pty Ltd (2007) 230 CLR 89
Graham *v*. Minister for Immigration and Border Protection (2017) 91 ALJR 890
Greyhound Racing Authority (NSW) *v*. Bragg (2003) NSWCA 388
Haoucher *v*. Minister for Immigration and Ethnic Affairs (1990) 169 CLR 648
International Finance Trust Co Ltd *v*. New South Wales Crimes Commission (2009) 240 CLR 319
Kable *v*. Director of Public Prosecutions (NSW) (1996) 189 CLR 51
Kioa *v*. West (1985) 150 CLR 550
Kirk *v*. Industrial Court (New South Wales) (2010) 239 CLR 531
McCawley *v*. R [1920] AC 619
Minister for Immigration and Border Protection *v*. WZARH (2015) 256 CLR 326
Minister for Immigration and Citizenship *v*. Li (2013) 249 CLR 332
Minister for Immigration and Citizenship *v*. SZMDS (2010) 240 CLR 611
Minister for Immigration and Ethnic Affairs *v*. Teoh (1995) 183 CLR 273
Momcilovic *v*. R [2011] HCA 34
Plaintiff M61/2010E *v*. Commonwealth (Offshore Processing Case) (2010) 243 CLR 319
Plaintiff M64/2015 *v*. Minister for Immigration and Border Protection (2015) 258 CLR 173
Plaintiff M79/2012 *v*. Minister for Immigration and Citizenship (2013) 252 CLR 336
Plaintiff S10/2011 *v*. Minister for Immigration and Citizenship (2012) 246 CLR 636

Plaintiff S157/2002 *v.* Commonwealth (2003) 211 CLR 476
Potter *v.* Minahan (1908) 7 CLR 277
Public Service Association (SA) *v.* Federated Clerks' Union (1991) 173 CLR 132
Public Service Board (NSW) *v.* Osmond (1986) 159 CLR 656
R *v.* Kirby; Ex parte Boilermakers' Society of Australia (1956) 94 CLR 254
R *v.* Richards; Ex parte Fitzpatrick and Browne (1955) 92 CLR 157
Re Becker and Minister for Immigration and Ethnic Affairs (1979) 1 ALD 158
Re Judiciary and Navigation Acts (1921) 29 CLR 257
Re Minister for Immigration and Multicultural Affairs; ex parte Miah (2001) 206 CLR 57
Re Minister for Immigration and Multicultural and Indigenous Affairs; ex parte Lam (2003) 214 CLR 1, 195 ALR 502
Re Refugee Review Tribunal; Ex parte Aala (2000) 204 CLR 82
Saeed *v.* Minister for Immigration and Citizenship (2010) 241 CLR 252
Shi *v.* Migration Agents Registration Authority (2008) 235 CLR 286
State of New South Wales *v.* Kable (2013) 252 CLR 118
Toy *v.* Musgrove (1888) 14 VLR 349
Toy *v.* Musgrove [1891] AC 272
Union Steamship Co of Australia Pty Ltd *v.* King (1988) 166 CLR 1
Wilson *v.* Minister for Aboriginal and Torres Strait Islanders Affairs (1996) 183 CLR 1

BANGLADESH

Abdul Bari Sarkar *v.* Bangladesh (1994) 46 DLR (AD) 37
Abdul Latif Mirza *v.* Government of Bangladesh 31 DLR (AD) 33
Abdul Mannan Bhuiyan *v.* State (2008) 60 DLR (AD)
Abdul Mannan Khan *v.* Bangladesh, Civil Appeal No 139 of 2005
Abdul Mannan Khan *v.* Bangladesh [2012] 64 DLR (AD) 169
Agrani Bank *v.* Khandoker Badrudduza (2004) 56 DLR 136
Akbar Ali *v.* Raziur Rahman (1966) 18 DLR (SC) 426
Aminul Haque Helal *v.* Justice Sultan Hossain Khan (2007) 15 BLT 1
Anisul Islam Mahmud *v.* Bangladesh (1992) 44 DLR
Anwar Hossain Chowdhury *v.* Bangladesh (1989) BLD (Spl) (AD) 1
Anwar Hossain Khan *v.* Speaker Jativa Sangsad (Parliament Boycott) 47 DLR (1995) 42
Arif Sultan *v.* DESA (2008) 60 DLR (HCD) 431
Aruna Sen *v.* Government of Bangladesh (1975) 27 DLR (HCD) 122
Ayub Ali Chowdhury *v.* BD (2005) 57 DLR 578
Bangladesh *v.* Advocate Asaduzzaman Siddiqui (Civil Appeal No. 06 of 2017)
Bangladesh *v.* Ahmed Nazir (1975) 27 DLR (AD) 41
Bangladesh *v.* AK Al-Mamun, (1997) BLD (AD) 77
Bangladesh *v.* Idrisur Rahman [2010] 7 LG (AD) 137
Bangladesh *v.* Mahbubuddin Ahmed (1998) 18 BLD (AD) 87
Bangladesh *v.* Rowshan Ara (2009) 17 BLT (AD) 65
Bangladesh Retired Government Employees Welfare Association *v.* Bangladesh 46 (1994) DLR (HCD) 426
Bazlur Rahman *v.* Bangladesh (2010) 62 DLR 360
CCB Foundation *v.* Government of Bangladesh 5 CLR (HCD) (2017)

Ekushey Television v. Dr Mahmood Hasan Court (2003) 55 DLR (AD) 26
Engineer Mahmudul Islam v. Bangladesh (2003) 55 DLR 171
Faruq Hasan v. Titas gas Transmission and Distribution Co (2006) 58 DLR 316
Fazal Din v. Lahore IT (1969) 21 DLR (SC) 225
Government of Bangladesh and Others v. Sontosh Kumar Shaha and Others 2016(1) LNJ (AD) 61
Halima Khatun v. Bangladesh (1978) 30 DLR (AD) 207
Hamidul Huq Chowdhury v. Bangladesh (1981) 33 DLR (HCD) 381
Idrisur Rahman v. Shahiduddin Ahmed 19 (1999) BLD (AD) 203
Jabbar Jute Mills v. Abdul Kashem (2007) 59 DLR (AD) 152
Jamal Shah v. Election Commission PLD 1966 SC 1
Jamil Haque v. Bangladesh (1981) DLR (AD) 125
Jibendra Kishore v. East Pakistan (1957) 9 DLR (SC) 21
Kazi Mukhlesur Rahman v. Bangladesh (1973) 25 DLR (HCD) 335
Khandkar Mostaque Ahmed v. Bangladesh (1982) 34 DLP (AD) 22
Kumudini Welfare Trust v. East Pakistan PLD 1963 Dac 136
Luthfunnessa v. Bangladesh (1990) 42 DLR (AD) 86
M H Chowdhury v. Titas Gas Transmission and Distribution Company Ltd (1981) 33 DLR (AD) 186
Maulvi Tamizuddin Khan v. Federation of Pakistan PLD 1955 Sind 96
Md Mustakin Ali v. Abdul Mutaleb (1993) 45 DLR 733
Mir Hassan & Another v. State, 1969 Lah Pak LD 786 (Pak 1969)
Mohammad Mahbubur Rahman v. Bangladesh (2017) 37 BLD (HCD) 104
Mohiuddin Farooque v. Bangladesh (1997) 17 BLD (AD)
Moulana Md. Abdul Hakim v. Bangladesh (2014) 34 BLD (HCD) 129
Mujibur Rahman v. Bangladesh (1992) 44 DLR (AD) 189
Mustafa Ansari v. Deputy Commissioner (1965) 17 DLR (Dacca) 553
Mustafa Kamal v. Commissioner of Customs (1990) 51 DLR (AD) 319
New India Tea Co Ltd v. Bangladesh (1978) 2 BD SCR 185
Queen v. Burah [1878] 3 AC 889
Rama Rani v. Bangladesh (1997) 49 DLR 364
Rezaul Haque v. Bangladesh (2010) 15 BLC 572
Ruhul Quddus v. Justice MA Aziz (2008) 60 DLR 511
Sajeda Parvin v. Bangladesh (1988) 40 DLR (AD) 178
Secretary, Ministry of Finance v. Masdar Hossain (1999) 52 DLR (AD) 82
Shafiq Ahmed v. BCIC (1993) 45 DLR 95
Shahdeen Malik v. Secretary, Ministry of Law, Justice and Parliamentary Affairs, WP No 2088/2005
Shamsul Huq Chowdhurv v. Justice Md Abdur Rouf 49 DLR (1997) 176
Shamsur Rahman v. Bangladesh (2010) 15 BLC 482
Sonali Bank v. Ruhul Amin Khan (1994) 46 DLR (AD) 85
Special Reference No 1 of 1995, (1995) 47 DLR (AD) 111
State v. Dosso (1958) PLD (SC) 533
Sultan Ahmed v. Chief Election Commissioner (1978) 30 DLR (HCD) 291
Syed SM Hasan v. Bangladesh (2008) 60 DLR (AD) 1
Tariq Transport v. Sargodha-Vera Bus Service (1959) 11 DLR (SC) 140
Unique Hotels and Resorts Ltd v. Bangladesh (2010) 15 BLC 770

University of Dhaka *v.* Zakir Ahmad PLD 1966 SC 105
Usif Patel *v.* Crown PLD 1955 FC 387

CANADA

Baker *v.* Canada (Citizenship and Immigration) [1999] 2 SCR 817
Bell *v.* Ontario Human Rights Commission [1971] SCR 756
Bernard *v.* Canada (Revenue Agency) 2015 FCA 263
Canada *v.* Kabul Farms Inc 2016 FCA 143
Canada (Attorney General) *v.* Canadian Human Rights Commission 2013 FCA 75
Canada (Attorney General) *v.* Igloo Vikski Inc [2016] 2 SCR 80
Canada (Citizenship and Immigration) *v.* Khosa [2009] 1 SCR 339
Canada (Minister of Transport, Infrastructure and Communities) *v.* Jagjit Singh Farwaha 2014 FCA 56
Canada Labour Relations Board *v.* Paul L'Anglais Inc [1983] 1 SCR 147
Canadian Union of Public Employees *v.* New Brunswick Liquor Corporation [1979] 2 SCR 227
Catalyst Paper Corp *v.* North Cowichan (District) [2012] 1 SCR 5
Chippewas of the Thames First Nation *v.* Enbridge Pipelines Inc [2017] 1 SCR 1099
Clyde River (Hamlet) *v.* Petroleum Geo Services Inc [2017] 1 SCR 1069
Crevier *v.* Attorney-General (Quebec) [1981] 2 SCR 220
Delgamuukw *v.* British Columbia [1997] 3 SCR 1010
Delios *v.* Canada (Attorney General) 2015 FCA 117
Doré *v.* Barreau du Québec [2012] 1 SCR 395
Dr Q *v.* College of Physicians and Surgeons of British Columbia [2003] 1 SCR 226
Dunsmuir *v.* New Brunswick [2008] SCC 9, [2008] 1 SCR 190
Forest Ethics Advocacy Association *v.* Canada (National Energy Board) 2014 FCA 245
Harelkin *v.* University of Regina [1979] 2 SCR 561
Hodge *v.* the Queen (1883) 9 AC 117
Kanthasamy *v.* Canada (2015) 41 BHRC 679
Loyola High School *v.* Quebec (Attorney General) [2015] 1 SCR 613
Metropolitan Life Insurance Co *v.* International Union of Operating Engineers [1970] SCR 425
Mobil Oil Canada Ltd *v.* Canada-Newfoundland Offshore Petroleum Board [1994] 1 SCR 202
National Corn Growers *v.* Canada (Import Tribunal) [1990] 2 SCR 1324
Newfoundland and Labrador Nurses' Union *v.* Newfoundland and Labrador (Treasury Board) [2011] 3 SCR 708
Nicholson *v.* Haldimand-Norfolk Regional Police Commissioners [1979] 1 SCR 311
Nova Scotia (Workers' Compensation Board) *v.* Martin; Nova Scotia (Workers' Compensation Board) *v.* Laseur [2003] 2 SCR 504
Paul *v.* British Columbia (Forest Appeals Commission) [2003] 2 SCR 585
Pushpanathan *v.* Canada (Minister of Citizenship and Immigration) [1998] 1 SCR 982
Quebec (Attorney General) *v.* Canada (Attorney General) [2015] 1 SCR 693
R *v.* Conway [2010] 1 SCR 765
R *v.* Hape 2007 SCC 26
R *v.* Oakes [1986] 1 SCR 103

Re Regional Trust and Superintendent of Insurance [1987] 2 FCR 271
Re Sound *v.* Canadian Association of Broadcasters 2017 FCA 138
Reference Re Canada Assistance Plan (BC) [1991] 2 SCR 525
Reference re Pan-Canadian Securities Regulation 2018 SCC 48
Reference re Secession of Quebec [1998] 2 SCR 217
Rio Tinto Alcan Inc *v.* Carrier Sekani Tribal Council [2010] 2 SCR 650
Roncarelli *v.* Duplessis [1959] SCR 121
Russel *v.* the Queen (1882) 7 AC 829
Saskatchewan (Human Rights Commission) *v.* Whatcott [2013] 1 SCR 467
Service Employees' International Union, Local No 333 *v.* Nipawin District Staff Nurses Association [1975] 1 SCR 382
Smith *v.* Alliance Pipeline [2011] 1 SCR 160
Suresh *v.* Canada 2002 SCC 1 (Supreme Court)
Syndicat des employés de production du Québec et de l'Acadie *v.* Canada Labour Relations Board [1984] 2 SCR 412
Toronto (City) *v.* Canadian Union of Public Employees, Local 79 [2003] 3 SCR 77
UES, Local 298 *v.* Bibeault [1988] 2 SCR 1048
Valente *v.* The Queen [1985] 2 SCR 673
Vavilov *v.* Canada (Citizenship and Immigration) 2017 FCA 132
Wilson *v.* Atomic Energy Agency of Canada [2016] 1 SCR 770
Windsor (City) *v.* Canadian Transit Co [2016] 2 SCR 617
Workplace Health, Safety and Compensation Commission *v.* Allen 2014 NLCA 42

EUROPEAN COURT OF HUMAN RIGHTS (ECTHR)

Ali *v.* United Kingdom (2016) 63 EHRR 20
Soering *v.* United Kingdom (1989) 98 ILR 270
Tsfayo *v.* United Kingdom (2009) 48 EHRR 18

EUROPEAN COURT OF JUSTICE (ECJ)

Case C-69/10 Diouf *v.* Ministre du Travail, de l'Emploi et de l'Immigration

HONG KONG SAR

AG *v.* Lee Kwong Kut (1993) 3 HKPLR 72
Anderson Asphalt Ltd *v.* Town Planning Board [2007] 3 HKLRD 18
Attorney-General *v.* Ng Yuen Shiu [1983] 1 HKC 23 (Privy Council)
Attorney General *v.* Yau Kwok-Lam Johnny [1988] HKCU 421
C *v.* Director of Immigration (2013) 16 HKCFAR 280
Chan To Foon *v.* Director of Immigration [2001] 3 HKLRD 109
Chim Sui Ping *v.* Housing Authority (HCAL 139/2009, [2012] HKEC 1268)
China Field Ltd *v.* Building Appeal Tribunal (No 2) (2009) 12 HKCFAR 342
Choi King Fung *v.* Hong Kong Housing Authority [2017] HKEC
Chong Fung Yuen *v.* Director of Immigration [2000] 2 HKCU 580
Chow Wai Hung *v.* The Hong Kong Government [1983] 2 HKC 537
Comilang Milagros Tecson *v.* Commissioner of Registration [2012] HKEC 869
Comilang Milagros Tecson *v.* Director of Immigration [2018] 2 HKLRD 534

De Lasala *v.* De Lasala [1979] HKLR 214
Democratic Party *v.* Secretary for Justice [2007] 2 HKLRD 807
Democratic Republic of the Congo *v.* FG Hemisphere Associates LLC (No 1) (2011) 14 HKCFAR 95
Designing Hong Kong Ltd *v.* Town Planning Board [2018] HKCFA 16
FG Hemisphere Associates LLC *v.* Democratic Republic of the Congo [2010] 2 HKLRD 66
Fok Chun Wa *v.* Hospital Authority [2012] HKEC 471
GA *v.* Director of Immigration (2014) 17 HKCFAR 60
Gurung Bhakta Bahadur *v.* Director of Immigration [2001] 3 HKLRD 225
HKSAR *v.* Ma Wai Kwan David [1997] HKLRD 761 [1997] 2 HKC 315 (CA)
HKSAR *v.* Ng Kung Siu & Another [1999] 3 HKLRD 907 (CFA)
Kong Yunming *v.* Director of Social Welfare (2013) 16 HKCFAR 950
Lam Siu Po *v.* Commissioner of Police (2009) 12 HKCFAR 237
Lau Kong-yung *v.* Director of Immigration [1999] 2 HKCFAR 300
Leung *v.* Secretary for Justice [2006] 4 HKLRD 211
Luk Ka Cheung *v.* Market Misconduct Tribunal [2009] 1 HKLRD 114
MA *v.* Director of Immigration [2011] 2 HKLRD F6 (Court of First Instance), [2011] HKEC 28 (CFI)
Ming Pao Newspapers Ltd *v.* AG of Hong Kong [1996] AC 907
Mok Chi Hung *v.* Director of Immigration [2001] 2 HKLRD 125
Ng Ka Ling *v.* Director of Immigration (1999) 2 HKCFAR 4
Ng Siu Tung *v.* Director of Immigration (2002) 5 HKCFAR 1
Ng Siu Tung & Others *v.* Director of Immigration [2002] HKCU 13
Oriental Daily Publisher Ltd *v.* Commissioner for Television and Entertainment Licensing Authority [1998] 4 HKC 505
Po Fun Chan *v.* Winnie Cheung [2008] 1 HKLRD 319 (CFA)
Prabakar *v.* Secretary for Security [2002] HKEC 1451 (Court of Appeal)
QT *v.* Director of Immigration [2016] 2 HKLRD 583 (Court of First Instance)
QT *v.* Director of Immigration [2018] HKCFA 28 (Court of Final Appeal)
R *v.* Sin Yau-ming [1992] 1 HKCLR 127 (CA)
R *v.* Town Planning Board, ex parte Kwan Kong Company (1995) 5 HKLPR 261
Re Tran Quoc Cuong *v.* Khuc The Loc [1991] 2 HKLR 312 (HC)
Re Tran Quoc Cuong *v.* Khuc The Loc [2007] 3 HKLRD 18 (CA)
Right to Inherent Dignity Movement Association *v.* Hong Kong SAR Government [2008] HKCU 1692
RV *v.* Director of Immigration [2008] 4 HKLRD 529
Secretary for Justice *v.* Wong Ho Ming [2018] HKCA 173
Secretary for Security *v.* Prabakar (2004) 7 HKCFAR 187 (Court of Final Appeal)
Smart Gain Investment Ltd *v.* Town Planning Board [2007] HKCU 1817
Solicitor (24/07) *v.* Law Society of Hong Kong (2008) 11 HKCFAR 117
Stock Exchange of Hong Kong Ltd *v.* New World Development Co Ltd (2006) 9 HKCFAR 234
Ubamaka *v.* Secretary for Security (2012) 15 HKCFAR 743
W *v.* Registrar of Marriages [2010] 6 HKC 359
W *v.* Registrar of Marriages (2013) 16 HKCFAR 112
Zestra Asia Ltd *v.* Commissioner for Transport [2007] 4 HKLRD 722
ZN *v.* Director of Immigration [2017] 1 HKLRD 559 (CFI)

ZN *v.* Director of Immigration [2018] HKCA 373 (CA)
ZN *v.* Secretary for Justice [2018] 3 HKLRD 778 (CA)

INDIA

Ajay Hasia *v.* Khalid Mujib Sehravardi (1981) 1 SCC 722
AK Kraipak *v.* Union of India AIR 1970 SC 150
BALCO Employees Union *v.* Union of India (2002) 2 SCC 333
Bharat Bank Ltd Delhi *v.* The Employees of the Bharat Bank Ltd Delhi AIR 1950 SC 188
Chairman, All India Railway Recruitment Board *v.* K Shyam Kumar (2010) 6 SCC 614
Chinnappa *v.* Union of India AIR 2002 SC 724
East Coast Railway & Anor *v.* Mahadev Appa Rao & Ors 2010 AIR SCC 4210
EP Royappa *v.* State of Tamil Nadu 1974 AIR 555
Gramophone Company of India *v.* Birendra Bahadur Pandey [1984] 2 SCR 673
Indian Express Newspapers (Bombay) *v.* Union of India AIR 1986 SC 515
Jolly George Verghese *v.* Bank of Cochin [1980] 2 SCR 913
Kasturi Lal Lakshmi Reddy *v.* State of Jammu and Kashmir AIR 1980 SC 1992
KCG Narayan Deo *v.* State of Orissa AIR 1953 SC 375
Kesavannada Bharati *v.* State of Kerala AIR 1973 SC 1461
Kumari Shrilekha Vidyarthi *v.* State of Uttar Pradesh & Ors AIR 1991 SC 537
M/S Sharma Transport Rep By Shri DP Sharma *v.* Government Of AP & Ors AIR 2002 SC 322, 2002 2 SCC 188
Maharashtra Ekta Hawkers Union *v.* Municipal Corporation, Greater Mumbai (2014) 1 SCC 490
Minerva Mills Ltd and Ors *v.* Union Of India and Ors AIR 1980 SC 1789
Mohini Jain *v.* State of Karnataka AIR 1992 SC 1858
New Horizons Ltd *v.* Union of India AIR 1994 Del 126
Om Kumar *v.* Union of India in Delhi Development Authority 2000 SCC 1993
Queen *v.* Burah [1878] 3 AC 889
R. D. Shetty *v.* International Airport Authority AIR 1979 SC 1628, (1979) 3 SCC 489
State of UP *v.* Vijay Kumar Tripathi AIR 1995 SC 1130
Tata Cellular *v.* Union of India AIR 1996 SC 11
The State of Andhra Pradesh and another, etc *v.* Nalla Raja Reddy and others Etc AIR 1967 SC 1458, 1967 AIR Supreme Court 1458, AIR 1960 Mad 543, [1968] 1 MLJ 6
Union of India *v.* G Ganayutham AIR 1997 SC 3387
Union of India *v.* Tulsiram (1985) Sup 2 SCR 382
Unni Krishnan *v.* State of Andhra Pradesh AIR 1993 SC 2178
Visaka *v.* State of Rajasthan [1997] 3 LRC 361
Y Srinivasa Rao *v.* J Veeraiah AIR 1993 SC 929
Zenit Mataplast P Ltd *v.* State of Maharashtra & Ors (2009) 10 SCC 388

INTER-AMERICAN COURT OF HUMAN RIGHTS

Advisory Opinion OC-3/83, Inter-American Court of Human Rights Series A No 3 (8 September 1983)

IRELAND

AAA *v.* Minister for Justice [2017] IESC 80

BFO *v.* Governor of Dóchas Centre [2005] 2 IR 1
Blehein *v.* Minister for Health and Children [2009] 1 IR 275
Bode *v.* Minister for Justice, Equality and Law Reform [2008] 3 IR 663
Brady *v.* Donegal County Council [1989] ILRM 282
Byrne *v.* Ireland [1972] IR 241
Carroll *v.* Minister for Agriculture and Food [1991] 1 IR 230
CE *v.* Minister for Justice, Equality and Law Reform [2012] IEHC 3
Cityview Press Ltd *v.* An Comhairle Oiliúna [1980] IR 381
Clinton *v.* An Bord Pleanála [2007] 4 IR 701
Cork County Council *v.* Shackleton [2007] IEHC 241
Cromane Seafoods Ltd *v.* Minister for Agriculture, Fisheries and Food [2016] IESC 6, [2017] 1 IR 119
Dellway Investments *v.* National Asset Management Agency [2011] 4 IR 1
Donegan *v.* Dublin City Council [2012] 3 IR 600
Dublin City Council *v.* Williams [2010] 1 IR 801
Dunmanus Bay Mussels Ltd *v.* Aquaculture Licences Appeals Board [2014] 1 IR 403
East Donegal Co-operative Livestock Mart Ltd *v.* Attorney General [1970] IR 317
Farrell *v.* Attorney General [1998] 1 ILRM 364
Flanagan *v.* University College Dublin [1988] IR 724
Gallagher *v.* Revenue Commissioners (No 2) [1995] 1 IR 55
Geoghegan *v.* Institute of Chartered Accountants [1995] 3 IR 86
Georgopoulos *v.* Beaumont Hospital Board [1998] 3 IR 132
Harvey *v.* The Minister for Social Welfare [1990] 2 IR 232
Heaney *v.* Ireland [1994] 3 IR 593
Howard *v.* Commissioners of Public Works [1994] 1 IR 101
In re Article 26 and the Illegal Immigrants (Trafficking) Bill 1999 [2000] 2 IR 360
International Vessels Ltd *v.* Minister for Marine (No 2) [1991] 2 IR 93
Irish Permanent Building Society *v.* Caldwell [1981] ILRM 242
John Grace Fried Chicken *v.* The Labour Court [2011] 3 IR 211
K *v.* An Bord Altranais [1990] 2 IR 396
Kavanagh *v.* Governor of Mountjoy Prison [2002] IESC 13
Keady *v.* Commissioner of an Garda Siochánna [1992] 2 IR 197
Kiely *v.* The Minister for Social Welfare [1977] IR 267
Killeen *v.* Director of Public Prosecutions [1998] 1 ILRM 1
Kirwan *v.* Minister for Justice [1994] 1 ILRM 333
Kivlehan *v.* Éireann [2016] IEHC 88
Laurentiu *v.* Minister for Justice [1999] 4 IR 26
Leen *v.* President of the Executive Council [1925] IR 456
Lett & Co *v.* Wexford Borough Council [2014] 2 IR 198
M *v.* Medical Council [1984] IR 485
Macauley *v.* Minister for Posts and Telegraphs [1966] IR 345
Mallak *v.* Minister for Justice, Equality and Law Reform [2012] 3 IR 297
McDonald *v.* Bord na gCon [1965] IR 217
McGee *v.* Attorney General [1974] IR 284
McGowan *v.* Labour Court [2013] 3 IR 718
McKernan *v.* Employment Appeals Tribunal [2008] IEHC 40
Meadows *v.* Minister for Justice, Equality and Law Reform [2010] 2 IR 201

Mone *v*. An Bord Pleanála [2010] IEHC 395
Murray and Murray *v*. Ireland [1991] ILRM 465
NM (DRC) *v*. Minister for Justice, Equality and Law Reform [2016] IECA 217
O'Brien *v*. Bord na Móna [1983] IR 255
O'Donnell *v*. Corporation of Dún Laoghaire [1991] ILRM 302
O'Keeffe *v*. An Bord Pleanála [1993] 1 IR 39
Peter Whelan *v*. Minister for Justice, Equality and Law Reform [2008] 2 IR 142
Prendergast *v*. Higher Education Authority [2009] 1 ILRM 47
R (Martin) *v*. Mahoney [1910] 2 IR 695
Re Haughey [1971] IR 217
Re Solicitors Act 1954 [1960] IR 239
Royal Dublin Society *v*. Revenue Commissioners [2000] 1 IR 270
Ryan *v*. Attorney General [1965] IR 294
Ryanair *v*. Labour Court [2007] 4 IR 199
Satke *v*. An Bord Pleanála [2009] IEHC 230
SFA *v*. Minister for Justice and Equality [2015] IEHC 364
Shell Limited *v*. McGrath [2013] 1 IR 247
State (Abenglen Properties Ltd) *v*. Dublin Corporation [1984] IR 381
State (Davidson) *v*. Farrell [1960] IR 438
State (Holland) *v*. Kennedy [1977] IR 193
State (Lynch) *v*. Cooney [1982] IR 337
Stroker *v*. Doherty [1991] 1 IR 23
Tormey *v*. Attorney General [1985] IR 289
Webb *v*. Ireland [1988] IR 353
White *v*. Dublin City Council [2004] 1 IR 545

ISRAEL

Abir Company Ltd *v*. Inspector-General of Police and Prisons, HC 76/39; 7 PLR 31 (1940)
Academic Center for Law and Business *v*. Minister of Finance, HCJ 2605/05; 63(2) PD 545 (2009)
Attorney General *v*. M Dizengoff & Co (Navigation) Ltd, CA 311/57; 13 PD 1026 (1959)
Bejerano *v*. Minister of Police, HCJ 1/49; 2 PD 80 (1949)
Ben-Ami *v*. Local Council Kfar Yona, HC 3/42; 9 PLR 75 (1942)
Ben-Atiyah *v*. Minister of Education, Culture and Sports, HCJ 3477/95; 49(5) PD 1 (1996)
Berman *v*. Minister of Interior, HCJ 3/58; 12 PD 1493 (1958)
Binnenboim *v*. Municipality of Tel-Aviv, HCJ 21/51; 6 PD 375 (1952)
Binui Vepituch Banegev Ltd *v*. Minister of Defense, HCJ 101/74; 28(2) PD 449 (1974)
Dapei Zahav Ltd *v*. Broadcasting Authority, HCJ 389/80; 35(1) PD 421 (1981)
Deri *v*. Committee of Releases, HCJ 598/77; 32(3) PD 161 (1979)
Eisenberg *v*. Minister of Building and Housing, HCJ 6163/92; 47(2) PD 229 (1993)
El-Karboutly *v*. Minister of Defense, HCJ 7/48; 2 PD 5 (1948)
Federman *v*. Sir Ronald Storrs, District Commissioner, Jerusalem – Southern District, HC 69/25; 1 PLR 57 (1920–1933)
Ganor *v*. Attorney General, HCJ 935/89; 44(2) PD 485 (1990)
Havkin *v*. Inspector General of Police and Prisons, HC 78/38; 7 PLR 35 (1940)
Jabotinski *v*. Weitzman, HCJ 65/51; 5 PD 801 (1951)

Kirshenbaum *v.* Major-General EL Bols, HC 86/47; 14 PLR 423 (1947)
Kol Ha'am Ltd. *v.* Minister of Interior, HCJ 73/53; 7 PD 871 (1953)
Lazarovitz *v.* Food Comptroller, Jersualem, HCJ 105/54; 10 PD 40 (1956)
Leon *v.* The Acting Commissioner of the Urban Area of Tel-Aviv (Yehoshua Gubernik), HCJ 5/48; 1 PD 58 (1948)
Microdaf *v.* Electricity Company of Israel Ltd, HCJ 731/86; 41(2) PD 449 (1987)
Miller, Engineering (Agency and Export) Ltd *v.* Minister of Transport, HCJ 311/60; 15 PD 1989 (1961)
Movement for Quality in Government in Israel *v.* Government of Israeli, HCJ 3094/93; 47(5) PD 404 (1993)
Municipality of Petach-Tikva *v.* Tachan, CA 183/69; 23(2) PD 398 (1969)
Ressler *v.* Minister of Defense, HCJ 910/86; 42(2) PD 441 (1988)
Rokach *v.* General Officer Commanding British Troops in Palestine and Trans-Jordan, HC 40/47; 14 PLR 154 (1947)
Sarid *v.* Knesset Speaker, HCJ 652/81; 36(2) PD 197 (1982)
Schnitzer *v.* Chief Military Censor, HCJ 680/88; 42(4) PD 617 (1989)
Sci-tex Corporation Ltd *v.* Minister of Commerce and Industry, HCJ 135/75; 30(1) PD 673 (1975)
Segal *v.* Minister of Interior, HCJ 217/80; 34(4) PD 429 (1980)
Sheib *v.* Minister of Defense, HCJ 144/50; 5 PD 399 (1951)
Shimel *v.* Authorized Authority, HCJ 174/54; 9 PD 459 (1955)
Trudler *v.* Elections Officer to the Agricultural Committees, HCJ 77/63; 17 PD 2503 (1963)
United Mizrahi Bank Ltd *v.* Migdal Cooperative Village, HCJ 6821/93; 49(4) PD 221 (1995)
Weinberg *v.* District Commissioner, Jerusalem District, HC 9/38; 5 PLR (1938)
Yehoshua *v.* Appeals Tribunal Under the Invalids (Pensions and Rehabilitations) Law, 1949, HCJ 176/54; 9 PD 617 (1955)
Zeev *v.* The Acting Commissioner of the Urban Area of Tel-Aviv (Yehoshua Gubernik), HCJ 10/48; 1 PD 85 (1948)
Zerubavel *v.* Appeals Tribunal Under the Families of Fallen Soldiers Law, HCJ 5/53; 7 PD 182 (1953)

KENYA

Alex Malikha Wasubwa & 7 others *v.* Elias Nambkha Wamita & 4 others [2012] eKLR
Daniel Nyongesa and others *v.* Egerton University College [1990] KLR 692
Dry Associates Limited *v.* Capital Markets Authority & another [2012] eKLR
Elizabeth Wainaina and others *v.* Board of Governors of Pangani Girls School, Misc. Civil Case No. 818 of 1992
Fauzia Tariq Zubedi *v.* Athman Hassan Awadh & 3 others [2013] eKLR
Geoffrey Mwangi Kariuki *v.* University of Nairobi, Misc Application No 4788 of 1992 (unreported)
Gilbert Hezekiah Miya *v.* Advocates Disciplinary Committee [2015] eKLR
Irungu Kangata and others *v.* University of Nairobi, Misc. Civil Application No. 40 of 2001 (unreported)
Jotham Mulati Welamondi *v.* Chairman, Electoral Commission of Kenya [2002] 1 KLR 486
Kasuli *v.* AG [1971] EA 423
Kenya African National Union *v.* Mwai Kibaki [2005] eKLR

Khobesh Agencies Limited & 32 others *v.* Minister of Foreign Affairs & International Relations & 4 others [2013] eKLR
Kibaki *v.* Moi and 2 others (No 2) (2008) 2 KLR 308; (2008) 2 KLR 351
Koinange Mbiu *v.* Rex (1951) 24(2) KLR 130
Martin Nyaga Wambora *v.* County Assembly of Embu and 37 others [2015] eKLR
Meshack Ageng'o Omondi *v.* Eldoret Municipal Council and another [2012] eKLR
Michael Mungai *v.* Attorney General & 9 others [2015] eKLR
Municipal Board of Mombasa *v.* Kala (1955) 22 EACA 319
Mwangi *v.* R (1950) 24 (1) KLR 72
Nation Media Group Limited *v.* Cradle – the Children's Foundation Suing through Geoffrey Maganya [2016] eKLR
Ndegwa *v.* Nairobi Liquor Licensing Court (1957) EA 709 (Kenya)
Patel *v.* Plateau Licensing Court (1954) 27 KLR 147
Peter Muchai Muhura *v.* Teachers Service Commission [2015] eKLR
R *v.* the Staff Disciplinary Committee of Maseno University and others ex parte Prof. Ochong' Okello, Kisumu Misc. Application No 227 of 2003
Re Marle's Application [1958] EALR 153
Republic *v.* Director of Public Prosecutions & another ex parte Chamanlal Vrajlal Kamani & 2 others [2015] eKLR
Republic *v.* Funyula Land Disputes Tribunal Busia Principal & 2 others [2014] eKLR
Republic *v.* Kahindi Nyafula & 3 others ex parte Kilifi South East Farmers Cooperative [2014] eKLR
Republic *v.* Minister for Information & Broadcasting and Ahmed Jibril, ex parte East African Television Network Limited, Nairobi High Court Misc Civ App No 403 of 1998 (unreported)
Shah *v.* AG (No 2) [1970] EA 523
Sheikh Brothers *v.* Hotels Authority (1949) 23(2) KLR 1
Suchan Investment Limited *v.* Ministry of National Heritage and Culture [2016] eKLR (4 March 2016)
Taib A Taib *v.* Minister for Local Government [2006] eKLR
University Academic Staff Union *v.* Registrar of Societies, Nairobi High Court Civil application No 20 of 1994
Wangari Maathai *v.* The Kenya Times Media Trust, Nairobi High Court Civil Case No 5403 of 1989 (unreported)

MALAYSIA

A Child & Ors *v.* Jabatan Pendaftaran Negara & Ors [2017] 7 Current Law Journal 533 (Court of Appeal)
Commissioner for Religious Affairs *v.* Tengku Mariam [1970] Malayan Law Journal 222 (Supreme Court)
Dalip Kaur *v.* Pegawai Polis Daerah, Balai Polis Daerah, Bukit Mertajam & Another [1992] 1 Malayan Law Journal 1 (Supreme Court)
Indira Gandhi a/p Mutho *v.* Pengarah Jabatan Agama Islam Perak [2013] 5 Malayan Law Journal 552 (High Court)
Indira Gandhi a/p Mutho *v.* Pengarah Jabatan Agama Islam Perak & Ors and Other Appeals [2018] 3 Malayan Law Journal 545 (Federal Court)

Jabatan Agama Islam Wilayah Persekuthuan *v.* Berjaya Books Sdn Bhd [2015] 3 Current Law Journal 461 (Court of Appeal)

Kamoo *v.* Thomas Turner Bassett [1808–1894] 1 Kyshe 1

Karam Singh *v.* Menteri Hal Ehwal Dalam Negeri (Minister of Home Affairs) Malaysia [1969] 2 MLJ 129

Kassim @ Osman bin Ahmad *v.* Dato' Seri Jamil Khir bin Baharom Menteri di Jabatan Perdana Menteri (Hal Ehwal Agama Islam) [2016] 5 Malayan Law Journal 258

Kassim @ Osman bin Ahmad *v.* Dato' Seri Jamil Khir bin Baharom Menteri di Jabatan Perdana Menteri (Hal Ehwal Agama Islam) [2016] 7 Malayan Law Journal 669

Lim Beh & Ors *v.* Opium Farmer [1808–1894] 3 Kyshe 10

Lina Joy *v.* Majlis Agama Islam Wilayah Persekutuan & Anor [2004] 6 Current Law Journal 242 (High Court)

Lina Joy *v.* Majlis Agama Islam Wilayah Persekutuan [2005] 6 Malayan Law Journal 193 (Court of Appeal)

Lina Joy *v.* Majlis Agama Islam Wilayah & Anor [2007] 4 Malayan Law Journal 585 (Federal Court)

Lina Joy *v.* The Federal Territory Islamic Council & Ors [2007] 3 AMR 693

Majlis Agama Islam dan Adat Melayu Perak Darul Ridzuan *v.* Mohamed Suffian bin Ahmad Syazali & Anor [2014] 3 Malayan Law Journal 74 (Court of Appeal)

Mamat bin Daud *v.* Government of Malaysia [1988] 1 Malayan Law Journal 119, 120 (Supreme Court)

Md Hakim Lee *v.* Majlis Agama Islam Wilayah Persekutuan, Kuala Lumpur [1998] 1 Malayan Law Journal 681 (High Court)

Mohd Faizal Musa *v.* Minister of Home Affairs [2017] 7 Current Law Journal 352 (High Court)

Pathmanathan a/l Krishnan (also known as Muhammad Riduan bin Abdullah) *v.* Indira Gandhi a/p Mutho [2016] 4 Malayan Law Journal 455 (Court of Appeal)

Semenyih Jaya Sdn Bhd *v.* Pentadbir Tanah Daerah Hulu Langat & Another Case [2017] 3 Malayan Law Journal 561

Shamala a/p Sathiyaseelan *v.* Dr Jeyaganesh a/l C Mogarajah [2004] 2 Malayan Law Journal 241 (High Court)

Shamala a/p Sathiyaseelan *v.* Dr Jeyaganesh a/l C Mogarajah (also known as Muhammad Ridzwan bin Mogarajah) [2011] 2 Malayan Law Journal 281 (Federal Court)

SIS Forum (M) *v.* Jawatankuasa Fatwa Negeri Selangor & Ors [2018] 3 Malayan Law Journal 706 (Court of Appeal)

Soon Singh *v.* Pertubuhan Kebajikan Islam Malaysia (PERKIM) Kedah [1999] 1 Malayan Law Journal 489 (Federal Court)

Subashini a/p Rajasingam *v.* Saravanan a/l Thangathoray and Other Appeals [2008] 2 Malayan Law Journal 147 (Federal Court)

Sukma Darmawan Sasmitaat Madja *v.* Ketua Pengarah Penjara Malaysia & Anor [1999] 1 Malayan Law Journal 266 (Court of Appeal)

Titular Roman Catholic Archbishop of Kuala Lumpur *v.* Menteri Dalam Negeri & Co [2014] 4 Malayan Law Journal 765 (Federal Court)

Viran Nagapan *v.* Deepa Subramaniam and Other Appeals [2016] 3 Current Law Journal 505 (Federal Court)

Zaina Abidin bin Hamid @ S Maniam & Others *v.* Kerajaan Malaysia & Others [2009] 6 Malayan Law Journal 863

NAMIBIA

Katofa *v.* Administrator-General for South West Africa 1985 (4) SA 211 (SWA)

NEW ZEALAND

Astrazeneca Ltd *v.* Commerce Commission [2009] NZSC 92, [2010] 1 NZLR 297
Attorney-General *v.* Ngati Apa [2003] 3 NZLR 643 (CA)
Attorney-General *v.* Ririnui [2015] NZCA 160
Auckland Casino Ltd *v.* Casino Control Authority (HC Auckland, M 81/94, 13 July 1994, Robertson J)
Bailey *v.* Christchurch City Council [2013] NZHC 1933, [2013] 3 NZLR 679
Barton-Prescott *v.* Director-General of Social Welfare [1997] 3 NZLR 179
Budget Rent A Car Ltd *v.* Auckland Regional Authority [1985] 2 NZLR 414 (CA)
Bulk Gas Users Group *v.* Attorney-General [1983] NZLR 129 (CA)
Charter Holdings Ltd *v.* Commissioner of Inland Revenue [2016] NZCA 499, (2016) 27 NZTC 22
Comptroller of Customs *v.* Terminals (NZ) Ltd [2012] NZCA 598, [2014] 2 NZLR 137
Daganayasi *v.* Minster of Immigration [1980] 2 NZLR 130 (CA)
Director of Maritime New Zealand *v.* Survey Nelson [2011] NZSC 61
Environmental Defence Society *v.* South Pacific Aluminium (No 3) [1981] 1 NZLR 216 (CA)
Glaxo Group Ltd *v.* Commissioner of Patents [1991] 3 NZLR 179 (CA)
Green *v.* Racing Integrity Unit Ltd [2014] NZCA 133, [2014] NZAR 623
GXL Realties Ltd *v.* Minister of Energy for New Zealand [2010] NZCA 185
H *v.* Refugee Protection Officer [2019] NZSC 13
Hawke's Bay Regional Investment Co Ltd *v.* Royal Forest and Bird Protection Society of New Zealand Inc [2017] NZSC 106, [2017] 1 NZLR 1041
Helu *v.* Immigration and Protection Tribunal [2015] NZSC 28, [2016] 1 NZLR 298
Hoani Te Heu Heu Tukino *v.* Aotea District Maori Trust Board [1941] NZLR 590 (PC)
Hu *v.* Immigration and Protection Tribunal [2017] NZHC 41, [2017] NZAR 508
Huakina Development Trust *v.* Waikato Valley Authority [1987] 2 NZLR 188 (HC)
Institute of Chartered Accountants of NZ *v.* Bevan [2003] 1 NZLR 154 (CA)
Kim *v.* Minister of Justice of New Zealand [2019] NZCA 209
Lewis *v.* Wilson & Horton Ltd [2000] 3 NZLR 546 (CA)
Maddaver *v.* Umawera School Board of Trustees [1993] 2 NZLR 478
Maori Council *v.* Attorney-General [1996] 3 NZLR 140
Martin *v.* Ryan [1990] 2 NZLR 209 (HC)
McGrath *v.* Accident Compensation Corporation [2011] NZSC 77, [2011] 3 NZLR 733
Minister of Justice *v.* Kim [2019] NZSC 100
Ministry of Transport *v.* Noort; Police *v.* Curran [1992] 3 NZLR 260
Moonen *v.* Film and Literature Board of Review [2000] 2 NZLR 9
New Zealand Airline Pilots' Association Inc *v.* Attorney-General [1997] 3 NZLR 269
New Zealand Association for Migration and Investments Inc *v.* Attorney-General [2006] NZAR 45 (HC)
New Zealand Maori Council *v.* Attorney-General [1987] 1 NZLR 641 (CA)
New Zealand Maori Council *v.* Attorney-General (Broadcasting Assets) [1994] 1 NZLR 513 (PC)
New Zealand Maori Council *v.* Attorney-General (Mighty River Power) [2013] NZSC 6, [2013] 3 NZLR 31

New Zealand Maori Council *v.* Attorney-General (Te Arawa Cross Claim Case) [2007] NZCA 269, [2008] 1 NZLR 318
New Zealand Rail Ltd *v.* Employment Court [1995] 3 NZLR 179 (CA)
Ngai Tahu Maori Trust Board *v.* Director-General of Conservation [1995] 3 NZLR 553 (CA)
Ngāi Tai Ki Tāmaki Tribal Trust *v.* Minister of Conservation [2018] NZSC 122
Ngaronoa *v.* Attorney-General [2017] NZCA 351, [2017] 3 NZLR 643
Ngaronoa *v.* Attorney-General [2018] NZSC 123
Nicholls *v.* Registrar of the Court of Appeal [1998] 2 NZLR 385 (CA)
Northland Regional Council *v.* Rogan [2018] NZCA 63
Osborne *v.* Worksafe New Zealand [2017] NZSC 175
Powerco Ltd *v.* Commerce Commission HC Wellington CIV-2005–485-001066, 9 June 2006
Quake Outcasts *v.* Minister of Canterbury Earthquake Recovery [2017] NZCA 332, [2017] 3 NZLR 486
Quilter *v.* Attorney-General [1998] 1 NZLR 523
R *v.* Hansen [2007] NZSC 7, [2007] 3 NZLR 1
R *v.* Pora [2001] 2 NZLR 37 (CA)
R *v.* Poumako [2000] 2 NZLR 695 (CA)
Rahman *v.* Minister of Immigration (26 September 2000) AP 56/99; CP 49/99, HC
Rajan *v.* Minister of Immigration [1996] 3 NZLR 543 (CA)
Reid *v.* Rowley [1977] 2 NZLR 472 (CA)
Ririnui *v.* Landcorp Farming Ltd [2014] NZHC 1128
Ririnui *v.* Landcorp Farming Ltd [2016] NZSC 62, [2016] 1 NZLR 1056
Seaton *v.* Minister for Land Information [2013] NZSC 42, [2013] 3 NZLR 157
Secretary for Justice *v.* Simes [2012] NZCA 459, [2012] NZAR 1044
Sellers *v.* Maritime Safety Inspector [1999] 2 NZLR 44 (CA)
Stininato *v.* New Zealand Boxing Association Inc [1978] 1 NZLR 1 (CA)
Survey Nelson Ltd *v.* Maritime New Zealand [2010] NZCA 629
Takamore *v.* Clarke [2011] NZCA 587, [2012] 1 NZLR 573 (CA)
Takamore *v.* Clarke [2012] NZSC 116, [2013] 2 NZLR 733
Tannadyce Investments Ltd *v.* Commissioner of Inland Revenue [2011] NZSC 158, [2012] 2 NZLR 153
Tavita *v.* Minister of Immigration [1994] 2 NZLR 257 (NZCA)
Taylor *v.* The Chief Executive of the Department of Corrections [2015] NZCA 477, [2015] NZAR 1648
Terminals (NZ) Ltd *v.* Comptroller of Customs [2013] NZSC 139, [2014] 1 NZLR 121
Tukaki *v.* Commonwealth of Australia [2018] NZCA 324
Webster *v.* Auckland Harbour Board [1987] 2 NZLR 129 (CA)
Wellington City Council *v.* Minotaur Custodians Ltd [2017] NZCA 302, [2017] 3 NZLR 464
Wellington International Airport Ltd *v.* New Zealand Air Line Pilots' Association Industrial Union of Workers Inc [2017] NZSC 199
Winther *v.* Housing Corporation of New Zealand [2010] NZCA 601, [2011] 1 NZLR 825
Wislang *v.* Medical Practitioners Disciplinary Committee [1974] 1 NZLR 29
Wolf *v.* Minister of Immigration [2004] NZAR 414 (HC)
Wool Board Disestablishment Company Ltd *v.* Saxmere Co Ltd [2010] NZCA 513, [2011] 2 NZLR 442
Ye *v.* Minister of Immigration [2009] NZSC 76, [2010] 1 NZLR 104
Zaoui *v.* Attorney General [2005] 4 LRC 557

Zaoui *v.* Attorney-General (No 2) [2005] NZSC 38, [2006] 1 NZLR 289

PAKISTAN

Akbar Ali *v.* Raziur Rahman (1966) 18 DLR (SC) 426
Fazal Din *v.* Lahore IT (1969) 21 DLR (SC) 225
Jamal Shah *v.* Election Commission PLD 1966 SC 1
Jibendra Kishore *v.* East Pakistan (1957) 9 DLR (SC) 21
Maulvi Tamizuddin Khan *v.* Federation of Pakistan PLD 1955 Sind 96
Mir Hassan & Another *v.* State, 1969 Lah Pak LD 786 (Pak 1969)
Muhammad Aboo *v.* Province of East Pakistan PLD 1960 SC 154
Mustafa Ansari *v.* Deputy Commissioner (1965) 17 DLR (Dacca) 553
State *v.* Dosso (1958) PLD (SC) 533
Tariq Transport *v.* Sargodha-Vera Bus Service (1959) 11 DLR (SC) 140
University of Dhaka *v.* Zakir Ahmad PLD 1966 SC 105
Usif Patel *v.* Crown PLD 1955 FC 387

SINGAPORE

Abdul Nasir bin Amer Hamsah *v.* Public Prosecutor [1997] 2 SLR(R) 842
Borissik Svetlanta *v.* Urban Redevelopment Authority [2009] 4 SLR(R) 92
Chan Hiang Leng Colin *v.* Minister for Information and the Arts [1996] 1 SLR(R) 294
Chee Siok Chin *v.* Minister for Home Affairs [2006] 1 SLR(R) 582
Cheong Chun Yin *v.* Attorney-General [2014] 3 SLR 1141
Chiu Teng @ Kallang Pte Ltd *v.* Singapore Land Authority [2014] 1 SLR 1047
Chng Suan Tze *v.* Minister for Home Affairs [1988] 2 SLR(R) 525
De Souza Kevin Desmond *v.* Minister for Home Affairs [1988] 1 SLR(R) 464
Jeyaretnam Kenneth Andrew *v.* Attorney-General [2013] 1 SLR 619 (HC)
Jeyaretnam Kenneth Andrew *v.* Attorney-General [2014] 1 SLR 345 (CA)
Lee Hsien Loong *v.* Review Publishing Co Ltd [2007] 2 SLR(R) 453
Lee Mau Seng *v.* Minister for Home Affairs [1971–1973] SLR(R) 135; [1971] SGHC 10
Lim Meng Suang *v.* Attorney-General [2013] 3 SLR 118 (HC)
Lim Meng Suang *v.* Attorney-General [2015] 1 SLR 26 (CA)
Madan Mohan Singh *v.* Attorney-General [2015] 2 SLR 1085
Manjit Singh s/o Kirpal Singh *v.* Attorney-General [2013] 4 SLR 483
Mohammad Faizal bin Sabtu *v.* Public Prosecutor [2012] 4 SLR 947
Muhammad Ridzuan bin Mohd Ali *v.* Attorney-General [2015] 5 SLR 1222
Nagaenthran a/l K Dharmalingam *v.* Attorney-General [2018] SGHC 112 (HC)
Nagaenthran a/l K Dharmalingam *v.* Attorney-General [2019] SGCA 37 (CA)
Ong Ah Chuan *v.* Public Prosecutor [1979–1980] SLR(R) 710
Per Ah Seng Robin *v.* Housing and Development Board [2016] 1 SLR 1020, [2015] SGCA 62
Prabagaran a/l Srivijayan *v.* Public Prosecutor & Other matters [2017] 1 SLR 173
Rajeevan Edakalavan *v.* Public Prosecutor [1998] 1 SLR(R) 10
Ramalingam Ravinthran *v.* Attorney-General [2012] 2 SLR 49
Re Application by Yee Yut Ee [1977–1978] SLR(R) 490
Re Raffles Town Club Pte Ltd [2008] 2 SLR(R) 1101
Re Siah Mooi Guat [1988] 2 SLR(R) 165

SOUTH AFRICA

Grey's Marine Hout Bay (Pty) Ltd *v*. Minister of Public Works 2005 (6) SA 313 (SCA)
Hira *v*. Booysen 1992 (4) SA 69 (A)
In re Insolvent Estate of Brink (1828) 1 Menzies 340
Johannesburg Consolidated Investment Co *v*. Johannesburg Town Council 1903 TS 111
Judicial Service Commission *v*. Cape Bar Council 2013 (1) SA 170 (SCA)
Katofa *v*. Administrator-General for South West Africa 1985 (4) SA 211 (SWA)
KZN Joint Liaison Committee *v*. MEC for Education, KwaZulu-Natal 2013 (4) SA 262 (CC)
Law Society of South Africa *v*. President of the Republic of South Africa 2019 (3) SA 30 (CC)
Minister of Defence and Military Veterans *v*. Motau 2014 (5) SA 69 (CC)
Minister of Health *v*. New Clicks South Africa (Pty) Ltd 2006 (2) SA 311 (CC)
Minister of Justice and Constitutional Development *v*. Southern Africa Litigation Centre 2016 (3) SA 317 (SCA)
Minister of Law and Order *v*. Hurley 1986 (3) SA 568 (A)
Mohlomi *v*. Minister of Defence 1997 (1) SA 124 (CC)
Ndlwana *v*. Hofmeyr 1937 AD 229
Offit Enterprises (Pty) Ltd *v*. Coega Development Corporation 2010 (4) SA 242 (SCA)
Oos-Kaapse Administrasieraad *v*. Rikhoto 1983 (3) SA 595 (A)
Oudekraal Estates (Pty) Ltd *v*. City of Cape Town 2004 (6) SA 222 (SCA)
Pepcor Retirement Fund *v*. Financial Services Board 2003 (6) SA 38 (SCA)
Pharmaceutical Manufacturers Association of SA: In re Ex parte President of the Republic of South Africa 2000 (2) SA 674 (CC)
President of the Republic of South Africa *v*. South African Rugby Football Union 2000 (1) SA 1 (CC)
Pretoria City Council *v*. Modimola 1966 (3) SA 250 (A)
Pretorius *v*. Transport Pension Fund (2018) 39 Industrial Law Journal 1937 (CC)
Sachs *v*. Dönges NO 1950 (2) SA 265 (A)
Shidiack *v*. Union Government (Minister of the Interior) 1912 AD 642
Southern Africa Litigation Centre *v*. Minister of Justice and Constitutional Development 2015 (5) SA 1 (GP)
Staatspresident *v*. United Democratic Front 1988 (4) SA 830 (A)
State Information Technology Agency Soc Ltd *v*. Gijima Holdings (Pty) Ltd [2015] ZAGPPHC 1079 (18 May 2015)
State Information Technology Agency Soc Ltd *v*. Gijima Holdings (Pty) Ltd 2017 (2) SA 63 (SCA)
State Information Technology Agency Soc Ltd *v*. Gijima Holdings (Pty) Ltd 2018 (2) SA 23 (CC)
Union Government (Minister of Lands) *v*. Estate Whittaker 1916 AD 194
Union Government (Minister of Mines and Industries) *v*. Union Steel Corporation (South Africa) Ltd 1928 AD 220
Van der Linde *v*. Calitz 1967 (2) SA 239 (A)
Walele *v*. City of Cape Town 2008 (6) SA 129 (CC)
Zondi *v*. MEC for Traditional and Local Government Affairs 2005 (3) SA 589 (CC)

SRI LANKA

Singarasa *v*. Attorney General SC SPL (LA) No 182/99 (2006)

UNITED KINGDOM

A *v.* Secretary of State for the Home Department [2005] 2 AC 68
Ahmed and Others *v.* HM Treasury [2010] UKSC 5, [2010] 2 AC 534
Airedale NHS Trust *v.* Bland [1993] AC 789
Anisminic Ltd *v.* Foreign Compensation Commission [1969] 2 AC 147 (HL)
Ashley *v.* Scottish Football Association [2016] CSOH 78
Assets Co Ltd *v.* Bain's Trustees (1904) 6 F 692
Associated Provincial Picture Houses Ltd *v.* Wednesbury Corporation [1948] 1 KB 223
Attorney-General of St Christopher, Nevis and Anguilla *v.* John Joseph Reynolds [1980] AC 637
AXA General Insurance Company Ltd *v.* Lord Advocate [2011] UKSC 46
B *v.* Auckland District Law Society (New Zealand) [2003] 2 AC 736
Bank Mellat *v.* Her Majesty's Treasury (No 2) [2013] UKSC 39; [2014] AC 700
Beggs *v.* Scottish Ministers, 2007 SLT 235
Belfast City Council *v.* Miss Behavin' Ltd [2007] UKHL 19, [2007] 1 WLR 1420
Board of Education *v.* Rice [1911] AC 179
Boddington *v.* British Transport Police [1999] 2 AC 143
Braganza *v.* BP Shipping Ltd [2015] UKSC 17
British Railways Board *v.* Glasgow Corporation, 1976 SC 224
Brown *v.* Hamilton District Council, 1983 SC (HL) 1
Bugdaycay *v.* Secretary of State for the Home Department [1987] AC 514 (HL)
Burnip *v.* Birmingham City Council [2013] PTSR 117
Bushell *v.* Environment Secretary [1981] AC 75
Calvin *v.* Carr [1980] AC 574 (PC)
Cardiffe Bridge case (1700) 1 Ld Raym 580
Case of Proclamations (1611) Co Rep 74
Champion *v.* Chief Constable of Gwent [1990] 1 WLR 1
Chundawadra *v.* Immigration Appeal Tribunal [1988] Imm AR 161
Cocks *v.* Thanet District Council [1983] 2 AC 286
Connor *v.* Strathclyde Regional Council, 1986 SLT 530
Cooper *v.* Booth (1785) 3 Esp 135
Cooper *v.* Wandsworth Board of Works (1863) 14 CB (NS) 180
Council of Civil Service Unions *v.* Minister for the Civil Service [1985] AC 374
Crédit Suisse *v.* Allerdale BC [1997] QB 306
Crocket *v.* Tantallon Golf Club, 2005 SLT 663
CWS *v.* Highland Council [2008] CSOH 28
D & J Nicol *v.* Dundee Harbour Trustees, 1915 SC (HL) 7
Dante *v.* Assessor for Ayr, 1922 SC 109
Davidson *v.* Scottish Ministers (No 1), 2006 SC (HL) 41
Davy *v.* Spelthorne Borough Council [1984] AC 262
De Freitas *v.* The Permanent Secretary of Ministry of Agriculture, Fisheries, Lands and Housing and Others (Antigua and Barbuda) [1998] UKPC 30, [1999] 1 AC 69 (PC)
Dominus Rex *v.* Randall (1795) 2 Salk 470
E *v.* Chief Constable of the Royal Ulster Constabulary [2009] 1 AC 536
E *v.* Secretary of State for the Home Department [2004] EWCA Civ 49, [2004] QB 1044, [2004] 2 WLR 1351

Earl of Kinnoull *v.* Presbytery of Auchterarder (1838) 16 S 661
Eba *v.* Advocate General for Scotland [2012] 1 AC 710
Edwards (Inspector of Taxes) *v.* Bairstow [1956] AC 14 (HL)
Entick *v.* Carrington [1765] EWHC KB J98
Estate and Trust Agencies *v.* Singapore Investment Trust [1937] AC 898
Evans *v.* Attorney-General [2015] UKSC 21
Falconer *v.* South Ayrshire Council, 2002 SLT 1033
Forbes *v.* Underwood (1886) 13 R 465
Ghaidan *v.* Godin-Mendoza [2004] UKHL 30, [2004] 2 AC 557
Gordon of Lougart *v.* Earl of Buchan (1499) Acts of the Lords of Council in Civil Causes, Vol 2 (1918), p 347
Graham *v.* Ladeside of Kilbirnie Bowling Club, 1990 SC 365
Gray *v.* Braid Logistics (UK) Ltd [2014] CSIH 81
Gunstone *v.* Scottish Women's Amateur Athletic Association, 1987 SLT 611
Hall and Co Ltd *v.* Shoreham-by-Sea Urban District Council [1964] 1 WLR 240
HM Treasury *v.* Ahmed [2010] UKSC 5
Holmes Oil Co Ltd *v.* Pumpherston Oil Co Ltd (1891) 18 R (HL) 52
Huang *v.* The Home Secretary [2007] UKHL 11
Ingle *v.* Ingle's Trustee, 1999 SLT 650
Inland Revenue Commissioners *v.* National Federation of Self-Employed and Small Businesses Ltd [1982] AC 617
Inter Inhabitan. King's Norton in Wigorn (1795) 2 Salk 481
Inter the Inhabitants of the Parish of Chittinston and Penhurst (1795) 2 Salk 475
JH Rayner (Mincing Lane) Ltd *v.* Department of Trade and Industry [1990] 2 AC 418
Jones (Caldwell) *v.* First Tier Tribunal [2013] 2 AC 48
Kennedy *v.* Charity Commission (Secretary of State for Justice intervening) [2014] UKSC 20, [2015] AC 455
Kennedy *v.* Information Commissioner [2014] UKSC 20, [2014] 2 WLR 808
The King *v.* The Commissioners of Sewers for Tower Hamlets (1830) 1 B & Ad 232
The King *v.* The Inhabitants of Denbigh (1804) 5 East 333
King *v.* The Justices of Essex (1816) 5 M & S 513
The King *v.* The Justices of the West Riding of Yorkshire (1834) 5 B & Ad 1003
The King *v.* The Trustees of the Cheshunt Turnpike Road (1833) 5 B & Ad 438
Khairandish *v.* Secretary of State for the Home Department 2003 SLT 1358
Kruse *v.* Johnson [1898] 2 QB 91
Liversidge *v.* Anderson [1942] AC 206
Lloyd *v.* McMahon [1987] AC 625
Lord Livingstone *v.* Lord Erskine (1482) Acts of the Lords of Council in Civil Causes, Vol 2 (1918), p ciii
Lord Prestongrange *v.* Justices of the Peace of Haddington, 1756 Mor 7350
Lumsdon & Ors, R (on the application of) *v.* Legal Services Board [2015] UKSC 41
M *v.* Law Society of Scotland [2013] CSOH 28
MacCormick *v.* Lord Advocate, 1953 SC 396
Mahon *v.* Air New Zealand Ltd [1984] AC 808 (PC)
Malloch *v.* Aberdeen Corporation, 1971 SC (HL) 85, [1971] 1 WLR 1578
McCawley *v.* R [1920] AC 619
McCue *v.* Glasgow City Council [2014] CSOH 124

McInnes *v.* Onslow-Fane [1978] 1 WLR 1520
McLaughlin *v.* Governor of the Cayman Islands [2007] UKPC 50
McMillan *v.* Free Church of Scotland (1861) 23 D 1314
Middleton *v.* Anderson (1842) 4 D 957
Mitchell *v.* Cable (1848) 10 D 1297
Moohan *v.* Lord Advocate [2014] UKSC 67
Mortimer *v.* Ogilvie (1497) Acts of the Lords of Council in Civil Causes, Vol 2 (1918), p 139
Moyna *v.* Secretary of State for Work and Pensions [2003] 1 WLR 1929
Naik *v.* University of Stirling, 1994 SLT 449
Nyali Ltd *v.* Attorney-General [1956] KB 1
O'Neill *v.* Scottish Joint Negotiating Committee for Teaching Staff, 1987 SC 90
O'Reilly *v.* Mackman [1983] 2 AC 237
Osborn *v.* Parole Board [2013] UKSC 61, [2014] AC 1115
Osmond *v.* Widdicombe (1818) 2 B & Ald 48
Padfield *v.* Minister of Agriculture, Fisheries and Food [1968] AC 997
Pearlman *v.* Keepers of Harrow School [1979] QB 56
Pham *v.* Secretary of State for the Home Department [2015] 1 WLR 1591
Prohibitions del Roy (1607) 12 Co Rep 63, [1607] EWHC KB J23, 77 ER 1432
PTOA Ltd *v.* Renfrew District Council, 1997 SLT 1112
R *v.* Cambridge Health Authority, ex p B [1995] 1 WLR 898
R *v.* Chief Constable of Sussex, ex parte International Trader's Ferry [1999] 2 AC 418
R *v.* Chief Immigration Officer, ex p Salamat Bibi [1976] 1 WLR 979
R *v.* Criminal Injuries Compensation Board ex parte A [1999] 2 AC 330
R *v.* Director of Public Prosecutions, ex p Kebilene [2000] 2 AC 326
R *v.* East Sussex County Council Ex Parte Reprotech (Pebsham) Ltd [2003] 1 WLR 348
R *v.* Environment Secretary, ex parte Hammersmith and Fulham London Borough Council [1991] 1 AC 521
R *v.* Fernandes (1980) WL 619001 (Court of Appeal)
R *v.* Gough [1993] AC 646
R *v.* Hillingdon London Borough Council, ex parte Royco Homes Ltd [1974] QB 720
R *v.* Home Secretary, ex parte Fayed [1998] 1 WLR 763
R *v.* Home Secretary ex p Khawaja [1984] AC 74
R *v.* Home Secretary, ex parte Pierson [1997] UKHL 37; [1998] AC 539
R *v.* Hull University Visitor, ex p Page [1993] AC 682
R *v.* Inland Revenue Commissioners, ex parte Preston [1985] 1 AC 835
R *v.* Inland Review Commissioners, ex parte The National Federation of Self-Employed and Small Business Ltd [1982] AC 617
R *v.* Investigatory Powers Tribunal, ex parte Privacy International [2018] 1 WLR 2572
R *v.* Justice of the Peace for Nottingham (1755) Sayer 216
R *v.* Lambert [2002] 2 AC 545
R *v.* Legal Aid Board, ex p Hughes (1992) 24 HLR 698 (July 1992)
R *v.* Liverpool Corporation ex parte Liverpool Taxi Fleet Operators Association [1972] 2 All ER 589, [1972] 2 QB 299 (CA)
R *v.* Lord Chancellor ex p Witham [1998] QB 575 (DC)
R *v.* Lord President of the Privy Council Ex p Page [1992] UKHL 12
R *v.* Lyons [2002] UKHL 44
R *v.* Medical Appeal Tribunal, ex p Gilmore [1957] EWCA Civ 1; [1957] QB 574

R (Nicklinson) *v.* Ministry of Justice [2015] AC 657
R (on the application of Cart) *v.* Upper Tribunal [2009] EWHC 3052 (Admin); [2010] 2 WLR 1012
R (on the application of Tekle) *v.* Secretary of State for the Home Department [2008] EWHC 3064
R (Privacy International) *v.* Investigatory Powers Tribunal [2017] EWCA Civ 1868, [2018] 1 WLR 2572
R (Privacy International) *v.* Investigatory Powers Tribunal [2019] UKSC 22
R (Public Law Project) *v.* Lord Chancellor [2016] UKSC 39, [2016] AC 1531
R (Quila) *v.* Home Secretary [2011] UKSC 45
R (Rotherham Metropolitan Borough Council) *v.* Secretary of State for Business, Innovation and Skills [2015] UKSC 6
R (SB) *v.* Governors of Denbigh High School [2006] UKHL 15, [2007] 1 AC 100
R (SG) *v.* Secretary of State for Work and Pensions [2015] 1 WLR 1449
R (Sinclair Collis Ltd) *v.* Secretary of State for Health [2012] QB 394
R (Unison) *v.* Lord Chancellor [2017] UKSC 51
R (Unison) *v.* Monitor [2009] EWHC 3221 (Admin), [2010] PTSR 1827
R (Yam) *v.* Central Criminal Court [2016] AC 771
Racal Communications Ltd, Re [1980] UKHL 5, [1981] AC 374
Rape Crisis Centre *v.* Secretary of State for the Home Department, 2000 SC 527
Raymond *v.* Honey [1983] 1 AC 1 (HL)
Re L [2003] 2 AC 633
Rederiaktiebolaget Amphitrite *v.* R [1921] 3 KB 500
Reid *v.* Walker (1826) 5 S 140
Rex *v.* Smith & Others Commissioners of Sewers (1670), 1 Modem Reports
Ridge *v.* Baldwin [1964] AC 40
Ridge *v.* Garlick (1818) 8 Taunt 424
Roy *v.* Kensington and Chelsea and Westminster Family Practitioner Committee [1992] 2 WLR 239
Russell *v.* Duke of Norfolk [1949] 1 All ER 109
Safeway Food Stores Ltd *v.* Scottish Provident Institution, 1989 SLT 131
Scottish Old People's Welfare Council, Petitioners, 1987 SLT 179
Secretary of State for Education and Science *v.* Tameside Metropolitan London Borough Council [1977] AC 1014
Smith *v.* East Elloe Rural District Council [1956] AC 736
Smith *v.* Nairn Golf Club [2007] CSOH 136
Somerville *v.* Scottish Ministers, 2007 SC 140
South East Asia Fire Bricks Sdn Bhd *v.* Non-Mettalic Mineral Products Manufacturing Employees Union and others [1980] UKPC 21; [1981] AC 363
St Johnstone Football Club Ltd *v.* Scottish Football Association Ltd, 1965 SLT 171
Tait *v.* Central Radio Taxis (Tollcross) Ltd, 1989 SC 4
Tehrani *v.* Argyll and Clyde Health Board (No 2), 1989 SC 342
Tesco Stores *v.* Secretary of State for the Environment [1995] 1 WLR 759
Tweed *v.* Parades Commission of Northern Ireland [2007] 1 AC 650
Watkins *v.* Secretary of State for the Home Department [2006] UKHL 17, [2006] 2 AC 395
West *v.* Secretary of State for Scotland, 1992 SC 385
Wheeler *v.* Leicester [1985] AC 1054

UNITED STATES

ZIMBABWE

Table of Legislation

AUSTRALIA

BANGLADESH

CANADA

EUROPEAN UNION

FIJI

GHANA

HONG KONG

Art 5
Art 24
Art 30
Art 35
Art 39
Art 54–56
Art 54
Art 60
Art 66–79
Art 81–82
Art 84
Art 158
Art 160
Annex I Art 2
Bill of Rights Ordinance (BORO)
s 11
Court of Final Appeal Ordinance
s 3
Interpretation and General Clauses Ordinance
s 3
Letters Patent and Royal Instructions to the Governor 1843
Marriage Ordinance
s 40

INDIA

Constitution 1949
Art 14
Art 19
Art 19(1)(g)
Art 21
Art 73
Art 51(c)
Government of India Act 1935
Pension Rules 1972
Right to Information Act 2005

INTERNATIONAL CONVENTIONS

American Convention on Human Rights
Art 4(2) and 4(4)
Convention against Torture and Other Cruel, Inhuman or Degrading Treatment or Punishment 1975 (CAT)
Art 3
Art 3(1)
European Convention on Human Rights (ECHR)
Art 6

IRELAND

ISRAEL

KENYA

NAMIBIA

NEW ZEALAND

PAKISTAN

SCOTLAND

SINGAPORE

SOUTH AFRICA

UGANDA

UNITED KINGDOM

UNITED STATES

ZIMBABWE

Abbreviations

AAT	Administrative Appeals Tribunal (Australia)
AD	Appellate Division (Bangladesh)
ADJR Act	Administrative Decisions (Judicial Review) Act (Australia)
AG	attorney-general
AJ	administrative judge (US)
AL	Awami League (Bangladesh)
ALJ	administrative law judge (US)
APA	Administrative Procedure Act 1946 (US)
ARC	Administrative Review Council (Australia)
BDRA	Births and Deaths Registration Act (Malaysia)
BORO	Bill of Rights Ordinance (Hong Kong)
CAT	Convention against Torture and Other Cruel, Inhuman or Degrading Treatment or Punishment, 1975
CFA	Court of Final Appeal (Hong Kong)
CFI	Court of First Instance (Hong Kong)
CG	caretaker government
CLTPA	Criminal Law (Temporary Provisions) Act (Singapore)
CPR	Civil Procedure Rules (UK)
CRC	Convention on the Rights of the Child
DG	director-general
ECHR	European Convention on Human Rights
ECtHR	European Court of Human Rights
EU	European Union
FAAA	Fair Administrative Action Act 2015 (Kenya)
FOIA	Freedom of Information Act 2000 (UK)
GATT	General Agreement on Tariffs and Trade
GNI	gross national income
HCD	High Court Division (Bangladesh)
HKSAR	Hong Kong Special Administrative Region, China
HRA	Human Rights Act 1998 (UK)
HRC	Human Rights Committee
ICCPR	International Covenant on Civil and Political Rights
ICESCR	International Covenant on Economic, Social and Cultural Rights
ISA	Internal Security Act

JAKIM	Jabatan Kemajuan Islam Malaysia (Islamic Development Department)
JAWI	Federal Territories Religious Department (Malaysia)
JP	Justice of the Peace
JSC	Judicial Service Commission (Kenya)
KADU	Kenya African Democratic Union
KANU	Kenya National African Union
MDA	Misuse of Drugs Act (Singapore)
MHA	Ministry of Home Affairs (Singapore)
MP	member of parliament
NGO	non-governmental organization
NRD	National Registry Department (Malaysia)
NZ	New Zealand
NZBORA	New Zealand Bill of Rights Act 1990
OECD	Organisation for Economic Co-operation and Development
PAJA	Promotion of Administrative Justice Act 3 of 2000 (South Africa)
PAP	People's Action Party (Singapore)
PAS	Parti Islam se-Malaysia
PIL	public interest litigation
POAS	Principal Officials Accountability System (Hong Kong)
PP	public prosecutor
PRC	People's Republic of China
QC	Queen's Counsel
ROC	Court of Session Rules (Scotland)
SIS	Sisters in Islam (Malaysia)
SJC	Supreme Judicial Council (Bangladesh)
SOE	state-owned enterprise
UDF	United Democratic Front (South Africa)
UDHR	Universal Declaration of Human Rights
UK	United Kingdom of Great Britain and Northern Ireland
UNECE	United Nations Economic Commission for Europe
UNHCR	United Nations High Commissioner for Refugees
US, USA	United States of America
USC	University of Southern California
VCAT	Victorian Civil and Administrative Tribunal (Australia)
VOC	*Vereenigde Geoctroyeerde Oost-Indische Compagnie* (Dutch East India Company)
WTO	World Trade Organization

PART I

Introduction

1

What's So Common about "Common Law" Approaches to Judicial Review?

Swati Jhaveri

1.1 INTRODUCTION

In the field of comparative public law, the focus has typically been on constitutional law.[1] A range of explanations can be offered for this imbalance. Primarily, there may be a concern that meaningful comparison may not be possible in the field of administrative law. Harlow and Rawlings observe that '[b]ehind every theory of administrative law there lies a theory of the state'.[2] Prospective comparativists might feel that there is too much variance in the make-up of different states for there to be a realistic prospect of comparison in systems of administrative law.[3] However, these objections persist even in the field of comparative constitutional law, manifesting, for example, as a concern that the parochially value-laden norms that make-up a particular jurisdictions' domestic constitutional law are not amenable to comparison or transfer.[4] Nonetheless, comparative constitutional law has been able to overcome these hurdles to thrive much more strongly as a field of study as is evident from the proliferation of research in the field.[5]

[1] The distinction between 'constitutional' and 'administrative' law is complex: see John Gardner, 'Can There Be a Written Constitution?' *Oxford Studies in Philosophy of Law* (Oxford University Press, 2011), chapter 5. There are various ways of formulating the distinction: constitutional as the macro context for the state's powers and administrative as the micro application of the macro; or administrative law as 'applied' or 'concretised' constitutional law. This chapter and the book take as 'administrative law' the norms and institutions that specifically check the executive arm based on common law norms, regulations, or statute (while broadly justified on meta-constitutional ideas like the rule of law or separation of powers).

[2] Carol Harlow and Richard Rawlings, *Law and Administration* (Cambridge University Press, 2009, 3rd edition), 1. See also Cheryl Saunders, 'Apples, Oranges and Comparative Administrative Law' 2006 Acta Juridica 423, 424, 426.

[3] John Ohnesorge, 'Administrative Law in East Asia: A Comparative Historical Analysis' in Susan Rose-Ackerman and Peter L Lindseth (eds.), *Comparative Administrative Law* (Edward Elgar 2011) 78 at 78–9; Janina Boughey, 'Administrative Law: The Next Frontier for Comparative Law' (2013) 62 *International and Comparative Law Quarterly* 55 at 61–62.

[4] Cheryl Saunders, 'The Use and Misuse of Comparative Constitutional Law' (2006) 13 *Indiana Journal of Global Legal Studies* 37.

[5] A further reason offered for the growth of comparative constitutional law as a field of study has been the growth and spread of constitutionalism and judicial review as a tool for the protection and advancement of constitutionalism. The corresponding administrative law 'product' (namely, (a) law as a tool for framing the way individuals and organisations test and challenge the legitimacy of the modern state outside of the electoral process and the constitution; (b) protecting citizens against an enlarged state and to provide checks on the accountability and competence of the state; and (c) most importantly, 'judicial review' as the primary mechanism for achieving these ends of the law) has not been the subject of such widespread export outside the common law. This is largely because of the larger role played by non-law frameworks and mechanisms (politics, internal bureaucratic accountability, civil society, etc.) in achieving these ends of 'administrative law'. The 'constitutionalism' product (at least the Anglo legal-liberal paradigm version of it) is said to be a more contained and adaptable product

This may be changing. There has been renewed interest in undertaking broad comparative administrative law studies across a wider range of jurisdictions on a wider range of issues.[6] The field has benefited from this renewed interest in understanding the design of different systems of administrative law and justice. However, the scope of comparison remains relatively narrow in the specific context of common law studies. This chapter analyses various existing comparative endeavours in the common law world, with a view to looking at how the field can progress further in its comparative work. It proposes that one area ripe for further study is to refine our understanding of 'common law' systems of administrative law. In current comparative studies, common law systems are typically identified as a family of systems that share a range of characteristics. Typically these characteristics include: a role for the ordinary courts in holding executive bodies to account; the nature of the court's role (review on the grounds of the 'legality' versus the 'merits' of a decision, with the latter being the preserve of the executive or administrative tribunals); grounds of judicial review that manifest this distinction between legality and merits-based review (jurisdictional error, procedural fairness, 'legality')[7]; the institutions outside of the courts used to achieve the ends of administrative law (tribunals, ombudsmen, independent anti-corruption commissions); the aims of administrative law (coalescing around broadly shared understandings of 'legitimacy', transparency, compliance with statutory frameworks for decision-making, 'fair' and inclusive decision-making processes that engage relevant stakeholders (civic, expert, political)); and a sense of how courts and political branches are supposed to interact in the overall administrative law industry (with different systems plotting themselves along different points of a spectrum in the balance of power between courts and the political branches). There will be differences of opinion on the optimal design of a common law system of administrative law but the designs will, in common, utilise these features.

The aim of this volume is to push back on the view that common law systems tend to coalesce around this group of concepts and ideas.[8] There is a significant amount of variance that it is necessary to explore and which only becomes apparent when specifically considered from the perspective of divergence. This volume specifically considers the issue of divergence by asking how far different common law jurisdictions have deviated from their original English law roots of administrative law. The contributors to this volume investigate the continued utilisation of English law across common law systems that traditionally imported,

capable of such widespread export. See, e.g., Ran Hirschl, *Comparative Matters: The Renaissance of Comparative Constitutional Law* (Oxford University Press 2014), especially chapter 5.

6 See, e.g., Tom Ginsburg and Albert H. Y. Chen, *Administrative Law and Governance in Asia* (Routledge 2009); Susan Rose-Ackerman and Peter L Lindseth (eds.), *Comparative Administrative Law* (Edward Elgar 2011 and 2017); John Bell, Mark Elliott, Jason N. E. Varuhas, and Philip Murray (eds.), *Public Law Adjudication in Common Law Systems: Process and Substance* (Hart Publishing 2016), and Mark Elliott, Jason N. E. Varuhas, and Shona Wilson Stark (eds.), *The Unity of Public Law: Doctrinal, Theoretical and Comparative Perspectives* (Hart Publishing 2018); Peter Cane, *Controlling Administrative Power: An Historical Comparison* (Cambridge University Press 2016); Boughey, above n 2; Hugh Corder, 'Comparing Administrative Justice across the Commonwealth: A First Scan' 2006 Acta Juridica 1; Peter Cane, Peter Lindseth, and Herwig Hoffman (eds.), *The Oxford Handbook of Comparative Administrative Law* (Oxford University Press, forthcoming).

7 On which, see S. Jhaveri, 'Revisiting Taxonomies and Truisms in Administrative Law in Singapore' (2019) *Singapore Journal of Legal Studies* 351–76.

8 A common observation in Peter Cane, 'Theory and Values in Public Law' in Paul Craig and Richard Rawlings (eds.), *Law and Administration in Europe: Essays for Carol Harlow* (Oxford: Oxford University Press 2003); Paul Daly, 'Administrative Law: A Values-Based Approach' in John Bell, Mark Elliott, Jason N. E. Varuhas, and Philip Murray (eds.), *Public Law Adjudication in Common Law Systems: Process and Substance* (Hart Publishing 2016), especially at 24–31; and Cheryl Saunders, 'Common Law Public Law: Comparative Reflections' in John Bell, Mark Elliott, Jason N. E. Varuhas, and Philip Murray (eds.), *Public Law Adjudication in Common Law Systems: Process and Substance* (Hart Publishing 2016) at 354.

or were modelled on, English law. The contributors consider the origins of English law within the jurisdiction (doctrines, concepts, structures, constitutional underpinnings); the range of adaptations made to English law and the autochthonous forces that influenced this adaptive process. The objective is to evaluate not just the continuing impact of the English law transplant in a multitude of common law jurisdictions, but also the broad range of causal factors and agents that influence the development of the common law. This conversation will be assisted with input from the perspective of a wide range of common law jurisdictions, including those outside the traditional focus of comparative administrative law in the common law world (outside Australia, New Zealand, England, US, and Canada to include South Africa, India, Singapore, Malaysia, Israel, Bangladesh, Scotland, Kenya, Republic of Ireland, and Hong Kong).

Such a conversation will help develop a much more refined and robust understanding of 'common law' administrative law that is not skewed towards an understanding coming out of the usual jurisdictions of comparison, especially for the benefit of 'newer' common law jurisdictions which are undergoing a more nascent development of administrative law and looking for inspiration on modes of development. It will also provide a more refined definition of 'common law' approaches to judicial review for studies cutting across the common law and civil law divide, which have until now tended to be driven by a 'unitary' or narrow understanding of 'common law' systems as a, more or less, unified group of systems with certain shared characteristics.[9] This chapter first engages with these restrictions in existing studies. It then moves on to look at specific questions that may be used to explore the degree of difference and diversity in approaches to judicial review in the common law world. The chapter concludes that multiple categories of common law systems are apparent once common law systems are studied from the perspective of divergence. While common law systems may share a common vocabulary, there is greater variance and nuance in the approach to judicial review that needs to be appreciated. The conclusion maps out a possible typology of common law systems.

1.2 LIMITATIONS OF EXISTING COMPARATIVE ADMINISTRATIVE LAW STUDIES ACROSS THE COMMON LAW WORLD

This section outlines four existing major 'centres' for comparative administrative law in the common law world. It highlights what may be gained by these studies, but also the significant gaps.

1.2.1 *Comparative Studies of Common Law Systems*

Hugh Corder organised a comparative administrative law workshop motivated by the need to develop post-apartheid South African administrative law and to 'examine trends in administrative law, compare problems and solutions, learn from each other and develop a collaborative agenda for the future'.[10] This was one of the first major studies on the nature of common law administrative law since the work of Dicey[11] and

9 See, for example, Rose-Ackerman and Lindseth, above n 6, chapter 1.

10 Saunders, above n 3, 424.

11 Albert Venn Dicey, *An Introduction to the Study of the Law of the Constitution* (Macmillan Press 1959, 10th edition). Dicey's focus is to use English 'administrative law' (or rather the absence thereof) to critique administrative law of France.

Goodnow.[12] There was broad coverage from across the Commonwealth, with parts of Africa and the Caribbean being the only omissions.[13] The comparative work stretched across five broad areas: (a) a broad outline of the powers and modes of accountability of the executive within each system; (b) the impact of 'administrative justice' on the working of democratic government within the systems;[14] (c) access to judicial review (whether through setting boundaries of reviewability or rules of standing); (d) the scope of judicial review (including discussions of review versus appeal and bearing in mind the growth in administrative tribunals engaging in merits review); and (e) analysis of the grounds of review, including codified grounds.[15]

In a reflective piece on the contributions to the workshop, Cheryl Saunders acknowledged the concern that comparison is inhibited in administrative law by the difficulties of understanding other systems at the level of their institutional and political set-up and against their particular socio-economic and political backgrounds.[16] However, Saunders also observed that unlike comparison across legal families as is the case in the European Union and across cultural families (African, Asian, Islamic, European, or Western), comparison across the Commonwealth is less inhibited through the use of a shared legal language (including concepts, principles and procedures) with broadly shared understandings on these matters as a matter of historical development and theory. While there are such shared similarities, Saunders also celebrates the plurality of the commonwealth systems that make comparison nonetheless fascinating or of interest to comparative lawyers and this is possible because of the broad geographical spread of Commonwealth systems.[17] Divergence is also apparent in the historical conditions that influenced the development of administrative law, once it was received from, its parent jurisdiction to the home jurisdiction.[18] However, despite these observations, Corder's own conclusion from the study was that there still exists a substantial degree of overlap in the contours of administrative law in the various national systems, despite their independence from the English legal system for a generally significant period of time. All systems appear to adopt varying degrees of judicial review that are expanded or contracted flexibly by courts in response to political conditions (such as the health of democracy and performance legitimacy on the part of the legislature and executive). This could be the result of an increasing use of precedent from other jurisdictions across the Commonwealth.[19] While an ambitious study in its comparative approach, the work did not continue. This is where Section 1.3 of this chapter picks up and proposes continuing comparative work across the common law world, as will be further discussed in the following section. In particular, Section 1.3 seeks to interrogate this view of overall convergence.

A second centre of study has been the work of Susan Rose-Ackerman and Peter Lindseth's. The aims of their study are twofold: to encourage research across jurisdictions and to stimulate research across disciplines in the comparative endeavour (most notably economics, law, and political science).[20] The former is ambitious in stretching across comparative divides (common law versus civil law; regional versus domestic systems).

12 Frank Goodnow, *Comparative Administrative Law: An Analysis of the Administrative Systems, National and Local, of the United States, England, France and Germany* (G. P. Putnam's Sons 1893).

13 Corder, above n 6, 5.

14 Corder, above n 6, 2.

15 Corder, above n 6, 7–8.

16 Saunders, above n 3, 424, 426.

17 Saunders, above n 3, 427–8.

18 Ibid.

19 Corder, above n 6, 8.

20 Rose-Ackerman and Lindseth, above n 6. See also Peter Cane, Peter Lindseth, and Herwig Hofmann (eds.), *Oxford Handbook of Comparative Administrative Law* (Oxford University Press, 2019).

The contributors are drawn from a broad range of jurisdictions: Europe (East and West); East Asia (China, Japan, South Korea, and Taiwan), the major jurisdictions in Africa; South Africa; South America; North America (extending to Mexico); and Canada. They identify a number of comparative topics for investigation, bearing in mind their preference for an inter-disciplinary approach to study: (a) administrative law's historical development across continental and Anglo-American traditions, and Eastern and Western systems; (b) the interplay and interaction between constitutional texts and structures and administrative law (acknowledging that this may not give a complete picture of administrative justice in a system given the largely invisible constitutional identity of the administrative state); (c) the issue of administrative independence and administrative law and particularly the tension between the design and structure of modern administration (its use of independent agencies and bureaucracy-level organs of decision-making) and traditional democratic sources of legitimacy via elections; (d) the issue of control over policy content and choices as well as participation in policy-making (contrasting the approach under the Administrative Procedure Act in the US with that in common law systems where there is little *legal control* versus political input on policy choices); (e) the issue of caution or deference when exercising control via administrative law[21]; (f) the role of the judiciary in reviewing policy-making activities, recognising that a key concern in designing the judicial role is the tension between achieving the ends of justice and facilitating administration[22]; (g) the boundaries of the state and the distinction between public and private law and the specific challenges posed to the task of drawing this boundary as a result of privatisation and contracting out of traditionally state-run government tasks;[23] and (h) the boundaries of the state in the context of transnational regulatory bodies which have regulatory authority within a state but originate outside of the state (such as the EU, WTO, and GATT).

The breadth of their comparative enterprise is prompted by observations on the growing complexity of the work of the state and government policy-making, the growth of the regulatory state (and the resultant growth in political mechanisms of rule-making and accountability), and the increasing fragmentation of the work of the state domestically (between public and private spheres) and between domestic and transitional realms, in a way that means law cannot avoid confronting politics. They intentionally adopt a 'broad conception' of the field to facilitate a rich exchange across jurisdictions and disciplines.[24]

However, a real concern here is that, in its ambition for geographical breadth and interdisciplinarity, it is perhaps over-broad. This is apparent from a consideration of the chapters in the volumes coming out of the conference. Few chapters in the volume breach the divide between common law and civil law or between disciplinary methods of study.[25] Without this inter-linking between the chapters – either jurisdictionally or from a disciplinary perspective – it is difficult to extract themes or trends or understand how discussions in certain jurisdictional contexts or certain categories of legal system are illuminating of others. The collection, therefore, provides an excellent array of comparators but without a yardstick to draw the various comparators together.

21 Susan Rose-Ackerman and Peter L Lindseth, 'Comparative Administrative Law: Outlining a Field of Study' 28 *Windsor Yearbook of Access to Justice* 435 (2010) at 442.

22 Rose-Ackerman, above n 21, 444.

23 Rose-Ackerman, above n 21, 445.

24 Rose-Ackerman, above n 21, 448–9.

25 One exception being, for example, Paul Craig's chapter in the 2nd edition in 2017: looking at judicial review in Canada, England, the US, and the EU ('Judicial Review on Questions of Law: A Comparative Perspective').

A third centre of comparative study across common law systems comes out of the series of thematically oriented biennial conferences organised by the Centre for Public Law at the University of Cambridge. Introduced in 2012, the conferences aimed at bringing together common lawyers from a range of jurisdictions.[26] Each biennial conference focused on a central theme. The first explored the divide between process and substance and, in particular, the way in which distinctions between the two sound in public law adjudication across common law systems. Authors sought to address this from a theoretical perspective (including, for example, whether administrative law can be gathered around certain substantive[27] or procedural[28] ideals or values) and more doctrinal approaches (looking at different grounds of judicial review).[29] The second conference considered the theme of the 'unity' (or otherwise) of public law. The volume included contributions engaging with the theme again from both a doctrinal and theoretical perspectives.[30] Chapters considered the possibility of identifying an overarching framework for public law, with others tackling the need to recognise plurality in the field of public law. A number of chapters analysed the idea of unity more topically, considering the possibility of identifying taxonomies for standing, proportionality, human rights, and remedies. While the programme of the Conference indicated some consideration of systems beyond domestic common law systems to look at the work of regional, subnational, and international bodies, the focus was squarely on the former.[31] Indeed while ambitious in scope, the resulting volume of papers published from the two conferences focused on England, Australia, Canada, US and New Zealand.

As noted by Saunders in reflecting on the most recent volume, broadening the comparative base beyond these key jurisdictions would 'introduce a more complex set of variables into the endeavour to understand the current state of common law public law: more diverse constitutional settings; other mixed legal systems; new social, economic, political and cultural conditions. … [T]here is a case for being more ambitious, in terms of both jurisdictions and the range of issues covered.'[32] Feldman further reflects in the volume that '[t]here is a superficial similarity between the structures of judicial review in England and Wales, Scotland, Canada, Australia and other parts of the world which came under the sway of English common law. They share concepts such as jurisdictional error, natural justice and unreasonableness. On the other hand, there is a difference between concepts, which are general, and conceptions, which are a particular … system's articulation or instantiation of the concept.'[33] These comments point to broadening the base for comparison to add complexity to the concepts, pushing past superficial similarities. This is the ambition of this volume.

[26] John Bell, Mark Elliott, Jason N. E. Varuhas, and Philip Murray, 'Introduction' in John Bell et al., above n 6 at p1.

[27] Daly, above n 7.

[28] Jerry L. Mashaw, 'Public Reason and Administrative Legitimacy' and Jason N. E. Varuhas, 'The Public Interest Conception of Public Law: Its Procedural Origins and Substantive Implications' in Bell et al., above n 6.

[29] For example, Philip Murray, 'Process, Substance and the History of Error of Law Review' and Alan Robertson, 'Is Judicial Review Qualitative' in John Bell, Mark Elliott, Jason N. E. Varuhas, and Philip Murray (eds.), *Public Law Adjudication in Common Law Systems: Process and Substance* (Hart Publishing 2016).

[30] Elliott et al., above n 6.

[31] https://resources.law.cam.ac.uk/public_law_conference/PLC_full_programme_2016.pdf (last accessed 19 October 2017).

[32] See Saunders, above n 7 at 354, 364–5.

[33] David Feldman, 'Comparison, Realism and Theory in Public Law' in John Bell, Mark Elliott, Jason N. E. Varuhas, and Philip Murray (eds.), *Public Law Adjudication in Common Law Systems: Process and Substance* (Hart Publishing 2016) at 374.

A fourth centre of study is the recent work of Peter Cane. In *Controlling Administrative Power: An Historical Comparison*,[34] Cane compares the administrative justice systems of the US (at the federal level), Australia (also at the federal level), and England and Wales. In doing so, Cane reverses his usual starting point ('providing an account of administrative law as a normative framework for public administration') to consider 'the idea of public administration as the institutional framework or context of administrative law'.[35] Cane posits that similarities and differences between 'control regimes' (i.e., institutions, norms and practices concerned with controlling public administrative power) are partly explained by similarities and differences in 'systems of government' (i.e., institutions, norms and practices concerned with the allocation and distribution of public power, including administrative power). Cane does not purport to offer a prescriptive tool of how things ought to be or even a causal tool to demonstrate that if 'x' conditions exist, then 'y' system will exist in a particular jurisdiction. Rather, his own claim is to provide a tool that can be used to describe and understand particular set-ups with a jurisdiction.[36] Cane identifies particular aspects of the control regimes within those jurisdictions to undertake the comparative work – not to achieve a comprehensive coverage of the system – but rather because those aspects present especially pronounced forums for understanding points of similarity and difference that can help illuminate the relationship between control regimes and systems of government that Cane is interested in studying.

Cane's schema has two metrics for comparing administrative justice systems. First, the system of government (there being two identifiable models of distributing power: diffusion and concentration[37]). Second, the kind of control regimes (there being two kinds of regimes: 'checks and balances' based and 'accountability' based). With respect to systems of government, 'diffusion' refers to the division of power between various institutions, giving each one a share in the exercise of power. Concentration, on the other hand, involves a more complete division of power between institutions whereby each one then exercises power unilaterally without the need for consent or action on the part of any other institution (although not without being accountable to the others). In studying control regimes, Cane looks at political, legal, and bureaucratic controls of administrative power. In his words, '[p]olitical control is concerned with the policy objectives and outcomes of administration; legal control addresses the question of whether or not administration is being conducted in accordance with law; and the concerns of bureaucratic control may be summarised in the classic "three Es" of public auditing (economy, efficiency and effectiveness), and process values such as fairness, consistency and responsiveness'.[38] With respect to control regimes, the typical regime for diffusion-based systems is, Cane observes, a horizontal, mostly prospective, multipolar system of 'checks-and-balances' among and between other power sharers checking the other in terms of progress and on the exercise of their power. Contrastingly, with concentration-based systems, control is typically through a vertical, bipolar and largely, retrospective form of 'accountability'. Cane's thesis is thus that there is an interrelationship between the two metrics – whether a system of government is based on a diffusion or concentration of power is determinative of whether the control regime will be one based on the idea of 'checks-

34 Cane, above n 6.

35 Cane, above n 6, xiii.

36 Cane, above n 6, p 6 fn 15.

37 Cane, above n 6 at 6. Cane here departs from his own use of the separation of powers as a normative tool of analysis in comparison in an earlier work: Peter Cane, *Administrative Tribunals and Adjudication* (Hart Publishing 2010).

38 Cane, above n 6, at 147.

and-balances' or 'accountability'. A few caveats apply: Cane himself acknowledges that these are not watertight categories. Therefore, for example, any system of government may contain elements of both diffusion and concentration of power. As Cane puts it, '[t]he two constitutional techniques are better envisaged as two coordinates of a field in which various systems of government can be located according to the particular combinations of the two techniques that they display'.[39]

Cane describes his approach in various ways: (a) 'structural' in its approach to comparison (looking at the structure of systems of government and control regimes)[40] versus comparative on the basis of 'normative preferences and cultural and ideological values ... constitutional and political values, and cultural and intellectual trends'[41]; (b) 'descriptive and explanatory, not evaluative';[42] (c) one that is focused not on administrative law as the vantage point but on public administration as the relevant vantage point;[43] 'historical institutionalism'[44] with the 'methodological assumption [being] that every system is a unique product of its history ... the value of the historical approach lies partly in its capacity to reveal how deeply embedded in society and culture ("path-dependent" or "sticky") certain governmental characteristics can become over long periods of time';[45] (d) 'formal-legalist ... comparative, historical and inductive';[46] and (e) 'formalist and realist'[47] in its focus on both the formal aspects of institutions and systems and the actual practical operation of those institutions.

Cane's comparative methodology is applied to what he calls '*sufficiently similar*' yet '*sufficiently different*' systems: namely, federal US, federal Australia, and England.[48] The similarity in question is their membership of the common law family of legal systems with a shared heritage that has impacted on the development of their contemporary systems of government and corresponding control regimes. A further similarity is a shared political environment of '*two-party competition rather than multi-party consensus*'.[49] The sufficient differences between the three jurisdictions come from their constitutional modes of distributing power: variances in whether they adopt a diffusion or concentration model with the US system apparently being strongly diffusive and the English system being highly concentrated and the Australian a hybrid of the two (in Cane's view). From this starting point, Cane proceeds to analyse a number of features of the control regimes of the three jurisdictions: judicial control of statutory interpretation, judicial review of fact-finding and policy-making; administrative rule-making; administrative adjudication; private law controls such as tort and contract law; and freedom of information within government and between the government and the public. In Cane's own words, his hypothesis about the connections between systems of government (diffusion versus concentration of power) and control regimes (checks-and-balances versus accountability) do not necessarily explain the make-up of all of the features. For example, the relationship does not bear out in the context of freedom of information

39 Cane, above n 6, 6.
40 Cane, above n 6, 2.
41 Cane, above n 6, 11.
42 Cane, above n 6, 6, 18.
43 Cane, above n 6, xiii.
44 Cane, above n 6, 13, 507.
45 Cane, above n 6, p 12, fn 26, 19. See also at 510.
46 Cane, above n 6, 14, 507.
47 Cane, above n 6, 15.
48 Cane, above n 6, 13, following the approach suggested in comparative constitutionalism (see Ran Hirschl on 'the "most similar cases" logic':'The Question of Case Selection in Comparative Constitutional Law' (2005) 53 *American Journal of Comparative Law* 125, 133–9).
49 Cane, above n 6, 13.

between government and the public where the three jurisdictions are quite similar despite their different systems of government.[50] As with the Cambridge forum, Cane's comparative study is a significant advance in the field, especially from a methodological perspective and its coverage of all aspects of a system of administrative justice. However, given its comparative base of the standard catchment of jurisdictions (Australia, UK, and US), it needs to be built on and tested across a broader range of systems.

1.2.2 *Conclusion*

This volume picks up on the specific issue of breadth across the common law world in the studies conducted thus far. It takes as its aim the need to interrogate the use of 'common law' as a description of a family of administrative law systems (to contrast such systems with, for example, 'civil law' systems).[51] Even when comparing across such common law systems, academics highlight in the above studies that there is a degree of assumed 'doctrinal and institutional similarity' based on an adherence to 'the essentials of the common law' with a shared language and the use of similar legal concepts.[52] This volume starts with the opposing assumption: that despite such a shared heritage and similarity, there is much diversity in common law systems that is worth exploring for a richer understanding of the plurality of 'common law administrative law'. Section 1.3 broadens the comparative base from the studies considered above, looking in particular at how doctrine and ideas of administrative law from English law have been treated on its export to and import by a number of systems.

There are several points to note about the proposed methodology of the volume. First, it is impossible to survey all of the common law jurisdictions in a single study.[53] The focus, therefore, is on comprehensive *variance* versus comprehensiveness per se in the coverage of common law jurisdictions. The chapter looks at a spread across Asian versus non-Asian jurisdictions; mixed legal systems versus 'pure' common law systems; Westminster versus non-Westminster constitutional systems; relatively recently decolonised systems versus long-standing decolonised systems. Converse to the problem of not going too far into the common law world is the usual methodological concern in comparative studies of selecting systems that, while different, have enough in common to allow meaningful comparison. It is for this reason that the jurisdictions studied have been selected on the basis that they are all systems that have inherited or modelled judicial review on English administrative law with a study of their journey from that inception point. The systems selected as 'common law' are on the basis that they have received the system of common law precedent; judicial decision-making as a source of law; the way in which the courts and the executive engage and interact with each other (with a general shared understanding of barriers to the courts' role, for example, in the review of the merits or content of decision-making) and a sense of what legitimacy (as judged through judicial review) involves (compliance with legislation and/or concepts grounded in the rule of law). It is the variance in the use of these concepts that is the subject of study.

50 Cane, above n 6, 22.

51 Mark Van Hoecke and Mark Warrington, 'Legal Cultures, Legal Paradigms and Legal Doctrine: Towards a New Model for Comparative Law' (1998) 47 *International and Comparative Law Quarterly* 495.

52 Saunders, above n 3, 427.

53 As to these systems, see: http://saint-claire.org/wp-content/uploads/2016/01/Legal-Systems-of-the-World.pdf (last accessed 11 October 2017).

Second, to ensure coherence across the study, the chapters use the same yardstick question for comparison: namely, the continuing use of English law principles of judicial review. The paper takes as 'English grounds of judicial review' the original and classic grounds,[54] as well as evolutions in those grounds (including, for example, proportionality and the doctrine of substantive legitimate expectations). So temporally, English law is taken holistically to mean past, present positions as received and adopted and then abandoned or indigenised in the various systems. Some of the jurisdictions studied have tracked the 'classic' grounds of review (illegality, irrationality, and procedural fairness) from *GCHQ* much more closely but not the subsequent developments in English law (instead, devising their own alternative grounds of review). Other jurisdictions have referred to those concepts (e.g., 'reasonableness') but without the same conscious adoption of structure and content of those 'classic' grounds or subsequent developments.

Third, the comparative focus is on the grounds of review used by courts to judicially review executive action under statute. This could be criticised for being a narrow focus for a comparative 'administrative law' study in not extending to broader aspects of the administrative justice system.[55] A lot can be gleaned from looking at the balance struck between the different tools of accountability in different jurisdictions. The precise design of a system of administrative justice can be viewed as a product of the trade-offs made by a system in electing to balance the system in a particular way between the different models of administrative decision-making. The scope of judicial review is an important vantage point for understanding these trade-offs in different jurisdictions. The ambition of this project lies in its comparative base rather than its coverage of system-wide issues across each jurisdiction.

1.3 TOPICS FOR COMPARISON ACROSS COMMON LAW SYSTEMS

This section proposes multiple metrics that can be used to help understand the degree of divergence and departure from English law in different common law systems' approach to judicial review.[56] Our understanding of these issues needs to be refined across a broader base of systems to better understand the diversity of approaches to judicial review inherent in common law systems of administrative law.

1.3.1 *Relationship between 'the C(c)onstitution' and Administrative Law*

There are several issues explored on this theme in the various chapters. First, the precise constitutional principles that inform a particular system's approach to administrative law are now more varied between different common law jurisdictions. Second, there are points of difference in the extent to which constitutional law norms and values fertilise administrative law (and, in particular, the impact of human rights norms) in the different jurisdictions. Third, the advent of the constitutional entrenchment of judicial review in a written constitution has also had an impact on the content and operation of common law administrative law principles.

54 *Council of Civil Service Unions* v. *Minister for the Civil Service* [1985] AC 374 at pp. 407–13 (namely, illegality, irrationality, and procedural impropriety).

55 Even the definition of 'judicial review' is increasingly pluralising: for example, Richard Rawlings, 'Modelling Judicial Review' 61 (2008) *Current Legal Problems* 95.

56 The chapters in the volume discuss these in more detail.

1.3.1.1 Constitutional Foundations of Administrative Law

The impact of Dicey on English administrative law is well-documented.[57] Dicey's emphasis on parliamentary sovereignty and the rule of law (equality of all before the law) explains many of the restraints built into the English approach to judicial review that the courts have gradually eroded over time. This includes, for example, the struggle with tribunals as a separate and specialised system of administrative justice (versus the use of the ordinary courts),[58] the application of the private law of contract to government contracts,[59] and the extent of substantive review permitted on the part of courts.[60] However, the Diceyan heritage does not explain the development of administrative law across the breadth of common law systems. As further explained in Sections 1.3.2 and 1.3.3 in the following section, contrasting emphases on other constitutional principles, involving the separation of powers and the thicker values embodied in the rule of law (including democratic values of participation and accountability), point to other directions in the development of administrative law. Thus, a first step to contrasting common law systems will be to consider the constitutional backbone of administrative law within that system. And secondary to this, it will be necessary to consider whether it promotes the expansion or contraction of administrative law (versus politics) in promoting and achieving good governance.

A specific jurisdictional context that provides a suitable forum for analysing this issue is Australia, which, as Groves and Weeks argue in their chapter, has seen a growing influence of the Australian Constitution (versus legislative intent and the related principle of legality) as a tool for deciding on the scope of judicial review. This has been prompted, to a large extent, by the entrenchment of the right to judicial review in the Australian Constitution. This raises the question of what the new foundation for judicial review is in Australia: the ultra vires doctrine, the rule of law, or some other constitutional principles (founded in ideas of 'abuse of power').[61] This increased attention to the constitutional foundations of judicial review take place against the backdrop of an earlier effort at codifying judicial review via statute (the Administrative Decisions (Judicial Review) Act 1977). The move from placing judicial review from the common law to a statutory footing (subject to parliamentary amendment and interpretation by reference to parliamentary intent) and then to a constitutionally entrenched position has led to multiple changes in the nature of administrative justice in Australia over time, prompting these broader constitutional conversations. This further provokes a consideration of whether this stronger foundation for judicial review through entrenchment necessarily means more judicial review, or whether the separation of powers which also runs through the Australian constitutional landscape places brakes on any advances in the scope of review arising from the entrenchment of judicial review.[62]

Interestingly, while the above debate may be considered one between the 'usual suspects' of broad meta-constitutional ideas (rule of law, parliamentary sovereignty, and the separation

[57] See, for example, Harry W. Arthurs, 'Rethinking Administrative Law: A Slightly Dicey Business' *Osgoode Hall Law Journal* 17(1) (1979), 1.

[58] Cane, above n 37, section 5 in particular.

[59] Boughey, above n 2.

[60] Mark Aronson, 'The Growth of Substantive Review: The Changes, Their Causes and Their Consequences' in John Bell, Mark Elliott, Jason N. E. Varuhas, and Philip Murray (eds.), *Public Law Adjudication in Common Law Systems: Process and Substance* (Hart Publishing 2016).

[61] See Christopher Forsyth (ed.), *Judicial Review and the Constitution* (Hart Publishing 2000), chapters 1, 2, and 5 in particular.

[62] See Hon Stephen Gageler, 'The Constitutional Dimension' in Matthew Groves (ed.), *Modern Administrative Law in Australia: Concepts and Context* (Cambridge University Press 2014).

of powers), debates have also started to shift to the constitutionally subcutaneous realm in some jurisdictions. This is especially in the context of the recognition of newer grounds of judicial review (like the doctrine of substantive legitimate expectations), as is considered in the chapter on Hong Kong. These more contemporary conversations have started to engage broader ideas of trust and promise-keeping as ideals of good governance. These are virtues of governance that may be borne out of broad constitutional ideals or values of a system relating to accountability and governance, but are more specific in nature and not always referenced back to constitutional ideas.[63]

1.3.1.2 Variance in the Influences on Administrative Law

The academic discussions on the impact of constitutional law norms on administrative law has been primarily focused on the impact of human rights norms found in written constitutions and constitutional instruments. For example, South Africa's constitution has a written framework for the protection of socio-economic rights that provide additional grounds of review for the invalidation of government action.[64] In other systems, courts have argued that rights listed in legislation or constitutions are relevant considerations that an administrative body is bound to take into account, and a failure to do so amounts to a reviewable error of law.[65]

The Israeli context provides a possibly broader view of the impact of rights on administrative law, outside of the usual conversations on proportionality and substantive review. The chapter on Israel engages with these issues. In 1992 two 'basic laws' were enacted to further the protection of human rights as part of the gradual progression towards the enactment of a formal constitution. This was also, however, highly influential on administrative law. Most notably, and perhaps in a way unique to Israel within the common law universe, the basic laws are *generative* of duties – imposing a general and positive duty on administrative authorities to exercise powers to advance the protection of rights. The basic laws are also generative of a duty of fairness and efficiency: the precise contours of which are the subject of incremental extension.[66] This could be a result of a broadening comparative basis in Israeli administrative law, with courts looking to European jurisdictions (like Germany) and the US for inspiration.

1.3.1.3 Impact of Constitutional Entrenchment on Administrative Law

Unlike the English legal system, which has no written constitution, a number of other common law systems have entrenched and constitutionalised administrative law through their written constitution.[67] This includes jurisdictions like Australia and South Africa and provides an interesting contrast with non-entrenched systems, where administrative law could

63 See Matthew Groves and Greg Weeks (eds.), *Legitimate Expectations in the Common Law World* (Hart Publishing 2016), chapters 1 and 7.

64 Melanie Murcott, 'The Role of Administrative Law in Enforcing Socio-Economic Rights: Revisiting Joseph' *South African Journal on Human Rights* 29(3) (2013), 481–95.

65 E.g., *Tavita* v. *Minister of Immigration* [1994] 2 NZLR 257 (NZCA).

66 The Basic Laws, while legislation, were given constitutional status by the Israeli Supreme Court – *HCJ 6821/93 United Mizrachi Bank Ltd* v. *Migdal Cooperative Village* 49(4) PD 221; *Misrachi Bank* v. *Migdal* (Gal Amendment) – translated extracts with commentary in (1997) 31 *Israel Law Review* 754.

67 See also Boughey, above n 2 at 68–9, 77.

arguably be more at the mercy of political forces or legislative erosion (through, e.g., ouster clauses).

Within the various entrenched systems, there is a further comparative question on the impact of entrenchment on the scope and operation of administrative law and the utilisation of English law to develop administrative law. This is considered in the chapters on Hong Kong, Ireland, Kenya, and South Africa. For example, in South Africa, in 1994 a right to lawful, reasonable, and procedurally fair administrative action was included in Section 24 of the Interim Constitution, followed by a similar provision in Section 33 of the current 1996 Constitution. This was to strengthen judicial review against political erosion. The constitutionalisation of judicial review arguably gave it a new and stronger constitutional justification. The Section 33 entrenchment was actualised through more detailed legislation via the Promotion of Administrative Justice Act 3 of 2000 (PAJA). PAJA includes an all-encompassing list of grounds of review, with considerable scope for substantive review.[68] While a strong step towards realising the constitutional entrenchment of judicial review, the barriers to its flourishing have been the technical aspects of the legislation. This includes barriers to access to judicial review under PAJA (e.g., it only applies to 'administrative' action, which raises difficult questions about what this may include). A further question that remains is whether the PAJA grounds of review will influence and impact the development of the common law grounds of review, which continue to apply where PAJA does not.[69] This discussion thus raises the general theme of the continuing relevance of the common law where there has been some constitutionalisation or codification of administrative law.[70] The chapter on Ireland makes the argument that the constitutionalisation of Irish law gave judges the confidence to strike out and depart from settled English principles, most notably in the area of substantive review. The chapter on Kenya similarly discusses the emboldening of judges: this time, to enforce constitutional principles of leadership and integrity. Finally, in England, too, there has been something of an awakening to the notion that the constitutional foundation of judicial review may be shifting away from the narrowly conceived *ultra vires* doctrine to one that locates constitutional principles in the common law, marking the advent of 'UK constitutionalism on the march' as Lady Hale described it, referencing the renewed emphasis on using the common law principle of legality as a basis for judicial review.[71]

Aside from formal entrenchment, the provisions of the written constitution have been utilised by some jurisdictions to ground administrative law, more generally. As is considered on the chapter in India, the Supreme Court has used a multitude of provisions to legally justify judicial review. This includes constitutional provisions such as Article 73, which sets out the general scope of executive powers,[72] and/or the fundamental rights provisions, especially, Article 14 (on equality). The latter has been used to extrapolate 'arbitrariness' as an all-encompassing ground and standard of review for the review of executive decision-making, even beyond the specific equality context.[73] The precise scope and impact of this on the common law grounds of review is unclear in the cases, and the authors of the chapter on

68 Section 6(2)(i) of the Promotion of Administrative Justice Act is the most broad, allowing review where 'the action is otherwise unconstitutional or unlawful'.

69 See also *Bato Star Fishing (Pty) Ltd* v. *Minister of Environmental Affairs* (2004)(4) SA 490, 504 per O'Regan J.

70 Ibid.

71 Lady Hale, 'UK Constitutionalism on the March', *Constitutional and Administrative Law Bar Association Conference*, 12 July 2014.

72 *M/S Sharma Transport Rep. By Shri D.P.Sharma* v. *Government Of A.P. & Ors*. AIR 2002 SC 322, 2002 2 SCC 188.

73 *The State of Andhra Pradesh and another, etc* v. *Nalla Raja Reddy and others, Etc* AIR 1967 SC 1458, 1967 AIR Supreme Court 1458, A.I.R. 1960 Mad. 543, [1968] 1 MLJ 6.

India argue that there is a pressing need to clarify the inter-relationship between the Constitution and common law for reasons relating to access to justice. The 'constitutionalisation' of administrative justice in the Indian context has led to a crowded and over-burdened constitutional docket before the courts, with significant delays in the resolution of cases. The re-invigoration of the common law grounds of judicial review will allow applicants to utilise the court's ordinary jurisdiction through the lower courts to resolve state-citizen disputes, alleviating the burden on the constitutional writ jurisdiction.

1.3.2 *Suspicion of Executive Power*

Judicial review of executive action has been 'the most striking feature of the development of the common law'.[74] The rise of such review, despite Dicey's reservations, could be seen as a response to Parliament's inability to supervise acts of the executive with the rise of party-based politics that coincided with a general growth in the regulatory state (and thus powers of the executive). The suspicion of executive power, however, varies across jurisdictions. Within some systems, there is a lower acceptance of bad governance by citizens, and citizens utilise the courts to undertake more intense and involved review.[75] However, in other systems, like Singapore, courts have traditionally been reluctant to engage in strong judicial review – largely on the basis of a perceived democratic and performance legitimacy on the part of the state.[76] This can also be explained on the basis that Singapore has always placed an emphasis on collective versus individual interests and the need to resolve dispute through consultation and consensus.[77] As the chapter on Singapore discusses, even though the courts in Singapore have recently stepped up the degree of review (incrementally and gradually), this is not because of any perceived decrease in the legitimacy of the state or quality of governance, but because of a perceived need on the part of the courts to contribute, as a 'co-equal' participant, its unique institutional perspective on matters of governance and accountability.[78]

1.3.3 *Balance between Courts and the Executive*

The equilibrium point between the courts and the executive, and the tools used to strike this balance, will clearly vary across jurisdictions. These include a range of legal doctrines relating to the grounds of review (demarcation of non-justiciable areas of decision-making, developed concepts of 'deference', distinction between reviewing the 'legality' versus the 'merits' of a decision, the permissible scope of substantive review), rules of access to judicial review (restricting scope of locus standi to exclude public interest cases that may draw the courts into the political arena, rules governing the enforcement of ouster clauses in legislation), and through the scope of remedies. In the routine comparative analyses between the 'usual suspect' jurisdictions, the balance is typically reduced to one between two constitutional imperatives: the rule of law (which calls for accountability) and the separation of powers (with an emphasis on the 'separation' of powers versus the need for checks and balances).[79]

74 *Mahon* v. *Air New Zealand Ltd* [1984] AC 808 (PC) at 816.

75 Saunders, above n 3, 443.

76 Thomas W. Merrill, 'The Origins of American-style Judicial Review' in Susan Rose-Ackerman and Peter L. Lindseth (eds.), *Comparative Administrative Law* (Edward Elgar 2010), chapter 23.

77 *Shared Values White Paper*, Cmmd 1 of 1991, Singapore Parliament at para 52.

78 See also Swati Jhaveri, 'Localising Administrative Law in Singapore: Embracing Inter-Branch Equality' (2017) 29SAcLJ 828.

79 *Dunsmuir* v. *New Brunswick* [2008] 1 SCR 190 at [27].

However, casting the net wider to other common law jurisdictions indicates that the balance may be attributable to a broader range of facts. One further factor includes the use of the courts to achieve developmental ends for a particular jurisdiction, on the back of state failure to achieve these same ends. The courts are used instrumentally and as proxies for political arms of government in the face of systemic inaction and/or incompetence by those organs. For example, as the chapter on India demonstrates, the Supreme Court of India is largely seen as an active court in response to a perceived failure on the part of the State to effectively provide for the socio-economic developmental needs of its citizens.[80] The Supreme Court views *itself* (versus the political branches) as a 'social transformer, sentinel of democracy ... protector of the market economy'.[81] The Court's strong form review extends not just to quashing executive decisions or policies. Remedially, it also frequently involves the issue of directive declaratory remedies and structural injunctions that prescribe what the political branches need to do in order to meet standards of good governance. The Court has appropriated a large amount of political space through these remedies.[82]

This use of judicial review as a tool for broader change mirrors the experience discussed in the chapter on Bangladesh, which looks at how courts have similarly made use of directive and structured remedies to achieve systemic political change. The Supreme Court of Bangladesh, in the landmark case of *Secretary, Minister of Finance* v. *Masdar Hossain*,[83] issued significantly expansive directive remedies to mandate the establishment of a judicial services commission that would eventually lead to the separation of the lower courts from the executive (something which had raised serious separation of power concerns up until then in the transition of Bangladesh to a democratic system of government). In doing so, the Supreme Court consciously utilised law and precedent from the region (particularly, India) rather than English law. As the author argues, this was a move towards 'decolonising' administrative law and its content in Bangladesh.

In Hong Kong, the problematic and stunted post-colonial transition to democratic rule means a general lack of democratic legitimacy on the part of the executive. The courts have sought to enhance procedural and participatory rules of administrative law in judicial review to plug this gap, pending broader democratic reform and the establishment of a more representative executive arm of government. The courts have been used as tools for legislative and policy-based reform in a broad range of areas including education, town planning, environmental protection, and political reform.[84] In order to do so, the courts have had to sometimes take stronger positions than are available in contemporary English administrative law.

80 Sujit Choudhry, Madhav Khosla, and Pratap Bhanu Mehta, 'Locating Indian Constitutionalism' in Sujit Choudhry et al. (eds.), *The Oxford Handbook of Indian Constitutional Law* (Oxford University Press 2016) at p 10.

81 Chintan Chandrachud, 'Constitutional Interpretation' in Sujit Choudhry et al. (eds.), *The Oxford Handbook on the Indian Constitution* (Oxford University Press 2016) at 86. See also Po Jen Yap, 'New Democracies and Novel Remedies' *Public Law* (January 2017), pp. 30–45, who refers to the 'managerial' or 'catalytic' position of the Supreme Court.

82 See Yap, above n 81.

83 *Secretary, Ministry of Finance* v. *Masdar Hossain* (1999) 52 DLR (AD) 82.

84 See generally Swati Jhaveri, 'Reconstitutionalising Politics in the Hong Kong SAR' (2017) *Asian Journal of Comparative Law* 1–31; Swati Jhaveri and Anne Scully-Hill, 'Executive and Legislative Reactions to Judicial Declarations of Constitutional Invalidity in Hong Kong: Engagement, Acceptance or Avoidance?' (2015) 13 *International Journal of Constitutional Law* 2, 507–29.

1.3.4 *Scope of Substantive Review by Courts*

Common law systems emphasise, in common, the need for courts to maintain a distance from the substance of an executive decision. While all systems maintain this view, the boundaries of substantive review will be drawn differently. Any analysis of this involves considering a family of judicial doctrines and tools used to delineate when and how much the courts can review the substance of a decision: deference, justiciability, varying standards or intensity of review, proportionality, and fact-law distinctions. It is in this context that the constitutional tussle between courts and the executive can be the most acute. Broadening the range of jurisdictional responses to substantive review will provide a more refined understanding of the operation of these tools, in particular on the extent to which more robust tools for substantive review necessarily translate into more positive outcomes for applicants in judicial review proceedings.

Substantive review of executive decision-making has been the subject of significant advancements in the English context, largely influenced by the enactment of the Human Rights Act. It is fair to say that this statutory rights regime has had, in the words of Lord Bingham, a 'persuasive and pervasive' influence on English judicial review, both in mandating a strong interpretive presumption of statutory compatibility and the application of proportionality – a concept once thought foreign and heretical to the common law judge in England.[85] Other jurisdictions, with equally strong, human rights instruments, have experienced similar, if not more far-reaching developments in substantive review. For example, the constitutional and political setup in Hong Kong does not necessarily restrict the development and evolution of substantive review in the same way as it does in the English context (the former is a system of constitutional versus parliamentary supremacy post-Handover, which has had a liberating effect on the courts). Hong Kong courts have demonstrated a greater degree of comfort with more involved forms of substantive review through varying standards of irrationality review, proportionality review for administrative acts (which in the English context only happened as a result of a HRA prompt), and the doctrine of substantive legitimate expectations (with the Court of Final Appeal of Hong Kong being the first apex appellate court to recognise the doctrine in the common law world).[86] The Hong Kong courts have also expanded the scope of substantive review through the use of concepts of 'fairness' (previously restricted to just procedural fairness) and the doctrine of substantive legitimate expectations.[87] However, there can sometimes be a sharp distinction between the strong rhetoric of these substantive grounds of review and the actual utilisation of them to quash executive decisions.

This can be contrasted with New Zealand, where the courts have been reluctant to adopt some of the advances on substantive review seen in the English context (notably heightened irrationality review, proportionality, substantive legitimate expectations, and review for errors of fact). In addition, the courts have not utilised Section 6 of the New Zealand Bill of Rights 1990 in as interventionist manner as its parallel, Section 3 of the Human Rights Act 1996, in

85 *R* v. *Lyons* [2002] UKHL 44, at [13] (Lord Bingham).

86 See Swati Jhaveri et al., *Hong Kong Administrative Law* (LexisNexis 2013, 2nd edition), Chapters 9–12.

87 See Swati Jhaveri, 'Transforming 'Fairness' as a Ground of Judicial Review in Hong Kong'; (2013 May) 11 *International Journal of Constitutional Law* 2; Swati Jhaveri 'Contrasting Responses to the "Coughlan" Moment: Legitimate Expectations in Hong Kong and Singapore' in Matthew Groves and Greg Weeks (eds.), *Legitimate Expectations in the Common Law World* (Hart Publishing 2017), 267–92.

the English context. Similarly, in Singapore, the courts, in adopting a predominantly green-light approach to judicial review have been reluctant to expand substantive review.[88] As discussed above, the courts in India have been willing to breach the legality-merits divide in order to provide remedial responses to widespread and systemic administrative failure.

1.3.5 *Impact of Multiple Legal Orders on Administrative Law*

A further issue apparent on the broadening of the sample group of common law jurisdictions is the impact of parallel or separate legal orders within a system. These sites of clash, or conversely, augmentation between the multiple legal orders can help provide an understanding of how the common law is moulded to accommodate the relevant legal principles of such parallel legal orders within a jurisdiction.

One example is the interplay between Syariah law (a formal source of law in Malaysia) and administrative law discussed in the chapter on Malaysia. Cases like *Lina Joy* v. *The Federal Territory Islamic Council & Ors*[89] exemplify one possible influence. In that case, the court held that the requirement by the National Registration Department for the applicant to obtain an apostasy certificate from the Syariah authorities before deleting the entry of Islam in her identity card (following her conversion to Christianity) was 'lawful' and 'reasonable', despite the absence of any specific legislative guidelines permitting such a requirement. The content of the common law administrative law principles (principle of legality and reasonableness) were read in a way that accommodated the special position of Syariah law in the Constitution of Malaysia. The majority's approach can be contrasted with the dissenting judgment: Justice Richard Malanjum recognised the special constitutional position of Syariah law but was unable to hold that this mandated the modification of the content and application of the common law grounds of review. He accordingly held that the National Registration Department's policy of requiring apostasy certificates, in singling out Muslims for additional procedural hurdles, was 'Wednesbury unreasonable'; the Department had acted 'illegally' in misconstruing the Regulations as permitting them to make such a request in line with Syariah law; had considered irrelevant considerations (namely, whether the applicant had 'properly converted'); had acted 'irrationally' in abnegating its discretionary power to an outside religious body; and had failed to give her a fair hearing. Syariah law, in this way, exerts an influence at these clash sites, while not really impacting on the remainder of administrative law. The chapter on Malaysia looks at how this may be changing in more recent cases.

Another context for considering the interplay of common law and 'indigenous' legal systems is dealt with in the chapter on New Zealand. The place of the Treaty of Waitangi in New Zealand's constitutional arrangements continues to be a complex legal and political issue. Recent cases highlight the possibility of utilising the Treaty as a tool of legislative interpretation: where courts should presume that Parliament intends to legislate consistently with the principles of the Treaty.[90] There would be a restraint on the power of New Zealand's executive under such presumptively interpreted legislation. This question will be the subject of ongoing refinement, especially with the relatively recent establishment of the Supreme Court of New Zealand in 2004. Section 3(1)(a)(ii) of the Supreme Court Act 2003 states that

88 Daniel Tan, 'An Analysis of Substantive Review in Singaporean Administrative Law' (2013) 25 *SAcLJ* 296; See Jhaveri, above n 79.

89 [2007] 3 AMR 693.

90 *New Zealand Maori Council* v. *Attorney-General* [2013] NZSC 6, [2013] NZLR 31.

one of the Act's purposes is 'to enable important legal matters, including legal matters relating to the Treaty of Waitangi, to be resolved with an understanding of New Zealand conditions, history, and traditions'. Influence is also apparent from sources outside of the domestic legal system: most notably, international law. The traditional strict dualist approach to international law in the English context is adopted to varying degrees in the remainder of the common law world (e.g., New Zealand[91] and Israel).[92] The different directions in which international law-infused common law principles may develop therefore needs to be calibrated across these jurisdictions.

1.3.6 *Style of Judicial Reasoning*

In the English context, courts have demonstrated different ways of reasoning through their decisions on the availability and scope of judicial review. Different 'waves' or trends are apparent over time.[93] First, there was a focus on categories of decisions and whether they are susceptible to review and on what grounds (e.g., natural justice principles only extended to 'adjudicative' bodies; the distinction between jurisdictional versus non-jurisdictional errors with the latter being non-reviewable; the use of the 'source' test to determine whether a body was 'public' and therefore susceptible to judicial review). A second wave involved abandoning this categorical approach to the question of reviewability and the related opening up of the grounds of review,[94] liberalising rules on standing[95] and opening up review to a wider range of decision-making bodies.[96] A third wave of cases sees the influence of the Human Rights Act on administrative law, most notably on substantive review in administrative law (shown by a more general embrace of reasonableness as a malleable ground of review to achieve constitutional goals of the rule of law and accountability). A fourth wave sees a growth and expansion in review to more areas of the merits of decision-making outside of the HRA context.[97] This is the subject of discussion in the chapter by Christopher Forsyth, who argues that the abandonment of a principled mode of reasoning more recently in English jurisprudence has impacted on its exportability across the commonwealth. This can be contrasted with the historical position, discussed in Paul Craig's chapter, where the nature and development of English administrative law made it aptly suitable for export and transplant.

91 Alice Osman, 'Demanding Attention: The Roles of Unincorporated International Instruments in Judicial Reasoning' (2014) 12 *New Zealand Journal of Public and International Law* 345.

92 Domestic jurisdictions are also increasingly broadening the comparative base of common law jurisdictions to enhance domestic administrative law: Margit Cohn, 'Pure or Mixed? The Evolution of Three Grounds of Judicial Review of the Administration in British and Israeli Administrative Law', *European Journal of Comparative Law & Governance* (2013) 1.

93 These are not sequential waves – they may co-exist or occur in tandem but touch on different areas of restriction in review.

94 *Ridge* v. *Baldwin* [1964] AC 40 (natural justice/procedural fairness); *Anisminic* v. *Foreign Compensation Commission* [1969] 2 AC 147 (errors of law); *Padfield* v. *Minister for Agriculture, Fisheries and Food* [1968] AC 997 (subjective/discretionary powers).

95 *R* v. *Inland Review Commissioners, ex parte The National Federation of Self-Employed and Small Business Ltd* [1982] AC 617.

96 See, e.g., *R* v. *Panel on Takeovers and Mergers, ex parte Datafin plc* [1987] QB 815.

97 See, e.g., *Upper Cart* v. *Tribunal* [2011] UKSC 28; *Keyu* v. *Secretary of State for Foreign and Commonwealth Affairs & Anor* [2015] UKSC 69 and *Pham* v. *Secretary of State for the Home Department* [2015] 1 WLR 1591 (on the application of proportionality review more broadly in administrative law outside of the Human Rights Act 1998 and the European context).

The different modes of judicial reasoning or judicial posturing either have not been adopted elsewhere or jurisdictions are at different stages of 'progression'[98] along these waves. For example, Singapore remains at the cusp of the second wave of review, as does Australia: both jurisdictions are only just on the brink of opening up the previous categories or classifications that existed to restrict and ring fence judicial review's reach.[99]

Canada, on the other hand, while opening up beyond the second wave has followed a different track – for its subsequent stage of development. It has preferred a structured, almost formulaic approach to determine questions of the scope of review, especially in the context of substantive review.[100] The most authoritative statement on the structure of substantive judicial review in Canada comes from *Dunsmuir* v. *New Brunswick*.[101] It creates a two-step test for deciding on the approach standard of substantive review (correctness and reasonableness). The first step involves examining past cases to see if the court has authoritatively determined the applicable standard of review for any particular category of case. If the case does not fall into any of these categories of cases, then the courts will undertake an analysis of a range of factors to help identify the applicable standard of review. This includes the existence of ouster or preclusion clauses (which is a strong indication of reasonableness review; i.e., democracy-based); whether the decision is one of fact, discretion or policy where deference will apply 'automatically'; i.e., expertise-based); and whether a tribunal or decision maker is interpreting 'its own statute or statutes closely connected to its function, with which it will have particular familiarity' (i.e., expertise-based), where reasonableness will generally be used.[102] Despite the court's formulaic style of judicial reasoning to decide this difficult question and its effort to propose a streamlined two-step methodology, debates following *Dunsmuir* demonstrate the lack of clarity and coherence in the workings of the methodology. Several questions persist. Is the first stage – involving surveying settled jurisprudence on the applicable standard of review to a particular category of decision or decision-maker – determinative? Do the factors identified by the courts displace previous categories? How are previous categories to be revisited? These issues are considered in the chapter on Canada. Studying the different styles of judicial reasoning or methodologies to deal with difficult questions on the scope of review can provide a broader menu of approaches that can be borrowed or used to evaluate a particular jurisdiction's approach.

1.4 CONCLUSION: CREATING A TYPOLOGY OF COMMON LAW SYSTEMS

Based on the above overview of the kinds of issues this volume will explore, it is possible to start to map out a typology of common law systems based on how they position themselves on the above issues. At least five such subcategories are apparent:

(a) Modified Westminster systems. These are systems that, while highly referential of concepts and doctrines from English administrative law, have tweaked the law with different degrees of retention of 'Diceyan' distinctions (law versus merits; degree of embrace of substantive review; degree of distinctiveness in dealing with, e.g., private

98 'Progression' here is used to highlight which wave/stage a jurisdiction is at versus a comment on the desirability of adopting the particular judicial approach to review of that stage.

99 Jhaveri, above n 79, and Tan, above n 91.

100 The position on procedural fairness is more settled: see Gus Van Harten et al., *Administrative Law: Cases, Texts and Materials* (Emond Publishing 2015, 7th edition), part II, generally.

101 [2008] 1 SCR 190. See also *Canada (Citizenship and Immigration)* v. *Khosa* [2009] 1 SCR 339 at 50.

102 *Dunsmuir* v. *New Brunswick* [2008] 1 SCR 190 at [27], [48], [49], [50]–[59].

law issues involving public bodies; balance struck between courts and the executive). They also differ in whether they adopt these distinctions for 'red-light' or 'green-light' reasons.[103]

(b) Constitutionalised systems. These are systems where judicial review is on a stronger and more visible/written constitutional footing, where the latter informs the scope of judicial review significantly. Jurisdictions like South Africa, India, Kenya, Ireland, and Australia fall into this category. These jurisdictions deal with additional issues relating to the overlap/conflicts between any such constitutionalisation or codification and the common law – which impact on the scope of cases that come before the courts and the grounds utilised at common law.

(c) 'Multi-layered' legal systems. These are jurisdictions where the common law co-exists with other systems (Syariah, indigenous, international law) or where there is a stronger influence from international law through a monist approach or a soft(ening) and thin(ning) dualist approach to international law. There is then the question of how much the separate system fertilizes the common law (with thick or thin influences being apparent across these jurisdictions). Malaysia and New Zealand are examples of these systems.

(d) Systems influenced by systemic 'transition' or development issues. These are jurisdictions where the common law is under pressure to be a tool to assist in transitional or development deficiencies in the broader system of governance. Jurisdictions in this category include Bangladesh, Kenya, India, and Hong Kong.

(e) A possible fifth category is apparent if we consider the US. This creates a further class of common law systems: non-derivative common law systems. As argued in Peter Cane's chapter, the 'common law' found in the US is different in nature: while the style of judicial reasoning follows the common law tradition or style of reasoning and the outcome of adjudicative processes in the courts are binding sources of law, there are differences in the framework of administrative law (governed largely by the Administrative Procedure Act and agency autonomy over interpretation via the *Chevron* doctrine). American administrative law, while using overlapping conceptual vocabulary on occasion (deference, reasonableness), has not tracked or tethered itself to English administrative law for content. It sits apart.[104]

This is just one proposal for possible subcategories as is the subject of exploration in the concluding chapter by Margit Cohn. There are a number of questions that will need to be explored in future studies. Two such questions are immediately apparent. First, there is a degree of porosity between the categories where certain jurisdictions can be classified under multiple headings. For example, India can be considered part of categories (b) and (d). Similarly, Hong Kong could be categorised under (a) or (d). A second issue is the need to further stratify the categories. For example, with the 'Westminster' inspired systems (category (a)), Singapore differs vastly from other systems in its conservative green light approach to judicial review generally. Similarly, in the context of 'constitutionalised' systems, there is a difference in the extent to which this has indeed led to a greater intensity in judicial review. (South Africa and the broader base for judicial review through socio-economic rights that impact on the breadth of values that inform administrative law can be contrasted with

[103] See Harlow and Rawlings, above n 3, chapter 1.

[104] See Adrian Vermeule, 'Our Schmittian Administrative Law' (2009) 122 *Harv. L. Rev.* 1095 and Paul P. Craig, 'The Legitimacy of US Administrative Law and the Foundations of English Administrative Law: Setting the Historical Record Straight' (on file with author).

Australia, where there is an absence of a bill of rights to provide a counter-weight to separation of powers concerns.) These issues will need to be worked through further. The above is just a start at subclassifying common law systems. This is the ambition of the volume: to expose the diversity of common law systems by illuminating the multi-event, multi-author, and multi-causal nature of the development of common law administrative law in a broader catchment of common law systems than has been studied to date.

PART II

Origins and Adaptations of Judicial Review in England

2

English Administrative Law History: Perception and Reality

Paul Craig

2.1 INTRODUCTION

The history of administrative law remains to be written. It is a task of considerable magnitude, given that it requires understanding of case law, regulatory legislation, government and politics spanning a period of circa 450 years. The task is more especially daunting given the range of different areas that were subject to governmental regulation broadly construed. It is, therefore, unsurprising that the intellectual task has not been fulfilled. This has not, however, translated into a dearth of opinion as to English administrative law history. To the contrary, as will be seen in the following section, there are views in this regard, and some are strongly held. There is, as in any intellectual endeavour, the danger of an inverse relationship between the strength of a person's conviction and the depth of their knowledge.

This chapter is not a history of English administrative law, since that would, as noted, require a book in itself. It does, however, offer a lens through which to view two different conceptions of that history, which are termed perception and reality. These terms are admittedly tendentious, in the sense that they convey, by their very semantic meaning, my view as to the more accurate picture of administrative law as it developed over time. There is, however, nothing special in the use of language in this regard, since those who adhere to the opposite position deploy language that is equally tendentious.

The discussion in this chapter is part of the larger study concerning the export and reception of administrative law in other common law jurisdictions. The effect of the disjunction between perception and reality on such export is interesting. The causation is contestable and does not necessarily always pull in the same direction. Thus, perception of administrative law as being relatively modern may have hampered its development elsewhere, and at the same time encouraged other jurisdictions to feel freer in adapting its precepts to local circumstance.

The essence of the argument presented over the following pages is as follows. The commonly held view about English administrative law is that it is of recent origin, some dating it from the mid-twentieth century, some venturing back to the late nineteenth century. This view, when unpacked, is premised on assumptions concerning doctrinal case law and regulation. There is an empirical and a normative foundation underlying both assumptions. This 'intellectual package' constitutes the commonly accepted picture of administrative law as it unfolded in England. This, then, is the perception, grounded in four central constructs concerning case law and regulation, viewed from an empirical and normative perspective. It is set out in the first part of the chapter.

The discussion thereafter is concerned with what I term the reality. It mirrors the discourse concerning perception, insofar as it considers case law and regulation from both an empirical and normative perspective. It will be argued that the commonly held view does not cohere empirically with reality concerning case law or regulation, and that the normative assumptions underlying the perceived view do not square with the general approach of the legislature or the courts during the foundational period of administrative law, which runs from the mid-sixteenth century onwards, with earlier origins. This disjunction between perception and reality could have had an impact on the ultimate exportability of English administrative law. The chapter concludes with a sketch of the implications for comparative study of other jurisdictions. These implications are the subject of discussion in the remaining chapters of the volume.

2.2 PERCEPTION: FOUR CENTRAL CONSTRUCTS

2.2.1 *Judicial Review Doctrine*

2.2.1.1 Empirical Dimension

The empirical dimension that underpins the common perception of administrative law history is grounded in assumptions concerning the case law. Put briefly, these are as follows: there was simply not much case law in quantitative terms; the doctrinal reach of this jurisprudence was limited, in the sense that it embraced only very limited forms of judicial oversight; and that it had little effect, as judged from the perspective of the individual litigant and in terms of its impact on the way in which government was conducted. These themes are evident in the secondary literature.

They provided the factual foundation for Dicey's account of the rule of law and the contrast that he drew between France and the UK. For Dicey, the very words 'administrative law', which he took to be the most natural rendering of the French *droit administratif*, 'are unknown to English judges and counsel, and are in themselves hardly intelligible without explanation'.[1] This absence of language was, said Dicey, significant: 'the want of a name arises at bottom from our non-recognition of the thing itself', such that in England the 'system of administrative law and the principles on which it rests are in truth unknown'.[2] The reasoning underlying the Diceyan account thereafter is well-known, insofar as it was predicated on suppositions as to how *droit administratif* functioned in France. The principal characteristic was said to be that the individual was treated disadvantageously because of the specially privileged position of the state, and its officials, with disputes settled by a different set of rules than those that pertained as between private citizens and adjudicated independently of the ordinary courts. The flawed nature of this account has been oft-related[3] and will not be repeated here.[4]

1 AV Dicey, *The Law of the Constitution*, J Allison (ed.) (Oxford University Press, 2013) p. 235.

2 Dicey (n 1) 235.

3 See, e.g., A Mestre, 'Droit Administratif' (1929) 3 *CLJ* 24; M Letourneur and CJ Hamson, 'The Control of Discretionary Executive Powers in France' (1952) 11 *CLJ* 258; P Weil, 'The Strength and Weakness of French Administrative Law' (1965) 26 *CLJ* 242; M Lewans, 'Rethinking the Diceyan Dialectic' (2008) 58 *UTLJ* 75.

4 For an instructive accounts of what underpinned Dicey's reasoning, and changes thereto, see M Walters, 'Public Law and Ordinary Legal Method: Revisiting Dicey's Approach to *Droit Administratif*' (2016) 66 *UTLJ* 53; M Walters, *A.V. Dicey and the Common Law Constitutional Tradition: A Legal Turn of Mind* (Cambridge University Press, 2020) ch. 11.

The salient point for present purposes is, however, the descriptive foundation for the asseveration that there was nothing that could be termed administrative law in the UK. Dicey, drawing on the definition of *droit administratif*, conceptualized the subject as being concerned with the liabilities of state officials, the rights and liabilities of private individuals in their dealings with government officials, and the procedure through which these should be enforced.[5] The Diceyan legacy, to the effect that there was no administrative law in England, was thus grounded on the assumption that we had no analogous body of law dealing with such issues[6] and found forceful expression in the statement that there was no recognition of the concept itself.

This was, moreover, how the reasoning was viewed by later generations, including, possibly, those importing or influenced by the principles of English administrative law in developing their own administrative law doctrine. This defective reading of the French system, combined with ignorance of the domestic jurisprudence, cast a long shadow over administrative law in the UK, and it is likely that it negatively influenced recognition of the subject in other common law jurisdictions. UK scholars recognized Dicey's mistaken characterization of the French system, but the view that administrative law only existed as a discrete body of law from the mid-twentieth century proved far more resilient.

It found voice in Mitchell's writings. He was, by way of contrast to Dicey, very positive about the French regime, and disparaged the UK for having no system of administrative law. For Mitchell, the causes of this malaise were eclectic, including the absence of separate public law courts. The principal rationale was, however, that 'we have no system of public law because reliance upon parliamentary redress (a reliance fostered both by the growth of Parliament and the reticence of the courts) has made development of such a system impossible'.[7] The consequences, for Mitchell, were a very narrow conception of what the subject might be about, this being confined to tribunals and delegated legislation, principles of judicial review that were unduly narrow and the absence of any conception of public contracts.

The idea that administrative law is a recent development is central to Varuhas's account.[8] He contends that, by way of contrast to private law, recognition of administrative law was very late in coming, only gaining acceptance in the second half of the twentieth century. For Varuhas, this was in part because of the Diceyan objection to any special body of rules dealing with government and, in part, because of the absence of a systematic text explicating the dimensions of the subject. He acknowledges that public officials were subject to legal regulation, through tort actions and the prerogative writs. However, Varuhas regards tort actions as indicative of reliance on private law to regulate public power and hence as reinforcing the difficulty in conceptualizing administrative law as a discrete subject, and he argues that although the prerogative writs operated as a control on public power, they were not 'generally recognized, collectively, as comprising a discrete field of public or administrative law until at least the middle of the twentieth century'.[9]

5 Dicey (n 1) 237.

6 This was more especially surprising, given that Dicey had a significant practice at the Bar, where he argued a number of public law cases involving, inter alia, mandamus; Walters, *Dicey* (n 4).

7 JDB Mitchell, 'The Causes and Effects of the Absence of a System of Public Law in the United Kingdom' [1965] *PL* 95, 104. See also JDB Mitchell, 'The Constitutional Implications of Judicial Control of the Administration in the Nineteenth Century' (1967) 26 *CLJ* 46 and 'The State of Public Law in the United Kingdom' (1966) 15 *ICLQ* 133.

8 Jason Varuhas, 'Taxonomy and Public Law', in M Elliott, J Varuhas and S Wilson Stark (eds.), *The Unity of Public Law? Doctrinal, Theoretical and Comparative Perspectives* (Hart Publishing, 2018) pp. 39, 41–4.

9 Varuhas (n 8) 42.

Cane's analysis speaks to similar themes concerning the limited role played by the English courts.[10] He depicts the courts as a 'subordinate judiciary', betokening the idea that they are 'marginal actors in the system of government and subordinate agents of the sovereign legislature in relation to which their main function is to interpret and apply statute law'.[11] While the courts have more recently adopted, or been accorded, a greater constitutional role, they 'were marginalized post the Glorious Revolution'.[12]

The preceding views are premised on contestable assumptions concerning a plethora of issues, including the body of primary case law that existed, its effect and the relationship between primary materials and secondary literature in the recognition of a legal subject. These issues will be considered in due course, but the focus now turns to the normative assumptions underlying the commonly accepted historical picture of judicial review.

2.2.1.2 The Normative Dimension

It would be impossible within the scope of this chapter to convey the plethora of different conceptions of public law within the existing literature. Nor is this the purpose of the present inquiry. It is the nature of these debates that is apposite here. The feature that predominates is contestation concerning visions of administrative law, between those who are said to conceive administration to be dangerous, such that it should be carefully confined and controlled through administrative law, and those who regard administration in a more positive light, as the vehicle for delivery of valuable social policy, with the consequence that the focus of administrative law should be to facilitate attainment of such legislative objectives.

This duality is evident in much of the literature, notwithstanding the fact that the nomenclature chosen to represent the two sides varies. Thus for Harlow and Rawlings, the main characters in the red-light/green-light discourse are commentators, principally academics, with Wade and Dicey exemplifying the red-light approach and Robson, Jennings and Griffith fulfilling this role for the green-light school of thought.[13] For Loughlin, the conservative vision of public law is epitomized by Oakeshott, Dicey and Wade; the liberal by Hayek, Dworkin, Allan and Jowell; and the functionalist by Griffith, Mitchell and Robson.[14] For Poole, the meaning of common law constitutionalism is scripted from Allan, Laws, Craig, Jowell and Oliver, while the tenets of political constitutionalism are drawn from Loughlin, Tomkins and Poole himself.[15]

Debate concerning the nature and purpose of administrative law is valuable and to be encouraged. It is, moreover, unsurprising that there should be differences of view in this respect, in the same way that there are vibrant debates as to the foundational values that underpin subjects such as contract, tort, property and crime.

It is, nonetheless, noteworthy that the general assumption, explicit or implicit, in much of this discourse is that the courts are distrustful of the administration and thus adhere to a red-

[10] Peter Cane, *Controlling Administrative Power: An Historical Comparison* (Cambridge University Press, 2016) p. 220. See also Peter Cane's contribution to this volume.

[11] Cane (n 10) 220.

[12] Cane (n 10) 225.

[13] C Harlow and R Rawlings, *Law and Administration* (Weidenfeld and Nicolson, 1984), ch. 1–2.

[14] M Loughlin, *Public Law and Political Theory* (Clarendon Press, 1992).

[15] T Poole, 'Back to the Future? Unearthing the Theory of Common Law Constitutionalism' (2003) 23 *OJLS* 453; 'Questioning Common Law Constitutionalism' (2005) 25 *Legal Studies* 142; 'Legitimacy, Rights and Judicial Review' (2005) 25 *OJLS* 697.

light perspective, or something analogous thereto, when engaging in judicial review. They are felt to be antipathetic to regulation, seeking to crab and confine the 'dangerous' administration, when it seeks to effectuate the legislative mandate accorded to it. It would be interesting to consider how far this normative vision accompanied the development of administrative law in other common law jurisdictions. The answer to this inquiry may well vary between different systems.[16] The soundness of this perception, and its match with reality, will be considered in the following section. Suffice it to say for the present that the very idea that there is stark dichotomy between these two visions of administrative law, and the attendant assumption that red light visions predominated in the courts, would have had negative implications for the perception of administrative law in systems that drew on the UK.

2.2.2 *Regulation*

2.2.2.1 Empirical Dimension

The focus now shifts to perceptions of regulation and the interrelationship between this and the emergence of administrative law. The standard view of UK administrative law is grounded not only on assumptions concerning the existence, or lack thereof, of case law pertaining to judicial review. It is also founded on empirical suppositions concerning the need, or lack thereof, for any such body of doctrine. The core empirical hypothesis was that we did not need administrative law until the turn of the twentieth century, because it was only then that state regulation became significant. The advent of the welfare state, epitomized by legislation of the Liberal government in 1906–1910, was felt to signal the birth of administrative law as developed thereafter by the courts. The logic was simple: such regulation was not particularly prevalent hitherto, which explained the absence of anything that should be recognized as administrative law; the outpouring of such regulation in the twentieth century was the catalyst for the development of a jurisprudence that was fit for purpose.

Dicey contended that regulation of a kind that had not existed hitherto was the reason for the beginnings of something akin to administrative law in the UK.[17] Lord Reid exemplified judicial invocation of this logic, when he opined that 'we do not have a developed system of administrative law – perhaps because until fairly recently we did not need it'.[18] The remainder of the paragraph, to which this sentence was appended, tells a rather different story, as will be seen in the following section, but the sentence itself was oft-quoted. Cane exemplifies academic invocation of the same reasoning. He acknowledges that he applies his historical method concerning control over administrative power asymmetrically. Thus, while there is historical analysis of change in the governmental regimes studied in the UK, US and Australia, there is much less attention given to change in administrative law over time.[19] Cane's rationalization for this asymmetry is that administrative law regimes have a much shorter history than the regimes of government in which they are embedded. Administrative law is related to growth in the regulatory state, which is said to have occurred in the last 150 years.[20]

16 Indeed, other chapters in this volume also consider this.

17 AV Dicey, 'Development of Administrative Law in England' (1915) 31 *LQR* 148.

18 *Ridge* v. *Baldwin* [1964] AC 40, 72.

19 Cane (n 10) 16.

20 Ibid.

2.2.2.2 Normative Dimension

There are two aspects to the normative dimension of regulation, the first of which concerns the subject matter to be regulated, the second the mode by which this should be done.

There is, firstly, an inherently normative dimension as to what aspects of life should be subject to state regulation, or to regulation the delivery of which is contracted out to private parties. Views in this respect have altered over time, and will continue to do so. The choice is quintessentially made by the legislature, with application of the resultant legislation being subject to judicial review. The judicial attitude to such regulatory legislation is, as seen above, central to the normative dimension of judicial review, as attested to by the secondary literature, wherein positive or negative attitudes to administrative law were explicated by the relative like or dislike of the regulatory legislation to which it applied.

There is, secondly, an inherently normative dimension, in terms of contestation as to the optimal way in which to conduct such regulation. There is a rich and vibrant literature concerning different modes of regulation, ranging from command and control to self-regulation, with many variants betwixt the two. This is not the place to engage in such debates that are not directly pertinent to the present inquiry. Suffice it to say the following, that is apposite in the present context. The more explicit recognition of administrative law in the last fifty years has occurred in tandem with growing academic specialization, such that public law and regulation are regarded as related but distinct disciplines. This has meant that public lawyers rarely read statutes that deal with regulatory subject matter, unless they contain a specific point concerning judicial review. The understanding of statutory architecture as it pertains to any particular area is thereby diminished. The implicit assumption on which most people would proceed is, moreover, that we are far more sophisticated than our predecessors when it comes to the design and maintenance of regulatory regimes. This is, as will be seen in the following section, not quite so obvious.

2.3 REALITY: FOUR CENTRAL CONSTRUCTS

2.3.1 *Judicial Review Doctrine*

2.3.1.1 Empirical Dimension

There is room for debate as to the yardsticks for deciding when a subject 'exists'. The two principal criteria in this respect are the primary materials, case law and statute, and secondary materials that reflect thereon, such as texts and the like. The ensuing argument is premised on the assumption that the primary materials are indeed of prime importance, and that commentary reflecting thereon is secondary in this respect.

This methodology is not premised on stipulation; it does not deny the significance of the secondary material; nor does it ignore the symbiotic interaction that can exist betwixt the two. The methodology is based on the assumption that to proceed in the converse manner, and accord primary significance to the secondary literature, is methodologically unsound. The fact that what are now regarded as standard texts came later is relevant, but not determinative, more especially because there was literature on central issues such as the scope of the prerogative writs.[21] The

[21] See, e.g., Thomas Tapping, *The Law and Practice of the High Prerogative Writ of Mandamus, as It Obtains in England and Ireland* (Benning, 1848); C Gray, *The Writ of Prohibition, Jurisdiction in Early Modern English Law* (Oceana Publications, 1994).

relative scale of such literature does not signify the absence of the primary material, nor does it in any way undermine the reality of its existence. It may well be true that 'administrative law' as an organizing concept for teaching and research is a relatively recent phenomenon, but this should be kept firmly in perspective.

The legal reality is that we have had a body of legal rules concerned directly with the legal constraints that should be placed on the administration broadly conceived for at least four hundred years, and many of the core concepts that we use today would be recognized by our judicial forbears, such as Coke, Holt, Hale, Abbott, Blackstone, Mansfield and Kenyon, because they created them. The rules were part of relations between individual and state, thereby forming the foundations for classic administrative law review, and were central also to relations between the arms of government, thereby operating as a form of structural constitutional review. The development of this jurisprudence was not fortuitous. To the contrary, the rich case law developed, as will be seen in the following section, precisely because of the extensive regulatory regime that existed in Tudor and Stuart England. How much the courts were doing as adjudged by the volume of the case law, its doctrinal reach, and efficacy are, therefore, the principal considerations in deciding when it is meaningful to speak of administrative law developing in England and thereafter in the UK. When viewed from these perspectives there is no doubt that judicial review as a central facet of administrative law existed from the mid-sixteenth century at the latest.

Consider *case law volume*. Between 1220 and 1867 there were 6,637 separate citations to certiorari, 5,563 to prohibition and 7,111 to mandamus. The very great majority of this judicial activity occurred from the late sixteenth century onwards.[22] There were in addition 2,512 citations to *quo warranto*, which was the action used to challenge the entitlement of a person to hold office. These figures are approximate,[23] but they are nonetheless telling. The figures do not cover collateral challenges, where the claimant used an action in, for example, tort to challenge an illegality. These challenges were often used even after the birth of the prerogative writs because the plaintiff wished to secure a monetary remedy or because there might be a *no certiorari* clause in the statute. Some figures concerning just two of the principal administrative authorities that were active during this time, Commissioners and justices of the peace, can help put matters in perspective.[24] The figures for cases involving Commissioners are trespass, 3,200; trover, 1,942; action on the case, 1,138; and replevin, 1,001. The figures for cases involving justices of the peace are trespass, 1,308; trover, 534; action on the case, 470; and replevin, 392.[25]

These figures do not touch the many collateral challenges to other administrative authorities, such as tortious actions against municipal corporations for illegality and abuse of power. The preceding figures also do not, by definition, include the number of unreported cases. Law reporting was private, and did not cover all cases. There might have been no reporter at a particular case, or it might have been felt that the case raised no new legal point and

22 There were, for example, 1,169 cases involving poor law guardians, 1,028 cases involving turnpike trustees and 408 involving inspectors.

23 This is partly because there can be more than one digital citation to the same case, the consequence of their being more than one report, and partly because the same passage can on occasion be cited under more than once.

24 A further caveat in addition to that mentioned in the previous note is that the case citations in these figures can sometimes inadvertently run together – for example, a mention of 'trespass' in one case and 'Commissioners' in another.

25 These latter figures are almost certainly too low, since in many cases the citation is simply to 'justices' rather than 'justices of the peace', but a search framed in terms of 'justices' can also bring in citations to judges and thus be too high. It is nonetheless interesting for the record to note that the search couched in terms of 'justices' reveals the following figures: trespass, 7,605; trover, 2,883; action on the case, 1,964; and replevin, 2,498.

therefore did not warrant a report, although such cases would still be important for an overall picture of the incidence of judicial review. It is difficult to obtain accurate information on the ratio between reported and unreported cases, but it is unlikely that it was greater than 60 per cent over time.

When reflecting on the historical incidence of judicial review it is noteworthy that the population at the turn of the seventeenth century was circa 4.8 million, 6 million at the beginning of the eighteenth century and 16.3 million by the nineteenth century. It is not, therefore, self-evident that judicial review was less used then than now, more especially if one removes the very large number of immigration/asylum cases from current figures,[26] and if one takes account of the fact that the preceding figures were for decided cases, since leave was not required until 1933.[27] It is also important to factor in the limited number of judges. King's Bench was staffed by the Chief Justice and three other justices, with the number rising to five in the nineteenth century. The numbers of judges in Common Pleas and Court of Exchequer were similarly limited.[28] This limited number of judges would, moreover, deal with a whole range of legal business in addition to judicial review. The preceding figures concerning the incidence of judicial review, approximate though they may be, are an important corrective to the view that we never had any administrative law before the 1960s, since the incidence thereof in 1670 was as high as in 1970, when calibrated for population size, and this is so only when taking account of reported cases.

Consider now *legal doctrine*. The doctrinal regime cannot be described in detail here. Suffice it to say the following. The foundational doctrine of administrative law was framed by constitutional principles elaborated by the courts, which shaped the relationship between the executive and the courts and between the executive and Parliament.[29] Within this constitutional frame, the courts developed many of the central concepts of judicial review with which we are familiar today. There was well-established case law on review of fact and law. There was doctrine dating back to the sixteenth century on legal control of discretion, which was cast in terms of propriety of purpose, rationality review and also what was termed *proportionability*. There was jurisprudence on due process and damages liability. There was doctrine on principles of good administration, as exemplified by case law limiting the ability of a person who possessed a de facto or de jure monopoly to charge whatever prices he liked. The courts reasoned that such property was imbued with a public interest that limited the normal capacity to charge what the market would bear. The case law also tackled the consequences of invalidity, and determined that it was, in principle, retrospective.[30]

26 In 1974, there were 160 applications for judicial review. This had risen to circa 11,000 in 2011, but 75 per cent concerned asylum and immigration, Judicial Review: proposals for reform, Cm 8515, 2012, paras. 28–9.

27 Administration of Justice (Miscellaneous Provisions) Act 1993, s.5. The number of cases decided at a substantive hearing in 2011 was circa 400, Judicial Review: proposals for reform, para. 30.

28 J Sainty, *The Judges of England, 1272–1990: A List of Judges of the Superior Courts* (Selden Society, 1993).

29 *Prohibitions del Roy* (1607) 12 Co. Rep. 63; *Case of Proclamations* (1611) Co. Rep. 74. The cases established that the courts would determine the existence and extent of prerogative power, and that the royal prerogative did not extend according to the monarch adjudicative power, nor did it afford the monarch any general economic regulatory power.

30 The relevant case law is considered in E Henderson, *Foundations of English Administrative Law* (Harvard University Press, 1963); P Craig, *UK, EU and Global Administrative Law: Foundations and Challenges* (Cambridge University Press, 2015) pp. 29–44; P Craig, 'The Legitimacy of US Administrative Law and The Foundations of English Administrative Law, Setting the Historical Record Straight', *SSRN* 2802784; P Craig, 'English Foundations of US Administrative Law: Four Central Errors', *SSRN* 2852835; P Craig, 'Proportionality and Judicial Review: A UK Historical Perspective', in S Vogenauer and S Weatherill (eds.), *General Principles of Law, European and Comparative Perspectives* (Hart, 2017) ch. 9.

The doctrine was given force through judicial creativity in relation to remedies. The amplification of grounds for review took place within, and was framed by, the evolution of adjectival law. Direct and collateral challenge were the vehicles for this development, the former through the prerogative writs of certiorari, prohibition and mandamus, the latter primarily, albeit not exclusively, through tort actions. The courts transformed mandamus, certiorari and prohibition, thereby creating the remedial mechanisms to effectuate the procedural and substantive doctrines of judicial review. The prerogative writs had existed from medieval times, but were not used to control administration in the manner that became the norm from the seventeenth century onwards. The judicial creativity matches anything found in more modern doctrine.[31] While the prerogative writs were the principal medium for direct challenge, a very considerable number of actions were brought collaterally, via tort claims. Plaintiffs used actions for trespass, case, replevin, trover, false imprisonment, nuisance and negligence to challenge administrative action, more especially where they sought damages, which were not available through the prerogative writs, or where a preclusive clause purporting to exclude review rendered recourse to such a writ more difficult.[32]

There was then an extensive body of legal doctrine that regulated exercise of public power from the mid-sixteenth century onwards. Judicial review was composed of discernible heads of procedural and substantive review, backed up by a remedial regime designed to effectuate the grounds of illegality developed by the courts. It constituted the core of administrative law, and was worthy of that appellation. There is nothing in the preceding argument to the effect that administrative law doctrine as it developed from the mid-sixteenth century was pristine. This is not a Whig version of history. There were, of course, decisions and doctrine that were open to criticism, as in all areas of the law. It is, moreover, no answer to say that the courts have created some novel doctrinal concepts since then. They have indeed done so. If this is, however, the touchstone, then it should serve to deny recognition of, for example, a 'system of tort liability' in the seventeenth century, since the difference between that body of law and the existing regime exceeded the differences between administrative law then and now. Similar caution should be exercised when viewing claims to the effect that there might have been conceptual tensions in some judicial review doctrine in the seventeenth and eighteenth centuries.[33] The extent to which this was so is itself debatable, but if pristine conceptual clarity is the benchmark for recognition of a body of law, then no part of private law would qualify. There are three misapprehensions about the preceding jurisprudence, which are related but distinct.

It is common to regard the case law as 'principally remedies driven'. This was true in a reductionist sense, since if there was no available remedy, then there would be little point in bringing an action. This is, however, equally true in relation to any area of the law. The remedial dimension was important, since it attested to the courts' concern to ensure that relief was available, but it should not be taken to signify the absence of developed grounds of review.

It is equally common to regard the case law as a wilderness of single instances, which was only reduced to order through the efforts of twentieth century scholarship. The scholarship was valuable, but the premise is nonetheless wrong. The case law was not a wilderness of single instances. To the contrary, there were established grounds of procedural and substantive review that were readily discernible from the cases for those who read them.[34] The

31 Henderson (n 30) 46–58, 112; Craig (n 30) 51–62.

32 A Rubinstein, *Jurisdiction and Illegality* (Oxford University Press, 1975) ch. 4; Craig (n 30) 59–62.

33 See, e.g., Varuhas (n 8) 42–3.

34 There could, of course, be contestation as to the application of established grounds of review in a given case or the precise application of a particular prerogative writ.

principal grounds of review flowed naturally from the very subject matter being reviewed. Judicial review developed from complaints concerning the plethora of regulatory legislation enacted from the fifteenth century onwards. It was natural for the courts that created the doctrinal principles to inquire whether the administrative authority strayed beyond the area assigned to it – hence the foundational categories of review for law and fact. It was natural also for the courts to exercise some control over the way in which the discretion accorded to such bodies was exercised – hence the review for propriety of purpose, rationality and proportionability. The courts necessarily determined the consequences of invalidity, and it took no great normative imagination to require the basic tenets of due process before power was exercised.

It is, moreover, common to contend that administrative law in the UK was only worthy of that appellation because of seminal judicial decisions in the 1960s. Many of the chapters reference these decisions when considering the English law product that was imported into the relevant jurisdiction. The argument based on the twentieth-century case law does not, however, withstand examination. There is, as stated above, nothing in the preceding argument to the effect that administrative law doctrine as it developed from the mid-sixteenth century was pristine. It should, moreover, be recognized that the seminal decisions of the 1960s largely removed impediments that had been imposed in the early twentieth century, such as the right-privilege distinction, that between administrative and quasi-judicial proceedings, and far-reaching conceptions of public interest immunity. In removing such limitations, the courts often drew on the more liberal jurisprudence from earlier centuries.

It is instructive in this regard to return to Lord Reid's quote from *Ridge*.[35] The reality is that the first sentence concerning the fact that administrative law was only a recent development in the UK has been taken out of context from the remainder of the paragraph and the judgment more generally. This is more especially paradoxical, since the fulcrum point on which Lord Reid's judgment turned in order to modernize the law relating to natural justice was the older case law, dating from the eighteenth and nineteenth century. His Lordship reviewed this case law and gave three reasons why the law had become confused: natural justice could have only a limited application in the context of the wider duties or discretion imposed upon a minister, but the courts had mistakenly applied these limits to other areas where the constraints were unnecessary;[36] the principle had only limited application during the war, but such considerations should not affect the ambit of natural justice now; and there was conceptual confusion between rights and remedies evident in the requirement of a superadded duty to act judicially for certiorari, and the way that this had stilted the development of natural justice.[37] It was in this context that Lord Reid opined that the courts should be wary of applying principles to situations for which they were not intended. However, his Lordships reaffirmed the earlier case law, stating that 'I see nothing in that to justify our thinking that our old methods are any less applicable today than ever they were to the older types of case, and if there are any dicta in modern authorities which point in that direction, then, in my judgment, they should not be followed'.[38]

Consider the third dimension of legal doctrine sketched above, which is *efficacy*. The effectiveness of judicial review, as judged in terms of impact, is controversial in relation to the modern law. Methodological issues abound, including the nature of the relevant empirical

35 *Ridge* (n 18) 71–2.
36 Ibid.
37 *Ridge* (n 18) 72–8.
38 *Ridge* (n 18) 73.

evidence, the determination of causality and the relative importance of judicial review as a determinant of administrative behaviour.[39] These difficulties are endemic and apply a fortiori to evaluation of impact two or three hundred years ago. I make no claims in this respect, since the relevant research is not, in general forthcoming. I do, however, make the following more modest point, which relates to the economics of litigation. Litigants brought cases in the numbers set out above, which did not represent the totality of such litigation, since the figures do not cover unreported cases. They would not have done so if review had generally been inefficacious.

It follows that they were able to do so, notwithstanding the costs of litigation. This is a point of some importance, since we naturally think of trial costs in Dickensian terms as being potentially prohibitive. Whatsoever the truth of this might be for some causes of action, it must be qualified in terms of judicial review. This is because such cases were regularly brought where the sums at stake were not large, and where the claimant was not a repeat player, eager to establish a precedent that would be beneficial going forward. Thus, for example, there were large numbers of cases dealing with liability for poor relief, where the claimant alleged that a person or persons were not resident in that parish, which should not therefore bear the liability; there were similar numbers of cases dealing with turnpike trustees, where the claimant would contest the amount charged for passage along a highway; and there were frequent actions against justices of the peace where the sums at stake were small.[40]

It follows also that the claimants thought that it was worthwhile pursuing an action for judicial review as a mode of seeking relief for their grievance. It is important to recognize that the claimants' range of options in this respect were often circumscribed and dependent on the particular administrative regime. There might be some recourse to internal administrative review, most notably in the context of excise; there might also be the possibility of challenging the initial decision through a tribunal, more especially from the nineteenth century onwards. Such options were, nonetheless, very much a patchwork quilt, dependent on the terms of the enabling legislation. The salient point for present purposes is that judicial review was perceived to be an option worth considering for those aggrieved by administrative action. This was so notwithstanding that adjudication was generally concentrated in the King's Bench located in London, at a time when travel and communication were a good deal more difficult than they are now. The preceding argument does not, however, serve to deny the fact that people also resolved disputes with the government by means other than traditional litigation.[41]

2.3.1.2 Normative Dimension

The previous section began by noting the room for debate concerning the criteria as to whether a legal subject exists and, if it does, the date from which it is meaningful to accord it

[39] See, e.g., S Halliday, *Judicial Review and Compliance with Administrative Law* (Hart, 2004); M Hertogh and S Halliday (eds.), *Judicial Review and Bureaucratic Impact, International and Interdisciplinary Perspectives* (Cambridge University Press, 2004).

[40] See, e.g., *Cardiffe Bridge* case (1700) 1 Ld. Raym. 580; *R* v. *Justice of the Peace for Nottingham* (1755) Sayer 216; *Inter the Inhabitants of the Parish of Chittinston and Penhurst* (1795) 2 Salk. 475; *Inter Inhabitan. King's Norton in Wigorn* (1795) 2 Salk. 481; *The King* v. *The Inhabitants of Denbigh* (1804) 5 East 333; *Ridge* v. *Garlick* (1818) 8 Taunt 424; *Osmond* v. *Widdicombe* (1818) 2 B. & Ald. 48; *The King* v. *The Trustees of the Cheshunt Turnpike Road* (1833) 5 B. & Ad. 438; *The King* v. *The Justices of the West Riding of Yorkshire* (1834) 5 B. & Ad. 1003.

[41] Harry Arthurs, *'Without the Law': Administrative Justice and Legal Pluralism in Nineteenth Century England* (University of Toronto Press, 1985).

such status. The respective role played by the primary and secondary materials, and the reasons for according the former priority, were adumbrated above when addressing the empirical dimension of judicial review.

These rationales are reinforced when we consider the normative dimension to such review. Contestation in the secondary literature as to the nature and purpose of administrative law is, as noted earlier, to be encouraged. This is, however, subject to an important caveat. We should not make assumptions in the secondary literature concerning the primary materials, case law, legislation and the like, which are not firmly grounded in those primary materials. To do so is to convey a picture of those materials on assumptions as to their content that is not tested and is wrong.[42]

The risks are exacerbated when we make such suppositions knowing that the particular writer had not examined the relevant case law or was unaware of its existence. Thus, to assume that the Diceyan vision of administrative law represented the judicial attitude of the courts that developed the principles of judicial review does not withstand examination. We should, in more general terms, be very cautious about assuming that contestation between writers as to the purpose of administrative law maps directly onto or reflects the primary materials. To put the same point in another way, if you wish to write an intellectual account of how writers have perceived administrative law, then that is fine, but do not imagine that it coheres with reality, when there is scant evidence that the account was premised on what courts or Parliament were doing. This point holds true for evaluation of any legal subject from a temporal perspective, including administrative law. It is all the more important when making assumptions as to how the courts regarded the administration when developing the foundational principles of administrative law from the sixteenth century onwards. The reality of administrative law as it unfolded during these years is not captured by a dichotomy between red-light and green-light approaches.

The reality was, rather, as follows. Over the course of four centuries, Parliament enacted a very great deal of social and economic legislation that was regarded as valuable, subject to normal political contestation as to the desirable direction of policy. It readily used a plethora of institutions to discharge policy, there being no general animadversion to any particular administrative form. Those charged with administration would normally discharge their task with care, but things could go wrong; hence the need for mechanisms of accountability, which were an admixture of political, administrative and legal.

The legal contribution, in the form of emerging principles of judicial review, was predicated on the normative assumption that constraints were warranted to control such public power. There was, however, nothing specific about public law in this respect, since control was also central to many rules of private law. The legal contribution was not premised on the assumption that administration was something dangerous in the manner conveyed by red-light theory, nor does the evidence support the conclusion that courts generally ignored the social value of the regulatory legislation that they were interpreting. To the contrary, they were mindful of this and sought to effectuate it when interpreting the regulatory legislation. This is apparent from the case law concerning different subject matter areas in which the courts exercised powers of review, where they would routinely

[42] Philip Hamburger, *Is Administrative Law Unlawful?* (University of Chicago Press, 2014) advanced an argument to the effect that US Administrative law should be perceived to be 'unlawful' or 'extra-legal' and sought to rely on evidence from early English administrative law to support this claim. The argument is untenable in normative terms and is not supported by the case law or legislation; see Craig, 'The Legitimacy of US Administrative Law and The Foundations of English Administrative Law, Setting the Historical Record Straight' (n 30) and Craig 'English Foundations of US Administrative Law: Four Central Errors' (n 30).

find against the claimant and interpret the legislation in the manner best designed to effectuate statutory purpose.[43]

This same duality is evident in the present day. It has not changed. The reasons for misapprehension in this respect are not complex. It is, in part, because scholars pay less attention to cases where the claimant fails than where the claim is successful, and it is, in part, because they pay almost no attention to the statistically very significant body of judicial review claims that simply turn on interpretation of the relevant statute, where no issue of doctrinal principle is centre-stage at all.[44] Claims will commonly fail because the court reads the legislation purposively so as to attain the legislative objectives.

The courts did of course err, and this was true in the foundational period of administrative law and in the modern day. All institutions are imperfect. It is true that some judges evinced a preference for the common law over legislation, but this was in relation to areas that had been developed by the common law. The courts did not, by way of contrast, feel that they should be devising broad regulatory schemes relating to the poor, land use, trade regulation, tax and the like. Nor did the courts regard such regulatory legislation in terms akin to being engulfed by some unnatural administrative leviathan. To the contrary, this was the ordinary nature of things in the world they inhabited, the existence of such measures being the norm from the fifteenth century onwards, although their incidence would perforce vary over time. The courts might, just as in the modern day, be inclined to interpret a regulatory statute more narrowly where they felt that its terms were unduly harsh.

2.3.2 *Regulation*

2.3.2.1 Empirical Dimension

The empirical assumptions that underlie the standard perception of the historical case law on judicial review are misguided. This is mirrored by erroneous assumptions concerning regulation. There is a proximate connection between state regulatory activity and the emergence of judicial review. The latter emerges because of alleged errors made pursuant to exercise of regulatory power. The mistake in the standard account is thus not conceptual but temporal. It misses the temporal mark by four hundred years. The reality was that there was a very great deal of regulation from the fifteenth century onwards, which was the catalyst for the emergence of the doctrinal and remedial principles of judicial review. The emergence of judicial review was not therefore fortuitous. It was driven by disputes that arose precisely because of state regulation, the scope of which was very significant.

We commonly think of government before the twentieth century as having limited responsibility, as doing a whole lot less than now. There is some truth in this, but misapprehension nonetheless exceeds veracity.[45] We must distinguish between centralization of state authority and decentralization of administration. England was highly centralized compared to its continental neighbours, more especially from the Tudors onwards. Social[46] and

[43] Craig, *UK, EU and Global Administrative Law* (n 30) 65–95. See, e.g., *King* v. *The Justices of Essex* (1816) 5 M. & S. 513; *Dominus Rex* v. *Randall* (1795) 2 Salk. 470; *Cooper* v. *Booth* (1785) 3 Esp 135; *The King* v. *The Commissioners of Sewers for Tower Hamlets* (1830) 1 B. & Ad. 232.

[44] Sarah Nason, *Reconstructing Judicial Review* (Hart, 2016) ch. 6–7.

[45] For analysis of the significant volume of public legislation in the eighteenth century, see Joanna Innes, *Inferior Politics, Social Problems and Social Policies in Eighteenth Century Britain* (Oxford University Press, 2009) pp. 21–47.

[46] See, e.g., Paul Slack, *Poverty and Policy in Tudor and Stuart England* (Longman, 1988).

economic legislation occupied a great deal of time in Elizabethan Parliaments[47] and 'was considered, after the granting of taxation, to be the primary function of the House of Commons'.[48]

Adam Smith's free market ideas were two centuries away, and there was statutory regulation of diverse matters, including trades such as leather, alcohol, iron and cloth; wages; bankruptcy; poverty, unemployment and vagrancy; land use; tax; flood defences; roads; shipping and morality. There was in addition much legislation pertaining to police powers broadly conceived. The later advent of free market principles led to some diminution in trade regulation, but there was also increased regulation in areas such as factories, health and the like, which is the backdrop to continuing historical debates as to whether the nineteenth century really ever was an era of laissez-faire.[49]

The fact that these measures were enacted by Parliament did not mean that they were initiated by central government departments.[50] Moreover, while the legislation was enacted from the centre, the general pattern of administration was decentralized. Central departments of government with generalized administrative responsibility as understood in the twentieth century were not the norm in earlier centuries. A catalyst for their development was the growth of the fiscal-military state towards the end of the seventeenth century, which prompted increased departmentalization in central government.[51]

Administrative responsibilities were commonly assigned to a wide range of bodies, with justices of the peace and commissioners performing prominent roles. Justices of the peace had judicial, administrative and regulatory responsibilities.[52] So too did Commissioners, which were the forerunners of modern agencies, with adjudicatory, decisional and rule-making powers. The concept of commission captured the idea of an authority and duty granted by the Crown, the terms of which could vary significantly. While the commission derived ultimately from the Crown, the person who did the appointing varied: in some instances it might be the monarch, in others the Lord Chancellor or someone from the Privy Council. Commissioners were not part of the judiciary, nor were they organized according to some homogenous institutional format. To the contrary, they were marked by institutional heterogeneity, although there were common features. They were integral to policy delivery in a plethora of areas. There were commissioners of sewers, excise, inclosure, tithes, improvement, bankruptcy and railways, to name but the principal examples, and that is without mention of bodies such as turnpike trustees, which undertook analogous functions in relation to roads; the guardians of the poor, who oversaw the poor law; and factory inspectors.[53]

Commissioners bestrode the land. They were the chosen medium for administration across diverse areas, they made decisions and regulations that impacted directly on the citizen, and they were, therefore, not surprisingly the subject of judicial review, direct and

[47] See, e.g., Geoffrey Elton, *The Parliament of England, 1559–1581* (Cambridge University Press, 1986); David Smith, *The Stuart Parliaments 1603–1689* (Arnold, 1999).

[48] R Sgroi, 'Elizabethan Social and Economic Legislation', www.historyofparliamentonline.org/periods/tudors/elizabethan-social-and-economic-legislation.

[49] See, e.g., Arthur Taylor, *Laissez-faire and State Intervention in Nineteenth-Century Britain* (Macmillan, 1972).

[50] For important insights as to who initiated legislation in the eighteenth century, see Innes (n 46).

[51] PGM Dickson, *The Financial Revolution in England: A Study in the Development of Public Credit, 1688–1756* (Macmillan, 1967); John Brewer, *The Sinews of Power, War, Money and the English State 1688–1783* (Routledge, 1988); Joanna Innes, 'Governing Diverse Societies', in Paul Langford (ed.), *The Eighteenth Century, 1688–1815* (Oxford University Press, 2002) pp. 119–20.

[52] Charles Beard, *The Office of Justice of the Peace in England in Its Origin and Development* (Macmillan, 1904).

[53] Sidney and Beatrice Webb, *English Local Government: Statutory Authorities for Special Purposes* (Cass, 1922); Brewer (n 52).

collateral. Many such bodies were later incorporated into either central or local government in the nineteenth century,[54] in large part because Parliament desired a greater degree of control than was possible when the activity was undertaken by a board, commission or agency. Tribunals, which performed adjudicative functions, came to assume increased importance in the nineteenth century[55] and have remained central to the administrative landscape since then.

There were political, administrative and legal mechanisms to ensure accountability. The courts were not all-important in this respect, but they did play a significant role, which varied depending, inter alia, on the existence and efficacy of political and administrative modes of accountability. It is equally important to understand that administrators, and the schemes they administered, were not approached with some inherent suspicion. The regulatory schemes were enacted to attain valuable social purposes broadly conceived, even if some were contestable, and courts, while seeking to ensure legal accountability, also strove to attain regulatory efficacy, much as they do today.[56]

2.3.2.2 Normative Dimension

The twin normative aspects of regulation that permeate modern thought were considered above: what should be regulated and how this should be done? These issues were also central to regulation as it developed from the fifteenth century to the nineteenth century.

It is unsurprising that there were shifts in legislative policy over time as to what should be regulated. It would, moreover, be mistaken to regard legislative policy as unitary in this regard at any one point in time. The balance between public and private legislation was quite different in the seventeenth and eighteenth centuries than it is now. There were, in addition, significant differences in relation to the catalyst for public legislation. Thus, even after the advent of cabinet government in the eighteenth century, public legislation would often be sponsored by a particular MP, rather than being the product of official governmental policy. All of which contributed to the fact that the rationales for regulation were eclectic. There were, nonetheless, broader trends that could be discerned, such as mercantilism. There was a subsequent shift away from mercantilism, under the influence of ideas promulgated by Adam Smith and David Hume, and a corresponding increase in regulation over issues such as factories, child labour and the like.

What is more surprising is the sophistication of the regulatory techniques used during this period. There was, of course, nothing akin to the detailed scholarship on regulatory techniques that currently exists. It would, nonetheless, be mistaken to regard statutory regulatory regimes in the fifteenth to the nineteenth century as unsophisticated. The legislative provisions concerning investigation and deterrence were commonly multilayered and reinforcing. This is exemplified by legislation concerning collection of excise. There were thirteen Commissioners, any four of whom could constitute a Board, with authority to exercise all powers given by the legislation. The Commissioners were authorized to appoint officers, who would collect the excise duties. There were strict rules preventing Commissioners or officers

[54] David Roberts, *Victorian Origins of the British Welfare State* (Yale University Press, 1960); Henry Parris, *Constitutional Bureaucracy: The Development of British Central Administration since the Eighteenth Century* (Allen and Unwin, 1969); Sir Daniel Norman Chester, *The English Administrative System 1780–1870* (Clarendon Press, 1981).

[55] Chantal Stebbings, *Legal Foundations of Tribunals in Nineteenth Century England* (Cambridge University Press, 2006).

[56] Craig, *UK, EU and Global Administrative Law* (n 30) 69–95.

from taking bribes, or colluding with those liable to pay excise, with penalties of £500 for any such offence, a very considerable sum in nineteenth century terms. The same penalties were imposed on the private party attempting to bribe. The deterrent nature of these provisions was reinforced by what was in effect a prisoner dilemma clause: if such collusion had taken place, the party that informed on the other would be indemnified, the penalty falling solely on the party that had not confessed.[57]

While regulatory techniques differed from area to area, certain common features stand out, one of the most important of which was the iterative nature of legislative initiatives. Parliament literally learned by doing. Subsequent legislatures learned from the shortcomings revealed by the operation of the earlier legislation and repeatedly filled gaps. These gaps might be substantive, they might be procedural or they might be remedial.

Thus, to take but one example, bankruptcy was regarded as a social, not primarily a private concern from the fifteenth to the nineteenth century. There were major pieces of legislation dealing with bankrupts in 1542, 1571, 1603, 1625, 1705, 1706, 1731, 1745, 1763, 1772, 1783, 1821 and 1822, with the law being consolidated in 1824.[58] The initial legislation was enacted in 1542 by Henry VIII.[59] It assigned regulatory competence to high officials such as the Lord President, the Lord Treasurer and judges of the King's Bench, who were accorded broad discretion to effectuate the principles contained therein. This regime lasted but thirty years until 1571, when statute enacted during the reign of Elizabeth I laid the pattern for regulatory enforcement thereafter. The new legislation stated at the outset that 'notwithstanding the Statute made against Bankrupts in the thirty-fourth Year of the Reign of our late Sovereign Lord King Henry the Eighth, those Kind of Persons have and do still increase into great and excessive Numbers, and are like more to do, if some better Provision be not made for the Repression of them'.[60]

The 'better Provision' took the form of a new enforcement mechanism, whereby regulatory authority was given to commissioners. This was unsurprising. It had become readily apparent in the years after 1542 that high officials such as the Lord President and judges of the King's Bench did not have the time to devote to the task at hand. The Commissioners were given the power to determine bankruptcy, deal with the person of the bankrupt and seize his goods. These powers were complemented by detailed provisions concerning the legal consequences of the bankrupt seeking to evade capture by leaving his normal abode and hiding elsewhere.[61] The 1571 legislation also made due provision for those who sought to evade the rigours of the statute by assigning goods that were liable to be seized to a third party, and then reclaiming them later on payment of some due recompense. The persons making the complaint of bankruptcy could if they knew, suspected or supposed that goods or debts of the bankrupt were in the hands of others make this known to the Commissioners, who were given broad investigative discretion, backed up by penalties that were sharp and peremptory: if a person failed to take the oath, or tell the truth when examined by Commissioners, then they risked forfeiting double the value of the goods that they had concealed.

The shift from the Tudors to the Stuarts betokened change in many respects, but not in this area. There is indeed a sense of modernity in much legislation enacted during this period, manifest in the willingness to revisit a regulatory domain and render it more efficacious where

57 Excise Management Act 1827, 7 & 8 Geo. 4, c. 53, s 13.
58 Bankruptcy (England) Act 1824, 5 Geo. 4, c. 98.
59 Statute of Bankrupts Act 1542, 34 & 35 Henry VIII, c. 4.
60 Statute of Bankrupts Act 1571, 13 Eliz I, c. 7.
61 Statute of Bankrupts Act 1571, 13 Eliz I, c. 7, ss 2, 9.

experience had revealed deficiencies. Thus it was in the very first year of James I of England (VI of Scotland) that Parliament enacted the Bankrupts Act 1603.[62] The statute broadened the definition of bankrupt, closing gaps revealed in the earlier definition, and applied the Commissioners' remedial powers to the new regulatory order.[63] Where the bankrupt sought to avoid creditors by disposing of the goods to family or other persons, the Commissioners' powers were strengthened, since they could now sell such goods as if they were still owned by the bankrupt.[64] The Commissioners could also imprison alleged confederates who refused to be sworn on oath or refused to answer the questions posed. The legislation strengthened the Commissioners' investigative powers and authorized them to issue arrest warrants and increased the punishment for those found of guilty of perjury by a court of record – the consequence being that the bankrupt 'shall stand upon the Pillory in some publick Place by the Space of two Hours, and have one of his Ears nailed to the Pillory and cut off',[65] a provision that reveals some limits to the modernity of legislation in this area.

The bankruptcy legislation continued to be amended and fine-tuned over the next 250 years, in response to shortcomings revealed in the status quo ante, and as a result of changes in the manner of doing business that generated novel opportunities for playing commercially fast and loose to the detriment of creditors.

The same pattern is apparent in other regulatory areas. Thus, to take but one further example, it is evident in the regulation of flood defences. The centrality of the problem was explicable because much of England was composed of vast fens and marshes[66] – hence the attention given to drainage and defences against the sea, leading to the Statute of Sewers 1531,[67] which gave statutory foundation for the Commissioners of Sewers and the Courts of Sewers. They resembled, in many respects, justices of the peace for the counties, albeit with a specialized jurisdiction over rivers, sewers, ditches, bridges, locks, weirs, sea defences and the like. Their jurisdiction was akin to that of a modern environmental agency. This analogy can be pressed further, insofar as the Commissioners of Sewers 'combined in themselves, judicial, executive and even legislative powers'.[68]

The Statute of Sewers 1531 authorized Commissioners of Sewers to undertake flood defences broadly conceived, and gave them extensive powers to fulfil this remit. They could make individual decisions concerning repairs that were needed to river banks, sea walls, streams, ditches, gutters and the like, and apportion the costs.[69] They were also authorized to make rules. The Commissioners could use the laws and customs of Romney Marsh as a boilerplate, or devise provisions according to their own discretion.[70] The Commissioners' powers were further augmented in the Elizabethan era, extending their tenure, increasing their rule-making power and strengthening their remedial authority.

There is force in the Webbs' comment that 'truly, the Parliaments of Henry the Eighth and Elizabeth weighed out powers to the King's Commissioners with no niggard hand.'[71] The regime inaugurated by the legislation of Henry VIII and Elizabeth I continued with

62 Bankrupts Act 1603, 1 Ja. 1, c. 15.
63 Bankrupts Act 1603, 1 Ja. 1, c. 15, ss 2–3.
64 Bankrupts Act 1603, 1 Ja. 1, c. 15, s 5.
65 Bankrupts Act 1603, 1 Ja. 1, c. 15, s 9.
66 Sidney and Beatrice Webb (n 54) 13.
67 Statute of Sewers Act 1531, 23 Henry 8, c. 5.
68 Sidney and Beatrice Webb (n 54) 21.
69 Statute of Sewers Act 1531, 23 Henry 8, c. 5, s 3.
70 Statute of Sewers Act 1531, 23 Henry 8, c. 5, ss 3, 7.
71 Sidney and Beatrice Webb (n 54) 24.

modification for over three hundred years,[72] although the relevant focus of the Commissioners' action perforce differed in rural and urban settings.[73] The rule-making powers accorded to the Commissioners in 1571 were reaffirmed in 1833.[74]

2.4 PERCEPTION AND REALITY, EXPORT AND RECEPTION

This volume is concerned, inter alia, with the export and reception of UK administrative law in other common law jurisdictions. It is fitting, therefore, to return to the relationship between the history of administrative law, as articulated in this chapter, and the development of administrative law in other common law jurisdictions. A number of points can be made in this respect. These themes are explored in other chapters in this volume.

First, there is no a priori reason why the effect of that disjunction (between perception and reality) would necessarily pull in the same direction in different countries. Thus, as noted at the outset, the perception of administrative law as being relatively modern may have hampered its development elsewhere and, at the same time, encouraged other jurisdictions to feel freer in adapting doctrinal precepts to local circumstance. The effect of mistaken assumptions concerning administrative law can, therefore, only be determined by those with detailed knowledge of other common law regimes, and even then the consequences may well be contested.

Second, it is interesting, when reflecting on the answer to the previous inquiry, to consider whether misperceptions as to the empirical dimension of administrative law, concerning both the incidence of judicial review, and the relationship between this and regulation, were more significant than misconceptions linked to the normative dimensions of judicial review and regulation. The answer may well be unknowable, since it may not be possible to disaggregate the two when reflecting on the reception of UK administrative law in other common law jurisdictions. It is, nonetheless, an interesting line of inquiry for administrative law scholars in those jurisdictions.

Third, both types of errors that plagued the understanding of UK administrative law could have had a marked impact on reception and development elsewhere. Thus, it would be important to know how far failure to perceive the foundational empirical connection between the prevalence of regulation and the emergence of judicial review existed elsewhere. The centrality of this connection cannot be underestimated, since it shapes much that follows thereafter. It is doubly significant. This very connectedness reveals the valuable social purposes pursued through regulation, and that is so notwithstanding the possibility of contestation as to what more precisely the state should seek to regulate. The empirical connectedness reveals also the need for some judicial controls over the power thereby accorded to the organs of the administrative state, as manifest in the basic doctrines of judicial review but does not, in any way, lead to the conclusion that the courts ignored the purposes of the regulatory schema that they scrutinized.

Fourth, the same inquiry is equally apposite in relation to the normative dimension of the story of administrative law in the UK. The failure to appreciate the empirical dimension of UK administrative law shaped the normative dimension of the subject matter, although the

[72] See, e.g., London Watercourses (Commissioners of Sewers) Act 1605, 3 James 1, c. 14; Commissioners of Sewers (City of London) Act 1708, 7 Ann., c. 9; Commissioners of Sewers Act 1708, 7 Ann., c. 10; Sewers Act 1833, 3 & 4 Will. 4, c. 22.

[73] Sidney and Beatrice Webb (n 54) 13-106.

[74] Sewers Act 1833, 3 & 4 Will. 4, c. 22, s. 7.

latter transcended its factual grounding. It would, therefore, be interesting to know how far the predominant Diceyan negative 'take' on administrative law affected the export and reception of the subject thereafter in other common law jurisdictions. Insofar as the Diceyan vision cast administrative law in this negative light, the salient issue would be how far other common law jurisdictions transcended that normative vision, or whether it clouded their initial, or continuing, perception of the subject.

2.5 CONCLUSION

Administrative law history is, in relative terms, in its infancy. Legal history is commonly left to legal historians in this age of increased specialization. Their expertise is invaluable, but the historical terrain is vast, the numbers of specialist legal historians are limited and the subject matter coverage uneven. There are perforce large gaps, as exemplified by the historical landscape of administrative law. Public lawyers know relatively little about legal development in this area, and the regulatory environment from which it grew, as attested to by the nostrum that the UK had no regime of administrative law until the mid-twentieth century. The judges who created and applied that regime in the seventeenth and eighteenth century might beg to differ. They would also take issue with the commonly accepted normative vision of administrative law that underpins the empirical assumptions. Facts do not literally speak for themselves; they require interpretation. Knowledge of the facts is, nonetheless, a condition precedent to reasoned interpretation and a fortiori to normative evaluation.

3

Modern Threats to English Administrative Law and Implications for Its Export

Christopher Forsyth

3.1 INTRODUCTION

This chapter critiques the contours of contemporary English administrative law. It argues that English administrative law is moving from its classical principled and conceptual form of legal reasoning towards a pragmatic mode of reasoning in which judicial discretion is paramount. This development is likely to render English administrative law less influential on the development of administrative law in the common law world than it has been in the past.

English administrative law was made by English judges with few external influences. It is indigenous to England and in no need of indigenisation. Even so, it has proved profoundly influential in the common law world. As many of the other chapters in this book attest, English administrative law was to a greater or lesser extent received into many common law legal systems. In part, this was doubtless simply a reflection of the fact that England was by far the biggest common law jurisdiction. Its deep pool of relevant precedent (some of it binding) lay close at hand to assist the judge searching for a solution to a novel administrative law problem. But much of this influence is surely also the result of the quality of classical administrative law developed by the English judges. It provided the conceptual furniture for the extension of the rule of law to the exercise of discretionary powers. Clear, principled and vigorous, it could lay claim to universal transfer and applicability; it had something to teach, whatever the constitutional background. A move to a less principled, more pragmatic form of administrative law that can be seen in more recent jurisprudence threatens this universal appeal of English law. This chapter first examines classical administrative law, and the basis of its universal appeal, before exploring the undermining of this appeal in contemporary administrative law.

3.2 CLASSICAL ADMINISTRATIVE LAW

3.2.1 *Doctrinal Features of Classical Administrative Law*

This section briefly sets out the principles of classical administrative law.[1] In 1982, in one of his last speeches in the House of Lords, Lord Diplock said that the progress made towards a comprehensive system of administrative law 'was the greatest achievement of the English

[1] By 'classical', this chapter refers to the 'big bang' moments of the 1960s that moved administrative law past formalistic distinctions to a more open-principled approach to governmental accountability. See Paul Craig and Peter Cane's contributions to this volume for alternative views on the dating of 'classical administrative law' (Chapters 2 and 7, respectively).

courts in my judicial lifetime'.[2] Here, he was referring to the way in which the law of judicial review then was an ever-present safeguard against the abuse of governmental power.

In the 1950s, 'an atmosphere of depression and defeatism hung over public law. The great accretion of discretionary power to the state during the [Second World] War and during Attlee's reforming government thereafter had left many to conclude that the common law had lost the power to control the executive'.[3] But in a series of bold judgments, made mostly during the 1960s, the English courts cast the mantle of the rule of law over the exercise of discretionary power. In two cases decided fifty-two years ago (*Anisminic*,[4] *Padfield*[5]) and one decided fifty-five years ago (*Ridge* v. *Baldwin*[6]), the foundations were laid for the modern administrative law. With the addition of the famous *Wednesbury* case from an earlier era, the conceptual foundations were complete.[7]

The organising principle was jurisdiction: did the decision maker act within or outside the decision-making power granted by Parliament?[8] If the decision maker acted outside the powers granted, the decision was legally non-existent and void (and thus not caught by ouster clauses reasonably interpreted as applying only to valid decisions). (This may be traced to *Anisminic*, but it is much older.[9])

Once it was determined that the decision maker had the power to act, the question was whether that decision was made in a procedurally fair manner. The duty to act fairly now applies to practically anyone who decides practically anything. If a decision was not made fairly, it was once more invalid and void. (This is all traced (with some hiccups) to *Ridge* v. *Baldwin*.) Similarly, the statute under which the power arises grants that power for a purpose, express or implied. When the decision maker acts for some other purpose, he or she acts invalidly and the decision is void. Since statutory power is always given for a purpose, it follows that there is no such thing as an unfettered discretion. (This is all traced to *Padfield*.)

Thus far there has been no intrusion by the courts into the merits of an administrative decision. The courts are concerned with the legality of the decision, not with whether it is a wise or unwise decision. The decision maker was accountable to the courts for the legality of the decision and to Parliament for the merits of the decision. But where a decision is so grossly unreasonable that it may be inferred there was something wrong with the decision-making process, then the courts may intervene. This is the *Wednesbury*[10] principle. A decision so unreasonable that no reasonable decision maker could have made it is also invalid and void.

From these simple ideas, classical administrative law was constructed. Today it is the case, with very few exceptions, that any person or body exercising public power may be called to

[2] Lord Diplock in *R* v. *Inland Revenue Commissioners, ex p. National Federation of Self Employed and Small Businesses* [1982] A.C. 617 at 641.

[3] From my obituary of Sir William Wade. *The Times*, 24 March 2004.

[4] *Anisminic Ltd* v. *Foreign Compensation Commission* [1968] UKHL 6.

[5] *Padfield* v. *Minister of Agriculture, Fisheries and Food* [1968] AC 997.

[6] *Ridge* v. *Baldwin* [1964] AC 40.

[7] *Associated Provincial Picture Houses Ltd.* v. *Wednesbury Corporation* [1948] 1 KB 223.

[8] This classical statement of the ultra vires doctrine is controversial; many scholars prefer to find the basis of judicial review in the common law. This has been the subject of a vigorous debate on England. The leading contributions will be found in C. Forsyth (ed.), *Judicial Review and the Constitution* (London: Hart, 2000).

[9] See, for instance, *Rex* v. *Smith & Others Commissioners of Sewers (1670)*, 1 Modem Reports, at 45, *Callis on Sewers*, 4th ed., 342. Kelynge CJ said, 'you cannot oust the jurisdiction of this Court without particular words in an Act of Parliament. There is no jurisdiction that is uncontrollable by this Court'. See the full discussion by Denning LJ in *R* v. *Medical Appeal Tribunal, ex p. Gilmore* [1957] EWCA Civ 1; [1957] QB 574 at 584.

[10] *Wednesbury*, note 7.

account to the law for its exercise. This was a great judicial achievement.[11] The judicial review court – or, to be technically accurate, the administrative court – today stands as the guarantor that all public power will be fairly and reasonably exercised. And this was achieved through the development of these classical principles.

These simple ideas also provided a straightforward measure which other common law jurisdictions might react to or reject as they indigenised their administrative law. As such, it is believed that these classical principles had an influence across the common law world that was generally beneficial, as several chapters in this volume suggest.[12] To be sure, there is much to discuss about these principles, but they form the conceptual furniture of modern administrative law. This common conceptual furniture provides the means whereby different common law jurisdictions can learn from each other as they develop their own systems of administrative law.

3.2.2 *Theoretical Foundations of Classical Administrative Law*

The ultra vires doctrine was a crucial part of this story of the scope and philosophy of classical administrative law. Where Parliament is sovereign (as it is in the UK),[13] then the ultra vires doctrine (or something very like it) necessarily provides the justification for judicial review. What is it that justifies an unelected official (a judge) in quashing a decision made by an elected Minister of the Crown accountable to Parliament? In oft-cited words, Professor L. G. Baxter puts it this way: 'the self-justification of the ultra vires doctrine is that its application consists of nothing other than an application of the law itself, and the law of Parliament to boot.'[14] If an official acts beyond his legal power, then his act is legally non-existent or void. And there is nothing exceptional (although it is very important) that a court should uphold the law and declare that act void. This is nothing more than the rule of law at work.

Of course, statutes are often silent or uncertain, and it is implausible to suppose that Parliament intends every nuance or point of detail that may arise in the application of the statute. But as Lord Steyn said in *R* v. *Home Secretary, ex parte Pierson*: 'Parliament does not legislate in a vacuum. Parliament legislates for a European liberal democracy founded on the principles and traditions of the common law. And the courts may approach legislation on this initial assumption. But this assumption only has prima facie force. It can be displaced by a clear and specific provision to the contrary.'[15] This is the so-called modified ultra vires doctrine, in which it is presumed that Parliament, unless it makes the contrary intent clear, intends that powers should be exercised in accordance with the principles of good administration. When decision makers do not exercise their powers according to those principles, they act ultra vires and their respective decisions may be quashed.

The ultra vires doctrine, even in this modified form, is not found convincing by all. Pointing to the acknowledged artificialities of the doctrine, some scholars find the basis of judicial review in the common law.[16] But there are adverse consequences to the

[11] And I would add an academic achievement for the writings of Professor Stanley de Smith and Professor Sir William Wade – both Cambridge writers – played a crucial role.

[12] See, e.g., Chapters 8 and 17.

[13] We will consider this in more detail later.

[14] L. G. Baxter, *Administrative Law* (Kenwyn: Juta & Co., 1984), p. 303.

[15] [1997] UKHL 37; [1998] AC 539, at 587.

[16] See, for instance, P. Craig, 'Ultra Vires and the Foundations of Judicial Review' (1998) 57(1) *Cambridge Law Journal* 63. For my defence of ultra vires, see C. Forsyth 'Of Fig Leaves and Fairy Tales: The Ultra Vires Doctrine, the Sovereignty of Parliament and Judicial Review' (1996) 55(1) *Cambridge Law Journal* 122.

abandonment of ultra vires, well illustrated by the 1988 *UDF* case[17] in South Africa. The central point of the case is that the logic of *Anisminic* is rejected and ouster clauses become effective to exclude from judicial review many decisions that the rule of law calls to be subject to judicial review. In this case, the ultra vires doctrine, previously considered the basis of judicial review in South African law, was abandoned by that country's highest court with consequences that every thoughtful critic has considered disastrous.[18] The *UDF* case stands as proof positive that the debate over the foundations of judicial review is not some idle past time of academicians but that these conceptual issues have real consequences. The *UDF* case also exemplifies that any export of administrative law principles without an awareness of the normative principles they rest on can lead to constitutionally problematic outcomes.

Why, then, is reconciliation of the competing foundations of judicial review so difficult? Behind the technical arguments is a fundamental question about the constitutional position of the judiciary. Are the judges (like everyone else) ultimately subject to the law, or are they masters of the common law? Surely the position is that the law is the judges' only master.[19] After all, judges swear an oath when taking office to 'do right to all manner of people after the laws and usages of this realm, without fear or favour, affection or ill will'.[20] The law, of course, needs to be developed to account for changing needs. Fidelity to the law – founded in the oath – means that any changes that judges introduce are interstitial, incremental and in accordance with recognised doctrine. The craft and challenge of the judicial office is to adapt the law to the challenges of today while staying within the overlapping constraints of the law and the constitution. Sometimes, of course, the judge finds it frustrating to proceed incrementally when it is clear that justice requires an immediate and broad reform. But classical administrative law, extending the benison of the rule of law far into practically all exercise of public power, is an eloquent demonstration of what can be achieved by the incremental approach.

17 *Staatspresident en andere* v. *United Democratic Front en 'n ander* 1988(4) SA 830(A).

18 The case concerned a challenge to several emergency regulations made by the State President in terms of the Public Safety Act 1953. During the several states of emergency declared under the 1953 Act during the 1980s, the State President made far-reaching emergency regulations controlling many aspects of everyday life. The United Democratic Front sought to challenge the regulations on the grounds that the concept of 'unrest' was so vague as to render the regulations null and void. All the emergency regulations made by the State President were apparently protected by an ouster clause, to be found in section 5B of the 1953 Act, providing that 'no court shall be competent to enquire into or to give judgment on the validity of any proclamation made under section 3' of the 1953 Act and the regulations attacked purported to be made under that section. On classic *Anisminic* principles, it was clear that if the regulations were ultra vires, judicial review would not be precluded by the ouster clause. Ultra vires regulations, the argument ran, were not made 'under section 3' of the 1953 Act and so were not protected from review by the ouster clause. This had been accepted in the first instance court. But on appeal, Rabie ACJ took a rather different view. The ACJ accepted the appellants' submission that, even if the regulations were vague, they were still made 'under section 3' and thus protected from review by the ouster clause. The doctrine of ultra vires was rejected in terms. The acting chief justice said the ultra vires approach 'was unjustified. In my opinion, it is artificial and false' (my translation).

19 The phrase comes from H. Hahlo and E. Kahn, *The South African Legal System and Its Background* (Cape Town: Juta Publishing, 1968), p. 39. But see, to like effect, Grundgesetz für die Bundesrepublik Deutschland, art 97(1): 'Die Richter sind unabhängig und nur dem Gesetze unterworfen' ('Judges are independent and subject only to the law'). This description of the judicial task is drawn from my description of Minerva J, 'a judge with preternatural abilities, wise beyond all telling, with unparalleled impartiality and unrivalled compassion rooted in her soul': C. Forsyth, 'Blasphemy against Basics', in J. Bell, M. Elliott, P. Murray (eds.), *Public Law Adjudication in Common Law Systems: Process and Substance* (London: Hart, 2016).

20 The words cited come from the Promissory Oaths Act 1868, section 4.

3.3 THREATS TO CLASSICAL ADMINISTRATIVE LAW: UNDERMINING EXPORT

3.3.1 *Threats to Parliamentary Supremacy, Direct and Indirect*[21]

The classical structure and form of administrative law just described developed in a context in which the Westminster Parliament was sovereign. But in the 1990s, it became common for some judges and academics frustrated by the failings of the elected legislature – chiefly that the executive dominated the legislature – to express the view that if Parliament (at the behest of the executive) did something sufficiently outrageous (such as abolishing judicial review), the judges would step in and 'disapply' the offending statute.

As we have already seen, judges will rightly strain to interpret legislation in a way that is consistent with the rule of law.[22] But when the will of Parliament is clear, even if inconsistent with the principles of the rule of law, judges must bow to that will. Courts have frequently affirmed that '[w]hat is at stake [here] is the location of the ultimate decision-making authority – the right to the "final word" in a legal system'.[23] Generally, any conflict between judiciary and legislature can be avoided by sensible construction of the relevant statute since, on the whole, Parliament will intend to comply with the rule of law. But if the judiciary, frustrated by the failings of the elected legislature, was to assert a power to hold Acts of Parliament invalid, it would be stepping from law into politics, and the outcome of its efforts would be impossible to predict.

So the suggestions that the judges might dispose of parliamentary sovereignty were always overbold. After all, all the judges who heard the *Miller* case (the Brexit judicial review) were emphatically orthodox.[24] At first instance,[25] the principle of parliamentary supremacy is unequivocally and unconditionally affirmed by the Lord Chief Justice, the Master of the Rolls and Sales LJ.[26] Dicey's famous dictum that Parliamentary sovereignty means that Parliament has 'the right to make or unmake any law whatever; and, further that no body or person is recognised by the law . . . as having a right to override or set aside legislation of Parliament' is cited with approval, as is Lord Bingham's remark in *Jackson* that 'the bedrock of the British constitution is the supremacy of the Crown in Parliament'.[27] In the Supreme Court,[28] their Lordships were equally forthright: 'Parliamentary sovereignty is a fundamental principle of the UK constitution'.[29] Their Lordships drew from the famous summary of the principle by Professor Dicey, noting that Parliament has 'the right to make or unmake any law whatsoever; and further, no person or body is recognised by the law as having a right to override or set aside the legislation of Parliament'.[30] While judges may always change their

21 This section draws, in part, from W. Wade and C. Forsyth, *Administrative Law*, 11th ed. (London: Oxford University Press, 2014), pp. 19–25, especially pp. 22–3, and R. Ekins and C. Forsyth, 'Judging the Public Interest: The Rule of Law vs. The Rule of Courts', *Policy Exchange*, 3 December 2005, available at https://policyexchange.org.uk/publication/judging-the-public-interest-the-rule-of-law-vs-the-rule-of-courts/.

22 See Section 3.2.

23 J. Goldsworthy, *The Sovereignty of Parliament: History and Philosophy*, (Oxford: Clarendon Press, 1999), p. 3.

24 *R (Miller)* v. *Secretary of State for Exiting the European Union* [2017] UKSC 5.

25 *R (Miller & Anor)* v. *The Secretary of State for Exiting the European Union* [2016] EWHC 2768 (Admin).

26 *Miller*, note 26, at paras. [20]–[23].

27 *Miller*, note 26, at paras. [22]–[23], citing *R (Jackson)* v. *Attorney General* [2005] UKHL 56; [2006] 1 AC 262, at para. [9].

28 *Miller*, note 25.

29 *Miller*, note 25, at [43] (per Lord Neuberger, Lady Hale, Lord Mance, Lord Kerr, Lord Clarke, Lord Wilson, Lord Sumption and Lord Hodge).

30 *Miller*, note 25.

mind and while one should never underestimate academics' ability to argue that judges in fact mean the precise opposite of what they said, a frontal attack on the supremacy of Parliament is now unlikely following *Miller*.

But judges sometimes pay lip service to supremacy but, in fact, do not heed the clear purpose of the legislature. And some of the judges contributing to the majority in *Evans v. Attorney-General* did not heed the clear intent of the legislature.[31] Here one sees imaginative and sophisticated approaches to interpretation being deployed to deny Parliament's will. This replaces the rule of law with the rule of judges.[32]

Perhaps we can devote a few paragraphs to this disconcerting case. We start with Section 53(2) of the Freedom of Information Act 2000 ('FOIA'):

> A decision notice or enforcement notice to which this section applies shall cease to have effect if ... the accountable person [a minister of the Crown] ... gives the Commissioner a certificate signed by him stating that he has on reasonable grounds formed the opinion that, in respect of the request or requests concerned, there was no failure falling within [section 53] subsection (1)(b). [This relates to a failure to communicate information as required by the Act (section 1(1)(b).]

This is the executive override that was exercised by the Attorney General in an attempt to prevent the disclosure under the FOIA of the Prince of Wales's correspondence with Ministers. But the AG's executive override was itself quashed by the Supreme Court. The fundamental point is contained in Lord Wilson's dissent. He said:

> It is helpful to notice the circumstances in which section 53 [the veto provision] came to be included in FOIA. The version of the Bill printed on 10 February 2000 included nothing analogous to it. But under that version the applicant had no *right* to disclosure of such information as was subject to qualified exemptions. Clause 13(4) of it merely conferred a *discretion* on the public authority to disclose such information and clause 13(5) required that, in exercising the discretion, it should have regard to the desirability of disclosing it wherever the public interest in doing so outweighed the public interest in not doing so. In the event that disclosure was refused, clause 48 empowered the Commissioner only to *recommend* that it be given. He could not overrule the authority by *ordering* disclosure. At the Commons Report stage, however, the text of the Bill came, instead, to impose enforceable obligations on public authorities to disclose such information as was subject to qualified exemptions unless (reversing the weighting originally canvassed) the public interest in maintaining the exemption outweighed the public interest in disclosing the information. But, if the discretion of public authorities in this respect was to be eliminated, there needed, so Parliament decided, to be a closely circumscribed power of public authorities at the highest level to override the evaluation of public interests by the Commissioner or by tribunals or courts in ensuing appeals. This was clause 52 of the text of the Bill printed on 6 April 2000 and it became section 53 of FOIA. It is a central feature of the Act.[33]

The executive override thus forms a central part of the legislative compromise that led to the enactment of 2000 Act in its current form; it is a central feature of the Act. One might take the view that the executive override is unnecessary or redundant but what cannot be gainsaid is that it is the result of a deliberate legislative choice by the sovereign Parliament. It is not an

31 [2015] UKSC 21.

32 See Ekins and Forsyth, note 21, from which the following paragraphs are drawn.

33 *Evans*, note 32, at para. [170].

error or an omission by the legislator; it is what Parliament chose. That choice must be accepted by those who administer the law.

It is also important to note that issue on which the Upper Tribunal and the Attorney-General took different views, and which provoked the application for judicial review of the Attorney-General's decision to issue a certificate, was not a point of law on which the Upper Tribunal might be thought to have particular expertise. It was, rather, an assessment of where the balance of public interest lies. The actual provision in contention is section 2(2)(b) of the 2000 Act which is in these terms: '[whether] in all the circumstances of the case, the public interest in maintaining the exemption outweighs the public interest in disclosing the information'.

Lord Wilson is, once more, spot on:

> A power of executive override of determinations of the Commissioner, or of tribunals or courts in ensuing appeals, on issues of *law* would have been an unlawful encroachment upon the principle of separation of powers: see the classic judgment of Sir Edward Coke, Chief Justice, in *Prohibitions del Roy*[1607] EWHC KB J23, 77 ER 1342, upon the claim of King James 1 to determine issues of law. But issues relating to the *evaluation of public interests* are entirely different. In the words of Lord Hoffmann in *R (Alconbury Developments Ltd) v Secretary of State for the Environment, Transport and the Regions* [2001] UKHL 23, [2003] 2 AC 295, at para 69, the principle is that 'in a democratic country, decisions as to what the general interest requires are made by democratically elected bodies or persons accountable to them'. This was the principle reflected in the first version of the Bill. In the later version Parliament sanctioned departure from it but, in enacting section 53, it no doubt continued to have in mind that the evaluation of public interests was not an exercise in relation to which the Commissioner, the tribunals and the courts, could claim any monopoly of expertise. With respect to Lord Neuberger, I cannot agree with his observation at para 96 above that in this context it is hard to differentiate between the findings of fact and conclusions of law traditionally reached by tribunals and courts, on the one hand, and their occasional excursions into evaluating the potency of rival public interests on the other.[34]

Compare this with Lord Neuberger:

> [W]here, as here, a court has conducted a full open hearing into the question of whether, in the light of certain facts and competing arguments, the public interest favours disclosure of certain information and has concluded for reasons given in a judgment that it does, *section 53 cannot be invoked effectively to overrule that judgment merely because a member of the executive, considering the same facts and arguments, takes a different view.*[35]

But is that not exactly what section 53(2) provides for?

The meaning of the statute is not to be invented by the court at its pleasure but is there to be found in what Parliament has already done. As we have seen, section 53 was a crucial part of the legislative compromise that Parliament enacted. Lord Wilson was right to say:

> I agree that Parliament will not be taken to have empowered a member of the executive to override a decision of a court unless it has made such an intention explicit. I agree that courts are entitled to act on the basis that only the clearest language will do this. In my view, however, Parliament has plainly shown such an intention in the present instance.[36]

34 *Evans*, note 32, at para. [171].
35 *Evans*, note 32, at para. [59].
36 *Evans*, note 32, at para. [159].

There can be little doubt that here the Supreme Court took to itself the power to override the clear intent of Parliament, thereby subverting the ultra vires doctrine and the classical structure of administrative law.[37]

3.3.2 *The Replacement of Law with Judicial Discretion*

There is also a distinct tendency in the Supreme Court not to lay down clear rules that can be followed in the future by lower courts and individuals seeking a guide to their conduct or, more importantly, for the purposes of this volume, by other common law systems seeking guidance in the development of their administrative law. Instead the outcome of legal disputes is made dependent upon the exercise of judicial discretion to the detriment of legal certainty and sound doctrine. A spectacular example of this is *Cart* v. *The Upper Tribunal*.[38] If the approach of this case is applied generally the question of whether a decision maker has power to make a particular decision (i.e., whether that decision is within jurisdiction becomes a matter of judicial discretion). In effect, law is replaced with judicial discretion and classical administrative law disappears.[39]

What had happened was that a claimant had been refused permission by the Upper Tribunal to appeal to it from a decision of the First-tier Tribunal and had sought judicial review of that refusal. Although there was, in many circumstances, a right of appeal to the Court of Appeal from a decision of the Upper Tribunal, this decision – the refusal of permission to appeal to the Upper Tribunal – was one of the occasions on which there was no right of appeal.[40] Any remedy that the claimant had would be by way judicial review. But was the Upper Tribunal, by statute 'a superior court of record',[41] subject to judicial review?

Since *Anisminic* there had been growing support for the proposition that all errors of law of administrative bodies (including the unreformed tribunals) were jurisdictional, so any error of law took the body outside its legal powers and rendered the decision in question liable to be quashed on judicial review.[42] But as far as courts were concerned, clear dicta from several House of Lords' decisions (most prominently *Racal*[43] and *Page*,[44] which were not mentioned

[37] There are other similar examples though not quite so strong. See, e.g., *R (Unison)* v. *Lord Chancellor* [2017] UKSC 51 (fees ordered payable by Lord Chancellor for use of employment tribunals pursuant to a power 'to prescribe fees payable' unlawful since they denied access to the courts). For comment, see M. Elliott, 'The Rule of Law and Access to Justice: Some Home Truths', (2018) 77(1) *Cambridge Law Journal* 5, and Sir Stephen Laws, 'Second-Guessing Policy Choices: The Rule of Law after the Supreme Court's UNISON Judgment', *Policy Exchange*, 14 May 2018, at www.policyexchange.org.uk/publication/second-guessing-policy-choices-the-rule-of-law-after-the-supreme-courts-unison-judgment/.

[38] [2011] UKSC 28; [2012] 1 AC 663. I have written about this at greater length in Forsyth, 'Blasphemy against Basics', note 19, which the following account draws from.

[39] It must be frankly admitted that others take a less critical approach to *Cart*.

[40] Tribunals, Courts and Enforcement Act 2007, s. 13(1) provides for an appeal to the Court of Appeal with permission of the Upper Tribunal or the Court of Appeal 'on any point of law arising from a decision made by the Upper Tribunal other than an excluded decision'. But s. 13(8) provides that an 'excluded decision' includes 'any decision of the Upper Tribunal on an application under section 11(4)(b) (application for permission or leave to appeal [from a decision of the First Tier Tribunal])'. Thus Parliament attempted to ensure that decisions of the Upper Tribunal, refusing permission to appeal to the Court of Appeal were not themselves subject to appeal: *interest reipublicae ut sit finis litium*.

[41] Tribunals, Courts and Enforcement Act 2007, section 3(1). At first instance (*R. (on the application of Cart)* v. *Upper Tribunal* [2009] EWHC 3052 (Admin); [2010] 2 W.L.R. 1012), Laws LJ rejected the proposition that the status of being a superior court of record was sufficient to exclude judicial review.

[42] *Anisminic*, note 4.

[43] *Racal Communications Ltd, Re* [1980] UKHL 5, [1981] AC 374, at paras. [14]–[15].

[44] *R* v. *Lord President of the Privy Council Ex p. Page* [1992] UKHL 12.

in the Supreme Court in *Cart*[45]) indicated that the position was different. It all depended upon the construction of the relevant statute. This is made crystal clear by Lord Diplock in *Racal*.[46]

So a court deciding whether the Upper Tribunal was subject to judicial review should – if it were taking the existing law as its starting point – consider whether it was dealing with a court or an administrative body. The Upper Tribunal was, after all, by statute a court of record. And it is surely uncontroversial that the changes introduced by the Tribunals, Courts and Enforcement Act 2007 (e.g., the guarantee of judicial independence extended to tribunal members) meant that the tribunals were now a fully fledged part of the judicial system.[47]

If the Upper Tribunal was a court then it might have been the intention of Parliament that some of the errors of law which the Upper Tribunal might make – such as an error over whether to grant permission to appeal – might be non-jurisdictional and so not subject to judicial review. This question would be the starting point in any inquiry into whether the Upper Tribunal was subject to judicial review. But this starting point at least requires the recognition of the possibility that some of those errors might be non-jurisdictional (i.e., that the pre-*Anisminic* distinction between jurisdiction and other errors still had some purchase).

The Supreme Court in *Cart*, however, rejected in terms any return to the pre-*Anisminic* law, which, it said, would 'lead us back to the distinction between jurisdictional and other errors which was effectively abandoned [in that case]'.[48] There was in the relevant legislation 'no clear and explicit recognition that the Upper Tribunal is to be permitted to make mistakes of law. Certain decisions are unappealable [such as the decision to refuse permission to appeal] and for the most part there are obvious practical reasons why this should be so. But this does not mean that the tribunal must always be permitted to make errors of law when making [such unappealable decisions].'[49]

This makes plain that all errors of law by the Upper Tribunal are jurisdictional – that is, any material error of law made by the tribunal renders its decision void.[50] But the Supreme Court also made it clear that the Upper Tribunal would only rarely be subject to judicial review and certainly not for any material error of law.

There is no clarity in the judgments of the Supreme Court as to what the doctrinal basis of this restriction on the reach of judicial review was. Instead, the court restricts the availability of judicial review on pragmatic but not principled grounds. The court (in Baroness Hale's

45 Also not mentioned in the Supreme Court in *Cart* is the leading Privy Council decision on jurisdiction of *South East Asia Fire Bricks Sdn. Bhd* v. *Non-Metalic Mineral Products Manufacturing Employees Union and others* [1980] UKPC 21; [1981] AC 363. It seems that the Supreme Court overlooked every decision of the House of Lords and the Privy Council on jurisdiction (except *Anisminic)*.

46 The crucial words from Lord Diplock's speech were that 'there is no ... presumption that where a decision-making power is conferred by statute upon a court of law, parliament did not intend to confer upon it power to decide questions of law as well as questions of fact. Whether it did or not and, in the case of inferior courts, what limits are imposed on the kinds of questions of law they are empowered to decide, depends upon the construction of the statute unencumbered by any such presumption'. *Racal*, note 44, at 382–3.

47 See Wade and Forsyth, note 21, at p. 768 for discussion. The effect of the changes wrought by the 2007 Act was much discussed by the Supreme Court: see, e.g., *Cart*, note 39, at para. 54.

48 The distinction was not abandoned in terms in *Anisnimic* and subsequent cases as far as courts were concerned.

49 *Cart*, note 39, at para. [40]. But this remark takes no account of the fact that the Upper Tribunal is made 'a superior court of record' and that the 2007 Act carefully excluded the decision to refuse permission from the scope of any appeal. Did Parliament intend notwithstanding these restrictions to allow judicial review on the precise matters on which it had excluded appeal?

50 See, for instance, *Anisminic*, note 4, at [170]; *Ridge* v. *Baldwin*, note 6, at para. [80]; *Crédit Suisse* v. *Allerdale BC* [1997] QB 306; *Boddington* v. *British Transport Police* [1999] 2 AC 143 at para. [158]; and *McLaughlin* v. *Governor of the Cayman Islands* [2007] UKPC 50.

lead judgment) makes a profoundly pragmatic case, after a tour through the alternatives, that permission to apply for judicial review of the Upper Tribunal should only be granted when the stringent 'second tier appeal criteria' – namely, whether judicial review 'would raise an important point of principle or practice; or . . . there is some other compelling reason for the Court of Appeal to hear it' were met.[51] The Supreme Court thus, while establishing in principle the general availability of judicial review of the Upper Tribunal (because all errors of law are jurisdictional), has carved away so much of that principle that only rarely (i.e., when some important point of principle or practice is engaged) will judicial review lie against decisions of the Upper Tribunal. When a statute has made provision for a second appeal, (i.e., an appeal to the Court of Appeal from the decision of the Upper Tribunal, in addition to an appeal from the first-tier tribunal to the Upper Tribunal), these stringent appeal criteria apply by statute. The effect of *Cart* is to fashion in the exercise of discretion to grant judicial review a form of redress from an error made by the Upper Tribunal, a form of redress which Parliament chose not to create. More positively, it can be said that *Cart* 'should ensure that important points of principle or practice do not become fossilised within the Upper Tribunal'.[52]

Does *Cart* portend then the abandonment of jurisdiction as the organising principle of administrative law and its replacement by the court allowing judicial review on a discretionary basis when it is 'rational and proportionate' to do so (which would be a revolutionary change)? This may be implied from Baroness Hales' dictum that

> the scope of judicial review is an artefact of the common law whose object is to maintain the rule of law – that is to ensure that, within the bounds of practical possibility, decisions are taken in accordance with the law, and in particular the law which Parliament has enacted, and not otherwise. Both tribunals and the courts are there to do Parliament's bidding. But we all make mistakes. No-one is infallible. The question is, what machinery is necessary and proportionate to keep such mistakes to a minimum? In particular, should there be any jurisdiction in which mistakes of law are, either in theory or in practice, immune from scrutiny in the higher courts?[53]

The consequences of this pragmatic approach are profound. The rejection of all distinctions between errors of law that went to jurisdiction and those that did not mean all courts[54] – except presumably the High Court as a court of unlimited jurisdiction – stray outside their jurisdiction when they make errors of law. It follows on classical principle, supported by innumerable decisions from the most authoritative courts, that any material error of law renders the decision void (i.e., legally non-existent).

It can hardly be supposed that the courts would accept that any error by the Upper Tribunal in practice rendered the decision of the tribunal void. But in order to avoid that consequence, they will need to return to a more orthodox analysis in which principle rather than pragmatism carries the day. Doubtless there would be a tendency to accept that any error of law

51 *Cart*, note 39, at para. [27].

52 See Mark Elliott and Robert Thomas, 'Cart and Eba – The New Tribunals System and the Courts', 10 May 2011, UK Constitutional Law Association, available at www.ukconstitutionallaw.org/2011/10/05/mark-elliott-and-robert-thomas-cart-and-eba%E2%80%94the-new-tribunals-system-and-the-courts/. For other more positive views of Cart, see J. Bell, 'The Relationship between Judicial Review and the Upper Tribunal: What Have the Courts Made of Cart v. Upper Tribunal?' [2018] Public Law 394.

53 *Cart*, note 39, at para. [31].

54 After all if the Upper Tribunal – by statute a 'superior court of record' – was subject to judicial review, then so too must other inferior courts yield to the same logic and be subject to judicial review.

rendered the decision void but then seeks to use remedial discretion to avoid the logical consequences.

Adherents of classical administrative law would surely be much dismayed by the abandonment of doctrine in *Cart*. Was the law of jurisdiction and all the learning and wisdom of the past to be set on one side with its place taken by the modern judge's estimate of what was 'proportionate'? The judges, even of the Supreme Court, should recognise the law as their master.

3.3.3 *The Manufacture of Uncertainty: Human Rights and the Doctrine of Proportionality*[55]

The enactment of the Human Rights Act 1998, though doubtless worthy, has led to great uncertainty. The reality of human rights adjudication in a liberal democratic state such as the UK is one in which the judiciary is primarily concerned with striking a balance between conflicting rights (for instance, should a tabloid newspaper's right to 'freedom of expression' under article 10 outweigh a celebrity's right to 'respect for his private and family life' under article 8?) or pronouncing upon whether the limitation of a particular right – say 'freedom of expression' – is justified, in the words of the European Convention on Human Rights, as 'necessary in a democratic society in the interests of national security, public safety or the economic well-being of the country, for the prevention of disorder or crime, for the protection of health or morals, or for the protection of the rights and freedoms of others'.[56]

To be sure, courts across the common law world have developed the doctrine of proportionality to assist them in the difficult task of striking these balances.[57] But the reality is that the outcome of these decisions is essentially a matter of judicial discretion – that is, the judiciary decides on the merits of these difficult decisions, which are often questions upon which reasonable men and women may take different views. When dealing with such questions then, the issue is not whether the decision maker reached the right answer or not – there is no right answer to many of these questions – but whether the decision maker had legitimate authority to make that decision. It is not clear that judges are inherently better placed – especially when acute issues of social and political policy are involved – to make such judgments than elected decision makers or officials accountable to elected representatives.

No reproach is due to the judiciary for the considerable uncertainty introduced by the necessity to strike these balances. This is because it was the legislature in the guise of the Human Rights Act 1998 that gave the judiciary these tasks. But the impact on classical

55 This account draws on Wade and Forsyth, note 21, at p. 306–12, especially p. 310–12.

56 Article 8(2) of the Convention for the Protection of Human Rights and Fundamental Freedoms, Nov. 4, 1950, Europ.T.S. No. 5; 213 U.N.T.S. 221.

57 Often, striking the balance requires 'the weighing of apples against pears', in which it is not plain that the judicial judgment is to be preferred to that on the responsible officials. See *R (Quila)* v. *Home Secretary* [2011] UKSC 45, where a small infringement of the human rights of a certain number of individuals had to be weighed against the grave infringement of the human rights of a smaller uncertain number of individuals. Lord Brown in dissent said at para. [91]: 'The extent to which the rule will help combat forced marriage and the countervailing extent to which it will disrupt the lives of innocent couples adversely affected by it is largely a matter of judgment. Unless demonstrably wrong, this judgment should be rather for government than for the courts. Still more obviously, the comparison between the enormity of suffering within forced marriages on the one hand and the disruption to innocent couples within the 18–21 age group whose desire to live together in this country is temporarily thwarted by the rule change, is essentially one for elected politicians, not for judges.'

administrative law is none the less profound. What is emerging (or in the view of some has emerged) is a culture of rights in which the crucial question will be whether a restriction of a right is justified.[58] As I have argued elsewhere,[59] in this flood of enthusiasm for rights-based judicial review, some sense of perspective should be retained. Classical administrative law questions will often arise even in prominent human rights cases and may be determinative of the outcome.[60] Even so, there can be little doubt that rights based judicial review and its concomitant, the doctrine of proportionality, introduces uncertainty and undermines classical administrative law.

But one point particularly relevant to the theme of this book should be noted. The structured test of proportionality[61] is undeniably a judicial creation. But it emerges from dialogue between the courts of several common law jurisdictions. First the Supreme Court of Canada broke the ground in *R* v. *Oakes*,[62] laying down a three-limbed 'proportionality test'. Relying on South African and Zimbabwean jurisprudence, the Privy Council in *de Freitas* v. *The Permanent Secretary of Ministry of Agriculture, Fisheries, Lands and Housing and Others (Antigua and Barbuda)*[63] adopted a slightly different three limbed test. Then, in *R* v. *The Home Secretary ex parte Daly*,[64] the House of Lords followed *de Freitas*. But, then, in *Huang* v. *The Home Secretary*,[65] the fourth element of the test is added – whether a fair balance has been struck between the rights of the individual and the interests of the community. And this is now the orthodox test.[66]

The structured test leaves the law very uncertain. A four-stage test with each stage requiring a separate judgment would generate uncertainty, even if it were not the case that each of those judgments was itself difficult to make and unpredictable. The answer to the question of whether a limitation on a fundamental right is justified in certain circumstances may vary from jurisdiction to jurisdiction, reflecting deep cultural and social divides. Moreover, then the further uncertainty of the degree of deference has to be considered. Such uncertainty is not in the broader public interest, but there is no easy remedy for it.

58 For a stimulating discussion, see T. Poole, 'Between the Devil and the Deep Blue Sea: Administrative Law in an Age of Rights', *LSE Law, Society and Economy Working Papers* 9/2008, available at www.lse.ac.uk/collections/law/wps/. See also T. Poole, 'The Reformation of English Administrative Law' (2009) 68 *Cambridge Law Journal* 142, and M. Taggart, 'Reinventing Administrative Law', in N. Bamforth and P. Leyland, *Public Law in a Multi-Layered Constitution* (London: Hart 2003), at pp. 331–4. For a critical discussion, see J. Varuhas, 'The Reformation of English Administrative Law? "Rights", Rhetoric and Reality' (2013) 72(2) *Cambridge Law* Journal 369 (drawing attention to the conceptual weakness of these views and their vagueness).

59 Wade and Forsyth, note 21, at pp. 139–40, from which this account is drawn.

60 See, for instance, the points of classical administrative law raised (in addition to the human rights points) in the 'control order' cases in the House of Lords. See C. Forsyth, 'Control Orders, Conditions Precedent and Compliance with Article 6(1)' (2008) 67 *Cambridge Law Journal* 1.

61 Wade and Forsyth, note 21, at p. 307: 'Under the "structured test" there are four questions which the decision-maker must address. The questions are cumulative in that everyone must be satisfactorily answered if the decision is to survive scrutiny. The questions are: (1) Whether the legislative objective is sufficiently important to justify limiting a fundamental right; (2) Whether the measures designed to meet the legislative objective are rationally connected to it; (3) Whether the means used to impair the right or freedom are no more than is necessary to accomplish the objective. (This is the "necessity question".); (4) Whether a fair balance has been struck between the rights of the individual and the interests of the community which is inherent in the whole of the Convention. (This is sometimes called "narrow proportionality".).'

62 [1986] 1 SCR 103 (reverse onus of proof provision held not proportionate).

63 [1998] UKPC 30.

64 [2001] UKHL 26.

65 [2007] UKHL 11.

66 *Bank Mellat* v. *Her Majesty's Treasury (No 2)* [2013] UKSC 39; [2014] AC 700 and *Lumsdon & Ors, R (on the application of)* v. *Legal Services Board* [2015] UKSC 41.

3.4 CONCLUSION

It would be wise to make no firm predictions as to the future of classical administrative law both within England and as a matter of export to elsewhere. But what all the threats identified herein have in common is a seemingly inexorable rise in the role of judicial discretion to be exercised on pragmatic grounds. *Cart* is the paradigm case in which judicial discretion now determines whether a public authority is subject to judicial review and where the boundary is to be found between law and fact. Even *Evans* turns on the judicial estimation not of a question of law but on where the balance of the public interest lies. The proportionality cases turn on the judicial estimation of whether a limitation of a fundamental right is justified by a range of utilitarian or pragmatic considerations. If this is right – and there are sufficient orthodox decisions to make one sceptical – two observations may be made in ending.

First, the current uneasy tension between the judiciary and the other branches of government is exemplified by the cases considered earlier in this chapter. How might this tension be resolved? It may be that the Supreme Court asserts itself more forcibly as the guardian of the constitution and effectively gains unchallenged control over the merits of major decisions. But this will surely call forth a legislative response. Perhaps that response to the growth in judicial power will be to make the appointment of the higher judiciary subject to Parliamentary approval. If the judiciary wish to assert a power to make important political decisions, they must anticipate that the political process will seek to hold them accountable.

Second, and most important from the point of view of this volume, is the likely decline in influence of English administrative law as comparative precedent; it will become less relevant to other common law jurisdictions. The invention of the classical administrative law (by English lawyers) provided a datum (which all except tyrants should accept) against which other common law jurisdictions reacted and adapted themselves. But post-classical English administrative law that is dominated by its own pragmatic concerns inevitably provides less guidance. Pragmatic assessments of where the limits of judicial review should lie may not be the same everywhere.

3.5 POSTSCRIPT

When the proofs of this book were in an advanced stage of preparation the United Kingdom Supreme Court handed down its judgement in *Privacy International*, R *(on the application of)* v. *Investigatory Powers Tribunal & Ors* [2019] UKSC 22. This will now become the leading case on the interpretation of ouster clauses displacing *Anisminic* [1969] 2 AC 147 from that position. The headline is that a divided Supreme Court held that a clause that ousted judicial review from 'determinations, awards and other decisions of the [Investigatory Powers Tribunal (including decisions as to whether they have jurisdiction)' (section 67(8) of Regulation of Investigatory Powers Act 2000) was ineffective to prevent judicial review if the IPT made an error of law. Thus, the decision may be seen as a strong assertion of judicial power to impose the values of the rule of law.

The decision confirms some of the trends identified in this chapter. In particular, para 144 of Lord Carnwath's judgment is in these terms:

> I see a strong case for holding that, consistently with the rule of law, binding effect cannot be given to a clause which purports wholly to exclude the supervisory jurisdiction of the High Court to review a decision of an inferior court or tribunal, whether for excess or abuse of jurisdiction, or error of law. In all cases, *regardless of the words used, it should remain*

> *ultimately a matter for the court to determine the extent to which such a clause should be upheld*, having regard to its purpose and statutory context, and the nature and importance of the legal issue in question; and to determine the level of scrutiny required by the rule of law. (emphasis added)

These emphasised words contain a clear challenge to the supremacy of Parliament since they deny Parliament the 'final word' on this issue of ouster. This paragraph undermines the classical administrative law. But it should be noted that only two judges (Lady Hale and Lord Kerr) agree with Lord Carnwath. (Lord Sumption (with whom Lord Reed agrees) dissented as did Lord Wilson. Lord Lloyd Jones wrote a separate judgement agreeing with Lord Carnwath but not addressing the para. 144 issues.) So, this challenge to supremacy does not enjoy majority support, but it would be idle to deny that the whole tenor of Lord Carnwath's judgment is to take judicial supremacy – at least on the issue of ouster – for granted.

There is much more that could be said about this case but one issue relevant to this chapter should be mentioned. The criticism I have made in this chapter and elsewhere of *Cart* to the effect it replaces the law of jurisdiction with judicial discretion is considered and answered by Lord Carnwath. It is recognised that this was what was happening, but the judge said (para 131) a:

> more flexible approach to the relationship between the legislature and the courts is in my view wholly consistent with the modern constitutional settlement . . . and recognised by this court in *Miller*. Against that background, the judgments of this court in *Cart* point the way to an approach which . . . is both pragmatic and principled. The critical step taken by this court in *Cart* was to confirm, what was perhaps implicit in some of the earlier cases, that it is ultimately for the courts, not the legislature, to determine the limits set by the rule of law to the power to exclude review.

Classical administrative law is crumbling.

4

International Influences on English Judicial Review and Implications for the Exportability of English Law

Michael Ramsden

4.1 INTRODUCTION

The central theme of this volume is that any comparative analysis on the differences that have emerged between common law jurisdictions on the principles of judicial review, and the extent to which 'importing' jurisdictions have departed from their English roots, is attributed to multiple pressures occurring within an indigenous legal order (including historical, constitutional, socio-economic, political and democratic), as explored at a macro level in Chapter 2. But alongside these indigenous considerations, there has been increasing recognition that international factors are also coming to bear on the scope and application of domestic judicial review principles.

The principle of dualism, that international law and domestic law are separate legal systems, has a distinct British constitutional and philosophical lineage.[1] Through colonial links, dualism came to be applied throughout the common law world.[2] Yet the traditional rationale that supports dualism, including that of legal self-determination, is increasingly questioned in an era of closer international regulation of problems common to humanity and the attendant rise of individuals as subjects of international law.[3] These developments have prompted common law jurisdictions to think hard about ways in which to make use of international law. In the context of administrative law, it has led some common law courts to embrace international human rights law as a positive statement of the values that enshrine the rule of law, but has led others, fearing the erosion of its national identity against the 'incoming tide', to reassert the dualist structure of its legal system in relation to the application of unincorporated international norms.[4]

The objective of this chapter, in this regard, is to survey the extent to which English judicial review has remained faithful to the dualist principle, drawing upon comparative developments from other common law jurisdictions. This analysis is pertinent both in consideration of the continued relevance of English judicial review in other jurisdictions (i.e., its 'exportability'), at a time when vertical pressures from international law are coming to bear on courts throughout the common law world. The analysis in this chapter is also relevant in considering

[1] H. Koh, 'Why Do Nations Obey International Law?' (1997) 106 *Yale Law Journal* 2599, at 2609.

[2] For example, *Minister for Immigration and Ethnic Affairs* v. *Teoh* (1995) 183 CLR 273, at [26] (Mason CJ and Brennan J) (Australia); *Glenister* v. *President of the Republic of South Africa* (CCT 48/10) [2011] ZACC 6 (CC), at [98] (Ngcobo CJ) (South Africa); *Gramophone Company of India* v. *Birendra Bahadur Pandey*, [1984] 2 SCR 673 (Reddy J) (India); *Singarasa* v. *Attorney General* SC SPL (LA) No. 182/99 (2006) (Sri Lanka).

[3] R. Jennings, 'An International Lawyer Takes Stock' (1990) 39 *International and Comparative Law Quarterly* 513.

[4] See also Chapter 18.

how close or far apart the English courts are from others in the common law world on the dualist question, which in turn potentially affects the reception of comparative judicial review principles, concerning unincorporated international law, in the English courts (i.e., 'importability'). It will focus in particular on the use of unincorporated international human rights law (be it conventional or customary) as a means to develop common law rights and principles of judicial review. To say 'international human rights law' in the English public law context is, of course, often seen as synonymous with the European Convention on Human Rights (ECHR) – such is the pervasive influence it has had on the jurisprudence, even before its incorporation. But the UK's precarious relationship with the European legal order also raises questions about the future of the Human Rights Act (HRA). This hypothetical scenario has provoked interesting and thoughtful debate already as to the capacity of the common law to draw upon its own sources and values to carry out the same functions as the HRA.[5]

But there is one variable that has received less attention in this debate: whether the capacity of the English common law to perform analogous HRA-functions is affected by the nature and extent of the dualist principle. Prior to the introduction of the HRA, the ECHR exerted a significance influence over the development of common law principles of review and the willingness of judges to speak of 'fundamental rights' as inhering in the common law. Recently, talk of common law rights has been in the ascendency, with an emphasis placed on distinctive British constitutional values in shaping these rights. The politically autochthonous environment in which this resurgence has taken place may end up seeing the English courts place less reliance on the ECHR and a corresponding assertion of normative autonomy via indigenous common law rights. However, as noted in this chapter, an indigenous turn might deprive the English common law of valuable external norms for its development; indigenous common law rights, while offering a more extensive conception of rights protection in certain instances, can lack the normative weight of rights that are underpinned by international obligations. This chapter thus proceeds to consider whether the English courts can profit from progressive approaches towards the use of international law found in the common law world so as to augment the development of its common law rights jurisdiction. The chapter will then conclude with some general observations on the potential effect that the approach currently adopted by the English court to dualism might have on the exportability of English judicial review precedents to other common law jurisdictions in the future.[6]

4.2 DUALISM IN ENGLISH ADMINISTRATIVE LAW

The modern story of dualism in English administrative law begins with the quest to give judicial effect to the ECHR, intertwined with a sub-plot over the common law's capacity to protect individual freedoms against the expanding administrative state. These themes stimulated a rich body of extra-judicial writings, which can only be summarised here. Lord Browne-Wilkinson preferred to draw upon 'our indigenous common law', rather than to give effect to the ECHR by judicial 'infiltration'; he argued that the courts should uphold its long-established jurisdiction to protect freedoms through strict statutory construction.[7]

[5] See, e.g., M. Elliott, 'Beyond the European Convention: Human Rights and the Common Law' (2015) 68 *Current Legal Problems* 85 (and citations therein).

[6] See also Chapter 3.

[7] N. Browne-Wilkinson, 'The Infiltration of a Bill of Rights' (1992) *Public Law* 397, at 403–4, 408.

Concerned about common law revisionism, Sedley LJ hoped that English law would not place singular emphasis on the ECHR with its 'inevitable historical limitations' but would continue in the direction of a 'new catholicity' of judicial review that draws upon a range of international and comparative sources.[8] Similarly, Laws LJ treated the ECHR as a source for common law development given its moral persuasion; he hoped that protection of the ECHR could be achieved by 'judicial development', in finding 'harmony between the common law', justifying a sliding scale of review.[9] Scarman LJ. went further; the common law could not ignore adverse Strasbourg rulings placing the UK in violation of its international obligations.[10] The solution was for the English courts to return to its historic origins and 'curb' Parliamentary excesses.[11] Lord Irvine, on the other hand, while appreciating the 'significant impact' of the ECHR on the 'theory and practice' of English judicial review, argued that this did not justify a conceptual shift from *Wednesbury*.[12] Other judges were not so optimistic that the common law could fill the gaps. Lord Bingham attributed judicial failings in protecting rights to the ECHR's lack of Parliamentary transformation of this instrument into law.[13] Lord Woolf, too, lamented the 'significant differences' between English and Strasbourg judicial review, to the detriment of the individual.[14]

This survey of extra-judicial opinion, finding solutions both 'within' and 'without', goes to support a central point here: the general judicial recognition that the ECHR was exerting greater pressure on English public law. It reflects Lord Bingham's observations that the ECHR had 'a persuasive and pervasive influence on judicial decision-making' even prior to incorporation.[15] Judges did not always agree on the ECHR's role in English law.[16] Early administrative law authority saw robust uses of the ECHR in curbing discretions. Scarman LJ, unsurprisingly given his extra-judicial views, regarded the ECHR to be a mandatory consideration: resolving statutory 'ambiguity or *omission*' by giving effect to the ECHR.[17] This, however, represented a high point and was soon reigned in with a new-found skepticism about holding the executive to 'vague' standards.[18] Other judges preferred to speak of indigenous common law rights.[19] However, the sense that the common law had yet to fully evolve to embrace all rights under the ECHR, coupled with the more progressive uses of the ECHR in other areas of law, left major question marks over the use of this instrument in administrative law.

An answer (of sorts) was provided by the House of Lords in *Brind*.[20] This decision confirmed that statutory 'ambiguity' remained the basis to presume that Parliament intended

8 S. Sedley, 'Human Rights: A Twenty-First Century Agenda' (1995) *Public Law* 386, at 395, 401.

9 J. Laws, 'Is the High Court the Guardian of Fundamental Constitutional Rights' (1993) *Public Law* 59, at 63, 69; J. Laws, 'Law and Democracy', (1995) *Public Law* 72, at 82.

10 L. Scarman, *Hamlyn Lectures (26th Series): English Law – The New Dimension* (London: Stevens, 1974), at 10, 19.

11 Scarman, at 20.

12 A. Irvine, 'Judges and Decision-Makers: The Theory and Practice of Wednesbury Review' (1996) *Public Law* 60, at 73.

13 T. Bingham, 'The European Convention on Human Rights: Time to Incorporate' (1993) 109 *Law Quarterly Review* 390.

14 H. Woolf, 'Droit Public – English Style' (1995) *Public Law* 57, at 59; H. Woolf, *Hamlyn Lectures (41st Series): Protection of the Public – A New Challenge* (London: Stevens, 1990), at 120.

15 *R* v. *Lyons* [2002] UKHL 44, at [13] (Lord Bingham).

16 See generally M. Hunt, *Using Human Rights Law in English Courts* (Oxford: Hart, 1997), at chapter 6.

17 *R* v. *Secretary of State for the Home Department, ex p Phansopkar* [1976] QB 606, at 626 (Scarman LJ).

18 *R* v. *Chief Immigration Officer, ex p Salamat Bibi* [1976] 1 WLR 979, at 984 (Lord Denning); *R* v. *Fernandes* (1980) WL 619001 (Court of Appeal).

19 *Wheeler* v. *Leicester* [1985] AC 1054, at 1065 (Lord Browne-Wilkinson).

20 *R* v. *Secretary of State for the Home Department, ex p Brind* [1991] 1 AC 696.

to act compatibly with international obligations; crucially, the statutory conferral of wide administrative discretions did not generate 'ambiguity'.[21] But there is also a curious duality itself to *Brind*: while the House of Lords was indigenous in its approach to statutory construction (in the sense of generally excluding the ECHR), *Wednesbury* was opened to international influences. Lord Bridge acknowledged the possibility that a violation of the ECHR would support a finding of unreasonableness.[22] On the other hand, Lord Bridge outlined a formulation that he previously coined in *Bugdaycay* as 'anxious scrutiny', noting that any restriction on freedom of expression would have to be justified 'and nothing less than an important competing public interest will be sufficient to justify it'.[23] The significance of *Brind*, to most administrative lawyers, is its consideration but ultimate rejection of proportionality as a general ground of judicial review. But the backstage presence in this analysis was the extent to which the courts were able to give effect to the ECHR. This reflects the fact that incorporation (direct or indirect) would not only entail the application of substantive rights but also an adjudicatory technique apparently forbidden in English administrative law.[24]

Brind is thus something of a double-edged sword, indigenous in statutory application but welcoming to outside norms in its appreciation of *Wednesbury* review: this curious 'duality' made *Brind* an instrument of both judicial activism and restraint. In particular, the emphasis on finding statutory 'ambiguity' made the definition of indigenous common law rights a proxy battlefield for the dualist debate. By framing a right under the ECHR as one that already inheres in the common law, a stronger interpretive principle materialises: the principle of legality.[25] 'Parliament must', as Lord Hoffman noted in *Simms*, 'confront what it is doing and accept the political cost. Fundamental rights cannot be overridden by general or ambiguous words'.[26] In many decisions, then, rights under the ECHR merely 'confirmed' a conclusion on the status of a fundamental right under the common law.[27] Laws J in *B* noted that a 'developing feature' of the English common law is that 'certain rights, broadly those occupying a central place in the ECHR' do not merely enjoy a legal status 'upon the international plane' but are 'to be vindicated as sharing with other principles the substance of the English common law'.[28] Finally, given that the ECHR could not generally find expression through statutory language, attention shifted to other doctrines of administrative law. Before the Australian High Court in *Teoh* developed its ratification theory in the doctrine of legitimate expectations,[29] the English courts had rejected a similar argument several years previously, before a later softening in some post-*Brind* decisions.[30] A potentially more significant development, that never ultimately came to be fully tested in the context of the ECHR given the imminent passage of the HRA, was the House of Lords' finding in *Launder*:

21 *Brind*, at 748 (Lord Bridge), at 761 (Lord Ackner).

22 *Brind*, at 748–9 (Lord Bridge).

23 *Brind*, at 748–9 (Lord Bridge), also at 757 (Lord Ackner); *Bugdaycay* v. *Secretary of State for the Home Department* [1987] AC 514, at 531 (Lord Bridge).

24 *Brind*, at 767 (Lord Lowry) See also *R.* v. *Secretary of State for the Environment, ex p* NALGO [1993] Admin. LR 785, at 798 (Neill LJ).

25 See, e.g., *R* v. *Secretary of State for the Home Department, ex p Leech* [1994] QB 198.

26 *R* v. *Secretary of State for the Home Department, ex p Simms* [2000] 2 AC 115, at 131 (Lord Hoffman).

27 *Leech*, above note 25, at 217E–F (Steyn LJ); *Raymond* v. *Honey* [1983] 1 AC 1 (HL), at 10F (Lord Wilberforce).

28 *R* v. *Cambridge Health Authority, ex p B* [1995] 1 WLR 898.

29 *Teoh*, above note 2.

30 *Chundawadra* v. *Immigration Appeal Tribunal* [1988] Imm AR 161. For a recent survey of the *Teoh* doctrine, see *R. (JS)* v. *Secretary of State for Work and Pensions* [2015] UKSC 16, at [246] (Lord Kerr) (noting it to be 'controversial').

that the voluntary consideration of the ECHR in an administrative policy justified the court in holding the executive to a 'correct' understanding of the treaty provision.[31]

A corollary of these developments was that the so-called monolithic *Wednesbury* standard came under renewed pressure. Fundamental rights should be subject to closer scrutiny by the courts, as per Lord Bridge's iteration in *Brind*.[32] But some judges continued to maintain that 'fundamental rights' did nothing to modify *Wednesbury*.[33] Lord Bingham, on the other hand, stated the ECHR as 'background' to irrationality, which was to be modified according to the now-famous 'anxious scrutiny' formulation: 'the more substantial the interference with human rights, the more the court will require by justification before it is satisfied that the decision is reasonable'.[34] This formulation has, inevitably, prompted debate, both as to its method and substance. Some have argued that it is in effect a permutation of proportionality review in that it requires the court to identify and assign priority to the respective interests for it to make any scrutiny meaningful.[35]

The wider point here though is that the ECHR did much in the pre-HRA period to stimulate consideration as to the efficacy of English judicial review in addressing unwarranted state intrusion into individual freedom. Some judges, however, questioned the legitimacy of these pre-HRA judicial techniques: to Lord Rodger, in asserting 'constitutional rights', 'judges were more or less explicitly, looking for a means of incorporation avant la lettre, of having the common law supply the benefits of incorporation without incorporation'.[36] A more sympathetic account is offered by the author here: many judges, concerned about the resilience of the common law to address contemporary threats, were empowered by a source external to itself to update the principles of judicial review. The ECHR was an instrument of particular moral persuasion because its values also inhered in the common law (even if the full catalogue of rights had yet to), and because it imposed international obligations on the UK, of geo-political significance, which in turn would offer English judges a measure of security in taking steps towards a more pronounced common law rights jurisdiction.

The HRA, at least initially, brought to an end the need to directly challenge the dualist principle. The ECHR was now a direct source of law in the English courts. Of equal significance, the English courts were also now required under Section 2 of the HRA to 'take into account' the jurisprudence of the European Court of Human Rights. In doing so, the effect was to obviate the need to revisit *Brind* outside the context of the HRA, given the expansive nature of rights interpretation under the ECHR. It is an indelible feature of Strasbourg jurisprudence that it treats the ECHR as a 'living instrument' and, increasingly, as indivisible from other sources of international human rights law.[37] In turn, the English courts, following influential Strasbourg jurisprudence, have made use of a range of sources,

[31] *R.* v. *Secretary of State for the Home Department, ex p Launder* [1997] 1 WLR 839 (HL), at 867F (Lord Hope).

[32] Not all judges recognise the place of the ECHR in supporting the emergence of anxious scrutiny: e.g., Lord Sumption, 'Anxious Scrutiny', *Administrative Law Bar Association Annual Lecture*, 4 November 2014 (available at www.supremecourt.uk/docs/speech-141104.pdf) (anxious scrutiny 'was a response to the recognition that, quite apart from modern international human rights law, there were certain rights which at common law should be regarded as fundamental').

[33] *NALGO*, above note 24, at 798 (Neill LJ); *R* v. *Ministry of Defence, ex p Smith* [1996] QB 517, at 536–41 (Brown J).

[34] *Smith*, above note 33, at 554 (Bingham MR); *Bugdaycay*, above note 23, at 531 (Lord Bridge).

[35] Hunt, above note 16, at 217; Laws, above note 8, 'Guardian of Rights', at 69 (anxious scrutiny represents 'a conceptual shift away from Wednesbury unreasonableness').

[36] See also *Watkins* v. *Secretary of State for the Home Department* [2006] UKHL 17, [2006] 2 AC 395, at [64] (Lord Rodger).

[37] E.g., *Soering* v. *United Kingdom* (1989) 98 I.L.R. 270, at [88].

unincorporated in English law, in the contextual interpretation of HRA rights.[38] Conversely, where such unincorporated instruments have been invoked outside the context of the HRA, they have often met with little success, which may reflect a preference to channel all international human rights through the HRA as the authoritative, self-contained, source of rights that derive from the international plane.

Outside the realm of the HRA, some case law, in fact, shows a toughening of approach to dualism than was perhaps typical in the era immediately preceding the HRA.[39] A reflection of the possible preference to define common law rights in indigenous terms, despite there being persuasive international authority, is *Moohan*, concerning the right of prisoners to vote in the Scottish independence referendum. Specifically, the Supreme Court found that there was no common law right to vote given that the universal franchise was created and developed by legislation.[40] Lord Hodge perfunctorily rejected the relevance of Article 25 of the International Covenant on Civil and Political Rights (ICCPR) to the case as inconsistent with the dualist theory of treaties.[41] Further, a reversal of pre-HRA attempts to mitigate *Brind* dualism is seen in *Corner House*.[42] The *Launder* principle, which held promise as a device to give greater expression to the ECHR in administrative law, was heavily qualified once the executive's voluntary consideration of an international instrument switched from the ECHR to another: the OECD Convention. According to *Corner House*, there is a need for a treaty regime to produce a clear body of jurisprudence on the provision that was taken into account by the executive, effectively limiting *Launder* to sophisticated supranational regimes such as the ECHR.[43] Finally, the customary international law doctrine of incorporation, which treats custom as a source of the common law, remains underdeveloped by the courts and still has no role in regulating broad conferral of statutory discretion.[44] Indeed, there was also a suggestion by Lord Mance in *Keyu* that any human rights custom would have to be taken subject to the limitations of the ECHR, once again reinforcing the monopoly on the applicability of international human rights norms that the Convention assumes in English law.[45]

4.3 FACTORS AFFECTING 'EXPORTABILITY' OF ENGLISH DUALISM IN COMMON LAW JUDICIAL REVIEW

The analysis proposed in the previous section demonstrates the difficulties that English judges faced in coming to terms with the growing pressure to take into account international human rights law in the development of domestic principles of judicial review, but these pressures, of course, were by no means exclusive to the English jurisdiction. Many other common law courts at the same time would be compelled to address the relevance of their state's international obligations on the scope of administrative law. It will be seen, in this regard, that some of the techniques used by the English courts to 'soften' dualism in judicial

38 A v. *Secretary of State for the Home Department* [2005] 2 AC 68, at 117–21 (Lord Bingham); *JS*, above note 30, at [83]–[87] (Lord Reed); *ZH (Tanzania)* v. *Secretary of State for the Home Department* [2011] UKSC 4, at [33] (Lady Hale); *Burnip* v. *Birmingham City Council* [2013] PTSR 117, at [22] (Maurice Kay LJ).

39 See section 4.4.

40 *Moohan* v. *Lord Advocate* [2014] UKSC 67, at [56] (Lord Hodge).

41 *Moohan*, at [29] (Lord Hodge) (although also see [35]).

42 *R (Corner House Research)* v. *Director of the Serious Fraud Office* [2009] 1 AC 756.

43 *Corner House*, at 845 (Lord Bingham).

44 *R* v. *Secretary of State for the Home Department, ex p Thakrar* [1974] QB 684 (CA), at 708 (Orr LJ). See further E. Bjørge, 'Common Law Rights: Balancing Domestic and International Exigencies' (2016) 75(2) *Cambridge Law Journal* 220, at 238–42.

45 *R (Keyu)* v. *Secretary of State for Foreign and Commonwealth Affairs* [2015] UKSC 69, at [151] (Lord Mance).

review (anxious scrutiny, presumption of compatibility, etc.) were successfully exported to other jurisdictions, sometimes with suitable adaptation. In equal measure, however, the narrowness of the English approach, crystallised in *Brind*, came in for much criticism and in turn hindered the exportability of English techniques for the use of unincorporated international norms in administrative law. The following section will thus consider approaches to dualism in judicial review across the common law world and the extent to which English jurisprudence has influenced such approaches.

At the outset, any comparative assessment of the dualist principle in the common law has to acknowledge the degrees to which these jurisdictions have constitutional or constitutionalised systems of public law. Express constitutional provisions provide the clearest entry point: the Indian Constitution 'obligates the State to foster respect for international law and treaty obligations' and the South African courts 'must consider international law' when interpreting the Bill of Rights, justifying its weighty use at least in the realm of constitutional interpretation.[46] Another clear entry point for international human rights law is in the contextual interpretation of analogous constitutional rights, often to resolve ambiguities, which has become a routine occurrence in constitutionalised systems in the common law world. Waters, having surveyed extensive comparative jurisprudence, observed that common law courts have increasingly used international human rights treaties in the contextual interpretation of domestic constitutions as part of a broader comparative common law discussion.[47] It may also be viewed more generally within Vicki Jackson's 'engagement model', where transnational sources are 'seen as interlocutors, offering a way of testing understanding of one's own traditions and possibilities by examining them in the reflection of others'; such sources inform but do not control another nation's legal norms.[48]

The issue is thus whether the use of international law in constitutional rights interpretation has a broadening down effect, to also influence the principles of administrative law. Or to put it another way, if constitutional values increasingly come to embody international values, then how big is the leap to say that administrative law also embodies the same, and to what extent? The Canadian Supreme Court's decision in *Baker* is instructive.[49] *Baker* was not a Charter case, but it certainly had an 'off-stage presence'.[50] Justice L'Heureux-Dube for the majority noted the orthodox dualist position, but also the important role that international human rights law has played as an aid in interpreting domestic law in other common law countries and its 'critical influence on the interpretation of the scope of the rights included in the Charter'.[51] Justice L'Heureux-Dub noted that 'children's rights, and attention to their interests, are central humanitarian and compassionate values in Canadian society', deducing these values from 'international instruments', ministerial statements and legislation.[52] It is also interesting that, in contrast to *Launder*, which only regards a treaty to be relevant where it is explicitly taken into account by the authority, *Baker* presumed treaty relevance more generally from the humanitarian nature of the discretion at the administrator's disposal. In

46 Article 51(c), Constitution of India; *Visaka* v. *State of Rajasthan* [1997] 3 LRC 361; *Jolly George Verghese* v. *Bank of Cochin* [1980] 2 SCR 913, 922; Section 39(1), 1996 South African Constitution.

47 M. Waters, 'Creeping Monism: The Judicial Trend towards Interpretive Incorporation of Human Rights Treaties' 107(3) (2007) *Columbia Law Review* 628, at 672–9.

48 V. Jackson, 'Constitutional Comparisons: Convergence, Resistance, Engagement' (2005) 119 *Harvard Law Review* 109, at 112.

49 *Baker* v. *Canada* [1999] 2 SCR 817.

50 D. Dyzenhaus, M. Hunt and M. Taggart, 'The Principle of Legality in Administrative Law: Internationalisation as Constitutionalisation' (2001) 1 *Oxford University Commonwealth Law Journal* 5, at 32.

51 *Baker*, above note 49, at [70] (L'Heureux-Dube J).

52 *Baker*, above note 49, at [67] (L'Heureux-Dube J).

other words, given that the discretion concerns 'humanitarian and compassionate' considerations, it necessarily includes consideration of child well-being under the CRC in the exercise of it.[53] It is also significant that the Supreme Court found the weighing of the child's interest to have been inadequate in the impugned decision: 'the failure to give serious weight and consideration to the interests of the children constitutes an unreasonable exercise of the discretion'.[54] This is not to discount the other domestic (non-CRC) factors that came to bear on this reasonableness assessment, but the Supreme Court's venture into weighing considerations clearly was influenced by the obligation under the CRC to give 'primary consideration' to the interests of the child.[55] The suggestion here, then, is that the identification of international norms as being congruent with national values, in constitutionalised systems, may in turn support the norm's use in a more rigorous way in administrative law than contemplated in *Brind*.[56]

But constitutionalism may go in the other direction. It has been used to crystallise autochthonous approaches to public law in post-colonial, constitutional settlements.[57] This is particularly so in Asia. The Hong Kong constitution, for example, is declaratory of the dualist position that pertained during colonial times, thereby affording less latitude for the fertilisation of unincorporated norms in administrative law.[58] In Singapore, dualist reasoning denied the utility of international human rights law in the interpretation of constitutional rights that addressed issues of moral sensitivity (such as the death penalty and caning).[59] Further, while dualism in the English tradition was based on the premise of liberal constitutional values (democratic legitimacy of Parliament and separation of powers), it has been used for less than benevolent effects. Dualism was invoked, as Dugard noted, by the South African courts during apartheid to reinforce its isolation from the world.[60] Further, the Sri Lankan Supreme Court, citing the English origins of the principle, took the extraordinary step of employing dualism to find that the executive acted unconstitutionally in ratifying the ICCPR Optional Protocol, given that it had no authority to outsource a judicial function.[61] Sri Lankan judges embraced a strict form of dualism, and one that not even its English originators would countenance today, as a means to guard its function from external influence and scrutiny.[62]

53 Compare *Baker* to the approach in Hong Kong, where the immigration authority's election to take into account 'humanitarian' and 'compassionate' considerations did not bring into play international human rights law: *Comilang Milagros Tecson* v. *Commissioner of Registration* [2012] HKEC 869, at [83] (Lam J); M. Ramsden, 'Immigration Judicial Review in Hong Kong: The Developing Legal Framework', (2019) 33(2) *Journal of Immigration, Asylum and Nationality Law* 177.

54 *Baker*, above note 49, at [65], [67] (L'Heureux-Dubé J).

55 See confirmation of this interpretation of *Baker* in *Kanthasamy* v. *Canada* (2015) 41 BHRC 679, at [37]–[38] (Abella J, with whom McLachlin CJ, Cromwell, Karakatsanis and Gascon JJ agreed).

56 Although see *Suresh* v. *Canada* 2002 SCC 1 (Supreme Court), at [36] (that the minister's discretion in *Baker* was 'self-imposed', thereby entitling the court to engage in more rigorous review).

57 See generally, with a focus on Caribbean states, D. Pollard, 'Unincorporated Treaties and Small States' (2007) 33(3) *Commonwealth Law Bulletin* 389.

58 See Article 39 Hong Kong Basic Law; *GA* v. *Director of Immigration* (2014) 17 HKCFAR 60, at [83] (Chan PJ); M. Ramsden, 'Reviewing the United Kingdom's ICCPR Immigration Reservation in Hong Kong Courts' (2014) 63(3) *International and Comparative Law Quarterly* 635.

59 *Yong Vui Kong* v. *Public Prosecutor* [2015] SGCA 11, at [45] (Menon CJ) (Court of Appeal).

60 J. Dugard, 'The South African Judiciary and International Law in the Apartheid Era' (1998) 14 *South African Journal of Human Rights* 110.

61 *Singarasa*, above note 2, at 15–17.

62 F. De Londras, 'Dualism, Domestic Courts, and the Rule of International Law', in M. Sellers and T. Tomaszewski, *The Rule of Law in Comparative Perspective* (London: Springer, 2010), at 234.

While common law jurisdictions have remained, at a theoretical level, faithful to the dualist structure, there has been a gradual softening of approach over time to augment the legitimacy of the various 'indirect' entry points of international law in judicial review. The principle of statutory construction that regards international law to only be relevant where textual 'ambiguity' is found has met with both acceptance and resistance in the common law world. To be sure, the 'ambiguity' requirement continues to be the torch-bearer in many jurisdictions: the *Bangalore Principles*, which famously encouraged common law judges to make greater use of international human rights law, affirmed it.[63] On the other hand, the New Zealand Court of Appeal in *Sellers* noted that compatibility (with customary international law) should be achieved even where it 'might appear to be difficult to reconcile with the seemingly generally applicable wording' of the statutory provision.[64] This approach was subsequently applied by the Supreme Court in *Zaoui*, where clear statutory wording was required to take away the right under Article 31(2) of the Refugee Convention for a detained asylum seeker to challenge their detention in court.[65] The New Zealand approach, outside the context of constitutional rights no less, supports a method of interpretation that is markedly different to the *Brind* ambiguity requirement in permitting the court to strain plain language to ensure compatibility.[66]

Being able to read international human rights law into legislation represents the strongest form of control, but other challenges have been made to the *Brind* unfettered discretion orthodoxy. New Zealand, once again, presents an alternative. In *Tavita*, the executive argued that using the ICCPR and CRC to constrain immigration discretion contravened *Brind*.[67] Cooke J openly challenged the persuasiveness of this House of Lords authority: *Brind* was 'in some respects a controversial decision'.[68] Cooke J considered the *Brind* unfettered discretion principle as 'an unattractive argument, apparently implying that New Zealand's adherence to the international instruments has been at least partly window-dressing'.[69] This point was heightened by the fact that New Zealand had ratified the Optional Protocol to the ICCPR, which made it, 'in a sense', part of 'this country's judicial structure'.[70] The implication was that the provisions of the ICCPR and CRC were mandatory considerations and not merely voluntary (as per *Launder*). Still, if the extent of *Tavita* was to place, on an ad hoc basis, an additional constraint on the immigration authority then the departure from *Brind* was not too dramatic. What is significant, then, is the High Court's subsequent finding in *Rahman* that the *Tavita* principle is a 'general one, not dependent upon the particular instruments concerned'.[71] New Zealand's obligations under the ICESCR also acted as a constraint on

63 See, e.g., M. Kirby, 'The Australian Use of International Human Rights Norms: From Bangalore to Balliol – A View from the Antipodes' (2003) 16 *University of New South Wales Law Journal* 363, at 374.

64 *Sellers* v. *Maritime Safety Inspector* [1999] 2 NZLR 44 (Keith J). See further T. Dunsworth, 'Hidden Anxieties: Customary International Law in New Zealand' (2004) 2 *New Zealand Journal of Public and International Law* 67.

65 *Zaoui* v. *Attorney General* [2005] 4 LRC 557, at 647 (Elias CJ, Gault, Keith, Blanchard and Eichelbaum JJ). The Supreme Court also based its finding on the 'ancient common law jurisdiction' over the liberty of the individual but given that it cited *Sellers* it arguably treated Article 31(2) as a separate basis for invoking the strong interpretive principle.

66 See further Chapter 18. For Canada, see *R* v. *Hape* 2007 SCC 26, at [53] (McLachlin CJ, LeBel, Deschamps, Fish and Charron JJ) (presumption of conformity is rebutted only where there is 'an *unequivocal legislative intent* to default on an international obligation').

67 *Tavita* v. *Minister for Immigration* [1994] 2 NZLR 257, at 266 (Cooke J).

68 *Tavita*, at 266 (Cooke J).

69 ibid.

70 ibid.

71 *Rahman* v. *Minister of Immigration* (26 September 2000) AP 56/99; CP 49/99, H.C., at [52]–[54] (McGechan J).

administrative discretions, despite common law iterations in New Zealand tending to treat socio-economic rights as non-justiciable.[72]

Still, the most discussed counter to *Brind* orthodoxy in the common law world is presented by the Australian High Court in *Teoh*, where it was held that the State's ratification of a treaty was capable of generating a legitimate expectation 'absent statutory or executive indications to the contrary'.[73] Inspired by *Tavita*, the High Court of Australia found it equally 'unattractive' to accept that 'no regard need to be paid to Australia's acceptance of international obligations' in defining the limits of discretionary powers.[74] That said, *Teoh* has caused political controversy within Australia and subsequent jurisprudence has equivocated on the soundness of the principle.[75] In *Lam*, Justices McHugh and Gummow doubted whether a treaty could give rise to an expectation on the premise that an individual would not subjectively hold the view that a transaction outside of Australia would entitle them to anything. They noted that *Teoh* accepted the established doctrine that international obligations 'are not mandatory relevant considerations', but rather affect the standard of procedural fairness applicable to an individual.[76]

Teoh remains controversial in Australia but has done much in the common law world to stimulate debate about the dualist principle in administrative law. First, *Teoh* has inspired domestic constitutional interpretation but also been excluded by it. The Indian Supreme Court, for example, drew upon *Teoh* to support the muscular principle of interpretation that, where possible, international human rights conventions should be used 'to enlarge the meaning and content' of the constitution.[77] The Irish Supreme Court, on the other hand, rejected *Teoh* on the basis that Australian public law does not replicate the dualist rule 'with anything like the constitutional rigour with which it is embodied' in the Irish Constitution.[78] Second, *Teoh* has been invoked to support an approach not even available in Australia: that of a substantive expectation. Most strikingly, the Zimbabwe High Court used the state's acceptance of a treaty body's jurisdiction on the international plane as meaning that 'it would comply with the requirements of the Treaty and abide by the decisions of the Tribunal'.[79] Thomas J in the New Zealand Court of Appeal, finding *Teoh* 'compelling', was prepared to give relevant socio-economic provisions in the Treaty of Waitangi substantive effect, reflecting its status as the 'country's fundamental constitutional document'.[80] Third, while *Teoh* has been accepted, its effects have been considerably tempered and qualified. The Scots Court of Session regarded *Teoh* to be good law, subject to 'three major qualifications': (1) that it does not give rise to a 'binding rule of law' (i.e., it only produces procedural effects); (2) that it may be negated by statutory or executive indications to the contrary; (3) that not all treaties are

[72] *Rahman*, at [54] (McGechan J). In the Hong Kong context, see M. Ramsden, 'Using the ICESCR in Hong Kong Courts' (2012) 42(3) *Hong Kong Law Journal* 839.

[73] *Teoh*, above note 2, at 365 (Mason CJ, Deane, Toohey and Gaudron JJ).

[74] *Teoh*, above note 2, at 372 (Mason CJ, Deane, Toohey and Gaudron JJ).

[75] M. Allars, 'International Law and Administrative Discretion', in B. Opeskin and D. Rothwell, *International Law and Australian Federalism* (Melbourne: Melbourne University Press, 1997), at 262–9.

[76] *Re Minister for Immigration and Multicultural Affairs, ex p Lam* 195 ALR 502, at 527 (McHugh and Gummow JJ).

[77] *Vishaka* v. *Rajasthan* [1997] 3 LRC 361, at 367.

[78] *Kavanagh* v. *Governor of Mountjoy Prison* [2002] IESC 13, at [25] (Fennelly J). Article 26(6) of the Irish Constitution provides: 'No international agreement shall be part of the domestic law of the state save as may be determined by the Oireachtas'.

[79] *Gramara (Private) Limited* v. *Government of Zimbabwe* HH 169/2009 (ZW 2010), 29 January 2010 (High Court) (Patel J), at [48] (although the expectation was defeated by an overriding public interest).

[80] *Maori Council* v. *Attorney-General* [1996] 3 NZLR 140, at 184–5 (Thomas J).

capable of generating legitimate expectations, only those that 'clearly intended to affect the rights of individuals'.[81]

The second qualification mentioned by the Scots Court of Session above has arguably led some common law judges to avoid the unnecessary baggage of *Teoh* altogether; recall that after the Australian High Court's decision the executive and legislature gave such resounding 'indications to the contrary'.[82] Fear of a similar backlash may, in turn, lead courts to refashion these treaty norms as indigenous common law principles so as to avoid dualist controversies altogether. The long struggle to establish a refugee screening mechanism in Hong Kong is instructive in this regard. Hong Kong is a party to the Convention Against Torture (CAT) but had yet to incorporate Article 3 (*non-refoluement* principle) in domestic law. The argument was made that Hong Kong had to observe Article 3 because of, among other reasons, *Teoh*.[83] The executive had a practice of allowing asylum seekers to temporarily remain in the territory for their CAT claims to be processed. The essence of the complaint was that the executive should conduct this assessment and not leave it to the UNHCR. The Court of Appeal accepted the possibility of a legitimate expectation flowing from Article 3 and executive acknowledgments that it observes this provision in a policy.[84] However, the Court of Final Appeal's reasoning on the source of executive obligation was purposefully under-theorised: Chief Justice Li noted that '[f]or the purposes of this appeal, the Court will assume without deciding that the Secretary is under a legal duty to follow the policy as a matter of domestic law'.[85] In doing so, it is arguable here that the court created space for itself to give effect to the *non-refoulement* principle in the Hong Kong common law, with the Chief Justice noting that the determination of a torture claim 'is plainly one of momentous importance to the individual concerned. To him, life and limb are in jeopardy and his fundamental human right not to be subjected to torture is involved.'[86] The under-theorised suggestion that the *non-refoulement* principle inheres in the common law rather than as a legitimate expectation may then account for an indigenisation of treaty norms, so as to avoid the type of executive and legislative countermeasures taken in Australia in the aftermath of *Teoh*.[87]

On a final point, common law courts have also embraced *Smith* anxious scrutiny review or otherwise benchmarked the reasonableness of executive decisions against unincorporated international law. The Supreme Court of Canada in *Baker* has explained the abstract relevance of treaties, in that they 'help show the values that are central in determining whether [a particular] decision was a reasonable exercise [of power]'.[88] The Supreme Court of India required the executive to 'keep in view' the Convention on Biological

[81] *Khairandish* v. *Secretary of State for the Home Department* 2003 SLT 1358, at [11]–[12] (Lord Drummond Young).

[82] See further A. Downer, 'Executive Statement on the Effect of Treaties in Administrative Decision-Making' (1997) 8 *Public Law Review* 120.

[83] See further M. Ramsden, 'Hong Kong's "High Standard of Fairness" and New Statutory Torture Screening Mechanism' (2013) *Public Law* 232.

[84] *Prabakar* v. *Secretary for Security* [2002] HKEC 1451 (Court of Appeal), at [24] (Rogers VP).

[85] *Secretary for Security* v. *Prabakar* (2004) 7 HKCFAR 187 (Court of Final Appeal), at [4] (Li CJ).

[86] *Prabakar*, at [44]. At that time, it was accepted that individuals could not invoke constitutional rights to challenge immigration decisions. The Chief Justice's reference to the 'fundamental human right to be tortured' has to therefore be based on the common law (be it influenced by international law or not).

[87] Especially as the previous Chief Executive of Hong Kong, CY Leung, indicated a desire to withdraw from the Torture Convention following major court rulings (an effect which would obviously undercut any *Teoh* expectation): J. Ngo and C. Leung, 'Hong Kong Could Quit Torture Convention, Says CY', *South China Morning Post*, 14 January 2016. See also M. Ramsden, 'Dualism in the Basic Law: The First 20 Years' (2019) 49(1) *Hong Kong Law Journal* 239.

[88] *Baker*, above note 49, at [71].

Diversity, 'unless there are *compelling* reasons to depart therefrom'.[89] The point of interest here, then, is the adoption of close scrutiny review beyond rights that Lord Bridge regarded as 'fundamental' – here, unincorporated environmental rights. Similarly, in Hong Kong, the right to work under the ICESCR was an 'important right' that supported anxious scrutiny in relation to the executive's stringent refugee work authorisation policy.[90] Commenting on the emergence of the doctrine in English law, Cheung J in *MA* noted that this was 'why after the enactment of the Human Rights Act in 1998, the need for the UK courts to resort to the anxious scrutiny approach has greatly diminished'.[91] But in Hong Kong, Lord Bridge's formulation was used to support the review of restrictions on unincorporated socio-economic rights.

There is, evidently, a rich variety of approaches to dualism in comparative administrative law. These examples show the continued influence of classic English dualism in certain jurisdictions but also the impact of pre-HRA approaches, such as anxious scrutiny, which have supported common law courts engaging in closer review on the basis of international instruments. But another trend has been to reject *Brind*, with novel approaches such as those presented in *Teoh* and *Tavita* gaining currency in many jurisdictions as a viable alternative to the English conception of dualism. Another possibility apparent from other jurisdictions is to avoid the dualist debate altogether and to construct any such right as inhering in the common law. The variety of approaches suggests that there will continue to be a stimulating comparative conversation as to the use of unincorporated norms in common law judicial review, informed by domestic constitutional imperatives, but also defined in relation to the narrow approach espoused by the House of Lords in *Brind*.

4.4 COMPARATIVE APPROACHES TO DUALISM AND THEIR RECEPTION IN THE ENGLISH COURTS

Having considered the 'export' of English judicial review principles in relation to unincorporated international norms, the purpose of the following section is to pose the question of whether the English courts are able to gather, from looking to other common law courts in the future, whether there are any suitable approaches for 'import' in the reformulation of dualism in English judicial review. This 'future' is not a mere hypothetical but may arise as a real issue as the full consequences of a post-Brexit legal and constitutional architecture become clear.

In this respect, the variety of comparative approaches to dualism in administrative law inevitably means that caution needs to be exercised in treating one approach as particularly suitable for adoption in English law. Evidently, the British constitution does not provide a particularly clear directive to the courts to apply international law, as is the case in South Africa and India. Nor does English judicial review reflect the activist social justice culture of other jurisdictions such as South Africa and India, which partially reflects the need to correct historic injustices; in these jurisdictions, a constitutional declaration as to the importance of universal human rights and sources of international law is viewed as an important means of both recognising the lessons of the past but also protecting the constitution from domestic exigencies in the future. There are also important doctrinal differences between English

89 *Chinnappa* v. *Union of India* AIR 2002 SC 724, at [42] (Justice Pasayat).

90 MA v. *Director of Immigration* [2011] 2 HKLRD F6 (Court of First Instance), at [97]–[99] (Cheung J). For a critique, see M. Ramsden and L. Marsh, 'The 'Right to Work' of Refugees in Hong Kong: MA v. Director of Immigration' (2013) 25(3) *International Journal of Refugee Law* 574.

91 *MA*, at [92] (Cheung J).

administrative law and some of these comparative approaches, which in turn bears upon the impact of making use of international law in judicial review. In particular, a common law court can afford to be bullish in drawing upon international law where local administrative law doctrine only provides for it to have limited effects. The *Teoh* doctrine, in this respect, represented an important departure from *Brind* in Australia, yet the potential impact of the relevant treaty in that case (i.e., the CRC) was curtailed by the fact that the courts only protected procedural expectations. By contrast, the English courts do recognise substantive legitimate expectations, which raises the concern that the treaty would be given direct effect through this doctrine. There are also other minor considerations that affect ratification: whereas Australia ratified the CRC only five years prior to *Teoh*, most of the human rights instruments that the UK ratified came at a much earlier stage, when it would not be reasonable to rely upon ratification as a basis for an expectation. This point was not lost on Lord Bingham, who noted that the ECHR could not possibly give rise to a legitimate expectation as the UK ratified it in 1951,[92] before the doctrine had even been conceived in English law, let alone as justifying an individual to look back to such ratification retrospectively as inducing an expectation on their part.

A broader point of difference between English judicial review and some of the more expansive inroads into *Brind* orthodoxy may also reflect the different degrees of international regulation that each jurisdiction is subject to, alongside geopolitical considerations. It is perhaps unsurprising that New Zealand, a small, geographically remote state, would see virtue in making international law effective in its domestic courts.[93] This is not to say that the UK has failed to appreciate the imperatives of observing international law or forging international relationships. Rather, the point is that the judicial inroads into dualism in the English courts generally did not extend beyond the ECHR, as noted above. By contrast, the *Tavita* principle is regarded to be one of general application to all international human rights instruments: no obligation can be 'window dressed'. Linked to this, the nature and degree of enforceability of international obligations may also affect the extent to which they are used in administrative law. There are, in this respect, differences between the European Court of Human Rights and Human Rights Committee, both in adjudicatory technique and sophistication, as well as normative reach of their interpretations.[94] A jurisdiction can perhaps be welcoming of rights under, say, the ICCPR or CRC, insofar as these treaty regimes remain relatively decentralised in their interpretation and application. This may potentially explain why the English courts pre-HRA did not go as far as some of the progressive common law courts did in qualifying the dualist principle, as to do so would effectively place the force of Strasbourg jurisprudence on the domestic plane in a way that would curtail judicial discretions in administrative law.

This is not to say, however, that these comparative developments bear no relevance to English judicial review; the question is always what purpose these comparisons are being made. The need to revisit *Brind* is, in large measure, tied to the political destiny of the HRA. Politically, the government has threatened to withdraw the UK from the ECHR, repeal the HRA and replace it with a 'homegrown' bill of rights.[95] This may seem improbable, at least while the executive is distracted with Brexit, but it remains on the table and is inevitably

92 *R* v. *Director of Public Prosecutions, ex p Kebilene* [2000] 2 AC 326, at 338 (Lord Bingham).
93 Dunsworth, above note 64, at 78.
94 See, e.g., D. McGoldrick, 'A Defence of the Margin of Appreciation and an Argument for Its Application by the Human Rights Committee' (2016) 65(1) *International and Comparative Law Quarterly* 21.
95 See Commission on a Bill of Rights, *A UK Bill of Rights: The Choice before Us*, December 2012.

connected to the UK's broader relationship with the European legal order. Comparative approaches to dualism, which are explained at least in part by factors grounded in international relations and geopolitics, as with New Zealand developments, may therefore become particularly instructive as the UK re-evaluates its relationship with Europe. As part of an effort to avoid isolation from the international system, the English courts might attempt to take more forceful steps to give effect to the foundational international human rights treaties and relevant justiciable provisions of the UN Charter, these instruments taking on renewed legal significance as the UK forges a new global identity outside of the European order.

Equally, there has been a trend of late for the courts to place less emphasis on rights under the HRA so as to prioritise rights under the common law in the first instance. There have been many pointed statements by senior judges to this effect: 'it was not the purpose of the Human Rights Act 1998 that the common law should become an ossuary';[96] '[h]uman rights continue to be protected by our domestic law, interpreted and developed in accordance with the [HRA] when appropriate';[97] and '[t]he development of the common law did not come to an end on the passing of the Human Rights Act 1998. It is in vigorous health and flourishing in many parts of the world which share a common legal tradition'.[98] This trend has been explained as representing a judicial desire to use the common law to offer a more expansive conception of rights than currently available under the ECHR. This might be because Strasbourg has yet to speak on an issue, or because international law protects rights less than under domestic law (e.g., because of the supremacy of Security Council resolutions over conflicting obligations, including the UK's obligations under the ECHR).[99]

However, the resurgence of common law rights has also been motivated by judicial frustration of Strasbourg overreaching and/or the sense that UK constitutionalism has been eclipsed by consideration of the requirements under the HRA. There are, much like in pre-HRA times, a rich source of extrajudicial writings that provide some explanation of the trend to look 'within' the common law, with a renewed emphasis on its 'constitutionalised' features. Lady Hale has described this recent trend as 'UK constitutionalism on the march', noting that there is 'emerging a renewed emphasis on the common law and distinctively UK constitutional principles as a source of legal inspiration'.[100] John Laws, once a proponent for the use of the ECHR in developing the common law, has come to see its unqualified importation as undermining the 'catholicity and restraint' of the common law; if the courts can make human rights 'truly our own', then it will quell the fears of an incoming tide.[101] Similarly, the notion that European-derived human rights law has become 'too big' has remained a theme of Lord Hoffman, who believes that human rights are 'universal in abstraction but national in application', lamenting Strasbourg's 'living instrument' doctrine as introducing 'wholly new concepts' into the ECHR.[102] The ECHR, to Lord Sumption, has unjustifiably moved beyond the oppression of minorities that the post-war instrument was drafted to address; it exposes the democratic deficit in the Strasbourg court's judicial law-making.[103] This analysis may support

96 *Kennedy* v. *Information Commissioner* [2014] UKSC 20, [2014] 2 WLR 808, at [133] (Lord Toulson).

97 *Osborn* v. *Parole Board* [2013] UKSC 61, [2014] AC 1115, at [57] (Lord Reed).

98 *R (Guardian News)* v. *City of Westminster Magistrates Court* [2013] QB 618, at [88] (Toulson LJ).

99 See, e.g., *HM Treasury* v. *Ahmed* [2010] UKSC 5.

100 Lady Hale, 'UK Constitutionalism on the March', *Constitutional and Administrative Law Bar Association Conference*, 12 July 2014.

101 Lord Justice Laws, 'The Common Law and Europe', *Hamlyn Lectures*, 27 November 2013, at [8].

102 Lord Hoffman, 'The Universality of Human Rights', *Judicial Studies Board Annual Lecture*, 19 March 2009.

103 Lord Sumption, 'The Limits of Law', *27th Sultan Azlan Shah Lecture*, 20 November 2013.

the proposition that, unlike common law approaches that seek to use international law to empower judges in administrative law, the English courts are looking to its indigenous common law as a means either to secure human rights or to offer a counterpoise to possible future interpretations in Strasbourg. The irony is that the English courts have come full circle: whereas they once used the ECHR as a source of guidance and inspiration to develop common law principles of judicial review, there is now a trend towards avoiding it so as to create a space for common law rights to emerge from the shadows.

However, there are also reasons to be cautious about pushing the indigenisation agenda too far. First, there is evidently a gap in the normative reach of common law rights compared to that of the ECHR, at least *at present*. This goes some way to explaining the formulation of pre-HRA fundamental rights in the English courts, which drew upon rights under the ECHR. This does not mean that the common law, consistent with its values, is unable to extend its protections in the directions that the expanding administrative state takes it. This would proceed, however, at an incremental pace, and there would remain lingering doubts about the scope and effect of common law rights in this lengthy process of norm crystallisation. There is a lot of force then in judicial recitations of the ECHR (and other instruments for that matter) as reflecting the values and catalogue of rights found in the common law. The basis for these judicial iterations, however, should not derive from statutory compliance with the HRA but rather from the ECHR as a source of international obligations. Second, and of equal importance, the focus on indigenous common law rights also ignores the potential significance of characterising a norm as being underpinned by an international obligation. This characterisation provides the courts with a powerful tool of legality; to not only find that the executive violated domestic law but that it committed an internationally wrongful act. The same point may be made with some caution in relation to the relative strength of norms under the HRA compared to those under the indigenous common law. There is, of course, debate about the normative reach, and constitutional powers of judges, under the common law versus the HRA. But leaving this aside, there is another dimension to this debate: as Elliott notes, the existence of an international obligation invests 'adjudication under the HRA with a degree of legal bite that adjudication at common law appears to lack'.[104] The significance of a finding under the HRA thus makes judicial decisions taken under it more resilient to Parliamentary challenge; indigenous common law rights, on the other hand, occupy the same domestic constitutional space as the doctrine of Parliamentary sovereignty.[105]

Admittedly, obligations under the ECHR may not now have the same moral purchase in a post-Brexit environment as they held in less autochthonous times. Equally, judges may also feel a sense of Strasbourg 'fatigue' and see the development of common law rights as a refreshing and flexible alternative to the increasing 'over-legalisation' of the ECHR. It is here, then, that some progressive approaches in other jurisdictions become useful. In particular, the English courts could also seek guidance from other sources of international human rights obligation while retaining normative autonomy to adapt such norms to cohere with national values. Or in Lord Hoffman's words (noted previously), the courts are able to espouse human rights as universal in abstraction, but national in their implementation. The courts may therefore look beyond the supranational 'European' to the (relatively) decentralised 'International', infusing the common law with greater references to foundational human rights instruments, particularly the ICCPR, in addition to customary international law, which

[104] Elliott, above note 5, at 108.
[105] Elliott, above note 5, at 111.

is most certainly declaratory of these foundational rights.[106] A broader approach of this kind is seen in Lord Bingham's majority opinion in *Roma Rights*, where he held that the UK's extraterritorial asylum screening operation at Prague Airport violated various UK's obligations, including under the ICCPR.[107] This obviously represents a rare example: the ICCPR remains under-utilized in English judicial review, which is hardly surprising given the dominant role that the ECHR has assumed via the HRA. But if the assumption here is to find a counterpoise to the ECHR, an alternative source of international obligation to augment the development of civil and political rights in the English common law, then resort to the ICCPR provides advantages. An important derivative benefit is that greater use of the ICCPR in English judicial review would also facilitate commonwealth dialogue on the nature and scope of such rights, the ICCPR in particular already given effect in other common law jurisdictions through constitutional recognition or via departures from *Brind* dualism (as noted previously). The notion of greater commonwealth rights engagement defined through foundational international human rights instruments would be appealing to some English judges frustrated with Strasbourg case law, which, as Lord Toulson once remarked, deflects from 'insightful and penetrating' common law analysis.[108]

To achieve this, though, the sovereigntist foundations upon which *Brind* rests have to be reappraised. The dualist principle was noted in *Miller* to be 'a necessary corollary of Parliamentary sovereignty'.[109] This suggests that there is less latitude to creatively evolve the dualist principle, given that it is tied to Parliamentary powers. In this respect, the challenge to *Brind* in other common law jurisdictions (e.g., New Zealand and Australia) can be viewed as a broader disaffection with the proposition that legislative intent should remain so central in defining the scope of judicial review, or at least that general legislative intent encompasses a broader set of (internationalist) values than permitted by *Brind*. Of all common law jurisdictions, New Zealand is closest to the UK in its commitment to Parliamentary sovereignty, but even this jurisdiction has not seen it as constitutional heresy to place a greater onus on the legislature to make plain its intention to violate international law. This same point may also be derived from the Canadian Supreme Court's observations in *Baker*, in that Parliament is assumed to share the same 'compassionate and humanitarian values' as the rest of Canadian society, such as to regard the rights of the child as the utmost administrative importance. The adoption of a presumption that Parliament intended to observe its international obligations, both in its statutory formulations and conferral of discretions, unless clearly stated otherwise, would also equally respect the final word of Parliament in the event that it was to express as much.

It is possible, though, that the English courts opt to retain the ambiguity requirement set out in *Brind* but instead find other indirect routes to giving greater expression to international human rights law: this would certainly be in keeping with pre-HRA jurisprudence. It may be that *Teoh*, for example, is revisited in English law. This is a possibility, especially as the Court

[106] As to the potential relevance of the ICCPR, see F. Klug, K. Starmer and S. Weir, 'The British Way of Doing Things: The United Kingdom and the International Covenant of Civil and Political Rights, 1976–94' (1995) *Public Law* 504.

[107] *R (European Roma Rights Centre)* v. *Immigration Officer at Prague Airport* [2004] UKHL 55, [2005] 2 A.C. 1, at 46–7 (Lord Bingham); at 64–6 (Lady Hale). This finding, though, was only operative via Section 1(1) of the Race Relations Act 1976.

[108] Lord Toulson, 'International Influence on the Common Law', *Lecture to the London Common Law and Commercial Law Bar Association*, 11 November 2014 (www.supremecourt.uk/docs/speech-141111.pdf).

[109] *R (Miller)* v. *Secretary of State for Exiting the European Union* [2017] UKSC 5, at [57] (Lord Neuberger, Baroness Hale, Lord Mance, Lord Kerr, Lord Clarke, Lord Wilson, Lord Sumption, Lord Hodge).

of Appeal has produced opposite conclusions on this doctrine.[110] Yet aside from the differences already identified between English and Australian approaches to legitimate expectations, there is a need to be circumspect in using *Teoh*: for a start, it distracts from more fruitful common law methods to give effect to international obligations in administrative law. Admittedly, any common law method that tries to draw significance from international obligations will have some basis in estoppel logic; if the executive assumes obligations, then there are good reasons to hold them to it. *Tavita*, in this respect, was also based on an estoppel logic, Cooke J finding it not to be right that New Zealand is able to 'window-dress' its obligations. But a crucial difference between *Teoh* and *Tavita* is that the latter was not as beholden to a domestic change of executive policy. Rather, the logic of *Tavita* was that if the executive wanted to avoid such obligations, then they should face the international political cost and withdraw from the treaty. This difference, in turn, makes the use of the international obligation in administrative law more resilient in the face of domestic exigencies. Conversely, *Teoh* does not provide a particularly strong foundation for the fertilisation of a norm in domestic law, allowing international obligations to be reduced to naught by a simple executive advice 'to the contrary'. *Teoh* may also promote obfuscation as to the origin of a common law norm, as *Prabakar* illustrates in the previous discussion.

More generally, though, comparative common law inroads into *Brind* dualism are able to provide guidance, with respect to the *values* which inhere in the common law. Irrespective of the doctrines used to give effect to international human rights treaties in *Tavita* and *Teoh*, both decisions provide support for the proposition that respect for international human rights law forms part of the rule of law as a common law value. The rule of law is, of course, something of a nebulous concept, but Lord Bingham prominently included within his definition the observance of international obligations.[111] Related to this, both *Tavita* and *Teoh* certainly stand for the proposition that there are normative similarities between international human rights law and the common law, in that they are both underpinned by a universal practice rooted in morality. This is also the apparent view of Lord Kerr who noted that Article 3 of the CRC was presumed to be the 'product of extensive and enlightened consideration' and therefore directly enforceable; presumably a reference to the common law's faith in human reason, which human rights treaties also share as reflecting the 'non-contingent interests' of States.[112] Finding value congruence, then, between the common law and international human rights obligations provides a more principled way in which to approach the dualist question and to which progressive comparative authority, such as *Teoh* and *Tavita*, is best able to support English judicial reconsideration of *Brind*. In short, comparative authority offers teleological support, but it is still necessary for the English courts to engage with this question based on British constitutional principles. This was, again, the view of Lord Kerr, who while citing *Teoh* to illustrate the importance of giving effect to human rights treaties went on to postulate a theory that such instruments form an exception to dualism – a proposition that arguably finds historical support on a careful reading of pre-*Brind*

[110] R. v. *Secretary of State for the Home Department ex p Behluli* [1998] INLR 594, at 602 (Beldam LJ); *R* v. *Secretary of State for the Home Department, ex p Ahmed and Patel* [1998] INLR 570, at 583 (Lord Woolf); *R* v. *Director of Public Prosecutions; ex p Kebilene* [2000] 2 AC 326, at 354 (Laws LJ); *R* v. *Uxbridge Magistrates' Court, ex p Adimi* [2001] QB 667, at 691 (Newman J).

[111] T. Bingham, 'The Rule of Law' (2006) 66(1) *Cambridge Law Journal* 67, at 81–2.

[112] A. Brudner 'The Domestic Enforcement of International Covenants on Human Rights: A Theoretical Framework' (1985) 35 *University of Toronto Law Journal* 219; Hunt, above note 16, at 35.

dualist cases.[113] The English courts might then re-evaluate dualism on the basis of the logic of long-standing British prerogative powers and buttress it with progressive comparative authority that recognises international human rights law to be an important component of the rule of law as a common law value. A fuller argument on this, however, is for another day.

4.5 CONCLUSION

This chapter has considered the scope of dualism, in the context of administrative law, in the English legal system and common law world. It has noted that there is no unitary account of the dualist principle in the common law; this too represents a spectrum of possibilities, from autochthonous leanings (Sri Lanka and Singapore) to legal cosmopolitanism (South Africa and India). It has suggested that a number of factors will ultimately shape the extent to which dualism is adhered to: constitutional foundations of judicial review; state identity and historical human rights legacies (or abuses); cultural relativism; geopolitical imperatives to engage with an international regime; the scope and intensity of existing principles of judicial review to which such norm will be 'received'; and the extent of international regime control over national legal systems. It has suggested that a rich comparative conversation is ongoing as to the proper scope and purpose of the dualist principle in common law judicial review. In turn, it has shown that the English approach to dualism in judicial review, illustrated in *Brind*, has garnered both opponents and supporters in other common law jurisdictions; in some instances, it has been 'exported', but at the very least it has fostered a rich comparative dialogue and competing approaches in cases such as *Teoh* and *Tavita*. At the same time, it was argued that the English courts can benefit from 'importing' more progressive approaches to unincorporated norms but that the indigenous turn in rights discourse may lead to an English assertion of normative autonomy from attempts at securing progressive convergence on the dualist question.

[113] *JS*, above note 30, at [247]–[257] (Lord Kerr). In addition to *Brind*, another dualist case used to support a restrictive approach is *JH Rayner (Mincing Lane) Ltd* v. *Department of Trade and Industry* [1990] 2 AC 418.

PART III

Origins and Adaptations in the British Isles

5

The Influence of English Judicial Review on Scots Judicial Review

A Tale of Resemblance and Distinctiveness

Stephen Thomson

When Scotland and England were dissolved as sovereign states and reconstituted in the United Kingdom of Great Britain by the Treaty of Union 1707, England[1] would be the dominant political and economic player in the United Kingdom in the centuries to come. The UK Parliament sat in England and was primarily composed of English members. The seat of UK Government was in England and primarily comprised English members.[2] Certain aspects of English constitutional law prevailed over those of Scots constitutional law. Notably, the doctrine of parliamentary supremacy was said to be an English principle with no counterpart in Scots constitutional law; the doctrine was, additionally, not provided for in the Treaty of Union.[3] As Lord President Cooper pointed out in *MacCormick* v. *Lord Advocate*:

> The principle of the unlimited sovereignty of Parliament is a distinctively English principle which has no counterpart in Scottish constitutional law. It derives its origin from Coke and Blackstone, and was widely popularised during the nineteenth century by Bagehot and Dicey, the latter having stated the doctrine in its classic form in his Law of the Constitution. Considering that the Union legislation extinguished the Parliaments of Scotland and England and replaced them by a new Parliament, I have difficulty in seeing why it should have been supposed that the new Parliament of Great Britain must inherit all the peculiar characteristics of the English Parliament but none of the Scottish Parliament, as if all that happened in 1707 was that Scottish representatives were admitted to the Parliament of England. That is not what was done.[4]

English law has nevertheless commanded a high degree of authority, influence and prestige in Scotland. It has served as a powerful force of convergence, not least because the two

1 For brevity, 'England' shall mean England and Wales, and 'English' shall mean English and Welsh, unless context dictates otherwise. This does not detract from, or imply a view on, the arguments in favour of (and against) Wales being recognised as a jurisdiction in its own right – see Timothy H. Jones and Jane M. Williams, 'Wales as a Jurisdiction' [2004] Public Law 78.

2 From 1885 until 1999, the year in which the Scottish Parliament was established, the Scottish Office was a department of the UK Government administering a wide range of governmental functions relating to Scotland. There remains an Office of the Secretary of State for Scotland, though this does not perform the wide-ranging governmental functions of the Scottish Office.

3 The Treaty of Union merely provided in Art. III that the 'United Kingdom of Great Britain be represented by one and the same Parliament, to be stiled, The Parliament of Great Britain'.

4 *MacCormick* v. *Lord Advocate*, 1953 SC 396, p. 411. On the Crown in Scots law, see *Davidson* v. *Scottish Ministers (No 1)*, 2006 SC (HL) 41; *Beggs* v. *Scottish Ministers*, 2007 *SLT* 235; and Adam Tomkins, 'The Crown in Scots Law' in Aileen McHarg and Tom Mullen (eds.), *Public Law in Scotland* (Avizandum, 2006).

jurisdictions have shared a common, sovereign legislature[5] and (in essence) a supreme court of civil jurisdiction.[6]

However, the Treaty of Union provided that Scotland would retain its own distinct laws and legal system[7] – albeit that both the law and legal system of Scotland are part of the law and legal system of the UK[8] – and there was a significant degree of continuity in the law and legal system of Scotland pre- and post-Union. The distinct body of law and legal system of Scotland would serve as a structural and cultural counterweight to forces of convergence, allowing aspects of institutional, legal and jurisprudential distinctiveness to be maintained and, indeed, developed.

Focusing specifically on judicial review, Scotland already had a rudimentary law of judicial review by the time of the Union, and its principal institution of judicial review – the Court of Session – had been in place since 1532. There was no wholesale importation into Scotland of English law or practice in the field of judicial review, though in some areas there is substantial alignment between the two, notably in the grounds of review.[9] In some aspects of Scots judicial review, there is a high degree of distinctiveness, where English influence has been weakened or resisted. This is at its most pronounced in the scope of judicial review and the question of who or what is amenable to review, particularly as it relates to doctrinal foundations. The central principle of judicial review in Scotland has not developed on the contours of a public/private distinction, but instead on the principle of confining bodies to their jurisdiction – regardless, in principle, of their public or private nature. It is quite possible under the law of Scotland for a private person performing private law functions to be successfully judicially reviewed (subject to various qualifications).[10]

Scottish courts have resisted English legal principle not only on issues of scope and amenability to review, but also in relation to remedies. There is no discrete class of (common law) public law remedies in Scotland comparable to the English prerogative writs/orders, and the remedies that are available on a petition for judicial review in Scotland are substantially the same remedies that are available in an ordinary action in vindication of private law rights.[11] Not only is there no equivalent to the English prerogative orders/writs; there does not

5 Noting the major constitutional development with the enactment of the Scotland Act 1998, which inter alia established the Scottish Parliament in 1999 and served as a key milestone in the process of Scottish devolution.

6 The House of Lords, and the UK Supreme Court, would technically sit as Scottish or English courts depending on whether they were hearing appeals from, respectively, a Scottish or English court. Though authority in (for example) a UK Supreme Court decision in an English appeal was highly persuasive in a UK Supreme Court case in a Scottish appeal, it would not be binding. Nevertheless, the two emanations of the court shared judicial personnel, and significant cross-fertilisation has occurred. It is important to note, however, that it is the Court of Session (though note the Tribunals, Courts and Enforcement Act 2007, s. 20), not the House of Lords or UK Supreme Court, that has been the main forum for resolution of petitions for judicial review in Scotland.

7 Treaty of Union 1707, Arts. XVIII–XIX.

8 On the 'legal system' differences between Scotland and other parts of the UK, see C. M. G. Himsworth, 'Devolution and Its Jurisdictional Asymmetries' (2007) 70(1) *Modern Law Review* 31.

9 It has been said that there is no substantial difference between the grounds of judicial review in Scotland and England and that reference may be made in Scotland to English cases to determine whether there has been excess or abuse of jurisdiction, power or authority or a failure to do what it requires – *West* v. *Secretary of State for Scotland*, 1992 SC 385, p. 413, per Lord Hope of Craighead; a similar point had been made in *Brown* v. *Hamilton District Council*, 1983 SC (HL) 1, p. 42, per Lord Fraser of Tullybelton.

10 Though this is far from common, it has occurred without encountering the kinds of doctrinal difficulties this would pose in England. As will be noted in the following section, one of the areas in which judicial review doctrine was developed in Scotland was in relation to arbitration, including contractually appointed arbiters.

11 Namely reduction, declarator, suspension, interdict, implement, restitution and payment (whether of damages or otherwise) – Rules of Court of Session, r. 58.13(3). There can nevertheless be other procedural considerations which apply to the choice of remedy or remedies sought by the petitioner.

seem to be a general, perceived need or desire to emulate them. There is, already in this survey, evidence of both resemblance and distinctiveness in a comparison of Scots and English judicial review.

However, the relationship between the two bodies of law is not static, and despite the distinctiveness of the scope and remedies of Scots judicial review, recent years have seen increasing convergence in relation to procedure. Notable were recommendations made in the Report of the Scottish Civil Courts Review of 2009[12] to bring Scots judicial review procedure into line with English procedure in relation to standing, time limits and leave. In Scotland, the courts used a title and interest test to determine standing to sue, rather than a sufficient interest test. There was no fixed time limit within which a petition for judicial review had to be made, the respondent instead being able to enter the common law plea of *mora*, taciturnity and acquiescence. There was also no distinct leave or permission stage. Statutory reforms in 2014 brought Scots judicial review procedure into line with its English counterpart, with little exhibition of innovation. Intriguingly, those reforms were enacted by the Scottish Parliament, demonstrating that devolution of legislative competence need not result in divergence in the substantive law; in this case, the devolved legislature served as an agent of convergence.

This chapter will examine the relationship between Scots and English judicial review through a consideration of distinctiveness of scope and procedural convergence. It is in these areas – rather than the (common law) grounds of judicial review – that distinctiveness has been at its most pronounced in Scotland.[13] It will then consider potential reasons why the Scottish courts have sought to retain distinctiveness in Scots judicial review from its English counterpart and why that distinctiveness has manifested in some areas rather than others.

5.1 DISTINCTIVENESS OF SCOPE AND AVAILABILITY OF JUDICIAL REVIEW

Though the grounds of judicial review are largely aligned in Scotland and England,[14] there are significant differences in scope, including the question of who or what is amenable to review. This is where the distinctiveness of judicial review is at its most pronounced between the two jurisdictions. It is grounded in a key difference of emphasis in the doctrinal foundations of judicial review. In England, the law of judicial review is primarily aimed at public bodies and bodies performing public functions, as a matter of legal doctrine.[15] In Scotland, though public bodies and bodies performing public functions comprise the bulk of respondents in petitions for judicial review, the core doctrine is one of confinement of bodies to their jurisdiction or controlling excess of jurisdiction. Those bodies need not be public bodies, nor need they be performing a public function. Whereas in England bodies or decisions lacking some 'public' or 'public law' element (however that is to be defined) have tended to fall outside the scope of judicial review, in Scotland a number of bodies and decisions lacking a notably public (law) element have been subject to review, and uncontroversially so.

[12] Court of Session, *Report of the Scottish Civil Courts Review* (Vol. 2) (2009).

[13] There are differences in the grounds of judicial review in the context of particular statutory regimes, such as those headed by the Human Rights Act 1998 and the Scotland Act 1998.

[14] Though see the discussion on error of law in *Ashley* v. *Scottish Football Association* [2016] CSOH 78, paras. 20–25.

[15] It is encouraged by the principle of procedural exclusivity, which has two juridical bases: (i) interpretation of the relevant statutory provisions on remedies; and (ii) abuse of process. See C. F. Forsyth, 'Beyond O'Reilly v. Mackman: The Foundations and Nature of Procedural Exclusivity' (1985) 44(3) *Cambridge Law Journal* 415. Many of the cases in this area are now well-known, particularly in the *O'Reilly* v. *Mackman* [1983] 2 AC 237 and *R* v. *Panel on Take-overs and Mergers, ex parte Datafin plc* [1987] QB 815 lines of cases.

Judicial review[16] has, since its earliest forms in Scotland, rarely been doctrinally expressed as directed at the control of public power. A major aspect of the distinctiveness of Scots judicial review has been that it has not used a public/private distinction on which to develop its core doctrinal approach to the question of reviewability.[17] In fact, a public/private distinction has in relative terms barely featured at all in the long development of the central doctrine of judicial review in Scotland, and it is only in more recent times that it has featured to any material extent, with the exception of a handful of cases in the 1980s,[18] which were later 'corrected'.[19]

To understand the doctrinal pedigree of judicial review in Scotland, it is necessary to give a brief overview of its historical development.[20] The Court of Session was established as the first centralised civil court in Scotland in 1532[21] but inherited a significant part of its jurisdiction from predecessor institutions, in particular from the so-called sessions of various manifestations of the King's Council and parliamentary committees. The judges of the Court continued to act with the authority of the King's Council and are still styled as 'Lords of Council and Session' to the present day. The sessions exercised what can loosely be described as a supervisory jurisdiction, it seems, primarily over inferior courts and judicial officers. Thus there are examples of proceedings in inferior courts being struck down or diverted by reason of irregularity[22] or judicial partiality[23] as early as in the latter part of the fifteenth century. The College of Justice Act 1532 served as a conduit for the inheritance by the new court of this supervisory jurisdiction.

In the decades and centuries that followed, the Court of Session asserted an increasingly general and comprehensive jurisdiction, assisted by the enactment of statutes that resulted in its absorption of the jurisdiction of other courts. Substantial inheritance of jurisdiction occurred with an Act of 1706[24] transferring to the Court the jurisdiction of the Commissions of Plantation of Kirks and Valuation of Teinds, and perhaps more significantly the Court of Session Act 1830, which transferred to the Court admiralty and consistorial jurisdiction. The Exchequer Court (Scotland) Act 1856 then transferred exchequer jurisdiction to the Court. This enlargement and generalisation of jurisdiction coincided with an increasing assertiveness of the Court's juridical power, and, from a long-term perspective, it was in the nineteenth century that the jurisprudence on judicial review was perhaps at its most rapidly developing.[25] Whereas in the sixteenth

16 Which did not, of course, go by that name throughout most of its history.

17 David Edward, 'Administrative Law in Scotland: The Public Law / Private Law Distinction Revisited' in Deirdre Curtin and David O'Keeffe (eds.), *Constitutional Adjudication in European Community and National Law* (Butterworths, 1992), p. 295. See also *Ashley* v. *Scottish Football Association* [2016] CSOH 78; cf. Aileen McHarg, 'Border Disputes: The Scope and Purposes of Judicial Review' in Aileen McHarg and Tom Mullen (eds.), Public Law in Scotland (Avizandum, 2006), pp. 233–6. It is notable that such a distinction is now appearing in relation to standing (as discussed later in this chapter); however, the public/private distinction has not manifested as a core doctrine of reviewability in Scotland; see Stephen Thomson, 'The Doctrinal Core of the Supervisory Jurisdiction of the Court of Session' [2016] Public Law 670.

18 *Connor* v. *Strathclyde Regional Council*, 1986 *SLT* 530; *Safeway Food Stores Ltd* v. *Scottish Provident Institution*, 1989 *SLT* 131. See also *Brown* v. *Hamilton District Council*, 1983 SC (HL) 1.

19 *West* v. *Secretary of State for Scotland*, 1992 SC 385, p. 405 (per Lord President Hope); reaffirmed in *AXA General Insurance Company Ltd* v. *Lord Advocate* [2011] UKSC 46, para. 57 (per Lord Hope).

20 A more thorough account is given in Stephen Thomson, 'The Doctrinal Core of the Supervisory Jurisdiction of the Court of Session' [2016] Public Law 670.

21 College of Justice Act 1532.

22 *Mortimer* v. *Ogilvie* (1497) *Acts of the Lords of Council in Civil Causes*, Vol.2 (1918), p. 139.

23 *Lord Livingstone* v. *Lord Erskine* (1482) *Acts of the Lords of Council in Civil Causes*, Vol. 2 (1918), p. ciii; *Gordon of Lougart* v. *Earl of Buchan* (1499) *Acts of the Lords of Council in Civil Causes*, Vol. 2 (1918), p. 347.

24 APS xi, 433, c. 10.

25 Of course, major developments have occurred in judicial review in more recent decades, particularly in relation to the Human Rights Act 1998, the Scotland Act 1998 and European Union law.

and seventeenth centuries the Court seems largely to have been exercising its supervisory jurisdiction over inferior courts and judicial officers, it appears to have increasingly asserted its jurisdiction over ecclesiastical courts in the eighteenth and nineteenth centuries. Ecclesiastical cases had generally been considered off limits for the temporal Court of Session, but it came to characterise the determination of the limits of ecclesiastical jurisdiction as a matter of civil jurisdiction, and thus the Court policed the boundaries of ecclesiastical jurisdiction.[26] The eighteenth and nineteenth centuries also witnessed a considerable exertion of supervisory jurisdiction over arbiters, notably including contractually-appointed arbiters.[27] The Court's exertion of jurisdiction over such entities was not restrained by a notion that judicial review (or the processes that could now be characterised as judicial review) was a check on excess of public or governmental power or directed at bodies performing a public (law) function.

It is true that a concept of 'publicness' had not necessarily taken full shape in these earlier periods, and that inferior courts, ecclesiastical courts and arbiters all performed a judicial function or one capable of being analogised with a judicial function. However, it is important to emphasise the broad nature of the supervisory jurisdiction asserted by the Court over an increasingly wide array of entities. When public and administrative bodies proliferated in the nineteenth and early twentieth centuries with the emergence of the modern state, the Court's supervisory jurisdiction – broad and doctrinally generalised[28] – was already in place, namely to ensure the confinement of bodies to their jurisdiction. There was not necessarily an 'historically consistent line of authority',[29] but the doctrinal core of judicial review is supported by a 'tradition of very long standing'.[30] It was even recently opined to be 'uncontroversial that the decisions of decision-makers whose powers have been conferred by private contract . . . are amenable to [judicial review]'.[31] As this author concluded elsewhere of the central doctrine of judicial review in Scotland,

> [t]he historical pedigree of the supervisory jurisdiction is more plausibly explained by a doctrinal core of confining bodies to jurisdiction, than one in which a public-private distinction has proved decisive. This is supported by the institutional, conceptual, jurisprudential and remedial veins that have carried the lifeblood of judicial review, each contributing to the doctrinal core of review throughout centuries of piecemeal development. There is little evidence of a definitive public-private distinction throughout the long pedigree of judicial review, and its adoption would redefine the doctrinal core of the supervisory jurisdiction.[32]

It was claimed by Lord Hope in *West* v. *Secretary of State for Scotland* that amenability to judicial review in Scotland was determined on the basis of a tripartite relationship test, namely whether there was an entity (A) conferring jurisdiction on another entity (B) to be exercised in

26 Watershed cases included *Earl of Kinnoull* v. *Presbytery of Auchterarder* (1838) 16 S 661; *Middleton* v. *Anderson* (1842) 4 D 957; and *McMillan* v. *Free Church of Scotland* (1861) 23 D 1314.

27 See, for example, *Mitchell* v. *Cable* (1848) 10 D 1297; *Forbes* v. *Underwood* (1886) 13 R 465; and *Holmes Oil Co Ltd* v. *Pumpherston Oil Co Ltd* (1891) 18 R (HL) 52.

28 This is not to say that the Scottish courts have been untroubled by issues of categorisation. For example, classification of decisions as administrative, judicial or quasi-judicial was a problematic and essentially rejected taxonomy – *Brown* v. *Hamilton District Council*, 1983 SC (HL) 1; see also *The Laws of Scotland: Stair Memorial Encyclopaedia*, para. 14.

29 Aileen McHarg, 'Border Disputes: The Scope and Purposes of Judicial Review' in Aileen McHarg and Tom Mullen (eds.), *Public Law in Scotland* (Avizandum, 2006), p. 228.

30 Chris Himsworth, 'Further West? More Geometry of Judicial Review' (1995) *SLT* 127, p. 129.

31 *Ashley* v. *Scottish Football Association* [2016] CSOH 78, para. 20, per Lord Brodie.

32 Stephen Thomson, 'The Doctrinal Core of the Supervisory Jurisdiction of the Court of Session' [2016] Public Law 670, p. 689.

relation to a third entity (C).[33] Though this test continued to be applied by the Scottish courts,[34] it does not appear to find any explicit, historical foundation in the jurisprudence. The doctrinal principle, as gradually formulated by the Scottish courts over centuries of jurisprudence, became one of confining bodies to their jurisdiction or correcting excess of jurisdiction. It does not appear to have been expressed in tripartite terms. The language of 'ultra vires' was in use in Scots judicial review by the 1750s in relation to inferior courts, reinforcing the idea of supervision according to the parameters of jurisdiction.[35] The term *ultra vires* may have been used in relation to arbiters from at least 1777 but certainly from the early nineteenth century.[36] The term was used in cases on ecclesiastical jurisdiction from at least 1838.[37] The tripartite relationship test attracted some scepticism,[38] including on the basis that it was overbroad: for example, would the tripartite relationship between a company's articles of association, its board of directors and its members be captured by the test? Would the relationship between a truster, trustee and beneficiary be captured by it? Did it include bodies that many would argue should not ordinarily be subject to judicial review (particularly when viewed through a public/private law lens), such as sporting associations[39] and golf clubs?[40] Conversely, would the test adequately capture exercise of prerogative power?[41]

Though these phenomena have tested the characterisation of the supervisory jurisdiction as directed at tripartite relationships, there has been no significant perception in Scotland that the doctrinal core of confining bodies to their jurisdiction should yield to the English approach to reviewability. Lord Hope stated that 'use of the expressions "private law" and "public law" is of recent origin and . . . must be used with caution', and that 'Scots law does not find it easy in practice to recognise the boundaries between these two concepts'.[42] However, the public law dimension is not wholly absent even from the Scottish position. Lord Hope himself stated that '[c]ontractual rights and obligations, such as those between employer and employee, are not as such amenable to judicial review'.[43] Neither this point, nor the rationale for it, has been greatly elaborated in the case law, perhaps because it might not sit comfortably with the contention that judicial review is not defined in relation to public law in Scotland. It could, however, be explained that resort should be had to other remedies

33 *West* v. *Secretary of State for Scotland*, 1992 SC 385.

34 *M* v. *Law Society of Scotland* [2013] CSOH 28; *Gray* v. *Braid Logistics (UK) Ltd* [2014] CSIH 81. It was applied with some reservation in *Naik* v. *University of Stirling*, 1994 *SLT* 449.

35 *Lord Prestongrange* v. *Justices of the Peace of Haddington*, 1756 Mor 7350.

36 Henry Home (Lord Kames), *Elucidations Respecting the Common and Statute Law of Scotland* (William Creech, 1777 / 2nd edition 1800). For usage in the context of a live case, see *Reid* v. *Walker* (1826) 5 S 140, p. 143 (per Lord Glenlee).

37 As, for example, in *Earl of Kinnoull* v. *Presbytery of Auchterarder* (1838) 16 S 661, pp. 735 and 739 (per Lord President Hope and Lord Gillies); *Middleton* v. *Anderson* (1842) 4 D 957 (inter alia) pp. 977–8 (per Lord President Boyle); and *McMillan* v. *Free Church of Scotland* (1861) 23 D 1314, p. 1340 (per Lord Ivory).

38 See, e.g., Wilson Finnie, 'Triangles as Touchstones of Review' (1993) *SLT* (News) 51; Chris Himsworth, 'Further West? More Geometry of Judicial Review' (1995) *SLT* 127; Aileen McHarg, 'Border Disputes: The Scope and Purposes of Judicial Review' in Aileen McHarg and Tom Mullen (eds.), *Public Law in Scotland* (Avizandum, 2006), pp. 231–2.

39 *St Johnstone Football Club Ltd* v. *Scottish Football Association Ltd*, 1965 *SLT* 171 (decided before *West*).

40 *Crocket* v. *Tantallon Golf Club*, 2005 *SLT* 663; *Wiles* v. *Bothwell Castle Golf Club*, 2005 *SLT* 785; *Smith* v. *Nairn Golf Club* [2007] CSOH 136. The fact that the overbroad nature of the tripartite relationship test generated so much scepticism, particularly as it related to private bodies and/or the performance of private functions, suggests that the conception of judicial review as a branch of law concerned with public bodies and public functions had seeped into the Scottish legal psyche.

41 Cf. *Council of Civil Service Unions* v. *Minister for the Civil Service* [1985] 1 AC 374.

42 *Davidson* v. *Scottish Ministers (No 1)*, 2006 SC (HL) 41, para. 42.

43 *West* above note 33, at p. 413. See also *Tehrani* v. *Argyll and Clyde Health Board (No 2)*, 1989 SC 342; distinguishing *Malloch* v. *Aberdeen Corporation*, 1971 SC (HL) 85.

before applying for judicial review, and that this includes contractual remedies where appropriate.[44] This would allow judicial review to retain its generalised doctrinal foundation without becoming a standard mechanism for transacting private law disputes. The general reluctance, and sometimes the refusal, of the Scottish courts to demarcate the boundaries of judicial review along public/private law contours nevertheless serves to highlight the distinctive approach of Scots law to questions of scope and amenability to review.

5.2 REMEDIES: MORE DISTINCTIVENESS

Another significant difference from English law is that Scots law has had no comparable system of prerogative writs/orders. The prerogative writs of certiorari, mandamus and prohibition (now quashing orders, mandatory orders and prohibiting orders[45]) have been directed primarily at public law wrongs in modern times.[46] The so-called public law remedies in England emphasised the extent to which judicial review was overtly calculated at public law wrongs.

In Scotland, by contrast, there had never been a corresponding class of remedies directed at public law wrongs. Instead, the remedies of judicial review have substantially been the same remedies that were capable of being sought using ordinary procedure in unequivocally private law actions, namely reduction, declarator, suspension, interdict, implement, restitution and payment (whether of damages or otherwise).[47] Reduction, which is broadly equivalent to certiorari or a quashing order,[48] could be used not only to strike down an act or decision of a public body, but also that of a trust or private company, or even to annul the legal effect of a document (including in a private law context). Reduction could be used for the judicial annulment of acts ranging from the 'unlawful decision of a public body' to the 'contested will of a private individual'.[49] J. D. B. Mitchell had referred in this regard to the 'formlessness' and generality of Scots judicial review, describing it as having a relatively generalised basis in lacking specialised procedures[50] and in using relatively formless and general remedies, with specific reference to reduction.[51]

This stood in contrast with the position in English law, where the 'scope of judicial review was . . . largely determined by the forms of action' and in particular the more restricted scope

44 See *Dante* v. *Assessor for Ayr*, 1922 SC 109; *British Railways Board* v. *Glasgow Corporation*, 1976 SC 224; *O'Neill* v. *Scottish Joint Negotiating Committee for Teaching Staff*, 1987 SC 90; *Ingle* v. *Ingle's Trustee*, 1999 *SLT* 650; *Falconer* v. *South Ayrshire Council*, 2002 *SLT* 1033; and *McCue* v. *Glasgow City Council* [2014] CSOH 124. It is stated in Rule of Court 58.3(1) that a 'petition may not be lodged in respect of an application if that application could be made by appeal or review under or by virtue of any enactment'.

45 CPR 54.2.

46 Though Dawn Oliver pointed out that they were not always conceived as public law remedies and to some extent traversed the public/private divide – Dawn Oliver, 'Public Law Procedures and Remedies – Do We Need Them?' [2002] Public Law 91, pp. 100–3.

47 ROC 58.13.

48 David Edward regarded English law as having 'no precise equivalent' to reduction, and regarded advocation (a remedy abolished in 1868) as the 'true parallel' to certiorari in Scotland – David Edward, 'Administrative Law in Scotland: The Public Law / Private Law Distinction Revisited' in Deirdre Curtin and David O'Keeffe (eds.), *Constitutional Adjudication in European Community and National Law* (Butterworths, 1992), p. 286. Advocation was, along with suspension and reduction, part of a powerful triumvirate of remedies that, broad in reach and flexible in nature, could be used to attack a wide range of decisions of both a 'public' and 'private' nature.

49 David Edward, 'Administrative Law in Scotland: The Public Law / Private Law Distinction Revisited' in Deirdre Curtin and David O'Keeffe (eds.), *Constitutional Adjudication in European Community and National Law* (Butterworths, 1992), p. 287. See also Tom Mullen, 'Standing to Seek Judicial Review' in Aileen McHarg and Tom Mullen (eds.), *Public Law in Scotland* (Avizandum, 2006), p. 241.

50 J. D. B. Mitchell, *Constitutional Law* (1st edition) (W. Green, 1964), pp. 250–1.

51 Mitchell, *Constitutional Law* (1st edition), pp. 210–11.

of the three prerogative writs of certiorari, mandamus and prohibition.[52] Remedies thus seem to be an area in which Scots judicial review has been more insulated from English influence than in relation to the grounds of review.[53] However, a Scottish judge in the House of Lords suggested that there might be advantages to Scotland developing a special procedure for dealing with public law questions 'comparable to the English prerogative orders'.[54] Whereas the English approach can be characterised as remedy-driven, in that the choice of remedy bears on the form of action,[55] in Scotland the approach has in comparative terms been less amenable to such a characterisation, in that the choice of remedy bears less on the form of action.[56] In other words, one does not select the form of action purely or principally due to the remedies made available thereby. The latter approach has been defended in Scotland. Whereas Mitchell described the Scottish approach as one of 'formlessness', he contrasted it with an English position of 'formalism',[57] and there does not seem to have been any significant movement for adopting the English approach towards remedies in judicial review procedure.

5.3 PROCEDURAL CONVERGENCE

In addition to the scope and remedies of judicial review, the procedure of judicial review was marked by significant differences between the two jurisdictions. The differences between the respective procedures have narrowed, however, with recent reforms implemented in Scotland that have sought to align Scottish procedure with that of England.[58] This is seen in three principal contexts. First, the Scottish courts previously applied a title and interest test instead of a sufficient interest test in relation to standing. The title and interest test was, with some judicial assistance, replaced by a test of sufficient interest. There was also no fixed time limit in Scotland, the courts instead applying common law rules on *mora*, taciturnity and acquiescence. However, a 'fixed' time limit has now been introduced in Scotland in line with the English position. Finally, there was no distinct leave stage in Scotland, and a leave stage has now been introduced. Each of these examples of procedural convergence between Scots and English judicial review shall be briefly discussed to illustrate a possible reduction in the distinctiveness of certain aspects of Scots judicial review.

Sufficient interest is not solely a procedural consideration but also has substantive, doctrinal elements. Nevertheless, it has tended to manifest or be considered in Scotland as a preliminary matter. In Scots law, the petitioner had to be capable of demonstrating title and interest, which was seen to have its roots in private law. The leading authority on title and interest, namely *D & J Nicol* v. *Dundee Harbour Trustees*,[59] was characterised as an extension

[52] Mitchell, *Constitutional Law* (1st edition), p. 250.

[53] Though see *Davidson* v. *Scottish Ministers (No 1)*, 2006 SC (HL) 41 on alignment of the law in Scotland with that in England on the availability of coercive remedies against the Crown.

[54] *Brown* v. *Hamilton District Council*, 1983 SC (HL) 1, p. 49, per Lord Fraser of Tullybelton; notably concurrent with *O'Reilly* v. *Mackman* [1983] 2 AC 237, and *Cocks* v. *Thanet District Council* [1983] 2 AC 286.

[55] CPR 54.2, which states that judicial review procedure must be used in a claim for judicial review where the claimant is seeking a mandatory order, a prohibiting order, a quashing order or an injunction under section 30 of the Senior Courts Act 1981 (restraining a person from acting in any office in which he is not entitled to act).

[56] ROC 58.1, which states that an application to the supervisory jurisdiction of the Court of Session must be made by petition for judicial review.

[57] Mitchell, *Constitutional Law* (1st edition), p. 250.

[58] Courts Reform (Scotland) Act 2014. See Tony Kelly, 'The Potential Impact of the Courts Reform (Scotland) Act 2014 on Judicial Review' (2015) *Juridical Review* 385.

[59] *D & J Nicol* v. *Dundee Harbour Trustees*, 1915 SC (HL) 7.

of the ultra vires concept in company law to acts by a public corporation.[60] Though Lord Dunedin was not disposed to 'risk . . . a definition of what constitutes title to sue', it 'may fairly be said that for a person to have such title he must be a party (using the word in its widest sense) to some legal relation which gives him some right which the person against whom he raises the actions either infringes or denies'.[61]

No attempt was made to define interest, though in a more recent case, it was said to be dependent on context but broader than the older approach referring to pecuniary rights and status.[62] If a petitioner had title but not interest, or interest but not title, he would lack standing. The accepted position was that the petitioner must be capable of demonstrating both title and interest for standing to be established. The title aspect arguably made the test more restrictive than the interest aspect,[63] though there were also examples of petitions failing where title existed but interest had not been sufficiently established.[64]

The two Scottish judges in *AXA General Insurance* v. *Lord Advocate* in the UK Supreme Court sought to consign the title and interest test to the history books as it related to 'public law' applications. Lord Hope made a distinction between public law and private law (a distinction that had not often been made in the context of Scots judicial review) and opined that it was difficult to see what justification there could be for applying the title and interest test, which was 'rooted in private law', to proceedings lying in the field of public law.[65] The 'time ha[d] come to recognise that the private law rule that title and interest has to be shown has no place in applications to the court's supervisory jurisdiction that lie in the field of public law'.[66] The term 'standing' would be more appropriate and should be based on the concept of interests rather than rights, but he (like Lord Dunedin) 'would not like to risk a definition of what constitutes standing in the public law context'.[67] That this distinction between public law and private law was made by Lord Hope was significant, as he delivered the judgment in *West* v. *Secretary of State for Scotland* in which it was stated that the

> competency of the application [for judicial review] does not depend upon any distinction between public law and private law, nor is it confined to those cases which English law has accepted as amenable to judicial review, nor is it correct in regard to issues about competency to describe judicial review . . . as a public law remedy.[68]

He had nevertheless expressed doubts, extra-judicially, about the title and interest test.[69]

Lord Reed noted that the title and interest test had been unpredictable in practice[70] and cited previous criticism by A. W. Bradley that the 'resulting state of the law places an unnecessary pitfall in the way of voluntary organisations and other bodies that have a serious reason for seeking judicial scrutiny of the legality of government policies'.[71] The

60 *AXA General Insurance Company Ltd* v. *Lord Advocate* [2011] UKSC 46, para. 165 (per Lord Reed).
61 *D & J Nicol* v. *Dundee Harbour Trustees*, 1915 SC (HL) 7, pp. 12–13.
62 *Scottish Old People's Welfare Council, Petitioners*, 1987 *SLT* 179, p. 186.
63 See, e.g., *Rape Crisis Centre* v. *Secretary of State for the Home Department*, 2000 SC 527; *PTOA Ltd* v. *Renfrew District Council*, 1997 *SLT* 1112.
64 *Scottish Old People's Welfare Council, Petitioners*, 1987 *SLT* 179.
65 *AXA General Insurance Company Ltd* v. *Lord Advocate* [2011] UKSC 46, para. 58.
66 *AXA*, para. 62.
67 *AXA*, paras. 62–3.
68 *West* v. *Secretary of State for Scotland*, 1992 SC 385, p. 413.
69 Lord Hope of Craighead, 'Mike Tyson Comes to Glasgow: A Question of Standing' [2001] Public Law 294.
70 *AXA General Insurance Company Ltd* v. *Lord Advocate* [2011] UKSC 46, para. 169.
71 A. W. Bradley, 'Applications for Judicial Review: The Scottish Model' [1987] Public Law 311, p. 319.

Report of the Scottish Civil Courts Review had also noted that the law on title and interest led to public law issues which had arisen in Scotland sometimes being litigated in the English courts where the rules on standing were clearer and less restrictively applied.[72] The example had been given of Greenpeace's decision to bring judicial review proceedings in England rather than Scotland in relation to the disposal of the Brent Spar oil platform in Scottish waters, on the basis of an opinion from a Scottish QC on problems they would encounter in demonstrating standing in Scotland.[73] That the English approach to standing was more liberal than the Scottish approach was described by Chris Himsworth as 'almost certain', especially in relation to NGOs.[74] Lord Reed concluded in his analysis in *AXA* that

> the time has come when it should be recognised by the courts that Lord Dunedin's *dictum* pre-dates the modern development of public law, that it is rooted in private law concepts which are not relevant in the context of applications to the supervisory jurisdiction, and that its continuing influence in that context has had a damaging effect on the development of public law in Scotland. This unsatisfactory situation should not be allowed to persist. The time has also come when the courts should cease to use the inappropriate terminology of title and interest in relation to such applications, and should refer instead to standing, based upon a sufficient interest.[75]

The Scottish position therefore moved into broader alignment with the English position on the question of standing, apparently on pragmatic grounds. The older test of title and interest was seen to be behind the times and unjustifiably obstructive to judicial review proceedings, whereas the English approach to sufficient interest was seen to be less restrictive and to compare favourably.[76] There had also been concerns that the restrictive title and interest test used in Scotland interfered with the UK's obligations under the UNECE Aarhus Convention[77] and European Union law.[78] The sufficient interest test was given a statutory footing, along with the requirement that the application have a real prospect of success.[79]

The second area in which procedural convergence is found is in the introduction of a three-month time limit within which an application to the supervisory jurisdiction must be made. Previously in Scots judicial review, there was no fixed time limit, though a respondent could bring a plea of *mora*, taciturnity and acquiescence. *Mora* generally described delay, taciturnity described a failure to assert one's claim or right, and acquiescence described silence or passive assent to the impugned act or decision. For the plea to be sustained, all three elements – *mora*, taciturnity and acquiescence – had to be present.[80] It remained unclear, however, whether prejudice or reliance were necessary elements of the plea.[81] The Report of the Scottish Civil Courts Review took the following view of the existing rule:

72 Court of Session, *Report of the Scottish Civil Courts Review* (vol. 2) (2009), p. 27.

73 Scott Blair and Scott Martin, 'Judicial Review 20 Years On – Where Are We Now?' (2005) *SLT* (News) 173.

74 C. M. G. Himsworth, 'Devolution and Its Jurisdictional Asymmetries' (2007) 70(1) *Modern Law Review* 31, pp. 50–1.

75 *AXA General Insurance Company Ltd* v. *Lord Advocate* [2011] UKSC 46, para. 171.

76 See Court of Session, *Report of the Scottish Civil Courts Review* (vol. 2) (2009), pp. 28–9 (though it did not appear to consider the approach adopted in overseas jurisdictions on this point).

77 Convention on Access to Information, Public Participation in Decision-Making and Access to Justice in Environmental Matters (adopted 25th June 1998; effective 30th October 2001).

78 Court of Session, *Report of the Scottish Civil Courts Review* (vol.2) (2009), p. 28.

79 Court of Session Act 1988, s. 27B, as amended by the Courts Reform (Scotland) Act 2014, s. 89.

80 *Somerville* v. *Scottish Ministers*, 2007 SC 140; and see *Assets Co Ltd* v. *Bain's Trustees* (1904) 6 F 692, pp. 705–6.

81 *CWS* v. *Highland Council* [2008] CSOH 28, para. 58.

> We consider that the common law plea of *mora*, taciturnity and acquiescence is not particularly well suited to a procedure designed to provide a speedy and effective remedy to challenge the decisions of public bodies. In such cases there is a public interest in challenges being made promptly and resolved quickly. Accordingly, we are of the view that a time limit should be introduced within which petitions for judicial review must be presented. If there is good reason for delay in making an application, or where the court is satisfied that injustice would result if a petition presented outwith the time limit was not allowed to proceed, the court should have discretion to allow a late petition to proceed.[82]

There did not seem to be a general view that a fixed time limit was necessary or desirable in Scotland, with just over 20 per cent of respondents to the public consultation associated with the Scottish Civil Courts Review, considering that a time limit should be introduced.[83] Nevertheless, the Review recommended the introduction of a three-month time limit in a fairly unimaginative adoption of the English position. It is questionable whether that was a sound recommendation to make. Not only did almost 80 per cent of respondents to the public consultation not consider that a time limit was necessary – indicating that the plea of *mora*, taciturnity and acquiescence did not cause significant problems in practice, even if its formulation could have been improved – the so-called fixed time limit of three months will likely introduce problems that have been felt elsewhere. In Hong Kong, for example, which also has a three-month time limit within which to apply for leave to apply for judicial review, there are so many exceptions made to the rule that it can barely be considered a time limit in the ordinary sense. This not only includes extensions of time beyond the three-month period, but the requirement for promptness can mean that applications for leave may still be refused, even within the three-month period, where promptness has not been demonstrated.[84] The concerns raised about uncertainty under the old rules[85] are therefore not necessarily resolved by the introduction of a 'fixed' time limit (which, in reality, is not fixed). These issues do not seem to have been considered in any substantial way, at least on the basis of the published Report. The statutory provision that introduced the three-month time limit stated:

> An application to the supervisory jurisdiction of the Court must be made before the end of –
>
> (a) the period of 3 months beginning with the date on which the grounds giving rise to the application first arose, or
> (b) such longer period as the Court considers equitable having regard to all the circumstances.[86]

This did not import the English requirement (also found in Hong Kong) that the claim must be made promptly, in addition to being made no later than three months after the grounds for making the claim first arose.[87] It suggests either that the courts will give petitioners in Scotland a clear three-month period within which to apply for leave, without an additional requirement for promptness (in which case petitioners might not be sufficiently incentivised to apply for leave significantly within the three-month period), or that the court

82 Court of Session, *Report of the Scottish Civil Courts Review* (vol. 2) (2009), p. 32.
83 Court of Session, *Report*, p. 30.
84 See Stephen Thomson, *Administrative Law in Hong Kong* (Cambridge University Press, 2018), pp. 42–51; and Stephen Thomson, 'Leave without Delay: The Requirement to Make Prompt Application for Leave to Apply for Judicial Review' (2015) 45(2) *Hong Kong Law Journal* 449.
85 Court of Session, *Report of the Scottish Civil Courts Review* (vol. 2) (2009), p. 30.
86 Court of Session Act 1988, s. 27A(1), as amended by the Courts Reform (Scotland) Act 2014, s. 89.
87 CPR 54.5.

retains discretion to refuse an application (or withhold relief) where the petitioner has delayed, though applying for leave within the three-month time period, which would to some extent be a continuation of the common law rules on *mora*. Whereas the rules on standing appear to have been more closely aligned with those in England for pragmatic reasons, in particular due to the alleged deficiency of the title and interest test, it is less clear why it was thought necessary to adopt the English position on time limits, particularly where the application of a 'fixed' time limit brings its own challenges. This raises questions about the motives for doing so, particularly as there appeared to be such little appetite in the consultation responses for convergence in this area. It is notable that the recommendation was effectively for convergence with the English position on time limits, even though the Report noted varying provisions in other jurisdictions such as Ireland, New Zealand, British Columbia, Alberta and South Australia.[88] Not only was there no significant elaboration on the perceived superiority of the English position, but there was no real explanation given for declining to adopt the position in any of these other jurisdictions.

Finally, procedural convergence was seen in the introduction of a leave or permission stage in Scots judicial review. Previously, Scots judicial review procedure did not have a distinct leave or permission stage, and it was regarded by some to be unnecessary due to the procedure for granting first orders. However, this was also considered to result in the lack of a proper mechanism for filtering out unmeritorious petitions, and the Report of the Scottish Civil Courts Review again recommended that the English model[89] be adopted by introducing a requirement to obtain leave to proceed with an application for judicial review. This included a requirement that the application was deemed to have a real prospect of success. The Report cited practical justifications for this change, such as the leave requirement helping to encourage early concessions by respondents in cases that are well founded and in preventing unmeritorious claims from proceeding, thus creating additional capacity in the court programme;[90] the motivations for this particular reform thus appear to have been pragmatic in nature. The Review's recommendations were enacted in the same round of statutory reforms.[91] It can therefore be seen that, while Scots judicial review has a high level of distinctiveness from English judicial review in terms of scope and remedies, it has recently lost some of its distinctiveness in matters of procedure. The remainder of this chapter will explore potential reasons for the distinctiveness of Scots judicial review and why it has manifested in some areas rather than others.

5.4 REASONS FOR DISTINCTIVENESS FROM ENGLISH LAW

While the Scottish courts have largely followed English law on the grounds of judicial review, they have tended to emphasise the distinctiveness of Scots law on questions of scope, remedies and (until recently, at least) procedure. The areas of similarity and confluence may seem easier to explain, as the powerful forces of convergence bear down on the constituent jurisdictions of the UK, and England offers a rich and developed law and legal system on which to draw. However, a major constitutional development in recent decades has been devolution, which could potentially act as a counterweight to forces of convergence. As

88 Court of Session, *Report of the Scottish Civil Courts Review* (vol. 2) (2009), pp. 31 and 171–2.
89 CPR 54.4.
90 Court of Session, *Report of the Scottish Civil Courts Review* (vol. 2) (2009), p. 35.
91 Court of Session Act 1988, s. 27B, as amended by the Courts Reform (Scotland) Act 2014, s. 89.

Himsworth noted, divergence may be (more) readily permitted in relation to devolved matters, while greater care should be taken in relation to reserved matters;[92] though even that would produce difficulties for Scots judicial review with different rules on devolved and reserved matters being run in parallel.[93] It is nevertheless intriguing to note that one of the most significant statutory reforms of judicial review made by the Scottish Parliament, the Courts Reform (Scotland) Act 2014,[94] introduced one of the greatest instances of legal convergence in Scots judicial review in modern times.[95] Devolution does not guarantee divergence, though it still offers an additional structural opportunity for divergence to occur.

There is nothing inherently objectionable about either convergence or divergence, though there may be matters of principle or practical concern that commend one or the other, depending on the precise issue. There is no reason in principle why Scots law should not adopt principles and procedures from its English counterpart where these are thought beneficial to adopt. The fact that both jurisdictions are part of the same state is also an underlying justification for convergence, as it may seem incongruous for one body to be subject to judicial review in one part of the state but not in another part, or for one party to be able to demonstrate standing in one part of the state but not in another, and so on. That may especially be the case where reserved matters are in issue, or where a body with UK-wide powers or jurisdiction is being judicially reviewed. However, there is also nothing intrinsically wrong with diversity in the rules and procedures of judicial review between the two jurisdictions. Scotland has never been unified with England into a single jurisdiction; its legal institutions, legal system and body of law have to a great extent remained distinct from the Treaty of Union 1707 to the present day. There is no inherent reason why Scots law must abandon that distinctiveness by adopting English ideas and practices at every turn. The English approach would be unlikely to be superior or more fitting in every case.

One explanation for the differences in scope, remedies and (until recently) procedure is that it may be thought that those aspects of Scots law are, in doctrinal or practical terms, normatively superior to their counterparts in England. Lord Hope referred to 'some confusion [in Scotland] about the proper use in this field of English terminology and case law'.[96] He was particularly concerned about the 'influence of English law on decisions about the competency of procedure', citing two Scottish cases[97] that had been essentially contaminated with English doctrine and could therefore not be regarded as correct.[98] The concerns were partly practical in nature, namely the introduction into

92 See Scotland Act 1998, s.29. Under the Sewel Convention, the UK Parliament does not normally legislate on devolved matters in Scotland without the consent of the Scottish Parliament, which is given by way of a legislative consent motion – Scotland Act 1998, s. 28 (as amended by Scotland Act 2016, s. 2) and Schedule 5; Scottish Parliament, *Standing Orders* (5th edition, 6th revision) (9 May 2018), chapter 9B.

93 C. M. G. Himsworth, 'Devolution and Its Jurisdictional Asymmetries' (2007) 70(1) *Modern Law Review* 31, p. 51.

94 Another major piece of legislation on judicial review enacted in the post-devolution period was the Tribunals, Courts and Enforcement Act 2007, though this was enacted by the UK Parliament.

95 See Section 5.3. There are other examples of convergence, such as procedure in relation to the Prevention of Terrorism Act 2005, which mandated parity of implementation; see C. M. G. Himsworth, 'Devolution and Its Jurisdictional Asymmetries' (2007) 70(1) *Modern Law Review* 31, pp. 52–3; and Act of Sederunt (Rules of the Court of Session Amendment No 4) (Prevention of Terrorism Act 2005) 2005, SSI 2005, No 153. Under some statutory regimes, such as the Human Rights Act 1998 and the Scotland Act 1998, special considerations apply in the context of judicial review.

96 *West* v. *Secretary of State for Scotland*, 1992 SC 385, p. 405.

97 *Connor* v. *Strathclyde Regional Council*, 1986 *SLT* 530; *Safeway Food Stores Ltd* v. *Scottish Provident Institution*, 1989 *SLT* 131.

98 *West* v. *Secretary of State for Scotland*, 1992 SC 385, p. 405.

Scotland of a test that had proved difficult in England;[99] noting in particular that the test of reviewability in *R* v. *Panel on Takeovers and Mergers, ex parte Datafin plc*[100] would not trouble Scots judicial review as its procedure (allegedly) recognised no difference between public law and private law.[101] There were 'obvious disadvantages in attempting to follow English authority in this field'.[102] Lord Hope seemed to regard the Scottish approach simply to be better than the English approach. Counsel even implied the moral superiority of the Scottish approach: whereas English law had adopted a case-by-case approach to the issue of competency, such a method was 'not the Scottish approach' where it would instead be determined on the basis of principle.[103] The Scottish rejection of a public/private divide in matters of reviewability therefore seems to be a matter of claimed normative superiority; Lord Brodie stated that there was a 'lack of any obvious good reason why there should be any difference as between the grounds for exercise of the supervisory jurisdiction in the public law sphere . . . and the grounds for its exercise in the private law sphere'.[104] This line of thought has not been without sympathy in England.[105]

Another explanation for the differences in approach is concern about pedigree. It was noted that the *ratio* of a particular decision 'would be in conflict with [a] long line of authority in Scotland'.[106] Pedigree is important, and not just for reasons of tradition or nostalgia. Lord Wilberforce had stated that 'English law fastens, not upon principles but upon remedies',[107] but as Lord Hope observed, 'Scots law, in contrast to English law, tends to fasten not upon remedies but upon principles'.[108] The idea was that English judicial review was (and is) much more remedy-driven: the choice of remedy could and still can determine the form of action in England, noting that judicial review procedure must be used where the claimant is seeking a mandatory order, a prohibiting order, a quashing order or an injunction under section 30 of the Senior Courts Act 1981.[109] While the remedy did not always determine the form of action in England (for example, where a declaration was sought), it did when one of the prerogative writs/orders was sought, and was a key aspect of procedural exclusivity.[110]

In Scotland, by contrast, the remedy would less commonly determine the form of action, as the remedies available by way of judicial review procedure were substantially the same

99 *West* v. *Secretary of State for Scotland*, 1992 SC 385, p. 408; citing *Davy* v. *Spelthorne Borough Council* [1984] AC 262, p. 276 on the 'importation' of the expressions 'public law' and 'private law' into English law.

100 *R* v. *Panel on Takeovers and Mergers, ex parte Datafin plc* [1987] QB 815.

101 *West* v. *Secretary of State for Scotland*, 1992 SC 385, p. 410.

102 Ibid.

103 *West* v. *Secretary of State for Scotland*, 1992 SC 385, p. 412.

104 *Ashley* v. *Scottish Football Association* [2016] CSOH 78, para. 24.

105 See notably Dawn Oliver, 'Common Values in Public and Private Law and the Public/Private Divide' [1997] Public Law 630; Dawn Oliver, *Common Values and the Public-Private Divide* (Cambridge University Press, 1999); Dawn Oliver, 'Review of (Non-Statutory) Discretions' in Christopher Forsyth (ed.), *Judicial Review and the Constitution* (Hart Publishing, 2000), 307. Sir William Wade and Christopher Forsyth argued that in Scotland '[j]ustice can . . . be done in cases which lie beyond the reach of the rigid English system with its misguided public and private law dichotomy, and procedural obstacles and dilemmas are avoided'; William Wade and Christopher Forsyth, *Administrative Law* (Oxford University Press, 11th edition, 2014), p. 545. Note also Lady Hale's observation that '[t]here are signs . . . that the contractual implied term is drawing closer and closer to the principles applicable in judicial review'; *Braganza* v. *BP Shipping Ltd* [2015] UKSC 17, para. 28.

106 *West* v. *Secretary of State for Scotland*, 1992 SC 385, p. 408.

107 *Davy* v. *Spelthorne Borough Council* [1984] AC 262, p. 276.

108 *Davidson* v. *Scottish Ministers (No 1)*, 2006 SC (HL) 41, para. 42. Lord Hope also stated that the 'Scottish approach is based essentially upon principle' – *West* v. *Secretary of State for Scotland*, 1992 SC 385, p. 409.

109 CPR Part 54.2 (and the predecessor provision in Order 53).

110 As noted previously in this chapter.

remedies that could be obtained on other forms of action, including in private law claims.[111] One sought judicial review rather than other forms of action, not because of the remedy sought, but because judicial review was doctrinally deemed the appropriate procedure where one sought to challenge excess of jurisdiction by a reviewable body. In other words, judicial review was selected as the mode of proceeding not necessarily because of the remedy sought, but the principle underlying the supervisory jurisdiction: this is especially, but not exclusively, seen where remedies available in judicial review have been obtained outside judicial review proceedings.[112] Pedigree is related to perceived normative superiority, however, not least because courts in Scotland would probably not have adhered to their doctrinal position in the face of such a different English approach unless they thought it advantageous to do so. With the many problems generated by English law's remedy-driven approach and its overt focus on publicness as a test of reviewability,[113] there has been much to warn against emulation of this model in Scotland.

One cannot rule out, as another explanation for the differences in approach, distinctiveness for its own sake. While identity can be expressed as a claimed identity, it can also be expressed as the rejection of another identity. It is worth considering to what extent the identity of Scots law and the Scottish legal system is asserted as the rejection of an English legal identity. In general terms, there have been numerous instances of Scots claiming (usually historical) shared identity with non-English communities almost to emphasise that Scottishness is distinct from Englishness; thus, depending on the context, shared identity is sometimes expressed with Ireland, Continental Europe[114] and Nordic countries. Often these are expressed in terms of shared historical struggles and solidarity.[115]

In terms of legal identity, Scotland is sometimes categorised as of the Civilian tradition, though this is truer of private law than it is of public law. Scots lawyers have laid claim to being one of the 'original' mixed jurisdictions, fusing Common law and Civil law traditions,[116] along with Louisiana, Quebec, South Africa and Sri Lanka. Some have claimed that Scotland is the only such legal system in Europe[117] (though writers in other European jurisdictions such as Cyprus and Malta can and do disagree[118]); others claim it is the oldest of

111 Of course, procedural considerations applied and continue to do so. For example, the level of court in which an action is commenced is relevant to the issue of remedies.

112 *Gunstone* v. *Scottish Women's Amateur Athletic Association*, 1987 *SLT* 611; and *Graham* v. *Ladeside of Kilbirnie Bowling Club*, 1990 SC 365. See also *Tait* v. *Central Radio Taxis (Tollcross) Ltd*, 1989 SC 4.

113 See Stephen Thomson, 'Judicial Review and Public Law: Challenging the Preconceptions of a Troubled Taxonomy' (2017) 41(2) *Melbourne University Law Review* 890.

114 It should be noted that Scots lawyers often received their legal education in Continental Europe, particularly at Dutch and French universities, in the seventeenth and eighteenth centuries (see, for example, John W. Cairns, 'Importing our Lawyers from Holland: Netherlands' Influences on Scots Law and Lawyers in the Eighteenth Century' in Grant G. Simpson (ed.), *Scotland and the Low Countries, 1124–1994* (Tuckwell Press, 1996), pp. 136–53.

115 These are not necessarily without truth, though vary in terms of historical accuracy.

116 More specifically, T. B. Smith described it as 'basically a civilian system that had been under pressure from the Anglo-American common law and has in part been overlaid by that rival system of jurisprudence'. T. B. Smith, 'The Preservation of the Civilian Tradition in "Mixed Jurisdictions"' in A. N. Yiannopoulos (ed.), *Civil Law in the Modern World* (Louisiana State University Press, 1965), pp. 2–3. Niall Whitty described it as usually comprising a 'civilian system overlaid by the common law'; Niall R. Whitty, 'The Civilian Tradition and Debates on Scots Law' (1996) *Tydskrif vir die Suid-Afrikaanse Reg* 227, p. 232.

117 Hector L. MacQueen, 'Mixed Jurisdictions and Convergence: Scotland' (2001) 29 *International Journal of Legal Information* 309, p. 310.

118 In any event, Scotland's 'mixture' of legal traditions does not merely encompass Common law and Civil law, but as this author has argued elsewhere, other traditions including those of the Scottish Common law, feudal law, canon law, Udal law, Celtic law, Biblical law, foreign maritime law and, in the modern age, European Union

such jurisdictions.[119] In line with these assertions of distinctiveness, there might be an inclination to retain differences in the scope and remedies of judicial review simply because they are different from their counterparts in England. Issues of pedigree will again arise in this context. Nevertheless, the recent importations from English judicial review procedure cast doubt on the extent to which distinctiveness for its own sake underlies the Scottish position. Lord Hope stated in *Davidson* v. *Scottish Ministers (No 1)* that '[t]here are occasions when those of your Lordships who come from Scotland feel justified in defending Scots law and the Scottish legal system against what are perceived to be alien influences', but, in relation to the law on the availability of coercive remedies against the Crown, 'this is not one of them'.[120]

In short, there are a number of possible reasons why Scots judicial review, on questions of scope, remedies and procedure, has retained distinctiveness from that of England. While it is possible that the courts have sought to retain distinctiveness for its own sake, the evidence would suggest that it is more likely explained by a blend of practical and normative considerations. There are advantages to be had by adopting aspects of English law that seem to work better in practice or which appear more cogent or principled, but it is also healthy for the legal system to retain the self-confidence to reject those aspects of English law that seem less desirable as a matter of principle and practice. McHarg described the Scottish courts' 'acceptance of English authority on the grounds of review though rejecting that on scope [as] plain incoherent, since both are influenced by prevailing attitudes to the role and foundations of judicial review'.[121] Although the Scottish approach does not seem to be driven purely by ideology or pragmatism, it is legitimate to raise the issue of coherence. One can question, for example, the apparent rejection of a public/private distinction in relation to scope, while admitting of the distinction in relation to standing. It will be intriguing to see if and how the courts reconcile these two positions or, indeed, if the admission of the public/private distinction in relation to standing is the beginning of the end of Scots judicial review's apparent abstention from drawing public/private distinctions. Long-established though Scots judicial review may be, its doctrinal narrative continues to unfold, and on this specific question, it is too early to tell.

5.5 CONCLUDING REMARKS

A comparison of judicial review in Scotland and England is characterised by both resemblance and distinctiveness. While the grounds of review are substantially aligned in the two jurisdictions, there are major doctrinal differences in the scope (and remedies) of review, in particular the possibility of judicial review in Scotland of private bodies performing private functions. The picture is not, however, static, and in recent years there has been increasing convergence of judicial review procedure, primarily due to statutory (and judicial) reforms in Scotland.

English law commands a great deal of authority in Scots judicial review and continues to be a major influence in that regard. Sometimes this manifests in Scots law following the English approach or aligning itself with English law or practice. This has occurred both by

law and the law on the European Convention on Human Rights; Stephen Thomson, 'Mixed Jurisdiction and the Scottish Legal Tradition: Reconsidering the Concept of Mixture' (2014) 7(1) *Journal of Civil Law Studies* 51.

119 Vernon V. Palmer, *Mixed Jurisdictions Worldwide: The Third Legal Family* (Cambridge University Press, 2001), p. 5.

120 *Davidson* v. *Scottish Ministers (No 1)*, 2006 SC (HL) 41, para. 38.

121 Aileen McHarg, 'Border Disputes: The Scope and Purposes of Judicial Review' in Aileen McHarg and Tom Mullen (eds.), *Public Law in Scotland* (Avizandum, 2006), p. 239.

way of statutory and judicial innovation. However, it can sometimes be discerned in a rejection of the English position, with the view that the Scottish approach is advantageous or practically or normatively superior, and that English authority is not to be followed. The influence of English law (and the structure of the system of laws and institutions in which English law and Scots law coexist) therefore simultaneously results in a powerful force of convergence and an increased resolution that aspects of distinctiveness should be maintained where this is thought apposite. Self-awareness and self-critique are valuable traits in a legal system and legal culture.

It is important, however, that when Scotland chooses to adopt or converge with English law or practice – and, in particular, where it chooses not to adopt or converge with the law or practice of other jurisdictions – that it does so for clear, justifiable reasons. It can be questioned whether the recent examples of procedural convergence, where Scots judicial review has been reformed to substantially align with English procedure, were pursued on the basis that the English rules were superior to the variety of alternative rules that exist in other jurisdictions. Perhaps the focus on English law is at times too singular; the fact that Scotland and England are constituent parts of a common state may serve as a powerful force for convergence but not an absolute force. It is hoped that the institutions of the Scottish legal system will continue to draw on the experiences of English law for the improvement of Scots law but also be more prepared to draw on the experiences of other jurisdictions in addition to retaining a willingness to assert a distinctive position where principle or practice commends.

Nevertheless, the state and status of judicial review must be considered in the current, turbulent political context: in particular, the recent surge in popular support for Scottish independence, and friction between the UK and Scottish Parliaments and the UK and Scottish Governments over the manner and extent of the UK's withdrawal from the European Union. These have the potential to significantly alter the dynamics of convergence and divergence between the law and practice in Scotland, and the law and practice in the unions of which it is currently a part. However, even when the dust has settled, a comparison of Scots and English judicial review will likely continue to be a tale of resemblance and distinctiveness.

6

The Constitutionalisation of English Judicial Review in Ireland

Continuity and Change

Paul Daly

INTRODUCTION

Ireland has its own body of administrative law, separate and distinct from the law developed by the English courts. Similarities abound, as one would expect given the geographical proximity of the two jurisdictions and the close historical ties between them. Yet the constitutionalisation of Irish public law – first on independence in 1922 and then in 1937 on the adoption of the Irish Constitution – has had a marked effect on the development of Irish administrative law. This is not to say that every aspect of the Irish law of judicial review of administrative action now bears a distinctively constitutional hue – the Constitution, as we shall see, demands continuity as well as change. However, the adoption of the Constitution has been hugely influential and may even have prompted Irish judges not to adopt some important orthodoxies of contemporary English administrative law.[1]

The objectives of the chapter are, first, to describe the constitutional influences on the development of Irish administrative law and, second, to demonstrate that Ireland has an indigenous administrative law. Section 6.1 begins with a brief historical introduction before moving in Section 6.2 to a discussion of the influence of the Constitution. In some areas, notwithstanding the adoption of the Constitution, legal life has gone on as before. The supervisory role of the superior courts has continued mostly unaltered, despite constitutional language that might be thought to justify a more intrusive judicial review jurisdiction. The law in relation to procedural fairness has been constitutionalised – and has a bespoke term, 'constitutional justice' – but is not markedly different in substance from the English equivalent. However, there have been some important changes. With sovereignty residing in the People, rather than the Crown, the prerogative has been held not to have survived the transition to a new constitutional order. The permissible scope of delegation of power by the legislature has also been circumscribed. The constitutionalisation of judicially enforceable fundamental rights, meanwhile, meant that Irish administrative lawyers followed a 'rights-based' approach before their counterparts elsewhere in the common law world began to think in such terms. Finally, even though the supervisory role of the superior courts remains intact, it now has constitutional protection, such that limitations on access to judicial review are strictly policed and, potentially, unconstitutional.[2]

[1] To facilitate the reader, I will refer generally to the 1937 Constitution. But several of the innovations discussed in the following section have their origins in the 1922 document: the demise of the royal prerogative; provision for judicially enforceable fundamental rights and the emergence of a non-delegation doctrine.

[2] With the consequence that they are void *ab initio*. An Irish court would thus not need to engage in the interpretive and intellectual gymnastics characteristic of the English courts' approach to ouster clauses: *Anisminic* v. *Foreign*

In Section 6.3, I will hypothesise that the existence of the Constitution, and thus of an identifiably indigenous Irish administrative law, has prompted Irish judges to be self-confident enough to refuse to follow settled English law. There are some important areas where Irish administrative law has not tracked English administrative law, most notably in relation to error of law and procedural exclusivity (which has had a particular effect on the development of the law of legitimate expectations). In these areas, the Irish courts have operated in the shadow of English law but have sought to develop an indigenous approach.

6.1 HISTORICAL OVERVIEW

In a piece of this nature, it is impossible to do justice to the tangled history of Ireland and Britain – political, economic, social, cultural, literary, legal and much else besides. Nonetheless, some introductory remarks may be helpful to the reader. In accordance with the terms of the Anglo-Irish Treaty 1921, Ireland left the United Kingdom in 1922, subsequent to the War of Independence, a (mostly) guerrilla struggle fought between 1919 and 1921. The effect was to reverse, as far as Ireland was concerned, the Acts of Union 1800, and give the country an equivalent status to Canada.[3] The Treaty settlement was gradually dismantled in the 1920s and (especially) the 1930s,[4] leading to the adoption of a new Constitution in 1937.

The judiciary did not survive this period of turbulence entirely unscathed. Prior to independence, the Irish legal system greatly resembled the English.[5] Ireland had its own common law courts (Common Pleas, Exchequer, King's Bench and a Court of Chancery), with a system of local administration presided over by assistant barristers and justices of the peace. Subsequent to the passage of the Judicature (Ireland) Act 1877, and after the fashion of the times, the common law courts – and law and equity – were fused into one Supreme Court, which itself had two distinct organs, a High Court and Court of Appeal. Since 1801, there had been an onward appeal to the House of Lords.

Revolution interfered with the administration of justice. The old courts, tainted by their association with the Crown, were supplanted to a significant extent by a set of revolutionary courts established by those rebelling against English rule as a precursor to the anticipated dismantling of colonial governance structures.[6] Post-independence changes were inevitable. But they had greatest effect at the local level, where District and Circuit Courts replaced the inefficient and unloved system of local justice.[7] The centralisation of English justice in the superior courts of record was maintained, with a High Court and Supreme Court sitting in

Compensation Commission [1969] 2 AC 147; *R (Privacy International)* v. *Investigatory Powers Tribunal* [2017] EWCA Civ 1868; [2018] 1 WLR 2572.

3 Leo Kohn, *The Constitution of the Irish Free State* (George Allen & Unwin: London, 1932), p. 50.

In substance this implied full internal self-government, unrestricted fiscal autonomy, the right to maintain an Irish police force and an Irish army subject only to the control of the Irish Parliament. In the sphere of external relations, it involved the concession of the new international status of the British dominions, the right to enter into agreements with foreign states, freedom from obligations arising from treaties not specifically approved by the Irish Parliament, full discretion in the matter of Irish participation in British wars and, lastly, membership of the League of Nations. In form, it connoted the conclusive recognition of Irish internal sovereignty.

4 See generally Nicholas Mansergh, *The Irish Free State: Its Government and Politics* (George Allen & Unwin: London, 1934).

5 See generally W. N. Osborough, 'The Irish Legal System 1796–1877' in *Studies in Irish Legal History* (Four Courts Press: Dublin, 1999).

6 See generally David Foxton, *Revolutionary Lawyers: Sinn Féin and the Crown Courts* (Four Courts Press: Dublin, 2008); Mary Kotsonouris, *The Winding Up of the Dáil Courts, 1922–1925: An Obvious Duty* (Four Courts Press: Dublin, 2004).

7 See generally the Courts of Justice Act 1924.

the capital to hear the cases of the greatest moment. Significantly, from an administrative law perspective, the prerogative writs were the exclusive preserve of the High Court and Supreme Court.

Yet, even in the post-independence era, administrative law was underdeveloped in the academy. The first lectures in the subject were only delivered in Trinity College Dublin after the Second World War; administrative law only became part of the syllabus in University College Cork, one of the country's largest law schools, at the end of the 1970s. In the 1950s, a comparative law scholar remarked that '[a] study of the use of the prerogative writs in Ireland is long overdue'.[8] Textbooks dedicated to the study of Irish administrative law would not roll off the printing presses until the 1980s.[9]

Thus, in 1937, when the Constitution was adopted, first by the national legislature sitting as a Constituent Assembly and then by plebiscite, Irish administrative law was no more developed than its English equivalent. Inasmuch as it existed, it existed in the interstices of the prerogative writs, issued by the High Court against inferior courts and analogous bodies.[10] Of course, the Irish courts 'were prepared on occasion to take action on lines differing from the English decisions',[11] but on the whole there was no recognisably Irish body of administrative law.

6.2 THE CONSTITUTION: CONTINUITY AND CHANGE

I will begin this section by setting out the ways in which the Constitution sought to guarantee continuity on the one hand and change on the other. Understanding the tension between continuity and change is crucial to understanding the development of Irish administrative law.

In some ways, the Constitution represents a radical break from the past – replacing the Crown as Sovereign with popular sovereignty and providing for judicially enforceable fundamental rights – but in others it preserves important components of the colonial legal order. The key constitutional provision in this regard is Article 50.1:

> *Subject to this Constitution and to the extent to which they are not inconsistent therewith*, the laws in force in Saorstát Éireann immediately prior to the date of the coming into operation of this Constitution *shall continue to be of full force and effect* until the same or any of them shall have been repealed or amended by enactment of the Oireachtas.[12]

The highlighted portions demonstrate how the drafters attempted to strike a compromise between the demand for continuity on the one hand and the desire for change on the other. The underlined portion, familiar in its terms to many of the 'reception' statutes enacted in British colonies,[13] establishes continuity as the status quo. In time, the Oireachtas will make Irish laws for Irish conditions. But until then, those laws previously in force 'shall continue'.

[8] A. G. Donaldson, *Some Aspects of Irish Comparative Law* (University of North Carolina Press: Durham, 1957), p. 204.

[9] Ronald Stout, *Administrative Law in Ireland* (Institute of Public Administration: Dublin, 1985); Gerard Hogan and David Gwynn Morgan, *Administrative Law in Ireland* (Sweet and Maxwell: London, 1986).

[10] See generally S. A. de Smith, *Judicial Review of Administrative Action* (Stevens & Sons: London, 1959).

[11] A. G. Donaldson, *Some Aspects of Irish Comparative Law* (University of North Carolina Press: Durham, 1957), p. 204.

[12] Emphasis added. Saorstát Éireann (Irish Free State) came into existence in 1922; the Oireachtas is the equivalent of Parliament, comprising a lower house (Dáil Éireann) and an upper house (Seanad Éireann).

[13] See generally Bruce McPherson, *The Reception of English Law Abroad* (Brisbane: Supreme Court of Queensland Library, 2007).

However, the italicised portion indicates that although continuity is to be presumed, the adoption of the Constitution has nonetheless altered the fundamental precepts of the legal order. Where once an all-mighty Westminster Parliament ultimately reigned supreme, the Constitution is now the supreme norm (something which has obvious implications for administrative law given the importance of legislative intent in the justification and development of judicial review of administrative action).[14]

This brief overview should serve as a frame for the ensuing discussion, alerting the reader to the likelihood of significant changes in some areas but cautioning that in other areas continuity should be expected, with familiar concepts taking on a constitutionalised form but retaining most or all of their (English) substance.

6.2.1 *Supervisory Jurisdiction*

The judicature provisions of the Constitution are contained in Articles 34 to 37. Three aspects are particularly pertinent. First, Article 34.3.1 states that the High Court is 'invested with full original jurisdiction in and power to determine all matters and questions whether of law or fact, civil or criminal'. Second, however, Article 34.3.4 envisages 'Courts of local and limited jurisdiction with a right of appeal as determined by law' and, third, Article 37 allows for the vesting of 'limited functions and powers of a judicial nature' in non-judicial bodies. The effect of these provisions is that while the High Court plainly has general jurisdiction, inferior courts and other administrative bodies will – equally plainly – exercise significant decision-making authority.

In interpreting these provisions, the Irish courts have largely preserved the status quo, permitting the Oireachtas to designate the inferior courts as the default venues for all but the most high-stakes civil litigation, including family law matters.[15] In according the legislature a significant degree of choice, the Irish system is the mirror image of the British. Moreover, notwithstanding the expansive language of Article 34.3.1, the Irish courts have cleaved just as closely as their British counterparts to the distinction between jurisdiction and merits.[16] Rather than finding in Article 34.3.1 a justification for more wide-ranging review of factual and legal matters considered by inferior courts and administrative bodies, the Irish courts have interpreted it as carrying over the 'inherent supervisory jurisdiction over inferior tribunals':[17]

> [I]f there has been ... a devolution [of decision-making power] on an exclusive basis, the High Court will not hear and determine the matter or question, but its full jurisdiction is there to be invoked – in proceedings such as *habeas corpus*, *certiorari*, prohibition,

[14] See generally Christopher Forsyth (eds.), *Judicial Review and the Constitution* (Oxford: Hart, 2000), and his contribution to this volume. Cf. my comments on parliamentary sovereignty, Canada-style, in my chapter on Canada in this volume.

[15] Most of the litigation has focused on the effects of legislation on the High Court's original jurisdiction in civil matters: is the jurisdiction residual, or central, and when can decisional authority be vested exclusively in an inferior court subject only to a right of appeal?

[16] See e.g. *R* v. *Somerset County Council, ex parte Fewings* [1995] 1 All ER 513, 515, *per* Laws J:

> The court does not ask itself the question, 'Is this decision right or wrong?' Far less does the judge ask himself whether he would himself have arrived at the decision in question. ... The only question for the judge is whether the decision taken by the body under review was one which it was legally permitted to take in the way that it did.

For an Irish equivalent, see *Stroker* v. *Doherty* [1991] 1 IR 23.

[17] *Farrell* v. *Attorney General* [1998] 1 ILRM 364, 377, per Keane J.

> *mandamus, quo warranto*, injunction or a declaratory action – so as to ensure that the hearing and determination will be in accordance with law.[18]

In extending the judicial review jurisdiction to errors of fact and errors of law, the Irish courts have been very cautious,[19] certainly more cautious than the language of the judicature provisions of the Constitution requires,[20] with its capacious reference to 'all matters and questions whether of law or fact'. Here, a traditional function of the superior courts – stretching back into the mists of time and the now-hazy institution of the *Curia Regis* – was already well established by the time of the adoption of the Constitution and the Irish courts, perhaps understandably, were loath to depart from settled practice and, in any event, were not pushed to do so.

There is an important constitutional corollary of the approach in *Tormey*. It is a 'necessary inference' from Article 34.3.1 that a citizen must have access to the High Court to challenge allegedly unlawful government action.[21] Any legislative attempt to oust the judicial review jurisdiction of the High Court is therefore constitutionally dubious: 'In the final analysis, of course, no statute can preclude [the High Court] from addressing the lawfulness of a decision when made.'[22] Even statutory provisions that provide for extremely brief time limits in which challenges must be brought to certain types of administrative decision are constitutionally dubious[23] and have been upheld only where the legislation empowers the High Court to extend the period of time within which an application can be brought.[24] The basis for so holding is that such provisions constitute a disproportionate interference with the right of access to the courts, part of which includes the supervisory jurisdiction.

The Irish courts have analysed such provisions in terms of 'the balancing of conflicting considerations' – the right of individual access to the courts versus the public interest in short limitation periods in some instances – rather than in terms of the underlying nature and constitutional foundations of administrative law.[25] This might be thought to mark Ireland out from other Commonwealth jurisdictions where judicial review of administrative action is entrenched by a written constitution and where ouster clauses prompt high-level discussion of

18 *Tormey* v. *Attorney General* [1985] IR 289, 297, *per* Henchy J.

19 See e.g. Paul Daly, 'Judicial Review of Factual Error in Ireland' (2008) 30 *Dublin University Law Journal* 187; *Donegan* v. *Dublin City Council* [2012] 3 IR 600.

20 It would not be fruitful, in the context of the present project, to drag the reader through the morass of case law on the meaning of 'limited functions and powers of a judicial nature'. The test to identify 'judicial' power was set out by Kenny J in *McDonald* v. *Bord na gCon* [1965] IR 217. See Eoin Carolan, 'Separation of Powers and Administrative Governance' in Eoin Carolan and Oran Doyle (eds.), *The Irish Constitution: Governance and Values* (Thomson Roundhall: Dublin, 2008), p. 195. As to whether a judicial power is 'limited' (and can thus safely be vested in a non-judicial body), the main source of litigation has been professional disciplinary functions, as in *Re Solicitors Act 1954* [1960] IR 239, a case which suggests that serious sanctions against members of a regulated profession can only be imposed by courts. For qualifications, see *M* v. *Medical Council* [1984] IR 485; *K* v. *An Bord Altranais* [1990] 2 IR 396; *Keady* v. *Commissioner of an Garda Siochánna* [1992] 2 IR 197.

21 *Macauley* v. *Minister for Posts and Telegraphs* [1966] IR 345, 358, per Kenny J. The right of access to the courts was also said to be 'one of the personal rights of the citizen' protected by Article 40.3 of the Constitution. Although *Macauley* concerned the right of access to the High Court to make a constitutional challenge, it is now accepted that its logic extends to judicial review of administrative action generally. See e.g. *Dunmanus Bay Mussels Ltd* v. *Aquaculture Licences Appeals Board* [2014] 1 IR 403.

22 *Satke* v. *An Bord Pleanála* [2009] IEHC 230, per Hanna J. See e.g. *Blehein* v. *Minister for Health and Children* [2009] 1 IR 275. See generally Gerard Hogan, 'Reflections on the Supreme Court's Decision in *Tormey* v. *Attorney General*' (1986) 8 *Dublin University Law Journal* 31.

23 See e.g. *Brady* v. *Donegal County Council* [1989] ILRM 282; *White* v. *Dublin City Council* [2004] 1 IR 545.

24 *In re Article 26 and the Illegal Immigrants (Trafficking) Bill 1999* [2000] 2 IR 360 (14-day time limit on immigration judicial reviews).

25 *White* v. *Dublin City Council* [2004] 1 IR 545 at 569, per Denham J.

the features of the supervisory jurisdiction.[26] However, the difference in focus may simply arise from the fact that the Irish courts have been called upon to address the validity of partial ouster clauses, not full ouster clauses. Given the strength of the constitutional objections to ouster clauses in the Irish context – of which the legislature and potential litigants are well aware – this focus is unsurprising.

6.2.2 *Constitutional Justice*

Natural justice, the twin rules of *nemo iudex in sua causa* and *audi alteram partem*, was 'reincarnated as constitutional justice'[27] in Ireland in *McDonald* v. *Bord na gCon*: 'In the context of the Constitution, natural justice might be more appropriately termed constitutional justice and must be understood to import more than the two well-established principles that no man shall be judge in his own cause and *audi alterm partem*.'[28]

The source from which constitutional justice springs is Article 40.3.1 of the Constitution, which obliges the State to 'protect as best it may from unjust attack and, in the case of injustice done, vindicate the life, person, good name, and property rights of every citizen'. This is 'a guarantee to the citizen of basic fairness of procedures'.[29]

Despite the sweeping rhetoric, however, there is, in substance, little to distinguish Ireland's native 'constitutional justice' from the modern doctrine of fairness familiar to courts around the common law world, the scope of which is very broad,[30] but the application of which depends on context.[31] Indeed, not long after *McDonald*, the Supreme Court adopted the well-known dictum of Tucker LJ in *Russell* v. *Duke of Norfolk*[32] on the context-sensitive nature of the modern law of natural justice. In Ireland, just as elsewhere, the procedural protections owed to the individual depend on 'the circumstances of the case, the nature of the inquiry, the rules under which the tribunal is acting, the subject matter that is being dealt with, and so forth'.[33] When litigants have attempted to convince the Irish courts that constitutional justice encompasses procedural rights additional to those available at common law, they have been tersely rebuffed.[34] Moreover, even Irish judges now tend to use the terms 'natural justice', 'constitutional justice' and 'fair procedures' more or less interchangeably.[35] The following passage, rendered in a recent case relating to the right to reasons for administrative decisions, is illustrative of the Irish approach to fairness in administrative law:

26 See e.g. *Crevier* v. *Attorney-General (Quebec)* [1981] 2 SCR 220; *Kirk* v. *Industrial Court (New South Wales)* (2010) 239 CLR 531.

27 Gerard Hogan and David Morgan (with Paul Daly), *Administrative Law in Ireland* (Roundhall: Dublin, 2010), p. 583.

28 [1965] IR 217, 242, per Walsh J. 'Bord na gCon' is the Greyhound Board.

29 *Re Haughey* [1971] IR 217, 263, per Ó Dálaigh CJ. It is also to be interpreted broadly, such that life, person, good name or property rights need not literally be at stake. See generally David Kenny, 'Fair Procedures in Irish Administrative Law: Towards a Constitutional Duty to Act Fairly in Dellaway Investments v. NAMA' (2011) 33 *Dublin University Law Journal* 47.

30 See e.g. *Dellway Investments* v. *National Asset Management Agency* [2011] 4 IR 1 (transfer of assets from a bank to a state-run 'bad bank' for 'toxic assets' in the wake of the global financial crisis held to require fair procedures).

31 See e.g. *Flanagan* v. *University College Dublin* [1988] IR 724; *International Vessels Ltd* v. *Minister for Marine (No. 2)* [1991] 2 IR 93; *Gallagher* v *Revenue Commissioners (No. 2)* [1995] 1 IR 55.

32 [1949] 1 All ER 109.

33 [1949] 1 All ER 109, at 118, approved in *Kiely* v. *The Minister for Social Welfare* [1977] IR 267 at 281.

34 See e.g. *Carroll* v. *Minister for Agriculture and Food* [1991] 1 IR 230 (right of appeal against adverse administrative decisions); *Kirwan* v. *Minister for Justice* [1994] 1 ILRM 333 (access to legal aid in administrative proceedings); *Georgopoulos* v. *Beaumont Hospital Board* [1998] 3 IR 132 (enhanced standard of proof in disciplinary proceedings).

35 See e.g. *BFO* v. *Governor of Dóchas Centre* [2005] 2 IR 1.

> The general principles of natural and constitutional justice comprise a number of individual aspects of the protection of due process. The obligation to give fair notice and, possibly, to provide access to information or, in some cases, to have a hearing are intimately interrelated and the obligation to give reasons is sometimes merely one part of the process. The overarching principle is that persons affected by administrative decisions should have access to justice, that they should have the right to seek the protection of the courts in order to see that the rule of law has been observed, that fair procedures have been applied and that their rights are not unfairly infringed.[36]

Were these words uttered in an Australian, Canadian or English accent, members of the audience would be unlikely to raise their eyebrows, still less any objections.

It is true that the constitutionalisation of procedural fairness means that it cannot be ousted even by clear statutory language,[37] but the practical effect of this change on the content of procedural protections is limited. For one thing, there is the venerable principle, long central to the common law as developed in England, that courts may, to ensure fairness, 'supply the omission of the legislature'.[38] For another thing, common law judges have long demonstrated a ferocious judicial reluctance to accept that statutory language is sufficiently clear to oust procedural protections, even where there are no constitutional concerns.[39]

6.2.3 *Prerogative Power*

One of the most ancient dogmas of the common law – and probably one of the most misunderstood[40] – is that the Crown is immune from suit. This is said variously (and not always consistently) to be an aspect of the royal prerogative, caused by the incongruity of suing the Crown in its own courts, or based in the idea that the 'king can do no wrong'. Whatever its precise origins, the dogma is evidently predicated on the existence of a monarch. This proved to be fatal for its prospects in independent Ireland.

In *Byrne* v. *Ireland*,[41] the Supreme Court held that immunity from suit did not survive the adoption of a Constitution based on popular sovereignty, a new order in which power derives from the People. Indeed, the royal prerogative, based on the 'King [as] the personification of the State' was 'quite inconsistent' with the forthright statement in the Constitution 'that all the powers of government and all authority, legislative, executive and judicial, in Ireland were derived from the people of Ireland'.[42] It has been strongly argued that this conclusion was inconsistent with the original understanding of the drafters of the Constitution,[43] but the Irish

36 *Mallak* v. *Minister for Justice, Equality and Law Reform* [2012] 3 IR 297, 316, per Fennelly J.

37 See e.g. *O'Brien* v. *Bord na Móna* [1983] IR 255, 270–1, per Keane J.

38 *Cooper* v. *Wandsworth Board of Works* (1863) 14 CB (NS) 180, 194, per Byles J.

39 See generally Matthew Groves, 'Exclusion of the Rules of Natural Justice' (2013) 39(2) *Monash University Law Review* 285.

40 See Harry Street, *Governmental Liability: A Comparative Study* (Cambridge University Press: New York, 1953), chapter 1.

41 [1972] IR 241. It is worth noting that no equivalent to the Crown Proceedings Act 1947 had been enacted in Ireland. Although legislation had been mooted, none was ever introduced: *Programme of Law Reform* (January 1962), p. 7. See also, 215 *Dáil Debates* Col. 1858 (20 May 1965).

42 [1972] IR 241, 272, per Walsh J. The question in *Byrne* was resolved on the basis that the royal prerogative had not survived the enactment of the 1922 Constitution of Saorstát Éireann and thus could not form part of the body of law transferred into independent Ireland by the 1937 Constitution. Article 2 of the 1922 Constitution is materially identical to Article 6.1 of the 1937 Constitution. Both locate sovereignty in the Irish People.

43 John Kelly, 'Hidden Treasure and the Constitution' (1988) 10 *Dublin University Law Journal* 5.

courts have persisted in the view that the continuance of the royal prerogative was incompatible with the creation of a 'brand new sovereign State'.[44]

Yet the Irish courts have nonetheless managed to find ways of placing old prerogatives on solid constitutional foundations. When a pair of treasure hunters dug up the celebrated Derrynaflan Horde, handed the artefacts over to the National Museum for safe keeping, but sued when the compensation provided by the State proved unacceptably low, the Supreme Court determined that the royal prerogative of treasure trove survived 'not as a right derived from the Crown but rather as an inherent attribute of the sovereignty of the State':

> It would, I think, now be universally accepted, certainly by the People of Ireland, and by the people of most modern states, that one of the most important national assets belonging to the people is their heritage and knowledge of its true origins and the buildings and objects which constitute keys to their ancient history. If this be so, then it would appear to me to follow that a necessary ingredient of sovereignty in a modern state and certainly in this State, having regard to the terms of the Constitution, with an emphasis on its historical origins and a constant concern for the common good is and should be an ownership by the State of objects which constitute antiquities of importance which are discovered and which have no known owner. It would appear to me to be inconsistent with the framework of the society sought to be created and sought to be protected by the Constitution that such objects should become the exclusive property of those who by chance may find them.[45]

Recognising prerogative power would be incompatible with the constitutional order. But recognising functional equivalents would not necessarily be.[46] One could not ask for a more vivid illustration of the tension between continuity and change. Indeed, the Irish courts have even suggested that there are inherent executive powers,[47] analogous to the 'administrative powers' of the Crown familiar to English lawyers,[48] thereby recognising a functional equivalent of a capacity which one might have thought to be unique to jurisdictions in which sovereignty resides in the monarch. Moreover, in the area of parole – treated as a purely 'executive' function – the Irish courts have held that decisions are largely unreviewable,[49] an approach arguably even more ungenerous than the contemporary English approach to the review of prerogative powers.[50]

6.2.4 *Fundamental Rights*

To say that the adoption of the Constitution ushered in a new era of rights protection would be an overstatement. Although Articles 40 to 44 create a plethora of judicially enforceable rights – relating to matters such as the family unit, private property and religion[51] – Irish

44 *Webb* v. *Ireland* [1988] IR 353, 382, per Finlay CJ. See also *Howard* v. *Commissioners of Public Works* [1994] 1 IR 101 (application of statutes to the State).

45 *Webb* v. *Ireland* [1988] IR 353, 383, per Finlay CJ. See also *Geoghegan* v. *Institute of Chartered Accountants* [1995] 3 IR 86, 118, per O'Flaherty J.

46 See also *Leen* v. *President of the Executive Council* [1925] IR 456 (public interest immunity).

47 See e.g. *Bode* v. *Minister for Justice, Equality and Law Reform* [2008] 3 IR 663; *Prendergast* v. *Higher Education Authority* [2009] 1 ILRM 47.

48 See generally Adam Perry, 'The Crown's Administrative Powers' (2015) 131 *Law Quarterly Review* 652.

49 *Murray and Murray* v. *Ireland* [1991] ILRM 465; *Peter Whelan* v. *Minister for Justice, Equality and Law Reform* [2008] 2 IR 142.

50 See e.g. *R* v. *Secretary of State for the Home Department, ex parte Bentley* [1994] QB 349.

51 Backed up by Articles 15.4.1 ('The Oireachtas shall not enact any law which is in any respect repugnant to this Constitution or any provision thereof') and 34.3.2 ('the jurisdiction of the High Court shall extend to the question of the validity of any law having regard to the provisions of this Constitution, and no such question shall be raised

practitioners, versed in the British legal tradition, were reluctant to weaponise them in litigation.[52] It was not until the 1960s that constitutional litigation really took off, prompted perhaps by high-profile developments in the United States during the Chief Justiceship of Earl Warren.[53] Indeed, the Irish courts soon came to enthusiastically embrace the concept of 'unenumerated rights', those constitutional rights not specifically set out in the document but nonetheless judicially enforceable against the State.[54] In the 1960s and 1970s, the courts recognised rights to personal integrity[55] and marital privacy;[56] recognition of the latter resulted in a declaration that a prohibition on the purchase of contraceptives was unconstitutional, mirroring the analysis and outcome in the American case of *Griswold* v. *Connecticut*.[57]

The consequences for administrative law were significant. The *East Donegal* case was a watershed.[58] The occasion was provided by the introduction of a licensing scheme for livestock marts, a controversial matter in a country with a largely agrarian economy. New legislation gave the Minister for Agriculture and Fisheries sweeping powers to attach conditions to licences. This legislation, having been introduced after 1937, was presumed to be constitutional.[59] But this presumption of constitutionality was – viewed from the perspective of the State – a double-edged sword. On the one hand, it could be used to fend off challenges to the constitutionality of legislation. On the other hand, however, it could be wielded by judges to cut down the scope of statutory powers, by requiring 'that proceedings, procedures, discretions and adjudications which are permitted, provided for, or prescribed by an Act of the Oireachtas are to be conducted in accordance with the principles of constitutional

(whether by pleading, argument or otherwise) in any Court established under this or any other Article of this Constitution other than the High Court, the Court of Appeal or the Supreme Court').

52 See e.g. John Kelly, 'Fundamental Rights and the Constitution' in Brian Farrell (eds.), *De Valera's Constitution and Ours* (Gill & MacMillan: Dublin, 1988), p. 163:

> [The] bill of rights was slow in making itself felt. This perhaps was partly due to the fact that the older generation of judges, those who sat in the High Court and Supreme Court in the 1940s, were men educated in the old, British tradition, which regarded the parliament as sovereign and which considered that civil liberties and decent standards of government were sufficiently protected by the moderation and good sense of the members of that parliament.

See also Donal Barrington, 'The Constitution and the Courts' in Frank Litton (eds.), *The Constitution of Ireland:* 1937–1987 (Institute for Public Administration: Dublin, 1988), p. 110.

53 On the regular, long-running private correspondence between Justice Brian Walsh, a long-serving member of the Irish Supreme Court, and Justice William Brennan of the United States Supreme Court, see Ruadhán Mac Cormaic, *The Supreme Court* (Penguin Books: Dublin, 2016).

54 The hook was provided by Article 40.3.2: 'The State shall, *in particular*, by its laws protect as best it may from unjust attack and, in the case of injustice done, vindicate the life, person, good name, and property rights of every citizen' (emphasis added). If, the reasoning went, these rights are protected *in particular*, then other rights must also be protected. The *locus classicus* is *Ryan* v. *Attorney General* [1965] IR 294. For a summary of the contemporary state of the law on unenumerated rights, see Conor O'Mahony, 'Unenumerated Rights: Possible Future Directions after NHV?' (2018) 40 *Dublin University Law Journal* (forthcoming).

55 *Ryan* v. *Attorney General* [1965] IR 294.

56 *McGee* v. *Attorney General* [1974] IR 284.

57 381 US 479 (1965). Irish administrative law has, by contrast, not been obviously influenced by American trends. The law relating to constitutional justice might be thought to resemble the concept of procedural due process developed by the United States Supreme Court, with *Goldberg* v. *Kelly* 397 US 254 (1970) and *McDonald* as the high watermarks before judicial enthusiasm ebbed away in *Mathews* v. *Eldridge* 424 US 319 (1976) and *Kiely*. Otherwise, given that much of American administrative law is statutory, revolving around the detailed and sometimes arcane provisions of the Administrative Procedure Act, and has (for all practical purposes) supplanted the constitutional concept of substantive due process, it is unsurprising that its influence has not been felt in Ireland.

58 *East Donegal Co-operative Livestock Mart Ltd* v. *Attorney General* [1970] IR 317.

59 *McDonald* v. *Bord nag Con* [1965] IR 217. See generally, Brian Foley, *Deference and the Presumption of Constitutionality* (Institute for Public Administration: Dublin, 2009).

justice'.[60] In the *East Donegal* case, the sword was used in the latter sense, to cabin the discretionary powers vested in the Minister, in particular by subjecting their use to the constraints of procedural fairness. In spite of the broad language used in the statute, the Minister was required to act 'fairly and judicially in accordance with the principles of constitutional justice'.[61]

Admittedly, the outcome here could have been reached on ordinary common law grounds, allowing the courts to supply the procedural protections omitted by the legislature. However, the presumption of constitutionality has been a powerful tool for the imposition of fundamental rights norms on administrative decision-making. Invoking it 'will usually have the effect of narrowing the power of a public body and so making its action ultra vires the governing statute under which it was purporting to act'.[62] A useful example is *State (Lynch) v. Cooney*,[63] a case decided during the period of civil war in Northern Ireland. Here, legislation provided that where the Minister for Posts and Telegraphs 'is of the opinion' that a broadcast would be likely to promote or incite crime or undermine the authority of the state, the Minister could issue an order forbidding the national broadcaster from carrying the broadcast.[64] The Minister issued such an order in respect of a candidate representing the Sinn Féin party – the political wing of the Irish Republican Army – in a general election. Having regard to its interference with 'the fundamental rights of citizens to express freely their convictions and opinions', for the legislation to function in a constitutional manner, 'any opinion formed by the Minister thereunder must be one which is bona fide held and factually sustainable and not unreasonable'.[65] On the facts, the Minister had sufficiently 'cogent grounds' for issuing the order,[66] but plainly his room for manoeuvre had been restricted by the operation of the *East Donegal* principle.[67]

The Irish approach, with its distinctively constitutional hue, predates the modern revolution in English administrative law, which has been typically described as 'a rights-based approach',[68] but which more recently has been cast in terms of 'public

60 *East Donegal Co-operative Livestock Mart Ltd* v. *Attorney General* [1970] IR 317, 341, per Walsh J.

61 *East Donegal Co-operative Livestock Mart Ltd* v. *Attorney General* [1970] IR 317, 343–4, per Walsh J.

62 Gerard Hogan and David Morgan (with Paul Daly), *Administrative Law in Ireland* (Roundhall: Dublin, 2010), p. 452.

63 [1982] IR 337.

64 Broadcasting Authority Act 1960, s. 31(1), as amended by the Broadcasting Authority (Amendment) Act 1976:

> Where the Minister is of the opinion that the broadcasting of a particular matter or any matter of a particular class would be likely to promote, or incite to, crime or would tend to undermine the authority of the State, he may by order direct the Authority to refrain from broadcasting the matter or any matter of the particular class, and the Authority shall comply with the order.

65 [1982] IR 337 at 360. At first instance, the High Court held that 'this far-reaching power' was an unconstitutional interference with freedom of expression ([1982] IR 337 at 347), but as the Supreme Court observed on appeal, this conclusion was predicated on the false premise that the legislation permitted the Minister 'to act in an unfettered and unreviewable manner' (at 359).

66 [1982] IR 337 at 365.

67 Of course, there are English cases in which the courts arrived at similar conclusions. See e.g. *Secretary of State for Education and Science* v. *Tameside Metropolitan London Borough Council* [1977] AC 1014 but note that the analysis there was premised solely on the interpretation of the statutory language at issue. See also Lord Atkin's spirited dissent in *Liversidge* v. *Anderson* [1942] AC 206 but note that the analysis there was based on common law principles, not constitutional considerations.

68 Tom Poole, 'The Reformation of English Administrative Law' (2009) 68 *Cambridge Law Journal* 142. A particularly far-reaching variant of this approach is espoused by David Dyzenhaus, Murray Hunt and Michael Taggart, 'The Principle of Legality in Administrative Law: Internationalisation as Constitutionalisation' (2001) 1 *Oxford University Commonwealth Law Journal* 5, who argue for an explicitly rights-based approach to public law adjudication. They claim that administrative decision-making should conform to a 'principle of legality', which requires 'a more or less intrusive standard of review ... depending

interest',[69] 'values'[70] and standards of public administration.[71] While English administrative lawyers fiercely debated the pertinence of the 'ultra vires' doctrine in the modern world,[72] their Irish counterparts looked on, bemused, happy to invoke the doctrine to keep administrative bodies within the boundaries of the powers accorded to them by the Oireachtas, but adept at supplementing these with written and unwritten constitutional limitations: the constitutional foundations of Irish administrative law are to be found in the Constitution, not the common law. Of course, this is not to suggest that the English law of judicial review remained static while the Irish equivalent was bounding ahead. With constitutional rights to the forefront, the Irish courts had little or no interest in developing variable standards of review for abuse of discretion – when the English courts were experimenting with concepts such as 'anxious scrutiny'[73] and 'sub-*Wednesbury*' review,[74] their Irish counterparts clung doggedly to traditional formulations of *Wednesbury* unreasonableness,[75] at least where a statute or decision issued under statute raised constitutional concerns.[76]

Nonetheless, there has been a degree of convergence in recent years. The adoption of the Human Rights Act 1998 has had an important effect on English administrative law, permitting rights-based challenges to legislation and administrative action,[77] adding further momentum to the development of a set of constitutional principles derived from the common law[78] and giving context-sensitive substantive review pride of place in the judicial review lexicon.[79] Meanwhile, the Irish courts have also tentatively endorsed proportionality as a tool for judicial review of administrative action in all cases.[80] Perhaps curiously, the endorsement of proportionality was self-consciously non-constitutional in nature, a development of the existing (though stunted) common law principles,[81] even though proportionality is a concept familiar to Irish judges, who have long embraced it as a tool for the analysis by courts of official action infringing upon

on a variety of context-dependent factors ... a duty on administrative decision-makers to give reasons for their decisions, and judges to defer to the extent that they find that the justification meets the applicable standard'. See also T. R. S. Allan, *Constitutional Justice: A Liberal Theory of the Rule of Law* (Oxford University Press: Oxford, 2001); *The Sovereignty of Law: Freedom, Constitution and Common Law* (Oxford University Press: Oxford, 2013).

69 Jason Varuhas, 'The Public Interest Conception of Public Law: Its Procedural Origins and Substantive Implications' in John Bell, Mark Elliott, Jason Varuhas and Philip Murray (eds.), *Public Law Adjudication in Common Law Systems: Process and Substance* (Hart Publishing: Oxford, 2016).

70 Paul Daly, 'Administrative Law: A Values-Based Approach' in John Bell, Mark Elliott, Jason Varuhas and Philip Murray (eds.), *Public Law Adjudication in Common Law Systems: Process and Substance* (Hart Publishing: Oxford, 2016); 'Administrative Law: Characteristics, Legitimacy, Unity' in Mark Elliott, Jason Varuhas and Shona Stark (eds.), *The Unity of Public Law? Doctrinal, Theoretical and Comparative Perspectives* (Hart Publishing: Oxford, 2017).

71 Hilary Biehler, 'Upholding Standards in Public Decision-Making: Getting the Balance Right' (2017) 47 *Irish Jurist* 94.

72 See generally Christopher Forsyth (eds.), *Judicial Review and the Constitution* (Hart Publishing: Oxford, 2000).

73 *R* v. *Secretary of State for the Home Department, ex parte Bugdaycay* [1987] AC 514 at 531, per Lord Bridge.

74 See e.g. *R* v. *Environment Secretary, ex parte Hammersmith and Fulham London Borough Council* [1991] 1 AC 521.

75 See especially *O'Keeffe* v. *An Bord Pleanála* [1993] 1 IR 39.

76 See e.g. *Clinton* v. *An Bord Pleanála* [2007] 4 IR 701 at 723, refusing to apply *Wednesbury*-style review to an alleged interference with the constitutional right to property.

77 *R (Daly)* v. *Home Secretary* [2001] 2 AC 532.

78 *Kennedy* v. *Charity Commission (Secretary of State for Justice intervening)* [2015] AC 455.

79 *Pham* v. *Home Secretary* [2015] 1 WLR 1591.

80 *Meadows* v. *Minister for Justice, Equality and Law Reform* [2010] 2 IR 201. See Paul Daly, 'Standards of Review in Irish Administrative Law after *Meadows*' (2010) 32 *Dublin University Law Journal* 379.

81 Oran Doyle, *The Constitution of Ireland: A Contextual Analysis* (Hart Publishing: Oxford, 2018) 174–5.

constitutional rights.[82] The most obvious drivers for change[83] were the influences of European Human Rights law[84] and European Union law,[85] as well as (like in England) the pressures of reviewing immigration decisions where important interests, falling short of constitutionally protected rights, are often at stake.[86] Traditional formulations of *Wednesbury* unreasonableness are no longer good law.[87]

On the whole, that the willingness of the Irish courts to use fundamental rights to limit the scope for official action predated the 'reformation' of English administrative law[88] has had marked consequences on the development of administrative law in the two jurisdictions. The fact that Irish and English administrative law have developed along different tracks has not precluded some convergence. But this should not be overstated, because the different sources relied upon by judges for inspiration – the Constitution in Ireland and the common law in England – bring with them different ways of thinking and prompt different questions about the legitimacy of judicial control of administration. Moreover, it bears noting that the legitimacy of reliance by English courts on the common law as a source of fundamental values remains controversial,[89] whereas Irish courts can – when pressed[90] – display a constitutional warrant for decisions limiting the executive's freedom of action, as in *State (Lynch)* v. *Cooney*. Ireland is much less likely to suffer a 'legitimacy crisis' as a result of overly intrusive judicial review of administrative action.[91]

6.2.5 *Delegation of Power*

Pursuant to Article 15.2.1 of the Constitution, the 'sole and exclusive' law-making power of the state is vested in the Oireachtas. An important implication of this provision is that the Oireachtas cannot delegate its law-making power to another body. Vesting broad authority in a body other than the Oireachtas would 'constitute a purported exercise of legislative power by an authority which is not permitted to do so under the Constitution'.[92] This conclusion flows not just from the letter of Article 15.2.1 but from the spirit of the Constitution: 'in accordance with the democratic basis of the Constitution, it is the people's representatives who make the law, who determine the principles and policies'.[93]

For a statute to survive constitutional challenge for breach of the non-delegation doctrine, the Oireachtas must set out the 'principles and policies' governing the exercise of the statutory

82 See e.g. *Heaney* v. *Ireland* [1994] 3 IR 593.

83 See generally, Paul Daly, 'Substantive Review in the Common Law World: AAA v. Minister for Justice [2017] IESC 80 in Comparative Perspective' [2019] *Irish Supreme Court Review* 105.

84 See e.g. *Donegan* v. *Dublin City Council* [2012] 3 IR 600, on the influence of Article 6 of the European Convention on Human Rights, which has the effect of requiring more intensive judicial review of administrative decision makers who are not sufficiently independent. See generally *Tsfayo* v. *United Kingdom* (2009) 48 EHRR 18; *Ali* v. *United Kingdom* (2016) 63 EHRR 20.

85 See e.g. *AAA* v. *Minister for Justice* [2017] IESC 80, on the influence of the European Union law concept of an effective remedy, which may require more intensive judicial review in some circumstances. See generally Case C-69/10 *Diouf* v. *Ministre du Travail, de l'Emploi et de l'Immigration*.

86 See e.g. *Meadows* v. *Minister for Justice, Equality and Law Reform* [2010] 2 IR 201.

87 See e.g. *Kivlehan* v. *Éireann* [2016] IEHC 88; *NM (DRC)* v. *Minister for Justice, Equality and Law Reform* [2016] IECA 217; *AAA* v. *Minister for Justice* [2017] IESC 80.

88 Tom Poole, 'The Reformation of English Administrative Law' (2009) 68 *Cambridge Law Journal* 142.

89 See e.g. Tom Poole, 'Questioning Common Law Constitutionalism' (2005) 25 *Legal Studies* 142.

90 See e.g. David Gwynn Morgan, *A Judgment Too Far? Judicial Activism and the Constitution* (Cork University Press: Cork, 2001).

91 See e.g. Jason Varuhas, *Judicial Capture of Political Accountability* (Policy Exchange: London, 2016) pp. 50–1.

92 *Cityview Press Ltd* v. *An Comhairle Oiliúna* [1980] IR 381, 399, per Finlay CJ [*Cityview*].

93 *Laurentiu* v. *Minister for Justice* [1999] 4 IR 26, 61.

authority it has created: 'if the law is laid down in the statute and details only are filled in or completed by the designated Minister or subordinate body ... there is no unauthorised delegation of legislative power'.[94] The non-delegation doctrine has waxed and waned over the years and the case law is notoriously difficult to rationalise,[95] but it has had an impact on Irish law, having operated recently to strike down provisions in immigration[96] and labour relations law.[97] This, of course, is a doctrine unknown to English law, where at most broad delegations can be interpreted narrowly on judicial review,[98] and it has the systemic effect of requiring that the Oireachtas set out with clarity the terms on which it delegates power to the executive.

In addition, Henry VIII clauses contained in primary legislation have been held to pose serious problems of constitutional validity. Given that the Oireachtas is the 'sole and exclusive' law-making organ of government, regulations that modify primary legislation are necessarily ultra vires: 'for the Minister to exercise a power of regulation granted to him by these Acts so as to negative the expressed intention of the legislature is an unconstitutional use of the power vested in him'.[99] In principle, Henry VIII clauses are unconstitutional per se (unless they can be saved by benevolent judicial construction) because the Oireachtas 'is constitutionally prohibited from abdicating its power'.[100] Again, this is in contradistinction to the position in England, where Henry VIII clauses are constitutionally controversial,[101] and narrowly interpreted by the courts,[102] but not invalid. Here, the Constitution, as interpreted by the courts, has required a marked change in Irish law. Rather than simply setting fetters on the bounds of statutory power, as English courts do, Irish judges can and do say that the Oireachtas has failed to place sufficient fetters on the bounds of statutory power. With Article 15 of the Constitution to call on in support, Irish judges have much more authority in respect of broad delegations of power than their English counterparts.

6.3 IN THE SHADOW OF THE CONSTITUTION? ERROR OF LAW AND PROCEDURAL EXCLUSIVITY

As I have explained in the previous sections, the result of some of the tensions between change and continuity created by the adoption of the Constitution has been a distinctive body of Irish administrative law, different in key respects in its content and evolution from the English law of judicial review of administrative action. However, the whole process of indigenisation of Irish administrative law cannot be traced solely to specific constitutional provisions. Articles 15, 34, 40 and 50 are important components in the gradual development of a distinctively Irish body of administrative law, but it is worth also considering some other important areas of administrative law untouched by constitutional concerns, in order to determine whether differences have also arisen there.

94 *Cityview*, 399.

95 See the discussion in *John Grace Fried Chicken* v. *The Labour Court* [2011] 3 IR 211.

96 *Laurentiu*.

97 *McGowan* v. *Labour Court* [2013] 3 IR 718.

98 See e.g. *R (Public Law Project)* v. *Lord Chancellor* [2016] AC 1531.

99 *Harvey* v. *The Minister for Social Welfare* [1990] 2 IR 232, 244, per Finlay CJ.

100 *Laurentiu* v. *The Minister for Justice, Equality & Law Reform* [1999] 4 IR 26, 61.

101 See e.g. Nick Barber and Alison Young, 'The Rise of Henry VIII Clauses and the Implications for Sovereignty' (2003) *Public Law* 112; Igor Judge, 'Ceding Power to the Executive; the Resurrection of Henry VIII' (King's College London, 6 April, 2016).

102 See e.g. *R (Public Law Project)* v. *Lord Chancellor* [2016] UKSC 39.

Sure enough, in the areas of error of law and procedural exclusivity, the Irish approach has been markedly different from the English. Identifying reasons for the differences in approach would be a hazardous undertaking. But it is reasonable to hypothesise that the important changes wrought by the constitutionalisation of Irish law gave Irish judges the confidence to strike out on a different path from their English counterparts. This is a tentative suggestion – for one cannot look into the hearts and minds of Irish judges to determine what has motivated them to reject English orthodoxy on error of law and procedural exclusivity – but a plausible one. In any event, whatever the underlying reasons, the differences in approach underscore the extent to which Ireland has developed an indigenous administrative law.

6.3.1 *Error of Law*

In England, the accepted mantra is that the decision of the House of Lords in *Anisminic* v. *Foreign Compensation Commission*[103] swept away the old distinction between jurisdictional and non-jurisdictional error, rendering any errors of law reviewable by the superior courts. In Ireland, however, *Anisminic* has never been enthusiastically embraced by the judiciary. A word of caution is in order before going any further. The present state of Irish law on jurisdictional error is 'in an unsatisfactory, uneven and dated condition' and awaits 'a reserved Supreme Court judgment which will definitively review the present state of the law dealing with jurisdictional error'.[104] Nonetheless, and notwithstanding the present author's previous efforts to demonstrate the Irish courts' preference for an *Anisminic*-type approach,[105] there are distinctively indigenous features of the Irish law on jurisdictional error.

Whereas English administrative law underwent serious reform in the 1960s and 1970s – moving Lord Diplock to comment, 'Any judicial statements on matters of public law if made before 1950 are likely to be a misleading guide to what the law is today'[106] – Ireland has never had such a clean break with the past. Preoccupied with constitutional issues in the fertile period of the 1960s and 1970s (and not faced, as their English counterparts were, with the need to perform intellectual gymnastics to circumvent ouster clauses[107]), members of the Irish legal profession never really turned their attention to jurisdictional error. Accordingly, some comparatively ancient authorities remain good, and frequently cited, law,[108] relevant to the scope of review for error of law, fact and jurisdiction. Many of these authorities originated in the inferior courts and relate to criminal law and procedure[109] (and even, albeit rarely, civil procedure).[110] Their relevance to administrative bodies such as regulators, tribunals and ministers might be thought to be limited, on the basis that there is a great difference between lower-court judges' decisions on the management of individual cases in the criminal process and regulators' decisions on general policy matters. But as a matter of practice and, indeed, of precedent, authorities relating to the availability of certiorari in respect of criminal law matters are relevant to the scope of review of administrative decision-making.

103 [1969] 2 AC 147.
104 James O'Reilly, 'Errors of Fact and Errors of Law as Grounds for Judicial Review' (2012) 48 *Irish Jurist* (N.S) 1 at 5.
105 Paul Daly, 'Judicial Review of Errors of Law in Ireland' (2006) 41 *Irish Jurist* (N.S.) 60.
106 R v. *Inland Revenue Commissioners, ex parte National Federation of Self-Employed and Small Businesses Ltd* [1982] AC 617 at 640.
107 See e.g. *Anisminic* v. *Foreign Compensation Commission* [1969] 2 AC 147.
108 See e.g. *R. (Martin)* v. *Mahoney* [1910] 2 IR 695 (and see Kevin Costello, '*R. (Martin)* v. *Mahoney*: The History of a Classical Certiorari Authority' (2006) 27 *Journal of Legal History* 267).
109 See e.g. *State (Holland)* v. *Kennedy* [1977] IR 193; *Killeen* v. *Director of Public Prosecutions* [1998] 1 ILRM 1.
110 See e.g. *State (Davidson)* v. *Farrell* [1960] IR 438.

Jurisdictional error remains a key component of Irish administrative law doctrine, with courts happy to intervene on a jurisdictional matter, raising issues of law, fact or mixed law and fact.[111] It follows, however, that unreviewable errors within jurisdiction – anathema to the contemporary English mind – must also be possible. Non-jurisdictional error of law retains a tenacious hold on the Irish legal imagination, especially in non-criminal cases.[112] For instance, in *State (Abenglen Properties Ltd)* v. *Dublin Corporation*,[113] where the issue was whether the Corporation had 'asked itself the wrong question' by misconstruing a development plan, Henchy J responded that if the Corporation could be said to have erred, it 'erred within jurisdiction'.[114] It also follows that the doctrine – defunct in England – of error of law on the face of the record retains some vitality.[115] Strikingly, those Irish decisions that most fulsomely embrace *Anisminic*-type review are concerned with criminal procedure and, thus, personal liberty,[116] an important constitutional value;[117] they seem to have carried less precedential weight in circumstances in which the stakes were lower.[118] There are, perhaps, affinities here with the approach to jurisdictional error taken in cognate jurisdictions.

One interesting feature of the Irish case law is a willingness on the part of the judges to entertain the possibility that judges will exercise their discretion *not* to quash some decisions tainted by an error of law:[119] in *Irish Permanent Building Society* v. *Caldwell*, Barrington J openly refused to entertain the quashing of a decision on the basis that doing so would cause administrative chaos.[120] More mildly, there have been references to the idea that only 'severe' errors of law are capable of justifying judicial intervention.[121] But even this would no doubt confound English administrative lawyers reared in the post-*Anisminic* era. It is interesting to note, therefore, that one of the central tenets of modern English administrative law has not won unqualified acceptance in a neighbouring common law jurisdiction.

6.3.2 *Procedural Exclusivity*[122]

Another English innovation that has not fared well in Ireland is the procedural exclusivity rule set out in *O'Reilly* v. *Mackman*.[123] In the leading Irish case, *O'Donnell* v. *Corporation of Dún Laoghaire*,[124] Costello J refused pointedly to follow

111 See e.g. *Ryanair* v. *Labour Court* [2007] 4 IR 199.

112 See e.g. *Killeen* v. *Director of Public Prosecutions* [1998] 1 ILRM; *SFA* v. *Minister for Justice and Equality* [2015] IEHC 364.

113 [1984] IR 381.

114 [1984] IR 381, at p. 400.

115 See e.g. *Mone* v. *An Bord Pleanála* [2010] IEHC 395.

116 *State (Holland)* v. *Kennedy* [1977] IR 193; *Killeen* v. *Director of Public Prosecutions* [1998] 1 ILRM 1.

117 Habeas corpus was constitutionalised by Article 40.4 of the Constitution, which sets out in significant detail the procedure for applying for the writ.

118 Though see *Royal Dublin Society* v. *Revenue Commissioners* [2000] 1 IR 270, 280, where the effect of an erroneous licensing decision on the applicant's right to earn a living was said to militate in favour of *Anisminic*-type review.

119 *CE* v. *Minister for Justice, Equality and Law Reform* [2012] IEHC 3; *SFA* v. *Minister for Justice and Equality* [2015] IEHC 364.

120 [1981] ILRM 242, 269–70.

121 See e.g. *Cork County Council* v. *Shackleton* [2007] IEHC 241; *McKernan* v. *Employment Appeals Tribunal* [2008] IEHC 40.

122 See Stephen Thomson's contribution on Scotland in this volume.

123 [1983] 2 AC 237.

124 [1991] ILRM 302, approved by the Supreme Court in *Dublin City Council* v. *Williams* [2010] 1 IR 801 and *Shell Limited* v. *McGrath* [2013] 1 IR 247.

O'Reilly. Even though there is a distinct procedure for judicial review applications in Ireland,[125] this is not 'exclusive'; it will not automatically be the case that seeking declaratory or injunctive relief against a public authority in private-law proceedings will amount to an abuse of process.[126]

Not too much should be made of the rejection of *O'Reilly* in Ireland. On the one hand, *O'Reilly* has been defanged to a large extent by the English courts, who were soon persuaded to adopt a more relaxed approach to procedural exclusivity.[127] On the other hand, the Irish courts have also accepted that it may sometimes be inappropriate to raise public law matters otherwise than by way of judicial review.[128]

But there is at least one area in which the absence of a strict public-private divide has allowed the Irish courts to develop the law in a more adventurous manner than their English counterparts. In the area of legitimate expectations, there remains significant cross-fertilisation between public and private law, with legitimate expectations and promissory estoppel operating almost interchangeably. Most significantly, there is now an impressive body of Irish authority for the proposition that damages are available as a remedy for breaches of legitimate expectations engendered by the promises or practices of a public body. In *Lett & Co* v. *Wexford Borough Council*, a case brought by mussel farmers whose operations were impeded by the installation of a sewerage pipe by a local authority, O'Donnell J commented in expansive terms:

> [I]t seems to me in principle at least, and indeed by analogy with the position in estoppel in private law, that the issue for the Court is that once a legitimate expectation or estoppel has been identified, it is necessary to make good the equity so found, and that in such circumstances again in principle, the Court can make an order, whether characterised as damages or restitution, in order to make good the breach identified.[129]

Lett & Co was not an especially difficult case, because it involved a promise for compensation, which did not conflict with any statutory function performed by the Council. To note, however, that the case might have been resolved on straightforward contractual grounds is to overlook the reasoning employed by O'Donnell J. There is no suggestion of a neat distinction between the territory of public law and that of private law: O'Donnell J was quite happy to reason 'by analogy' across the public/private divide, and he expressly associated the public law concept of legitimate expectation with the private law concept of 'making good the equity so found'.[130] This is a clear example of cross-fertilisation, with equitable seeds being allowed to flourish in the territory of public law. Such radical developments would be difficult to countenance in England, where estoppel and legitimate expectations have been confined to separate hermetically sealed compartments.[131]

[125] With the typical provisions relating to time limits and the seeking of leave.

[126] [1991] ILRM 302, 314.

[127] See e.g. *Roy* v. *Kensington and Chelsea* and Westminster Family Practitioner Committee [1992] 2 WLR 239.

[128] See e.g. *Dublin City Council* v. *Williams* [2010] 1 IR 801; *Shell Limited* v. *McGrath* [2013] 1 IR 247 and note Costello J's observation in *O'Donnell* that 'if the plenary action is not brought within three months from the date on which the cause of action arose the court would normally refuse relief unless it is satisfied that had the claim been brought [in judicial review proceedings], time would have been extended' ([1991] ILRM 302, 314).

[129] [2014] 2 IR 198. See also *Cromane Seafoods Ltd* v. *Minister for Agriculture, Fisheries and Food* [2016] IESC 6, [2017] 1 IR 119.

[130] Hilary Biehler, 'Legitimate Expectation: An Odyssey' (2013) 47 *Irish Jurist* 40.

[131] *R* v. *East Sussex County Council Ex Parte Reprotech (Pebsham) Ltd* [2003] 1 WLR 348.

6.4 CONCLUSION

Using the theme of continuity and change, I have described the most important components in the indigensation of English administrative law in Ireland. My primary objectives have been to describe the influence constitutional change has had on the development of Irish administrative law and to demonstrate that Ireland has its own body of administrative law, distinctively Irish and separate from English administrative law. As we saw in Section 6.2, there has been a tension between continuity and change, between retaining the status quo and making a radical break with the past. Nonetheless, there have been important changes, resulting in the development of a distinctively Irish body of administrative law.

First, in Irish administrative law there is evidently a tension between continuity and change, best appreciated in the context of the royal prerogative. Second, some areas of Irish administrative law have been untouched by constitutional considerations: the supervisory jurisdiction is as it is in England, and the law of procedural fairness will, in spite of its constitutional nomenclature, be familiar to English administrative lawyers (and, indeed, others from around the Commonwealth). Third, there have, however, been some significant changes. Constitutionalising fundamental rights has had a marked effect on the evolution of Irish administrative law, for instance, and judicial control of delegations of authority is on a constitutional footing that it does not enjoy in England. It seems fair to conclude that administrative law in Ireland has been heavily influenced by constitutional considerations, so much so that it has become significantly different from English administrative law, and can comfortably and confidently be described as an indigenous *Irish* administrative law.

Moreover, as explained in Section 6.3, Irish judges have departed from English orthodoxy in important areas of administrative law, the confidence to do so coming (perhaps) from the distinctively Irish developments resulting from the adoption of the Constitution. Citation to English authorities is comparatively rare in the field of administrative law, even though Irish judges have typically been prepared to look to foreign jurisprudence to inform their thinking.[132] As a consequence, it is difficult now to deny the existence of an indigenous Irish administrative law.

[132] See generally Bruce Carolan, 'The Search for Coherence in the Use of Foreign Court Judgments by the Supreme Court of Ireland' (2004) 12 *Tulsa Journal of Comparative and International Law* 123.

PART IV

Origins and Adaptations in North America and Canada

7

Divided by the Common Law

Controlling Administrative Power in England and the United States

Peter Cane

[I]t is not an accident that common-law principles, as they were fashioned in the age of Coke, have attained the highest and most complete logical development in America, and that in this respect we are and long have been more thoroughly a common-law country than England herself.

Roscoe Pound (1921)[1]

George Bernard Shaw described England and the United States as two nations divided by a common language. I would adapt that to say that we have two legal systems divided by the common law. . . . The heritage of English law in this country is now thin. Except for a strange period between 1880 and 1920, the trend since 1783, or at least since the early federal period, has been to drift further and further apart. . . . What has changed most dramatically is the role of law.

Robert Stephens (1985)[2]

7.1 INTRODUCTION

This chapter is about the 'migration' of what we would now call 'administrative law' from England to the American colonies in the seventeenth and eighteenth centuries, its adaptation to local conditions in the nineteenth century and the evolution of American administrative law, in the twentieth, into a species quite distinct from its English ancestor. In what follows, for the period before 1789, 'US' and 'America' refer to the American colonies; after 1789, they refer to the United States of America – the Union, not the States. Considerations of space (at least) counsel against extension beyond the US federal system.

The term 'administrative law' is used here very broadly to refer to legal norms that frame creation, exercise and control of the powers and duties of entities belonging to the executive/bureaucratic arm of government and their non-governmental delegates. Administrative law is what Bruce Wyman called the 'internal' law of administration or, in other words, law about the administration.[3] It has three main sources: the legislature, the judiciary and the 'administration' itself (the executive, broadly understood). Administrative law may be hard or soft, and

[1] R Pound, *The Spirit of the Common Law* (Boston: Marshal Jones Company, 1921), p. 42.

[2] R Stephens, 'Basic Concepts and Current Differences in English and American Law' (1985) 6 *Journal of Legal History* 336, 346.

[3] B Wyman, *The Principles of the Administrative Law Governing the Relations of Public Officers* (St Paul: Keefe-Davidson Company, 1903). The US Constitution contains very little administrative law, unlike some more recent constitutions, such as that of South Africa (see Cora Hoexter's chapter in this volume).

it may or may not be enforceable by a court.[4] Left out of the definition are the laws about civil society that the administration implements – in Wyman's terms, the 'law of the land' or the 'external' law of administration. External law of the administration has the same three sources as internal law. (Internal) administrative law is law about how the (external) law of the land is implemented by the administration.

The main argument of this chapter may be summarily expressed: writing sixty years after Pound, Stephens (perhaps unsurprisingly) gets closer to the truth about contemporary English and US administrative law. The argument is built on an assumption that there is a significant relationship between the way public power is distributed among the various organs of government and the way power (particularly including administrative power) is controlled.[5] This assumption implies that we can expect structural differences between the systems of government in the US and England to be reflected in differences in the ways (administrative) power is controlled in the two systems respectively – or, put differently, in the administrative law (broadly understood) of the two systems respectively. Judicial review of administrative decisions, on which later chapters focus, is one important element of administrative law. The analysis that follows includes, but is not confined to, judicial review. Connecting to the theme of this volume, it is concerned, more broadly, with the 'life and times' of English administrative law in the US.

Another implication of the assumption is that the distinction between constitutional law (sometimes conceived as being concerned chiefly with the structure of government) and administrative law (sometimes conceived as being concerned chiefly with control of administrative power) is of no particular relevance to the analysis. Both categories of law are concerned with 'constituting' (creating and distributing) as well as controlling public power, including administrative power. The focus of the analysis is on the interaction between the structure of power and control of its exercise.

7.2 ENGLISH 'ADMINISTRATIVE LAW' IN THE EARLY EIGHTEENTH CENTURY

Under British colonial law, the American colonies (like the later-established Australian colonies, for instance) were treated as having been 'settled' rather than 'conquered' or 'ceded'. This meant that the settlors took English law with them as an aspect of their English heritage. Existing local law was absorbed, displaced or ignored. Although the story of such processes is complicated, the restoration of the monarchy in 1660 proved a turning point. It marked the adoption by the British of a policy of imposing English law more systematically on North America at the expense, for instance, of local custom, the legal practices of the indigenous inhabitants, Dutch law in New York and Puritan law in New England.[6] By the beginning of the eighteenth century English law was formally established in the various colonies that would come together, later in the century, to form the United States

4 Wyman's distinction is sometimes identified with the distinction between hard and soft law, or between law made by the administration and law made by other law-makers: e.g., GE Metzger and KM Stack, 'Internal Administrative Law' (2017) 115 *Michigan Law Review* 1239.

5 See generally P Cane, *Controlling Administrative Power: An Historical Comparison* (Cambridge: Cambridge University Press, 2016).

6 WE Nelson, *The Common Law in Colonial America: Volume I: The Chesapeake and New England, 1607–1660* (Oxford: Oxford University Press, 2008); *Volume II: The Middle Colonies and the Carolinas, 1660–1730* (Oxford: Oxford University Press, 2013); *Volume III: The Chesapeake and New England, 1660–1750* (Oxford: Oxford University Press, 2016).

of America. Under colonial law, English law applied in the colonies subject to modifications justified by differences between local conditions and those in England, and locally made law was valid to the extent that it was consistent with applicable English law.[7]

The modern concept of 'administrative law' is a creation of the late nineteenth and early twentieth centuries. This is not to say, of course, that at the beginning of the eighteenth century, English law did not regulate 'constitution' and control of administrative power. The aim of this section is to provide a brief and somewhat speculative account of English 'administrative law' in the early eighteenth century – by which time, as already noted, English law was formally in place in the American colonies. The account provides the foundation for the analysis in later sections of how that law was developed and adapted, first in the American colonies and later in the legal system of the US, and of the speciation of American administrative law in the twentieth century.

As a result of the Glorious Revolution of 1689, central executive power in England was concentrated in the hands of the monarch. Central government was concerned almost exclusively with defence and foreign affairs, and the raising of revenue to support these activities. By modern standards, the central bureaucracy was very small. Beyond what we would now call Westminster and Whitehall, local administration (in areas such as law and order, regulation and welfare) in parishes, villages, towns, boroughs and counties was conducted, notionally at least, on behalf and in the name of the monarch. From the mid-fourteenth century, the most important institution of local public administration was the Justice of the Peace (JP). From the time of the Tudors, JPs were 'the pillars of local government and the favourite agents of the central government in the localities'.[8] In addition, various appointed commissions and boards played important roles in local administration, dealing with matters such as drainage and sewerage, and the relief of poverty. For about a century, until 1641, conciliar courts (notably Star Chamber) exercised significant control over central and local government. Following their abolition, central control of local administration rested chiefly in the hands of the Court of King's Bench until the nineteenth century, when Parliament started creating 'tribunals' and inspectorates to monitor and control the implementation of statutory regimes of regulation and welfare.[9]

Early in the seventeenth century, the Court of King's/Queen's Bench began adapting the existing administrative writs of *certiorari*, *mandamus* and prohibition as new judicial mechanisms for controlling local administration in the name of the monarch. The writs were intended, in part, to make up for deficiencies of actions for damages. One problem was that such actions lay only against Crown officials, the Crown itself being liable neither personally nor vicariously for wrongs committed in its name. Moreover, damages actions did not lie against JPs in respect of their judicial activities.[10] At local level, a degree of judicial control was exercised over administration by way of appeals from initial decisions to the Justices meeting at Quarter Sessions.

The basic contours of the substantive law of control of administration were unaffected by the Glorious Revolution.[11] They can be summed up in three propositions: (1) the monarch

7 Among a large literature, see, e.g., SM Bilder, 'English Settlement and Local Governance' in M Grossberg and C Tomlins (eds.), *The Cambridge History of Law in America, Volume 1, 1580–1815* (Cambridge: Cambridge University Press, 2008).

8 SB Chrimes, *English Constitutional History*, 3rd ed. (London: Oxford University Press, 1965), p. 137.

9 FJ Port, *Administrative Law* (London: Longmans, Green & Co, 1929), p. 54.

10 EG Henderson, *Foundations of English Administrative Law: Certiorari and Mandamus in the Seventeenth Century* (Cambridge: Harvard University Press, 1963), pp. 34–5.

11 For a suggestive, late nineteenth century account of the 'administrative jurisdiction' in the eighteenth century, see R Gneist, *The History of the English Constitution*, 2nd ed. (trans. PA Ashworth) (London: William Clowes and Sons Ltd, 1889), ch. XLVIII.

could be sued (in contract and tort, for instance), only if royal immunity from suit was waived; (2) individual royal officials were amenable to suit for private wrongs done in exercise of their powers and performance of their duties, but the monarch was not vicariously liable for their wrongs; and (3) the Court of King's Bench had jurisdiction to issue prerogative writs against local administrative officials and bodies acting in a judicial mode ('exercising judicial power'). In the interstices of the remedially oriented writs, the basic grounds of judicial review, recognised today, were taking shape.[12] The basic justification for central-court intervention was to ensure that decision-makers acted legally, within jurisdiction. Errors within jurisdiction could be effectively challenged only if obvious 'on the face of the record'.[13] Although criminal trials generated quite-detailed records, those of non-criminal (administrative) proceedings tended to be spare, going little beyond the complaint and the decision.

So far as political control of administration is concerned, 'the 18th-century Commons had two main functions: holding ministers to account; and redressing the people's grievances. ... In the years which immediately followed the revolution ... [m]uch energy in parliament was devoted to examining the activities of the executive government'.[14] At first, appointed commissions were the vehicles for such scrutiny; but when these fell out of favour, Parliamentary committees took their place. 'Committees of enquiry grew in number during the [eighteenth] century, and in scope and ambition. One reason was their flexibility as a ... political tool; another was the growing trend towards the systematic collection of data and information as a tool of government.'[15] Also, 'from the 1760s the practice of asking questions of individual ministers grew'.[16] Nevertheless, George III's reign made clear the continuing capacity of the Crown to act as it chose despite opposition in Parliament. A proto-ministry developed in the eighteenth century, but it was not until well into the nineteenth that it became effectively responsible to Parliament rather than the monarch, thus finally ending the competition between the monarch and the legislature.[17]

7.3 MIGRATION: 'ADMINISTRATIVE LAW' IN THE COLONIAL PERIOD IN AMERICA

Detailed consideration of the development of administrative law in the thirteen colonies (and in the states after the American Revolution) is outside the scope of this chapter as it is, indeed, outside the scope of mainstream, scholarly, administrative-law literature in the US, which focuses heavily on the federal system. However, one might speculate that the basic substantive contours of the eighteenth-century English administrative law summarised above were replicated in the colonies if only because the basic distribution of public power in the

[12] For a general discussion, see P Craig, *UK, EU and Global Administrative Law: Foundations and Challenges* (Cambridge: Cambridge University Press, 2015), pp. 25–95.

[13] P Murray, 'Process, Substance and the History of Error of Law Review' in J Bell, M Elliott, JNE Varuhas and P Murray (eds.), *Public Law Adjudication in Common Law Systems* (Oxford: Hart Publishing, 2016). See also n 48 in the following section.

[14] B Harris, 'The House of Commons, 1707–1800' in C Jones (ed.), *A Short History of Parliament* (Woodbridge: Boydell Press, 2009), p. 176; see also P Jupp, *The Governing of Britain, 1688–1848: The Executive, Parliament and the People* (London: Routledge, 2006), ch. 3.

[15] Harris, 'The House of Commons, 1707–1800' (n 14 above), p. 179. See also PDG Thomas, *The House of Commons in the Eighteenth Century* (Oxford: Clarendon Press, 1971), ch. 14.

[16] Harris, 'The House of Commons, 1707–1800' (n 14 above), p. 177; Thomas, *The House of Commons in the Eighteenth Century* (n 15 above), p. 30.

[17] Jupp, *The Governing of Britain, 1688–1848* (n 14 above), chs. 1 and 5; Port, *Administrative Law* (n 9 above), pp. 56–73.

colonies was similar to that in England at the time. Nevertheless, political and social conditions in the colonies were significantly different from those in England, and this inevitably affected the way colonial governmental power was exercised and controlled.

The majority of the North American colonies were established not by the British government but by private entrepreneurs (for profit) or civil-society groups (for political, religious and social reasons). Nevertheless, most received some form of documentary royal support in the form, for instance, of a charter. In the frontier conditions of the early settlements and in the absence of an organised legal profession, legal development was typically informal, haphazard and pragmatic. As already noted, however, by the first half of the eighteenth century, English law formally or effectively formed the basis of the law of all thirteen of the North American colonies, subject to a general principle allowing exceptions and qualifications to accommodate local conditions. The Privy Council, as the executive branch of the British government and the final appellate court for the colonies, played an important part in developing and applying the general principle. One important result of this arrangement was that colonial authorities and lawyers needed reliable information about English law, for which they were heavily dependent on imported, English legal literature,[18] particularly William Blackstone's *Commentaries on the Laws of England*.

Executive and higher judicial power in the colonies resided in the Governor and Council.[19] The government in London communicated with and attempted to control governors and government by written 'instructions'. Together, instructions to the Governor and the founding Charter represented a sort of written proto-constitution for a colony. Inferior courts, like JPs in England, were as much local administrators as repositories of what we could now call 'judicial power'.[20] In each colony, there was a legislative assembly (which, at certain times and places, also functioned as an appellate court) elected by an enfranchised group significantly larger than in England at the same time.[21] Control of the assembly by the Governor and Council varied from time to time and place to place. In general, however, a more- or less-competitive relationship existed between the executive, which (in theory, anyway) represented the metropolis, and the locally and popularly elected assembly. The colonial assemblies asserted much greater control over their local executives than Parliament could exert over the monarch in eighteenth-century England.[22] Moreover, whereas in England, local justices and juries tended to be thought of as agents of central government, in the colonies they were typically aligned with local rather than metropolitan interests, thus further undermining the authority of the Governor and Council.

All this suggests that the development of administrative law in the American colonies might have been influenced by the early emergence of ideas about popular sovereignty and democracy. In England, the common law (at least) was not significantly affected by democratisation until the nineteenth century.[23] It began as a tool of royal government, as did the

18 According to William Nelson, '[b]y 1760 not a single American law book had been printed': WE Nelson, *The Americanization of the Common Law: The Impact of Legal Change on Massachusetts Society, 1760–1830* (Cambridge: Harvard University Press, 1975), p. 2.

19 See generally LW Labaree, *Royal Government in America: A Study of the British Colonial System Before 1783* (New York: Frederick Ungar Publishing, 1958).

20 See, e.g., EC Surrency, 'The Courts in the American Colonies' (1967) 11 *American Journal of Legal History* 253.

21 M Kammen, *Deputyes and Libertyes: The Origins of Representative Government in Colonial America* (New York: Alfred A Knopf, 1969).

22 JP Greene, *The Quest for Power: The Lower Houses of Assembly in the Southern Royal Colonies 1689–1776* (Chapel Hill: University of North Carolina Press, 1963).

23 Extension of the franchise, beginning in the 1830s, triggered the development of responsible government and the 'constitutionalisation' of the monarchy, paving the way for the 'secularisation' (or 'constitutionalisation', or 'judicialisation') of the (formerly prerogative) writs and their application to central administration.

'prerogative' writs, brought into service (as we have seen) by the Court of King's Bench in the seventeenth century to control local, judicialised administration. The subjection of the common-law courts to the authority of Parliament as a result of the Glorious Revolution had little or nothing to do with democracy or popular power, but witnessed the shift of the institutional location of 'sovereignty' within government. The American colonies, by contrast, experienced early-onset democracy in the seventeenth and eighteenth centuries (although the process did not reach its end (universal adult suffrage) until much the same time as in England). In England, local, lay, judicialised administration provided monarchs with a relatively cheap way of extending control beyond the centre. Similarly, juries provided a relatively cheap mode of trial that tapped into local knowledge and attracted less suspicion than the King's judicial officials and servants. In America, too, the local magistracy and trial by jury were valued by the British government as economical tools of government. But Americans quite soon started to think of them as voices of the people that could be raised against the colonial authorities. In this and other ways, 'the common law' and 'the rights of Englishmen' that it had brought with it since Magna Carta and before (or so the story went) served as weapons of resistance and revolution, rather than tools of the regime.

7.4 ADAPTATION: THE US FEDERATION 1789–1880

7.4.1 *Distribution of Power*

As is well known, in the course of the eighteenth century Americans' increasing desire for local autonomy and the growth of democratic sentiment, set against the determination of the British to extract as much value as possible from the North American colonies, produced increasing tension between the metropole and the periphery, culminating in the Declaration of Independence of 1776. By the late 1780s, many Americans were suspicious of both executive power (as a result of their experiences with the British monarchy and colonial governors) and legislative power (as represented, first, by the House of Commons and later – ironically – by 'populist', post-Revolutionary representative assemblies).[24] As reflected in the *Federalist Papers*, both fears influenced the design of the federal government structure. Ironically, however, the arrangements finally settled upon by the former colonies to replace the confederation that had been formed to prosecute the war of independence against Britain bore striking resemblances to British governmental institutions at the time. In Montesquieu's by-then-famous account of British government, it was (in modern terms) an amalgam of mixed government and separation of powers.[25] The one (the monarch), the few (the House of Lords) and the many (the House of Commons) shared legislative power. At the same time, the institutional re-alignments of the seventeenth century had distanced the judiciary from the (monarchical) executive and the executive from the legislature.[26]

Under the new US Constitution, executive power was vested in a single official – the President. In *Federalist* 69, Alexander Hamilton went to great lengths to address fears that the

Democratisation of local government brought about the demise of judicialised administration by Justices of the Peace and led to the extension of judicial review to local administration, whether judicialised or not.

24 M Kammen, *Deputyes and Libertyes: The Origins of Representative Government in Colonial America* (n 21 above).

25 William Paley, *Principles of Moral and Political Philosophy* (Cambridge: Cambridge University Press, 2013), book 6, chapter 7, 478–82 (first published 1785).

26 For a helpful discussion, see D Lieberman, 'The Mixed Constitution and the Common Law' in M Goldie and R Wokler (eds.), *Cambridge History of Eighteenth-Century Political Thought* (Cambridge: Cambridge University Press, 2006).

President would resemble George III, by pointing out structural differences between the Presidency and the English Monarchy, the latter having emerged from the Glorious Revolution as the sole repository of executive power.[27] The main responsibility given to the Presidency was not to 'execute the laws faithfully' but rather 'to take care that the laws be faithfully executed'. To this end, the President was empowered to 'nominate, and with the Advice and Consent of the Senate, appoint, Judges of the Supreme Court, and all other Officers of the United States, whose Appointments are not herein otherwise provided for, and which shall be established by Law', with the proviso that Congress could vest in the President 'Appointment of such inferior Officers' as the President 'thinks proper'.[28] The President is authorised to 'require the opinion' of department heads and is required 'from time to time [to] give information to Congress about the state of the nation'.

Ambiguity in these provisions – particularly in recent times – has generated heated and ongoing debate about whether the President is properly a 'decider', or merely an 'overseer', vis-à-vis the bureaucracy.[29] In fact, the history of the office since 1789 has been one of accretion of power, particularly at the expense of Congress. Nevertheless, the power of the President vis-à-vis the civil service (the 'bureaucracy') is, even today, much less than that of the British government, let alone that enjoyed by the monarch in the eighteenth century. The bureaucracy in the US, and the powers of the President in relation to the bureaucracy, are mainly the product of Congressional legislation over which the President has only a qualified veto. It is accepted that the President has a certain amount of 'unilateral' power to manage the civil service, but only so much as Congress and the Supreme Court are prepared to confer or concede. In reality, the Presidency and the Congress are in constant competition for control of the bureaucracy (and, incidentally, the judiciary), as regularly illustrated by high-profile Senate confirmation hearings.[30] Congress can also qualify the President's basic power (established by Congress in 1789 but not recognised in the Constitution) to dismiss civil servants at will.[31] This provides the legal hook for the creation of 'independent' bureaucratic agencies,[32] which are contrasted with 'executive agencies'. By virtue of its initiative in the legislative process (including fiscal and budgetary matters), Congress can exercise much more control over the President and the bureaucracy than the English Parliament (in which legislative initiative belongs to the Government) can exercise over the executive or the civil service.

Beyond these provisions, the Constitution says nothing explicitly about the executive branch or the bureaucracy. In particular, it does not mention judicial review of either legislation or administration.[33] The possibility of both was established by *Marbury v. Madison* in 1803.[34] This decision made explicit what many believed to be implicit in the document, namely that the main (public-law) role of the Supreme Court is to enforce the

[27] There were pro- and anti-monarchist strands in revolutionary thinking. Eric Nelson argues that as a result of the Revolution, America acquired a monarchy without kings, whereas in England, there were to be kings without monarchy: E Nelson, *The Royalist Revolution: Monarchy and the American Founding* (Cambridge: Belknap Press, 2014).

[28] *US Constitution* Article II, §2.2.

[29] See e.g., PL Strauss, 'Overseer or "The Decider"? The President in Administrative Law' (2007) 75 *George Washington Law Review* 696.

[30] A Google search of 'Trump confirmation hearings', for instance, yields 8.85 million links.

[31] Cane, *Controlling Administrative Power* (n 5 above), p. 86.

[32] Cane, *Controlling Administrative Power* (n 5 above), pp. 88–9.

[33] This may seem surprising in light of the fact that the Privy Council frequently reviewed colonial legislation for 'repugnancy' to English law.

[34] 5 US (1 Cranch) 137 (1803).

Constitution, the 'laws of the United States made in pursuance thereof' and 'treaties made under the authority of the United States', on behalf of the People, against the Congress and the President, and against the States. Most of the jurisdiction of the Supreme Court is appellate, and the Constitution contemplated the creation of federal, 'inferior', trial courts (constituted, initially, by single Justices of the Supreme Court on circuit). Today, the bulk of federal public-law jurisdiction, at both original and intermediate appellate levels, is exercised by the Federal Court for the District of Columbia. The only writ mentioned in the Constitution (in Art I, § 9.2) is habeas corpus. This contrasts with the Australian Constitution (modelled, in significant respects, on the US Constitution), which (in s 75(v)) confers on the High Court of Australia *original* jurisdiction to issue 'writs' of prohibition and mandamus (as well as injunctions) against 'officers of the Commonwealth'. The Australian provision seems intended to confer on the High Court the 'inherent' ('common-law') jurisdiction of the Court of Queen's Bench to issue prerogative writs.[35] In *Marbury* v. *Madison*, the absence of such a provision from the Constitution was crucial to the Court's conclusion that it lacked jurisdiction to issue a writ of mandamus, thus implying that the Court had not inherited, and the Constitution had not conferred, original judicial review jurisdiction.

7.4.2 *The Constitution and the Common Law*

Turning from structural arrangements to substantive law, what was the status in the new federal system, under the Constitution, of the English common law that had been imported into the colonies? This issue arose and was settled in the wake of enactment of the Sedition Act in 1798. The Act prohibited seditious libel against the US Government, the President and either House of Congress, subject to a defence of truth. One of the arguments in favour of the constitutionality of the Act was that

> the common law carried over from the Revolution was the law of the land . . . seditious libel was a common law crime. . . . What the courts could reach under the common law, Congress could reach by statute, and the Sedition Act ameliorated the common law by making truth a defense and giving all issues to the jury.[36]

If it were correct that the federal legislative power was coterminous with the common law, the substantive limitations imposed on federal legislative power by the Constitution would be outflanked, thus completely upsetting the delicate federal/state balance established thereby. The Supreme Court rejected this untenable result in 1812.[37] In the US federal system, the Constitution rules, not 'the (common) law'. Put differently, in English law the constitution is based on the common law whereas in US law, the Constitution constrains judicial law-making and the common law.[38]

An important effect of the replacement of the common law by the Constitution as the root of the US legal system relates to the jurisdiction of the US Supreme Court. The Supreme Court has only such jurisdiction as is conferred by Article III of the Constitution (and statutes made under it). Only one of these heads of jurisdiction ('all cases of maritime and admiralty

35 See further the chapter by Matthew Groves and Greg Weeks in this volume.

36 LA Powe Jr, *The Supreme Court and the American Elite, 1789–2008* (Cambridge: Cambridge University Press, 2009), p. 35.

37 *United States* v. *Hudson and Goodwin* 11 US (7 Cranch) 32 (1812).

38 On this point, see the chapters on Australia, Ireland, Israel and South Africa in this volume.

jurisdiction') appears to imply that the Court may entertain cases that arise not under the Constitution, or the laws and treaties of the US, but under maritime and admiralty 'common law'.[39] In all other cases, it seems, the Court may entertain only cases that can be related in some way to the texts of the Constitution, statutes or treaties. By contrast, under English law 'common-law courts' may, and are obliged to, answer any question of law properly presented to them, regardless of whether it arises under a statute. Such 'inherent' jurisdiction reflects the historical and political fact that long before the development of Parliament as a legislative body, courts in England were making law, as agents of the monarch. In the US, most 'inherent' jurisdiction was inherited by state courts. Despite the massive contribution of federal courts to the body of US law, the standard view is that the power of federal judges to make law, outside the context of deciding an issue of constitutional or statutory interpretation and application, is very limited.[40]

Nevertheless, US federal courts make a lot of law, and some of this is sometimes referred to as (federal, as opposed to national) 'common law'. A crucial distinction between federal common law in the US and classic English common law is made clear by contrasting what US scholars have called 'constitutional common law' and the English concept of 'the common law constitution'. Although not usually articulated in this way, the category of constitutional common law seems to consist of rules and principles of constitutional law that cannot plausibly be described as 'interpretations' of the Constitution, understood in terms of standard canons of construction but which nevertheless are, in theory, exactly that: interpretations and applications. Illustrations include certain rules and principles made and established under the rubric of the due process and equal protection clauses of the Bill of Rights (such as 'substantive due process', a doctrine that flourished in the late nineteenth and early twentieth centuries, and was particularly protective of property and contract, and more recently, a right to privacy – protective of personal autonomy – on which the whole edifice of the Supreme Court's regulation of abortion (most famously in *Roe* v. *Wade*)[41] rests). By contrast, the English concept of 'the common-law constitution' implies that the constitution is rooted in the activities of courts. Put differently, while in the US the Supreme Court can (and, practically, must) fill gaps in the written Constitution, in the English system, things are the other way around: written law (statute) can be and is used to modify, supplement and even supersede the 'common law' constitution. In the US, both the courts and the legislature are delegates of the constituent assembly of the People; in England, there is no constituent assembly. 'Constitutional law' made by English courts is, of course, (more or less) subordinate to statute, but it is, for that, no less constitutional law.

A particularly apposite example of 'federal common law' in the US is provided by much of the law of judicial review built on the foundations of the Administrative Procedure Act 1946, which, by reason of its extremely tenuous connection, or even inconsistency, with the statutory text, may be called 'administrative common law'.[42] In the English system, by contrast, most of the general rules and principles of administrative law have resulted from exercise of the court's inherent jurisdiction to supervise the executive. In the English system,

39 For an explanation, see AR Amar, *America's Constitution: A Biography* (New York: Random House, 2005), 577.

40 See, e.g., TW Merrill, 'The Common Law Powers of Federal Courts' (1985) 52 *University of Chicago Law Review* 1.

41 (1973) 410 US 113.

42 G Metzger, 'Ordinary Administrative Law as Constitutional Common Law' (2010) 110 *Columbia Law Review* 479; KM Stack, 'The Statutory Fiction of Judicial Review of Administrative Action' in C Forsyth, M Elliott, S Jhaveri, A Scully-Hill and M Ramsden (eds.), *Effective Judicial Review: A Cornerstone of Good Governance* (Oxford: Oxford University Press, 2010).

too, judicial interpretations of statutes have the same status as the statute, regardless of how stretched they might be. In the US, federal system, 'common law' is understood as the product of judicial activism in applying and interpreting written texts. In US law, as in the English system, interpretations within the flexible boundaries of orthodoxy have the same status as the document being interpreted, but some scholars are distinctly queasy about according this status to highly stretched readings.

7.4.3 *Control of Administrative Power in Nineteenth-Century America*

The development of federal administrative law from 1789 to the end of the nineteenth century has been magisterially traced by Jerry Mashaw.[43] Unsurprisingly, in 1789, Congress immediately set about the task of constructing a bureaucracy, establishing both executive departments (such as Treasury) and non-executive agencies (such as the Patent Office).[44] By virtue of this legislative initiative given to Congress by the Constitution, Congressional scrutiny of and control over the bureaucracy is built into the very fabric of the US system of checks and balances. Mashaw's study focuses on mechanisms of management, scrutiny and control internal to the bureaucracy itself: administrative rule-making and adjudication. He explains this emphasis by pointing to the fact that judicial control of the bureaucracy in nineteenth-century America was very limited. As in England,[45] the main mechanisms of judicial control were actions for damages – in tort, for instance – and applications for the 'extraordinary writs' of *mandamus* and injunction.[46] However, about *mandamus* and injunction, Mashaw says that their 'availability was so restricted that relief was rarely available'.[47] Federal courts – it seems – adopted the jurisdictional theory on which English judicial review was based.[48]

According to Mashaw, Congress sometimes gave courts the 'ministerial, administrative' role of fact-finding preliminary to the making of an administrative decision – to impose a fine, for instance.[49] In this practice he finds the origins of the role of 'hearing officers' and (later) 'administrative (law) judges' (AJs and ALJs) within administrative agencies as preliminary fact finders. In due course, such officials would be given the power, in addition, to make an initial decision on fact and law, subject to appeal to (the head of) the agency. The Administrative Procedure Act 1946 placed ALJs behind Chinese walls within agencies. This opened the way for their use, in some contexts, as intermediate appellate bodies between initial decision-makers and the agency as final appellate body (subject to judicial review). In England, 'internal', appellate adjudicative bodies – 'tribunals' were introduced in the early nineteenth century to perform functions in relation to new statutory schemes of regulation and welfare

[43] JL Mashaw, *Creating the Administrative Constitution: The Lost One Hundred Years of American Administrative Law* (New Haven: Yale University Press, 2012).

[44] Mashaw, *Creating the Administrative Constitution*, n 43 above, ch. 2.

[45] Mashaw, *Creating the Administrative Constitution*, n 43 above, ch. 3. Mashaw speaks of 'the common law model' of judicial review.

[46] Mashaw, *Creating the Administrative Constitution*, n 43 above, ch. 4.

[47] Mashaw, *Creating the Administrative Constitution*, n 43 above, ch. 3.

[48] As developed in the seventeenth and eighteenth centuries, the mechanism of judicial review in England involved the delivery of the 'record' of the proceedings under review into the Court King's/Queen's Bench for examination. Records of criminal proceedings before Justices of the Peace at this time were quite full, but those in non-criminal proceedings often consisted of little more than the complaint and the final decision, without any account of evidence or reasons for decision. This gave the Court the opportunity to control a growing tide of judicial review claims by limiting review to errors of 'jurisdiction', unless the error 'appeared on the face of the record' – legality review, not merits review, as we might now say. See Murray, 'Process, Substance and the History of Error of Law Review' (n 13 above).

[49] Mashaw, *Creating the Administrative Constitution* (n 43 above), pp. 74–5.

for which the common-law courts were thought unsuitable. By the early twentieth century, concerns about their independence within the agency had been met by locating tribunals outside agencies rather than leaving them behind a Chinese wall inside the agency. Earlier this century, tribunals were integrated into the judicial system alongside courts.[50]

Marbury v. *Madison*[51] made it clear that federal courts had jurisdiction to review administrative action of federal (i.e., central government) officials – although it held that the Supreme Court itself (as opposed to inferior federal courts) did not have and could not be given original jurisdiction to issue a writ of *mandamus*. This decision represented a major departure from the situation in England, where judicial review was originally understood as an exercise of royal power over local, as opposed to central (judicialised) administration. Another major US departure from the English inheritance was relatively early abolition of the extraordinary writs, shifting the emphasis of the law from remedies to rules and principles, rights and duties. In private law, this process was complete in England by 1875, but in public law not until the late twentieth century (beginning in 1978).[52]

7.4.4 *Administrative Law and Democracy*

As in the colonies previously, the development of federal administrative law was significantly affected by democratisation. From the 1830s onwards, under the Jacksonian 'spoils system', many administrative and judicial posts were opened up to popular election or party-political patronage.[53] By the end of the century, many found increasingly problematic the corruption that was an inevitable part of such methods of appointment and recruitment. The path to depoliticisation of the bureaucracy was found in the contrast between 'politics' and 'administration'. One of the basic goals of civil service reform in the 1880s was that recruitment to the bureaucracy should be based on expertise, not politics.[54] This principle underpinned the idea that bureaucracy involved the application of means-end rationality, not politics, to solving the problems of the day.[55] Bureaucratic power came to be understood as separate and distinct from 'executive power', which was primarily concerned with establishing ends (or, in the parlance of modern administrative law, 'relevant considerations' or 'proper purposes'), not devising means. In this way of thinking, the bureaucracy assumed the identity of a 'fourth branch of government' that would, ideally, operate more or less 'independently' of its political masters. Of course, those masters – the President on the one side (by virtue of the obligation to see that the laws were faithfully executed) and Congress (by virtue of its role as creator of the bureaucracy) – could and would 'check and balance' the bureaucracy, but its role was not to serve either but, like the other organs of government, to serve the People – in the case of the bureaucracy, by performing its distinctive function of technocratic 'administration'.

Contrast the position of the civil service in the English system. English bureaucrats today retain the essential character of their forebears in earlier periods: they are servants of the executive and its political agenda. In *Yes Minister*, Sir Humphrey (the gentleman amateur) does not dazzle Jim Hacker with science that Jim cannot refute; rather, he beats the Minister at his own (political) game. True, nineteenth-century reforms of the process of recruitment to

50 See generally P Cane, *Administrative Tribunals and Adjudication* (Oxford: Hart Publishing, 2009).
51 5 US (1 Cranch) 137 (1803).
52 The catalyst was amendment of Order 53 of the Rules of the Supreme Court.
53 Political parties in the modern sense developed earlier in the US than in England.
54 See, e.g., WE Nelson, *The Roots of American Bureaucracy, 1830–1900* (Cambridge: Harvard University Press, 1982).
55 A seminal contribution was W Wilson, 'The Study of Administration' (1887) 2 *Political Science Quarterly* 197.

the civil service substituted merit for patronage as the basic criterion of appointment. However, these reforms were concerned more with efficiency and effectiveness than with changing the relationship between civil servants and politicians. The 'independence' of American bureaucratic agencies is designed primarily to protect bureaucratic decision-making from political contamination and has no direct counterpart in the case of English, non-departmental agencies except, perhaps, the Bank of England. Even the 'agencification' of British government in the 1980s and 1990s did not, and was not intended to, significantly undermine ministerial responsibility.[56]

Despite the demise of the spoils system in the late nineteenth century, ideas of democracy still play a much more significant role in US public law than in English. At the state level, there is a degree of popular, electoral input into the selection of many judicial and administrative officials. At the federal level, about 4,000 of the most senior bureaucratic posts are in the gift of the President, and the party-political patronage as a criterion of judicial appointment is (more or less) uncontroversial. There are ongoing debates in the public-administration literature about democratisation of the bureaucracy.[57] The very idea (prominent in *The Federalist Papers*) that the various branches of government are 'perfectly co-ordinate', equally agents of the People in performing their allocated functions, and in checking and balancing performance of each other's allocated functions, is now understood as an expression of the power of the *demos* rather than, as it was seen in the eighteenth century, an expression of republican (rather than democratic) ideals.

7.5 1880–1946: TRANS-ATLANTIC SCHOLARLY CONVERSATIONS ABOUT ADMINISTRATIVE LAW

7.5.1 *The English Voice*

The influence of English law, and the associated idea that US law was a modified version of what the settlers had brought with them, began to wane with the development of American legal literature and the declining use of Blackstone's *Commentaries* after the American Civil War. Nevertheless, the last two decades of the nineteenth century and the period up to World War II were marked by a small tsunami of trans-Atlantic conversations about the distribution and control of public power.[58] Prominent among the early English contributors were James Bryce[59] and AV Dicey.[60] According to HA Tulloch, both regarded 'American constitutionalism as the consummation of the English common law tradition'.[61] Above all, Dicey feared government unbridled by law. The common law, in his mind, stood precisely for constraint of public power. This explains his view (expressed as late as 1908, after he had corrected his original defective account of the French system) that the French '*droit administratif*' was

56 P Aucoin, 'The Political-Administrative Design of NPM' in T Christensen and P Laegreid, *The Ashgate Research Companion to the New Public Management* (Farnham, Surrey: Ashgate, 2011).

57 See, e.g., L Deleon, 'Public Management, Democracy and Politics' in E Ferlie, LE Lynn and C Pollitt (eds.), *The Oxford Handbook of Public Management* (Oxford: Oxford University Press, 2005).

58 Stephens, 'Basic Concepts and Current Differences' (n 2 above), pp. 342–3. See more generally DT Rodgers, *Atlantic Crossings: Social Politics in a Progressive Age* (Cambridge: Harvard University Press, 2000).

59 J Bryce, *The American Commonwealth* (New York: Macmillan, 1910).

60 AV Dicey, *Lectures Introductory to the Study of the Law of the Constitution*, JWF Allison (ed.) (Oxford: Oxford University Press, 2013), Lectures I and IV; *Lectures on Comparative Constitutionalism*, JWF Allison (ed.) (Oxford: Oxford University Press, 2013), esp. pp. 76–88, 233–48, 275–85, 296–8.

61 HA Tulloch, 'Changing British Attitudes towards the United States in the 1880s' (1977) 20 *Historical Journal* 825, 833–40.

'opposed in its fundamental principles to ideas that lie at the basis of English constitutional government':[62] for him, it represented law controlled by power, not power controlled by law. Ironically,[63] too, (as vividly illustrated by his views about Irish home rule), for Dicey parliamentary sovereignty, coupled with responsible government and democratic franchise, represented the apotheosis of power unconstrained by law. He admired the inflexibility and inherent conservatism of US governmental arrangements attributable to their documentary foundation,[64] the power of the judiciary over legislation, and the 'extra-parliamentary' nature of the US executive,[65] the last of which the Founders had designed precisely in order to guard against Congressional populism, and which was also a feature of pre-democratic, eighteenth-century English, governmental arrangements.

Dicey's writings track changes in 'the common-law tradition' in the nineteenth century. Blackstone's *Commentaries* were suffused with the spirit of an ancient, customary common law (identified and formulated, but not made, by judges) that sat above the governors as much as the governed, above courts and adjudication as much as Parliament and legislation. Dicey's *Law of the Constitution*, by contrast, is a product of nineteenth-century, utilitarian, positivist thinking, which understood common law as the product of judicial activity, so that using the common law to constrain government meant looking directly to the (common-law) courts rather than to pre-institutional custom. This focus on courts and judges helps explain why Dicey so disliked administrative adjudication and why, in the course of the nineteenth, twentieth and twenty-first centuries (and, we may speculate, under his influence) administrative tribunals ((re)invented in the early nineteenth century) have become increasingly more like courts.[66]

Administrative rule-making is a different matter. By the end of the nineteenth century it had already overtaken Parliamentary legislation, at least in volume if not also in significance. But for Dicey, the big problem was to constrain legislation, not administrative rule-making. Developments in England (responsible government and democracy) had made this very difficult, which explains Dicey's interest in and approval of the American 'extra-Parliamentary' executive. Growth of the power of the legislature in nineteenth-century England had effectively (although not technically) demoted the common law (judicial rule-making) from a position of pre-eminence to the role of subordinate, interstitial, adjudicative supplementation of statutory, programmatic rule-making. In the US, by contrast, the structural constraints on legislative rule-making imposed by the qualified, executive veto[67] (that accounted for the conservatism that Dicey so admired), encouraged the development of a forward-looking, instrumentalist understanding of judicial rule-making as a necessary

62 Allison (ed.), *The Law of the Constitution*, p. 367.

63 Because Dicey is often portrayed as *the* champion of Parliamentary sovereignty rather than its perceptive chronicler. Unfortunately, he says very little about courts in *Comparative Constitutionalism*, noting only the power of the US Supreme Court to invalidate legislation (9–10). 'La Porta et al show that a history of the common law explains the rise of judicial review [of legislation]': V Menaldo and NW Williams, 'Judicial Supremacy: Explaining False Starts and Surprising Successes' in R Hazell and J Melton (eds.), *Magna Carta and Its Modern Legacy* (Cambridge: Cambridge University Press, 2015), p. 177 citing R La Porta et al., 'Judicial Checks and Balances' (2004) 112 *Journal of Political Economy* 445. In this light, Menaldo and Williams attempt to explain why judicial review of legislation developed in America but not in England.

64 AV Dicey, *Lectures Introductory to the Study of the Law of the Constitution*, pp. 10–11.

65 JWF Allison, *Lectures on Comparative Constitutionalism*, pp. 10–12.

66 P Cane, *Administrative Tribunals and Adjudication* (Oxford: Hart Publishing, 2009), pp. 30–48.

67 In the US system, legislative initiative resides in Congress, not the President. In the English system, by contrast, legislative initiative resides, predominantly, in the executive.

alternative to gridlocked and deadlocked legislative processes.[68] Hence the standard image of the activist, American court.[69]

By the late 1920s in England, the inexorable and dramatic growth of administrative rule-making (delegated legislation) had raised in some (most notoriously Lord Hewart)[70] concerns analogous to those Dicey had had about administrative adjudication. However, such concerns were countered and allayed by the Report of the Committee on Ministers' Powers (the Donoughmore Committee)[71] and, to this day, administrative rule-making is subject to very little external control. In the US at this time, adjudication rather than rule-making was the preferred mode of bureaucratic decision-making. As a result, the Administrative Procedure Act 1946 has much more to say about adjudication than rule-making. The US rule-making revolution did not occur until the 1960s, when there was a mass conversion from adjudication to rule-making, on which federal courts imposed an elaborate set of legal controls.[72]

In 1929, the author of what appears to be the first English monograph on administrative law, FJ Port, included chapters on the US and French systems.[73] Port's observations about the US system lack Bryce's and Dicey's clear political and ideological agendas. He explained what he was doing by arguing that in England, the legislative and judicial powers had, 'in a sense', developed out of the administrative power[74] because, in his view, 'in ancient as well as in modern times, the administrative is, in the last resort, the most essential of State functions'.[75] However, by the time he was writing, Port argued, the legislative power had come to dominate both executive and judicial power which, in that sense, were derived from and subordinate to it. At the same time, Port detected a long historical arc in which judicial and legislative power had first, as a function of changing political and governmental practice and social demands, moved away from the executive, but in which, by 'statutory re-grant . . . during the last half century or so . . . a good deal of the territory surrendered long since' by the executive had been regained.[76] 'The United States', Port argued, 'presents an outstanding example of the theory that administrative power inevitably gathers to itself a preponderant share in the processes of government under modern conditions'[77] because of the administration's relative advantages of expertise, permanence and flexibility.[78]

In Port's mind (as in mine), understanding the relationship between the various powers of government was central to understanding administrative law. That relationship was different in France and the US from what it was in the UK. In his comparative discussion of the exercise of legislative and judicial power by the executive in the UK and the US,[79] Port

[68] Especially (but not only) in periods of 'divided government', when the President's party lacks control of either or both houses of Congress, the legislative process may grind to a halt as a result of Presidential vetoes of Congressional legislation coupled with inability of Congress to overturn them. This dynamic has been a notable feature of the Trump presidency.

[69] This might explain Ronald Dworkin's basic concern to find a theory of the judicial role that did not paint courts as doing essentially the same work as the legislature: RMD working, *Taking Rights Seriously* (London: Duckworth, 1987), p. 82.

[70] Lord Hewart, *The New Despotism* (London: Ernest Benn, 1929). See further Cane, *Controlling Administrative Power* (n 5 above), pp. 276–9.

[71] Cmd 4060, 1932.

[72] Cane, *Controlling Administrative Power* (n 5 above), 297–305

[73] Port, *Administrative Law* (n 9 above).

[74] Port, *Administrative Law* (n 9 above), at p. 18.

[75] Port, *Administrative Law* (n 9 above), at p. 327.

[76] Port, *Administrative Law* (n 9 above), at p. 328.

[77] Port, *Administrative Law* (n 9 above), at p. 331.

[78] Port, *Administrative Law* (n 9 above), at pp. 336–8.

[79] Port, *Administrative Law* (n 9 above), at ch. 6.

focused on the US Constitution and, particularly, the extent to which statutory delegation of legislative and judicial power to the executive was more constrained in the US than in the UK. Concerning legislative power, Port argued that the US non-delegation rule, based on the constitutional principle of separation of powers,[80] presented no significant, practical barrier to delegation of either legislative or judicial power. This position he saw as an inevitable, pragmatic adjustment of constitutional principle to the realities of modern, activist governance in areas such as regulation and welfare. On the other hand, he judged that the constitutional principle of due process (in the Fifth Amendment) did impose significant limitations on administrative adjudication such that in the US, '[t]he silent and almost unnoticed growth of extraordinary powers in the hands of administrative authorities, such as has recently taken place in England, is impossible'.[81] Port analogised constitutional limitations on legislation in the US to a medieval, English common law, which was 'anterior' to, and provided 'authority or basis' for, Parliamentary 'promulgation' of law.[82]

7.5.2 *The View from the US*

English observers of US public law in this period generally liked what they saw because it seemed to possess greater resources than English law for constraining administrative power. How did things look from the other side? During the 1930s, in reaction to the massive expansion of the federal government and bureaucracy under the New Deal,[83] the ideas of Dicey and his followers were called in aid by Roosevelt's opponents[84] and castigated by his supporters.[85]

In 1941, Roscoe Pound went so far as to say that American judges of the day were 'much in the position of the common-law judges under the Stuarts', guardians of the common-law rights of citizens against executive absolutism.[86] On the very first page of his 1927 monograph, *Administrative Justice and the Supremacy of Law in the United States*,[87] John Dickinson transported his readers back to the 'age of Coke'. His target was 'administrative adjudication', by which he meant the application of law to facts prior to and independently of any dispute. The growth of this practice, Dickinson argued, inevitably undermined individual rights by making them 'more flexible, and more responsive to uncertain factors of discretion, than when they are left to be defined by the more rigid processes of a court applying supposedly permanent rules of law'.[88] For this reason, administrative tribunals were to be 'feared' and courts 'favoured'.[89] For Dickinson, Dicey was the champion of the supremacy of law over government.[90] Just as Dicey looked longingly to the US, Dickinson considered a written

80 More particularly, the ideas that all three branches are coordinate delegates of the People and *delegatus non potest delegare*.

81 Port, *Administrative Law* (n 9 above), p. 291.

82 Port, *Administrative Law* (n 9 above), p. 290.

83 On the legal significance of the lack of an English New Deal, see Stephens, 'Basic Concepts and Current Differences' (n 2 above), p. 344.

84 E.g., JM Beck, *Our Wonderland of Bureaucracy* (New York: Macmillan, 1932), esp. ch. XII

85 E.g., F Frankfurter, 'Foreword' (1938) 47 *Yale Law Journal* 515.

86 R Pound, 'The Place of the Judiciary in a Democratic Polity' (1941) *American Bar Association Journal* 133, esp. 138–9.

87 J Dickinson, *Administrative Justice and the Supremacy of Law in the United States* (Cambridge: Harvard University Press, 1927), p. 3.

88 Dickinson, *Administrative Justice and the Supremacy of Law in the United States* (n 87 above), p. 29.

89 Dickinson, *Administrative Justice and the Supremacy of Law in the United States* (n 87 above), p. 76.

90 Dickinson, *Administrative Justice and the Supremacy of Law in the United States* (n 87 above), ch. 2.

constitution to be 'the most effective possible application of [Coke's] idea of a law sovereign over all laws which emanate merely from government'.[91] The law of a constitution is fixed, inflexible and rigid in a way that law made by administrators (and legislatures) is not. Like Coke's ancient, customary common law, it stands above and behind all law promulgated by governmental institutions. Just as Coke insisted on the power of the common-law courts to enforce that law against governmental institutions, so Dickinson insisted on the power of courts to enforce constitutional (and non-constitutional) law on administrative tribunals and other law-promulgating organs of government. What Dickinson explains at length,[92] and what Dicey had eventually to concede,[93] is that there must be 'practical limits' to the supremacy of law enforced by courts, in order to preserve the effectiveness, efficiency and vigour of the other branches of government. The power of the last word is ideally spread around.[94]

The sort of hankering that we have found in Dickinson, Pound and others, after a lost golden age of the common law, continues to the present day, exemplified most spectacularly in Philip Hamburger's *Is Administrative Law Unlawful?*. 'Historically', Hamburger's book 'places administrative law within the broader ebb and flow of irregular power'.[95] It argues that '[l]ike the English Crown before the development of English constitutional law, the American executive seeks to exercise power outside the door and the adjudications of courts. ... Administrative power thus returns to prerogative power and, as in the past, this absolute power threatens to evade a wide range of regular law, adjudication, institutions, processes, and rights'.[96] However, whereas, in the 1930s, such arguments presented a still-plausible point of view, Hamburger's work is widely considered not just historically inaccurate and ill-informed but downright mad.[97] American administrative law has left its historical roots far behind.

The legal warfare around the New Deal was not the only battle for the heart and soul of American administrative law waged across the turn of the nineteenth century. Leading proponents in the other long-running saga were Ernst Freund and Felix Frankfurter. Their skirmish revolved around a choice between 'common-law' and 'civil-law' models of bureaucracy.

The civil law model relied on centralised, agency-based, state administration aimed at the implementation of regulatory standards through expert legislators and bureaucrats. The common law model fundamentally distrusted bureaucratic administration, and as a consequence, identified courts as the proper locus for administrative governance.[98]

91 Dickinson, *Administrative Justice and the Supremacy of Law in the United States* (n 87 above), p. 96.

92 Dickinson, *Administrative Justice and the Supremacy of Law in the United States* (n 87 above), ch. 5.

93 AV Dicey, 'The Development of Administrative Law in England' (1915) 31 *Law Quarterly Review* 148.

94 Space prevents further discussion of the implications of such views for grounds of judicial review, for instance, and other aspects of substantive administrative law. See further Cane, *Controlling Administrative Power* (n 5 above), ch. 6 (on review for error of law), ch. 7 (on review for error of fact) and ch. 9 (on review for procedural unfairness).

95 P Hamburger, *Is Administrative Law Unlawful?* (Chicago: University of Chicago Press, 2014), p. 12.

96 Hamburger, *Is Administrative Law Unlawful?* (n 95 above), pp. 493–4.

97 See, e.g., A Vermeule, 'No' (2015) 93 *Texas Law Review* 1475; P Craig, 'The Legitimacy of US Administrative Law and the Foundations of English Administrative Law: Setting the Historical Record Straight', https://papers.ssrn.com/sol3/papers.cfm?abstract_id=2802784. For a completely different view, see G Lawson, 'The Return of the King: The Unsavoury Origins of Administrative Law' (2015) 93 *Texas Law Review* 1521.

98 N Morag-Levine, 'Common Law, Civil Law, and the Administrative State: From Coke to *Lochner*' (2007) 24 *Constitutional Commentary* 601, 604.

Both Freund and Frankfurter 'rejected the widely held dogma, most authoritatively pronounced by A.V. Dicey, that equated the Rule of Law with the freedom to challenge any administrators' [*sic*] deprivation of a private right in a proceeding conducted in "the ordinary legal manner before the ordinary Courts of the land". . . . For all that, the two disagreed fundamentally about administrative law.'[99] Whereas Freund (a German emigré) was suspicious of administrative discretion, which, he thought, should be tightly cabined by statutory law enforced by administrative courts along the lines of the Continental *rechtsstaat*, Frankfurter (who was a strong supporter of the New Deal) favoured freeing administrators as much as possible from judicial review and from detailed management by the legislature. Frankfurter (and other New Dealers) got their way over the latter when, in the 1930s, the Supreme Court more or less abandoned the non-delegation doctrine. In return, however, they were forced to accept procedural regulation of administrative rule-making and adjudication, enforced by the ordinary courts under standards of review of various degrees of intensity. This compromise was enacted in the Administrative Procedure Act 1946.

7.6 A *FIN-DE-SIECLE* CHANGE OF JUDICIAL DIRECTION

Contemporaneously with such trans-Atlantic scholarly interchanges around the role of judicially enforced administrative law in controlling administrative power, courts initiated the process by which the US law of judicial review of administrative action would cast off its English moorings. Consistently with the assumption underpinning the argument in this chapter (about the relationship between distribution and control of power), the change was arguably a reaction to the creation of the first 'independent' regulatory agency – the Interstate Commerce Commission – in 1887 and reforms designed to de-politicise the bureaucracy and put it in the service of instrumental rationality.[100] The now-accepted account of the process of change is that early in the twentieth century, US federal courts abandoned the theory of jurisdiction in favour of an 'appellate theory of judicial review'. Under this latter theory, the relationship between the reviewing court and the decision-maker is analogous to that between an inferior and an appellate court: appellate courts are much less willing to interfere with decisions on fact than with decisions on law. This shift (I would argue) reflects a fundamental difference between the role of courts in the US federal system and in the English system. In the US, the various organs of government are understood to be 'coordinate' in the sense that they all share in the exercise of the various powers of government and, in that way, can 'check and balance' each other. By contrast, in the English system, courts are not 'coordinate' with the other branches of government. Under the Revolution settlement of the late seventeenth century, courts are separated from the other organs of government and judicial power is distinguished and quarantined from both legislative and executive power. The role of courts is to exercise judicial power, not to exercise, or participate in the exercise of, executive or legislative power. When courts make law they do not 'legislate' as some sort of delegate of Parliament; rather, they make 'common law', which is subordinate to Parliamentary legislation. Similarly, when courts judicially review administrative action, the task they give themselves (as conceptualised in the seventeenth and eighteenth centuries) is to 'supervise'

[99] DR Ernst, 'Ernst Freund, Felix Frankfurter, and the American *Rechtsstaat*: A Transatlantic Shipwreck, 1894–1932' (2009) 23 *Studies in American Political Development* 171.

[100] TW Merrill, 'Article III, Agency Adjudication, and the Origins of the Appellate Review Model of Administrative Law' (2011) 111 *Columbia Law Review* 939. See also section 7.4.4.

rather than to hear an 'appeal' – to police limits on the jurisdiction of administrative decision-makers.

The idea of policing the limits of jurisdiction is deeply embedded in the history of the English common law. The common law grew out of the provision by the monarch of a forum, a procedure and remedies in competition with the procedures and remedies of local and seigneurial courts. Similarly, the distinction between common law and equity grew out of competition between the common-law courts and the Chancellor in the provision of 'justice services'. Again, the conciliar courts provided litigants with different procedures, rules of evidence and remedies than the common-law courts. Moreover, Parliament originally provided citizens dissatisfied by government action with a forum, additional to the royal courts, for hearing complaints and resolving disputes. Competition for 'judicial' power, not any particular set of rules or principles, was the defining characteristic of the mediaeval common law. The shift in US administrative law from the theory of jurisdiction to the appellate theory in the early twentieth century marked a break with that tradition. In England, the first major departure from the old approach did not occur until decades later, and involved expanding the concept of 'the record' and allowing evidence and reasons to be incorporated into the record after the proceedings were completed. More fundamental was the revolution sparked by the decision of the House of Lords, in *Anisminic* v. *Foreign Compensation Commission*,[101] to expand the concept of 'jurisdictional error' so much that it has now effectively been replaced by distinctions between law, fact and discretion. This shift has introduced important elements of the appellate theory into English law, but the basic principle remains that judicial review is supervisory, not appellate. This latter conceptualisation is underpinned by a robust understanding of the independence of the judiciary and the separation of judicial power – an understanding that reaches its apotheosis, perhaps, in the Australian legal system. In Australian law, the concept of jurisdiction and the distinction between jurisdictional and non-jurisdictional error are foundational components of the law of judicial review, and the distinction between legality review (based on ideas of jurisdiction) and merits review (analogous to an appeal) marks the boundary of the respective provinces of courts and tribunals.[102]

7.7 THE PARTING OF THE WAYS

Enactment of the Administrative Procedure Act 1946 (APA) was a watershed in American administrative law.[103] It marked the end of what we might call the War of the Agencies. The APA has come to be seen as a sort of (big-C) Constitution for the administrative state, supplementary to the meagre provisions about the executive and the administration in the 1789 Constitution. Its quasi-constitutional, 'super-statutory'[104] status is reflected in the facts, first, that although various provisions have been added to it over the years to strengthen regulation of the administrative process, its terms have been very little amended and, second, that the Supreme Court has applied quasi-constitutional modes of interpretation to some of its key provisions, producing (as we have noted) a 'common law' of judicial review that bears little relationship to the statutory text.[105]

101 *Anisminic* v. *Foreign Compensation Commission* [1969] 1 AC 247.
102 Cane, *Controlling Administrative Power* (n 5 above), pp. 215–31.
103 MJ Horwitz, *The Transformation of American Law, 1870–1960* (New York: Oxford University Press, 1992), ch. 8.
104 WN Eskridge Jr, 'America's Statutory "Constitution"' (2007) 41 *UC Davis Law Review* 1.
105 G Metzger, 'Ordinary Administrative Law as Constitutional Common Law' (2010) 110 *Columbia Law Review* 479; KM Stack, 'The Statutory Fiction of Judicial Review of Administrative Action' in C Forsyth, M Elliott,

The APA scheme has three main planks. The first is a restatement of the law of judicial review, including the grounds. The second is the separation of agency officials who exercise judicial power from policy and prosecutorial staff to provide them a significant measure of independence falling short, however, of the gold standard of judicial independence. The third is the proceduralisation of agency 'adjudication' and rule-making. The APA regulates the procedure for 'formal' adjudication and rule-making in much more detail than the procedure for 'informal' rule-making. In the 1960s and 1970s, federal courts built on (and, some would say, in conflict with) the APA to provide much more detailed regulation of the procedure for informal rule-making. The APA does not regulate 'informal' adjudication at all.[106] Informal adjudication includes what is referred to outside the US as 'decision-making'. Sources of procedural regulation, apart from the APA, are the due process clause of the Fifth Amendment and statutes dealing with adjudication in particular areas of administrative activity.

In Merrill's words, the APA represented a shift from a 'positivist' tradition to a 'process' tradition in US administrative law. Under the positivist tradition (which, he argues, predominated in the nineteenth century), judicial review was concerned primarily with whether decisions were authorised by law ('*intra vires*'). Under the process tradition, by contrast, it is concerned primarily with whether decisions are well-reasoned.[107] Richard Stewart famously referred to the positivist tradition as the 'transmission-belt theory' and conceptualised its competitor, in procedural terms, as 'interest-representation'.[108] Authority, rationality and procedure, we might say, are the three pillars of judicial-review law in both US and English law. Traditionally, the (English) common law focused on authority and, to a lesser extent, procedure. However, its procedural concern was primarily with fairness to individuals, not any wider concept of 'due process' that might underpin regulation of non-adjudicatory proceedings. Rationality has always been – and remains to a significant extent – marginal to judicial review in the (English) common-law tradition. It is in the distinctive balancing of these three pillars that we find many of the significant differences between the English and US 'common laws' of judicial review.

Part of the explanation for the emphasis of US law on procedure and rationality is to be found in the distinction between two images of bureaucracy explained earlier: the one that bureaucrats serve politicians and the other that they perform a distinct function of rational administration. Perhaps the most fundamental instance of this emphasis is found in the centrality of the administrative record and reasons to the US law of judicial review.[109] For instance, so-called hard-look review, on which many English scholars have lavished their undisguised admiration and envy, finds its rationale in the idea that decisions about means to ends should be based on arguments that plausibly link means and ends *instrumentally*.[110] There is ongoing debate among US judges and scholars about the extent to which bureaucrats ought to be allowed to take changes in government policy into account in the absence of

S Jhaveri, A Scully-Hill and M Ramsden (eds.), *Effective Judicial Review: A Cornerstone of Good Governance* (Oxford: Oxford University Press, 2010).

106 The reason for this omission is not obvious. For discussion see EL Rubin, 'Executive Action: Its History, Its Dilemmas and Its Potential Remedies' (2016) 8 *Journal of Legal Analysis* 1.

107 TW Merrill, 'Presidential Administration and the Traditions of Administrative Law' (2015) 115 *Columbia Law Review* 1953.

108 RB Stewart, 'The Reformation of American Administrative Law' (1975) 88 *Harvard Law Review* 1667.

109 P Cane, 'Records, Reasons and Rationality in Judicial Control of Administrative Action: England, the US and Australia' (2015) 48 *Israel Law Review* 309.

110 For discussion and critical analysis of this approach, see JL Mashaw, *Reasoned Administration and Democratic Legitimacy* (Cambridge: Cambridge University Press, 2018), esp. ch. 5.

sound arguments rooted in means-end rationality.[111] There is no equivalent debate in England because the relationship between the elected executive and the appointed bureaucracy is not understood in terms of a distinction between politics and expertise. To the extent that the British civil service embodies expertise, such expertise is to be used to support government policies, not compete with them in the name of instrumental rationality.

It can also be argued that the greater willingness of US courts, compared with their English counterparts, to 'defer' to statutory interpretations by bureaucrats is partly based on the supposed instrumental rationality of bureaucratic decision-making when compared with either political or legal decision-making. In this respect, there is no direct analogy with English and European concepts of 'deference' in the human-rights context, where it is concerned, I would suggest, as much with political choice of ends as with instrumental means-end rationality.

The enactment of the APA also affected Anglo-American public law scholarship. The second period of Atlantic crossings,[112] the conversations were participatory and took place more or less within a common tradition. The hot questions were how best to understand that tradition and whether it should be replaced by a different tradition. After World War II, interchange in both directions took an observational and comparative turn. This is no better illustrated than by Bernard Schwartz's and William Wade's *Legal Control of Government*, published in 1972.[113] The book conceptualises the two legal systems as parallel streams rather than tributaries of the same river and as competing sources of 'the best law'. The question is no longer how to understand a common heritage but, in the words of Judge Henry Friendly, how to interpret a common task: to 'protect the citizen from arbitrary exertions of the awesome power of government'.[114]

7.8 CONCLUSION

In an important sense, the APA represented the decisive break between US (administrative) law and its English, common-law inheritance. In the words of William Novak,

> the common law tradition, that had shaped and ruled so much of public and private life through the early 19th century, had been displaced as a principal tool of American governance. And a regime of constitutional law, positive legislation, and administrative regulation assumed prominence. That regime rested on a different conception of the nature of law.[115]

The shift from a common-law constitution to one contained in a canonical document fundamentally changes the role of courts in the governmental system. Instead of being guardians of a foundational tradition they become active participants in the governmental project of 'provision of public services in the interest of the public welfare'.[116] The

111 E.g., KA Watts, 'Proposing a Place of Politics in Arbitrary and Capricious Review' (2009) 119 *Yale Law Journal* 2.

112 See section 7.5.

113 B Schwartz and HWR Wade, *Legal Control of Government: Administrative Law in Britain and the United States* (Oxford: Clarendon Press, 1972). See also B Schwartz, *Law and the Executive in Britain: A Comparative Study* (New York: New York University Press, 1949); HWR Wade, 'Anglo-American Administrative Law: Some Reflections' (1965) 81 *Law Quarterly Review* 357. This is not to say that there were no earlier, truly comparative Atlantic crossings. Perhaps most notable is FJ Goodnow, *Comparative Administrative Law* (New York: Burt Franklin, 1903), which surveyed the US, England, France and Germany and started with the claim that as long as there had been administrative government, there had been administrative law.

114 Schwartz and Wade, *Legal Control of Government* (n 113 above), xxi.

115 WJ Novak, 'The Administrative State in America' in *The Max Planck Handbooks in European Public Law: Volume 1, The Administrative State* (Oxford: Oxford University Press, 2017), 110. See also section 7.4.2.

116 Novak, 'The Administrative State in America' (n 115 above), 116.

Constitution supersedes the common law as the embodiment of the nation's deepest commitments, which are expressed in documents, not in the activities of judges.[117] In this new world, the characteristic differences between legislative and adjudicatory law-making lie in the forum and the process.[118] The implications of this change for administrative law only started to become clear once the massive shift of power to the executive and bureaucracy in the century or so up to the end of the Second World War began the process of its maturation. In some sense, the US legal system is still a common-law system, but it is no longer an Anglo-common-law system. As Stephens puts it in the epigram at the top of this article, England and the US are two countries divided by the common law.

The adoption and ratification of the US Constitution forever changed the path of development of government and politics in the US from that in the UK. Whatever the similarities between the English system of government of the late eighteenth century and the new US system of government after 1789, the inherent flexibility of the English, common-law constitution and the inherent rigidity of the US, documentary constitution had the result that by the early twentieth century, the two systems of government had taken very different paths. The seeds of many of the divergences between contemporary English and US administrative law were sown in 1789, lay more or less dormant for about a century, then slowly sprouted and grew over a period of about seventy years. Since then, the two plants have borne flowers and fruit which clearly demonstrate that though the plants belong to the same genus, they are very different species.

117 ES Corwin, 'The "Higher Law" Background of American Constitutional Law' (1929) 42 *Harvard Law Review* 365.

118 This shift is under way in Australia: Cane, *Controlling Administrative Power* (n 5 above), pp. 231–5.

8

Divergence and Convergence in English and Canadian Administrative Law

Paul Daly

INTRODUCTION

Canadian administrative law contains important features that do not appear on the landscape of English administrative law. In Canada, administrative tribunals may fall under a duty to consult with First Nations about projects liable to interfere with Aboriginal rights[1] and, indeed, may be considered to be part of the Crown for these purposes;[2] administrative tribunals have the power to consider constitutional questions[3] and, in some circumstances, to grant remedies for breaches of fundamental rights;[4] and there is a bespoke judicial review and appellate jurisdiction in respect of federal administrative action,[5] which is reviewed in the Federal Courts and is generally not subject to the inherent jurisdiction of the provincial superior courts.[6] None of these features is especially surprising, given that Canada is a federation created on land largely held by Aboriginal peoples[7] and which now boasts a supreme, written constitution.[8] Indeed, they may be thought of as necessary features, bolted on to the framework for judicial review of administrative action.

For the most part, however, Canadian and English administrative law are strikingly similar. First, notwithstanding its federal structure, the Canadian court system has been, since Confederation, broadly similar to the English. From their English forebears, the superior courts of the Canadian provinces inherited inherent jurisdiction, of which the supervisory jurisdiction over inferior tribunals and statutory bodies forms a large part.[9] The Constitution Act 1867, the written constitution marking the Confederation of the Canadian provinces, assumes the continuity of existing judicial institutions and substantive law; conscious choices

1 See, e.g., *Rio Tinto Alcan Inc.* v. *Carrier Sekani Tribal Council* [2010] 2 SCR 650.

2 See *Clyde River (Hamlet)* v. *Petroleum Geo-Services Inc.* [2017] 1 SCR 1069; *Chippewas of the Thames First Nation* v. *Enbridge Pipelines Inc.* [2017] 1 SCR 1099.

3 See *Nova Scotia (Workers' Compensation Board)* v. *Martin; Nova Scotia (Workers' Compensation Board)* v. *Laseur* [2003] 2 SCR 504; *Paul* v. *British Columbia (Forest Appeals Commission)* [2003] 2 SCR 585.

4 *R* v. *Conway* [2010] 1 SCR 765.

5 Federal Courts Act RSC 1985, c F-7, especially ss. 18, 27 and 28.

6 See the discussion in *Canada Labour Relations Board* v. *Paul L'Anglais Inc.* [1983] 1 SCR 147 and *Windsor (City)* v. *Canadian Transit Co.* [2016] 2 SCR 617.

7 See, e.g., *Delgamuukw* v. *British Columbia* [1997] 3 SCR 1010.

8 See Constitution Acts 1867 to 1982, especially Constitution Act 1982, s. 52(1):

> The Constitution of Canada is the supreme law of Canada, and any law that is inconsistent with the provisions of the Constitution is, to the extent of the inconsistency, of no force or effect.

9 See generally Supreme Court Act RSC 1985 c S-26; Federal Courts Act RSC 1985 c F-7; Paul Daly, 'Section 96: Striking a Balance between Legal Centralism and Legal Pluralism' in Richard Albert, Paul Daly and Vanessa MacDonnell (eds.), *The Canadian Constitution in Transition* (Toronto: University of Toronto Press, 2018).

were made in the nineteenth century *not* to provoke a rupture with the past – indeed, the Canadian Constitution is said in its preamble to be 'similar in principle' to the English Constitution.[10] It is also notable that, a century or so later, when waves of judicial review reform swept the Commonwealth in the 1960s and 1970s, the Canadians were also carried along.[11]

Second, the Canadian approach to parliamentary sovereignty is worth noting, not least (as we shall see) because so much of the law of judicial review in Canada and in England turns on legislative intent. At the time of Confederation, no major change was effected to the traditional English approach: parliamentary sovereignty was simply divided between the federal and provincial levels of power,[12] with each level supreme on those 'matters that fall within their respective spheres of jurisdiction'.[13] Even after the adoption of a supremacy clause in the Constitution Act 1982, there is a distinctly English hue to parliamentary sovereignty in Canada. As long as the rights set out in the Charter of Rights and Freedoms entrenched by the Constitution Act 1982 are respected, legislatures remain supreme within their areas of competence.[14]

Third, it is difficult to identify significant differences between the English and Canadian approaches to procedural fairness. In both jurisdictions, what fairness requires depends on the context and is not to be modelled on courtroom procedures. True, the Canadian courts have made express reference to 'deference' to decision-makers' procedural choices in making a determination about the fairness of the administrative process whereas 'deference' is absent from the English procedural fairness lexicon, but healthy judicial attention to the importance of context ensures that oversight of the administrative process is conducted with respectful attention to considered procedural choices regardless of the language employed.[15]

Fourth, remedial discretion has a similar character in both jurisdictions. The range of remedies is the same; the starting point is that unlawful administrative action is invalid; but relief may be withheld for various reasons, such as where granting it would make no difference[16] and where adequate alternative remedies exist.[17] In both jurisdictions, lawyers have sought through legislation, delegated legislation and case law to reshape the common law's old remedies – the prerogative writs of certiorari, mandamus, prohibition and quo warranto – to the new realities of an expansive administrative state.[18]

Fifth, although the application for judicial review is encrusted, in both jurisdictions, with a variety of rules of granular detail – such that a practising lawyer from London, England, could not hope to step off the plane in London, Ontario, and effectively manage an

10 Preamble to the Constitution Act 1867, 30 & 31 Vict, c 3.

11 See generally David Mullan, 'Reform of Administrative Law Remedies: Method or Madness?' (1975) *Federal Law Review* 340.

12 Jeremy Webber, *The Constitution of Canada: A Contextual Analysis* (Oxford: Hart, 2015), pp. 63–4.

13 *Reference re Pan-Canadian Securities Regulation* 2018 SCC 48, [56].

14 See, e.g., *Reference Re Canada Assistance Plan (BC)* [1991] 2 SCR; *Quebec (Attorney General)* v. *Canada (Attorney General)* [2015] 1 SCR 693.

15 *Lloyd* v. *McMahon* [1987] AC 625; *Baker* v. *Canada (Citizenship and Immigration)* [1999] 2 SCR 817.

16 *Malloch* v. *Aberdeen Corporation* [1971] 1 WLR 1578; *Mobil Oil Canada Ltd* v. *Canada-Newfoundland Offshore Petroleum Board* [1994] 1 SCR 202.

17 *R* v. *Inland Revenue Commissioners, ex parte Preston* [1985] 1 AC 835; *Harelkin* v. *University of Regina* [1979] 2 SCR 561.

18 See, on the Canadian side, *First Report of the Royal Commission Inquiry into Civil Rights (McRuer Report)* (Toronto, 1968), followed by Ontario's Judicial Review Procedure Act 1971 (see JM Evans, 'Judicial Review in Ontario – Recent Developments in the Remedies – Some Problems of Pouring Old Wine into New Bottles' (1977) 55 *Canadian Bar Review* 148); and on the English side, English Law Commission, *Report on Remedies in Administrative Law* (Law Com. No. 77) (Cmnd 6407, 1976).

administrative law case – both jurisdictions have faced similar challenges in updating these rules to take account of the increased scope of judicial review of administrative action: for instance, English and Canadian courts have updated the definition of the 'record' for the purposes of judicial review in a cautious, incremental fashion.[19]

As with the features now bolted on to the Canadian law of judicial review of administrative action, these similarities are entirely unsurprising. The conscious choice at the time of Confederation to permit the common law and its accompanying institutions to continue in force created a high degree of path dependency for Canadian administrative law.

In the area of substantive review,[20] however, there are, at least at first glance, marked differences. Substantive review in Canada, where courts regularly defer to administrative decision-makers' interpretations of law and judicial review of administrative action, is organised around the concept of reasonableness, and seems very different to its equivalent in England, where courts do not defer to administrative interpretations of law and prefer to conceive of the justification for judicial oversight of administrative action in terms of vires-based grounds of review and jurisdictional error. One might think, based on this first glance, that the differences must be attributable to deep-seated disagreement about the nature of judicial power and the appropriate allocation of interpretive authority between the branches of government. One might even suspect that such disagreement must rest on long-settled historical foundations.[21]

In this chapter, however, I will make a positive case for comparative analysis of substantive review in Canadian and English administrative law. I will argue that the difference between Canadian and English administrative law is best explained by relatively recent accidents of history. They are bumps along a path-dependent road. Indeed, I will suggest, a prolonged period of divergence may be coming to an end, with the Transatlantic rise of reasonableness review – allied to the global march of proportionality – ushering in a new era of convergence.

I will develop this argument by tracing the pattern of divergence and convergence in Canadian and English administrative law from the 1970s to the present day. From the common starting point identified in Section 8.1, the two jurisdictions diverged dramatically between the 1970s and 2000s, as I will explain in Section 8.2. Since then, the administrative law of the two jurisdictions has converged to some extent, as outlined in Section 8.3. One of

19 *Tweed* v. *Parades Commission of Northern Ireland* [2007] 1 AC 650; *Bernard* v. *Canada (Revenue Agency)* 2015 FCA 263. See generally Paul Daly, 'Updating the Procedural Law of Judicial Review of Administrative Action' (2018) 51 *University of British Columbia Law Review* 705.

20 In this area, the issue is 'the extent to which review of the merits, traditionally limited to *Wednesbury* unreasonableness, should be expanded into more intensive reasonableness review, or new substantive grounds of review, or both'. Hanna Wilberg and Mark Elliott, 'Introduction' in *The Scope and Intensity of Substantive Review: Traversing Taggart's Rainbow* (Oxford: Hart, 2015), p. 1.

21 See, e.g., Peter Cane, *Controlling Delegated Power: An Historical Comparison* (Cambridge: Cambridge University Press, 2016); Peter Cane, 'The Common Law, the High Court of Australia, and the United States Supreme Court' in Paul Daly (ed.), *Apex Courts and the Common Law* (Toronto: University of Toronto Press, 2019) and in this volume, distinguishing between Anglo-Australian and American administrative law and explaining the differences between them the basis of institutional considerations, in particular the place of the judiciary in the different systems relative to other branches of government. Professor Cane does not discuss Canada. One might think that despite its geographical proximity to the United States, it is institutionally proximate to the Anglo-Australian tradition and, as such, deference in Canada poses something of a conundrum for Professor Cane. See, e.g., Paul Craig, 'Comparative Administrative Law and Political Structure' (2017) 37 *OJLS* 946. My analysis in this chapter suggests, first, that institutional considerations do not help explain divergence between English and Canadian administrative law but, second, that there are significant similarities between the two, which may become even more pronounced in the future (and could be explicable in terms of institutional considerations). My analysis thus neither strongly contradicts nor strongly supports Professor Cane's thesis.

the implications of my argument is, as I discuss in Section 8.4, is that further convergence in the future is possible.

There are three aspects to this chapter. First, and most simply, the chapter contains a description of the patterns of divergence and convergence between Canadian and English administrative law from their common starting point in the 1970s. Second, the chapter contains a discussion of the possibilities for fruitful Transatlantic dialogue on the future of substantive review, highlighting the extent to which both jurisdictions are facing similar contemporary challenges. Third, the chapter is designed to encourage those interested in administrative law to look at Canada and England from a comparative perspective. There has been little such work to date, as indeed there has been little comparative work on judicial review of administrative action.[22] This may be because too few administrative lawyers are confidently conversant in the details of administrative law in the two jurisdictions. In addition, contemporary legal academics might be sceptical about the utility of comparative legal research in general and of comparative public law analysis specifically, especially, in this case, because the points of difference between Canadian and English administrative law intuitively seem to be related to (if not caused by) fundamental philosophical or institutional differences. My message to those who fear –for whatever reason – that 'there be dragons' is that they can safely venture forward in an Anglo-Canadian comparative administrative law endeavour. A reader interested in undertaking comparative analysis might well conclude that the nature of judicial power, the appropriate allocation of interpretive authority and long-settled historical foundations are substantially similar in both jurisdictions.

8.1 A COMMON STARTING POINT

In the early 1970s, one would have been hard pressed to identify points of divergence between the English and the Canadian law of judicial review of administrative action. As is well known, in an important trilogy of 1960s cases, the House of Lords significantly reshaped administrative law:[23] *Ridge* v. *Baldwin*,[24] *Padfield* v. *Minister of Agriculture, Fisheries and Food*[25] and *Anisminic* v. *Foreign Compensation Commission*.[26] The effect of these decisions was, first, to dispense with a set of formal distinctions between judicial and administrative decision-making (*Ridge*) and jurisdictional and non-jurisdictional error (*Anisminic*) and, second, to confirm that administrative decisions were not immune from judicial oversight, regardless of whether they were policy-laden exercises of broadly drawn discretionary powers (*Padfield*) or sheltered by a privative clause (*Anisminic*). The courts would stand ready to correct errors of law, whether these arose by misinterpretation of a statutory provision (*Anisminic*) or misconstruction of the purpose of a statutory provision (*Padfield*), and to ensure the fairness of administrative decision-making processes having important effects on individual interests (*Ridge*). My précis of the trilogy is, as we shall see, oversimplified to some degree, particularly as to the effect of *Anisminic*, but it represents the orthodox account of the 1960s developments. To this should be added the well-known framework for review of discretionary power set out by Lord Greene MR in *Associated Provincial Picture Houses*

[22] See the introductory chapter to this volume. Janina Boughey, 'Administrative Law: The Next Frontier for Comparative Law' (2013) 62 *International and Comparative Law Quarterly* 55.

[23] See Chapter 3.

[24] [1964] AC 40.

[25] [1968] AC 997.

[26] [1969] 2 AC 147.

v. *Wednesbury Corporation*:[27] decision-makers must direct themselves properly in law, take into account relevant factors, ignore irrelevant factors and reach rational conclusions.[28]

In the following decade, the Supreme Court of Canada followed the same course as the House of Lords. There was no obvious equivalent to *Padfield*, though the influential 1950s decision in *Roncarelli* v. *Duplessis*[29] contains a reference, in Rand J's celebrated reasons, to the 'perspective' in which a statute operates.[30] In any event, *Metropolitan Life Insurance Co* v. *International Union of Operating Engineers*[31] and *Nicholson* v. *Haldimand-Norfolk Regional Police Commissioners*[32] were directly analogous to *Anisminic* and *Ridge*, respectively. In *Metropolitan Life*, the Ontario Labour Relations Board's misinterpretation of the statutory term 'members of a trade union' was fatal to the legality of its order certifying the Union as a bargaining agent, notwithstanding the presence of a privative clause.[33] Reference can also usefully be made to *Service Employees' International Union, Local No 333* v. *Nipawin District Staff Nurses Association*,[34] where Dickson J (as he then was) took an expansive review of the type of errors that would cause an administrative decision-maker to forfeit 'the protection of the privative or preclusive clause': 'acting in bad faith, basing the decision on extraneous matters, failing to take relevant factors into account, breaching the provisions of natural justice or misinterpreting provisions of the Act so as to embark on an inquiry or answer a question not remitted to it'.[35] Review of the exercise of discretionary powers was also indistinguishable from England's *Wednesbury* test, which could still be cited with approval in the 1980s.[36] Meanwhile, in *Nicholson*, Laskin CJ endorsed the emergence of a general duty of fairness in administrative law.[37]

In both England and Canada, jurisdictional error was the organising principle of judicial review of administrative action,[38] with a more expansive view taken in the 1970s than in previous eras of the jurisdictional conditions (of legality and fairness) that administrative decision-makers had to comply with. From this common starting point, however, the paths taken by the English and Canadian courts soon diverged. By the 2000s, English and Canadian administrative law had developed very differently.

8.2 DIVERGENCE: 1970S–2000S

8.2.1 *Canada*[39]

Soon after *Metropolitan Life* the Supreme Court of Canada began to strike off on a different path. Already in *Nipawin*, although Dickson J used language that would have been familiar to

27 [1948] 1 KB 223 [*Wednesbury*].
28 *Wednesbury* at 229.
29 [1959] SCR 121 [*Roncarelli*].
30 *Roncarelli* at 140.
31 [1970] SCR 425 [*Metropolitan Life*].
32 [1979] 1 SCR 311 [*Nicholson*].
33 *Metropolitan Life*, at 435.
34 [1975] 1 SCR 382 [*Nipawin*].
35 *Nipawin* at 389.
36 See, e.g., *Re Regional Trust and Superintendent of Insurance* [1987] 2 FCR 271.
37 *Nicholson* at 325.
38 See especially *Bell* v. *Ontario Human Rights Commission* [1971] SCR 756.
39 See generally Paul Daly, 'The Struggle for Deference in Canada' in Mark Elliott and Hannah Wilberg (eds.), *Traversing Taggart's Rainbow: The Scope and Intensity of Substantive Review* (Oxford: Hart, 2015); Mark D Walters, 'Jurisdiction, Functionalism, and Constitutionalism in Canadian Administrative Law' in

the reader of *Anisminic*, he also wrote: 'if the Board acts in good faith and its decision can be *rationally supported on a construction which the relevant legislation may reasonably be considered to bear,* then the Court will not intervene'.[40] Then, in *Canadian Union of Public Employees* v. *New Brunswick Liquor Corporation*,[41] a case involving the New Brunswick Public Service Labour Relations Board's interpretation of a prohibition on replacing 'striking employees with any other employee', the Court overtly advocated a deferential approach. In situations involving the review by the ordinary courts of specialised administrative tribunals protected by privative clauses, the following question had to be asked: 'was the ... interpretation so patently unreasonable that its construction cannot be rationally supported by the relevant legislation and demands intervention by the court upon review?'[42] However, jurisdictional error remained the organising principle. A reviewing court would only ask the foregoing question of an interpretation that was within the decision-maker's jurisdiction. Dickson J emphasised that it can be 'very difficult to determine' when a question is jurisdictional in nature and made a plea for epistemic humility: 'The courts, in my view, should not be alert to brand as jurisdictional, and therefore subject to broader curial review, that which may be doubtfully so.'[43] Jurisdiction was not discarded, but it soon became clear that on matters central to the mandate of an administrative decision-maker, a 'manifestly unreasonable' error would have to be identified in order to justify judicial intervention.[44]

Jurisdiction soon lost much of its analytical force, however, supplemented and ultimately supplanted by a 'pragmatic and functional analysis'. In *UES, Local 298* v. *Bibeault*,[45] Beetz J was openly sceptical of the utility of jurisdictional error.[46] Accordingly, he developed a multi-factor test to determine whether a court should take a deferential approach to reviewing a given administrative interpretation of law, pursuant to which a court should examine 'not only the wording of the enactment conferring jurisdiction on the administrative tribunal, but the purpose of the statute creating the tribunal, the reason for its existence, the area of expertise of its members and the nature of the problem before the tribunal'.[47]

The law in this area was characterised by important ebbs and flows over the years,[48] but came ultimately to be dominated by the pragmatic and functional approach. *Pushpanathan* v. *Canada (Minister of Citizenship and Immigration)*[49] represented its 'logical conclusion'.[50] For Bastarache J, the purpose of the pragmatic and functional approach was to identify those questions the legislature intended to reserve to the courts and to be answered on a 'correctness' standard. Whether any given question should be answered on a correctness standard or alternatively a deferential standard was to be determined by reference to four

Christopher Forsyth, Mark Elliott, Swati Jhaveri, Michael Ramsden and Anne Scully-Hill (eds.), *Effective Judicial Review: a Cornerstone of Good Governance* (Oxford: Oxford University Press, 2010).

40 *Nipawin* at 389. My emphasis.

41 [1979] 2 SCR 227 [*New Brunswick Liquor*].

42 *New Brunswick Liquor* at 237.

43 *New Brunswick Liquor* at 233.

44 *Syndicat des employés de production du Québec et de l'Acadie* v. *Canada Labour Relations Board* [1984] 2 SCR 412 at 422.

45 [1988] 2 SCR 1048 [*Bibeault*].

46 *Bibeault* at 1087.

47 *Bibeault* at 1088.

48 Claire L'Heureux-Dubé, 'The "Ebb" and "Flow" of Administrative Law on the "General Question of Law"', in Michael Taggart (ed.), *The Province of Administrative Law* (Oxford: Hart, 1997).

49 [1998] 1 SCR 982.

50 Daly, 'Struggle for Deference', at 309.

factors: the presence or absence of a privative clause or right of appeal; the expertise of the decision-maker; the purpose of the statutory framework; and the nature of the question at issue. This was an 'unrelentingly substantive' approach that eschewed categorical distinctions.[51] Moreover, the pragmatic and functional approach was expanded to cover review of discretionary powers,[52] creating a unified approach to judicial review of administrative action in which error of law and discretion were, analytically, treated as one.[53]

It is not necessary to elaborate at this point upon the complex superstructure that the Canadian courts established to permit the operation of the pragmatic and functional approach.[54] Suffice it to say for present purposes that, by the 2000s, Canada had developed a deferential approach to judicial review of questions of law, characterised by a focus on substance rather than form.

8.2.2 *England*

Anisminic was undoubtedly an important case when decided, as is evidenced by the flurry of commentary it immediately attracted.[55] The commentary also demonstrates, however, that *Anisminic's* legacy was contestable. All that could be said with certainty about the decision of the House of Lords was that it demonstrated that a misinterpretation of a statutory instrument could amount to a reviewable error of law.[56]

It is true that the speeches of the *Anisminic* majority contained important statements of principle giving a generous scope to judicial review, for instance that administrative decision-makers must 'confine themselves within the powers specially committed to them on a true construction of the relevant Acts of Parliament'.[57] This left open the route travelled by Lord Denning MR, who, a decade after *Anisminic*, trumpeted that the effect of their Lordship's decision was to vest the control of legal interpretation in the senior courts:

> [I]n truth the High Court has a choice before it whether to interfere with an inferior court on a point of law. If it chooses to interfere, it can formulate its decision in the words: 'The court in the following section had no jurisdiction to decide this point wrongly as it did'. If it does not choose to interfere, it can say: 'The court had jurisdiction to decide it wrongly, and did so.'[58]

Nonetheless, equally sweeping statements in *Anisminic* pointed towards a more restrained judicial role. Lord Wilberforce was careful to point that in determining the 'extent of the interpretatory power conferred upon the tribunal' by Parliament one should not begin with 'any necessary predisposition towards one that questions of law, or questions of construction,

[51] Paul Daly, 'The Unfortunate Triumph of Form over Substance in Canadian Administrative Law' (2012) 50 *Osgoode Hall Law Journal* 317 at 323.

[52] *Baker* v. *Canada (Citizenship and Immigration)* [1999] 2 SCR 817 at [51–6].

[53] See, e.g., *Dr Q* v. *College of Physicians and Surgeons of British Columbia* [2003] 1 SCR 226 at [24].

[54] See generally David J Mullan, 'Establishing the Standard of Review: The Struggle for Complexity?' (2004) 17 *Canadian Journal of Administrative Law & Practice* 59.

[55] E.g., SA De Smith, 'Judicial Review in Administrative Law: The Ever-Open Door?' (1969) 17 *Cambridge Law Journal* 161; HWR Wade, 'Constitutional and Administrative Aspects of the Anisminic Case' (1969) 85 *Law Quarterly Review* 198.

[56] See generally David Feldman, '*Anisminic Ltd* v. *Foreign Compensation Commission* (1968): In Perspective' in Satvinder Juss and Maurice Sunkin (eds.), *Landmark Cases in Public Law* (Oxford: Hart, 2017), p. 63.

[57] *Anisminic* at 194, per Lord Pearce. See similarly *Anisminic* at 207, per Lord Wilberforce. See similarly *R* v. *Northumberland Compensation Appeal Tribunal, Ex parte Shaw* [1952] 1 KB 338 at 346.

[58] *Pearlman* v. *Keepers of Harrow School* [1979] QB 56 at 70.

are necessarily for the courts'.[59] Ample scope existed,[60] in other words, for a deferential approach to emerge, along the lines of the pragmatic and functional approach developed by the Canadian courts (or, indeed, America's '*Chevron* doctrine')[61].

Be that as it may, the dominant view was that *Anisminic* abolished the distinction between jurisdictional and non-jurisdictional error, meaning that any error of law committed by an inferior tribunal was subject to correction by the High Court.[62] By the mid-1990s, it was possible for Lord Griffiths to state, in *R* v. *Hull University Visitor, ex p Page*,[63] that as a general principle, 'bodies other than courts ... are required to apply the law correctly'; should they fail to do so, 'judicial review is available to correct their error of law so that they may make their decision upon a proper understanding of the law'.[64] There are some exceptions to this rule, relating variously to inferior courts,[65] 'special' jurisdictions,[66] and (perhaps) the interpretation of vague statutory terms,[67] but they are decidedly limited in scope, notwithstanding academic attempts to expand their importance.[68] Unlike in Canada, in England, the courts had the last word on questions of law. Meanwhile, *Wednesbury* continued to dominate the analysis of discretionary powers, with added scope to review non-jurisdictional issues of fact.[69]

8.2.3 *Explaining Divergence*

The effect of the developments in England and in Canada in substantive review post-*Anisminic* and into the new century was to create a significant divergence between the two systems. First, in England, judges retained the last word on questions of law, whereas in Canada administrative decision-makers' interpretations of law were often entitled to deference such that they could be set aside only for manifest error. Second, in Canada, the overarching approach developed to separate those questions to be reviewed deferentially from those questions to be answered authoritatively by the courts became the dominant approach, whereas in England, the old *Wednesbury* framework survived (and the dominant question remained: did the decision-maker abuse its discretion in a *Wednesbury* sense?). It is difficult to perceive any deep-rooted institutional reasons for this divergence. The judiciary plays a similar role in the two jurisdictions – and federalism concerns have been notably absent from Canadian administrative law jurisprudence.

My brief introduction to the landscape of judicial review of administrative action in 1970s Canada should not be taken as suggesting that the landscape was much loved by members of the Canadian legal community. On the contrary, the Supreme Court of Canada's administrative law jurisprudence was regularly and roundly denounced by leading commentators. In

59 *Anisminic* at 209.

60 See , e.g., GL Peiris, 'Jurisdictional Review and Judicial Policy: The Evolving Mosaic' (1987) 103 *Law Quarterly Review* 66.

61 *Chevron USA Inc* v. *Natural Resources Defense Council* 467 US 837 (1984).

62 See also *R (Cart)* v. *Upper Tribunal* [2012] 1 AC 663, at [18] [*Cart*], per Baroness Hale of Richmond.

63 [1993] AC 682 [*Page*].

64 *Page* at 693.

65 *Re Racal Communications* [1981] AC 374 at 383–4.

66 *Page* at 693–5

67 *R* v. *Monopolies and Mergers Commission, ex p South Yorkshire Transport* [1993] 1 All ER 289 [*South Yorkshire Transport*].

68 See , e.g., Paul Daly, 'Deference on Questions of Law' (2011) 74 *Modern Law Review* 694.

69 See successively *Secretary of State for Education* v. *Tameside Metropolitan Borough Council* [1977] AC 1014; *R* v. *Criminal Injuries Compensation Board ex parte A* [1999] 2AC 330; *E* v. *Secretary of State for the Home Department* [2004] 2 WLR 1351.

Canada, the dominant critique of the Supreme Court of Canada, through the 1970s, was its over-interventionist approach to the review of administrative tribunals, especially labour relations tribunals. These tribunals were invariably staffed by experts – leading members of the bar and academy – who rendered careful decisions in an area that, because of the need to strike a balance between the interests of employers and employed, called for sensitive value judgements. Yet, on the *Metropolitan Life* approach, their decisions were subject to second-guessing by judges in judicial review proceedings. As we have seen, these criticisms did not fall on deaf ears. Tribunals were often staffed by expert arbitrators, among them Bora Laskin, who became Chief Justice of Canada in 1973. Labour cases featured heavily on the Supreme Court's administrative law docket, which meant that Laskin, and judges like Brian Dickson and Jean Beetz, had regular opportunities to preach for deference on questions lying with labour tribunals' expertise. Later on, Bertha Wilson[70] and Claire L'Heureux-Dubé[71] were able to take the strands of this case law and weave it into a coherent doctrinal framework.

Deference on questions of law never took hold in England. This was not inevitable. In the years after *Anisminic*, counsel could have pressed subsequent courts to reinvigorate the distinction between jurisdictional and non-jurisdictional error, certainly in cases where a privative clause did not pose a challenge to rule-of-law orthodoxy. There were also elegant academic pleas to seize upon the ambiguities in *Anisminic*.[72] The reasons these pleas went unheard have been recounted in fascinating detail by Sir Stephen Sedley:

> What happened was that it became the experience of counsel (of whom I was one) appearing during the 1970s in judicial review cases against government departments or official bodies to be told by Treasury counsel that no point was to be taken on the applicability of Anisminic. In other words, if the applicant could establish an error of law, it was not going to be argued by the Crown that it was justiciable only if it vitiated the decision-maker's jurisdiction. It was accepted in effect that if the tribunal's error in Anisminic truly went to its jurisdiction, as the law lords had decided it did, then the old divide between jurisdictional and non-jurisdictional error had collapsed. The goalposts had become the corner flags. This was not a trahison des clercs. It was a recognition that the orderly development of public law required a comprehensive approach to arguable abuses of power in place of the hair-splitting distinctions which had come to disfigure the law in the inter-war years; and it should be placed on record that it was from the successive standing counsel to the Treasury – first Gordon Slynn, then Harry Woolf, then Simon Brown, then John Laws–that these initiatives came.[73]

These efforts were supported by forthright judicial *dicta*, expressed at the highest level, most prominently by Lord Diplock, who wasted no opportunity to expound the mantra, first expressed extra-curially, that *Anisminic* 'renders obsolete the technical distinction between errors of law which go to "jurisdiction" and errors of law which do not'.[74] Deep-seated institutional reasons do not explain the course English law has taken since *Anisminic*. Historically contingent considerations predominate. Treasury Counsel – reflecting a widely-held view that authoritative judicial pronouncements on questions of law served the common good – did not resist the increasing scope of judicial review of errors of law. And it hardly hurt

70 *National Corn Growers* v. *Canada (Import Tribunal)* [1990] 2 SCR 1324.

71 *Baker*.

72 See, e.g., Jack Beatson, 'The Scope of Judicial Review for Error of Law' (1984) 4 *Oxford Journal of Legal Studies* 22.

73 'The Lion Beneath the Throne: Law as History', Sixteenth Annual Sir David Williams Lecture, University of Cambridge, 5 March 2016.

74 'Administrative Law: Judicial Review Reviewed' (1974) 33 *Cambridge Law Journal* 233 at 243.

those efforts that Lord Diplock – one of the most celebrated jurists of the twentieth century – expounded a similar view from the bench.

8.3 CONVERGENCE: 2000S TO PRESENT DAY

The period of post-*Anisminic* divergence had by the 2000s created two markedly different systems substantive of judicial review of administrative action. Since then, however, the systems have begun to converge. On the one hand, Canada's pragmatic and functional approach has evolved towards a one-size-fits-all reasonableness standard, which applies to almost all administrative interpretations of law, to exercises of discretionary power and even to some questions of constitutional law. On the other hand, European influences have prompted English judges to grapple with the framework for review of discretionary powers, wrestling in particular with the suggestion that *Wednesbury* unreasonableness could be supplanted by a proportionality test. As we shall see, English judges seem tempted by a one-size-fits-all reasonableness standard. The convergence to be charted in this section should not be overstated: it is at best halting, it covers only discretionary powers and it only portends future developments in respect of error of law in England. But it nonetheless underscores how convergence and divergence can be prompted and subsequently explained by historical happenstance.[75]

8.3.1 *England*

Several eminent scholars have advocated replacing *Wednesbury* with proportionality. The impetus here comes from the introduction to domestic law of proportionality through, first, European Union law (via the European Communities Act 1972) and, subsequently, the Human Rights Act 1998 (which incorporates many of the rights protected, at the international level, by the European Convention on Human Rights). It is variously said that the more structured methodology of proportionality is superior to the methodology of *Wednesbury*;[76] that the law would be simplified if proportionality, already used in European Union law cases and human rights adjudication, were adopted as the general common law ground of review;[77] and (more recently) that proportionality has deep historical roots in the common law.[78] It has been said in response that properly understood *Wednesbury* has its own structure;[79] that *Wednesbury* preserves an appropriate balance between decision-making autonomy and

75 From one perspective, proportionality's recent prominence might be seen as historical happenstance: it came along at a propitious moment in the development of Canadian and English administrative law. From another perspective, one might view the rise of proportionality as the real historical story, with the Canadian and English experiences as mere footnotes in a much broader narrative; indeed, developments in legal systems generally may merely be epiphenomena of broader cultural, intellectual, political and social shifts. See, e.g., Yves-Marie Morissette, 'Appellate Standards of Review Then and Now' (2017) 18 *Journal of Appellate Practice and Process* 55. My perspective is somewhere between these two. Canadian and English developments are important in their own right and would most likely have occurred with or without proportionality's emergence and rise. But proportionality's presence in both systems at least made the move towards more contextual substantive review more likely.

76 Jeffrey Jowell and Anthony Lester, 'Proportionality: Neither Novel nor Dangerous' in Jeffrey Jowell and Dawn Oliver (eds.), *New Directions in Judicial Review* (London: Stevens and Sons, 1988); Paul Craig 'Unreasonableness and Proportionality in UK Law' in Evelyn Ellis (ed.), *The Principle of Proportionality in the Laws of Europe* (Oxford: Oxford University Press, 1999), pp. 99–100

77 Paul Craig (eds.), *Administrative Law* (London: Sweet and Maxwell, 2012).

78 Paul Craig, 'Proportionality and Judicial Review: a UK Historical Perspective', *SSRN*, 16 June 2016.

79 Paul Daly, '*Wednesbury's* Reason and Structure' (2011) *Public Law* 238.

judicial intervention, which would be upset by the introduction of more intrusive proportionality review;[80] and that deferential *Wednesbury* review and less deferential proportionality review serve different functions.[81]

The judges have tended to equivocate.[82] Lord Steyn's discussion in *R (Daly)* v. *Secretary of State for the Home Department*[83] remains influential. In his *obiter* comments on the difference between common law review and proportionality review, Lord Steyn took the view that although there was 'some overlap' between the two, 'the intensity of review is somewhat greater under the proportionality approach' than under *Wednesbury*.[84] Yet although he suggested that, in general, proportionality review will be of greater intensity than *Wednesbury* review, he emphasised the role of context. He approved of Laws LJ's comment in *R (Mahmood)* v. *Secretary of State for the Home Department* to the effect that 'that the intensity of review in a public law case will depend on the subject matter in hand',[85] before adding: 'In law context is everything.'[86] Indeed, there are less-intense and more-intense variants of *Wednesbury*:[87] so-called super-*Wednesbury* review reserved for matters of high policy[88] and so-called sub-*Wednesbury* review requiring 'anxious scrutiny' of decisions having an impact on important rights.[89] As Lord Mance pithily summarised in *Pham* v. *Home Secretary*, 'Whether under EU, Convention or common law, context will determine the appropriate intensity of review.'[90]

Interestingly, however, although partisans in the substantive review debate typically advocate either that proportionality should sweep the board or that proportionality and *Wednesbury* (usually in a modified form) should both be retained and kept distinct, the United Kingdom Supreme Court seems poised to sanction a merger of *Wednesbury* and proportionality.

80 Lord Irvine of Lairg, 'Judges and Decision-Makers: The Theory and Practice of *Wednesbury* Review' (1996) *Public Law* 59.

81 Jason Varuhas, 'Against Unification' in Mark Elliott and Hanna Wilberg (eds.), *The Scope and Intensity of Substantive Review: Traversing Taggart's Rainbow* (Oxford: Hart Publishing, 2015), though see Paul Craig's rejoinder in *UK, EU and Global Administrative Law: Foundations and Challenges* (Cambridge: Cambridge University Press, 2015), pp. 260–71. See also Mark Elliott, 'The Human Rights Act 1998 and the Standard of Substantive Review' (2001) 60 *Cambridge Law Journal* 301 at 305, suggesting that the 'defining feature' of *Wednesbury* review is that a court 'may simultaneously conclude that a decision which infringes an individual's human rights is incoherent and lacking in adequate justification, but that it is not unlawful'. See also Swati Jhaveri, 'The Survival of Reasonableness Review: Confirming the Boundaries' (2018) 46 *Federal Law Review* 137, noting that reasonableness review might serve different functions in different jurisdictions.

82 In *R (Association of British Civilian Internees (Far East Region))* v. *Secretary of State for Defence*, the Court of Appeal appeared to think that *Wednesbury's* days were numbered, but that the House of Lords would have to perform *Wednesbury's* 'burial rites'. [2003] QB 1397 at [35], per Lord Dyson MR. But the Supreme Court recently refused to perform the burial rites when invited to do so in *Keyu* v. *Foreign Secretary* [2015] 3 WLR 1665 [*Keyu*].

83 [2001] 2 AC 532 [*Daly*].

84 *Daly* at [27].

85 [2001] 1 WLR 840 at [18].

86 *Daly* at [28]. See also at [32], per Lord Cooke of Thorndon.

87 See generally Sir John Laws, '*Wednesbury*' in Christopher Forsyth and Ivan Hare (eds.), *The Golden Metwand and the Crooked Cord* (Oxford: Oxford University Press, 1998), pp. 186–7.

88 See, e.g., *R* v. *Environment Secretary, ex parte Hammersmith and Fulham London Borough Council* [1991] 1 AC 521.

89 *R* v. *Secretary of State for the Home Department, ex parte Bugdaycay* [1987] AC 514 at 531, per Lord Bridge; *R* v. *Secretary of State for the Home Department, ex parte Brind* [1991] AC 696 at 748–9, per Lord Bridge; *R* v. *Ministry of Defence, ex parte Smith* [1996] QB 517; Paul Craig, 'Judicial review and anxious scrutiny: foundations, evolution and application' (2015) *Public Law* 60.

90 [2015] 1 WLR 1591 at [96] [*Pham*].

The catalyst is the apparent acceptance by the Supreme Court of Professor Craig's view of the conceptual similarity between *Wednesbury* and proportionality.[91] Consider the following *dictum* of Lord Mance in *Kennedy*: 'Both reasonableness review and proportionality involve considerations of weight and balance, with the intensity of the scrutiny and the weight to be given to any primary decision maker's view depending on the context.'[92] This was taken further in *Pham*, where it was said of Lord Mance's reasons in *Kennedy* that 'a majority of this court endorsed a flexible approach to principles of judicial review, particularly where important rights are at stake'.[93] Lord Mance himself (writing for a group of four judges on a seven-judge court) found it, in the context of a decision stripping a British national of citizenship (with the corollary that he would also lose the benefits of being a European Union national), 'improbable that the nature, strictness or outcome of such a review would differ according to whether it was conducted under domestic principles or whether it was also required to be conducted by reference to a principle of proportionality derived from Union law'.[94]

Lord Sumption, with whom three other judges agreed, was even more expansive. He noted that the use of proportionality in cases involving human rights and EU law but not domestic law produced 'some rather arbitrary distinctions between essentially similar issues'.[95] Here, for instance, the citizenship decision would be reviewed on domestic judicial review grounds, but if it had an EU law aspect would fall to be considered in accordance with the EU principle of proportionality. Nonetheless, despite the failure to embrace proportionality, English law 'has for many years stumbled towards a concept which is in significant respects similar, and over the last three decades has been influenced by European jurisprudence even in areas of law lying beyond the domains of EU and international human rights law'.[96] In commenting on Lord Steyn's discussion of *Wednesbury* and proportionality in *Daly*, Lord Sumption said:

> *It is for the court to assess how broad the range of rational decisions is in the circumstances of any given case.* That must necessarily depend on the significance of the right interfered with, the degree of interference involved, and notably the extent to which, even on a statutory appeal, the court is competent to reassess the balance which the decision-maker was called on to make given the subject-matter. The differences pointed out by Lord Steyn may in practice be more or less significant depending on the answers to these questions. In some cases, the range of rational decisions is so narrow as to determine the outcome.[97]

What will ultimately matter, Lord Sumption seems to suggest, is 'the strength of the justification or the breadth of the decision-maker's margin of judgment'.[98] On this emergent view – on which no '[f]inal conclusions' have been reached[99] – there is no great difference between *Wednesbury* and proportionality. Both involve questions of weight and balance,

91 Paul Craig, 'The Nature of Reasonableness Review' (2013) 66 *Current Legal Problems* 131.

92 *Kennedy* v. *Charity Commission (Secretary of State for Justice intervening)* [2015] AC 455 at [54], [*Kennedy*].

93 *Pham* at [60].

94 *Pham* at [98].

95 *Pham* at [104].

96 *Pham* at [105].

97 *Pham* at [107], emphasis added.

98 *Pham* at [109]. See also *R (Sinclair Collis Ltd)* v. *Secretary of State for Health* [2012] QB 394 at [200] (Lord Neuberger of Abbotsbury MR), cited by Lord Carnwath in *R (Rotherham Metropolitan Borough Council)* v. *Secretary of State for Business, Innovation and Skills* [2015] UKSC 6.

99 *Keyu* v. *Foreign Secretary* Keyu at [278], per Lord Kerr. See also *Youssef* v. *Foreign Secretary* [2016] 2 WLR 509 at [55], per Lord Carnwath, expressing his desire for an 'authoritative review' of academic and comparative material before reaching a final conclusion.

which fall to be assessed in the context of particular factual and legal matrices that create broader or narrower ranges of possible outcomes, depending on the circumstances. It is clear from the recent cases that the Supreme Court finds significant attraction in the concept, most clearly advocated by Lord Sumption, of a 'range of rational outcomes', which will be broader or narrower depending on all the circumstances.[100]

8.3.2 *Canada*

It has justly been said that Canadian administrative law resembles an on-going construction site.[101] By 2003, the pragmatic and functional approach featured four factors (noted previously) and three distinct standards of review: correctness, reasonableness *simpliciter* and patent unreasonableness. No sooner had the Supreme Court of Canada forged an apparent consensus on the structure of the pragmatic and functional approach, however, than cracks began to appear in the façade.[102] Faced with mounting unhappiness in the legal profession about the complexity of the pragmatic and functional analysis,[103] the Court took the opportunity presented by *Dunsmuir* v. *New Brunswick* to renovate Canadian administrative law doctrine.[104] The four factors, with their unerringly substantive focus, were replaced by a set of categories.[105] Of most interest for present purposes is the Court's move from three standards of review to two. Correctness remained, but Bastarache and LeBel JJ introduced a new definition of the reasonableness standard:

> A court conducting a review for reasonableness inquires into the qualities that make a decision reasonable, referring both to the process of articulating the reasons and to outcomes. In judicial review, reasonableness is concerned mostly with the existence of justification, transparency and intelligibility within the decision-making process. But it is also concerned with whether the decision falls within a range of possible, acceptable outcomes which are defensible in respect of the facts and law.[106]

Reasonableness has become the dominant standard of review in Canada.[107] It applies even to administrative decisions involving constitutional matters.[108] The details of the rise of

100 Note, however, that in *Kennedy*, Lord Carnwath confessed himself 'unpersuaded that domestic judicial review, even adopting the most flexible view of the developing jurisprudence, can achieve the same practical effect in a case such as the present as full merits review under . . . the HRA'. *Kennedy* at [267]. See also Lord Reed's doubts in *Pham* 'that the *Wednesbury* test, even when applied with "heightened" or "anxious" scrutiny, is identical to the principle of proportionality as understood in EU law, or as it has been explained in cases decided under the Human Rights Act 1998'. *Pham* at [115].

101 David Stratas, 'The Canadian Law of Judicial Review: A Plea for Doctrinal Coherence and Consistency' (2016) 42 *Queen's Law Journal* 27.

102 *Toronto (City)* v. *Canadian Union of Public Employees, Local* 79 [2003] 3 SCR 77 at [60–135]. For discussion, see Paul Daly, 'The Language of Administrative Law' (2016) 94 *Canadian Bar Review* 519.

103 My evidence here is anecdotal only. Interestingly enough, private criticism rarely manifested itself in the reasons of lower courts or the writings of scholars.

104 [2008] 1 SCR 190 [*Dunsmuir*].

105 *Smith* v. *Alliance Pipeline* [2011] 1 SCR 160 at [26].

106 *Dunsmuir* at [47]. The expansive language relating to the 'justification, transparency and intelligibility' of the decision-making process has subsequently been significantly qualified, such that it requires only a comprehensible basis for the decision. See *Newfoundland and Labrador Nurses' Union* v. *Newfoundland and Labrador (Treasury Board)* [2011] 3 SCR 708.

107 John Evans, 'Triumph of Reasonableness: But How Much Does It Really Matter?' (2014) 27 *Canadian Journal of Administrative Law & Practice* 101.

108 *Doré* v. *Barreau du Québec* [2012] 1 SCR 395. Save where the constitutional validity of a law is frontally attacked, in which case the administrative tribunal's conclusions will be subject to correctness review, as in *Saskatchewan (Human Rights Commission)* v. *Whatcott* [2013] 1 SCR 467.

reasonableness are not important for present purposes.[109] What matters is that the concept of a 'range' of reasonable outcomes is now central to Canadian administrative law. Cases subsequent to *Dunsmuir* teach that reasonableness 'takes its colour from its context';[110] and that the 'range will necessarily vary',[111] which is to 'be assessed in the context of the particular type of decision making involved and all relevant factors'.[112]

Much of the post-*Dunsmuir* jurisprudence, especially the decisions of lower courts, and academic literature have been concerned with fleshing out the concept of a 'range' and better understanding the importance of context.[113] It seems to be the case that context can be cabined by reference to the principles said in *Dunsmuir* to underlie Canada's law of judicial review: the rule of law and democracy.[114] These are very broad principles, of course, but in Canadian administrative law, they tend to equate to, respectively, the protection of constitutional fundamentals (including rights) and giving effect to legislative intent. Accordingly, in cases involving fundamental constitutional values or important individual interests, the range of reasonable outcomes will be narrower.[115] Prior judicial decisions on matters subsequently considered by an administrative tribunal will tend also to narrow the range of reasonable outcomes,[116] as will, potentially, the need to give effect to international obligations.[117]

Legislative intent also plays a role in setting the range of reasonable outcomes. The range of reasonable outcomes may be 'circumscribed' by reference to 'the rationale of the statutory regime',[118] or the legislature might have specified 'a recipe of factors to be considered', narrowing 'the range of options the decision-maker legitimately has'.[119] Equally, however, powers might have been granted in broad terms,[120] to a democratically accountable or expert decision-maker, such that the range of reasonable outcomes will be relatively large.[121] As a result, 'reviewing courts can afford the administrative decision-maker hardly any margin or no margin of appreciation, a moderate margin, or a broad margin'.[122]

The Canadian courts have also provided guidance about how to determine when a decision falls outside the permissible range. Briefly, there is a two-step process, involving the identification of a 'badge of unreasonableness',[123] which then must be assessed in light of the reasons and evidence contained in the record before the reviewing court:

109 See generally Paul Daly, 'Unreasonable Interpretations of Law' in Joseph T Robertson, Peter Gall and Paul Daly, *Judicial Deference to Administrative Tribunals in Canada: Its Past and Future* (Toronto: LexisNexis, 2014); Paul Daly, 'The Scope and Meaning of Reasonableness Review' (2015) 52 *Alberta Law Review* 799.

110 *Canada (Citizenship and Immigration)* v. *Khosa* [2009] 1 SCR 339 at [59].

111 *Wilson* v. *Atomic Energy Agency of Canada* [2016] 1 SCR 770 at [22] [*Wilson*].

112 *Catalyst Paper Corp* v. *North Cowichan (District)* [2012] 1 SCR 5 at [18] [*Catalyst Paper*].

113 It must be noted that the Supreme Court of Canada has resolutely avoided taking a position on the attempts of lower courts and commentators to firm up the analytical structure of reasonableness review. But see *Wilson*, where Abella J expressed some openness towards the possibility of applying reasonableness review in all circumstances; four other judges expressed their appreciation for her 'efforts to stimulate a discussion on how to clarify or simplify our standard of review jurisprudence to better promote certainty and predictability' (at [70]).

114 *Dunsmuir* at [27].

115 *Loyola High School* v. *Quebec (Attorney General)* [2015] 1 SCR 613, at [38].

116 *Canada (Attorney General)* v. *Canadian Human Rights Commission* 2013 FCA 75 at [16] and [18].

117 *Canada (Attorney General)* v. *Igloo Vikski Inc* [2016] 2 SCR 80, at [58], per Côté J, dissenting.

118 *Catalyst Paper* at [25].

119 *Canada (Minister of Transport, Infrastructure and Communities)* v. *Jagjit Singh Farwaha* 2014 FCA 56 at [91] [*Farwaha*].

120 See, e.g., *Re: Sound* v. *Canadian Association of Broadcasters* 2017 FCA 138 at [40].

121 *Re*: Sound at [40]. See also *Forest Ethics Advocacy Association* v. *Canada (National Energy Board)* 2014 FCA 245 at [69].

122 *Canada* v. *Kabul Farms Inc* 2016 FCA 143 at [24].

123 *Delios* v. *Canada (Attorney General)* 2015 FCA 117 at [27].

> Where a decision is indelibly tainted by a badge or badges of unreasonableness, judicial intervention will be more or less appropriate depending on the range of reasonable outcomes. For instance, the narrower the range, the more that will be required by way of explanation of the badge(s) of unreasonableness tainting the decision. Conversely, the wider the range, the less a reviewing court should require by way of explanation.[124]

8.3.3 *Explaining Convergence*

Just as historical happenstance provides the best explanation of the divergence between English and Canadian administrative law, accidents of history best explain the recent convergence. On the Canadian side, unhappiness in the legal community with the overly complex approach to administrative law developed by the Supreme Court of Canada led the Court to renovate Canada's law of judicial review of administrative action. Reasonableness has since become the central organising principle of Canadian administrative law. Given its centrality, it is unsurprising that Canadian courts and commentators have sought to develop their understanding of reasonableness. It can now fairly be said that reasonableness is an analytically robust feature of Canada's legal landscape. But there was nothing inevitable about the rise of reasonableness: the Court developed a new definition of reasonableness when decomplexifying its approach to administrative law in response to criticism from the legal community.

English judges and scholars' hesitant[125] embrace of the concept of a range of rational outcomes can also be understood as having been prompted by complexity. With the interrelationship of European Union law, European Human Rights Law and the common law, English administrative law has come to resemble a 'spaghetti junction'.[126] Anyone who has encountered the famous interchange in Birmingham will happily (or perhaps grudgingly) testify that it is very difficult to navigate – English judges have found the legal equivalent just as challenging. In cases such as *Pham*, where citizenship was at issue, it is quite possible that an applicant will be able to claim EU-law rights (to which the doctrine of proportionality applies), Convention rights (to which proportionality also applies, subject to the additional limitation of the 'margin of appreciation' at the European level and, perhaps, to a 'discretionary area of judgment' domestically[127]) and the protection of the common law (certainly *Wednesbury* unreasonableness and, in some circumstances, the principle of legality[128]). Categorising these different types of claim is difficult and the obvious overlaps create a significant risk that a claim will be assigned incorrectly, leading to the application of a more or less intrusive standard of review than appropriate. Advocates of a one-size-fits-all proportionality test have as yet been unable to convince other members of the legal community to adopt proportionality across the board. Recent judicial experience suggests that wide

124 Paul Daly, 'Struggling Towards Coherence in Canadian Administrative Law: Recent Cases on Standard of Review and Reasonableness' (2016) 62 *McGill Law Journal* 527 at 558. See also *Workplace Health, Safety and Compensation Commission* v. *Allen* 2014 NLCA 42 at [41]; *Delios* at [21–7].

125 Their hesitancy can perhaps be understood as arising from concern to leave well-enough alone, especially in the absence of a statutory basis to justify change. See generally Mark Elliott, 'The Human Rights Act 1998 and the Standard of Substantive Review' (2001) 60 *Cambridge Law Journal* 301, and especially Philip Sales, 'Rationality, Proportionality and the Development of the Law' (2013) 129 *Law Quarterly Review* 223.

126 Carol Harlow and Richard Rawlings (eds.), *Law and Administration* (Cambridge: Cambridge University Press, 2009) p. 677, fig. 15.5, 'Spaghetti junction'.

127 *R (Nicklinson)* v. *Ministry of Justice* [2015] AC 657 at [296], per Lord Reed.

128 *R* v. *Secretary of State for the Home Department, Ex p Simms* [2000] 2 AC 115 at 131.

application of the protean concept of proportionality would require the development of additional doctrinal tools (such as deference) in order to ensure that the proportionality test is applied with appropriate intensity across the wide spectrum of administrative law cases, ranging from fundamental rights on one end to purely economic interests at the other extreme. This, I submit, explains the recent interest in the concept of a range of rational outcomes.

Again, it is difficult to identify a deeply rooted distinction between the English and Canadian systems that would account for the halting convergence between the two over the last decade. Rather, in responding to complexity – judicially created in Canada, legislatively created in England – courts and commentators in each jurisdiction have found it useful to rely upon the concept of a range of rational outcomes.

8.4 THE FUTURE: FURTHER CONVERGENCE?

In Canada, the creative tension between the rule of law and democracy – constitutional principles recognised by the Supreme Court of Canada[129] – provides a crucible in which judicial review doctrine is formed. There is no ready equivalent in English administrative law, certainly none at present that would attract the consensus that Canadian constitutional principles enjoy. Nonetheless, there have been attempts to mark out the boundaries of substantive review in ways that may also be helpful in setting limits to ranges of rational outcomes. In an influential essay, Jeffrey Jowell set out two general reasons for deference, which he termed 'constitutional competence' and 'institutional competence'.[130] Similarly, Mark Elliott has argued that beneath the vocabulary of *Wednesbury* and proportionality lie normative values, 'a network of deeper considerations that determine what doctrinal instruments should be brought to bear in the circumstances of the case, and precisely what form those instruments should take given the particularities of context'.[131] In terms of constitutional competence, the identity of the decision-maker might have an effect on the range of rational outcomes. For instance, 'in a democracy a person charged with making assessments of this kind should be politically responsible for them. Ministers are politically responsible for the consequences of their decision. Judges are not'.[132] Similarly, it has been said, '[t]he formulation and the implementation of national economic policy are matters depending essentially on political judgment' such that the relevant decisions 'are for politicians to take' and to be debated 'in the political forum of the House of Commons'.[133] As a result, discretionary, policy-infused decisions taken by democratically elected and accountable politicians fall to be assessed against a broad range of rational outcomes. And as in Canada, broad statutory language (which has the imprimatur of Parliament) can empower decision-makers, making the range of rational outcomes relatively broader.[134] But constitutional competence is not a one-way ratchet. Statutory language will, when couched in objective terms, constrain

129 *Dunsmuir* at [27]. See also *Reference re Secession of Quebec* [1998] 2 SCR 217.

130 'Of *Vires* and Vacuums: the Constitutional Context of Judicial Review' (1999) *Public Law* 448 at 451.

131 'From Bifurcation to Calibration: Twin-Track Deference and the Culture of Justification' in Mark Elliott and Hanna Wilberg (eds.), *The Scope and Intensity of Substantive Judicial Review: Traversing Taggart's Rainbow* (Oxford: Hart, 2015), 61 at 65.

132 *R (Lord Carlile)* v. *Secretary of State for the Home Department* [2015] AC 945 at [32] [*Lord Carlile*].

133 R v. *Environment Secretary, ex parte Hammersmith and Fulham London Borough Council* [1991] 1 AC 521 at 597, per Lord Bridge of Harwich.

134 *South Yorkshire Transport.*

decision-makers and narrow the range of rational outcomes. And when rights or important individual interests are in play, the range of rational outcomes will be narrower.[135]

In terms of institutional competence, administrative decision-makers often have greater expertise relative to courts in respect of the subject matter falling within their jurisdiction. As Lord Slynn of Hadley put it in *R* v. *Chief Constable of Sussex, ex parte International Trader's Ferry*, where the Chief Constable had struck a balance in allocating police resources to quell disruptive protests, deference was due: 'He knows through his officers the local situation, the availability of officers and his financial resources [and] the other demands on the police in the area at different times.'[136] Similarly, a minister has access to the 'collective knowledge, experience and expertise of all those who serve the Crown in the department',[137] which helps explain why ministerial decisions on matters within departmental expertise are typically accorded significant deference by the courts. In such circumstances, the range of rational outcomes will be broader. Polycentricity,[138] according to which problems 'cannot be resolved independently and sequentially' but are 'interdependent and a choice from one set of alternatives has implications for preferences within other sets of alternatives',[139] will also enlarge the range of rational outcomes,[140] as will complex situations that require evaluative judgement on the part of decision-makers.[141] But on more strictly legal issues involving concepts with which judges are familiar, or are at least no less expert than the primary decision-maker, the range of rational outcomes will be narrower.[142]

Conceiving of ranges that are broader or narrower depending on circumstances involves an analytical exercise that is already familiar to English administrative lawyers. It is very similar to the operation of the 'anxious scrutiny' principle, whereby '[t]he more substantial the interference with human rights, the more the court will require by way of justification before it is satisfied that the decision is reasonable'.[143] It is also similar to the context-sensitive application of the rules of natural justice, whereby the content of procedural fairness increases in proportion to the importance of the decision to the individual concerned.[144] And an English public lawyer might derive badges of unreasonableness from the administrative law cases: for instance, one could say that failure to give sufficient weight to a fundamental right,[145] or inconsistent treatment of two similarly situated individuals, are badges of unreasonableness,[146] and that arbitrary or illogical decisions bear badges of unreasonableness.[147]

135 *R* v. *Home Secretary ex p Khawaja* [1984] AC 74; *R* v. *Secretary of State for the Home Department, ex parte Bugdaycay* [1987] AC 514 at 531; *R* v. *Secretary of State for the Home Department, ex parte Brind* [1991] AC 696 at 748–9; *R* v. *Ministry of Defence, ex parte Smith* [1996] QB 517 at 554; *Pham* at [108].

136 [1999] 2 AC 418 at 430.

137 *Bushell* v. *Environment Secretary* [1981] AC 75 at 95, per Lord Diplock.

138 Lon Fuller, 'The Forms and Limits of Adjudication' (1978) 92 *Harvard Law Review* 3553.

139 Anthony Ogus, *Regulation: Legal Form and Economic Theory* (Oxford: Clarendon Press, 1994), p. 117.

140 See, e.g., *R* v. *Cambridge Health Authority, ex parte B* [1995] 1 WLR 898 at 906.

141 See, e.g., *(Lord Carlile)* at [32]; *Youssef* v. *Secretary of State for Foreign and Commonwealth Affairs* [2016] 2 WLR 509 at [50].

142 See, e.g., *Vavilov* v. *Canada (Citizenship and Immigration)* 2017 FCA 132, at [36].

143 *R* v. *Ministry of Defence, ex parte Smith* [1996] QB 517, at 554, per Sir Thomas Bingham MR.

144 See, e.g., *McInnes* v. *Onslow-Fane* [1978] 1 WLR 1520 at 1529; *R* v. *Home Secretary, ex parte Fayed* [1998] 1 WLR 763.

145 See, e.g., *Hall and Co Ltd* v. *Shoreham-by-Sea Urban District Council* [1964] 1 WLR 240 and *R* v. *Hillingdon London Borough Council, ex parte Royco Homes Ltd* [1974] QB 720, both involving interference with interests in property.

146 See, e.g., *Re L* [2003] 2 AC 633.

147 See, e.g., *Champion* v. *Chief Constable of Gwent* [1990] 1 WLR 1.

Thus English courts and commentators might usefully draw from the Canadian experience with reasonableness review in order to better understand the concept of a range of rational outcomes. It may even be possible to expand the application of the concept beyond the domain of review of discretionary decisions. Take, for instance, the grounds of review of improper purposes and relevant considerations. In England, these have traditionally been treated as distinct from *Wednesbury* unreasonableness in the sense of a decision-maker who has acted irrationally: it is for the courts to determine the propriety of purpose and relevancy of consideration.[148] If reasonableness is a 'sliding scale' dependent on context, we can surely say that statutory purposes and statutory considerations form part of the context, limiting the range of potential outcomes.[149] Indeed, the same could be said of review for error of law: sometimes the statutory language will create a wide range of rational outcomes;[150] on other occasions, the range will be narrower, perhaps containing only one possible outcome.

Already, the English courts have signalled a limited retreat from the advances widely thought to have been accomplished by *Anisminic* – in *Cart* the UK Supreme Court did not employ the concept of jurisdictional error to determine how to control alleged illegalities committed by the Upper Tribunal and preferred to rely on pragmatic considerations to limit the scope of review.[151] Subsequently, Lord Carnwath suggested in *Jones (Caldwell)* v. *First Tier Tribunal*[152] that the distinction between law and fact – upon which close judicial control of administrative interpretations of law logically depends – does not accomplish significant analytical work. Rather, 'the division between law and fact in such classification cases is not purely objective, but must take account of factors of "expediency" or "policy"', including 'the utility of an appeal, having regard to the development of the law in the particular field, and the relative competencies in that field of the tribunal of fact on the one hand, and the appellate court on the other'.[153] The suggestion is noteworthy not only because it presages a future in which contextual considerations play a role in determining the appropriate level of judicial scrutiny of alleged errors of law (as they do in Canada) but also because it underscores how contingent change in administrative law doctrine can be. The decisions in *Cart* and *Jones* arose from cases involving the new tribunal structure introduced by the Tribunal, Courts and Enforcement Act 2007, which has required English courts to grapple with the limitations of jurisdictional error and the importance of context in determining the intensity of judicial review of administrative action. And the author of the noteworthy comments in *Jones* was, as Sir Robert Carnwath, the first Senior President of Tribunals appointed under the 2007 Act; in other words, due to historical happenstance, a jurist well placed to appreciate the effects of the 2007 Act found himself involved in a case raising important questions about jurisdictional error and was able to deliver a reasoned judgment that may well prove influential in the future development of English administrative law.[154]

148 *Tesco Stores* v. *Secretary of State for the Environment* [1995] 1 WLR 759.

149 See, e.g., Rebecca Williams, 'Structuring Substantive Review' (2017) *Public Law* 99.

150 *South Yorkshire Transport*.

151 See generally Christopher Forsyth, '"Blasphemy against Basics": Doctrine, Conceptual Reasoning and Certain Decisions of the UK Supreme Court' in John Bell, Mark Elliott, Jason Varuhas and Philip Murray (eds.), *Public Law Adjudication in Common Law Systems: Process and Substance* (Oxford: Hart, 2016), p. 145.

152 [2013] 2 AC 48 [*Jones*]. Lord Hope gave the leading judgment for a five-judge panel, but Lord Carnwath's 'brief comment on the course of the proceedings, having regard also to the new framework established under the Tribunals Courts and Enforcement Act 2007' (at [27]) attracted the accord of three other judges.

153 *Jones* at [46], citing Robert Carnwath, 'Tribunal Justice, A New Start' (2009) *Public Law* 48, at 63–4. See also *Moyna* v. *Secretary of State for Work and Pensions* [2003] 1 WLR 1929.

154 See Christopher Forsyth's contribution to this volume.

8.5 CONCLUSION

It is tempting for comparative public lawyers to focus on and even exaggerate difference while overlooking similarities. It makes for more interesting scholarship, for one thing.[155] Moreover, influential comparative public lawyers have been sceptical of cross-country comparisons, particularly on substantive review.[156] And, of course, there are theorists for whom any comparative study must inevitably collapse into a disquisition on difference.[157] I do not dispute the editors' observation in the Introduction that there is much difference to be explored in the common law world, and I accept that these explorations may yield a great deal of useful knowledge. As I have argued, however, differences in approach to substantive review might be the result of historical happenstance – bumps along a path-dependent road. This is likely to be especially true of jurisdictions with a shared legal heritage;[158] as is the case with England and Canada, abundant similarity is present in the law of judicial review of administrative action (notwithstanding the development of unique features in both). I have thus set out a positive case for further comparative study of substantive review in the two jurisdictions, notwithstanding the surface differences that portend deep disagreement. That administrative law in both countries springs from the same source helps explain why divergence has been relatively recent and the brightness of the prospects for future convergence.

155 Though see Janina Boughey, *Human Rights and Judicial Review in Australia and Canada: The Newest Despotism?* (Oxford: Hart, 2017).

156 See especially Cheryl Saunders, 'Apples, Oranges and Comparative Administrative Law' (2006) *Acta Juridica* 423; 'Constitution as Catalyst: Different Paths within Australasian Administrative Law' (2012) 10 *New Zealand Journal of Public and International Law* 143.

157 See, e.g., Pierre Legrand, 'The Same and the Different' in Roderick Munday and Pierre Legrand (eds.), *Comparative Legal Studies: Traditions and Transitions* (Cambridge: Cambridge University Press, 2003).

158 Han-Ru Zhou, 'A Contextual Defense of "Comparative Constitutional Common Law"' (2014) 12 *International Journal of Constitutional Law* 1034. Cf. Peter Cane, *Controlling Administrative Power: An Historical Comparison* (Cambridge: Cambridge University Press, 2016), noting profound differences between Anglo-Australian and American public law.

PART V

Origins and Adaptations in the Middle East and Africa

9

English Administrative Law in the Holy Land

Tradition and Independence

Daphne Barak-Erez

9.1 INTRODUCTION

The long-lasting influence of English administrative law on Israeli administrative law is one of the most enduring legacies from the British Mandatory rule of the area where Israel was later established, known at the time as Palestine. This period, 1917–1948, was relatively short in comparison to the length of time that the British had dominion over other territories (mostly in the more conventional colonial model), as well as in comparison to the long period of Ottoman rule in the land (approximately four hundred years). It was, however, very significant in terms of its long-lasting impact. British rule brought with it concepts of the 'rule of law' that proved to be crucial for the future development of law in Israel. This chapter begins by describing the process of absorbing English law into Israeli law. It then points out the most influential principles to have left their mark on the system. It then considers the process by which Israeli administrative law gradually acquired its independence in breaking away from English principles of administrative law. This discussion highlights the most significant departures from the traditional administrative law principles, as inherited from English law, as well as the significance of later developments in the Israeli legal sphere and constitutional arena. The implications for the potential directions for future development are then discussed.

9.2 INITIAL ABSORPTION DURING THE PERIOD OF THE BRITISH MANDATE

The process of adopting and transplanting the principles of English administrative law was based on two important provisions included in the Palestine Order in Council, 1922. First, article 46 of this Order in Council stated that when domestic courts are faced with legal questions to which there is no answer in local law, they should decide them by using the principles of English common law and equity.[1] In addition, article 43 of the same Order in

[1] Article 46 of the Palestine Order in Council stated: 'The jurisdiction of the Civil Courts shall be exercised in conformity with the Ottoman Law in force in Palestine on November 1st, 1914, and such later Ottoman Laws as have been or may be declared to be in force by Public Notice, and such Orders in Council, Ordinances and regulations as are in force in Palestine at the date of the commencement of this Order, or may hereafter be applied or enacted; and subject thereto and so far as the same shall not extend or apply, shall be exercised in conformity with the substance of the common law, and the doctrines of equity in force in England, and with the powers vested in and according to the procedure and practice observed by or before Courts of Justice and Justices of the Peace in England, according to their respective jurisdictions and authorities at that date, save in so far as the said powers, procedure and practice may have been or may hereafter be modified, amended or replaced by any other provisions. Provided always that the said common law and doctrines of equity shall be in force in Palestine so

Council established the Supreme Court of the land and authorized it to function as a 'High Court of Justice', based on the model of the High Court of Justice in the UK (even borrowing the name), with the power to issue prerogative orders against the government.[2] While called the High Court of Justice, interestingly, in Palestine this power was given to the Supreme Court and not to courts of first instance.[3] The adoption of this model of judicial review expressed itself not only in the content of judicial opinions, as the following discussion shows, but also in the importation of the procedures of judicial review – starting with the preliminary stage of issuing order nisi, and then - after evaluation - discharging the order nisi or deciding to make it absolute.[4] At the same time, it was held that the scope of the jurisdiction of the court is even wider than that of its English counterpart.[5]

The change brought about by the importation of English administrative law into the local legal system was dramatic, especially taking into consideration the nature of the legal regime in the Ottoman Empire. Ottoman law, as applied in then Palestine, was based upon principles of Muslim law and transplants from European legislation of the nineteenth century, and it was focused on the regulation of civil, criminal and family law. In contrast, during the years of the British Mandate, petitions against the government became a common phenomenon, and this process led to growing numbers of administrative law decisions, which gradually adopted principles of English administrative law and, thus, shaped local law in this area. These decisions included a wide range of doctrines from English administrative law, covering questions of the authorization to act (the ultra vires doctrine) and the appropriateness of administrative discretion and administrative process.[6] This process of importing

far only as the circumstances of Palestine and its inhabitants and the limits of His Majesty's jurisdiction permit and subject to such qualification as local circumstances render necessary.'

2 Article 43 of the Palestine Order in Council stated: 'There shall be established a Court to be called the Supreme Court of which the constitution shall be prescribed by Ordinance. The Supreme Court sitting as a Court of Appeal shall have jurisdiction subject to the provisions of any Ordinance to hear appeals from all judgments given by a District Court in first instance or by the Court of Criminal Azzize or by a Land Court. The Supreme Court sitting as a High Court of Justice, shall have jurisdiction to hear and determine such matters as are not causes or trials, but petitions or applications not within the jurisdiction of any other Court and necessary to be decided for the administration of justice'. On the basis of this, the powers of the court were defined also by the Courts Ordinance, enacted in 1924. Section 6 to this ordinance stated that '[t]he High Court of Justice shall have exclusive jurisdiction in the following matters – (a) applications (in nature of habeas corpus proceedings) for orders of release of persons unlawfully detained in custody; (b) orders directed to public officers or public bodies in regard to the performance of their public duties and requiring them to do or refrain from doing certain acts'.

3 For the historical background, see Yair Sagy, 'For the Administration of Justice: On the Establishment of the High Court of Justice' (2004), 28 *Tel Aviv University Law Review* 225 (in Hebrew).

4 See High Court Rules, 1937, Palestine Gazette Supp 2, 301. The current regulations (High Court of Justice Procedure Regulations, 1984) are based to a large extent on the historical rules.

5 HC 78/38 *Havkin* v. *Inspector General of Police and Prisons*, 7 PLR 35, 41 (1940) ('I think it is clear that this Court will exercise a wider jurisdiction, conferred upon it by law, than that of the Supreme Court of England, but that jurisdiction is discretionary, and remedies will not be given unless they are necessary in the interests of justice.').

6 See e.g. HC 69/25 *Federman* v. *Sir Ronald Storrs, District Commissioner, Jerusalem – Southern District*, 1 PLR 57 (1920–1933) (making absolute an order nisi in circumstances in which limitations were put on the sale of meat produced by slaughtering on the beach of Jaffa without the supervision of the Tel-Aviv Rabbinate because there was no legislative authorization to do so); HC 9/38 *Weinberg* v. *District Commissioner, Jerusalem District*, 5 PLR (1938) (making absolute an order nisi regarding a decision to cancel the petitioner's license as a petition writer without giving him the opportunity to answer an alleged charge of misconduct); HC 76/39 *Abir Company Ltd.* v. *Inspector-General of Police and Prisons*, 7 PLR 31 (1940) (the court discharged an order nisi in a petition that concerned future distribution of permits and explained that, while the licensing authority must act impartially in the future, the court could not make an order in this matter since there was nothing to justify the conclusion that the authority was intending not to do so); HC 3/42 *Ben-Ami* v. *Local Council Kfar Yona*, 9 PLR 75 (1942) (an order nisi was discharged in the case of a petitioner, who was refused a license to keep a café, because it was not established that the respondent had acted capriciously, with bias, or due to improper motives or other wrong reasons).

English administrative law was enhanced by what is now known as the 'Anglification' of the law of Palestine during that period, which also occurred in other branches of law. Generally speaking, new legislation reformed completely various areas of law, including criminal law, corporate law and more. In addition, the courts started to guide themselves by common law principles and precedents.[7]

An interesting aspect of the growing influence of English administrative law is the fact that, during the last decade of the British Mandate in Palestine, many judgments in this area concerned the use of emergency powers in matters involving the Jewish community's struggle for independence and against the continuation of the rule of the British Mandate. The judgments tended to dismiss petitions brought against decisions that were based on these emergency powers, stating that the decisions were intra vires and based on valid legal grounds.[8] It is, therefore, worthwhile noting that despite the results in many of these cases, the reference to English administrative law (as well as to emergency powers legislated by the British authorities) was very much welcomed after independence. The court adopted a clear distinction between the disappointing results during the time of the British Mandate (from a national perspective) and the desirability of the doctrines themselves – the doctrines of English administrative law in general as well as the emergency powers legislated during the time of the British Mandate .[9]

7 Daniel Friedman, 'The Effect of Foreign Law on the Law of Israel: Remnant of the Ottoman Period' (1975), 10 *Israel Law Review* 192; Daniel Friedman, 'The Effect of Foreign Law on the Law of Israel: Infusion of the Common Law into the Legal System of Israel' (1975), 10 *Israeli Law Review* 324. For more background on the legal system in Mandatory Palestine, see Ronen Shamir, *The Colonies of Law: Colonialism, Zionism, and Law in Early Mandate Palestine* (Cambridge: Cambridge University Press, 2000); Ron Harris, Alexandre Kedar, Pnina Lahav and Assaf Likhovski (eds.), *The History of Law in a Multi-Cultural Society: Israel 1917–1967* (Aldershot: Ashgate Publishing, 2002); Assaf Likhovi, *Law and Identity in Mandate Palestine* (University of North Carolina Press, 2006); Ron Harris and Michael Crystal, 'Some Reflections on the Transplantation of British Company Law in Post-Ottoman Palestine (2009), 10 *Theoretical Inquiries in Law* 561.

8 See e.g. HC 40/47 *Rokach* v. *General Officer Commanding British Troops in Palestine and Trans-Jordan*, 14 PLR 154 (1947) (dismissing a petition against the execution of underground member, Dov Gruner); HC 86/47 *Kirshenbaum* v. *Major-General E.L. Bols*, 14 PLR 423 (1947) (dismissing a petition against the forfeiture of houses based on Regulation 119 of the Defense (Emergency) Regulations, 1945, where some of their inhabitants had abetted an offence of violence against the British authorities). It is worthwhile to add that during these years, the courts in the UK itself also adopted a relatively narrow scope of judicial review, against the background of the Second World War. See *Liversidge* v. *Anderson* [1942] AC 206.

9 This included the use of emergency powers in contexts such as confiscation of property and administrative detentions. See HCJ 5/48 *Leon* v. *The Acting Commissioner of the Urban Area of Tel-Aviv (Yehoshua Gubernik)*, 1 PD 58, 68 (1948) ('We do not think that the legislature of a democratic state is precluded from passing a law which enables the making of Emergency Regulations. Laws such as these are to be found in the most democratic of Constitutions. ... The governing consideration here is not the existence of Emergency Regulations but the manner in which they are employed. There is no room today for the submission that Emergency Regulations made in the time of the Mandate are no longer in force because they were then used for anti-Jewish purposes.'); HCJ 10/48 *Zeev* v. *The Acting Commissioner of the Urban Area of Tel-Aviv (Yehoshua Gubernik)*, 1 PD 85 (1948). Both cases dismissed petitions against decisions to take possession of private apartments for the use of government officials based on special emergency powers (stipulated by the Defense Regulations, 1939, and the Defense (Emergency) Regulations, 1945). In HCJ 7/48 *El-Karboutly* v. *Minister of Defense*, 2 PD 5 (1948) the court accepted a habeas corpus petition in the matter of a person who was under administrative detention based on Regulation 111 of the Defense (Emergency) Regulations, 1945 – but the judgment was limited to the circumstances of the case. Since the advising committee of the Military Commander was not established, the court stated that the commander had no power to give an order of administrative detention (despite the fact that the committee was only authorized to advise and did not have the power to override a detention order).

9.3 ENGLISH ADMINISTRATIVE LAW AND THE FOUNDATIONS OF ADMINISTRATIVE LAW DURING THE FIRST YEARS AFTER INDEPENDENCE

The legacy of English administrative law has played an even more important role since Israel became independent in 1948. The reason for this can be attributed to the many challenges of setting up the foundations of a whole new legal system for a newly independent state.

Despite the fact that Israel perceived itself as an independent state that did not function as a continuation of Mandatory Palestine, for practical purposes, it made a decision to absorb the former system, subject to 'modifications as may result from the establishment of the State and its authorities'[10] (an exception that was supposed to serve as a 'safety valve' against the danger of being ruled by principles that do not match the needs or interests of the new state). The result was the almost total absorption of the law of Mandatory Palestine.[11]

In the area of public law, this decision proved to be especially crucial.[12] First, in contrast to various fields of private law,[13] public law was never codified.[14] Second, despite the original aspiration to eventually write a constitution for the state, due to several controversies around its possible content and other pressures of the time, Israel decided to follow (for the time being) the British tradition of an unwritten constitution.[15] Against this backdrop, with no formal constitutional guidelines, the principles of English administrative law proved to be even more important for setting the foundations of the system. Indeed, within a relatively short period, the Supreme Court – already the Supreme Court of Israel – implemented some of the most foundational principles of English administrative law in a way that left its mark for the decades to come. In general, rather than limiting itself to the case law of the Supreme Court of Palestine (such references are primarily found in the first few years after Independence), the more prevalent practice of the Israeli Supreme Court was to make direct references to leading precedents of the English courts.

It would be most informative to start describing the emergence of Israeli administrative law with early examples of the courts' use of the ultra vires principle (known also as the legality principle, as further defined in the following section) for the sake of limiting government power. In fact, this principle – most identified with the famous *Entick* v. *Carrington* case[16] – was cited in the first years

10 Section 11 of the Law and Administration Ordinance, 1948 stated: 'The law which existed in Palestine on the 5th Iyar, 5708 (14th May, 1948) shall remain in force, insofar as there is nothing therein repugnant to this Ordinance or to the other laws which may be enacted by or on behalf of the Provisional Council of State, and subject to such modifications as may result from the establishment of the State and its authorities.' See also the chapter on Hong Kong for a similar example of a modified, post-colonial, common law.

11 See also Assaf Likhovski, 'Between Mandate and State: On the Periodization of Israeli Legal History' (1998), 19(2) *Journal of Israeli History* 39.

12 The reasons for this are stated in the paragraph. However, this evaluation has not yet been studied empirically in the sense that so far empirical studies of Israeli law have concentrated on the influence of foreign law on the system without distinctions between branches of law. See Yoram Shachar, Ron Harris and Meron Gross, 'Citation Practices of Israel's Supreme Court, Quantitative Analysis' (1996) 27 *Mishpatim* 119, 151–9 (Hebrew).

13 The Israeli Ministry of Justice initiated an ambitious codification process, mostly in the area of private law that was based at the time on problematic combinations between Ottoman legislation and common law principles. This project was inspired mainly by continental legislation. This choice was influenced both by the fact that English law did not have a code that could serve as a model and the legal education of many of the leaders of the professional community (at the time) who came from continental Europe.

14 After many years, the Ministry of Justice initiated a bill that sought to codify the case law principles of administrative law. See Administrative Procedure (Agency Procedure and Rights of Citizens Addressing Administrative Agencies) Bill, 2014. As of writing this chapter, the bill has not been advanced.

15 Daphne Barak-Erez, 'From an Unwritten to a written Constitution: The Israeli Challenge in American Perspective' (1995), 26 *Columbia Human Rights Review* 309.

16 *Entick* v. *Carrington* [1765] EWHC KB J98.

of Israel's independence more times than it was in the UK during the same period.[17] The two cases considered in the following section involved, in substance, claims to rights and freedoms – more specifically, the freedom to work, discussed in Israel as 'freedom of occupation'. However, the analysis highlights the importance of administrative law principles in the judicial reasoning.

The ultra vires principle was at the center of the *Bejerano* case,[18] one of the very first judgments handed down by the Israeli Supreme Court after independence. The case concerned a petition brought by several people whose trade was to bring requests on behalf of citizens to the offices of the Department of Transportation. The new Israeli government, at the time, had decided to prohibit this practice in order to fight potential corruption. The petitioners argued against the legality of prohibiting them to continue their practice of representing their clients in their dealings with the department. While the motives and policies behind the prohibition were, therefore, proper or legitimate, the petition was accepted. The Supreme Court held that the government was not authorized to limit the possible ways of applying to the authorities, and therefore held that the principle of ultra vires mandated that the petition must be accepted. While, in substance, this case recognised the freedom to choose one's trade as a basic right, the formal basis for the decision was clearly the ultra vires principle, which served as the ground for judicial review.[19]

In another ground-breaking decision handed down during the state's formative years, the Israeli Supreme Court accepted the petition in the matter of *Sheib*.[20] This time, the petition was brought by a right-wing activist known for advocating extreme views. The Minister of Defense at the time, Prime Minister David Ben Gurion, ordered that a public school, which intended to hire the petitioner as a school teacher, should not do so. The petitioner challenged this decision and argued that he was persecuted because of his political views and activities. Once again, the petition was accepted. The court held that even though the goal of preserving a neutral political atmosphere in schools was a positive one, the Minister of Defense was not empowered to give orders that limit the freedom of occupation of otherwise deserving professionals.

In addition to the ultra vires principle, the Israeli Supreme Court referred to other principles of English administrative law – including the rules of natural justice[21] and the prohibition to take into account irrelevant considerations.[22] Another characteristic of the heavy reliance on English administrative law has been not only the reference to court cases but also the tendency to use the major English textbooks in the area.[23]

9.4 ENGLISH ADMINISTRATIVE LAW SUBJECT TO INDEPENDENCE: FROM DETAILS TO PRINCIPLES AND ADDITIONAL SOURCES OF INFLUENCE

Despite the fact that English administrative law served as the ultimate point of reference for the Israeli Supreme Court while developing its jurisprudence, the establishment of Israel as an independent state made these references subject to modifications as the system matured.

17 For an analysis of the nuances of the law in this area in the UK, see Margit Cohn, 'Medieval Chains, Invisible Inks: On Non-Statutory Powers of the Executive' (2005), 25 *Oxford Journal of Legal Studies* 97.

18 HCJ 1/49 *Bejerano* v. *Minister of Police*, 2 PD 80 (1949).

19 This decision referred to the *Federman* case (n 6 above), from the British Mandate period.

20 HCJ 144/50 *Sheib* v. *Minister of Defense*, 5 PD 399 (1951).

21 See e.g. HCJ 3/58 *Berman* v. Minister of Interior, 12 PD 1493 (1958) (the right to be heard); HCJ 174/54 *Shimel* v. *Authorized Authority*, 9 PD 459 (1955) (bias).

22 HCJ 105/54 *Lazarovitz* v. *Food Comptroller, Jersualem*, 10 PD 40 (1956).

23 Such as De Smith, *Judicial Review of Administrative Action* (various editions, starting from the first one published in 1959). The current edition, written by Lord Woolf and others, was published in 2016.

First, alongside the English influence, the Israeli system opened itself to inspiration from other legal systems. These influences were understandably natural in a country with a plural population composed of many immigrants and with a judiciary populated by judges who had been educated in other legal traditions.[24] For example, two landmark cases that signified the acceptance of US influence on public law during the first years of independence were the *Jabotinski* decision[25] that endorsed the justiciability or political question doctrine, and the *Kol Ha'am* decision,[26] which invalidated a decision by the Minister of Interior to temporarily shut down a newspaper (an administrative decision that did not give due weight to the right to freedom of speech when balanced vis-à-vis the keeping of public peace).[27] At the same time, it is accurate to state that the vast majority of cases that were being cited in the everyday practice of judicial review at the time were English precedents. The growing US impact on Israeli law developed later, more as a result of the general increase of US influence on the Israeli public arena (in politics and culture as well). It is manifested in the growing tendency to borrow models from US legislation, as well as to cite US precedents.[28]

Second, the court made it clear that it did not regard itself as being bound by the doctrinal details of English administrative law, but rather as guiding itself by its principles. Therefore, the court allowed itself to innovate and set new rules when certain English precedents were considered to be too rigid or unjust. Formally speaking, the court used to explain its ability to innovate by the fact that the authorizing legislation that defined its jurisdiction stated that it has the power to give remedies which are 'necessary . . . for the administration of justice'. The court also gave mention to the fact that even the Supreme Court of Mandatory Palestine construed its jurisdiction as being broader than that of the UK High Court. A representative decision informed by this spirit was handed down in the *Trudler* case,[29] where the Supreme Court of Israel went beyond English precedent and stated that judicial review of tribunals is not limited to cases in which the 'error' in the decision of the tribunal is clear 'on the face of the record', as that rule is unjust, prior to similar developments in England following *Anisminic*.[30] In fact, some Israeli case law even turned out to portend developments in English law, in the sense that some 'natural' changes materialized in Israeli law even before they were implemented in the UK itself. For example, in England, the court in *Ridge* v. *Baldwin*[31] acknowledged the right to be heard in administrative law matters not only in

24 See also E. Salzberger and F. Oz-Salzberger, 'The Secret German Sources of the Israel Supreme Court' (1998), 3(2) *Israel Studies* 159.

25 HCJ 65/51 *Jabotinski* v. *Weitzman*, 5 PD 801 (1951).

26 HCJ *Kol Ha'am Ltd.* v. *Minister of Interior*, 7 PD 871 (1953).

27 The Supreme Court referred here to US freedom of speech precedents, as well as to academic commentary on them. Another example in this direction is the shift in the area of government contracts from the relatively restrictive approach of the English precedent of *Rederiaktiebolaget Amphitrite* v. *R.* [1921] 3 KB 500 to a more flexible approach that recognizes the ability of government bodies to commit to contractual obligations (subject to exceptions). See HCJ 311/60 *Miller, Engineering (Agency and Export) Ltd.* v. *Minister of Transport* 15 PD 1989 (1961).

28 In addition, currently, American universities are the main target of Israeli law graduates who are interested in pursuing advanced degrees. See Pnina Lahav, 'American Moment(s): When, How and Why Did Israeli Law Faculties Come to Resemble Elite U.S. Law Schools' (2009), 10 *Theoretical Inquiries in Law* 653.

29 HCJ 77/63 *Trudler* v. *Elections Officer to the Agricultural Committees*, 17 PD 2503 (1963). See also Michael Asimow and Yoav Dotan, 'Open and Closed Judicial Review of Agency Action: The Conflicting US and Israel Approaches' (2016), 64 *American Journal of Comparative Law* 521, 541–2.

30 *Anisminic* v. *Foreign Comp. Comm.* [1969] 2 AC 147. The court explained that it was free to depart from English precedents with the aspiration that the law would suit local needs and do justice. See also Itzhak Zamir, 'Latent Errors of Law in Decisions of Administrative Tribunals' (1966), 1 *Israel Law Review* 162. See also Christopher Forsyth's chapter in this volume on the classical model of administrative law.

31 *Ridge* v. *Baldwin* [1964] AC 40.

judicial and quasi-judicial proceedings but also in 'purely' administrative decision-making. The Israeli Supreme Court introduced this rule – that is, the right to be heard irrespective of whether the proceedings are 'administrative', 'judicial' or 'quasi-judicial' – a few years earlier in the *Berman* case.[32] Similarly, on ouster clauses, the famous *Anisminic* decision, stated that courts are not precluded from judicial review of administrative decisions even if these are defined as 'final' by the relevant legislation. The Israeli Supreme Court announced a similar rule years before in the *Zerubavel* case[33] and the *Yehoshua* case.[34] Also, the Supreme Court of Israel applied a reasonableness review to regulations promulgated by government ministers before this had become the position in English case law.[35]

In other cases, the Supreme Court was also willing to develop new doctrines based on its own sense of fairness in government dealings with citizens, with no clear equivalent in English law. For example, in the *Sci-tex* case,[36] the court introduced a new doctrine regarding the duty to respect administrative promises that were made within the agency's power, based on the notion of 'trust' in government. This was an innovative new doctrine, which once again preceded the development of the principle of legitimate expectations (applicable also to administrative promises), which was just starting to crystalize in the UK during that time.[37] The decision was given with no reference to any comparative sources of inspiration.[38]

9.5 SIGNIFICANT DEPARTURES: THE 1980S ONWARD

Although Israeli administrative law was 'independent' from its very beginning (as the examples in the previous sections show), more robust signs of independence emerged later in the late 1970s and 1980s, with the accumulation of local case law and judicial experience in the time that passed since 1948. A quick look at the most significant changes that occurred at that time will show just how substantial this development was.[39] It is interesting to note that despite the fact that, at this stage, the Supreme Court had allowed itself to significantly depart from English doctrines, to a large degree it has done so while preserving the vocabulary of

32 *Berman* case (n 21 above). At the same time, the *Ridge* v. *Baldwin* case (n 31 above) was studied and cited in later Israeli case law as well. See e.g. CA 183/69 *Municipality of Petach-Tikva* v. *Tachan*, 23(2) PD 398 (1969). This case accepted the view that a decision to fire a public employee, without a hearing, is null and void, as was the view of the majority in the *Ridge* v. *Baldwin* case. The court was aware of different holdings but preferred that view. See also HCJ 598/77 *Deri* v. *Committee of Releases*, 32(3) PD 161 (1979).

33 HCJ 5/53 *Zerubavel* v. *Appeals Tribunal under the Families of Fallen Soldiers Law*, 7 PD 182 (1953).

34 HCJ 176/54 *Yehoshua* v. *Appeals Tribunal Under the Invalids (Pensions and Rehabilitations) Law*, 1949, 9 PD 617 (1955) (translation available in the VERSA website, Cardozo Law School).

35 CA 311/57 *Attorney General* v. *M. Dizengoff & Co. (Navigation) Ltd.*, 13 PD 1026 (1959). In England, at the time, reasonableness review was applied only to bylaws of municipalities following the precedent set in *Kruse* v. *Johnson* [1898] 2 QB 91.

36 HCJ 135/75 *Sci-tex Corporation Ltd.* v. *Minister of Commerce and Industry*, 30(1) PD 673 (1975).

37 The first important case in this regard in the UK was given around the same time by the Court of Appeals. See *R.* v. *Liverpool Corporation ex parte Liverpool Taxi Fleet Operators Association* [1972] 2 All E.R. 589. This decision was not mentioned by the Israeli Supreme Court in the *Sci-tex* case.

38 The judgment was authored by Justice Berenson, who was an especially innovative judge in the area of administrative law. He was writing for the court also in the *Trudler* case (n 29 above). In another decision, HCJ 101/ 74 *Binui Vepituch Banegev Ltd.* v. *Minister of Defense*, 28(2) PD 449 (1974), he was responsible for recognizing the possibility of awarding damages for illegal administrative action. In this decision, he quoted the view of French administrative law.

39 See also David Kretzmer, 'Forty Years of Public Law' (1990), 24 *Israel Law Review* 341; Itzhak Zamir, 'Administrative Law: Revolution or Evolution' (1990), 24 *Israel Law Review* 356; Itzhak Zamir and Allen Zysblat (eds.), *Public Law in Israel* (Clarendon Press, 1996).

English administrative law, as is most evident with the doctrine of reasonableness. The terminology has been retained even though the content changed.

9.5.1 *Relaxing Formal Barriers for Judicial Review*

The first significant development, which started in the second half of the 1970s, was the willingness to allow petitions for judicial review in cases that, according to traditional doctrine, should have been dismissed for preliminary reasons (without getting into their merits).[40] The most obvious examples of these are the barriers of standing and justiciability. In general, the Supreme Court of Israel emphasized that dismissing petitions due to lack of standing or non-justiciability may lead to leaving grave infringements untouched. Accordingly, the court was willing to look beyond the veil of the preliminary tests and accept petitions, despite concerns of standing and justiciability, if they raised important rule of law matters.

In the area of standing, for example, the court was willing to hear a petition against the refusal of the Minister of Interior to apply a 'daylight saving time' arrangement, despite the fact that the petitioner could not demonstrate that he had a particular stake in the matter.[41] The approach taken in this context was, once again, a development that also emerged in the years following this decision in English courts (as exemplified by Lord Diplock's famous dictum in the *National Federation of Self-employed and Small Businesses* case).[42]

A very influential decision in this area has been the *Ressler* case,[43] where the Supreme Court was willing to hear a petition against the policy of not drafting Yeshiva students – even though the petition was submitted by a public petitioner with no particular connection to the matter and despite the especially sensitive political context. In other words, this decision exemplifies the double effect of the broad approaches taken with regard to both standing and justiciability. It is interesting to note that the Supreme Court referred in this case to Lord Diplock's words in the relatively new decision in IRC case.[44] At the same time, the main source of inspiration regarding the limits of non-justiciability was the decision of the US Supreme Court in *Baker* v. *Carr*.[45]

This new approach, which has relaxed traditional barriers to judicial review, went hand in hand with a growing willingness to review decisions in areas that used to be outside the reach of traditional administrative law in the UK, such as judicial review of inner parliamentary proceedings[46] and appointments of high-level officials, including government ministers.[47]

40 Similar developments are apparent in Kenya and Scotland as discussed in the chapters by Migai Akech and Stephen Thomson (respectively) in this volume.

41 HCJ 217/80 *Segal* v. *Minister of Interior*, 34(4) PD 429 (1980).

42 R. v. *Inland Revenue Commissioners, ex parte National Federation of Self-employed and Small Businesses Ltd.* [1982] AC 617 (IRC case) ('It would, in my view, be a grave lacuna in our system of public law if a pressure group . . . or even a single public-spirited taxpayer . . . were prevented by outdated technical rules of [standing] from bringing the matter to the attention of the court to vindicate the rule of law and get the unlawful conduct stopped'). See also the Hong Kong chapter for similar liberal developments to *locus standi* after the House of Lords decision in *National Federation*.

43 HCJ 910/86 *Ressler* v. *Minister of Defense*, 42(2) PD 441 (1988).

44 IRC case (n 42).

45 *Baker* v. *Carr*, 369 US 186 (1961).

46 HCJ 652/81 *Sarid* v. *Knesset Speaker* 36(2) PD 197 (1982).

47 HCJ 6163/92 *Eisenberg* v. *Minister of Building and Housing*, 47(2) PD 229 (1993) (invalidating a decision to appoint as a general manager of the Ministry of Building and Housing a person who admitted the commission of offenses in the course of his service in the Israeli General Security Services); HCJ 3094/93 *Movement for Quality*

The result was that during these years, the regulation of improper decisions in the public realm has started to lean heavily on legal rules and less on codes of 'this is not done'.

9.5.2 *Substantive Review: Reasonableness and Proportionality*

The most notable development during the 1980s involved the emergence of the new reasonableness doctrine in Israeli case law. Indeed, the formal recognition of reasonableness as grounds for judicial review has always been part of Israeli administrative law, following English administrative law. However, as a consequence of *Kruse* v. *Johnson*[48] and *Wednesbury*, it was a relatively narrow ground for judicial review, which applied in cases of severe irrationality .[49] All this, however, changed with Justice Aharon Barak's decision in the *Dapei Zahav* case,[50] which introduced a new reasonableness doctrine. According to the new test – as presented by Barak – an administrative decision would be declared unreasonable if it severely distorted the proper balance between considerations that were all legal, as such. This standard obviously goes beyond the *Wednesbury* principle that was limited to a decision that no reasonable person could have made. Accordingly, the reasonableness test has become a much broader and more effective tool for the review of administrative decisions. In fact, within a few years, it developed from a relatively remote and rare ground for review to a central and influential doctrine in the area of administrative law.[51]

At the beginning of the 1990s, the Israeli Supreme Court started to apply a new standard for judicial review – proportionality.[52] This doctrine was not part of traditional administrative law in the UK and Israeli administrative law adopted this ground of review with no direct connection to its English roots (although, eventually, the two systems came to a similar conclusion in accepting and implementing this doctrine).[53] It was only adopted by English Courts after the enactment of the Human Rights Act 1998 as a result of the growing influence from Europe. The proportionality doctrine was adopted in Israel with reference to its three sub-tests as applied in other systems, such as Germany and Canada. More specifically, according to this doctrine, the court is expected to review whether there was a logical connection between the purpose of the administrative decision and the means adopted for achieving it, whether the administrative decision caused the least possible harm from the perspective of rights (considering the available options), and whether the balance between the benefit arising from the decision and the harm it caused can be justified (even when it is the least infringing alternative) – reflecting the view that the end does not justify all means.

In general, both doctrines present a bolder willingness to review administrative discretion. They certainly have things in common – in the sense that they are 'objective' grounds of review that assess the administrative decision, and therefore go beyond the subjective

in Government in Israel v. *Government of Israel*, 47(5) PD 404 (1993) (stating that the Prime Minister has to fire a government minister who was indicated for alleged commission of corruption offenses).

48 See n 35 above. See e.g. HCJ 21/51 *Binnenboim* v. *Municipality of Tel-Aviv* 6 PD 375, 386 (1952).

49 *Associated Provincial Picture Houses Ltd.* v. *Wednesbury Corporation* [1948] 1KB 223.

50 HCJ 389/80 *Dapei Zahav Ltd.* v. *Broadcasting Authority*, 35(1) PD 421 (1981).

51 See also HCJ 680/88 *Schnitzer* v. *Chief Military Censor*, 42(4) PD 617 (1989) (judicial review of a decision accepted by the military censorship); HCJ 935/89 *Ganor* v. *Attorney General*, 44(2) PD 485 (1990) (judicial review of a decision of the Attorney General not to indict).

52 See e.g. HCJ 3477/95 *Ben-Atiyah* v. *Minister of Education, Culture and Sports*, 49(5) PD 1 (1996).

53 See also Margit Cohn, 'Pure or Mixed? The Evolution of Three Grounds of Judicial Review of the Administration in British and Israeli Administrative Law' (2012), 6(1) *Journal of Comparative Law* 86; Margit Cohn, 'Legal Transplants Chronicles: The Evolution of Unreasonableness and Proportionality Review of the Administration in the United Kingdom' (2010), 58 *American Journal of Comparative Law* 583.

motivations and reasons behind it. They both consider the inner balance of the decision. They are not identical, however. The reasonableness doctrine focuses on the general balance between the different considerations that the administrative authority should have assessed. In contrast, the proportionality doctrine is based on more structured three sub-tests. For this reason, one may think that the proportionality doctrine is just the 'new stage' of judicial review, leaving the reasonableness doctrine redundant. Despite the prima facie attractiveness of this hypothesis, this is not the case. Indeed, the proportionality doctrine has become very common and useful in judicial decisions. It is designed, however, mainly for the review of decisions that have direct impact on human rights. There are other administrative decisions that do not fit this model – for example, decisions on levels of municipal taxes. In such cases, the reasonableness doctrine seems to be the more relevant one.

9.6 THE BIGGER PICTURE: INTERNATIONALIZATION, CONSTITUTIONALIZATION AND PRIVATIZATION

In addition to the doctrinal developments reviewed so far, it is important to examine three major changes that occurred beyond the arena of administrative law and are of important significance: the growing role of international law, the constitutionalization (at least partially) of Israeli law and the privatization trend.[54]

9.6.1 *International Law*

One important development that seems to be important has been the growing impact of international law. Indeed, formally speaking, Israel follows the traditional 'dualist' model of English law, meaning that norms of international law are not self-executed in domestic law and need to be adopted by legislation, unless these are customary norms.[55] However, in general, the Supreme Court of Israeli endorses a very open approach to international law.[56] First, it aspires to interpret Israeli law as much as possible in alignment with international law. In addition, it tends to be inspired by international instruments, even when they don't have a formal mandatory role vis-à-vis Israeli law. Another driving force is that regulation is currently very much inspired by international standards as adopted by international organizations.[57] In addition, as far as the occupied territories are concerned, international law applies since they are governed by the law of belligerent occupation.[58] Additionally, reference to international law provides another important source of inspiration to the judicial review of administrative action.[59]

54 Daphne Barak-Erez, 'Israeli Administrative Law at the Crossroads: Between the English Model and the American Model' (2007), 40 *Israel Law Review* 56.

55 See contributions by Michael Ramsden, and Hanna Wilberg and Kris Gledhill, on the growing role of international law on the common law.

56 Daphne Barak-Erez, 'The International Law of Human Rights and Domestic Law: a Case Study of an Expanding Dialogue' (2004), 2 *International Journal of Constitutional Law* 611.

57 See generally Daphne Barak-Erez and Oren Perez, 'Whose Administrative Law Is It Anyway? How Global Norms Reshape the Administrative State' (2013), 46 *Cornell International Law Journal* 455; Daphne Barak-Erez and Oren Perez, 'The Administrative State Goes Global', in Michael A. Helfand (ed.), *Negotiating State and Non-state Law: The Challenges of Global and Local Legal Pluralism*, (Cambridge: Cambridge University Press, 2015), p. 134

58 See also Daphne Barak-Erez, 'The Security Barrier – Between International Law, Constitutional Law, and Domestic Judicial Review' (2006), 4 *International Journal of Constitutional Law* 540.

59 Barak-Erez, *The International Law of Human Rights*, (n 56 above).

9.6.2 *Constitutionalization*[60]

In 1992, Israel enacted two basic laws dedicated to the protection of human rights as part of the gradual process intended to eventually lead to accepting a full and formalized constitution. In general, since its establishment, Israel enacted a series of basic laws, each dedicated to one of the issues that should be included in its constitution – with the intent to finalize its constitution based on these basic laws. The basic laws project started with basic laws that covered institutional aspects, and the enactment of two basic laws on human rights was a significant step ahead. Indeed, this step has been important first and foremost for the development of constitutional law. However, it was also highly influential on administrative law. Since the enactment of these basic laws, which secure the protection of human rights, vis-à-vis the state, administrative actions must also be assessed from the perspective of their compatibility with the standards of the basic laws. According to the basic laws, infringements of the basic rights protected by them must be based on 'express law' that has been enacted for a 'worthy cause' and meets the values of the state of Israel as a 'Jewish and democratic state' as well as the proportionality test. This standard implies some of the causes for judicial review – it refers to the question of statutory authorization (which lies at the heart of the ultra vires principle), evaluates the purpose of the action (that is, it refers also to the issue of irrelevant considerations) and focuses, to a large degree, on proportionality. Beyond these details, as a matter of principle, currently the protection of human rights is not only the result of the application of administrative law principles but rather part of the constitutional framework.[61]

9.6.3 *Privatization*

Another major development in the public arena in Israel has been the relatively broad acceptance of privatization policies. This is not a legal change, but it has proved to be very challenging for traditional administrative law, which had to adapt in order to review the privatization decisions themselves, as well as the decisions of some of the hybrid bodies that resulted from the process. Accordingly, the Israeli Supreme Court has developed doctrines that recognized the 'dual' nature of bodies that are neither completely private nor public in order to subject them to judicial review (although only concerning the basic 'principles' of administrative law, in contrast to its detailed rules).[62] It should be noted that, in addition, the Israeli Supreme Court has stated that in some cases, privatization initiatives may be subject to constitutional judicial review (as was the case with the initiative to establish a private prison which was enacted in a statute invalidated by the Supreme Court as unconstitutional).[63]

9.7 CONCLUSIONS AND DIRECTIONS FOR FURTHER DEVELOPMENT

Looking back on the decades that have passed since the establishment of the state of Israel, with its new and independent legal system, the great contribution of English administrative

60 See also the chapters on Kenya, South Africa, India, Australia and Ireland on the interplay between the 'Constitution' and administrative law.

61 See also Baruch Bracha, 'Constitutional Upgrading of Human Rights in Israel: The Impact on Administrative Law' (2001), 3 *University of Pennsylvania Journal of Constitutional Law* 581.

62 See e.g. HCJ 731/86 *Microdaf* v. *Electricity Company of Israel Ltd.*, 41(2) PD 449 (1987). See also the contribution by Stephen Thomson on Scotland in this volume.

63 See HCJ 2605/05 *Academic Center for Law and Business* v. *Minister of Finance*, 63(2) PD 545 (2009); Daphne Barak-Erez, 'The Private Prison Controversy and the Privatization Continuum' (2011), 5(1) *Law and Ethics of Human Rights* 137.

law is still prevalent and shining through in Israeli law. The ultra vires principle serves as a cornerstone, judicial review is based on prerogative orders and the causes of review are similar to those prevalent today in England. At the same time, as to be expected, Israeli law is now very different in its details from English doctrines. The Supreme Court blazed an independent course of development that displays no sense of obligation to follow English precedents formally. In addition, other legal systems, as well as international law, have become influential as well. Other processes, some of them external to administrative law, such as the enactment of basic laws on human rights and privatization policies, had their share of influence in reshaping Israeli law. Despite these differences, when English and Israeli legal scholars meet and discuss their respective administrative law frameworks, they understand each other very well as people proficient in two dialects of the same ancient language.

10

From Pale Reflection to Guiding Light

The Indigenisation of Judicial Review in South Africa

Cora Hoexter

10.1 INTRODUCTION

South Africa's legal system is of an unusual type: a mixed system that has become constitutionalised. The result of South Africa's colonial past is a Roman-Dutch legal substratum with a thick overlay of English law, a combination found also in Sri Lanka and, to a lesser extent, Scotland.[1] This interesting mixture explains why the old authorities of Roman-Dutch Law remain a source of common law.[2] In practice, however, judicial decisions are a far more important source. Scott rightly describes the adoption of the doctrine of precedent as 'the most significant and lasting legacy of English colonial rule'.[3]

The Roman-Dutch foundation is still evident in certain areas of South African private law, such as the law of delict (which still goes by that Roman name). However, it is barely evident in administrative law, except in judicial remedies and a few other areas.[4] In administrative law, as in South African public law more generally, the influence of English common law was dominant,[5] and from its earliest days, judicial review of administrative action was based on the common-law model. In essence, this meant that the superior courts exercised their supervisory jurisdiction by way of common-law grounds of review backed up by the ultra vires doctrine. However, judicial review developed indigenous features over time. Above all, it was shaped, or rather distorted, by the effects of the racial segregation and oppression practised officially in South Africa from 1948.

Apartheid and white minority rule both came to an end in April 1994, when South Africa's first democratic Constitution entered force. The Bill of Rights in that Constitution included rights to just administrative action, and these were subsequently given effect to by means of

1 See Stephen Thomson's contribution on Scotland in this volume.

2 See Helen Scott, 'The Death of Doctrine? Private-Law Scholarship in South Africa Today' in Jürgen Basedow, Holger Fleischer and Reinhard Zimmermann (eds.), *Legislators, Judges, and Professors* (2016) 223. The mixture was not always a harmonious one: the mid-twentieth century witnessed a contest between rival schools of purists, who saw themselves as the guardians of Roman-Dutch law and rejected any English influences, and modernists or pragmatists who regarded judicial precedent as the primary source of South African law. This rivalry was an aspect of a larger political divide between (white) Afrikaner nationalists and English-speaking liberals. See especially Proculus, 'Bellum Juridicum: Two Approaches to South African Law' (1951) 68 *South African Law Journal* 306.

3 Scott (n 2) 226.

4 Roman-Dutch authorities have been cited in relation to '[f]ailure to observe prescribed procedures, the finality of administrative acts, delegation of powers, the principles of fair procedure, compensation for interference with rights and judicial remedies'. Lawrence Baxter, *Administrative Law* (1984) 34.

5 See B Beinart, 'The English Legal Contribution to South Africa: The Interaction of Civil and Common Law' 1981 *Acta Juridica* 7.

constitutionally mandated legislation. In this way, what was essentially a common-law system of judicial review became both constitutionalised and codified, and thus transformed into a model that has been emulated in several other countries.[6] But notwithstanding these sweeping changes, the old connection with English law is still quite obvious and probably always will be.

This chapter begins with an outline of the constitutional history of South Africa and the implications of that history for administrative law and judicial review. It goes on to describe the indigenisation of judicial review in South African administrative law both before and after 1994, as well as its influence on other countries in recent years. Some prominent features of the indigenised system of judicial review are then identified. Finally, examples are given of the courts' reliance, both past and present, on English precedents and concepts, and explanations are suggested for the continuing influence of English law.

10.2 ADMINISTRATIVE-LAW MILESTONES

The 'pre-democratic era' is shorthand for a period spanning 342 years, from April 1652 to April 1994. This part identifies three major constitutional epochs during that period, each of which had distinct implications for the administrative law of the time.

10.2.1 *The Cape under the VOC*

The Cape of Good Hope, a peninsula about 140 miles from the southern tip of Africa, was an obvious stopping-off point for vessels of the Dutch East India Company, or VOC,[7] on the long voyage between Europe and the east. In April 1652 the VOC, an agency of the United Netherlands, landed three ships at the Cape with a view to establishing a refreshment station there – and those ships brought with them the common law of the province of Holland, Roman-Dutch law. Little is known of the customary law practised by the semi-nomadic Khoisan people they found there. The VOC did not recognise the unwritten customs of the Khoisan as law, and by the 1670s they were increasingly being assimilated into the colonial legal system.[8]

Initially a tiny settlement, the Cape grew into a colony and expanded into the interior. Farming became increasingly practicable after the arrival of the first shiploads of slaves in 1658.[9] However, public administration of the colony remained rudimentary, and administrative law undeveloped. As Baxter suggests, the view of the Cape colony as a mere staging post seems to have retarded the development both of administrative machinery and of controls against administrative abuse.[10]

10.2.2 *British Colonial Rule*

In 1795, the British laid claim to the Cape with the aim of securing the sea route to the east. After a brief reoccupation by the Dutch from 1803, the British resumed control in 1806 and

6 Since 2010, the constitutional provision has been adopted by Kenya, Zimbabwe and Fiji; and Kenya went on to model its Fair Administrative Action Act of 2015 on South Africa's Promotion of Administrative Justice Act 3 of 2000. See further in Section 10.5.

7 *Vereenigde Geoctroyeerde Oost-Indische Compagnie*.

8 See further Richard Elphick and V C Malherbe, 'The Khoisan to 1828' in Richard Elphick and Hermann Giliomee (eds.), *The Shaping of South African Society, 1652–1840* (1979) 3.

9 See further James C Armstrong and Nigel A Worden, 'The Slaves, 1652–1834' in Elphick and Giliomee (n 8) 109.

10 Baxter (n 4) 8.

remained the colonial power at the Cape for the next century and more. British policy was to respect the existing law of its colonies, which ensured the preservation of Roman-Dutch common law.[11] Nevertheless, steady anglicisation of the legal system took place, particularly after the arrival of five thousand British settlers in 1820. English became the official language of the colony in 1822.

In 1827, the First Charter of Justice established a Supreme Court modelled on English lines, whose judges were drawn from Britain. The penetration of English law was further encouraged by the English legal training of most practitioners and the accessibility of English legal texts and law reports. A legislature was set up in 1853, and responsible government was introduced in 1872. By then, the legal system was thoroughly anglicised and 'all the conditions for the adoption of the English system of administrative law ... were present'.[12] But judicial review of administrative action on common-law grounds actually began much earlier than this, almost at the inception of the Supreme Court,[13] and its justification by way of the ultra vires doctrine was more or less established by 1855.[14]

Meanwhile, three adjacent Boer or trekker republics had come into existence as a result of the Great Trek of the 1830s, during which descendants of the Dutch settlers moved into the hinterland. Natal, lying north-east of the Cape colony, was a Boer republic from 1839, but was annexed and proclaimed as a British colony just a few years later, in 1843. The other two republics, the Free State and the South African Republic, were annexed by Britain during the Anglo-Boer War of 1899–1902 and became Crown colonies: the Orange River Colony and the Transvaal Colony. The English constitutional and administrative model was adopted in these three colonies too, and their superior courts also practised judicial review in the English manner. Indeed, the classic statement of common-law review in South Africa remains that of Innes CJ in a judgment of the Transvaal Supreme Court in 1903.[15]

In parallel, African customary law was practised by indigenous people in all four colonies, and acknowledged and applied to a greater or lesser extent by the lower courts of the colonial regime as well as by chiefs and other traditional leaders. Natal, where there was a large Zulu population, had the most fully developed system of native courts, including a Native High Court from 1875.

10.2.3 *South Africa after Union*

In 1910, pursuant to a national convention, the Union of South Africa was created as a British dominion[16] and the four colonies became provinces of the new Union: the Cape, Natal, the Orange Free State and the Transvaal. The constitutional fundamentals are outlined immediately in the following section, but the period after Union also provided an important new

11 The Articles of Capitulation of 1806 specifically provided for the preservation of Roman-Dutch law: see further H R Hahlo and Ellison Kahn, *The South African Legal System and Its Background* (1968), chapter 17. The introduction of a civil code in Holland in 1809 came just three years too late to affect the law at the Cape.

12 Baxter (n 4) 29.

13 Examples cited by Baxter (n 4, 303) are *In re Insolvent Estate of Brink* (1828) 1 Menzies 340 and *Du Preez* v. *The Protector of Slaves* (1831) 1 Menzies 528.

14 *Central Road Board* v. *Meintjes* (1855) 2 Searle 165, especially in the judgment of Bell J at 175–6.

15 *Johannesburg Consolidated Investment Co* v. *Johannesburg Town Council* 1903 TS 111 at 115: 'Whenever a public body has a duty imposed on it by statute, and disregards important provisions of the statute, or is guilty of gross irregularity or clear illegality in the performance of this duty, this Court may be asked to review the proceedings complained of and set aside or correct them. This is no special machinery created by the Legislature; it is a right inherent in the Court.'

16 See further H R Hahlo and Ellison Kahn, *The Union of South Africa: The Development of its Laws and Constitution* (1960).

context for South African administrative law – so important that its characteristics are described in detail in Section 10.3.

As one would expect, the Westminster constitutional model was reflected in the Union Constitution, the South Africa Act of 1909. Disastrously, however, parliamentary sovereignty was combined with white minority rule; for the hegemony of whites was established long before racial segregation became official government policy in 1948 under the National Party government. Union was primarily about uniting English- and Afrikaans-speaking whites, who had been divided by the Anglo-Boer War of 1899–1902. People of colour had no say in it and were excluded from the franchise with one exception, and 'native affairs' were placed under the control of the Governor-General.

The exception was that a clause of the South Africa Act preserved the existing, qualified[17] but non-racial franchise in the Cape province. That clause was itself protected by an entrenching provision that made amendment or repeal of the clause dependent on achieving a two-thirds majority of both houses of Parliament sitting together. In spite of this special protection, black voters were removed from the common roll in 1936,[18] and 'coloured' or mixed-race voters more notoriously so in the early 1950s – a step that precipitated a constitutional crisis.[19] Under the Constitution of 1961,[20] when South Africa became a republic, only whites had the vote.

The 'tricameral' Constitution of 1983[21] was an experiment in political reform in which two minorities, coloureds and Indians, were each given their own legislative assembly alongside the white parliament. But this fooled no one,[22] for the black majority was still excluded from political participation. In fact, the grand design of apartheid was for all blacks to become citizens of so-called tribal homelands and to lose their South African citizenship altogether.[23]

By the mid-1980s it was clear that minority rule could not be sustained. The declaration of successive states of emergency failed to diminish political tension, and the government finally started a process of political reform. Key events in this process were the unbanning of the African National Congress and the release of Nelson Mandela in February 1990, which cleared the way for constitutional negotiation.[24] In 1994 South Africa became a constitutional democracy, initially under the temporary or interim Constitution of 1993[25] and then under its successor, the 'final' or 1996 Constitution.[26]

10.3 A PALE REFLECTION: JUDICIAL REVIEW AFTER UNION (1910–1993)

As a discipline, South African administrative law had a slow and unpromising start. In 1948 Beinart remarked that 'reared and nurtured in the traditional Diceyan concept of the rule of

17 Women were entirely excluded, and the Union franchise was extended to them only in 1930.

18 In terms of the Separate Representation of Natives Act 12 of 1936, whose validity was upheld in *Ndlwana v. Hofmeyr* 1937 AD 229.

19 See Christopher Forsyth, 'The Judiciary under Apartheid' in Cora Hoexter and Morné Olivier (eds.), *The Judiciary in South Africa* (2014) 26 at 33–8.

20 Republic of South Africa Constitution Act 32 of 1961.

21 Republic of South Africa Constitution Act 110 of 1983.

22 Least of all the international community, which repudiated the 1983 Constitution in Security Council Resolution 554 of August 1984.

23 In terms of the National States Citizenship Act 26 of 1970.

24 See further Richard Spitz with Matthew Chaskalson, *The Politics of Transition: A Hidden History of South Africa's Negotiated Settlement* (2000).

25 Constitution of the Republic of South Africa, Act 200 of 1993.

26 Constitution of the Republic of South Africa, 1996, which remains in force.

law and the individualistic conception of society, the South African lawyer like his English counterpart, is still wont to regard administrative law as an undesirable out crop, and has given it scant attention and rather Cinderella treatment'.[27]In the 1980s, the leading writer on administrative law characterised it as 'a pale reflection of the English law of a bygone age';[28] and another eminent academic suggested that this branch of the law was a 'dismal science'.[29]

These unflattering assessments are explained by two significant adaptations of the imported English common law. First, in South Africa judicial review was by far the most dominant safeguard in the administrative system: internal and other external controls were either ineffective or absent. Second, the courts' approach to the review of administrative action was influenced by the politics of the time. Accordingly, their application of the common-law grounds of review tended towards formalism and extreme deference, particularly after 1948.

10.3.1 *The Paucity of Other Safeguards and the Dominance of Judicial Review*

Formally, judicial review on administrative-law grounds followed the common-law model quite closely: it took place in the ordinary courts on grounds imported from the English common law and was explained and justified by the ultra vires doctrine. But here, unlike in other common-law jurisdictions, judicial review was virtually the only way of controlling official action, and *some* control was desperately needed in a political system that invited administrative abuse of human rights.[30] So, though constrained by parliamentary sovereignty and their own inhibitions, the courts inevitably played an exaggerated role in the system.

Political control over the executive, including ministerial responsibility, was very feeble. As Baxter described it, Parliament was a useful device for conferring wide powers on the executive, but ineffective when it came to disciplining those powers.[31] A sort of ombudsman, the Advocate-General, was created in 1979,[32] but the office was inaccessible to a population of legally unsophisticated people as complaints had to be submitted on affidavit.[33] It had, in any event, very limited jurisdiction: the misuse of public money. Internal controls such as administrative appeal mechanisms were underdeveloped and lacked independence, while other potential safeguards, such as freedom of information, did not exist because it would hardly have suited the government to introduce them. The government simply ignored calls for stronger administrative accountability – or rejected such calls as subversive criticism of the state.[34] In this 'strong anti-reformist atmosphere'[35] judicial review, though flawed, was generally the citizen's only hope against oppressive administrative conduct.

And there was plenty of that, particularly after 1948: the year in which the National Party came to power and started implementing its policy of racial segregation and systematic discrimination against 'non-whites'. Apartheid entailed classifying people racially at birth, allowing them to live only in the 'group areas' reserved for their particular race and allowing

27 B Beinart, 'Administrative Law' (1948) 11 *Tydskrif vir Hedendaagse Romeins-Hollandse Reg* 204 at 206.

28 Baxter (n 4) 34.

29 W H B Dean, 'Our Administrative Law: A Dismal Science?' (1986) 2 *South African Journal on Human Rights* 164.

30 See further Cora Hoexter, 'The Future of Judicial Review in South African Administrative Law' (2000) 117 *South African Law Journal* 484.

31 Baxter (n 4) 33.

32 The Advocate-General, regulated by the Advocate-General Act 118 of 1979.

33 Section 4(2). No doubt this helps explain why a mere 18 complaints were received during the period March 1985 to February 1987, as recorded in Laurence Boulle, Bede Harris and Cora Hoexter, *Constitutional and Administrative Law: Basic Principles* (1989) 213 fn 60.

34 Baxter (n 4) 293.

35 Baxter (n 4) 292.

them to use only the hospitals, schools and other facilities reserved for them – superior ones for whites and inferior ones for everyone else. All of these inroads on people's rights were enabled in general terms by statute[36] but had to be implemented by administrative officials; and in the absence of other reliable safeguards, people turned to the courts in the hope that the common law would mitigate some of the effects of the apartheid system. In practice, it did so often enough to sustain an enduring belief in the legal system and in the rule of law.[37] For instance, detention without trial was held to be unlawful in landmark cases in the Appellate Division,[38] as were restrictions on the freedom of movement of black people in urban areas.[39]

No wonder, then, that 'excessive attention' was given by South African administrative lawyers to judicial review in those days.[40] Journal articles on the subject all tended to call for the same thing: greater judicial intervention on wider grounds of review.[41] It is revealing, too, that when it was investigating administrative-law reform in the 1980s and early 1990s, even the Law Commission was unable to imagine a world beyond judicial review.[42]

10.3.2 *The Courts' Approach to Judicial Review*

In the pre-democratic era, the courts' approach to judicial review was progressive in some ways and retrogressive in others. A wide range of remedies was available, including some drawn from Roman-Dutch law, and the remedies taken from English administrative law tended to be free of the 'complex technicalities' for which the common law was notorious.[43] The South African courts also guarded their review jurisdiction jealously, so that ouster clauses were very seldom successful in practice even though they abounded in legislation.[44]

Yet those same courts enforced very restrictive rules of standing, a far cry from the *actio popularis* of Roman law, and their cautious and often parsimonious application of the common-law grounds of review suggested submissive deference to the legislature and executive. For instance, unreasonableness was not a ground of review in itself except in relation to delegated legislation. Instead, a highly deferential test of 'symptomatic' unreasonableness held sway: the unreasonableness had to be so gross as to suggest *mala fides*, ulterior motive or failure to apply the mind.[45] And in relation to abuse of discretion, the courts did not always

36 Key apartheid statutes were the Population Registration Act 30 of 1950, the Group Areas Act 41 of 1950 and the Reservation of Separate Amenities Act 49 of 1953.

37 See Jens Meierhenrich, *The Legacies of Law: Long Run Consequences of Legal Development in South Africa, 1652–2000* (2008).

38 See e.g. *Minister of Law and Order* v. *Hurley* 1986 (3) SA 568 (A).

39 See e.g. *Oos-Kaapse Administratsieraad* v. *Rikhoto* 1983 (3) SA 595 (A).

40 Baxter (n 4) 70.

41 See Hoexter, 'The Future of Judicial Review' (n 30) 486–8.

42 Two working papers, a report and a revised report were issued under Project 24 of the South African Law Commission between 1986 and 1994, and all essentially confined themselves to recommendations regarding the improvement and codification of the grounds of review in administrative law. The reform of the system of administrative appeals, though urgently needed, was not thought feasible.

43 Baxter (n 4) 675.

44 This was famously demonstrated by *Minister of Law and Order* v. *Hurley* (n 38), a judgment all the more remarkable because it was handed down during a state of emergency. A notable exception to the trend was *Staatspresident* v. *United Democratic Front* 1988 (4) SA 830 (A), where the Appellate Division applied a literal version of ultra vires – and concluded that an ouster clause prevented the setting aside of regulations on a *judge-made* ground, vagueness. The court declined to follow English law: see Nicholas Haysom and Clive Plasket, 'The War against Law: Judicial Activism and the Appellate Division' (1988) 4 *South African Journal on Human Rights* 303 at 316–27.

45 *Union Government (Minister of Mines and Industries)* v. *Union Steel Corporation (South Africa) Ltd* 1928 AD 220 at 234–5.

regard ulterior motives or even dishonesty as legally relevant provided a legitimate ostensible purpose had been made out.[46]

As this suggests, the courts were also strongly attracted to formalistic reasoning. Indeed, this was a characteristic of pre-1994 South African law more generally,[47] and it went far beyond the rather benign type of formalism that has been defended by Forsyth.[48] The prime example of this is the courts' addiction to a rigid and illogical classification of functions as a method for determining whether a decision had to be procedurally fair. So 'judicial' and quasi-judicial' decisions (i.e., decisions prejudicially affecting existing rights) attracted fairness while 'legislative' and 'purely administrative' ones did not – almost irrespective of their effect on existing rights. A decision to expropriate property under an apartheid statute, for instance, clearly affected existing property rights prejudicially but was still labelled 'purely administrative' because it affected an entire community and was not 'directed against any individual'.[49] As I have summed it up elsewhere,

> [P]arsimony combined with conceptualism in a way that was not only devastating for the victims of the system, but also for the development of judicial review. The courts' energies were largely directed towards a negative enterprise: finding ways to *restrict* the application of principles of good administration and their obverse, the grounds of review. . . . The courts' focus meant that the most fundamental, helpful and positive question was never asked: What does administrative justice require in this case?[50]

10.4 JUDICIAL REVIEW SINCE 1994: CONSTITUTIONALISATION AND CODIFICATION

Since 1994, the South African legal system has been transformed by the adoption of a supreme democratic Constitution with a justiciable and very extensive Bill of Rights. That charter includes rights to just administrative action, which have in turn brought about dramatic changes to administrative-law review.

Rights to just administrative action first appeared in section 24 of South Africa's interim Constitution[51] and, subsequently, in section 33 of the 1996 or 'final' Constitution. South Africa did not, however, lead the way in adopting such rights. Rather, it followed the example of its neighbour, Namibia (formerly South West Africa), which it had effectively possessed from 1915 to 1990.[52] That was the year in which Namibia achieved independence,

46 See e.g. *Broadway Mansions (Pty) Ltd* v. *Pretoria City Council* 1955 (1) SA 517 (A), and see further Cora Hoexter, 'Administrative Justice and Dishonesty' (1994) 111 *South African Law Journal* 700.

47 See further Cora Hoexter, 'Judicial Policy Revisited: Transformative Adjudication in Administrative Law' (2008) 24 *South African Journal on Human Rights* 281.

48 Christopher Forsyth, 'Showing the Fly the Way Out of the Flybottle: The Value of Formalism and Conceptual Reasoning in Administrative Law' (2007) 66 *Cambridge Law Journal* 325.

49 *Pretoria City Council* v. *Modimola* 1966 (3) SA 250 (A) at 262F.

50 Cora Hoexter, 'The Principle of Legality in South African Administrative Law' (2004) 4 *Macquarie Law Journal* 165 at 168–9.

51 Section 24 provided: 'Every person shall have the right to – *(a)* lawful administrative action where any of his or her rights or interests is affected or threatened; *(b)* procedurally fair administrative action where any of his or her rights or legitimate expectations is affected or threatened; *(c)* be furnished with reasons in writing for administrative action which affects any of his or her rights or interests unless the reasons for such action have been made public; and *(d)* administrative action which is justifiable in relation to the reasons given for it where any of his or her rights is affected or threatened.'

52 See further G J Naldi, *Constitutional Rights in Namibia: A Comparative Analysis with International Human Rights* (1995) 1–9.

simultaneously ridding itself of the South African apartheid legacy and becoming one of the first countries to include administrative-justice rights in its Constitution.[53]

Section 33 of South Africa's 1996 Constitution reads as follows:

> (1) Everyone has the right to administrative action that is lawful, reasonable and procedurally fair.
> (2) Everyone whose rights have been adversely affected by administrative action has the right to be given written reasons.
> (3) National legislation must be enacted to give effect to these rights, and must –
> (a) provide for the review of administrative action by a court or, where appropriate, an independent or impartial tribunal;
> (b) impose a duty on the state to give effect to the rights in subsections (1) and (2); and
> (c) promote an efficient administration.

These rights have effectively constitutionalised administrative-law review. For one thing, judicial review of administrative action is constitutionally justified and explained by the presence of section 33 within a supreme Constitution. Judicial review is also guaranteed by section 34, the right of access to court, and ultimately by the limitation clause, section 36, which prohibits the infringement of constitutional rights except where it can be regarded as 'reasonable and justifiable in a democratic society based on human dignity, equality and freedom'. Legislative provisions that place time limits on the availability of judicial review might pass this test,[54] or provisions that limit the grounds of review or the remedies available on review, but thoroughgoing ouster or privative clauses are unlikely to do so.[55]

In accordance with the constitutional mandate in section 33(3), the rights in section 33(1) and (2) were subsequently given effect by means of legislation, the Promotion of Administrative Justice Act 3 of 2000 (PAJA), so that judicial review now has a statutory basis. The Constitutional Court[56] has made it clear that the source of the courts' power of review is no longer the common law but the PAJA, and ultimately the Constitution.[57] There is no room now for the view, quite popular at one time, that a sphere of administrative-law review governed by the common law continues to exist alongside the constitutional sphere, effectively adding up to two systems of law.[58] Nevertheless, the common law still exists and, to the extent that it is constitutionally compliant, it may be (and is) used to inform the meaning of the PAJA and section 33.[59] Judgments from the common-law era are still regularly referred

53 Article 18, Constitution of Namibia imposes a duty on administrators to act 'fairly and reasonably and comply with the requirements imposed … by common law and any relevant legislation', and protects the right of aggrieved persons to seek redress before a competent court or tribunal. Very similar wording appears in article 23 of the Constitution of Ghana, 1992.

54 Some have been struck down while the constitutionality of others has been upheld: cf. e.g. *Mohlomi* v. *Minister of Defence* 1997 (1) SA 124 (CC) and *Brümmer* v. *Minister for Social Development* 2009 (6) SA 323 (CC).

55 See e.g. *Chief Lesapo* v. *North West Agricultural Bank* 2000 (1) SA 409 (CC) para 22.

56 The Constitutional Court, created as the guardian of the democratic Constitution, is now at the apex of the superior court structure, with various provincial and local divisions of the High Court below it. In between is the Supreme Court of Appeal, formerly the Appellate Division, which functions as an intermediate court of appeal (in spite of what is implied by its name).

57 *Bato Star Fishing (Pty) Ltd* v. *Minister of Environmental Affairs* 2004 (4) SA 490 (CC) ('*Bato Star*') paras 22 and 25.

58 *Pharmaceutical Manufacturers Association of SA: In re Ex parte President of the Republic of South Africa* 2000 (2) SA 674 (CC) para 44; Cora Hoexter, 'The Constitutionalisation and Codification of Judicial Review in South Africa' in Christopher Forsyth, Mark Elliott, Swati Jhaveri et al. (eds.), *Effective Judicial Review: A Cornerstone of Good Governance* (2010) 43 at 48–9.

59 *Bato Star* (n 57) para 22.

to in cases decided under the PAJA. For instance, they are quite prominent in areas such as sub-delegation and legitimate expectations, where the common law was well developed and well understood.[60]

The highest court has also made it clear that because the PAJA gives effect to and effectively codifies the rights in section 33, a litigant may not avoid the provisions of the PAJA by seeking to rely directly on section 33 itself.[61] That is not to deny the appropriateness of direct reliance in other circumstances, of course, typically where the constitutionality of original legislation is being challenged.[62] Section 33 also plays an important role in the interpretation of provisions of the PAJA, and has generally been used to expand the scope of the statute and of judicial review under it.[63]

The heart of the PAJA is the extensive list of grounds of review contained in section 6 of the Act. Here one finds almost all of the common-law grounds from the pre-1994 era, which are the chief legacy of English law in this area: grounds such as lack of authority, error of law, ulterior purpose, acting under dictation, irrationality, unreasonableness, bias and procedural unfairness. So the English legacy lives on in statutory form, but with a few idiosyncracies. For instance, a couple of well-known grounds of review are missing from the list. Grounds addressing both vagueness and fettering appeared in the Administrative Justice Bill proposed by the South African Law Reform Commission but were dropped at the committee stage of the legislative process.[64] Fortunately, the PAJA's catch-all ground of 'otherwise unconstitutional or unlawful' is able to compensate for such omissions.

Another South African peculiarity is that the common-law ground of failure to decide is given great prominence in section 6(2)(g) read with section 6(3) of the PAJA, which makes detailed provision for failure to act within a prescribed period and/or within a reasonable time. These provisions were intended to benefit the rural poor and disadvantaged: they were added at the committee stage as a result of submissions complaining of the dilatoriness of administrators in dealing with applications for benefits.[65] Delay does seem to be a problem endemic to the South African administration, unfortunately, and the response 'come back next week' remains a depressingly common one.[66]

10.5 A GUIDING LIGHT

South African administrative law, originally borrowed mainly from English law, has itself become something worth emulating. Over the last two decades, the South African model described above has come to be seen as an archetype of constitutionalised judicial review. It

60 On sub-delegation, see further Cora Hoexter, *Administrative Law in South Africa* 2 ed (2012) 265–73; and on legitimate expectations, see Cora Hoexter, 'The Unruly Horse and the Gordian Knot: Legitimate Expectations in South Africa' in Matthew Groves and Greg Weeks (eds.), *Legitimate Expectations in the Common Law World* (2017) 165.

61 *Minister of Health* v. *New Clicks South Africa (Pty) Ltd* 2006 (2) SA 311 (CC) ('*New Clicks*') paras 95–7.

62 As, for instance, in *Zondi* v. *MEC for Traditional and Local Government Affairs* 2005 (3) SA 589 (CC), where the original legislation in question was found to be compliant with section 33.

63 See e.g. *Grey's Marine Hout Bay (Pty) Ltd* v. *Minister of Public Works* 2005 (6) SA 313 (SCA) para 23; and see the liberal interpretation of the PAJA's *Wednesbury*-inspired ground of unreasonableness, discussed in Section 10.6.

64 See South African Law Reform Commission *Project 115: Administrative Justice Report* (August 1999) 15ff ('the SALRC draft Bill'). While the reasons for dropping these grounds do not emerge clearly from the deliberations, it appears that their import may not have been understood by the portfolio committee: see J R de Ville, *Judicial Review of Administrative Action in South Africa* (2003) 114 and 186.

65 See De Ville (n 64) 184–5.

66 See *Offit Enterprises (Pty) Ltd* v. *Coega Development Corporation* 2010 (4) SA 242 (SCA) para 27.

has become a guiding light in this regard, particularly in Africa, where South Africa's administrative-justice rights have inspired or helped inspire the inclusion of similar rights in other post-independence constitutions.

In southern Africa, at least, this lighting of the way recalls relationships established long before independence. As noted by Beinart,[67] in the post-Union era the South African legal system had already spread to a greater or lesser extent to her neighbours, South-West Africa (later Namibia),[68] Rhodesia (later Zimbabwe) and Bechuanaland (later Botswana), as well as to two former British protectorates located within South Africa's borders, Lesotho and Swaziland. It says much that even today, important judgments of the Namibian and Zimbabwean courts are considered for inclusion in the *South African Law Reports*.

South Africa's administrative-justice rights exerted some influence early on, under the interim Constitution. Section 43 of the Malawian Constitution of 1994 was adapted from section 24 of South Africa's first democratic Constitution, although it is evidently intended to apply more widely than its model did.[69] In contrast, the wording of article 42 of Uganda's Constitution of 1995 is more reminiscent of article 18 of the Namibian Constitution.[70] But section 33 of the 1996 Constitution has been more influential than its predecessor. It has served as the model for the rights to 'fair administrative action' in article 47 of Kenya's Constitution of 2010, for the rights to just administrative action in section 68 of the Zimbabwean Constitution adopted in 2013, and – moving far beyond Africa – for similar rights in the Constitutions of the Maldives (2008), the Cayman Islands (2009) and Fiji (2013).

Given the breadth of section 33, it is interesting to see that the trend has been towards ever more expansive formulations. In layout and wording, Kenya's article 47 is almost identical to section 33 but slightly more generous: the Kenyan provision requires administrative action that is 'expeditious' and 'efficient' as well as 'lawful, reasonable and procedurally fair', and the right to reasons extends to administrative action that is merely 'likely to' have an adverse effect on a right or fundamental freedom.[71] In the case of Fiji, article 16 is again more generous than section 33. Article 16(1)(a) requires both executive and administrative action to be 'lawful, rational, proportionate, procedurally fair, and reasonably prompt', while the right to reasons in (b) applies to 'every person who has been adversely affected by any executive or administrative action'.

The Zimbabwean provision is the most lavish of all: section 68(1) promises action that is 'lawful, prompt, efficient, reasonable, proportionate, impartial and both substantively and procedurally fair'. The reference to substantive fairness is especially arresting, for it takes the section 68(1) rights well beyond the normal scope of administrative justice – and does so notwithstanding the absence of a tradition of review on substantive grounds in Zimbabwean law.[72] It will be interesting to see, in years to come, whether these increasingly ambitious

67 Beinart (n 5) 8.

68 South Africa's influence was particularly strong here as a result of its long possession of the territory; see Section 10.4.

69 Section 43(1) compresses section 24(a), (b) and (d) into a single right to 'lawful and procedurally fair administrative action which is justifiable in relation to reasons given', while section 43(2) covers the right to reasons itself. In contrast with the different dosages used in section 24, however, the section 43 rights apply more universally where 'rights, freedoms, legitimate expectations or interests are affected or threatened'.

70 Article 42 provides: 'Any person appearing before any administrative official or body has a right to be treated justly and fairly and shall have a right to apply to a court of law in respect of any administrative decision taken against him or her.' Cf. article 38 of the Constitution of Burundi, 2005.

71 See Migai Akech's contribution on Kenya in this volume.

72 See G Feltoe, *Guide to Zimbabwean Administrative Law* (2012) 31.

formulations put pressure on the South African courts to interpret s 33 (or the PAJA) even more expansively.

The influence of the South African model has not been confined to constitutional provisions. Some countries, such as Namibia, are currently considering the enactment of legislation to give effect to their administrative-justice rights, while others have actually done so. Most notably, Kenya's Fair Administrative Action Act of 2015 (FAAA) was enacted pursuant to a mandate in article 47(3) and was modelled closely on the PAJA. The two statutes cover very much the same ground and the resemblance between them is striking.

Like the PAJA, the FAAA starts with a definition of administrative action, deals in some detail with the content of procedural fairness, fleshes out the right to reasons (even though that right did not feature in the article 47(3) mandate), has a detailed list of the grounds of review and deals explicitly with the duty to exhaust internal remedies. The remedies listed are also very similar to those in the PAJA. There are differences too, especially since the Kenyan drafters took note of the South African experience and sensibly chose to avoid some of the more flawed and problematic provisions of the South African legislation.[73] One apparently significant difference, the express preservation of the common law in section 12 of the FAAA, is probably more apparent than real; for the highest courts of both countries seem to agree that the extent to which the common law remains relevant is something to be determined on a case-by-case basis.[74] As already noted, the South African courts are very willing to refer to the pre-1994 common law where it is constitutionally compliant.

The South African case law on administrative-law review exerts considerable influence throughout southern Africa and is relied on to varying degrees in countries such as Botswana, Lesotho, Namibia, Swaziland and Zimbabwe. The Kenyan courts, too, have been known to borrow from the jurisprudence of the Constitutional Court, though not always with attribution.[75]

10.6 DISTINCTIVE FEATURES OF THE INDIGENISED SYSTEM

In spite of the sweeping changes described in this chapter, the most distinctive features of South Africa's indigenised administrative-law system are not primarily doctrinal in nature. They continue to be associated with the dominance of judicial review.

Although South African administrative law has acquired a range of safeguards beyond judicial review, in practice these have not done much to change the focus of the discipline. Instead, the courts have increasingly filled the accountability vacuum, and judicial review has become even more prominent as a remedy for maladministration. In this the courts have demonstrated their mastery of the common-law tradition of judicial law-making, a practice brought to the Cape in 1827 – and now facilitated by key provisions of a transformative Constitution.[76] In less than two decades, the courts have managed to expand the already quite

[73] See Cora Hoexter, 'Administrative Justice in Kenya: Learning from South Africa's Mistakes' (2018) 62 *Journal of African Law* 105 at 116–20. For example, the drafters of the FAAA rejected the narrow and overly complicated definition of administrative action in the PAJA; they avoided the unpopular outer limit of six months for bringing an application for review; and they chose not to replicate the PAJA's *Wednesbury*-like ground of unreasonableness.

[74] See e.g. *Bato Star* (n 57) para 22, a dictum echoed by the Kenyan Court of Appeal in *Suchan Investment Limited v. Ministry of National Heritage and Culture* [2016] eKLR (4 March 2016) para 54. See further Hoexter 'Administrative Justice in Kenya' (n 73) 110–11.

[75] For examples of such borrowing, see Hoexter 'Administrative Justice in Kenya' (n 73) 113–14.

[76] These include sections 38 and 172, which provide for generous standing and very liberal remedial powers. For further discussion of factors that encourage the South African courts to 'perform', see Cora Hoexter, 'A Rainbow

expansive list of grounds of review in the PAJA; and even more remarkably, they have developed an extensive constitutional safety net for cases not addressed by the PAJA. This second feat of judicial law-making can be likened to the (very rapid) creation of a new common law for the constitutional era.[77]

In spite of their readiness to intervene and their creativity, however, the South African courts have not abandoned the essential rhetoric of administrative law. References to the distinction between review and appeal, or legality and merits, probably remain as frequent and fervent as ever. Indeed, the courts' boldest moves have generally been coupled with statements about the importance of preserving that distinction.

10.6.1 *The Continuing Dominance of Judicial Review*

Beyond judicial review, the administrative-law system has been enriched by a number of constitutional innovations, including various 'Chapter 9' institutions created in support of constitutional democracy: the office of Public Protector, a Human Rights Commission, a Commission on Gender Equality and other such bodies. A right of access to information has been given legislative effect, and there is considerable scope for public participation in law-making processes.[78] Unfortunately, non-curial mechanisms such as these have often proved far less effective in practice than in theory,[79] and all too often their enforcement has required a court order. Requests for state-held information, for instance, are frequently ignored by government departments,[80] meaning that those asserting the right of access to information may well have to resort to litigation. Similarly, the recommendations of the Public Protector have sometimes had to be enforced in court.[81] The result is that judicial review has tended to remain the primary safeguard it has traditionally been.

This is consonant with the long South African tradition of relying on the courts to uphold the rule of law. The presidency of Jacob Zuma (May 2009–February 2018) witnessed a particular spate of judicial review applications in politically charged matters. This wave of 'lawfare' was facilitated by factors including generous constitutional provisions regulating standing and remedies, the courts' liberal approach to justiciability and the absence of a 'political question' doctrine.[82] But the more immediate impetus for the spike in judicial review applications was swiftly rising levels of public corruption, nepotism and, indeed, 'state capture':[83] devastating developments that the political branches proved unwilling or unable to curb by means of political processes. In the absence of proper oversight by political institutions, it is not surprising that opposition parties and NGOs seeking to uphold the rule of law were so ready to turn to the courts (which had largely managed to resist capture).

of One Colour? Review on Substantive Grounds in South African Law' in Hanna Wilberg and Mark Elliott (eds.), *The Scope and Intensity of Substantive Review: Traversing Taggart's Rainbow* (2015) 163 at 187ff.

77 See Cora Hoexter, 'South African Administrative Law at a Crossroads: The PAJA and the Principle of Legality', *Administrative Law in the Common Law World*, 28 April 2017, available at https://adminlawblog.org.

78 Particularly in terms of sections 59(1), 72(1), 118(1) and 160(4)(b) and (7) of the Constitution.

79 See Cora Hoexter, 'Administrative Justice and the Enforcement of the Constitution' in Hugh Corder, Veronica Federico and Romano Orrù (eds.), *The Quest for Constitutionalism: South Africa since 1994* (2014) 127 at 134–6.

80 See further Iain Currie, 'Freedom of Information: Controversies and Reforms' in Corder, Federico and Orrù (n 79) 169.

81 See especially *Economic Freedom Fighters* v. *Speaker, National Assembly* 2016 (3) SA 580 (CC).

82 See further Hugh Corder and Cora Hoexter, '"Lawfare" in South Africa and Its Effects on the Judiciary' (2017) 10 *African Journal of Legal Studies* 105 .

83 Tellingly, on 16 October 2017, the Pan South African Language Board announced that 'state capture' was the most prominent word or phrase of the year.

The courts have found against the government in any number of cases in recent years, from declaring unlawful its defiance of an International Criminal Court warrant for the arrest of President al-Bashir of Sudan[84] to striking down a pivotal decision to drop corruption charges against Jacob Zuma.[85] In another prominent example, an inconvenient National Director of Public Prosecutions was paid millions to vacate his (supposedly independent) office, leaving President Zuma free to appoint someone more pliable.[86] The sad reality is that, as the National Executive Committee of the majority party has acknowledged, under Zuma the government abdicated its governance responsibilities to the judiciary to a considerable extent.[87]

10.6.2 *Rapidly Expanding Grounds of Review*

The list of grounds of review in section 6 of the PAJA is an extensive one by any measure. Nevertheless, it has steadily been expanded by the courts to meet the apparently insatiable demand for more judicial review on ever wider grounds. In terms of jurisdiction, for instance, a decade ago the Constitutional Court rejected ipsedixitism in relation to subjectively phrased jurisdictional facts,[88] and more recently, it expanded the ambit of error of law to include an administrator's reliance on (binding) judicial precedent.[89] As regards substantive grounds, the most dramatic development in recent years has been the creation of non-jurisdictional 'material mistake of fact' as a ground of review. The expansion of the existing ground of unreasonableness, section 6(2)(h) of the PAJA, is also noteworthy.[90] Support for both of these developments was found in the dicta of English courts as well as in the South African Constitution.

At common law, non-jurisdictional mistakes of fact were reviewable only on the traditional grounds of abuse of discretion: mala fides, ulterior motive, failure to apply the mind or breach of an express statutory provision.[91] These grounds were difficult or impossible to establish, however, particularly where incorrect information had been placed before an unwitting administrator. In the *Pepcor* case of 2003, the Supreme Court of Appeal held that material mistake of fact ought to be a ground of review in itself – adding that it should not be applied so as to 'blur, far less eliminate', the crucial distinction between legality and merits.[92]

The court reasoned as follows:

> If legislation has empowered a functionary to make a decision, in the public interest, the decision should be made on the material facts which should have been available for the decision properly to have been made. And if a decision has been made in ignorance of facts

84 *Southern Africa Litigation Centre* v. *Minister of Justice and Constitutional Development* 2015 (5) SA 1 (GP), largely upheld on appeal in *Minister of Justice and Constitutional Development* v. *Southern Africa Litigation Centre* 2016 (3) SA 317 (SCA).

85 *Democratic Alliance* v. *Acting National Director of Public Prosecutions* 2016 (8) BCLR 1077 (GP). For further examples, see Corder and Hoexter (n 82).

86 *Corruption Watch NPC* v. *President of the Republic of South Africa* 2018 (10) BCLR 1179 (CC).

87 Secretary-General of the African National Congress, Gwede Mantashe, in a public statement made after a National Executive Committee meeting held on 24–25 March 2017.

88 *Walele* v. *City of Cape Town* 2008 (6) SA 129 (CC) para 60.

89 *Genesis Medical Aid Scheme* v. *Registrar, Medical Schemes* 2017 (6) SA 1 (CC); and see Paul Daly's contribution on Canada in this volume.

90 For more detail, see Hoexter 'A Rainbow of One Colour' (n 76) 166–74.

91 *Shidiack* v. *Union Government (Minister of the Interior)* 1912 AD 642 at 651–2 (Innes CJ).

92 Cloete JA for a unanimous court in *Pepcor Retirement Fund* v. *Financial Services Board* 2003 (6) SA 38 (SCA) ('*Pepcor*') para 48.

> material to the decision and which therefore should have been before the functionary, the decision should . . . be reviewable.[93]

This statement owed much to English authority, especially the opinion of Scarman LJ in the *Tameside* case[94] and that of Lord Slynn in *Ex parte* A.[95] The court in *Pepcor* quoted extensively from both.[96]

The PAJA was not applicable in this case, so this development took place under the principle of legality (discussed in the following section); but with an eye to the future, the court characterised the new ground as an extension of an existing ground in section 6(2)(e)(iii) of the PAJA (relevant and irrelevant considerations).[97] It also indicated that the application of the new ground in a particular case would depend on factors including the public interest and prejudice to any of the parties. These factors have not been used as a brake in practice, however, and the ground has been applied in several cases since *Pepcor*, both under the principle of legality and under the PAJA.[98] A more recent and more effective brake was applied in *Dumani*, where the Supreme Court of Appeal emphasised that the ground is capable of application only to facts that are uncontentious in the sense of being objectively verifiable.[99] That important qualification was borrowed, of course, from the judgment of Carnwath LJ in *E* v. *Secretary of State for the Home Department.*[100] It has meant, for instance, that mistake of fact was not applicable to a refugee officer's assessment of the political situation in Somalia.[101]

When one considers the far-reaching nature of some of the grounds of review in the PAJA, it seems odd that the legislature should have opted to model the ground of unreasonableness on *Wednesbury* – a test that has been more or less discredited throughout the common-law world. As Currie suggests, the retrogressive choice was almost certainly motivated by 'a desire to reduce the scope of judicial review'.[102] Section 6(2)(h) targets action that is 'so unreasonable that no reasonable person could have so exercised the power or performed the function'. Judicial interpretation using the touchstone of section 33 has considerably broadened the ground, however, with some help from English law. In *Bato Star*,[103] the Constitutional Court reasoned that the PAJA review ground had to be construed consistently with the Constitution, and since section 33(1) calls for action that is 'reasonable', it evidently contemplates review of action that is simply 'unreasonable'. With reference to the test prescribed by Lord Cooke in *Trader's Ferry*,[104] O'Regan J concluded that a decision would be reviewable under section 6(2)(h), where 'it is one that a reasonable decision-maker could not reach'.[105] This would

93 *Pepcor* (n 92) para 47.
94 *Secretary of State for Education and Science* v. *Tameside Metropolitan Borough Council* [1977] AC 1014.
95 *R* v. *Criminal Injuries Compensation Board, Ex parte A* [1999] 2 AC 330 at 344–5.
96 *Pepcor* (n 92) paras 33–9.
97 *Pepcor* (n 92) para 46.
98 Including *Government Employees Pension Fund* v. *Buitendag* 2007 (4) SA 2 (SCA), *Chairpersons' Association* v. *Minister of Arts and Culture* 2007 (5) SA 236 (SCA) and *Chairman, State Tender Board* v. *Digital Voice Processing (Pty) Ltd* 2012 (2) SA 16 (SCA).
99 *Dumani* v. *Nair* 2013 (2) SA 274 (SCA) ('*Dumani*') para 32.
100 [2004] QB 1044.
101 *Gorhan* v. *Minister of Home Affairs* [2016] ZAECPEHC 70 (20 October 2016) para 52.
102 Iain Currie, *The Promotion of Administrative Justice Act: A Commentary*, 2nd ed (2007) 169–70. It is worth noting that in the constitutional negotiations, the African National Congress (now the governing party) argued for a standard of 'such gross unreasonableness . . . as to amount to manifest injustice': see the ANC's draft Bill of Rights published in (1991) 7 *South African Journal on Human Rights* 110.
103 *Bato Star* (n 57).
104 *R* v. *Chief Constable of Sussex, ex parte International Trader's Ferry Ltd* [1999] 2 AC 418 at 452 ('*Trader's Ferry*').
105 Bato Star (n 57) para 44.

depend on the circumstances but would be guided by considerations including 'the nature of the decision, the identity and expertise of the decision-maker, the range of factors relevant to the decision, the reasons given for the decision, the nature of the competing interests involved and the impact of the decision on the lives and well-being of those affected'.[106]

Some of these considerations, especially the last two, lend themselves to a proportionality inquiry. That is not particularly surprising, for it is well understood in South African jurisprudence that proportionality is an aspect of reasonableness.[107] But it is interesting when one considers that an explicit ground of proportionality recommended by the Law Commission in its draft Bill[108] was rejected during the parliamentary process. In *Bato Star*, the Constitutional Court managed to reinstate it to some extent – again with the caveat that the distinction between appeal and review 'continues to be significant'.[109]

10.6.3 *Growth of 'Legality' Review and Sidelining of the PAJA*

The PAJA was enacted to give effect to the rights in section 33(1) and (2). However, its narrow and complicated definition of 'administrative action', among other provisions, has encouraged widespread avoidance of the statute in favour of what has come to be called 'legality review': judicial review under a constitutional principle of legality. The principle in question is held to be an aspect of the rule of law, which in turn is expressly listed in section 1(c) of the Constitution as a founding value of the Republic. Though legality review was conceived as a mere safety net for instances of non-administrative action, the grounds associated with it have proliferated remarkably in recent years and now resemble those listed in the PAJA.

When it was first identified by the Constitutional Court in 1998, South Africa's version of the principle of legality was held to imply merely that those exercising public power had to act within their powers.[110] But the principle soon evolved. Within a few months, the same court added that they also had to act in good faith and not misconstrue their powers.[111] Not long after that came the seminal judgment in *Pharmaceutical Manufacturers Association*, which laid down a minimum requirement of rationality: a rational connection between the exercise of a power and the purpose for which the power was given.[112]

This basic requirement proved to be hugely significant. In the *Simelane* case, the Constitutional Court maintained that not only the decision but also '*everything done in the process of taking that decision*, constitutes means towards the attainment of the purpose for which the power was conferred'.[113] This proposition spawned 'procedural rationality' as a companion to the 'substantive' rationality contemplated in *Pharmaceutical Manufacturers Association*, where the focus is on the decision itself. As the full bench of the High Court has put it, 'to determine procedural irrationality is to look at the process as a whole and determine whether steps in the process were rationally related to the end sought to be achieved; if not,

106 Bato Star (n 57) para 45.
107 As Sachs J remarked in a minority judgment in *New Clicks* (n 61) para 637.
108 Clause 7(1)(g) of the SALRC draft Bill (n 64) provided for review for 'disproportionality between the adverse and beneficial consequences of the action' and the existence of 'less restrictive means to achieve the purpose for which the action was taken'.
109 *Bato Star* (n 57) para 45.
110 *Fedsure* v. *Greater Johannesburg Metropolitan Council* 1999 (1) SA 374 (CC) paras 56, 58.
111 *President of the Republic of South Africa* v. *South African Rugby Football Union* 2000 (1) SA 1 (CC) para 148.
112 *Pharmaceutical Manufacturers Association* (n 58) para 85.
113 *Democratic Alliance* v. *President of the Republic of South Africa* 2013 (1) SA 248 (CC) para 36, my emphasis.

whether … a particular step is so unrelated to the end as to taint the whole process with irrationality'.[114]

Importantly, too, while procedural fairness is said not to be a requirement under the legality principle, a fair hearing or the giving of reasons[115] may nevertheless be required in a particular case as a matter of procedural rationality.[116] All this has made scrutiny for rationality very much more searching than it used to be – notwithstanding the court's assurance in *Simelane* that 'a rationality standard by its very nature prescribes the lowest possible threshold' for the review of executive decisions.[117]

The truth is that the principle of legality has burgeoned out of all recognition, although it has not (yet) come to encompass the ground of reasonableness, which includes proportionality. The legality principle has the advantage of applying to every exercise of public power, and its ability to mimic virtually any other ground of review in the PAJA has made it tremendously popular with litigants and, indeed, with the courts. This, in turn, has inspired avoidance of the PAJA in favour of legality review, which comes untrammeled by the difficult administrative action inquiry and which attracts gentler common-law versions of the unpopular procedural requirements found in section 7 of the PAJA: a strict deadline for launching review proceedings[118] and a rigorous duty to exhaust internal remedies. It is not so surprising, then, that there has been a rapidly growing tendency to rely on the principle of legality, even where it is not clear that the action being challenged is non-administrative action.

What is more surprising is the extent to which the courts have gone along with this tendency; for, as I have pointed out elsewhere, it effectively makes the PAJA redundant, thus disregarding some rather fundamental constitutional principles as well as the mandate in section 33(3).[119] The highest court went so far as to encourage the trend in a unanimous 2010 judgment,[120] and in a later one, the court merely recorded its apparent change of mind in a very brief footnote.[121]

In the *Gijima* case, both the High Court and the Supreme Court of Appeal disapproved of the trend, with the latter holding that litigants are not entitled to bypass the PAJA in favour of a principle that is supposed to be a measure of last resort.[122] On further appeal, however, the Constitutional Court focused on the identity of the applicant, an organ of state seeking to have its own decision reviewed.[123] The court concluded that since organs of state are not the

114 The full court in *Democratic Alliance* v. *Minister of International Relations and Cooperation* 2017 (3) SA 212 (GP) para 64.

115 See *Albutt* v. *Centre for the Study of Violence and Reconciliation* 2010 (3) SA 293 (CC) ('*Albutt*') paras 68, 70–2; *Judicial Service Commission* v. *Cape Bar Council* 2013 (1) SA 170 (SCA) paras 44–5.

116 In *Law Society of South Africa* v. *President of the Republic of South Africa* 2019 (3) SA 30 (CC) para 64 the Constitutional Court confined the meaning of 'procedural fairness' to hearing a person who is likely to be adversely affected by a decision. This narrow approach tends to contradict the court's previous jurisprudence, in which rationality or more informed decision-making often featured as one of the rationales for a fair hearing.

117 *Democratic Alliance* v. *President of the RSA* (n 113) paras 41–2.

118 The differences between the strict delay rule in the PAJA and the more flexible approach under the legality principle were highlighted in *Buffalo City Metropolitan Municipality* v. *Asla Construction (Pty) Ltd* 2019 (4) SA 331 (CC) ('*Asla Construction*'). More remarkably, the court confirmed that the court may still declare the action unlawful, even in the case of unreasonable delay that cannot be condoned; see paras 63–71.

119 See Hoexter 'SA Administrative Law at a Crossroads' (n 77). For a more detailed discussion of the problem of avoidance of the PAJA, see Hoexter, *Administrative Law in South Africa* (n 60) 131–7.

120 *Albutt* (n 115) paras 82–3.

121 *Minister of Defence and Military Veterans* v. *Motau* 2014 (5) SA 69 (CC) para 27 fn 28.

122 *State Information Technology Agency Soc Ltd* v. *Gijima Holdings (Pty) Ltd* [2015] ZAGPPHC 1079 (18 May 2015) and *State Information Technology Agency Soc Ltd* v. *Gijima Holdings (Pty) Ltd* 2017 (2) SA 63 (SCA) paras 38 and 44.

123 *State Information Technology Agency Soc Ltd* v. *Gijima Holdings (Pty) Ltd* 2018 (2) SA 23 (CC) ('*Gijima*').

primary beneficiaries of the section 33 rights, the PAJA is simply not available to them as applicants asking for review of their own decisions – and they are thus obliged to use the principle of legality.[124] The broader problem of sidestepping was thus itself sidestepped. Indeed, as two members of the court observed in a subsequent case, the approach in *Gijima* stands accused of aggravating the existing bifurcation of South African administrative law.[125]

But 'bifurcation' is an understatement, as the principle of legality is not the only way of avoiding the PAJA with impunity. In recent years the highest court has developed a public-law claim of unconscionable state conduct that closely resembles an administrative-justice claim but is nevertheless said to be based on rights *other than those in section* 33.[126] This device, another claim 'legitimately outside PAJA',[127] effectively allows the court to rescue deserving applicants who ought to have challenged administrative action via the PAJA but did not. The problem is that since virtually every administrative-justice case implicates a constitutional right or rights other than those in section 33 itself (rights to social security, for example, or property or fair labour practices), the scope for sidestepping section 33 and the PAJA seems considerable.

10.7 THE CONTINUING INFLUENCE OF ENGLISH ADMINISTRATIVE LAW

In spite of the thorough indigenisation of South African administrative law, its longstanding connection with English administrative law is still quite obvious and probably always will be. This is remarkable when one considers that English precedents have not been generally binding on South African courts since 1950[128] and that contemporary English law is now effectively foreign law. However, the historical link with Britain and the familiarity of English-law concepts and doctrines have ensured that English cases continue to be relied on as persuasive authority in many areas of South African law today – and administrative law is certainly one of those areas. The following discussion gives some sense of the nature and extent of this influence by referring to a few examples from the pre- and post-1994 eras.

A century ago, areas of especially strong English influence included the law relating to the prerogative as a source of administrative authority. In 1916, for instance, the prerogative was held to be as extensive in the province of Natal as in England, except to the extent that it had been modified or abandoned in either country.[129] Even in 1950, at a time when 'purist' views and Afrikaner nationalism[130] were dominant, the Appellate Division confirmed that 'in

124 *Gijima* (n 123) paras 29–32, 37. No reference was made to the principle of legality in any other jurisdiction: *Gijima* seems to have been an entirely home-grown affair.

125 Cameron and Froneman JJ in *Asla Construction* (n 118) para 112. This accusation is made, for instance, in Leo Boonzaier, 'A Decision to Undo' (2018) 135 *South African Law Journal* 642 at 655–6.

126 *KZN Joint Liaison Committee* v. *MEC for Education, KwaZulu-Natal* 2013 (4) SA 262 (CC) (concerning the right to education) as explained in *Pretorius* v. *Transport Pension Fund* (2018) 39 *Industrial Law Journal* 1937 (CC) paras 33–41 (implicating the right to social security).

127 *Pretorius* v. *Transport Pension Fund* (n 126) paras 40–41.

128 See Hahlo and Kahn *The Union of South Africa* (n 16) 31–4. Relevant decisions of the Judicial Committee of the Privy Council were absolutely binding on South African courts until appeals from the Appellate Division were abolished by the Privy Council Appeals Act 16 of 1950. After that, English judgments created no binding precedent in South Africa except in the law of evidence. Here decisions of the Supreme Court of Judicature continue to be followed to 30 May 1961, the day before South Africa became independent from Britain: *Van der Linde* v. *Calitz* 1967 (2) SA 239 (A), and see further Hahlo and Kahn *The South African Legal System* (n 11) 258–60.

129 *Union Government (Minister of Lands)* v. *Estate Whittaker* 1916 AD 194 at 202.

130 See n 2 above.

inquiring into the scope of the Royal Prerogative one must have regard to English and not Roman-Dutch authorities'.[131]

Another area notable for reliance on English case law was unreasonableness as a ground of review for delegated legislation: the test laid down by Lord Russell in *Kruse* v. *Johnson*[132] had already been applied at the time of Union and came to be accepted in a large number of cases. As Plasket and Firman explained many years later, the doctrine had special relevance for South Africa under apartheid, when discriminatory legislation was largely implemented by means of proclamations and regulations: 'To label the four legs of Lord Russell's test a "mini bill of rights of the common law" would not be to exaggerate the potency of *Kruse*.'[133]

In the area of procedural fairness, the English law was always influential. Dicta from classic cases such as *Board of Education* v. *Rice*[134] and *Russell* v. *Duke of Norfolk*[135] were referred to many times by South African courts, and indeed they continue to be cited quite regularly today. But the clearest instance of English influence in this part of the law is the adoption of the doctrine of legitimate expectations, which occurred officially in the *Traub* case of 1989.[136] Here Corbett CJ (a Cambridge graduate) took inspiration from the English law of the time and quoted extensively from the *CCSU* case.[137] The Chief Justice also made reference to another product of English law, the 'duty to act fairly'.[138] This duty had previously been alluded to in a few South African cases and had been hailed by Baxter as a way of escaping the classification of functions.[139]

The same Chief Justice reinvented the principles governing error of law a few years later, in *Hira* v. *Booysen*,[140] with reference to leading English cases including *Anisminic*[141] and *Re Racal Communications*.[142]

Interestingly, reliance on the concepts and doctrines of English administrative law seems to have increased rather than diminished since 1994. A factor that is thought to encourage the use of foreign jurisprudence is section 39(1) of the Constitution, which requires the courts to consider international law when they are interpreting the Bill of Rights and expressly permits them to consider foreign law. Another is the strong 'comparative law ethos' in this country.[143] Whatever the respective strength of these factors, the UK is certainly a prominent source of inspiration to the South African courts in relation to both section 33 of the Bill of Rights and the principle of legality.

As explained in Section 10.6, dicta from English cases were used to support the courts' interpretation of the PAJA ground of unreasonableness, as well as the recognition and

131 *Sachs* v. *Dönges NO* 1950 (2) SA 265 (A) at 288.
132 [1898] 2 QB 91 at 99–100.
133 C M Plasket and P L Firman, 'Subordinate Legislation and Unreasonableness: The Application of *Kruse* v. *Johnson* ([1898] 2 QB 91) by the South African Courts' (1984) 47 *Tyskrif vir Hedendaagse Romeins-Hollandse Reg* 416 at 418.
134 [1911] AC 179.
135 [1949] 1 All ER 109.
136 *Administrator, Transvaal* v. *Traub* 1989 (4) SA 731 (A) ('*Traub*'); Hoexter, 'The Unruly Horse and the Gordian Knot' (n 60).
137 *Council of Civil Service Unions (CCSU)* v. *Minister for the Civil Service* [1985] AC 374.
138 *Traub* (n 136) at 755D–E.
139 See Baxter (n 4) 595.
140 *Hira* v. *Booysen* 1992 (4) SA 69 (A).
141 *Anisminic Ltd* v. *Foreign Compensation Commission* [1969] 2 AC 147.
142 *Re Racal Communications Ltd* [1981] AC 374.
143 L W H Ackermann, 'Constitutional Comparativism in South Africa' (2006) 123 *South African Law Journal* 497 at 501.

development of material mistake of fact as a ground of review. Several other significant developments in South African law have leant on English ideas and precedents. For example, the *Datafin*[144] case was referred to in a number of South African judgments before 1994, and it continues to be cited quite regularly today in the context of public powers and functions: along with other prominent English cases, it featured in the leading case of *AAA Investments*[145] and has done so in many other judgments since then.

Another example is Forsyth's theory of the second actor.[146] This theory was crucial to the principles established by the Supreme Court of Appeal in the *Oudekraal* case of 2004[147] in relation to the status and effects of unlawful administrative action, just as the decision of the House of Lords in *Boddington*[148] illuminated the South African court's understanding of the nature and ambit of collateral challenge.[149] *Oudekraal* has, in turn, become one of the most pivotal administrative-law judgments of the constitutional era, and its citations to Forsyth, *Boddington* and other English cases have become embedded in South African law.

There can be no doubt, then, about the continuing utility of English case law to the South African courts' elaboration of principles of administrative law – and this notwithstanding obvious constitutional differences between the two systems. One might wonder whether this situation is likely to change in the future. Since the South African courts already seek inspiration sometimes from other constitutionalised systems such as India, they might perhaps start looking to constitutionalised jurisdictions that have actually borrowed from section 33 or the PAJA. Such a move not only would make logical sense but also would be consonant with current calls for the law to be decolonised.[150] But even then, one suspects that the connection with English law is simply too strong and too deep to be broken completely.

10.8 CONCLUSION

Once a pale reflection of the English common law, South African administrative law has been thoroughly indigenised by the constitutionalisation and codification of judicial review. The South African model has indeed come to be seen as an archetype of constitutionalised judicial review. Over the last two decades, the South African rights to just administrative action and the legislation giving effect to them, the PAJA, have been a guiding light for a number of other jurisdictions.

144 R v. *Panel on Take-overs and Mergers, ex parte Datafin plc* [1987] QB 815.

145 *AAA Investments (Pty) Ltd* v. *Micro Finance Regulatory Council* 2007 (1) SA 343 (CC) paras 32 and 120, and see further Cora Hoexter, 'A Matter of Feel? Public Powers and Functions in South Africa' in Mark Elliott, Shona Wilson Stark and Jason NE Varuhas (eds,), *The Unity of Public Law? Doctrinal, Theoretical and Comparative Perspectives* (2018) 149.

146 Christopher Forsyth, '"The Metaphysic of Nullity": Invalidity, Conceptual Reasoning and the Rule of Law' in Christopher Forsyth and Ivan Hare (eds.), *The Golden Metwand and the Crooked Cord: Essays on Public Law in Honour of Sir William Wade QC* (1998) 141; and see further Christopher Forsyth, 'The Theory of the Second Actor Revisited' 2006 *Acta Juridica* 209.

147 *Oudekraal Estates (Pty) Ltd* v. *City of Cape Town* 2004 (6) SA 222 (SCA) ('*Oudekraal*').

148 *Boddington* v. *British Transport Police* [1999] 2 AC 143, in which Lord Steyn referred to Forsyth's 'Metaphysic of Nullity' (n 146) with approval (at 172).

149 See *Oudekraal* (n 147) para 32, where the court quotes extensively from the opinions of Lord Irvine LC and Lord Steyn.

150 See e.g. Mapula Sedutla, 'NADEL Discuss Decolonisation of the Law at AGM' May 2017 *De Rebus* 6; C Himonga and F Diallo, 'Decolonisation and Teaching Law in Africa with Special Reference to Living Customary Law' (2017) 20 *Potchefstroom Electronic Law Journal* 1.

This chapter has sought to identify the most significant features of the South African system both before and after 1994, and to describe its influence on other jurisdictions. It has also pointed to examples of areas in which English cases and doctrines have been and continue to be relied on by the South African courts: evidence of a longstanding and perhaps unbreakable connection between the two systems.

11

Judicial Review in Kenya

The Ambivalent Legacy of English Law

Migai Akech

11.1 INTRODUCTION

Judicial review can, at least in theory, facilitate the attainment of democratic governance. Not only is judicial review a mechanism to control governmental power; it also provides a means through which individuals can participate in governance. This latter function is of particular importance in states with authoritarian or dominant-party rule. In common law jurisdictions, the principles and procedures of administrative law are a product of the English common law. Although these principles and procedures appear to be the same in most common law systems, they are often articulated differently owing to various historical, social and political reasons – as Kenya's experience will demonstrate.

This chapter considers the evolution of judicial review in Kenya, and the continued relevance of English law, in the broader context of the role of judicial review in facilitating the attainment of democratic governance. It argues that English law bequeathed to Kenya an ambivalent legacy that continues to shape the exercise of judicial review. In theory, law has promised to provide a bulwark against the abuse of governmental power. In practice, however, it has largely served to facilitate authoritarianism. Section 11.2 locates judicial review in the context of governance in colonial and postcolonial Kenya. Section 11.3 examines the nature and role of judicial review in the Kenya colony. Section 11.4 examines the nature and role of judicial review in Independent Kenya. Section 11.5 examines the nature and role of judicial review after the promulgation of the Constitution of Kenya 2010. Section 11.6 provides a conclusion.

11.2 GOVERNANCE IN COLONIAL AND POSTCOLONIAL KENYA

In order to understand the evolution of judicial review in Kenya, it is useful to examine it in the context of the dynamics of governance in both colonial and postcolonial times. How did the prevailing English notions of governance influence the colonial enterprise? Second, what role did these notions subsequently play in the governance of the independent state? Third, what role did law play in both contexts?

Throughout the colonial period, the subjugation and domination of the colonized characterized governance. The colonial polity was undemocratic, particularly for the African population. Africans were subjects, not citizens; the paternalistic and despotic colonial government decided what was best for Africans, without consulting them.[1] Asians fared better, as they came to enjoy rights that in some respects were comparable to the white settlers.[2]

Britain acquired control of Kenya in 1895, having decided to declare it a protectorate and take over from the Imperial British East Africa Company.[3] Prior to the declaration of the protectorate, Britain had enacted a Foreign Jurisdiction Act, which gave it the power to exercise jurisdiction over its colonized territories.[4] Among other things, this law gave Britain the power to promulgate regulations for the protectorate and hold courts.[5] Ironically, the inhabitants of the protectorate were not British subjects in the eyes of English law, yet were subject to the laws of the protecting power.[6] Thus, while the local inhabitants were treated as foreigners, the colonizer assumed power over them on the basis that it needed to ensure effective government in the protectorate.[7] It thus enacted laws that gave it power to establish courts with jurisdiction over the local inhabitants, the so–called native courts.[8] Law, therefore, played an instrumental role in enabling Britain to assume full governmental powers in the protectorate.[9]

In terms of governance, the protectorate was headed by a Commissioner (later Governor when Kenya became a colony in 1920) who was the chief executive officer of the territory and was only answerable to the Colonial Secretary, who was based at the Colonial Office in Whitehall, England. The Commissioner/Governor had extensive powers, including the powers to make laws, establish courts and appoint judicial officers.[10] A team of administrators – consisting of an executive council and local administrators – supported the Commissioner. In practice, however, there "was too little control of senior officials by Whitehall, and by senior officials of their juniors."[11] Administrators "often did not know what the law allowed or forbade them to do, or if they did, sometimes considered that it was unrealistic and ignored it."[12] A legislative council was subsequently introduced, although it did not exercise any real power, the colonial enterprise being based on the principle that the legislature was subordinate to the executive.[13] In fact, until 1948, the Commissioner/Governor was the Speaker of the Legislative Council.[14] The courts also lacked the will to control the administration.[15] For example, in *Nyali Ltd* v. *Attorney-General*, Lord Denning, asserted that "Once jurisdiction is exercised by the Crown the courts will not permit it to be challenged."[16]

1 Mahmood Mamdani, *Citizen and Subject: Contemporary Africa and the Legacy of Late Colonialism* (Princeton University Press, 1996).
2 Y. P. Ghai and J. P. W. B. McAuslan, *Public Law and Political Change in Kenya: A Study of the Legal Framework of Government from Colonial Times to Present* (Oxford University Press, 1970) 47–50, 163–166.
3 Ghai and McAuslan, at 3.
4 Ghai and McAuslan, at 15.
5 Ghai and McAuslan, at 16.
6 Ghai and McAuslan, at 18. While this may be typical of colonial governance, the unequal treatment is stark: residents denied citizenship rights and were subject to oppressive laws, such as the East Africa Order in Council 1897, S.R.O. 1575/1897.
7 Ghai and McAuslan, at 19.
8 Ghai and McAuslan, at 19–20.
9 Ghai and McAuslan, at 34.
10 Ghai and McAuslan, at 37.
11 Ghai and McAuslan, at 24.
12 Ghai and McAuslan, at 24.
13 Ghai and McAuslan, at 35.
14 J. B. Ojwang, *Constitutional Development in Kenya: Institutional Adaptation and Social Change* (ACTS Press, 1990) 31.
15 Ghai and McAuslan, at 24.
16 *Nyali Ltd* v. *Attorney-General* [1956] K.B. 1 at 15.

Throughout the colonial period the safeguards of the common law were only available to the privileged races, the citizens.[17] It was inconceivable that an African, a mere subject, however much aggrieved by governmental action, could have dared to file a judicial review action against the colonial state.[18] Such a litigant faced other formidable obstacles, including finding the resources to file a suit, and a lawyer who could take up the case. As an institution for the regulation of state power, judicial review was therefore constrained by its adversarial nature. In any case, and as we shall see, the grants of power to administrators were so broad that the courts found it difficult to invoke the ultra vires doctrine.[19] Far from being constrained by any notions of constitutionalism, the colonial state was highly authoritarian and was defined by control and coercion.[20] In turn, statutory laws characterized by high degrees of discretion enabled such control and coercion.[21]

For various reasons, independence did little to change this picture. Although Kenya became independent in 1963 under a liberal constitution with elaborate arrangements for the protection of minorities,[22] the independence government began undermining the constitutional arrangements that circumscribed majority power as soon as it assumed office. It reasoned that the independence constitution's structures were unworkable and that, as the principal agent of development, the government needed to be clothed with wide-ranging powers if it was to fulfill the expectations of the citizenry. A more plausible reason, however, is that having been properly schooled in colonialism, the new rulers thought that the autocratic structures of the colonial system of government were more attractive than the "restraints and delicate balances" of the liberal independence constitution.[23]

As far as governance was concerned, independence, for the most part, meant continuity, as the independence government sought to maintain the colonial edifice. The culture of authoritarianism, now taking the form of an "imperial presidency," persisted.[24] The inherited colonial laws, characterized by high degrees of discretion, came to the aid of the new government keen to consolidate and exercise despotic power. As Okoth-Ogendo has observed, "it was the [inherited] legal order, not the constitutional order, that offered African elites real power and the bureaucratic machinery with which to exercise it effectively."[25] These authoritarian statutory laws remained in force thanks to the common law's presumption of validity, until they were repealed or the courts overturned them.[26]

17 Sandra F. Joireman, "The Evolution of the Common Law: Legal Development in Kenya and India" (2006), Richmond School of Arts & Sciences, Political Science Faculty Publications, Paper 68, at 4.

18 See the contribution by Farrah Ahmed and Swati Jhaveri on India in this volume for an interesting parallel.

19 Robert B. Seidman, "Administrative Law and Legitimacy in Anglophonic Africa: A problem in the Reception of Foreign Law" (1970) 5 *Law & Society Review* 161 at 181.

20 H. W. O. Okoth-Ogendo, "Constitutions without Constitutionalism: Reflections on an African Paradox," in *Constitutionalism and Democracy in Transitions in the Contemporary World* (Douglas Greenberg et al., eds, Oxford University Press, 1993) 69.

21 Okoth-Ogendo at 77.

22 The provisions of the Independence Constitution for protection of minorities included: a federal system of government consisting of a national government, eight regional assemblies and a bicameral legislature; an independent judiciary; protection from the deprivation of property; and protection from discrimination on the grounds of race and ethnicity.

23 Yash Pal Ghai, "The Constitution and the Economy," Institute of Economic Affairs, Annual Lecture (January 28, 2002) 13.

24 See H. Kwasi Prempeh, "Presidents Untamed" (2008) 19 *Journal of Democracy* 109 at 110. "Imperial presidency" denotes presidential supremacy, created through the appropriation by the president of constitutional powers reserved to other branches of government.

25 Okoth-Ogendo at 71.

26 H. Kwasi Prempeh, "Marbury in Africa: Judicial Review and the Challenge of Constitutionalism in Contemporary Africa' (2006) 80 *Tulane Law Review* 1 at 27.

Accordingly, Kenya's political elite quickly embraced this familiar statutory order and in many ways reinforced it. Like their colonial predecessors, they considered the facilitation of state power to be the primary purpose of law.

Thus, English law has had an ambivalent legacy in Kenya. In theory, it promised to provide a bulwark against the abuse of governmental power. In reality, it has largely served to facilitate authoritarianism. In the colonial era, while the settlers could easily access the safeguards of the common law, other races faced formidable challenges in their endeavors to hold government accountable. After independence, the political elite simply replaced the privileged white settlers, with the result that the protections of English law, including judicial review, continued to be inaccessible for most citizens.

11.3 THE IRRELEVANCE OF JUDICIAL REVIEW IN THE KENYA COLONY, 1895–1962

As we have noted, Britain formally imposed the common law, including administrative law, on the Kenya colony. At the same time, an informal system of governance emerged during the colonial period. The role of judicial review, or lack thereof, in the colonial era thus needs to be examined in the context of the interactions of these formal and informal systems of governance.

The formal system of governance was, of course, derived from norms and practices then prevailing in England. Here, "the burgeoning welfare state" had occasioned the expansion of administrative law "in a country with an unwritten constitution, absolute parliamentary supremacy, and a ministerial system of administration."[27] The bureaucracy that administered this welfare state satisfied the requirements of a formally rational-legal bureaucracy in a number of respects.[28]

First, the bureaucracy was instrumental to the political institutions. In particular, the bureaucracy was subordinate to Parliament, the supreme policy-making body.[29] Second, administrative roles were defined narrowly in an attempt to preclude capriciousness in decision-making.[30] Third, "deeply entrenched traditions of the civil service" required administrators to consult affected groups before making decisions.[31] Court-enforced rules of natural justice supplemented these traditions.[32] Fourth, accountability institutions – including bureaucratic controls, Parliamentary control, and judicial review – sanctioned these norms.[33] Finally, lawyers were available to file judicial review applications.[34] Unfortunately, "[o]f these institutions, only the formal, court-enforced norms of administrative law made the long trip to Africa."[35]

These norms were to be enforced by a complex and desegregated judicial system. First, there was a system of superior courts that applied norms of English law. This system consisted of three classes of subordinate courts, three classes of subordinate native courts and a high court (later supreme court) to handle appeals from these courts and exercise "control,

27 Seidman, "Administrative Law and Legitimacy in Anglophonic Africa" at 164, 165.
28 Seidman, "Administrative Law and Legitimacy in Anglophonic Africa" at 164.
29 Seidman, "Administrative Law and Legitimacy in Anglophonic Africa" at 163.
30 Seidman, "Administrative Law and Legitimacy in Anglophonic Africa" at 163.
31 Seidman, "Administrative Law and Legitimacy in Anglophonic Africa" at 165.
32 Seidman, "Administrative Law and Legitimacy in Anglophonic Africa" at 165.
33 Seidman, "Administrative Law and Legitimacy in Anglophonic Africa" at 166.
34 Seidman, "Administrative Law and Legitimacy in Anglophonic Africa" at 166.
35 Seidman, "Administrative Law and Legitimacy in Anglophonic Africa" at 166.

supervision and revisional jurisdiction" over them.[36] The subordinate courts were invariably staffed by administrative officers, who simultaneously exercised executive and judicial power.[37] Appeals from the high court lay to the East African Court of Appeal and ultimately to the Judicial Committee of the Privy Council. These superior courts applied English law and "catered primarily for the immigrant communities who regarded English law as their law."[38] Additionally, the Governor established native tribunals, which primarily applied customary law, and whose decisions were subject to revision by administrative officers "where they saw good reason to do so."[39] There was also a system of courts for Muslims, which applied both Muslim and English law.[40] The three systems of courts were distinct, even if there were overlaps.[41]

The court-enforced norms of English law were soon accompanied by an informal system of governance that rendered the formal system virtually useless. The British faced two challenges in establishing effective government.[42] First, they did not have sufficient English administrators. Second, the protectorate consisted of a vast territory, with varying ecological and social conditions that were bound to make communicating over long distances extremely difficult. As the British saw it, these circumstances made decentralized administration inevitable. They thus established a system of indirect rule, consisting of the Commissioner/Governor who established the main lines of policy and was assisted by an executive council, and a team of district commissioners who were "in charge of interpreting, modifying, and implementing policy in light of local conditions."[43] In turn, coopted native chiefs working through native institutions assisted the district commissioners.[44]

As Mamdani noted, the district was the real locus of colonial administration, making it imperative for the district commissioner, as the "man on the spot," to "be carefully identified, groomed and placed."[45] The challenge of communication meant that the man on the spot would enjoy wide discretionary powers. Thus, in an effort to ensure that these individuals would be accountable to the centre, a system was designed to ensure the selection of self-disciplined individuals who could be trusted to pursue the interests of the colonial service.[46] By this system, individuals who had the "character and personality to deal with natives" were recruited from English public schools and Oxbridge.[47] The colonial service was looking for "men who considered it their birthright to rule, and who did so by habit."[48] This explains why these men were drawn from English upper-class society.

This system of appointment "gave rise to a common set of values and a ubiquitous informal organization."[49] This set of values was found in the shared public school ethic, which served as a "surrogate for detailed rules"; these officials could be trusted to pursue the goals of the

36 Ghai and McAuslan at 135.
37 Ghai and McAuslan at 130.
38 Ghai and McAuslan at 164, 172.
39 Ghai and McAuslan at 135.
40 Ghai and McAuslan at 164.
41 Ghai and McAuslan at 164. See the contributions on Malaysia and New Zealand in this volume for similarly legally pluralistic systems.
42 Mahmood Mamdani, *Citizen and Subject: Contemporary Africa and the Legacy of Late Colonialism* (Princeton University Press, 1996) 73–74.
43 Mamdani, *Citizen and Subject* at 74.
44 Mamdani, *Citizen and Subject* at 77.
45 Mamdani, *Citizen and Subject* at 77.
46 Seidman, "Administrative Law and Legitimacy in Anglophonic Africa" at 193.
47 Mamdani, *Citizen and Subject* at 77.
48 Mamdani, *Citizen and Subject* at 77.
49 Seidman, "Administrative Law and Legitimacy in Anglophonic Africa" at 194.

colonial enterprise without being micromanaged.[50] This system of selection produced a homogenous colonial service whose functionaries formed "an informal organization that ultimately became far more important than formal rules and bureaucracy."[51] Formal rules "setting out rational decision-making procedures and explicitly setting forth guides to discretion" were thus considered irrelevant.[52] In other words, these English gentlemen did not require any rules stipulating rational decision-making procedures, as they knew what was best for the African.[53] The colonial service firmly believed that the "collective wisdom" of these gentlemen would ensure a more efficient system of administration than a legal code ever could.[54]

Interestingly, other whites in the colony were also included in this informal organization.[55] For example, white settlers and English firms with subsidiaries or branches in Kenya "had no difficulty in finding informal channels of communication with officials, which in most cases served in the stead of formal control devices."[56] This informal organization was later formalized with the creation of boards to regulate industry and agriculture, which the settlers and expatriate entrepreneurs dominated.[57] Invariably, these boards enjoyed wide-ranging rule-making powers.[58] In these circumstances, the white settlers simply had to invoke the informal organization to protect their interests, and had no real need to resort to the formal, court-enforced norms of English law.[59] Despite much rhetoric to the contrary, Britain thus bequeathed to Kenya a culture of authoritarianism, not democracy. Robert B. Seidman aptly captures this legacy, when he writes:

> If the "British ideal" so carefully inculcated in the aristocratic family, the public school, and the university means anything, it must include the notion of the rule of law, the unceasing effort to govern by law, not by man alone. What the colonial service bequeathed to Africa was its precise opposite: a tradition that good government was made by good men, and a set of authoritarian institutions which were designed to give the widest possible scope to individual discretion, rather than an instrumental system with easy communication with the governed, narrowly defined roles, institutions for rational decision-making, and sanctioning devices to enforce the rules.[60]

The requirements of a rational-legal bureaucracy that in Britain served to ensure that the government exercised its powers according to the rule of law were absent in colonial Kenya. First, the administration was not answerable to the governed. Second, administrative roles were defined broadly, as the system trusted the judgment of the "man on the spot." Third, there were no accountability institutions to sanction maladministration. The legislature had no real oversight powers, and was in any case dominated by white interests as it for a long time consisted entirely of ex officio and appointed members.[61] Similarly, the judicial structures

[50] Seidman, "Administrative Law and Legitimacy in Anglophonic Africa" at 195.
[51] Seidman, "Administrative Law and Legitimacy in Anglophonic Africa" at 196.
[52] Seidman, "Administrative Law and Legitimacy in Anglophonic Africa" at 196.
[53] Seidman, "Administrative Law and Legitimacy in Anglophonic Africa" at 197.
[54] Seidman, "Administrative Law and Legitimacy in Anglophonic Africa" at 174.
[55] Seidman, "Administrative Law and Legitimacy in Anglophonic Africa" at 197.
[56] Seidman, "Administrative Law and Legitimacy in Anglophonic Africa" at 197.
[57] Seidman, "Administrative Law and Legitimacy in Anglophonic Africa" at 198.
[58] Seidman, "Administrative Law and Legitimacy in Anglophonic Africa" at 171.
[59] Seidman, "Administrative Law and Legitimacy in Anglophonic Africa" at 198.
[60] Seidman, "Administrative Law and Legitimacy in Anglophonic Africa" at 199.
[61] Steven B. Pfeiffer, "Notes on the Role of the Judiciary in the Constitutional Systems of East Africa Since Independence" (1978) 10 *Case Western Reserve Journal of International Law* 11 at 20.

largely protected white interests. Further, judicial officers had no security of tenure and served "at the pleasure of the Crown."[62]

In the colonial era, therefore, administrative law was "largely incompetent to correct abuses."[63] The overly broad grants of power confounded the ultra vires rule.[64] For example, the East African Order in Council 1902 gave the Commissioner the power to "make ordinances for the administration of justice, the raising of revenue, and generally for the peace, order and good government of all persons in East Africa." Further, courts largely disqualified themselves from reviewing administrative action on the reasoning that the decisions at hand were "executive" or "legislative," rather than "quasi-judicial."[65] In doing so, they followed English precedents.[66] While this approach made some sense in the English context where Parliament exercised political control over the administration, it made little sense in the Kenya Colony where the African majority was not even represented in the legislature.[67] Unlike its English counterpart, the legislature in the Kenya Colony had no meaningful oversight powers. It is also worth noting that the colonial judicial officers were members of the informal organization, given that they came from the same class and social backgrounds as the administrators. Thus, it was to be expected that they would find the authoritarian ideologies of the colonial service agreeable.[68] All these factors culminated in the absence of judicial control of the administration.[69] In every sense, therefore, the colonial system of governance was "a parody of English democracy."[70]

Things only started to change from the 1940s as African and Asian agitation for independence and equal treatment compelled the colonial government to start making concessions.[71] Middle-class Africans and Asians started using administrative law, also because a cadre of able and willing African and Asian lawyers was now available.[72] An example is *Koinange Mbiu* v. *Rex*.[73] Here, the relevant ordinance gave the Governor the power to limit coffee growing by areas. However, the Governor made regulations that sought to restrict Africans from growing coffee in particular areas. The court held that the Governor had acted ultra vires by purporting to determine the races that could grow coffee.

A second example is *Sheikh Brothers Limited* v. *Hotels Authority*[74], where the applicable regulations empowered the Hotels Authority to fix the percentage of accommodation for those residing in hotels on a monthly as opposed to a daily basis. Following a complaint by the residents of the applicant's hotel, the Hotels Authority purported to fix the percentage of accommodation for monthly residents at 100 percent. The applicants, who were middle-class Asian owners of a hotel aggrieved by this decision, brought an action to quash it. The court held that the Hotels Authority had exceeded its powers, reasoning that some "comparative

62 Pfeiffer at 26.
63 Seidman, "Administrative Law and Legitimacy in Anglophonic Africa" at 172.
64 Seidman, "Administrative Law and Legitimacy in Anglophonic Africa" at 175.
65 Seidman, "Administrative Law and Legitimacy in Anglophonic Africa" at 175.
66 See, for example, Re Marle's Application [1958] EALR 153, following *Smith* v. *East Elloe Rural District Council* [1956] AC 736.
67 Seidman, "Administrative Law and Legitimacy in Anglophonic Africa" at 178–179.
68 Robert B. Seidman, "Judicial Review and Fundamental Freedoms in Anglophonic Independent Africa" (1974) 35 *Ohio State Law Journal* 820 at 839.
69 Ghai and McAuslan at 302.
70 Seidman, "Administrative Law and Legitimacy in Anglophonic Africa" at 173.
71 See, for example, H. W. O. Okoth-Ogendo, "The Politics of Constitutional Change in Kenya Since Independence, 1963–69" (1972) 71 *African Affairs* 9.
72 See also *Municipal Board of Mombasa* v. *Kala* (1955) 22 EACA 319; *Patel* v. *Plateau Licensing Court* (1954) 27 KLR 147; *Mwangi* v. *R* (1950) 24 (1) KLR 72.
73 *Koinange Mbiu* v. *Rex* (1951) 24(2) KLR 130.
74 *Sheikh Brothers* v. *Hotels Authority* (1949) 23(2) KLR 1.

relation as may be considered reasonable must be maintained between accommodation fixed for monthly residents and other residents."[75]

Perhaps anticipating that applications for judicial review would become more common, the colonial government enacted the Law Reform Ordinance 1956. This law gave the High Court the power to issue the orders of mandamus, prohibition and certiorari in instances where the High Court of England could issue similar orders under the English Administration of Justice (Miscellaneous Provisions) Act 1938. The Law Reform Ordinance was later amended to empower the High Court to grant the above orders notwithstanding the availability of alternative remedies.[76]

Despite these late changes, however, we can safely conclude that constitutionalism, defined as government limited by law, was not practiced in the Kenya Colony. The colonial state was subject neither to popular control nor to effective judicial control.[77] Further, law played an instrumental role, namely facilitating the exploitation of the resources of the Colony while subjugating the African majority. The transferred common law played a significant role in this respect, largely serving as an instrument that the courts used to approve or ignore the actions of the colonial state while doing little to constrain its excesses.[78]

11.4 JUDICIAL REVIEW IN INDEPENDENT KENYA, 1963–2010

Although there were two main political parties (the Kenya National African Union or KANU and the Kenya African Democratic Union or KADU) when Kenya became independent in 1963, the country quickly joined the ranks of the one-party states when KADU was dissolved in 1964 and its members joined KANU.[79] The Independence Constitution of 1963 was quickly rendered useless through a series of amendments that consolidated power in the president.[80]

Kenya was to remain a de facto one-party state until 1982, when, following an announcement by a number of prominent government critics that they would form an opposition party, the legislature amended the constitution to legalize the one-party system.[81] Dissent was not tolerated in the one-party state, for the most part, and governance was characterized by oligarchic rule, with an imperial president at the helm.

The oligarchy prescribed a fairly narrow role for the judiciary, which itself played a significant role in protecting the interests of the oligarchy.[82] In many ways, this represented a continuation of the policies and practices of the colonial government.[83] This circumscription of the role of the judiciary was achieved through the establishment of constitutional rules that enabled the executive to control the judiciary,[84] remaining in place until the enactment of a radically different Constitution in August 2010.[85] In addition, the exercise of judicial

75 See also *Ndegwa v. Nairobi Liquor Licensing Court* (1957) EA 709 (Kenya).

76 Law Reform (Miscellaneous Provisions Amendment) Ordinance No. 16 of 1960.

77 James C. N. Paul, "Some Observations on Constitutionalism, Judicial Review and Rule of Law in Africa" (1974) 35 *Ohio State Law Journal* 851 at 862.

78 Paul at 862.

79 See Ojwang, *Constitutional Development in Kenya* at 46–47.

80 See Okoth-Ogendo, "The Politics of Constitutional Change in Kenya."

81 Republic of Kenya, Constitution of Kenya amended in 1982 (1969).

82 Kuria G. Kamau and J. B. Ojwang, "Judges and the Rule of Law in the Framework of Politics: The Kenya Case," (1979) Public Law 254.

83 See, for example, Gary Wasserman, "The Independence Bargain: Kenya Europeans and the Land Issue 1960–1962," (1973) *Journal of Commonwealth Political Studies* 99.

84 Kuria and Ojwang at 61.

85 Republic of Kenya, Constitution of Kenya 2010.

power in Kenya was at this time considerably influenced by a culture of judicial restraint.[86] This cautious approach may in part be explained by fear of the executive, which wielded immense power over the judiciary, including the power to appoint and dismiss judges.[87] This section considers some of the main factors that influenced the role of judicial review in independent Kenya.

11.4.1 *The Postindependence Period, 1963–1989*

On the basis that an impartial and independent judiciary would be required if the rule of law were to thrive in Kenya, section 184 of the independence constitution established a Judicial Service Commission (JSC) to regulate matters such as judicial appointments and discipline. Under section 172 of this constitution, the Chief Justice was to be appointed by the Governor-General, acting in accordance with the advice of the Prime Minister, while other judges were to be appointed by the Governor-General acting in accordance with the advice of the JSC. To further solidify the position of the judicial officers, this constitution provided that offices of judges could not be abolished when there was a substantive office holder.[88] Judges could only be removed from office for inability to perform functions or misbehavior, a determination that would be made by an impartial tribunal appointed by the Governor-General with appeal allowed to the Judicial Committee of the Privy Council whose decision the Governor-General would act on.[89] The JSC was also given the power to appoint other judicial officers, such as magistrates.

However, following numerous amendments to the independence constitution (now repealed), the power of appointing the Chief Justice vested in the president, who was no longer required to consult anybody. In addition, while the constitution required the president to consult the JSC in appointing judges, little if any consultation occurred in practice. Further, section 62 of this constitution provided that the President could dismiss the Chief Justice and other judges for inability to perform the functions of their office or for misbehavior, if an impartial tribunal recommended their removal. Unfortunately, this constitution did not spell out the ingredients of these offenses and did not establish due process mechanisms for transparent, objective, impartial and fair removal. Further, section 61(5) gave the President power to appoint judges in an acting capacity. All of this enabled the executive to control the judiciary to the detriment of judicial independence. Most of the judges that the president appointed were expatriates, who were well aware that their tenure was tenuous, and so were inclined not to upset the apple cart.[90]

The situation was made worse in 1989 when the judiciary was delinked from the public service and placed under the office of the Chief Justice.[91] The Chief Justice now possessed wide-ranging but unregulated administrative powers, including the power to determine which judges heard what cases; where litigants could file their cases and how;[92] supervising,

86 See, for example, *Kibaki* v. *Moi and 2 others* (No. 2) (2008) 2 KLR 308; (2008) 2 KLR 351.

87 See Migai Akech, "Abuse of Power and Corruption in Kenya: Will the New Constitution Enhance Government Accountability?," (2011) 18 *Indiana Journal of Global Legal Studies* 341.

88 Kuria and Ojwang at 267.

89 Kuria and Ojwang at 267.

90 Seidman, "Judicial Review and Fundamental Freedoms in Anglophonic Independent Africa" 841.

91 Paul Mwangi, *The Black Bar: Corruption and Political Intrigue within Kenya's Legal Fraternity* (Oakland Media Services, 2001) 114.

92 For example, the Chief Justice would issue circulars indicating the courts where litigants could file their cases or applications. One such circular stated that judicial review applications could only be filed in Nairobi: "Lawyers

disciplining and initiating the process of removing judges and other judicial officers; allocating office space, housing and cars to judicial officers; and transferring judicial officers from one geographic station to another. The exercise of these powers was not regulated, and they were often abused to the detriment of judicial independence and accountability. Thus, judges confronted with these powers could be inclined to do the bidding of the Chief Justice. Moreover, because the Chief Justice's appointment was a presidential prerogative, it is not difficult to imagine how the judiciary could have been deployed in regime maintenance schemes.

In these circumstances, the courts often adopted a conservative or self-censoring approach when adjudicating political questions, particularly those they considered to be within the purview of the executive. As Sir Charles Newbold, then President of the East African Court of Appeal, while espousing a preference for conservatism on the part of the judiciary, stated:

> The courts derive a considerable amount of their authority and perhaps, even more, the acceptance of their authority from their independence of the executive, from their disassociation from matters political. In a democracy . . . the determination of matters political . . . rests ultimately with the will of the people through the ballot box. For that purpose, people elect the executive and the legislature and it is on these two branches . . . that the primary responsibility rests. The third branch, the judiciary is not elected and should not seek to interfere in a sphere which is outside the true function of the judges . . . it is the function of the courts to be conservative, so as to ensure that the rights of the individual are determined by the rule of law.[93]

By drawing a distinction between law and politics, it is arguable that the courts had marginalized their role in public affairs. The courts had therefore been likely to accord deference to the position of the executive where the official action complained of was governed by a policy of the government, relating to, for example, the maintenance of public order.[94] This restrained approach was often adopted in cases concerning personal liberty, freedom of expression and freedom of movement.[95]

In these circumstances, judicial review did not play a significant role in checking executive power. The courts continued to apply English precedents and procedures in the post-independence period, pursuant to the Judicature Act.[96] The courts based their judicial review power entirely on English common law. In this regime, while the Law Reform Act[97] provided a basis for judicial review, the Civil Procedure Act[98] regulated its exercise. The Law Reform Act imported and vested in the High Court the power to issue the prerogative orders (of mandamus, prohibition and certiorari) in all cases in which the High Court of England could do so. This limited jurisdiction meant that the High Court could not grant remedies other than mandamus, prohibition and certiorari.[99] Further, the Law Reform Act empowered the judiciary to make rules prescribing procedures for judicial review applications.[100] The

Threaten Suit Against CJ," *Daily Nation*, Tuesday, June 22, 2004, available at www.nation.co.ke/news/1056–15322-117bmcj/index.html.

93 Sir Charles Newbold, 'The Role of a Judge as a Policy Maker', (1969) 2 *East African Law Review* 127 at 133.

94 J. B. Ojwang and J. A. Otieno-Odek, 'The Judiciary in Sensitive Areas of Public Law: Emerging Approaches to Human Rights Litigation in Kenya', (1988) 35 *Netherlands International Law Review* 29.

95 Ojwang and Otieno-Odek.

96 Judicature Act, Chapter 8, Laws of Kenya.

97 Law Reform Act, Chapter 26, Laws of Kenya.

98 Civil Procedure Act, Chapter 21, Laws of Kenya.

99 This limited jurisdiction meant that the High Court could not grant remedies other than mandamus, prohibition and certiorari. See, for example, Jotham Mulati *Welamondi* v. *Chairman, Electoral Commission of* Kenya [2002] 1 KLR 486.

100 Law Reform Act, section 9.

envisaged procedures were enacted as Order 53 of the Civil Procedure Rules, made under the Civil Procedure Act.

While the courts often reviewed the decisions of statutory tribunals and local authorities,[101] they construed the constitution restrictively and were careful not to "substitute their policy views for those of properly constituted government officials." In addition, few individuals were willing to confront the authoritarian and oppressive executive. Kenya's independence government sought to inherit the colonial administration's power edifice, and not to replace it.[102] Its objective was continuity, not revolution. Thus, the executive retained its hold on the judiciary, which therefore continued to be a useful instrument for regime maintenance.

11.4.2 *The Role of the Democracy Movement, 1990–2009*

Despite such exceptions, judicial review largely remained moribund until the dawn of multi-party democracy in the 1990s. An increasingly enlightened public – mostly the elite[103] – began to push back against state tyranny, and on occasion resorted to judicial review. For example, university student leaders, who were at the forefront of the clamor for democracy, were sometimes suspended or even dismissed by their universities, and consequently sought judicial review of these decisions.[104] University lecturers constitute another group of democracy activists that turned to the courts to confront state-induced tyranny.[105] For the first time, individuals even acquired the courage to question the decisions of the Boards of Governors of high schools.[106]

Although the courts exercised their common-law based power of judicial review and struck down numerous acts of government during this period,[107] their effectiveness to check the abuse of governmental power was constrained by three primary factors. First, Order 53 established restrictive and technical rules of procedure, whose effect was to limit access to judicial review. Courts insisted on strict adherence to the requirements and timelines of Order 53, with the result that many arguably meritorious applications were dismissed on technicalities.[108]

Second, the courts adopted a restrictive approach to standing, with the effect that applications were not always determined on the merits. On the one hand, courts should certainly discourage "meddlesome interlopers."[109] On the other hand, a person with an otherwise meritorious challenge to the validity of a governmental action should not be turned away on the mere ground that their rights or interests are not sufficiently affected by a decision.[110] In

101 See, for example, *Kasuli* v. A.G. [1971] E.A. 423; *Shah* v. A.G. (No.2) [1970] E.A. 523.

102 See, for example, Okoth-Ogendo, "Constitutions without Constitutionalism."

103 See, for example, *University Academic Staff Union* v. *Registrar of Societies*, Nairobi High Court Civil application No. 20 of 1994; *Kibaki* v. *Moi & 2 others* (No. 2) (2008) 2KLR 308.

104 See, for example, *Irungu Kangata and others* v. *University of Nairobi*, Misc. Civil Application No. 40 of 2001 (unreported); *Geoffrey Mwangi Kariuki* v. *University of Nairobi*, Misc. Application No. 4788 of 1992 (unreported).

105 See, for example, *Daniel Nyongesa and others* v. *Egerton University College* [1990] KLR 692; *R* v. *the Staff Disciplinary Committee of Maseno University and others ex parte Prof. Ochong Okello*, Kisumu Misc. Application No. 227 of 2003.

106 See, for example, *Elizabeth Wainaina and others* v. *Board of Governors of Pangani Girls School*, Misc. Civil Case No. 818 of 1992.

107 See, for example, Peter Kaluma, *Judicial Review: Law, Procedure and Practice* (Law Africa, 2009).

108 See, for example, *Republic* v. *Funyula Land Disputes Tribunal Busia Principal & 2 others* [2014] eKLR.

109 The Right Hon. Lord Woolf, Jeffrey Jowell, Andrew Le Sueur and Stanley Alexander de Smith, *De Smith's Judicial Review* (6th edition, Sweet & Maxwell, 2007) at 70.

110 Jowell et al. at 70.

this latter respect, the courts should not be merely concerned to redress individual grievances, but should, above all, aim to maintain the rule of law.[111] And maintaining the rule of law would mean encouraging public-spirited individuals to challenge unlawful administrative action.[112] But Kenyan courts tended to discourage such individuals, by insisting that they had to evince a concrete injury in the matter before the court.[113] The courts only began to depart from this rigid approach in the late 1990s.[114]

Third, judges lacked independence, with the result that the courts tended to adopt an unduly deferential and minimalist approach to exercising their powers, including judicial review, particularly when confronted with political questions.[115] Even where the courts struck down offending acts of government during this period, the executive tended to ignore the court orders. The case of *Kenya African National Union* v. *Mwai Kibaki*[116] illustrates this trend. The applicant, the Kenya African National Union sought orders to quash the government's decision to "repossess" a building that housed the applicant's headquarters and to restrain the government from taking possession of the building. The court obliged. However, the minister to whom the order was addressed simply defied the court. Likewise, in *Taib A. Taib* v. *Minister for Local Government*,[117] the applicant had been nominated to serve on, and was shortly thereafter elected mayor of, the Municipal Council of Mombasa. The Minister for Local Government revoked the nomination by a Gazette Notice. The court quashed this decision and prohibited the Minister from interfering with his exercise of the office of mayor. The Minister defied the court. No action was taken against such defiant ministers. This contributed to creating a perception among Kenyans that there was a "widespread culture of defiance of court orders."[118]

Therefore, just as in the colonial era, English law was, in the period 1963–2010, deployed effectively as an instrument of power despite the allure of judicial review. The legal system continued to be characterized by broad grants of poorly circumscribed discretionary powers, thereby bolstering authoritarianism.[119] Further, the Executive continued to straddle the divide between informalism and the realm of legal-rational norms, basing its actions on formal rules, informal considerations, or some combination of the two, as expediency dictated.[120] And so the fundamental problem remained that the formal rules – particularly the statutory laws that gave the Executive its vast discretionary powers – were still insufficiently institutionalized, meaning that they were all too often open-ended and neither transparent nor accountable.[121] They, therefore, availed authoritarian regimes as tools with which to subvert democracy and constitutionalism.[122] Accordingly, the challenge has been to transform the statutes that give the legal order its imperial or authoritarian character so that

111 Jowell et al. at 70.

112 Jowell et al. at 71.

113 See, for example, *Wangari Maathai* v. *The Kenya Times Media Trust*, Nairobi High Court Civil Case No. 5403 of 1989 (unreported).

114 See, for example, *Republic* v. *Minister for Information & Broadcasting and Ahmed Jibril, ex parte East African Television Network Limited*, Nairobi High Court Misc. Civ. App. No. 403 of 1998 (unreported).

115 See, for example, Migai Akech and Patricia Kameri-Mbote, "Kenyan Courts and the Politics of the Rule of Law in the Post-Authoritarian State from 1991 to 2010," (2012) 18 *East African Journal of Peace and Human Rights* 357.

116 *Kenya African National Union* v. *Mwai Kibaki* [2005] eKLR.

117 *Taib A. Taib* v. *Minister for Local Government* [2006] eKLR.

118 Winnie Mitullah et al., *Kenya's Democratisation: Gains or Losses?* (Claripress, 2005) 52–53.

119 See Migai Akech, "Constraining Government Power in Africa" (2011) 22 *Journal of Democracy* 96.

120 Akech, "Constraining Government Power in Africa" at 98.

121 Akech, "Constraining Government Power in Africa" at 102.

122 Akech, "Constraining Government Power in Africa" at 102.

this order conforms to the demands of constitutionalism. Let us now see whether the Constitution of Kenya 2010 addresses this challenge.

11.5 THE CONSTITUTION OF KENYA 2010: A GAME CHANGER?

The Constitution of Kenya 2010 affects judicial review in numerous respects: it seeks to enhance access to court, has permissive standing requirements and promotes judicial independence and accountability. More significantly, perhaps, it establishes a new basis for judicial review.[123] There are now three, parallel, bases for judicial review in Kenya: Order 53 of the Civil Procedure Rules, Article 47 of the Constitution of Kenya 2010, and the Fair Administrative Action Act (FAAA) of 2016. This new regime has created procedural complications that will need to be resolved if the Constitution is to have a broader impact on judicial review.

11.5.1 *The New Constitutional Petition Jurisdiction*

Article 47 of the Constitution of 2010 provides a new and comprehensive basis for judicial review: "Every person has the right to administrative action that is expeditious, efficient, lawful, reasonable and procedurally fair."[124] It further provides that a person whose right or fundamental freedom has been, or is likely to be, affected by administrative action has the right to be given written reasons for the action.[125] It then requires Parliament to enact legislation to give effect to these rights.[126] Clearly, it is no longer necessary for the courts to resort to the Law Reform Act.[127] Some argue that the Constitution impliedly repeals the Law Reform Act and Order 53 of the Civil Procedure Rules that are founded on it. As the discussion in the following section shows, however, the position is more complicated than this.[128] As the High Court observed, "Article 47 is intended to subject administrative processes to constitutional discipline hence relief for administrative grievances is no longer left to the realm of the common law or judicial review under the Law Reform Act ... but is to be measured against the standards established by the Constitution."[129]

Second, the Constitution establishes permissive standing requirements. In addition to persons acting in their own interests, the following categories of persons may institute court proceedings: persons acting on behalf of others who cannot act in their own names, persons acting as members of, or in the interests of, a group or class of persons, persons acting in the public interest, or associations acting in the interests of their members.[130] It also provides that rules of procedure governing the institution of proceedings should be kept to a minimum and

123 See the contributions on Australia and South Africa, which discuss the influence of a written Constitution on administrative law.
124 Constitution of Kenya 2010, Article 47(1).
125 Constitution of Kenya 2010, Article 47(2).
126 Constitution of Kenya 2010, Article 47(3).
127 See Danwood Mzikenge Chirwa, "Liberating Malawi's Administrative Justice Jurisprudence from its Common Law Shackles," (2011) 55 *Journal of African Law* 105 (arguing that the Constitution of Malawi 1994 had fundamentally altered the substantive law of judicial review, and that Order 53 of the Rules of the Supreme Court of England is subservient to section 43 of this constitution).
128 See Constitution of Kenya 2010, Sixth Schedule, Clause 7(1), which provides that "All law in force immediately before the effective date continues in force and shall be construed with the alterations, adaptations, qualifications and exceptions necessary to bring it into conformity with this Constitution."
129 *Dry Associates Limited* v. *Capital Markets Authority & another* [2012] eKLR, para. 62.
130 Constitution of Kenya 2010, Article 22(1) and (2).

should, where necessary, allow courts to entertain proceedings on the basis of informal documentation.[131] In this respect, the Chief Justice has promulgated Practice and Procedure Rules to govern constitutional petitions.[132] Under these Rules, a person who alleges that his or her constitutional right or fundamental freedom has been denied, violated or threatened may apply to the High Court by filing a petition (which may be supported by an affidavit) or making an oral application (which the court shall reduce into writing).[133] Further, these Rules require the petitioner to serve the respondents with the petition within fifteen days of filing it, or such time as the court may direct.[134] The Rules also allow the petitioner to apply for conservatory or interim orders,[135] by way of notice of motion or informal documentation.[136] The constitutional petition therefore offers an accessible, non-technical route for those seeking to vindicate their constitutional rights.

Third, the constitution expands the scope of remedies that courts can grant where it is established that a person's rights or fundamental freedoms have been denied, violated or threatened. It provides that the High Court may grant "appropriate relief," including a declaration of rights, an injunction, a conservatory order, a declaration that an offending law is invalid, an order for compensation and an order for judicial review.[137] Essentially, this means that a constitutional petition alleging the violation of Article 47 can seek the orders of certiorari, prohibition and mandamus.

11.5.2 *Two Parallel Jurisdictions: Constitutional Petitions and Applications for Judicial Review under Order 53*

As mentioned in the introduction to Section 11.5, there are multiple bases for judicial review. Seeking judicial review has rather been confusing since the promulgation of the Constitution of 2010. While some applicants approach the court by way of constitutional petitions (in which they seek all manner of orders, including judicial review orders[138]), others continue to approach the court via Order 53.[139] And the courts have continued to entertain both kinds of applications. In *Michael Mungai* v. *Attorney General*,[140] for instance, the court sought to draw a distinction between what it termed an application for "judicial review simpliciter" and a constitutional petition, but acknowledged that a person could apply for judicial review using either of these routes.[141] It went on to observe that an applicant who filed an application for judicial review simpliciter had to comply with the Order 53 requirements, including seeking prior leave and asking only for the prerogative orders (as contemplated by section 8,

[131] Constitution of Kenya 2010, Article 22(3).
[132] The Constitution of Kenya (Protection of Rights and Fundamental Freedoms) Practice and Procedure Rules 2013, L.N. 117/2013.
[133] The Constitution of Kenya (Protection of Rights and Fundamental Freedoms) Practice and Procedure Rules 2013, L.N. 117/2013, rule 10.
[134] The Constitution of Kenya (Protection of Rights and Fundamental Freedoms) Practice and Procedure Rules 2013, L.N. 117/2013, rule 14.
[135] The Constitution of Kenya (Protection of Rights and Fundamental Freedoms) Practice and Procedure Rules 2013, L.N. 117/2013, rule 23.
[136] The Constitution of Kenya (Protection of Rights and Fundamental Freedoms) Practice and Procedure Rules 2013, L.N. 117/2013, rule 24.
[137] The Constitution of Kenya (Protection of Rights and Fundamental Freedoms) Practice and Procedure Rules 2013, L.N. 117/2013, Article 23(1).
[138] Article 22(1) and 23(3)(f) of Constitution of Kenya 2010.
[139] See, for example, *Peter Muchai* v. *Teachers Service Commission* [2015] eKLR.
[140] *Michael Mungai* v. *Attorney General & 9 others* [2015] eKLR.
[141] *Michael Mungai* v. *Attorney General & 9 others* [2015] eKLR, at para. 6.

Law Reform Act).[142] As the applicant failed to seek prior leave, the court determined that his application was incompetent.[143]

A similar approach was adopted in *Khobesh Agencies Limited & 32 others* v. *Minister of Foreign Affairs & International Relations & 4 others*.[144] The applicants sought to rely on a ground that was not stated in their "statutory statement"; Rule 4(1) of Order 53 states that a party is not entitled to rely on any ground or seek any relief apart from the ones indicated in their statement accompanying their application for leave. The court ruled that the application was incompetent for this reason. In doing so, it noted that although the courts are bound to ensure adherence to the Constitution in determining judicial review applications, they do not have the power to change the nature of a judicial review application into a constitutional petition.[145] In the court's view, to do that would defeat the express provisions of sections 8 and 9 of the Law Reform Act, which make the judicial review jurisdiction special.[146] The Court of Appeal took the same approach in *Nation Media Group Limited* v. *Cradle – the Children's Foundation Suing through Geoffrey Maganya*,[147] where it stated that "in judicial review the special jurisdiction is invoked under Order 53 of the Civil Procedure Rules while the jurisdiction of the court to enforce fundamental rights is invoked under Articles 23 and 258 of the Constitution."[148]

Thus, although the Constitution now requires courts to administer justice without undue regard to procedural technicalities, some courts have ruled that failures to comply with the requirements of Order 53 are incurable. In *Republic* v. *Kahindi Nyafula & 3 others ex parte Kilifi South East Farmers Cooperative*,[149] for example, where the applicant filed a notice of motion out of time, the court determined that "The Law Reform Act, which is the substantive law dealing with prerogative orders, does not provide for the enlargement of time within which a party should file the motion."[150]

However, the courts' reasoning in *Khobesh Agencies Limited* and *Nation Media Group Limited* is difficult to comprehend. Article 23(1) of the Constitution gives the High Court jurisdiction to hear and determine applications for redress of a denial, violation or threat to a fundamental right or freedom in the Bill of Rights. The right to fair administrative action is one such fundamental right, and, for the avoidance of doubt, it is contained in the Bill of Rights. The courts no longer require a special judicial review jurisdiction for the simple reason that the Constitution has given them a general or universal jurisdiction to hear and determine applications for the redress of any violations of human rights, of which the right to fair administrative action is a core component. If such applications are required to take the form of constitutional petitions, there is thus no justification for mandating a different

[142] *Michael Mungai* v. *Attorney General & 9 others* [2015] eKLR, at 6 & 9.

[143] *Michael Mungai* v. *Attorney General & 9 others* [2015] eKLR, at para. 9.

[144] *Khobesh Agencies Limited & 32 others* v. *Minister of Foreign Affairs & International Relations & 4 others* [2013] eKLR.

[145] *Khobesh Agencies Limited & 32 others* v. *Minister of Foreign Affairs & International Relations & 4 others* [2013] eKLR, at para. 31.

[146] *Khobesh Agencies Limited & 32 others* v. *Minister of Foreign Affairs & International Relations & 4 others* [2013] eKLR, at para. 31.

[147] *Nation Media Group Limited* v. *Cradle – the Children's Foundation Suing through Geoffrey Maganya* [2016] eKLR.

[148] *Nation Media Group Limited* v. *Cradle – the Children's Foundation Suing through Geoffrey Maganya* [2016] eKLR, at para. 27.

[149] *Republic* v. *Kahindi Nyafula & 3 others ex parte Kilifi South East Farmers Cooperative* [2014] eKLR.

[150] *Republic* v. *Kahindi Nyafula & 3 others ex parte Kilifi South East Farmers Cooperative* [2014] eKLR, at para. 9.

procedure for judicial review applications where an applicant is challenging administrative action.

A number of courts have taken this approach.[151] In *Peter Muchiri Muhura* v. *Teachers Service Commission*,[152] the High Court reasoned that a person who has filed a constitutional petition is entitled to ask for "both compensatory relief and orders of judicial review in the same pleading."[153] According to this court, the Constitution had collapsed the ridge between judicial review proceedings and ordinary actions, thereby opening "avenues to access to justice and all stipulated remedies in the same proceedings."[154] Similarly, in *Meshack Ageng'o Omondi* v. *Eldoret Municipal Council and another*,[155] the court thought that "the new constitutional order prescribes and favours [a] universal approach towards the realization of the rights and fundamental freedoms."[156] And in *Alex Malikha Wasubwa & 7 others* v. *Elias Nambkha Wamita & 4 others*,[157] the High Court held that a party could apply for judicial review orders in a constitutional petition.

This reasoning resonates with the fact that the Constitution clearly grants the courts the power of judicial review in Article 47. Further, it confers on the courts the power to grant "appropriate relief" where a person alleges that Article 47 has been threatened or violated, including "an order of judicial review." How can the Law Reform Act then be considered the substantive law dealing with prerogative orders? And doesn't "an order of judicial review" that the constitution contemplates embrace all of the prerogative orders? The court then asserts that not even Article 159(2) of the Constitution – which mandates courts to administer justice without undue regard to procedural technicalities – can come to the aid of an applicant who has failed to observe the strictures of Order 53.[158] Given that the Constitution is the superior law, wouldn't it be sensible to either amend Order 53, or interpret it in a manner that makes it compatible with the Constitution? In these circumstances, it is evident that the constitutional petition promises better access to judicial review, and a need arises to abandon the so-called applications for judicial review simpliciter. The Constitution envisages a simple but clear petition that is unencumbered by technicalities (such as the need to obtain the leave of the court before filing an application, or restrictive time limits within which the substantive application can be made or judicial orders sought). For example, the need to obtain the leave arguably serves to prolong administrative injustices and prevents applicants from seeking timely remedies. In any case, the doctrines of justiciability and standing can always assist the courts to sift deserving cases from non-deserving ones, meaning that they are not likely to be inundated with judicial review applications.

In this regard, it should be noted that the High Court in *Gilbert Hezekiah Miya* v. *Advocates Disciplinary Committee* suggested that section 9 of the Law Reform Act should be amended "to provide for extension of time in cases where a strict adherence to the limitations manifests a miscarriage of justice for example where a decision is made and for some reasons the same is not made public with the result that the persons affected thereby are

151 But see *Republic* v. *Director of Public Prosecutions & another ex parte Chamanlal Vrajlal Kamani & 2 others* at para. 144 [2015] eKLR.

152 *Peter Muchiri Muhura* v. *Teachers Service Commission* [2015] eKLR.

153 *Peter Muchiri Muhura* v. *Teachers Service Commission* [2015] eKLR.

154 *Peter Muchiri Muhura* v. *Teachers Service Commission* [2015] eKLR.

155 *Meshack Ageng'o Omondi* v. *Eldoret Municipal Council and another* [2012] eKLR.

156 *Meshack Ageng'o Omondi* v. *Eldoret Municipal Council and another* [2012] eKLR.

157 *Alex Malikha Wasubwa & 7 others* v. *Elias Nambkha Wamita & 4 others* [2012] eKLR; see also *Fauzia Tariq Zubedi* v. *Athman Awadh & 3 others* [2013] eKLR.

158 *Republic* v. *Kahindi Nyafula & 3 others ex parte Kilifi South East Farmers Cooperative* [2014] eKLR at para. 10.

not aware of the decision until after the expiry of the said limitation period."[159] This was since the Law Reform Act was based on the premise that the High Court did not have inherent judicial review jurisdiction – hence the need to take an approach similar to that of England, where the High Court was given judicial review jurisdiction by section 7 of the Administration of Justice (Miscellaneous Provisions) Act of 1938.[160] In Kenya's case, Article 47 of the Constitution now gives the courts this jurisdiction, meaning that the Law Reform Act should be repealed altogether. Indeed, it is arguable that the Constitution repeals this colonial-order statute by implication.[161]

Further, the court in *Miya* rightfully suggests that "in order to uphold the values of the Constitution, the court would be perfectly entitled, where an Act of Parliament exhibits certain deficiencies which make it insufficient to properly realise the constitutional aspirations to 'read in' the omitted words so as to being the legislation in line with the constitutional aspirations without the necessity of declaring the entire legislation unconstitutional."[162] So that had the applicant made an application for the extension of time, the court would have been prepared to "read in" a provision for extension of time in Order 53, had it found the application deserving.[163] Likewise, in *Fauzia Tariq Zubedi* v. *Athman Hassan Awadh & 3 others*,[164] the court thought that the Constitution of Kenya 2010 has liberated applicants from the strictures of the Law Reform Act and the Civil Procedure Rules, by enabling them to apply for judicial review remedies in situations where they would have been caught up by the six months limitation.

11.5.3 The Role of the Fair Administrative Action Act 2016

Parliament has since enacted a law – known as the Fair Administrative Action Act, 2015 – to give effect to Article 47 of the Constitution, and which creates a third avenue for judicial review.[165] This Act adopts a broad definition of "administrative action," which it says includes "the powers, functions and duties exercised by authorities or quasi-judicial tribunals," and "any act, omission, or decision of any person, body or authority that affects the legal rights or interests of any person to who such action relates."[166] In the latter sense, the definition embraces both public and private administrative action, and the Act is clear that it applies to both state and non-state agencies.[167] Further, it defines "decision" to include not only administrative decisions already made, but also those proposed to be made.[168]

With respect to how applicants seeking judicial review remedies may approach courts, the Act provides that a person aggrieved by an administrative action may apply to the High Court (or a subordinate court upon which original jurisdiction has been conferred pursuant to Article 22(3) of the Constitution) for judicial review.[169] It does not establish timelines within which such applications are to be made, and only stipulates that they should be filed "without

159 *Gilbert Hezekiah Miya* v. *Advocates Disciplinary Committee* [2015] eKLR, at para. 19.

160 Law Reform Act, section 8(2).

161 See generally H. Kwasi Prempeh, "Africa's 'Constitutionalism Revival': False Start or New Dawn?" *International Journal of Constitutional Law* 469 (2007).

162 *Gilbert Hezekiah Miya* v. *Advocates Disciplinary Committee* [2015] eKLR, at para. 20.

163 *Gilbert Hezekiah Miya* v. *Advocates Disciplinary Committee* [2015] eKLR, at para 19.

164 *Fauzia Tariq Zubedi* v. *Athman Hassan Awadh & 3 others* [2013] eKLR.

165 See also the contributions on Australia and South Africa in this volume.

166 Fair Administrative Action Act, 2015, section 2.

167 Fair Administrative Action Act, 2015, section 3.

168 Fair Administrative Action Act, 2015, section 2.

169 Fair Administrative Action Act, 2015, section 9(1).

unreasonable delay."[170] Further, it provides that an application for review of an administrative action shall be heard and determined within ninety days of filing the application,[171] without undue regard to procedural technicalities.[172] It then empowers the Chief Justice to make rules to regulate judicial review procedure and practice.[173] Unfortunately, the Act fails to make any reference to the existing procedures (governing constitutional petitions[174] and applications for judicial review simpliciter). So it is not clear whether the intention of the Act was to repeal these existing procedures or to simply provide an alternative route. It thus fails to resolve the existing confusion on judicial review procedures, and arguably makes it worse. For example, the Act states that a person aggrieved by an administrative action may apply for judicial review "without unreasonable delay," while Order 53 prescribes timelines within which such applications may be made. Further, the practice and procedure rules governing constitutional petitions do not stipulate any such timelines, meaning that such a petition can be filed at any time.[175]

In these circumstances, are we to assume that the Act, being the later statute, supersedes the Law Reform Act and Order 53? And how do we reconcile the Act with the practice and procedure rules governing constitutional petitions?

Concerning the substance of judicial review, there is a need to unpack Article 47. Given the wording of Article 47, it is arguable that a person aggrieved by administrative action can apply for its review on the grounds that it is not expeditious, or that it is inefficient, or that it is unlawful, or that it is unreasonable, or that it is procedurally unfair. Of these, unlawfulness, unreasonableness and procedural unfairness are the familiar categories, and have been accepted by the courts as they are drawn from the inherited English common law. According to the Merriam-Webster Dictionary, the word *expeditious* means "acting or done in a quick and efficient way." Further, it defines the word *efficient* to mean "capable of producing desired results without wasting materials, time or energy." In which case it is arguable that Article 47 is tautologous when it talks of "expeditious and efficient" administrative action, for these terms mean the same thing.

A need therefore arises to clarify the grounds of judicial review mentioned in Article 47, if they are to be manageable by judicial standards. For example, it is arguable that unreasonableness subsumes actions and decisions that are inefficient or not expeditious. On this logic, inefficiency becomes an indicator of unreasonableness. Indeed, as applied in other common law jurisdictions, unreasonableness is a dynamic concept capable of expanding as judicial and social attitudes change.[176] For example, it can embrace the concept of proportionality, which requires courts to consider whether the decision maker has struck a fair balance between competing considerations.[177] As Woolf et al. have observed, "Proportionality in the sense of achieving a 'fair balance' has always been an aspect of unreasonableness."[178] The net result is that we would have three clear grounds of judicial review under the Constitution: unlawfulness, unreasonableness and procedural unfairness. The common

[170] Fair Administrative Action Act, 2015, section 9(1).
[171] Fair Administrative Action Act, 2015, section 8.
[172] Fair Administrative Action Act, 2015, section 10(1).
[173] Fair Administrative Action Act, 2015, section 10(2).
[174] See Constitution of Kenya (Protection of Rights and Fundamental Freedoms) Practice and Procedure Rules 2013, L.N. 117/2013.
[175] Fair Administrative Action Act, 2015, rule 4.
[176] Woolf et al., *De Smith's Judicial Review* at 554.
[177] Woolf et al., *De Smith's Judicial Review* at 545.
[178] Woolf et al., *De Smith's Judicial Review* at 546.

law can remain useful, and can be used to interpret or explicate these grounds of review.[179] And new grounds of judicial review can always be created by statute, provided of course they protect and promote the right to fair administrative action. But it should be noted that the Judicature Act,[180] which continues to list the English common law as one of the sources of Kenyan law, now requires review so that it conforms to the Constitution. If only as an expression of sovereignty and the growth of its legal system, Kenya now needs to be governed by indigenous laws, and which the people have participated in making, whether directly or indirectly. Ultimately, the concern should be to ensure that the grounds of judicial review are manageable by judicial standards in Kenya, for the simple reason that this approach enables courts to keep within the bounds of their authority and in a way that meets the needs of applicants and respondents in Kenya.

In this respect, the Fair Administrative Action Act lists numerous grounds of review.[181] For example, it specifies unreasonableness as a ground of review,[182] but then lists what are arguably indicia of unreasonableness as specific or distinct grounds of review – for example, the administrator failed to take into account relevant considerations,[183] or the administrative action or decision was made in bad faith.[184] Further, it lists procedural fairness,[185] bias[186] and denial of a hearing[187] as distinct grounds of review. Unpacking the grounds of review in this manner may, nevertheless, be useful from the perspective of administrators, in so far as they clarify the common law, which only lawyers seem to comprehend. This approach enables administrators to know, in advance, what is expected of them in terms of ensuring administrative justice while exercising power. In the future, promulgating guidelines on administrative decision-making could augment this approach.

11.5.4 *Reflecting on the Post-2010 Landscape*

Despite the apparent confusion in procedure, Kenya has seen an exponential growth in judicial review since the promulgation of the Constitution of 2010.[188] However, it remains unclear whether this growth in judicial review has meaningfully enhanced democracy and constitutionalism. While judicial review has considerably constrained the exercise of power by low-level bureaucrats and administrative agencies, and even the legislature,[189] the Executive remains unconstrained in significant respects. This could be attributed to the persistence of the inherited common law culture of judicial deference. It seems that judges remain fearful of engaging the Executive in high-octane political matters. In turn, this could be attributed to the fact that the Constitution of Kenya 2010 does not do a very good job of securing judicial tenure. It is arguable that this Constitution establishes a low threshold for the removal of judges, since judges can be removed from office on the ground of "incompetence,"[190] for example, meaning that the incompetence need not be gross, contrary

179 See, for example, Chirwa, "Liberating Malawi's Administrative Justice Jurisprudence" at 108.
180 Judicature Act, Chapter 8, Laws of Kenya, section 3(1).
181 Fair Administrative Action Act, 2015, section 7(2).
182 Fair Administrative Action Act, 2015, section 7(2)(k).
183 Fair Administrative Action Act, 2015, section 7(2)(f).
184 Fair Administrative Action Act, 2015, section 7(2)(h).
185 Fair Administrative Action Act, 2015, section 7(2)(c).
186 Fair Administrative Action Act, 2015, section 7(2)(a)(iv).
187 Fair Administrative Action Act, 2015, section 7(2)(a)(v).
188 See Migai Akech, *Administrative Law* (Strathmore University Press, 2016).
189 See, for example, *Martin Nyaga Wambora* v. *County Assembly of Embu and 37 others* [2015] eKLR.
190 Constitution of Kenya 2010, article 168(1)(d).

to international best practice.[191] In addition, the process of removing judges is not sufficiently protected by procedural safeguards. In particular, this process should be preceded by a preliminary investigation that respects due process. At present, however, there are no procedures to guide this investigation.[192]

Additionally, although the Constitution attempted to limit the influence of the executive over the Judicial Service Commission, the latter remains capable of influencing the composition of this commission, meaning that it can continue to influence the independence of judges. In the recent past, for example, the government has sought to further its interests in the JSC by appointing regime loyalists to the two positions of representatives of the public.[193] The President has even sought to influence the appointment of judges by refusing to appoint persons recommended by the JSC.[194] Although the constitution mandates the President to appoint persons recommended by the JSC, the President has interpreted the constitution as empowering him to vet such persons by carrying out "background checks."[195] In other words, the President is claiming a nonexistent power to review the recommendations of the JSC. Even the legislature is now claiming that it has the power to vet judges nominated by the courts to sit on the JSC.[196] We can, therefore, expect that these power games will continue in the foreseeable future. Their net effect is to undermine judicial independence.

The Constitution of 2010 also sought to rid the judiciary of regime actors, and provided a framework for the removal of "unsuitable" judicial officers, on the basis that the public had lost "faith in the Judiciary's ability to dispense justice fairly, impartially and without fear."[197] It consequently required Parliament to enact a law establishing mechanisms and procedures for vetting "the suitability of all judges and magistrates who were in office on the effective date to continue to serve in accordance with the values and principles set out in Articles 10 and 159."[198] More importantly for our purposes, the Constitution then stipulated in an ouster clause that: "A removal, or a process leading to the removal, of a judge, from office by virtue of the operation of legislation contemplated under subsection (1) shall not be subject to question in, or review by, any court."[199]

Parliament enacted this law in the form of the Vetting of Judges and Magistrates Act of 2011 (Vetting Act), and a Judges and Magistrates Vetting Board (the Board) established by this Act was constituted.[200] Unfortunately, the courts were not consistent in their approach to the constitutional ouster clause. While they defied it in some instances, in the majority of cases

191 See *Report of the Special Rapporteur on the Independence of Judges and Lawyers*, Gabriela Knaul, UN Doc A/HRC/26/32, 2014, para 87.

192 Akech, *Administrative Law* at 440–444.

193 See, for example, "What Jubilee's Judicial Service Commission Appointments Really Mean," *Sunday Nation*, 22 March 2015, available at www.nation.co.ke/news/politics/Judicial-Service-Commission-Appointments-Judiciary/-/1064/2661742/-/6xwcbpz/-/index.html.

194 See, for example, Geoffrey Mosoku, "LSK Files Petition Seeking to Compel President Uhuru Kenyatta to Swear in New High Court Judges," *Standard*, July 10, 2014, available at www.standardmedia.co.ke/article/2000127681/lsk-files-petition-seeking-to-compel-president-uhuru-kenyatta-to-swear-in-new-high-court-judges.

195 Mosoku, "LSK Files Petition Seeking to Compel President Uhuru Kenyatta to Swear in New High Court Judges."

196 See, for example, "Parliament Is Wrong on Warsame Vetting," *The Star*, April 21, 2018, available at www.the-star.co.ke/news/2018/04/21/parliament-is-wrong-on-warsame-vetting_c1747202.

197 Constitution of Kenya Review Commission, The Final Report of the Constitution of Kenya Review Commission 206 (2005).

198 Constitution of Kenya 2010, Schedule 6, clause 23(1).

199 Constitution of Kenya 2010, Schedule 6, clause 23(2).

200 Judges and Magistrates Vetting Act, No. 2 of 2011, section 6.

they deemed it inviolable.[201] On the rationale that the people of Kenya demanded a speedy vetting process, the Supreme Court took the approach that any consequential violations of the fundamental rights of affected judicial officers were but a small price to pay to uphold public confidence in the judiciary. And so, by largely refusing to assume jurisdiction to interrogate the Vetting Board's decision-making processes and decisions, the courts failed to interrogate the suitability of the vetting process to achieve its declared objectives. For example, the Vetting Act and its regulations did not establish a decision-making procedure.[202] In default, the Board made decisions by majority vote.[203] This was arguably a lottery, and it fell kindly on some judges, while condemning others.[204] What made it seem absurd was that where there was a tie in the Board's vote, the affected judicial officer was given the benefit of the doubt. One could therefore legitimately question the reasonableness of the Board's decision-making procedure by which a tied vote constituted a verdict of suitability. (Why wouldn't a tied vote constitute a verdict of unsuitability?) In these circumstances, it was difficult for the Board to defend itself against claims that, at least, some of its decisions were whimsical. More importantly, the message for judges was that their decisions could be revisited in the future with a view to securing their removal.

11.6 CONCLUSION

English law bequeathed to Kenya an ambivalent legacy that continues to shape the exercise of judicial review. On the one hand, Britain introduced a formal legal system, including a regime of common-law-based administrative law. On the other hand, an informal system of governance emerged during the colonial period. This chapter has examined the role of judicial review in enhancing democracy and constitutionalism in Kenya in the context of the interactions of these formal and informal systems of governance from colonial times to the present. The chapter has contended that a culture of making overly broad grants of power has not only enabled informalism in governance but also undermined judicial review. In this culture, law is merely seen as an instrument of power. The idea that judicial review can meaningfully constrain the Executive thus remains a mirage in significant respects. Although the Constitution of 2010 promises to bring the formal and informal governance systems closer, greater efforts need to be made to enhance judicial independence if the courts are to fearlessly confront Executive authoritarianism. Attention must also be given to the reform of the statutory law regime, so that it can conform to the requirements of the progressive Constitution of 2010.

201 See Akech, *Administrative Law* at 453–461.
202 Migai Akech, "Is the Vetting Process Really Fair to Judges?," *The Star*, June 21, 2012.
203 Akech, "Is the Vetting Process Really Fair to Judges?"
204 Akech, "Is the Vetting Process Really Fair to Judges?"

PART VI

Origins and Adaptations in Asia

12

The Evolution of Administrative Law in Singapore

From Adoption to Autochthonous Adaptation

Swati Jhaveri

12.1 INTRODUCTION – A PRAGMATIC START

As with other common law jurisdictions, administrative law in Singapore has its foundations in English law. The latter continued to exert an influence on local administrative law for a significant period of time. This can be partly explained by the constitutional genesis of Singapore in 1965. One of the most recent texts on constitutional law in Singapore describes it as an unlikely nation with an abrupt beginning.[1] When Singapore was ousted from the Malaysian federation, it was left in a constitutional vacuum. The state-level constitution that applied under the Malaysian Federal Constitution no longer extended to Singapore. Therefore, one of the first projects within the nation-building exercise should have been the filling of this gap. The then Prime Minister, Lee Kuan Yew, assured the citizens that this would be done. The Cabinet of Ministers at the time were advised to consult members of governments in the Commonwealth on questions of post-independence constitutional design.

However, soon after, the constitutional project was paused. In the words of Lee Kuan Yew, he felt the need to take a more considered and gradual approach to questions of constitutional design. There was a level of insecurity with entrenching a particular constitutional design at such an early stage in the nation's accidental founding, especially as political power had not been consolidated enough (in the hands of a clear majority of one political party) at a level that would allow swift economic, social and public order decisions to stabilise the nation.[2]

The approach was thus a pragmatic one – while having a constitutional document was considered important, it was not in itself normatively desirable or paramount at that stage in the nation's history. The Constitution was to be a tool for empowering government to carry out its functions in three respects: maintaining economic progress; managing ethnic relations (in particular, between the Malays and other races); and maintaining political dominance, which allowed the government to achieve the latter two imperatives.[3] And it was achieving success in these projects that was seen as the source of legitimacy of public power rather than

1 See K Tan, *The Constitution of Singapore: A Contextual Analysis* (Hart, 2015) at p 1. See also A Harding, 'Does the 'Basic Structure' Doctrine Apply in Singapore's Constitution? An Inquiry into Some Fundamental Constitutional Premises' in *Constitutional Interpretation in Singapore: Theory and Practice* (J Neo ed., Routledge 2016) p 32. Harding argues that the beginning of Singapore was not a 'moment' but 'a process of adjustment which may be regarded as ongoing even after fifty years' (at 36 and 39).

2 K Tan and L Thio, *Singapore: 50 Constitutional Moments That Defined a Nation* (Marshall-Cavendish, 2015) at pp 46–47.

3 K Tan, *The Constitution of Singapore: A Contextual Analysis* (Hart, 2015) pp 2–3.

compliance with a constitutional framework under which such decisions were made. The resulting Constitution was a patchwork document based on the previous state-level Constitution.

This pragmatic approach, grounded in striving for performance versus constitutional legitimacy informed much of administrative law for a significant period of time. Administrative *law* and judicial review were not going to be the primary tool used to control executive power. Political control via the executive and Parliament would be the primary forum for checking executive accountability and legitimacy. Due to this early peripheralisation of the law (versus political institutions – executive and parliamentary) as the main check on the executive, there was little renovation done of English administrative law, despite early suggestions to 'cut the Gordian Knot'.[4]

This chapter looks, however, at changes to this approach. Section 12.2 sets out the English principles of administrative law that informed local law at Singapore's independence. It further sketches out the reasons offered for rationalising a deferential approach to judicial review of executive action in Singapore on the back of these English law principles. Section 12.3 goes on to consider evidence that the courts may be stepping into a stronger and more articulated role in checking exercises of executive power. This is based, not on any perceived drop in the performance legitimacy of the executive but instead on the idea that the rule of law requires the co-equality of the judiciary and executive. In carrying out this analysis, the focus of the chapter is on changes in the use of comparative jurisprudence by the courts to inform their transition to a stronger and more articulated role on a range of issues. This includes, questions of justiciability, validity of ouster clauses, and scope of judicial review, especially substantive review and the approach to statutory interpretation for policing boundaries of executive power. It highlights how early references to English law principles are giving way to a more conscious development of local lines of precedent to justify the stronger role for the courts. These recent shifts mark the start of a more conscious autochthonous adaptation of English law principles in Singapore.

12.2 EARLY ADMINISTRATIVE LAW IN SINGAPORE: RATIONALISING A GREEN-LIGHT APPROACH TO JUDICIAL REVIEW

Singapore is administratively complex with the work of the State carried out by a multitude of government ministries, government corporations and statutory boards that regulate almost all aspects of life: from health care, education and housing to environmental planning, trade and business development and transport infrastructure.[5] Given the 'largeness' of the administrative state, scholars have argued that there are one of two responses open to the Judiciary in checking the executive branch through judicial review.

[4] Max Friedman, 'Unscrambling the Judicial Egg: Some Observations on Stare Decisis in Singapore and Malaysia' (1980) 22 *Mal. L.R.* 227; Walter Woon, 'Precedents that Bind – A Gordian Knot: Stare Decisis in the Federal Court of Malaysia and the Court of Appeal, Singapore' (1982) 24 *Mal. L.R.* 1; and, by the same author, 'Stare Decisis and Judicial Precedent in Singapore' in chapter 4 of *The Common Law in Singapore and Malaysia* (AJ Harding ed., 1985), as well as (more recently) 'The Doctrine of Judicial Precedent' in chapter 8 of *The Singapore Legal System* (Walter Woon ed., 1989); Andrew Phang, 'Stare Decisis in Singapore and Malaysia: A Sad Tale of the Use and Abuse of Statutes' (1983) 4 *Sing. L.R.* 155; Andrew Phang Boon Leong, "Overseas Fetters': Myth or Reality?' (1983) 2 *M.L.J.* cxxxix.

[5] See Jolene Lin, 'The Judicialization of Governance: The Case of Singapore' in *Administrative Law and Governance in Asia* (Tom Ginsburg and Albert Chen eds., Routledge, 2009) at p 287, and Jon ST Quah, *Public Administration Singapore Style* (Emerald Group, 2010) ch 11.

One is a 'green-light' approach based on trust in the Executive and its internal mechanisms for ensuring good governance and accountability. Alternatively, the Judiciary may be 'red light' in response to such a concentration of power and subject the exercise of executive power to more intense scrutiny.[6] This could be especially so in a Westminster-style system where the Executive is drawn from the elected members of Parliament and the latter, therefore, potentially becomes a relatively blunter tool of *independent* accountability. This may be mitigated, to some extent, in a bicameral parliamentary system like the English parliamentary system. This has been the prompt for instances of a red-light approach to judicial review in the English context.[7] It could be argued that a similar 'red-light' approach should be adopted in Singapore. It has a unicameral and dominant party-membership-based legislature, where the latter has been constituted by a strong majority from a single political party since Singapore's independence, leading scholars to query the capacity of the Legislature to act as an effective check.[8]

However, in Singapore, there have been a number of justifications offered for maintaining a green-light approach, notwithstanding Singapore's Westminster political system.[9] These are all grounded in the genesis of the Constitution in Singapore: the political arms of government were going to be primarily tasked with maintaining accountability, transparency and good governance. This is reinforced by the courts. The latter have observed how the state generally acts prophylactically in checking issues of legality prior to making decisions. Former Chief Justice, Chan Sek Keong, observed how government bodies in Singapore frequently consult the Attorney-General's Chambers for advice and, accordingly, the courts should exercise a light touch in carrying out any judicial review.[10] Second, there is a reliance on the Government's emphasis on governing 'honourably':[11]

> The concept of government by honourable men ... who have a duty to do right for the people, and who have the trust and respect of the population fits us better than the Western idea that a government should be given as limited powers as possible, and should always be treated with suspicion unless proven otherwise.

Finally, a further explanation provided for less invasive judicial review is that the administrative state in Singapore was created primarily for the purpose of advancing a benevolent collective national goal of economic success for all citizens and at a critical time in Singapore's history on the sudden expulsion of the latter from the Federation of

6 See generally Carol Harlow and Richard Rawlings, *Law and Administration* (Cambridge University Press, 3rd ed, 2009) ch 1 and at pp 22–31. See also Leigh Hancher and Matthias Ruete, 'Reviews: Forever Amber' (1985) 48 *Modern Law Review* 236.

7 See Albert Venn Dicey, *An Introduction to the Study of the Law of the Constitution* (Macmillan, 10th ed, 1970) ch 12 on the demands of the rule of law when it comes to power – the thrust of which is the need for limits on discretionary power.

8 See Chan Heng Chee, *The Politics of One Party Dominance: PAP at Grassroots* (Singapore University Press, 1976), and Thio Li-ann, 'Law and the Administrative State' in *The Singapore Legal System* (Kevin YL Tan ed., Singapore University Press, 1999) at p 3; 'Choosing Representatives – Singapore Does It Her Way' in *The People's Representatives: Electoral Systems in the Asia-Pacific Region* (Graham Hassall and Cheryl Saunders eds., Allen & Unwin, 1997) at pp 38–58.

9 Chan Sek Keong, 'Judicial Review – From Angst to Empathy' (2010) 22 *SAcLJ* 469 at 470–480; see also *Jeyaretnam Kenneth Andrew* v. *Attorney-General* [2014] 1 SLR 345 at [48]–[50], and Sundaresh Menon, 'The Rule of Law: The Path to Exceptionalism' (2016) 28 *SAcLJ* 413 at paras 24–25.

10 Chan Sek Keong, 'Judicial Review – From Angst to Empathy' (2010) 22 *SAcLJ* 469 at para 15.

11 See Singapore, Shared Values (White Paper, Cm 1, 1991) at para 41; see also Goh Chok Tong, 'Increasing Public Trust in Leaders of a Harmonious Society', speech at the Singapore-China Forum on Leadership (16 April 2010).

Malaysia, rather than as a way of appropriating power as may be the Diceyan suspicion elsewhere.[12]

The courts in Singapore have, therefore, for a long time maintained a conservative approach to the review of executive decision-making. This was done using the grounds from Lord Diplock's now famous exposition in *Council of Civil Service Unions* v. *Minister for the Civil Service*[13] – namely, illegality, irrationality and procedural impropriety.[14]

It was observed in 2011 by a local commentator that 'Singapore courts are generally conservative in their approach towards administrative law, drawing heavily from English case law in some respects but not engaging in innovative elaboration of the existing heads of judicial review'.[15] This continued a pre-independence trend.[16] There may be various reasons for this trend of relying on English law principles: most notably, the relatively recent severance of the Privy Council as the final appellate court. The continued role and influence of the Privy Council and the absence of a large body of home grown jurisprudence may explain the reliance on English law.[17] In addition, it is only recently that there has been an increase in the number of administrative law cases in a wider range of cases involving heavily localised issue. This includes (i) a challenge by a resident of a geographical constituency seeking a mandatory order to call a by-election on the abrupt resignation of Member of Parliament of that constituency;[18] (ii) a challenge by a member of an opposition political party of the constitutional vires of a loan made by the executive to an international funding body;[19] (iii) a challenge by members of the Hindu religion of a ban on the use of musical instruments during a religious procession;[20] and (iv) a challenge by a prison counsellor for members of the Sikh religion of a hair-grooming policy in prison that affected members of that religion.[21] These cases have prompted a re-think of the comparative (or otherwise) base for making decisions. The next section considers shifts, with a view to discussing the diminishing influence of English law – especially contemporary English law – in Singapore at the various points of expansion of judicial review.

12.3 AUTOCHTHONOUS ADAPTATIONS: THE DEVELOPMENT OF A LOCALISED ADMINISTRATIVE LAW

This section will consider contrasting pairs of cases to exemplify the shift to stronger judicial review by the courts. While, in Singapore, the courts have referenced constitutional principles like the 'rule of law' and 'separation of powers', in common with English courts, the operation of these principles has been influenced significantly by the local political

12 Jolene Lin, 'The Judicialization of Governance: The Case of Singapore' in *Administrative Law and Governance in Asia* (Tom Ginsburg and Albert Chen eds., Routledge, 2009) at pp 288–289.

13 *Council of Civil Service Unions* v. *Minister for the Civil Service* [1984] 3 WLR 1174 at 1196, per Lord Diplock.

14 See, S Jhaveri, 'Testing the Taxonomy of the Grounds of Judicial Review', [2019] *Sing J Leg Studies* (forthcoming).

15 Thio Li-ann, 'The Theory and Practice of Judicial Review of Administrative Action in Singapore', SAL Conference 2011 – Singapore Law Developments (2006–2010) 714 at 721.

16 *Estate and Trust Agencies* v. *Singapore Investment Trust* [1937] AC 898; *Sim Soo Koon* (1915) SSLR 57.

17 Andrew BL Phang, *The Development of Singapore Law: Historical and Socio-Legal Perspectives* (Butterworths 1990); Andrew Phang, 'Stare Decisis in Singapore and Malaysia: A Sad Tale of the Use and Abuse of Statutes' (1983) 4 *Sing. L.R.* 155; Andrew Phang Boon Leong, '"Overseas Fetters": Myth or Reality?', [1983] 2 *M.L.J.* cxxxix.

18 *Vellama d/o Marie Muthu* v. AG [2012] 2 SLR 1033; *Vellama d/o Marie Muthu* v. AG [2013] 4 SLR 1 (CA).

19 *Jeyaretnam Kenneth Andrew* v. AG [2013] 1 SLR 619 (HC); *Jeyaretnam Kenneth Andrew* v. AG [2014] 1 SLR 345 (CA)

20 *Vijaya Kumar s/o Rajendran* v. AG [2015] SGHC 244

21 *Madan Mohan Singh* v. AG [2015] 2 SLR 1085.

environment.[22] Therefore, 'the notion of a subjective or unfettered discretion [being] contrary to the rule of law'[23] has competed with varying concepts of the separation of powers: the latter manifesting itself through the exercise of judicial deference,[24] the identification of non-justiciable areas of review[25] and the extension of a presumption of legality to executive action.[26] In considering these shifts in key areas of the courts' judicial review jurisdiction, the focus of the discussion will be on the comparative reference points that the courts used to rationalise their position. This is with a view to assessing the continuing relevance of English law (both as at independence and thereafter) in Singapore.[27]

12.3.1 *Articulating the Judicial Role: From Judicial-Executive Separation to Judicial Co-equality*

The view that the courts maintain a completely green-light approach may be an oversimplification in light of some of the more recent pronouncements by the courts on their role in reviewing executive action.

This is evident most recently in the Court of Appeal's approach to judicial review in *Tan Seet Eng* v. *Attorney-General*[28] (*Tan Seet Eng*). The applicant in the case was challenging his detention under s 30 of the Criminal Law (Temporary Provisions) Act[29] (CLTPA). Under this section, the Minister for Home Affairs (with the consent of the Public Prosecutor) can detain a person without trial if they are suspected of being involved in activities of a criminal nature and if this is necessary in the interests of 'public safety, peace and good order'. The applicant sought to challenge his detention under s 30. Preventative detention is permitted under legislation other than the CLTPA. The most prominent is detention under the Internal Security Act (ISA).[30]

Judicial review of such detention orders has been a problematic area of review. In the late 1980s, there had been a number of detentions under the ISA, which had been the subject of review in the courts. In the famous case of *Chng Suan Tze* v. *Minister of Home Affairs*[31] (*Chng Suan Tze*), the Court of Appeal held that such detentions were subject to judicial review on

22 Singapore's indigenous rule of law has been the subject of extensive academic discussion: see Sundaresh Menon, 'The Rule of Law: The Path to Exceptionalism' (2016) 28 *SAcLJ* 413; Thio Li-Ann, 'Rule of Law within a Non-Liberal 'Communitarian' Democracy: The Singapore Experience' in *Asian Discourses of Rule of Law: Theories and Implementation of Rule of Law in Twelve Asian countries, France and the US* (Randall Peerenboom ed., Routledge, 2004) ch 6; Chan Sek Keong, 'The Courts and the "Rule of Law" in Singapore' [2012] *Sing JLS* 209; Thio Li-Ann, 'Between Apology and Apogee, Autochthony: The "Rule of Law" beyond the Rules of Law in Singapore' [2012] *Sing JLS* 269; Jack Tsen-Ta Lee, 'Shall the Twain Never Meet? Competing Narratives and Discourses of the Rule of Law in Singapore' [2012] *Sing JLS* 298; and Kasiviswanathan Shanmugam, 'The Rule of Law in Singapore' [2012] *Sing JLS* 357.

23 *Chng Suan Tze* v. *Minister for Home Affairs* [1988] 2 SLR(R) 525 at [86].

24 Daniel Tan, 'An Analysis of Substantive Review in Singaporean Administrative Law' (2013) 25 *SAcLJ* 296 at paras 62–70.

25 *Lee Hsien Loong* v. *Review Publishing Co Ltd* [2007] 2 SLR(R) 453 at [90].

26 *Ramalingam Ravinthran* v. *Attorney-General* [2012] 2 SLR 49 at [43]–[44]. A similar point was made by the Court of Appeal in *Yong Vui Kong* v. *Attorney-General* [2011] 2 SLR 1189 at [139]. The recent assertion of the stronger role discussed in this section does not equate with a red-light approach borne out of a distrust of power, but is also a departure from a green-light approach. The court's role is not premised on distrust but on the idea of co-equality and balance between the two branches.

27 See also Kenny Chng, 'The Theoretical Foundations of Judicial Review in Singapore' [2019] *Sing JLS* 294.

28 [2016] 1 SLR 779.

29 Cap 67, 2000 Rev Ed.

30 Cap 143, 1985 Rev Ed.

31 *Chng Suan Tze* v. *Minister for Home Affairs* [1988] 2 SLR(R) 525.

the usual grounds of review.[32] This judgment was quickly followed by a number of statutory and constitutional amendments, significantly restricting judicial review under the ISA to narrow technical grounds.[33]

One of the issues for the Court of Appeal in *Tan Seet Eng* was whether the approach in *Chng Suan Tze* to reviewing such detention orders continued to be 'good law' outside of the ISA context, given the amendments that followed that case. The Court of Appeal answered this in the affirmative.[34] The foundation for this was the rule of law, with judges being entrusted with the task of ensuring that executive power is exercised within legal limits.[35] The court built on both the rule of law and the separation of powers in setting out their role as co-equal with versus superior to the Executive. The detention orders were struck down and, remarkably, the government accepted the court's decision.[36]

This idea of co-equality is not new. However, until *Tan Seet Eng*, it was used to rationalise judicial deference. This is apparent from *Ramalingam Ravinthran* v. *Attorney-General*.[37] The applicant here challenged the Attorney-General's decision (as Public Prosecutor) to charge him and his co-accused with different charges under the Misuse of Drugs Act[38] in connection with the same criminal enterprise. The applicant's charge carried the mandatory death penalty. The applicant argued this infringed Art 12 (on equality) of the Constitution.[39] In deciding on the standard of review to adopt when reviewing the exercise of prosecutorial discretion for compatibility with Art 12, the court observed that[40]

> prosecutorial power is a constitutional power vested in the Attorney-General pursuant to Art 35(8) of the Constitution. *It is constitutionally equal in status to the judicial power set out in Art 93. . . . In view of the co-equal status of the two aforesaid constitutional powers, the*

[32] This is based on the grounds set out in *Council of Civil Service Unions* v. *Minister for the Civil Service* [1984] 3 WLR 1174 at 1196, per Lord Diplock (namely, illegality, irrationality and procedural impropriety).

[33] Constitutional challenges to these ouster-clause-type amendments to the Internal Security Act (Cap 143, 1985 Rev Ed) were unsuccessful: *Teo Soh Lung* v. *Minister for Home Affairs* [1989] 1 SLR(R) 461 (HC); [1990] 1 SLR(R) 347 (CA). It is possible that the court may review its position on the constitutionality of ouster clauses: see *Per Ah Seng Robin* v. *Housing and Development Board* [2016] 1 SLR 1020 at [65]; see also Chan Sek Keong, 'Judicial Review – From Angst to Empathy' (2010) 22 *SAcLJ* 469 at para 19 on the 'academic' possibility of such an argument. Cf. views expressed by the former Chief Justice in 'The Courts and the "Rule of Law" in Singapore' [2012] *Sing JLS* 209 at 223–224. See further discussion in Section 12.4.

[34] *Tan Seet Eng* v. *Attorney-General* [2016] 1 SLR 779 at [67]–[76]. This differs from the courts' position in earlier cases under the Criminal Law (Temporary Provisions) Act (Cap 67, 2000 Rev Ed); see, most notably, *Re Wong Sin Yee* [2007] 4 SLR(R) 676.

[35] *Tan Seet Eng* v. *Attorney-General* [2016] 1 SLR 779 at [1] and [90], per Sundaresh Menon CJ.

[36] Soon after the decision, the Ministry of Home Affairs issued a statement indicating that the '[ministry] respects and accepts the Court of Appeal's judgment'. It further stated that the ministry had sought to reissue detention orders with the consent of the Public Prosecutor, which would comply with the Court of Appeal's decision in *Tan Seet Eng*. In particular, the ministry stated that the orders will set out the impact of the applicant's match-fixing activities 'on public safety, peace and good order within Singapore' as per the Court of Appeal's interpretation of s 30 of the CLTPA: Ministry of Home Affairs, 'MHA Statement on Detention of Dan Tan Seet Eng' (5 December 2015). The applicant was rearrested less than a week later and the detention order was not challenged. In addition, the Ministry of Home Affairs released a further three detainees under the CLTPA on the basis that they had reviewed the detention orders of those persons following the judgment and come to the view that they also needed to be revoked. Once released, these detainees were not rearrested under fresh detention orders but instead subject to the lesser restraint of a police supervision order: Ministry of Home Affairs, 'MHA Statement on Three Members of Match-Fixing Syndicate Released from Detention and Placed on Police Supervision Orders' (18 January 2016).

[37] *Ramalingam Ravinthran* v. *Attorney-General* [2012] 2 SLR 49.

[38] Cap 185, 2001 Rev Ed.

[39] Constitution of the Republic of Singapore (1999 Reprint).

[40] *Ramalingam Ravinthran* v. *Attorney-General* [2012] 2 SLR 49 at [43]–[44].

> *separation of powers doctrine requires the courts not to interfere with the exercise of the prosecutorial discretion unless it has been exercised unlawfully*. (emphasis added)

The court accorded the Attorney-General a presumption of constitutionality and restricted their review to assess only whether the decision was based on an unbiased consideration of 'relevant' considerations (defined broadly to include the willingness of one offender to testify against others and 'other policy factors').[41] This can be compared with the approach in *Tan Seet Eng*, where co-equality was used to rationalise judicial review on the usual grounds of review and a more involved approach to interpreting the provisions of the CLTPA (as discussed further in Section 12.3.4).[42]

What is interesting are the comparative reference points for the courts in *Chng Suan Tze* and *Tan Seet Eng*, when setting out the imperatives of the rule of law and implications of the separation of powers. Both are decisions advocating a stronger role for the courts. However, the comparative base for the decisions differed. In the earlier case of *Chng Suan Tze* – in extending its role under the ISA – the Court of Appeal departed from Malaysian jurisprudence, which had applied until then.[43] However, it continued to be informed by the newer positions of the English courts on questions of reviewability. The most critical aspect of the judgement – the idea that all power has legal limits and the rule of law demands that the courts should be able to examine the exercise of discretionary power – was housed firmly within English case law.[44] There were some indicators of the court starting to broaden its approach. First, it also relied on decisions of the highest courts in many Commonwealth countries. This was on the back of 'extensive arguments' from the applicants' counsel.[45] The Court of Appeal relied on decisions from the Supreme Court of Zimbabwe and a Privy Council appeal from St Christopher, Nevis and Anguilla. More interestingly, the Court of Appeal was also persuaded by its *own* jurisprudence on the implications of liberty rights in the Constitution – which generally prohibited arbitrary exercises of detention.[46] *Tan Seet Eng* took this much further. The Court of Appeal was much more confident in asserting its role under the CLTPA. It relied on more general constitutional principles – such as the rule of law – to rationalise its role under the CLTPA.[47]

This can be contrasted with the comparative approach in *Ramalingam*. Here the courts sought support for the presumption of constitutionality from decisions of the US Federal Courts.[48] This is a surprising comparative reference point, especially as the court was convinced by the reasoning of the US courts on the specific issue of judicial non-

41 A similar point was made by the Court of Appeal in *Yong Vui Kong* v. *Attorney-General* [2011] 2 SLR 1189 at [139].

42 *Council of Civil Service Unions* v. *Minister for the Civil Service* [1984] 3 WLR 1174 at 1196, per Lord Diplock (namely, illegality, irrationality and procedural impropriety).

43 As set out in *Karam Singh* v. *Menteri Hal Ehwal Dalam Negeri (Minister of Home Affairs) Malaysia* [1969] 2 MLJ 129 applied in the earlier cases of *Lee Mau Seng* v. *Minister for Home Affairs* and *De Souza Kevin Desmond* v. *Minister for Home Affairs* [1988] 1 SLR(R) 464 in Singapore. *Karam Singh* was a decision of the Malaysian Federal Court involving a detention under s 8 of the Malaysian ISA, which is identical to s 8 of the ISA in Singapore.

44 *Chng Suan Tze* v. *Minister for Home Affairs* [1988] 2 SLR(R) 525 at [86] referring to *Inland Revenue Commissioners* v. *National Federation of Self-Employed and Small Businesses Ltd* [1982] AC 617 at 644 and *Padfield* v. *Minister of Agriculture, Fisheries and Food* [1968] AC 997.

45 *Chng Suan Tze* v. *Minister for Home Affairs* [1988] 2 SLR(R) 525 at [55]–[86] – relying on *Minister of Home Affairs* v. *Austin* (1987) LRC (Const) 567, *Katofa* v. *Administrator-General for South West Africa* 1985 (4) SA 211 (SWA) and *Attorney-General of St Christopher, Nevis and Anguilla* v. *John Joseph Reynolds* [1980] AC 637.

46 Relying on a Privy Council Decision (at the time the court was the final appellate court in Singapore): *Ong Ah Chuan* v. *PP* [1979–1980] SLR(R) 710.

47 Referring to *Chng Suan Tze* only: *Tan Seet Eng* v. *Attorney-General* [2016] 1 SLR 779 at [2]

48 *Ramalingam Ravinthran* v. *Attorney-General* [2012] 2 SLR 49 at [49]–[50].

interference as a result of the separation of powers doctrine. The Court of Appeal in *Ramalingam* did not rationalise their comparative choice or go into a detailed discussion on different political foundations to the separation of powers doctrine in the US versus Singapore. It also marks a break from the usual common law comparative base in decisions.

12.3.2 *Clawing Back Areas of Non-justiciability*

Another development in the court's jurisprudence has been a movement away from the view that there are areas of executive action that are *immune* from judicial review. Previously, in the case of *Lee Hsien Loong* v. *Review Publishing Co Ltd*,[49] the courts had to consider the question of whether certain writs to commence civil defamation proceedings had been properly served out of jurisdiction. This turned, inter alia, on whether service had been affected in the manner required under a treaty between China and Singapore. This raised the issue of whether executive actions taken under the treaty are justiciable. On this, Judicial Commissioner Sundaresh Menon (as he then was) observed that

> there are clearly provinces of executive decision-making ['high policy'] that are, and should be, immune from judicial review. This comes as no surprise and is merely a reflection of the constitutional doctrine of the separation of powers. The doctrine of the separation of powers, as seen from the *dicta* cited above, undoubtedly informs the constitutional structure of the Westminster model of governance, on which our own constitutional framework is based.

This was informed entirely by the English position on the existence and content of such areas of 'high policy'.[50]

This remained the approach for a significant period of time. However, *Tan Seet Eng* itself exemplifies a shift, where the Court of Appeal held that 'even for matters falling within the category of 'high policy', the courts can inquire into whether decisions are made within the scope of the relevant legal power duty and arrived at in a legal manner', so such areas are not entirely non-justiciable but subject to deference and a calibrated review instead.[51]

A starker example is the court's approach to the question of the justiciability of the President's power to decide a clemency petition in death penalty cases. In *Yong Vui Kong* v. *Attorney-General*,[52] the applicant sought to challenge the President's decision to refuse clemency. The Respondent's case was basically that the clemency power and/or its exercise (collectively referred to hereafter as 'the clemency power' for convenience) was not justiciable as the clemency power was 'an extra-legal, extra-judicial and extraordinary [power] . . . that [was] only invoked when the legal process ha[d] reached its final and ultimate conclusion': the manner in which the President exercised the clemency power and the decision which he made pursuant to that power would be outside the purview of the courts.[53]

On this, Chief Justice Chan Sek Keong concluded that

> [t]he Justiciability Issue can be seen as a subset of the broader question of whether there are any matters which are non-justiciable, *ie*, which the courts do not have jurisdiction to rule on. Where Singapore is concerned, I am of the view that by virtue of the judicial power vested in the Supreme Court under Art 93 of the Singapore Constitution, the Supreme Court has

49 [2007] 2 SLR(R) 453.
50 [2007] 2 SLR(R) 453 at [74]–[104].
51 *Tan Seet Eng* v. *Attorney*-General [2016] 1 SLR 779 at [105]–[106].
52 [2011] SGCA 9.
53 [2011] SGCA 9 at [12].

> jurisdiction to adjudicate on every legal dispute on a subject matter in respect of which Parliament has conferred jurisdiction on it, including any constitutional dispute between the State and an individual. In any modern State whose fundamental law is a written Constitution based on the doctrine of separation of powers (*ie*, where the judicial power is vested in an independent judiciary), there will (or should) be few, if any, legal disputes between the State and the people from which the judicial power is excluded.[54]

Following a broad survey on the question of justiciability of clemency powers in England, the Caribbean States, Canada, Australia, New Zealand, India, Hong Kong and Malaysia, Chief Justice Chan Sek Keong held that, while clemency powers are extraordinary executive powers (as they are an act of grace), this does not mean they are not amenable to judicial review. The Indian position appeared to be determinative on the matter.[55] While clemency decisions were not justiciable on the *merits* 'on the basis of the doctrine of separation of powers ... [and] on the basis of established administrative law principles ... the courts will subject the President's exercise of his clemency power to normal administrative law judicial review (illegality, irrationality and procedural fairness) on the basis that no legal powers are unfettered and beyond the purview of the courts. This is especially so in the present case, where there is an implication for the life and liberty of the individual concerned.'[56] The courts' broader comparative base in *Yong Vui Kong* was driven by counsels' arguments and its own concern to undertake such a survey at a critical point in the court's expansion of its powers.[57]

12.3.3 *Questioning the Enforceability of Ouster Clauses*

Privative or ouster clauses are found across the common law world. These clauses exclude or restrict the scope of judicial review of the executive's acts or decisions under that statute. Ousters may be full or partial. The latter may impose a strict time limit for the commencement of proceedings or restrict the grounds on which decisions may be challenged. The former seek to exclude all judicial review. Irrespective of form, these clauses bring into tension a number of constitutional principles: the need for courts to respect parliamentary intention, the separation of powers (the judiciary and the executive should have their domains respected) and rule of law concerns that require that all public power is held to account and that the aggrieved have a proper remedy for challenging decisions of public bodies. Courts across the common law world have adopted varying approaches to resolve this tension. They may recognise the ouster of judicial review, respecting the intention of the legislature. Alternatively, such clauses may be disregarded on the basis that they are an unconstitutional interference with judicial power or not sufficiently respectful of the rule of law and access to justice. Finally, courts have also sought to (re)interpret ouster clauses in a way that allows for some judicial review on traditional administrative law grounds of review: namely, illegality, irrationality and procedural impropriety. This section looks at the judicial consideration of the latter argument by the courts this year.[58]

54 [2011] SGCA 9 at [13].
55 [2011] SGCA 9 at [76].
56 [2011] SGCA 9 at [75], [77], [78] and [85].
57 [2011] SGCA 9 at [77], [83].
58 This section focuses on the courts' consideration of arguments in favour of interpreting ouster clauses to permit review on traditional administrative law grounds. The cases in this section also raise constitutional arguments against such clauses. For example, in *Prabagaran a/l Srivijayan* v. *Public Prosecutor and Other matters* [2017] 1 SLR 173, the applicant argued that section 33B(4) is contrary to the rule of law.

Following the introduction of ouster clauses in the Constitution after *Chng Suan Tze* (see Section 12.3.1), the courts took a modest approach to reviewing the validity of such clauses. There were routinely enforced.[59] Recent cases indicate an alternative stance.

First, the courts have been willing to entertain applications that challenge legislative encroachments on judicial power. In *Mohammad Faizal bin Sabtu* v. *PP*,[60] the applicant sought to challenge the constitutionality of legislative amendments to the Misuse of Drugs Act, which prescribed mandatory minimum punishments for convicted drug offenders. The applicant argued that this encroached on the judicial power of sentencing and was, therefore, in violation of the separation of powers. The applicant was unsuccessful as the court concluded that, historically speaking, sentencing was not an exclusively judicial power. However, in reaching this conclusion, the court demonstrated a willingness to guard its own jurisdiction under the separation of powers.[61] The court identified the separation of powers as part of the 'basic structure' of the Constitution, which thus fell within the purview of the court's role as guardian of the Constitution. The courts relied on constitutional jurisprudence from India to develop the concept of and identify aspects of the 'basic structure' of the Constitution that would inform judicial review (as discussed further in Section 12.3.4).

Second, in obiter, courts have indicated that they may start to push back on the enforceability of ouster clauses. In *Per Ah Seng & Another* v. *Housing Development Board & Another*,[62] the Court of Appeal acknowledged counsels' arguments that enforcing ouster clauses may run counter to the rule of law, in restricting the court's purview to declare legal limits on discretionary powers.[63] The Court of Appeal further observed that such clauses may be contrary to Article 93 of the Constitution, which states that '[t]he judicial power of Singapore shall be vested in a Supreme Court and in such subordinate courts as may be provided by any written law for the time being in force'.[64] As this was not a live issue, the court's discussion was brief. It will remain to be seen how the courts will approach this from a comparative point of view. In the earlier case of *Teo Soh Lung* v. *Minister for Home Affairs*,[65] the applicants sought to challenge the constitutional amendments following Chng Suan Tze (that essentially ousted the courts' jurisdiction under the ISA). In rejecting this argument, the Court of Appeal did not engage with English jurisprudence following Anisminic on ouster clauses. The applicants faced an uphill battle, given they were seeking to challenge a constitutional amendment, which had been duly passed as a matter of amendment process.[66]

This stance might be changing and in a way that did not rely on English jurisprudence under the *Anisminic* line of precedent. Recently, the courts have indicated that ousters may

59 With few exceptions in narrow circumstances: *Re Application by Yee Yut Ee* [1977–1978] SLR(R) 490 at [18] and [31], *Stansfield Business International Pte Ltd* v. *Minister for Manpower (formerly known as Minister for Labour)* [1999] 2 SLR(R) 866 at [21]–[22], *Re Raffles Town Club Pte Ltd* [2008] 2 SLR(R) 1101 at [5] and [8] but cf. *Borissik Svetlanta* v. *Urban Redevelopment Authority* [2009] 4 SLR(R) 92 at [29].

60 [2012] 4 SLR 947.

61 [2012] 4 SLR 947 at paras 11 and 12.

62 [2015] SGCA 62 – the court's comments were *obiter* as the respondent did not seek to rely on the ouster clauses in question.

63 [2015] SGCA 62 at [63].

64 [2015] SGCA 62 at [65].

65 [1990] 1 S.L.R.(R.) 347.

66 This is of course not a barrier in other jurisdictions; see Y Roznai, *Unconstitutional Constitutional Amendments* (Oxford University Press, 2017). Contrast this to the position in Hong Kong, where the constitutional right of access to court has not been used to render ouster clauses ineffective, with the courts instead continuing to cite *Anisminic*; see the chapter by Michael Ramsden on Hong Kong.

be interpreted in a way that does not completely exclude judicial review. This issue remains a live one in respect of the most litigated privative clause in recent times: the partial ouster of judicial review in Section 33B(4) of the Misuse of Drugs Act (Cap 185, 2008 Rev Ed) (**MDA**). This was introduced in 2013 as part of the broader amendments to the death penalty sentencing regime for certain drugs offences. Section 33B(1)(a) of the MDA provides that a court may sentence a person to life imprisonment instead of the death penalty if, inter alia, the Public Prosecutor certifies that 'the person has substantively assisted the Central Narcotics Bureau in disrupting drug trafficking activities within or outside Singapore'.[67] Section 33B(4) then provides that

> [t]he determination of whether or not any person has substantively assisted the Central Narcotics Bureau in disrupting drug trafficking activities shall be at the sole discretion of the Public Prosecutor and no action or proceeding shall lie against the Public Prosecutor in relation to any such determination unless it is proved to the court that the determination was done in bad faith or with malice.

In *Cheong Chun Yin* v. *Attorney-General*,[68] the respondent accepted that aside from bad faith and malice, an applicant can challenge the constitutionality of a determination by the Public Prosecutor under section 33B.[69] This was affirmed in *Muhammad Ridzuan bin Mohd Ali* v. *Attorney-General*.[70] The Court of Appeal in that case held that this reading of the section 'flows from the doctrine of constitutional supremacy . . . all executive acts must be constitutional and the court is conferred the power to declare void any executive act that contravenes the provisions of the Constitution'.[71]

In 2018, the debate relating to the scope of section 33B(4) was taken one step further: does this section also preclude judicial review on the traditional administrative law grounds of illegality, irrationality and procedural impropriety? In 2014, the applicant in *Cheong Chun Yin* sought to argue that section 33B(4) allowed judicial review on the grounds that the Public Prosecutor had made an error of law that took him out of his jurisdiction and, in these circumstances, the partial ouster clause embodied in section 33B(4) was not applicable. The clause does not oust the court's power to review a decision that has been made outside of the executive's jurisdiction. This argument has been successful elsewhere. For example, in the UK, in the case of *Anisminic* v. *Foreign Compensation Commission*, a majority of the House of Lords held that a clause purporting to oust the jurisdiction of the courts to review any 'determination' was ineffective if the relevant decision was tainted by legal error.[72] A 'determination' that did not comply with the principles of administrative law was a nullity and beyond the jurisdiction of the decision-maker. Accordingly, it was void and not a 'determination' for the purposes of the relevant ouster clause. Justice Tay Yong Kwang rejected the applicant's argument to this effect in *Cheong Chun Yin*.[73] The question was how far the Singapore courts should adopt the English position under *Anisminic*.

67 Section 33(2)(b) of the MDA.

68 [2014] 3 SLR 1141.

69 This was highlighted by the Minister of Law during parliamentary debates – Second Reading of the Bill, the Minister for Law, Mr K Shanmugam, Singapore Parliamentary Debates, Official Report (14 November 2012) vol 89: 'the Public Prosecutor's discretion is not unfettered. It is subject to judicial review, either on bad faith or malice, which is expressly provided for, and of course, unconstitutionality, which goes without saying.'

70 [2015] 5 SLR 1222.

71 [2015] 5 SLR 1222 at [35].

72 [1969] 2 AC 147.

73 [2015] 5 SLR 1222 at [31].

In 2015, in *Ridzuan*, the Court of Appeal was urged by the applicants to review the Public Prosecutor's decisions on grounds of procedural impropriety. The Court of Appeal indicated that this may not be possible on a plain reading of section 33B(4); however, ultimately concluded that 'it is an open question'.[74] This echoed views expressed earlier in the judgment on the possibility of review on other administrative law grounds. In particular, the Court of Appeal observed that 'where it has been shown that the PP has disregarded relevant considerations and/or failed to take relevant consideration [*sic*] into account … intuitively it seems inconceivable that the aggrieved person would be left without a remedy and that the decision of the PP should nevertheless stand'.[75] On both questions (review for procedural impropriety and taking account of relevant / irrelevant considerations), the Court of Appeal declined to express a definitive view in the absence of full argument on the issue by the parties.

The issue was revived in May 2018 in the case of *Nagaenthran a/l K Dharmalingam* v. *Attorney-General*.[76] The applicant in this case challenged the Public Prosecutor's refusal to issue a certificate of assistance on grounds of review that went beyond bad faith, malice and unconstitutionality. The applicant made several arguments. First, he argued that the Public Prosecutor had failed to take into account relevant considerations. Second, the Public Prosecutor had made a determination in the absence of a 'precedent fact' (namely in the absence of properly investigated information put forward by the applicant by way of assistance). Finally, the Public Prosecutor had acted irrationally. In addition to the constitutional challenges to section 33B(4), the applicant argued that, even if it is constitutional, that section does not oust the court's judicial review of a non-certification decision, where the latter is, in fact, a nullity. The applicant's argument revived the question of the scope and application of *Anisminic*-type arguments on ouster clauses in Singapore.[77]

The High Court in *Nagaenthran* concluded that

> although s 33B(4) … is a constitutionally valid ouster clause that expressly ousts the jurisdiction of the courts to review the Public Prosecutor's decision not to issue a certificate of substantive assistance except on the grounds of bad faith, malice or unconstitutionality, the ouster clause in principle does not exclude the review of the Public Prosecutor's determination on the grounds of other jurisdictional errors of law which render the ouster clause inapplicable.[78]

The applicant was ultimately, however, not able to satisfy the court that there was a prima facie case with respect to the various pleaded administrative law grounds and leave was refused. The High Court left open a number of questions that will need to be resolved by the Court of Appeal. The Court of Appeal in *Nagaenthran* had to resolve a number of connected questions. First, what is the true scope of the *Anisminic* argument in Singapore. There are a number of sub-issues that will emerge when answering this question. Are ouster clauses ineffective where the relevant decision is a nullity? Which decisions are to be regarded as nullity? Is there a distinction between jurisdictional errors (which render decisions a nullity)

74 [2014] 3 SLR 1222 at [76].

75 [2014] 3 SLR 1222 at [72].

76 [2018] SGHC 112 (High Court); [2019] SGCA 37 (Court of Appeal).

77 An issue which remains unsettled: *Re Application by Yee Yut Ee* [1977–1978] SLR(R) 490 at [18] and [31], *Stansfield Business International Pte Ltd* v. *Minister for Manpower* [1999] 2 SLR(R) 866 at [21]–[22], *Re Raffles Town Club Pte Ltd* [2008] 2 SLR(R) 1101 at [5] and [8] and *Teng Fuh Holdings Pte Ltd* v. *Collector of Land* Revenue [2006] 3 SLR(R) 507at [37]–[38]; but cf. *Borissik Svetlana* v. *Urban Redevelopment Authority* [2009] 4 SLR(R) 92 at [29]).

78 [2018] SGHC 112 at [43].

and non-jurisdictional errors (which do not)? How will we draw a distinction between jurisdictional and non-jurisdictional errors of law to determine when an ouster clause is applicable? This latter question was left open by the High Court in *Nagaenthran* because of the absence of argument on the matter by the respondent.[79] The High Court indicated it was minded to view the applicant's argument relating to the absence of a precedent fact as raising a possible jurisdictional error,[80] but all other grounds pleaded (improper accounting of relevant and/or irrelevant considerations and irrationality) were errors that did not go to jurisdiction.[81] The court ultimately, however, in reviewing these other grounds, proceeded on the assumption that all errors are jurisdictional errors of law and reviewable.[82]

On appeal, the Court of Appeal, however, took a completely different and autochthonous approach to the issue. The Court of Appeal did not consider the implications of Section 33B(2)(b) within the parameters of a typical *Anisminic* argument, as discussed in the preceding paragraph. The Court of Appeal instead characterised the provision as a clause that confers immunity on the Public Prosecutor from liability for decisions made without bad faith and malice. The court began with the observation that in a constitutional system of governance such as Singapore's, the courts are ordinarily vested with the power to adjudicate upon all disputes; judicial review forms a part of this power to adjudicate and concerns that area of law where the courts review the legality of government actions.[83] The court found that s 33B(4) was not an ouster clause, as it did not purport to exclude the jurisdiction of the courts to supervise the legality of the Public Prosecutor's decision not to issue a certificate of assistance. It only immunised the PP from suit save on certain exceptions as stated in s 33B (4).[84] The court noted that the inquiry whether an offender had substantively assisted the authorities in disrupting drug trafficking activities within or outside Singapore entailed a wide-ranging assessment going beyond the institutional competence of the courts, which was ultimately directed to the resolution of particular controversies.[85] In that light, it was entirely logical for Parliament to vest in the Public Prosecutor the responsibility for determining whether an offender had rendered substantive assistance to the authorities in disrupting drug trafficking activities and then to immunise the Public Prosecutor, save on excepted grounds, in respect of that determination. Without s 33B(4), an aggrieved offender might be tempted to bring suit against the PP challenging his determination, and thereby force the court into the unviable position of having to determine an issue that the court is inherently not capable of determining; yet, at the same time, the exceptions to the immunity granted by s 33B(4) serve to safeguard against abuse.[86]

79 [2018] SGHC 112 at [107]–[108] and [119]. The House of Lords in *Anisminic* came to different conclusions on this precise question (see *Nagaenthran* at [104]). There were many attempts to resolve this post-*Anisminic*: *R* v. *Lord President of the Privy Council, ex parte Page* [1993] AC 682; *R(Cart)* v. *Upper Tribunal (Public Law Project and Another Intervening)* [2012] 1 AC 663. It is a live issue at the moment in the UK: *R* v. *Investigatory Powers Tribunal, ex parte Privacy International* [2018] 1 WLR 2572; appeal to be heard before a seven-judge panel of the Supreme Court in December 2018.

80 Precedent fact review is the review of errors made in the assessment of evidence presented in support of facts that must objectively exist before a decision maker has the power to make a decision under relevant legislation. In the case of section 33B, the precedent fact is the information provided by him to the Central Narcotics Bureau, which is needed for the Public Prosecutor to make a decision on whether to issue a certificate of substantive assistance in favour of the applicant: [2018] SGHC 112 at [137].

81 [2018] SGHC 112 at [108].

82 [2018] SGHC 112 at [116].

83 [2019] SGCA 37 at [46].

84 [2019] SGCA 37 at [51].

85 [2019] SGCA 37 at [58].

86 [2019] SGCA 37 at [67].

Having found that s 33B(4) did not oust the jurisdiction of the courts to review the Public Prosecutor's non-certification decision, the court proceeded to determine the merits of the appeal. The court dismissed the second appeal on both grounds of review brought by the appellant. As to the first ground, the court was of the view that the appellant had not adduced a shred of evidence to show that the Public Prosecutor had failed to consider the effect of the appellant's information provided in his contemporaneous statements on the disruption of drug trafficking activities at that time.[87] As to the second ground, the court took the view that the Public Prosecutor's determination of whether an offender had rendered substantive assistance to the authorities in disrupting drug trafficking activities both within and outside Singapore was simply not a determination involving the exercise of an executive discretion that required a precedent fact to be established,[88] which meant that the appellant could not impugn the Public Prosecutor's non-certification decision on the grounds that the decision was reached in the absence of a precedent fact being established.

In making this decision, the Court of Appeal relied predominantly on its own previous jurisprudence and the legislative intention behind Section 33B as apparent through the parliamentary debates relating to the provision. With respect to its own previous jurisprudence, it relied on cases where the courts had interpreted similar provisions in Singapore in other legislation.[89] It also relied on its own articulation of the nature of the judicial function in Singapore set out in previous cases.[90]

12.3.4 *Approaches to the Interpretation of Text – Moving Away from a Literal-Positivistic Approach?*

The courts' approach to the review of executive action generally hangs on statutory interpretation: the courts' refer to text to ascertain limits on discretionary power. Here, again, the courts have demonstrated a change in their approach to text. First, in *Tan Seet Eng*, the court expressed the view that questions of statutory interpretation are 'centrally' for the courts. The applicant focused primarily on 'illegality' as his ground of review. This involved interpreting the provisions of the CLTPA to ascertain the scope of the power that had been delegated by Parliament to the Executive. Here, the Court of Appeal, echoing the views of the Court of Appeal in *Chng Suan Tze*, observed that this question was 'centrally' one for the Judiciary.[91] In carrying out the interpretation of the requisite provisions of the CLTPA (primarily the question of what was 'necessary ... in the interests of public safety, peace and good order' under s 30 of the CLTPA), the Court of Appeal paid close attention to parliamentary debates at the enactment and subsequent renewal of the CLTPA by the Legislature. However, it did not just defer to the interpretation provided by the Attorney-General but undertook its own interpretation of parliamentary debates.[92] This determined the outcome of the case that the

87 [2019] SGCA 37 at [79].

88 [2019] SGCA 37 at [84].

89 See also Benjamin Joshua Ong, 'The Constitutionality of Ouster Clauses: *Nagaenthran a/l K Dharmalingam* v. *Attorney-General* [2018] SGHC 112' (2019) *Oxford University Commonwealth Law Journal* 1–22.

90 *Mohammad Faizal bin Sabtu* v. *Public Prosecutor* [2012] 4 SLR 947 at [27] – discussed in Section 12.3.2.

91 *Tan Seet Eng* v. *Attorney-General* [2015] 2 SLR 453 at [134] (cf. *Chng Suan Tze* v. *Minister for Home Affairs* [1988] 2 SLR 525, where the Court of Appeal held that the boundaries of the decision maker's jurisdiction as conferred by an Act of Parliament is a question 'solely' for the courts).

92 This contrasts with the court's approach to statutory interpretation in the context of constitutional judicial review where they defer to the interpretation offered by the attorney-general as to the purpose of a statute (according it a presumption of constitutionality albeit to varying degrees): *Taw Cheng Kong* v. *Public Prosecutor* [1988] 1 SLR 943 (HC); [1998] 2 SLR 410 (CA); *Lim Meng Suang* v. *Attorney-General* [2013] 3 SLR 118 (HC); [2015] 1 SLR 26

grounds for detention were not demonstrably compliant with s 30 of the CLTPA.[93] In the court's view, the CLTPA must be interpreted to apply only to 'offences of sufficient seriousness'[94] and for activities that have a prejudicial effect on the public safety, peace and good order *of Singapore*,[95] and the applicant's global match-fixing activities did not appear to conform to this interpretation. Consequently, the Court of Appeal quashed the detention order. In reaching the position that the question of the scope of the power conferred on the Executive by the Legislature is centrally one for the Judiciary, the courts did not refer to similar debates on statutory interpretation elsewhere.[96] The courts instead based their decision on broad principles of the rule of law developed in local case law (discussed in Section 12.3.1).

Secondly, there is a general movement away from a strict positivistic approach to interpretation. Earlier cases show that the prevailing position was that the political branches had the final say on governance and constitutional matters. For example, in *Rajeevan Edakalavan* v. *Public Prosecutor*[97] concerning the right to counsel under art 9(3) of the Constitution, the then Chief Justice, Yong Pung How, sitting in the High Court, declined to rule that this included the right to be informed of one's right to counsel. According to the Chief Justice, art 9(3) merely states that an arrested person 'shall be allowed to consult' counsel and to say that this imposes a positive obligation to inform the accused of his right would be 'tantamount to judicial legislation'.[98] As he puts it, '[t]he duty of the judge is to adjudicate and interpret the laws passed by Parliament with the aim of ensuring that justice is upheld. He is in no position to expand the scope of or imply into the Constitution and other legislation his own interpretation of the provisions which is clearly contrary to Parliament's intention.'[99]This can be contrasted with more recent cases on constitutional interpretation. The courts' feel less restricted by the text and more driven by the values and structures that are inherent in the Constitution. This question has been addressed directly by the courts in Singapore in the form of a discussion on the 'basic structure' of the Constitution.

The language of the 'basic structure' or 'basic features doctrine' comes from Indian constitutional law jurisprudence, most notably the case of *Kesavannada Bharati* v. *State of Kerala*,[100] where the Supreme Court of India held that 'every provision of the Constitution can be amended provided in the result the basic foundation and structure of the Constitution remains the same'.[101] The Supreme Court of India has gone on in subsequent cases to identify such fundamental features of the Constitution of India that are beyond the reach of constitutional amendment.[102] The application of this doctrine was first tested in Singapore in the case

(CA). The court's more involved approach to statutory interpretation in *Tan Seet Eng* v. *Attorney-General* [2016] 1 SLR 779 can also be contrasted with the approaches taken elsewhere: see, eg, the more conservative approach to judicial interpretation of statute in the English context (largely driven by parliamentary supremacy): *R* v. *Monopolies and Mergers Commission, ex parte South Yorkshire Transport Ltd* [1993] 1 WLR 23; *R (British Broadcasting Corp)* v. *Information Tribunal* [2007] 1 WLR 2583; *R (Cart)* v. *Upper Tribunal* [2012] 1 AC 663; *Eba* v. *Advocate General for Scotland* [2012] 1 AC 710; *R (Jones)* v. *First-tier Tribunal* [2013] 2 AC 48.

93 *Tan Seet Eng* v. *Attorney-General* [2016] 1 SLR 779 at [146].

94 *Tan Seet Eng* v. *Attorney-General* [2016] 1 SLR 779 at [135].

95 *Tan Seet Eng* v. *Attorney-General* [2016] 1 SLR 779 at [137].

96 See contributions on Australia and Canada in this volume, for example.

97 *Rajeevan Edakalavan* v. *Public Prosecutor* [1998] 1 SLR(R) 10.

98 *Rajeevan Edakalavan* v. *Public Prosecutor* [1998] 1 SLR(R) 10 at [19].

99 *Rajeevan Edakalavan* v. *Public Prosecutor* [1998] 1 SLR(R) 10 (Rajeevan) at [19].

100 AIR 1973 SC 1461.

101 AIR 1973 SC 1461 at [316].

102 *Minerva Mills Ltd. and Ors.* v. *Union Of India and Ors* AIR 1980 SC 1789, where the court held that the limit on absolute power was a fundamental feature of the Constitution – therefore any constitutional amendment that

of *Teo Soh Lung* v. *Minister for Home Affairs*, where the High Court held that 'the Kesavananda doctrine is not applicable to our Constitution. Considering the differences in the making of the Indian and our Constitution, it cannot be said that our Parliament's power to amend our Constitution is limited in the same way as the Indian Parliament's power to amend the Indian Constitution'.[103]

This remained the position until the very recent decision of the Singapore Court of Appeal in the case of *Yong Vui Kong* v. *Public Prosecutor*.[104] The applicant in the case had been convicted for trafficking drugs under the Misuse of Drugs Act and received the mandatory sentence of the death penalty under that legislation.[105] The legislation was subsequently amendment to permit the imposition of a mandatory life sentence and no less than fifteen strokes of the cane. The applicant was re-sentenced under these legislative amendments. He sought to challenge the caning part of his re-sentence on the grounds that it was a form of torture and violated Article 9 (protection of liberty) as being a form of punishment that was contrary to 'law', and that caning was discriminatory in its application to men and therefore violated Article 12, which protected the equality of persons before the law. The relevant challenge for present purposes was the argument that (having failed to convince the court of his arguments under Articles 9 and 12) 'a prohibition against torture and inhuman punishment should be read into the Constitution because such practices violate "first principles of natural law"'.[106] The applicant sought to rely on an interim case – *Mohammad Faizal bin Sabtu* v. *PP*[107] – where the High Court referred to the principle of the separation of powers as part of the 'basic structure' of the Constitution.

The Court of Appeal accepted that this case had introduced the idea that certain aspects of the Constitution are part of its 'basic structure' into the jurisprudence of Singapore. To this, the Court of Appeal added that the right to vote may be part of the basic structure of the

sought to further enlarge the amendment powers of Parliament and limit judicial power to review that was unconstitutional.

103 *Teo Soh Lung* v. *Minister for Home Affairs* [1989] 1 SLR(R) 461 and [1990] 1 SLR(R) 347 at para 47 per FA Chua J (the Court of Appeal did not consider the issue on appeal). The High Court took a strict originalist interpretation of the origination of the Constitution to reach this conclusion positing that '[i]f the framers of the Singapore Constitution had intended limitations on the power of amendment, they would have expressly provided for such limitations'. The applicant had tried to argue that constitutional amendments which sought to immunise national security decisions from judicial review violated the basic structure of the Constitution as being in contravention of the rule of law and the separation of powers and in reliance on the Supreme Court of India's decision in *Minerva Mills* (n 103).

104 [2015] 2 SLR 1158.

105 The applicant sought to challenge that sentence (and the subsequent refusal to grant him clemency) in numerous unsuccessful constitutional challenges: *Yong Vui Kong* v. AG [2011] 2 SLR 1189, CA; *Yong Vui Kong* v. *PP* [2010] 3 SLR 489; *Yong Vui Kong* v. *PP* [2012] 2 SLR 872, CA.

106 [2015] 2 SLR 1158 at para 38.

107 [2012] 4 SLR 947: the High Court held that the principle of separation of powers is part of the 'basic structure' of the Constitution: 'The Singapore Constitution is based on the Westminster model of constitutional government ("the Westminster model"), under which the sovereign power of the State is distributed among three organs of state, viz, the Legislature, the Executive and the Judiciary . . . the sovereign power of Singapore is shared among the same trinity of constitutional organs, viz, the Legislature (comprising the President of Singapore and the Singapore parliament), the Executive (the Singapore government) and the Judiciary (the judges of the Supreme Court and the Subordinate Courts). The principle of separation of powers, whether conceived as a sharing or a division of sovereign power between these three organs of state, is therefore part of the basic structure of the Singapore Constitution. . . . All Constitutions based on the Westminster model incorporate the principle of separation of powers as part of their constitutional structure in order to diffuse state power among different organs of state' at paras 11 and 12 (the court went on to hold that constitutional supremacy and the exclusiveness of judicial power were part of this idea of the separation of powers). The court eventually concluded, however, that none of these principles were breached by a legislative provision that sought to structure the sentencing 'discretion' of the judges in the context of certain drug trafficking offences.

Constitution,[108] acknowledging their earlier decision on this right in the case of *Vellama d/o Marie Muthu* v. *AG*,[109] where the Court of Appeal held that citizens had a right to a representative in Parliament in the Westminster model of government that is part of the inherent framework of the Constitution. Using these examples, the Court of Appeal concluded in *Yong Vui Kong* that in order for something to be part of the basic structure of the Constitution, 'it must be something fundamental and essential to the *political system* that is established thereunder'.[110]

The courts have therefore assumed a stronger role on matters of text. They have done this by relying broadly on notions of the rule of law (without any comparative discussion but grounded in local case law) or, alternatively, jurisprudence from outside England (most, notably, India). And in referring to India, it sought to distinguish the 'basic features' doctrine – instead, creating Singapore's own version of the doctrine.

12.3.5 *Expanding the Scope of Substantive Review*

In Singapore, the courts have maintained a stricter distinction between reviewing the 'legality' and 'merits' of a decision, relative to other jurisdictions.[111] Irrationality has been used sparingly and with a high threshold for an applicant to overcome.[112] The courts also rejected proportionality as a ground for judicial review.[113] This remained the status quo until recently. The recent recognition of the doctrine of substantive legitimate expectations is a break away from this. The High Court's decision in *Chiu Teng @ Kallang Pte Ltd* v. *Singapore Land Authority*[114] (*Chiu Teng*) to recognise the doctrine of substantive legitimate expectations is

108 Relying on parliamentary debates where the Government acknowledged this to be the case – see Singapore Parliamentary Debates, Official Report (16 May 2001) vol 73 at col 1726 (Wong Kan Seng, Minister for Home Affairs and Leader of the House): 'While the Constitution does not contain an expressed declaration of the right to vote, I have been advised by the Attorney General, even before today, that the right to vote at parliamentary and presidential elections is *implied within the structure of our Constitution*. We have a parliamentary form of government. The Constitution provides for regular general elections to make up Parliament and establishes representative democracy in Singapore. So the right to vote is fundamental to a representative democracy, which we are, and that is why we have the Parliamentary Elections Act to give effect to this right' (emphasis added).

109 [2013] 4 SLR 1.

110 Above [2015] 2 SLR 1158 at para 70 relying on Calvin Liang and Sarah Shi, 'The Constitution of Our Constitution, A Vindication of the Basic Structure Doctrine' Singapore Law Gazette (August 2014) 12 at paras 38 and 46: 'The basic structure is intrinsic to, and arises from, the very nature of a constitution and not legislative or even judicial fiat. At its uncontentious minimum, a constitution sets out how political power is organised and divided between the organs of State in a particular society. In other words, the constitution is a power-defining and, therefore, power-limiting tool . . . the basic structure is a limited doctrine. It is arguable that fundamental rights are not a necessary part of the basic structure of a constitution. This is because fundamental rights relate to rights and liberties of citizens and do not define the limits to the powers of and checks on each organ of the State. What is not fundamental to a constitution cannot form part of its basic structure.' The court has stopped short of saying that it will use the 'basic structure' to invalidate *constitutional* amendments.

111 See *Jeyaretnam Kenneth Andrew* v. *Attorney-General* [2014] 1 SLR 345 at [56]. See also the chapters on Hong Kong, Australia and Canada on the development of stronger substantive review elsewhere in the common law world. But see S Jhaveri, 'Testing the Taxonomy of Grounds of Review: Revising the Legality: Merits Divide' [2019] *Sing J of Leg Studies*, forthcoming for an interrogation of the continuing utility of this divide.

112 See e.g. *Manjit Singh s/o Kirpal Singh* v. *Attorney-General* [2013] 4 SLR 483 at [7] and *Chee Siok Chin* v. *Minister for Home Affairs* [2006] 1 SLR(R) 582 at [125].

113 See e.g. *Chan Hiang Leng Colin* v. *Minister for Information and the Arts* [1996] 1 SLR (R) 294 at [38]–[47] and *Chng Suan Tze* v. *Minister for Home Affairs* [1988] 2 SLR 525 at [108]–[121]. This is largely on the basis that proportionality – in English law – is a European import and, therefore, of no application in Singapore.

114 [2014] 1 SLR 1047; see also Swati Jhaveri, 'The Doctrine of Substantive Legitimate Expectations: the Significance of *Chiu Teng @ Kallang Pte Ltd* v. *Singapore Land Authority*' [2016] Public Law 1; 'Contrasting Responses to the "Coughlan Moments": Legitimate Expectations in Hong Kong and Singapore' in Legitimate Expectations in the

significant. Prior to *Chiu Teng*, the courts were reluctant to recognise the doctrine, with little discussion on the reasons for this in the cases.[115] In *Chiu Teng*, the court recognised the application of the doctrine in Singapore and rejected the argument that this would offend the separation of powers:[116]

> The upholding of legitimate expectations is eminently within the powers of the judiciary . . . in deciding whether a legitimate expectation ought to be upheld, the court must remember that there are concerns and interests larger than the private expectation of an individual. . . . If there is a public interest which overrides the expectation, then the expectation ought not to be given effect to. In this way, I believe the judiciary can fulfil its constitutional role [to verify not only that the powers asserted accord with the substantive law created by Parliament but also that the manner in which they are exercised confirms with the standards of fairness which Parliament must have intended] without arrogating to itself the unconstitutional position of being a super-legislature or a super-executive.

Thus, in expounding the court's role in the area, the judge, while extending review into this new area, was also cautious to build in a sense of balance in the approach to be taken in upholding expectations. Even if an applicant can establish a 'legitimate' expectation (on the basis of a clear representation from a public body and reasonable reliance on that representation), the court will not enforce it if the public authority can show an overriding public interest to depart from it.[117]

The court's relatively muted role in balancing the expectation and the public interest also needs to be considered in the context of the remedies the court said it was prepared to utilise in enforcing a valid expectation in the absence of any overriding public interest. In appropriate cases the court would be prepared to issue a mandatory order to enforce the expectation.[118] In *Chiu Teng*, the Court felt unrestrained by the previous case law, which it felt had not considered 'head on' the issue of recognising the doctrine of substantive legitimate expectations as part of Singaporean administrative law.[119] It looked further afield than English law to also consider the law in Australia, Canada and Hong Kong in devising a doctrine to apply in Singapore. While the Court was influenced by the refusal of Australia and Canada to recognise the doctrine of *substantive* legitimate expectations, those jurisdictions did not have any impact on the way the Court eventually developed that doctrine.[120]

Common Law World (Matthew Groves and Greg Weeks eds., Hart, 2017) ch 12; Charles Tay, 'Substantive Legitimate Expectations: The Singapore Reception' (2014) 26 *SAcLJ* 609; and Zhida Chen, 'Substantive Legitimate Expectations in Singapore Administrative Law' (2014) 26 *SAcLJ* 237. The Singapore Court of Appeal has yet to definitively affirm or reject the doctrine. They stopped short of doing so in the recent case of *SGB Starkstrom Pte Ltd* v. *Commissioner for Labour* [2016] 3 SLR 598 (SGB Starkstrom). This was on the basis that the issue did not arise in the case, although the Court of Appeal ended its judgment flagging issues that may cause the courts to pause and reflect on the recognition of the doctrine in Singapore (SGB Starkstrom at [42], [55]–[63], per Sundaresh Menon CJ).

115 Chan Sek Keong, 'Judicial Review – From Angst to Empathy' (2010) 22 *SAcLJ* 469 at 478.

116 *Chiu Teng @ Kallang Pte Ltd* v. *Singapore Land Authority* [2014] 1 SLR 1047 at [113].

117 *Chiu Teng @ Kallang Pte Ltd* v. *Singapore Land Authority* [2014] 1 SLR 1047 at [119].

118 Ignoring changes elsewhere which only 'enforce' expectations as a relevant consideration: *R (Bibi)* v. *Newham London Borough Council (No 1)* [2002] 1 WLR 237 and *Ng Siu Tung* v. *Director of Immigration* (2002) 5 HKCFAR 1.

119 See e.g. *Re Siah Mooi Guat* [1988] 2 SLR(R) 165, *Borissik Svetlana* v. *Urban Redevelopment Authority* [2009] 4 SLR(R) 92 and *UDL Marine (Singapore) Pte Ltd* v. *Jurong Town Corp* [2011] 3 SLR 94; cf. *Abdul Nasir bin Amer Hamsah* v. *Public Prosecutor* [1997] 2 SLR(R) 842.

120 *SGB Starkstrom Pte Ltd* v. *Commissioner for Labour* [2016] 3 SLR 598 at [55]–[63].

12.4 CONCLUSIONS: WHY AUTOCHTHONISE?

The courts have started to break the connection with English law in advancing the reach of administrative law. Malaysian judgments (that largely tracked English case law) from the federation period also have less relevance. The discussion in Section 12.3 looked at various departures in different areas of administrative law. The role of lawyers in broadening the comparative and local base of pleadings is significant. However, it is also clear from the courts' approach that they are leaning on their own previous jurisprudence to inform and justify the expansion of their role. The reasons for this switch are not clear. Judgments reference the usual arguments relating to the limited relevance of foreign jurisprudence – developed in different socio-political contexts – to Singapore's unique context.[121] A further possible reason may be the court's articulation of the co-equality of the different branches: judicial and political branches. This articulation of a clearer and stronger (not necessarily strong) role for the courts would be more solidly initiated and consolidated if done using local jurisprudence, where the relevance cannot be disputed. There are a number of key cases currently on the courts' docket (on ouster clauses, the use of proportionality and standing in 'public interest' cases) that will be further testing ground for (i) how much further the courts are willing to advance the reach of judicial review and (ii) the local reference points for these extensions.

121 See Chan Sek Keong, 'Judicial Review – From Angst to Empathy' (2010) 22 *SAcLJ* 469 at 470–480.

13

Indigenous Interactions

Administrative Law and Syariah Law in Malaysia

Dian A. H. Shah and Kevin Y. L. Tan

13.1 INTRODUCTION

This chapter analyses the ways in which the common law has been applied in judicial review cases involving Syariah matters in Malaysia. Given the complex relationship between the civil courts and the Syariah courts, we will consider how key administrative law principles such as natural justice, reasonableness, and proportionality are applied in cases involving the administration of Syariah law. We begin with an overview of the constitutional and administrative law framework in Malaysia, focusing on the position of Islam as the religion of the Federation and the historical and contemporary significance of Syariah law. We will then briefly examine the series of reforms introduced in the 1980s and 1990s, as part of the state's quest to 'modernise' Islamic law and administration. Next, we examine several important cases to demonstrate the patterns of judicial review of cases implicating Islam and to tease out the impact of Syariah courts and institutions on the 'indigenising' of administrative law. We will show that while judges continued to refer to English precedents on administrative law, the application of these principles in cases involving Syariah has been affected and modified by particular exigencies surrounding the role of Islam in the political and legal order. Finally, we consider the broader consequences of the current and emerging trends in the deviation of Malaysian administrative law jurisprudence from its English roots. In particular, we posit that the reluctance of the civil courts to supervise the decisions of religious courts and bodies has rendered these institutions largely unaccountable. This reluctance has also had the effect of whittling away the protection of fundamental rights for Muslims and non-Muslims alike.

13.2 SYARIAH LAW AND COURTS: A HISTORICAL BACKGROUND

Anyone picking up a textbook on administrative law in Malaysia will immediately see how closely Malaysian administrative law principles mirror those of England.[1] This should come as no surprise since the British occupied the states comprising the Federation of Malaysia for over a century.[2] English law was introduced into two of the Federation's thirteen states – Penang and

1 See, for example, Damien HJ Cremean (ed.), *MP Jain's Administrative Law of Malaysia and Singapore*, 4th ed. (Petaling Jaya: LexisNexis, 2011); and Wan Azlan Ahmad and Nik Ahmad Kamal Nik Mahmod, *Administrative Law in Malaysia* (Petaling Jaya: Sweet and Maxwell, 2006).

2 On the reception of English law in Malaysia, see Wu Min Aun, *The Malaysian Legal System*, 3rd ed. (Petaling Jaya: Pearson, 2005) at 17–27; Wan Arfah Hamzah, *A First Look at the Malaysian Legal System* (Shah Alam: Oxford Fajar, 2009) at 115–19; and Tun Abdul Hamid Mohamad and Adnan Trakic, 'The Reception of English

Malacca – in 1826 through the Second Charter of Justice.[3] English law was then introduced to the Federated Malay States[4] in 1937 by section 2(1) of the Civil Law Enactment, and this was extended to the Unfederated Malay States[5] in 1951 by Civil Law (Extension) Ordinance.[6] In the Borneo states of Sarawak and Sabah, English law was received in 1928 and 1938, respectively.[7] It thus comes as no surprise that the local courts have, since their earliest days, issued prerogative writs in much the same way as the English courts did[8] and accordingly adopted English principles of administrative law generally.[9]

Prior to the formal introduction of English law into the Malay states, the prevailing law or *lex loci* was a mix of Malay *adat* (customary) law modified by principles of Islamic Law, or the Syariah.[10] Notwithstanding the introduction of English law in the Straits Settlements[11] and in the Malay states, its application did not affect the application of Syariah law in personal matters. In the Straits Settlements, the application of English law was subject to modifications 'so far as the several Religions, Manners and Customs of the inhabitants of the said Settlement and Places will admit',[12] and in the Malay States, Islamic law was regulated by ordinary legislation by the various state legislatures.[13] At the same time, the traditional state Syariah courts, which were under the direct jurisdiction of their respective Sultans, was reduced to an inferior civil court, with appeals to the magistrates courts.[14] By 1918, the British had determined that the Syariah courts would be constituted separately as part of customary tribunals like the Court of the Kathi and of a Penghulu, which had 'such powers in all matters concerning Muhammadan religion, marriage, and divorce, and all matters regulated by Muhammadan Law, as may be defined in its *kuasa*'.[15]

In 1948, with the creation of the Federation of Malaya, a new Courts Ordinance was enacted. Syariah courts were removed from the federal court structure and would henceforth be regulated by state legislation. The only provision in the Court Ordinance in which Islamic Religious Courts were mentioned was section 18(5) which provides for the execution by the Sessions Court of judgments or orders from any 'Islamic Religious Court having jurisdiction in the State in which the Sessions Court is situate'. This division of jurisdiction between civil courts and Syariah courts was maintained when the Federation of Malaya became independent from Britain in 1957, and then when it became the Federation of Malaysia in 1963. Article 121 of the Federal Constitution 1963 vested the 'judicial power of the Federation' in the three

Law in Malaysia and the Development of the Malaysian Common Law' (2015) 44(2) *Common Law World Review* 123–44, at 124–36.

3 Letters Patent Establishing the Court of Judicature of the Prince of Wales' Island, Malacca and Singapore, 27 November 1826 (Malacca: Mission Press, 1827).

4 The Federated Malay States were Perak, Pahang, Selangor, and Negri Sembilan.

5 The Unfederated Malay States were Kelantan, Terengganu, Kedah, Perlis, and Johor.

6 Ordinance 49 of 1951.

7 See Laws of Sarawak Ordinance 1928; and Civil Law Ordinance 1938.

8 See, for example, *Lim Beh and Ors* v. *Opium Farmer* [1808–1894] 3 Kyshe 10; *Kamoo* v. *Thomas Turner Bassett* [1808–1894] 1 Kyshe 1.

9 See *Halsbury's Laws of Malaysia: Administrative Law*, Vol 3(1) (2015 Reissue) (Petaling Jaya: LexisNexis, 2015) at 3–24.

10 Wan Arfah Hamzah (n 2) at 124.

11 The Straits Settlements comprised the states of Penang, Malacca, and Singapore and lasted between 1824 and 1946.

12 Second Charter of Justice, 1826.

13 Ahmad Ibrahim, *Islamic Law in Malaysia* (Singapore: Malaysian Sociological Research Institute, 1965) at 35–6. See also the chapter on Hong Kong on the adaptation of English law to suit local colonial circumstances.

14 See, for example, the Federated Malay States Enactment No 15 of 1905.

15 See Federated Malay States Enactment No 14 of 1918, section 65. The word *kuasa* means 'authority' or 'jurisdiction' in Malay.

High Courts of coordinate jurisdiction and status – the High Court in Malaya, the High Court in Borneo, and the High Court in Singapore. The Constitution further provided that matters of religion would be determined by the individual states. Among other things, List II of the Constitution's Ninth Schedule lists Islamic personal and family laws as matters strictly within the sovereign jurisdiction of the constituent states of the Federation. State legislatures are also entitled to create and punish offences against precepts of Islam.

While religion is a State matter, the Federal Constitution proclaims Islam to be the 'religion of the Federation'. However, there are specific constitutional limitations on the power of the states: laws punishing offences against the precepts of Islam apply only to Muslims, and state assemblies cannot legislate on offences that are technically against the precepts of Islam but that are already covered by federal jurisdiction (for example, murder, theft, robbery, rape, and incest). In addition, the punitive powers of state Syariah courts in matters within their criminal jurisdiction (for instance, consumption of alcohol or failure to observe fasting during Ramadhan) are limited by federal law. It is against this complex background that the 1988 amendment to the Federal Constitution has to be understood.

13.3 THE 1988 CONSTITUTIONAL AMENDMENT

In 1988, Malaysia's Parliament amended the Federal Constitution to separate the Syariah and civil jurisdictions, stripping the latter of jurisdiction in matters exclusively within the jurisdiction of the Syariah courts. This was done by amending Article 121 of the Federal Constitution by establishing two High Courts of co-ordinate jurisdiction – the High Court in Malaya and the High Court in Sabah and Sarawak – and providing that these courts 'shall have no jurisdiction in respect of any matter within the jurisdiction of the Syariah courts.'[16] The words 'judicial power' in the old Article 121 were also omitted. The initial motivations for the 1988 amendment were twofold. First, it was thought that questions involving Syariah law (in the limited areas where the law applies, as provided for in the Constitution) require the expertise of those trained in Islamic jurisprudence. Second, there were concerns at the time that the federal civil and state Syariah courts were issuing conflicting decisions. By segregating the Syariah courts from the civil courts and according them with a degree of autonomy, it was thought that these problems of legal conflict and uncertainty would be resolved.

However, the operation of Syariah laws within Malaysia's constitutional and administrative law framework has proven complicated and problematic, especially where key 'secular' issues are at stake, such as the fundamental liberties of Muslims and non-Muslims alike. Some examples include the arrest of a Muslim individual by the religious authorities for acting in contempt of a *fatwa*,[17] a ministerial decision prohibiting the Catholic Church from using the word 'Allah',[18] cases of conversions into and out of Islam,[19] and custody battles involving

[16] Article 121(1A), Federal Constitution.

[17] Fatwa is an authoritative legal opinion or learned interpretation issued by Islamic scholars.

[18] *Titular Roman Catholic Archbishop of Kuala Lumpur* v. *Menteri Dalam Negeri and Co* [2014] 4 *Malayan Law Journal* 765 (Federal Court). See also Dian Shah, 'The "Allah" Case: Implications for Religious Practice and Expression in Malaysia' (2015) 4 *Oxford Journal of Law and Religion* 141–6; and Jaclyn L Neo, 'What's in the Name? Malaysia's "Allah" Controversy and the Judicial Intertwining of Islam with Ethnic Identity' (2014) 12(3) *I•CON* 751–68.

[19] *Lina Joy* v. *Majlis Agama Islam Wilayah and Anor* [2007] 4 *Malayan Law Journal* 585 (Federal Court).

divorced Muslim and non-Muslim spouses.[20] Although these cases implicate crucial fundamental rights issues, they also raise questions about how common law principles are applied, especially with regard to how decisions are made by both secular and religious authorities. Take for example the case of a Muslim apostate. How do the civil courts treat questions of reasonableness in such cases? To put the question more broadly, how do civil courts exercise their judicial review powers in cases involving Syariah or Islamic matters? How useful are common law principles of administrative law in such cases?

13.4 ISLAM AND CIVIL LAW: THE 1980S REFORMS AND 'REVITALISATION'

13.4.1 *The Position of Islam and Syariah Law in Malaysia*

The role of Islam – and by extension, the role of Syariah institutions – in the Malaysian constitutional order has long been a centre of controversy. As mentioned above, Article 3(1) of the Federal Constitution recognises Islam – the religion of the majority – as the 'religion of the Federation', while at the same time acknowledging that 'other religions may be practised in peace and harmony in any part of the Federation'. In some respects, the role of Islam in Malaysian politics and governance is not new: Islam shaped Malay political thinking before colonial rule, especially through the institution of the sultanate as far back as the 1400s.[21] And in the nineteenth and early twentieth centuries, the Malay States recognised the special position of Islam by constitutionally requiring the sultan to be a Muslim and stipulating that he is the head of Islam in his state.[22] Even as British colonial rule began with the Pangkor Treaty in 1874, it was agreed that the British Resident would advise the sultan on all matters except those involving local customs (adat) and Islam. At the societal level, the practice of an acculturated version of Islam infused with adat (much of which had pre-Islamic influences) was prominent, and, likewise, governing laws reflected the intricate mix of Islamic laws and adat.[23] Thus, although English-derived law (including administrative law) dominated the Malaysian legal system for more than a century, the British colonial government nevertheless had to accommodate local customs and practices, which came – among others – in the form of adat and Muslim law. The British also co-opted the (informal) Muslim legal system within its system of governance. Kadis' courts (whose jurisdictions span Muslim personal law and Muslim morality crimes), for instance, were made part of the judicial hierarchy, although there was a system of appeals from these courts to the secular courts.

The constitutionalisation of Islam at independence, however, was not intended to entrench the supremacy of Islamic law over secular law. In fact, during the constitution-making process, the Malayan elites explicitly rejected the idea that Article 3 would create

20 *Indira Gandhi a/p Mutho* v. *Pengarah Jabatan Agama Islam Perak and Ors and Other Appeals* [2018] 3 *Malayan Law Journal* 545 (Federal Court).

21 AC Milner, 'Islam and Malay Kingship' (1981) 1 *Journal of the Royal Asiatic Society of Great Britain and Ireland* 46, 50–2.

22 Ahmad Ibrahim, 'The Position of Islam in the Constitution of Malaysia', in *The Constitution of Malaysia: Its Development: 1957–1977* (Tun Mohamed Suffian, HP Lee, and FA Trindade, eds, 1978), at 41–7. See also Andrew Harding, *Law, Government, and the Constitution in Malaysia* (Singapore: *Kluwer Law International*, 1996), at 13.

23 See generally MB Hooker, *Islamic Law in Southeast Asia* (Oxford: Oxford University Press, 1984); and Vincent JH Houben, 'Southeast Asia and Islam' (2003) 588 *Annals of the American Academy of Political and Social Science* 149. See also, Donald L Horowitz, 'The Qur'an and the Common Law: Islamic Law Reform and the Theory of Legal Change' (1994) 42(2) *American Journal of Comparative Law* 233, 254–5.

a theocratic state.[24] It was thought that the arrangement would model the British system with the establishment of the Church of England, but where full rights would nevertheless be secured for the minorities. In addition, the constitutional recognition of Islam came with an important qualification – the provision shall not 'derogate ... from other provisions in the Constitution'.[25] The constitution-making Reid Commission also emphasized the point that institutions set up to advise the Yang Di-Pertuan Agong (the king) or sultans on Islamic religious matters 'will not be entitled to interfere in any way with the affairs of people of other religious groups'.[26]

13.4.2 *The 1980s Islamic Reforms: The Resurgence of Syariah Courts and Islamic Law*

For more than two decades after independence, Malaysia's religious courts operated on the periphery of the justice system. Syariah courts were considered inferior administrative tribunals and the ordinary courts 'had the power to review, and quite regularly reviewed, the decisions of Syariah courts by certiorari'.[27] Society was, at this time, fairly secular in its orientation. However, things began to change in the early 1980s when the ruling Barisan Nasional coalition undertook a spate of 'reforms' in Islamic matters, largely in response to forces of Islamic revivalism and the serious political challenge posed by the rival Islamic political party, Parti Islam se-Malaysia (PAS). Although there was 'little sympathy' or enthusiasm for the implementation of a full panoply of Islamic laws (including Islamic criminal law punishments such as the hudud),[28] the government found it impossible to ignore these forces and their attendant demands.[29]

Among the myriad demands was the call for the government to 'upgrade' Islamic institutions. As a result, Kadis' courts – which were originally informally functioning institutions that administered personal laws and Muslim morality crimes since the British colonial period[30] – were restructured and upgraded in the 1980s. They were formally established at three levels – the Syariah Lower Court (*Mahkamah Rendah Syariah*), Syariah High Court (*Mahkamah Tinggi Syariah*), and Syariah Appeal Court (*Mahkamah Rayuan Syariah*). This 'modernization' effort also saw Kadis trained in both Islamic and civil rules of procedure and evidence.[31] Beyond that, the courthouses were also 'upgraded' and updated (i.e., formalised and corporatised), and staff appearance became more westernised, in the sense that they shifted from traditional Malay outfits to western-style suits.[32] In addition to all this, the

[24] See Joseph M Fernando, 'The Position of Islam in the Constitution of Malaysia' (2006) 37(2) *Journal of Southeast Asian Studies* 249–66, especially at 250–1.

[25] Federal Constitution of Malaysia, art 3(4).

[26] Constitutional Proposals for the Federation of Malaya, Cmnd 210 (Her Majesty's Stationery Office, 1957), para. 59.

[27] Per Gopal Sri Ram JCA in *Sukma Darmawan Sasmitaat Madja* v. *Ketua Pengarah Penjara Malaysia and Anor* [1999] 1 *Malayan Law Journal* 266 (Court of Appeal).

[28] See Horowitz (n 23) at 243; Khaled Abou El Fadl, 'The Islamic Legal Tradition' in Mauro Bussani and Ugo Mattei (eds.), *The Cambridge Companion to Comparative Law* (Cambridge: Cambridge University Press 2012), 295–312.

[29] Jason P Abbott and Sophie Gregorios-Pippas, 'Islamization in Malaysia: Processes and Dynamics' (2010) 16(2) *Contemporary Politics* 135–51.

[30] Abbott and Sophie Gregorios Pippas (n 29). See also Michael G Peletz, 'A Tale of Two Courts: Judicial Transformation and the Rise of A Corporate Islamic Governmentality in Malaysia' (2015) 42(1) *American Ethnologist* 144.

[31] Horowitz (n 23) at 237.

[32] See generally Peletz (n 30).

government, obsessed with centralising and controlling the discourse on Islam, expanded its religious bureaucracy – the Jabatan Kemajuan Islam Malaysia (JAKIM) or Islamic Development Department) – which was tasked to coordinate the development of Syariah. The expansion of Islamic laws then followed, including laws governing Islamic criminal offenses (now codified almost uniformly across all states), as well as Islamic family law.[33]

Crucial institutional and constitutional changes were made as the Malaysian state realised that its reforms would be useless without a clear system to enforce the boundaries between the two systems – common law and Syariah – of law. Government officials (such as those in the Religious Affairs Division) and lawmakers, who were bent on 'enhancing' the status of Syariah courts (and, as a corollary, Syariah judges) and clarifying the jurisdictional boundaries of the religious courts, engineered a constitutional amendment in the form of Article 121(1A), as noted previously. It is this institutional reform that precipitated the clashes discussed in the following section.

13.4.3 *Reforming Islamic Law: Interactions with Common Law*

The Islamic resurgence in the 1980s spurred the ruling Barisan Nasional party's effort to demonstrate its commitment to a programme of reinvigorating Islamic laws and institutions.[34] This task fell on the shoulders of experts (i.e., academics and lawyers) trained in and familiar with both Islamic law and English law, who – cognizant of the country's secular system and traditions – 'borrowed widely from English and foreign Islamic sources'.[35] Part of this programme involved Islamic law reform, which entailed efforts to ensure uniformity and standardisation of Islamic laws nationwide. During the colonial period, the different Malay states applied and enforced their own versions of Islamic law. But it is also worth noting that Islamic law did not operate in isolation; there were instances where English law displaced Islamic law even in the realms of personal law.[36] For this reason, it was perhaps unsurprising that the Islamic law statutes in a variety of areas (particularly procedural ones, such as evidence) that emerged after the reforms contained secular influences.[37] For example, Islamic rules on expert testimony, burden of proof, and relevancy were almost similar to the 'secular' Evidence Act 1950.[38] Likewise, with regard to family law matters such as divorce, the Administration of Islamic Family Law enactments lay out grounds for divorce that are largely similar to the grounds enumerated in the Law Reform (Marriage and Divorce) Act 1976, which applies to non-Muslims. This Act, in turn, drew heavily on the English Matrimonial Causes Act 1973.

As Horowitz's seminal study notes, the borrowing, transplantation, and adaptation of common law rules intermingled with Syariah reforms.[39] Indeed, the Syariah Technical Committee, whose task was to deliberate and prepare draft statutes to be adopted by states nationwide, comprised scholars and lawyers trained both in Islamic law and common law. Given the legal background of the Committee members, English law thus became one of the

33 Maznah Mohamad, 'Making Majority, Undoing Family: Law, Religion and the Islamization of the State in Malaysia' (2010) 39(3) *Economy and Society* 360, 366.

34 Horowitz (n 23) at 243.

35 Horowitz (n 23) at 243–4.

36 Horowitz cites a case in Penang where it was decided that a Muslim could dispose of all his property by will, despite the dominant view that such testamentary dispositions are contrary to Islamic norms and precepts. See Horowitz (n 23) at 256.

37 Horowitz (n 23) at 270.

38 Horowitz (n 23) at 272.

39 Horowitz (n 23).

models for Syariah legal reform, even if there was also evidence of borrowing and adaptation from other jurisdictions (notably India and Pakistan).

13.5 JURISDICTIONAL CLASHES AND AN INDIGENISING JUDICIAL REVIEW CULTURE

With the 1980s reforms and the amendment to the Constitution under which Article 121(1A) was introduced, the scene was set for over two decades of jurisdictional clashes between the civil and Syariah courts. This directly impacted the way in which administrative law principles were applied in matters involving Islamic law and institutions. As we will explore in this section, the prevailing political and institutional climate caused the civil courts to adopt an approach to administrative review that conceded considerable ground to the Syariah courts.

Before evaluating how the civil courts judicially reviewed cases involving Syariah law and authorities, we must first tackle the question: What is the consequence of Article 121(1A)? Only then can we determine other fundamental questions, such as the ability (and willingness) of civil courts to review decisions of religious authorities, as well as religious edicts (fatawa), along with the courts' competence to review matters where Islam is implicated, even if such matters overlap with 'secular' questions of fundamental rights.

The problem begins with the unfortunate drafting of Article 121(1A) itself. It simply stipulates that the High Court 'shall have no jurisdiction in respect of any matter within the jurisdiction of the Syariah courts'. Since the Constitution does not define the Syariah court's jurisdiction (except for providing a specific list of 'Islamic' matters that state assemblies are authorised to legislate), we need to look at individual state enactments to ascertain the jurisdictional limits of each Syariah court. And since the Syariah courts are referred to in the plural, this requires the High Court to look at all the Syariah courts in Malaysia's thirteen states to determine the extent of the jurisdictional terrain it may not trespass. There is one further problem: to what extent can state legislatures enact laws on Islamic matters, including matters on the jurisdiction of state Syariah courts? One view is that there is nothing to stop each state legislature from expanding the jurisdictional scope of its Syariah Court. This follows the position that if a legislation 'in pith and substance' deals with religion (i.e., an Islamic matter), then it is a law that only the state legislatures are empowered to enact.[40] Another view, however, sees the legislative powers of the states on Islamic matters as being limited by the Federal Constitution's Ninth Schedule, List II, paragraph I.[41] Furthermore, the Syariah Courts (Criminal Jurisdiction) Act 1965 imposes limits on the punitive powers of state-level Syariah courts – they are only allowed to impose a maximum of three years imprisonment, fine not exceeding 5000 Malaysian Ringgits, and/or six strokes of the cane. And if the court's jurisdiction is solely subject to the state legislature, it could hardly be a co-equal branch of government.

Taking this argument – that the court's jurisdiction may be determined solely by state law – to its logical conclusion, it would mean that the state legislature can, with impunity, enact law to oust the court's judicial review jurisdiction altogether. This has not yet happened, and the

40 This is the 'pith and substance test' adopted in *Mamat bin Daud* v. *Government of Malaysia* [1988] 1 *Malayan Law Journal* 119, 120 (Supreme Court).

41 See, for example, Shad Saleem Faruqi, 'Jurisdiction of State Authorities to Punish Offences against the Precepts of Islam: A Constitutional Perspective', *The Malaysian Bar* (28 September 2005), www.malaysianbar.org.my/constitutional_law/jurisdiction_of_state_authorities_to_punish_offences_against_the_precepts_of_islam_a_constitutional_perspective.html.

Malaysian High Court continues to exercise its supervisory jurisdiction over all inferior tribunals and administrative bodies in much the same way the High Court in England does. The main difference is where the Malaysian High Court has to deal with the knotty problem of competing jurisdictional claims in respect of matters within the purview of the Syariah Courts.

The intent of Article 121(1A) was to ensure that Syariah court decisions on matters exclusively within their own jurisdiction are conclusive and to protect such courts from undue interference from the civil branch.[42] The amendment does not oust the civil court's supervisory powers over the Syariah courts,[43] nor does it elevate the Syariah courts to a status that is on par with that of the civil courts. This is because they are creatures of state legislation with limited jurisdiction as defined in the Federal Constitution's Ninth Schedule, List II, paragraph I. Thus the general law in Malaysia remains secular even if a separate Syariah jurisdiction is carved out to address, among others, personal and family matters for 'persons professing the religion of Islam'.[44] State legislatures are also entitled to create and punish 'offences against precepts of Islam'. However, there are specific constitutional limitations on this power: laws punishing offences against the precepts of Islam are only applicable to Muslims, and in theory, state legislatures cannot legislate on matters that are exclusively within the federal jurisdiction.[45] In other words, crimes that are considered to be 'against the precepts of Islam' but are nonetheless are under the federal list of legislative power, such as murder, theft, robbery, rape, and incest, are beyond state legislative power and thus beyond the purview of the Syariah courts.

Although the rationale behind the separation of the civil and Syariah jurisdictions may seem clear, competing interpretations on what Article 121(1A) entails and increasingly expansive interpretations of the role of Islam in Malaysia's constitutional order have led to what Thio characterises as a 'jurisdictional imbroglio'[46] – a legal muddling of the relationship between Islam as the state religion, the 'civil' issue of religious freedom, and the Syariah jurisdictional autonomy. The view that state legislatures have no authority to enact just any laws concerning Islam (i.e., that their legislative power is limited to matters specified in List II of the Ninth Schedule) is – in practice – increasingly unpopular, if not ignored.[47] It also used to be the case that the jurisdiction of Syariah courts to adjudicate a matter falling within List II must be explicitly conferred by a statute.[48] However, the courts have also shown an inclination towards a different approach – one that grants jurisdiction to the Syariah courts by implication, even where no statute explicitly affords the Syariah courts such jurisdiction.[49]

42 Li-ann Thio, 'Jurisdictional Imbroglio: Civil and Religious Courts, Turf Wars and Article 121(1A) of the Federal Constitution' in Andrew Harding and HP Lee (eds.), *Constitutional Landmarks in Malaysia: The First 50 Years 1957–2007* (LexisNexis 2007), 202–3.

43 Shanmuga Kanesalingam, 'Article 121(1A) – What Does It Really Mean?', *The Malaysian Bar* (11 December 2006), www.malaysianbar.org.my/members_opinions_and_comments/article_1211a_what_does_it_really_mean_.html.

44 See, for example, *Zaina Abidin bin Hamid @ S Maniam and Others* v. *Kerajaan Malaysia and Others* [2009] 6 *Malayan Law Journal* 863.

45 Federal Constitution of Malaysia, Arts. 74 and 75.

46 Thio (n 42).

47 Shad Saleem Faruqi, *Document of Destiny: The Constitution of the Federation of Malaysia* (Petaling Jaya: Star Publications, 2008) 134.

48 *Dalip Kaur* v. *Pegawai Polis Daerah, Balai Polis Daerah, Bukit Mertajam and Another* [1992] 1 *Malayan Law Journal* 1 (Supreme Court); and *Majlis Agama Islam dan Adat Melayu Perak Darul Ridzuan* v. *Mohamed Suffian bin Ahmad Syazali and Anor* [2014] 3 *Malayan Law Journal* 74 (Court of Appeal).

49 *Md Hakim Lee* v. *Majlis Agama Islam Wilayah Persekutuan, Kuala Lumpur* [1998] 1 *Malayan Law Journal* 681 (High Court); *Soon Singh* v. *Pertubuhan Kebajikan Islam Malaysia (PERKIM) Kedah* [1999] 1 *Malayan Law Journal* 489 (Federal Court); and *Lina Joy* (n 19).

In the following sections, we look at how this jurisdictional confusion and clash manifested in different contestations between the civil courts and Syariah institutions.

13.5.1 *Religious Conversions*

13.5.1.1 The *Lina Joy* Litigation

One obvious area where jurisdictional battles and uncertainties have shaped the reviewability of decisions implicating Islam or Syariah is religious conversion. The case of *Lina Joy* v. *Majlis Agama Islam Wilayah Persekutuan*[50] (*Lina Joy*) best demonstrates the impact of Article 121(1A) and Syariah on mainstream constitutional and administrative law in Malaysia. In 1997, Lina Joy – a Muslim-born woman who had converted into Christianity – applied to the National Registry Department (NRD) to change her name and, subsequently, to remove the word 'Islam' from her national identity card. The NRD refused her application on the ground that she failed to follow procedures spelled out in the National Registration Regulations 1990 ('1990 Regulations'), namely, to supply the NRD with documentary evidence to support her application. Under Regulation 4(c)(x), an applicant is required to provide '[a]ny further documentary evidence as the registration officer may consider necessary to support the accuracy of any particulars submitted'. According to the presiding NRD officer, there was no authoritative documentary evidence stating that Joy had officially renounced Islam before converting to Christianity.[51]

To be sure, the NRD is not a religious authority and this was not a case about the reviewability of decisions by Syariah authorities. However, it is instructive in illustrating how civil or 'secular' authorities exercise their discretion in matters involving Islam. In the course of making its decision, the NRD deemed that the only satisfactory evidence of a renunciation of Islam was a certificate of apostasy from a state-level Syariah court or Religious Department.[52] This was despite the fact that the Administration of Islamic Law (Federal Territories) Act (1993) did not spell out any procedure for Muslim apostasy – that is, the relevant legislation did not confer explicit authority on Syariah courts to deal with questions or applications on apostasy.

At the High Court, a number of arguments were raised, including the appellant's right to the freedom of religion. In a long, incoherent judgment, Faiza Tamby Chik J held that Article 11(1) of the Federal Constitution – which guaranteed all persons the 'right to profess and practise his religion and . . . to propagate it' – had to be read subject to Article 3(1), which declares Islam to be the 'religion of the Federation'.[53] Article 11(1) was held to ensure religion freedom, 'but on the issue of conversion out of Islam, a Muslim is bound by the syariah law on the matter'.[54]

The Court went on to hold that the validity of a person's renunciation of Islam can only be determined by the Syariah Courts based on *hukum syarak*, or laws of Islam. Following Faiza Thamby Chik J's line of reasoning, a Muslim's freedom of religion rights are thus necessarily more restricted than that of persons of any other (or no) faith. A state Syariah court could, by

50 *Lina Joy* v. *Majlis Agama Islam Wilayah Persekutuan and Anor* [2004] 6 *Current Law Journal* 242 (High Court).

51 *Lina Joy* v. *Majlis Agama Islam Wilayah Persekutuan* [2005] 6 *Malayan Law Journal* 193, 202 (Court of Appeal).

52 *Lina Joy* (n 19) at 627. See also Mohamed Azam Mohamed Adil, 'Law of Apostasy and Freedom of Religion in Malaysia', (2007) 2(1) *Asian Journal of Comparative Law* 28.

53 *Lina Joy* (n 50) at 254, 257, 262.

54 *Lina Joy* (n 50) at 262.

refusing the grant of a Certificate of Renunciation, effectively snuff out a Muslim's religious freedom without any apparent recourse to a judicial remedy in the civil courts.

By the time the case reached the appellate courts, *Lina Joy*'s arguments focused on administrative (as opposed to purely constitutional) law questions. The question posed in the Court of Appeal was whether the Director-General of National Registration (DG) acted unreasonably in requiring Joy to produce a certificate or order from the Syariah Court. The legislative provision in contention was Regulation 14(2) of the 1990 Regulations, which required any person applying for a change of name to 'furnish the registration officer with a statutory declaration to the effect that he has absolutely renounced and abandoned the use of his former name'. Regulation 14(2) simply required a statutory declaration to effect the name change. However, the Court of Appeal (on a majority of 2–1)[55] relied on Regulation 4(c)(x) – which empowered the registration to request 'for any other documentary evidence' he 'may consider necessary to support the accuracy of any particulars submitted' – to uphold the DG's decision to require Joy to produce a certificate of apostasy. Abdul Aziz Mohammad JCA (with whom Arifin Zakaria JCA concurred) explained:

> [33] Renunciation of Islam is generally regarded by the Muslim community as a very grave matter. This is reflected in the very things reported in the newspapers that constituted one of the reasons that the appellant said it was necessary that her right to renounce Islam, and her position as no longer a Muslim, be recognised. The Muslim community regards it as a grave matter not only for the person concerned, in terms of the afterlife, but also for Muslims generally, as they regard it to be their responsibility to save another Muslim from the damnation of apostasy. The incidence of apostasy is therefore a highly sensitive matter among Muslims. Apart from the spiritual aspect, Muslims in this country, where Islam is the official religion, are subject to special laws that no other community is subject to. In particular there are statutory offences that are committable by Muslims as Muslims that are not committable by others.
>
> [34] Against that background must be mentioned the fact that whether a person has renounced Islam is a question of Islamic law that is not within the jurisdiction of the NRD and that the NRD is not equipped or qualified to decide. What the Islamic law on the matter is has not been ventilated in this appeal. One might be tempted to think that the fact that a person affirms in a statutory declaration that he is no longer a Muslim or the fact that he has been participating in a Christian form of worship, or the fact that he has been baptised is sufficient, according to Islamic law, this warrant others to treat him as having apostatized and as being no longer a Muslim. But is that so in Islamic law? The NRD would be right in taking the stand that it is not for it to decide. It may be according to Islamic law no Muslim may be treated as having apostatized, no matter what he may have done or failed to do, unless and until he has been declared an apostate by some proper authority. If the NRD were to accept that a person has apostatized merely on his declaration, and on that basis officially stamp him a non-Muslim by deleting the word 'Islam' from his identity cared, it runs the risk of mistakenly stamping a person a non-Muslim who according to Islamic law has not apostatized. It will also be making it easy for persons who are born and bred as Muslims simply to avoid being punished for committing the offences that I have mentioned. It will consequently be inviting the censure of the Muslim community. It is for these reasons that I believe that the NRD adopts the policy that a mere statutory declaration is insufficient for it to remove the word 'Islam' from the identity card of a Muslim.[56]

55 *Lina Joy* (n 51).

56 *Lina Joy* (n 51) at 208–9.

Gopal Sri Ram JCA dissented, holding that the regulation requiring documentary evidence is limited and qualified by Regulation 14(2):

> [58] All I have to do is look at the wording of reg 4(cc)(xiii) and see what it says. And it says that a request can be made 'for any other documentary evidence as the registration office may consider necessary to support the accuracy of any particulars submitted'. There can be no quarrel, I think, that the words 'particulars submitted' refer to the particular contained in the application already submitted by the appellant to the NRD. In her statutory declaration dated 21 February 1997 stated, among other matters: (i) that she had never professed or practised Islam as her religion; (ii) that she had embraced Christianity in 1990; and (iii) that she intended to marry a Christian. Her later statutory declaration dated 15 March 1999 affirmed in support of her application dated 3 January 2000 adds little to what she had previously declared. The form she attempted to submit on 3 January 2000 makes it clear in column 31 that she no longer wished to be a Muslim. In these circumstances, an order from the Syariah Court does nothing to support the accuracy of the particular that the appellant is a Christian. However the baptismal certificate dated 11 May 1998 produced by the appellant in evidence amply supports the accuracy of the particular that the appellant is a Christian. This conclusion is amply supported by examining the way in which reg 14(2) is constructed.[57]

Then, citing with approval the English decision of *Associated Provincial Picture Houses Ltd* v. *Wednesbury Corp*,[58] and the Indian Supreme Court case of *Bharat Bank Ltd Delhi* v. *The Employees of the Bharat Bank Ltd Delhi*,[59] Gopal Sri Ram JCA continued:

> [64] The principle that is to be distilled from these cases is that where a public decision-maker takes extraneous matters into account, his or her decision is null and void and of no effect. So here, the Director-General's decision in refusing to effect the amendment to the appellant's NRIC without an order/certificate of the Syariah Court is null and void and of no effect.[60]

Joy's appeal to the Federal Court[61] was dismissed again, by a majority of 2–1, with Ahmad Fairuz CJ (with whom Alauddin FCJ concurred) citing primarily the same reasons as the majority in the Court of Appeal in the following section. Fairuz CJ added:

> [16] *Soon Singh's* case clearly indicates that apostasy is within Syariah Court's jurisdiction. In paragraph (10) I have also referred to item 1, list 2, Schedule 9 of the Constitution to show that the key words used therein are 'matters' and because 'Islamic Law' is one of the 'matters' and when read against the backdrop of *Dalip Kaur's* case, it is especially noteworthy that apostasy is a matter relating to Islamic law and thus within the jurisdiction of the Syariah Court, and civil courts cannot intervene on account of Article 121(1A) of the Constitution.[62]
>
> . . .
>
> [17.2] What is clear in Article 11 is the use of the words ' . . . right to profess and practice his religion . . . ' As Abdul Hamid Mohamad HMR (then) said in the case of *Kamariah bte Ali* v. *Kelantan State Government, Malaysia* [2002] 3 MLJ 657 at 665: 'the words "has the right" apply to "profess" and "practise"'. According to the case of *Che Omar bin Che Soh* v. *Public Prosecutor* [1988] 2 MLJ 55, Islam is not just a set of dogmas and rituals but a complete way of life encompassing all fields of human, private or public activity, legal, political, economic, social, cultural, moral or judicial. And if we look at items 11(1), 74(2) and item 1 in list 2 in

57 *Lina Joy* (n 51) at 218.
58 [1941] 1 KB 223.
59 AIR 1950 SC 188.
60 *Lina Joy* (n 51) at 220.
61 *Lina Joy* (n 19).
62 *Lina Joy* (n 19) at 616 (translated by the authors from the original Malay text).

> Schedule 9 of the Constitution it would be obvious that Islam includes Islamic laws. Thus, ... if a Muslim wants to break out of Islam, he actually exercises his right within the context of the syariah law which has its own jurisprudence on apostasy. If a person professes and practices Islam, it is imperative that he follows Islamic law which stipulates how one enters Islam and how one leaves it ... I do not see how that action can be said to be contrary to Article 11(1) which necessitates compliance with the requirements of Islam before he can leave the religion. Of course, the adherence to and practice of Islam means conforming not only the theological aspects of the religion but also to religious law.[63]

In his dissent, Richard Malanjum CJ took a more traditional approach to administrative law. He first held that Regulation s 4(c)(iva) and 4(c)(x) – which, taken together, required Muslim applicants to state their religion and to go through 'additional procedural burdens' – was unconstitutional in violation of the equal protection clause under Article 8(1) of the Constitution.[64] In tackling the administrative law grounds, he then spelled out several reasons why the NRD's actions were, in his judgment, unreasonable. The first concerns illegality. Malanjum CJ held, citing *CCSU* v. *Minister for Civil Service*,[65] that the NRD acted ultra vires since its regulations did not authorise nor require it to add further requirements to ensure that she had been 'properly apostatized'.[66] In other words, the NRD acted beyond its statutory powers by seeking to ensure that a person had 'properly renounced the Islamic faith in accordance with the requirements set by the Islamic authorities'.[67] In addition, the NRD had excluded from its consideration a legally relevant factor – that is, *Lina Joy*'s statutory declaration and other accompanying documents demonstrating that she had renounced Islam.[68] Citing with approval the English landmark decision in *Anisminic Ltd* v. *Foreign Compensation Tribunal*,[69] Malanjum CJ held the NRD had abused its power by failing 'to take into consideration a legally relevant factor, namely the statutory declaration and the documents submitted by the appellant, preferring its policy of requiring a certificate of apostacy from the Federal Territory Syariah Court'.[70] The second point concerns the NRD's failure to properly exercise its discretion. Malanjum CJ opined that the NRD failed to exercise its discretion by 'abdicating its discretionary power to an outside religious body'.[71] Although a decision-making body could consult an external body, it has to make the final decision: here the NRD had allowed itself to be dictated by the decision of the Syariah authorities. Third, Malanjum CJ held that the certificate of apostasy requirement was 'unreasonable' in the *Wednesbury* sense, as the relevant statute did not confer the Syariah court with the power to adjudicate apostasy matters.[72] For Malanjum, the Syariah court's jurisdiction could not be assumed and the insistence for the certificate amounted to the requirement to '[perform] an act that was almost impossible to perform'.[73] Moreover, Malanjum argued that it would be unreasonable to expect Lina Joy to apply for a certificate of apostasy because it would be tantamount to self-incrimination. Finally, in addition to the grounds of illegality and irrationality, Malanjum CJ observed that the

63 *Lina Joy* (n 19) at 617 (translated by the authors from the original Malay text).
64 *Lina Joy* (n 19) at 627.
65 [1985] AC 374 (House of Lords).
66 *Lina Joy* (n 19) at 628.
67 *Lina Joy* (n 19) at 629.
68 *Lina Joy* (n 19) at 630.
69 [1969] 2 AC 147 (House of Lords).
70 *Lina Joy* (n 19) at 630–1.
71 *Lina Joy* (n 19) at 632.
72 *Lina Joy* (n 19) at 632.
73 *Lina Joy* (n 19) at 632.

failure to give the appellant a fair hearing and give reasons for the NRD's decision, contravened the principles of natural justice.[74]

13.5.1.2 The *Indira Gandhi* Case

Quite clearly, the *Lina Joy* cases left unsettled the jurisdictional conflict between civil courts and the Syariah courts, and it was not till the case of *Indira Gandhi a/p Mutho* v. *Pengarah Jabatan Agama Islam Perak*[75] (*Indira Gandhi*) a decade later that the Federal Court authoritatively reviewed the decision-making powers of a religious body. It is worth noting for a start that as in the *Lina Joy* case, *Indira Gandhi* – along with cases like *Shamala*,[76] *Deepa*,[77] and *Subashini*[78] – illustrate the jurisdictional conundrum created by Article 121(1A). These cases, however, involve child conversions. The women in these cases were previously party to a civil (non-Muslim) marriage governed by the Law Reform (Marriage & Divorce) Act 1976. During the marriage, their husbands decided to convert to Islam and, without their knowledge, convert their children to Islam as well. In the state of Perak, where the Indira Gandhi case emerged, conversion is a relatively simple matter, involving the *muallaf* (convert) appearing before the Registrar of converts and swearing the Affirmation of Faith or *Kalimah Shahadah* before the Registrar. When the respective marriages end in divorce, custody battles ensued. In all cases, the Muslim husbands successfully applied for and obtained custody of the children in the Syariah courts – again, without the knowledge of their erstwhile wives, who could never challenge the custody before the Syariah courts since they were not Muslims and therefore lacked standing.

The applicants in *Subashini*, *Indira Gandhi*, and *Deepa* went to the civil courts to obtain a custody order. In all three cases, the High Court granted custody to the three women. The erstwhile husbands, as well as the civil and religious law enforcement bodies, were thus faced with conflicting decisions from the civil and Syariah courts. It should be stated at this point that the Malaysian civil courts have consistently held that in divorce and custody proceedings, it is the High Court and not the Syariah courts that have ultimate jurisdiction, especially since the non-Muslim spouse would have no standing to challenge any matter raised before a Syariah court.[79] However, what was contested in *Indira Gandhi* and similar cases is the capacity of non-Muslim parents to challenge the conversion of their children.

More specifically, this raises the specific questions of how and on what grounds a non-Muslim parent can challenge religious conversions that were effected without their approval and knowledge in civil courts. This issue is made especially problematic by the words of Article 12(3) and 12(4) of the Constitution. Under Article 12(3), no person is 'required to receive instruction in or to take part in any ceremony or act of worship of a religion other than his own'. For these purposes, Article 12(4) stipulates that 'the religion of a person under the age of eighteen years shall be decided by his parent or guardian'. The reference to 'parent or

74 *Lina Joy* (n 19) at 633.

75 *Indira Gandhi* (n 20).

76 *Shamala a/p Sathiyaseelan* v. *Dr Jeyaganesh a/l C Mogarajah* [2004] 2 *Malayan Law Journal* 241 (High Court); *Shamala a/p Sathiyaseelan* v. *Dr Jeyaganesh a/l C Mogarajah (also known as Muhammad Ridzwan bin Mogarajah)* [2011] 2 *Malayan Law Journal* 281 (Federal Court).

77 *Viran Nagapan* v. *Deepa Subramaniam and Other Appeals* [2016] 3 *Current Law Journal* 505 (Federal Court).

78 *Subashini a/p Rajasingam* v. *Saravanan a/l Thangathoray and Other Appeals* [2008] 2 *Malayan Law Journal* 147 (Federal Court).

79 *Subashini* (n 78).

guardian', being in the singular, has been interpreted by the Court to mean that unilateral conversions are permissible under Article 12.[80]

This clause came up for interpretation in *Indira Gandhi* when the decision of the Registrar of Muallafs was challenged.[81] On her part, the applicant had successfully obtained a High Court order giving her custody over her three children. In the High Court, Lee Swee Seng JC held that Article 12(4) had to be read to refer to both parents and not any of the child's parents. Accordingly, Article 8 (equality) was violated if either parent were to be allowed the power to unilaterally convert the religion of his or her child, without the consent of the other parent.[82] In deciding that the children's certificates of conversion (issued by the Registrar of Muallafs – a religious body in the state of Perak) were null and void, the court took the position that the children's conversion – secured without their mother's consent – violated Article 11 of the Constitution (freedom of religion clause). The court also held that the issuing of the certificates of conversion had breached principles of natural justice, as the mother was deprived of her right to be heard.

This decision was reversed by the Court of Appeal.[83] It is apparent that the majority did not seriously consider the constitutional rights questions at stake, nor did it earnestly evaluate the reviewability of the Registrar of Muallaf's decision. As a matter of fact, counsel for the applicant had argued that the Registrar's statutory decision-making powers were purely administrative and thus amenable to judicial review. Instead, the court characterised the issue narrowly as one of the court's jurisdiction to adjudicate on the matter under Article 121 (1A) of the Constitution.[84]

In this regard, the Court of Appeal was content to hold that the validity of a conversion for persons professing the religion of Islam was a question that fell exclusively under the jurisdiction of the Syariah court – the same avoidance tactic that the Federal Court employed in *Lina Joy*. The majority also opined that the argument that the Registrar's decision was subject to judicial review was 'simplistic' and that any challenge to the decision must be done before the Syariah court.[85] The Court of Appeal did not appear the least bit concerned that such a holding would deny non-Muslims access to justice when their rights or those of their children have been violated.

In a landmark decision in 2018, the Federal Court overturned the Court of Appeal's decision and declared the unilateral conversion of Indira's children unlawful. Two crucial aspects of the decision are noteworthy. The first is significant with regard to the 'jurisdictional imbroglio' created by Article 121(1A), which has long plagued Malaysian jurisprudence. The court held that Article 121(1A) did not oust the jurisdiction of the civil courts to review the decisions of Syariah courts on administrative law grounds, nor does it remove the power of the civil courts to interpret the constitution and legislation, 'even where the determination of Islamic law is required for such interpretation'.[86] The Federal Court spent considerable time explicating the nature of Malaysia's 'judicial power'[87] and pointedly held that it was part of

80 See *Subashini* (n 78) at 171–2.

81 *Indira Gandhi a/p Mutho* v. *Pengarah Jabatan Agama Islam Perak* [2013] 5 *Malayan Law Journal* 552 (High Court).

82 *Indira Gandhi* (n 81) at 578.

83 *Pathmanathan a/l Krishnan (also known as Muhammad Riduan bin Abdullah)* v. *Indira Gandhi a/p Mutho* [2016] 4 *Malayan Law Journal* 455 (Court of Appeal).

84 *Pathmanathan* (n 83) at 469.

85 *Pathmanathan* (n 83) at 473.

86 *Indira Gandhi* (n 20) at 584–6.

87 *Indira Gandhi* (n 20) at 561–76. See also *Semenyih Jaya Sdn Bhd* v. *Pentadbir Tanah Daerah Hulu Langat and Another Case* [2017] 3 *Malayan Law Journal* 561, at 567.

the Constitution's Basic Structure. As such, the civil court's jurisdiction is not ousted merely because the subject matter involves Syariah law, especially since the civil courts' judicial powers encompass powers of judicial review and constitutional and statutory interpretation.[88] Zainun Ali FJ, delivering the decision of the court, held that Article 121(1A) 'does not oust the jurisdiction of the civil courts nor does it confer judicial power on the Syariah Courts. More importantly, Parliament does not have the power to make any constitutional amendment to give such an effect; it would be invalid, if not downright repugnant, to the notion of judicial power inherent in the basic structure of the constitution.'[89] This was grounded in 'settled law' based 'on the principles in *Anisminic*'.[90]

The Registrar of Muallaf's power to issue conversion certificates is governed by the Perak Administration of the Religion of Islam Enactment 2004 (Perak Enactment) and civil courts possess inherent powers to review the decision of a public body – including a religious body like the Registrar of Muallaf – to ensure that its power was exercised in accordance with the statute. Citing *Anisminic*,[91] the court stated that the existence of a finality clause in the Perak Enactment did not preclude judicial review of the legality of the Registrar's issuance of the certificate.[92] In the present case, the certificates were deemed null and void, because the statutory requirement (namely, that the children had to be present before the Registrar and utter the affirmation of faith) was not complied with.[93] While the exact holding is narrow, the dicta of the Court makes two things clear: first, that conversion of minors requires the consent of both parents on the basis of equality as required by Article 12 of the Federal Constitution and, second, that it was now prepared to return to the application of basic common law principles of administrative law so long as the matters under contention do not involve the actual interpretation of the Syariah itself.

13.5.2 *The Administrative Fiat of the Fatwa*

The Federal Court's decision in *Indira Gandhi* provides some cause for optimism, after three decades of the civil courts, self-inflicted allergy to adjudicating on any matter that might even vaguely be in the realm of Syariah. What remains to be seen is how courts will approach applications for judicial review that seek to challenge fatawa – a non-binding opinion of the Islamic authorities on a matter affecting Islam. Many fatawa are issued each year on any number of issues, and as a whole, they are not entirely coherent nor consistent. Prior to the amendment to Article 121 of the Constitution, civil courts had little reservation adjudicating on matters implicating Islamic Law. For example, in the 1970 case of *Commissioner for Religious Affairs* v. *Tengku Mariam*, the Federal Court held that the existence of a fatwa upholding the validity of a *wakaf* (charitable trust) did not preclude the civil court from adjudicating on the validity of the *wakaf*,[94] and rejected the argument that the Mufti of Terengganu's fatwa was binding on the court. But after the 1988 amendments and inclusion of Article 121(1A), the pendulum swung to the other end of the spectrum, such that the civil courts were not only unprepared to review challenges to fatawa but began treating them as having the force of law.

88 *Indira Gandhi* (n 20) at 587.
89 *Indira Gandhi* (n 20) at 584.
90 *Indira Gandhi* (n 20) at 595.
91 [1968] 2 AC 147.
92 [1968] 2 AC 147 at 594–6.
93 [1968] 2 AC 147 at 596–7.
94 *Commissioner for Religious Affairs* v. *Tengku Mariam* [1970] *Malayan Law Journal* 222, 224 (Supreme Court).

In *Mohd Faizal Musa* v. *Minister of Home Affairs*,[95] the applicant challenged a Ministerial order issued under section 7(1) of the Printing Presses and Publications Act 1984, prohibiting the printing, importation, production, reproduction, publishing, sale, issue, circulation, distribution, or possession of four of his books – *Sebongkah Batu di Kuala Berang*, *Karbala*, *Tiga Kali Seminggu*, and *Ingin Jadi Nasrallah*. Prior to the order being issued, the respondent Minister invited the applicant to attend a meeting together with the Department of Islamic Development (Jabatan Kemajuan Islam Malaysia (JAKIM)) for a discussion on the four books which JAKIM certified as being prohibited. The applicant refused to attend, arguing that there was no basis for the meeting and that, in any case, his four books had been in circulation for some years before the Minister banned them in 2015 after consulting JAKIM.

According to the Ministry, the books were deemed potentially prejudicial to public order, as they contained elements that could lead to 'confusion' among Muslims. It was also thought by the Ministry that the contents of the books promoted Shia teachings and contained provocative statements pitting Sunni Muslims against Shia Muslims. In these respects, the Ministry referred to a 1996 fatwa from the National Fatwa Council, stating that Muslims in Malaysia must adhere to Islamic principles based on the Sunni school of thought and that doctrines contrary to the Sunni school are prohibited. Although a large part of the decision focused on establishing threats to public order, what is interesting for our purposes was the court's approval of the use of a fatwa as a basis for the Minister's decision. For the court, the books implicated an 'Islamic law matter', and it was thus reasonable for the Minister to rely on a relevant fatwa in the course of making his executive decision.[96]

Mohd Faizal may need to be read in light of the case of *Kassim @ Osman bin Ahmad* v. *Dato' Seri Jamil Khir bin Baharom Menteri di Jabatan Perdana Menteri*,[97] which demonstrates quite clearly that the power play between religious authorities and the civil courts is a constantly evolving phenomenon. Kassim Ahmad, a well-known public intellectual, was arrested by the Federal Territories Religious Department (JAWI) in the state of Kedah for acting in contempt of a fatwa issued in the Federal Territories and then taken to Kuala Lumpur for interrogation and questioning. His speech at a seminar in the Federal Territory was considered by the religious authorities to have contravened a Federal Territories fatwa and insulted Islam. In the High Court, Kassim Ahmad argued that the fatwa in question, emanating as it did from the Federal Territories, did not apply to him, a Kedah resident. The trial judge refused to hear this argument on the grounds that it was 'rather premature' for him to raise this issue at the judicial review motion stage since it was a 'question of fact to be decided by the Syariah High Court'[98] and that he had failed to exhaust all remedies available in the Syariah courts. This decision was reversed by the Court of Appeal,[99] which had no compunction about reviewing the applicability of the fatwa to the appellant, holding that as the fatwa only applied to residents of the Federal Territories, and not to Kassim, since he was a resident of Kedah. The Court of Appeal did not, however, deal specifically with the legality of section 9 of the Syariah Criminal Offences (Federal Territories) Act 1997 (Act 559), which makes it an offence to act in contempt of a Federal Territories fatwa. This sidestepped the fundamental question as to how the administrative fiat of the fatwa was to be treated by the

95 *Mohd Faizal Musa* v. *Minister of Home Affairs* [2017] 7 Current Law Journal 352 (High Court).

96 *Mohd Faizal Musa* (n 95) at 364.

97 *Kassim @ Osman bin Ahmad* v. *Dato' Seri Jamil Khir bin Baharom Menteri di Jabatan Perdana Menteri (Hal Ehwal Agama Islam)* [2016] 7 *Malayan Law Journal* 669.

98 *Kassim* (n 97) at 695.

99 *Kassim @ Osman bin Ahmad* v. *Dato' Seri Jamil Khir bin Baharom Menteri di Jabatan Perdana Menteri (Hal Ehwal Agama Islam)* [2016] 5 *Malayan Law Journal* 258.

civil courts, and even at the Court of Appeal level, there was a seeming reluctance to supervise such administrative orders.

The legality of a fatwa will be argued in full in a case which the Federal Court recently remitted back to the High Court for hearing – *SIS Forum (M)* v. *Jawatankuasa Fatwa Negeri Selangor*.[100] In this case, Sisters in Islam (SIS), a civil society organisation for the promotion of women's rights within the frameworks of Islam and universal human rights, applied for a judicial review of a fatwa issued by the Selangor Fatwa Council labelling the organisation as 'deviant'.[101] In its first application in 2014, the High Court granted leave for the case to be heard on its merits. Asmabi J further dismissed objections that the High Court lacked jurisdiction to hear the case on the ground that it was a matter within the Syariah court's jurisdiction. However, before the substantive application could be heard, the conduct of the case was taken over by another judge, Hanipah Farikullah J. A second application – on the same question of the High Court's jurisdiction – was filed before the new judge who, in what now appears to be a familiar line of reasoning, dismissed the challenge on the basis that only the Syariah courts have exclusive jurisdiction to decide the validity of the fatwa. Invoking Article 121(1A), the court argued that the fact that SIS would have no remedy in the Syariah courts does not give civil courts jurisdiction to hear the case. The case was appealed all the way to the Federal Court, where a special bench of seven judges ordered the case to be remitted back to the High Court to be decided 'once and for all'.[102] In a four-point consent order, all those involved agreed for the judicial review application to be sent back to the High Court. Despite the *Indira Gandhi* decision and the recent political change in the country, the outcome of the High Court decision in August 2019 did not reflect the progressive gains made in reasserting judicial power. SIS had again argued that the fatwa was ultra vires, and it also asserted that the fatwa was unconstitutional for violating rules of natural justice and Article 10(2)(a) of the Constitution. SIS also argued, as it did in the 2014 application, that the civil courts have jurisdiction to hear the matter because it is a constitutional question. In a ruling reminiscent of *Lina Joy*, the High Court, however, held that pursuant to Article 121(1A), it did not have the jurisdiction to hear the judicial review application because fatwa implicates Syariah law questions and this fell under the exclusive jurisdiction of the Syariah court.[103]

13.5.3 *Drawing Jurisdictional Boundaries: Evolutions in the Implementation of Article 121(1A)*

Aside from the latest *Indira Gandhi* decision, the foregoing cases demonstrate how quickly the Malaysian civil courts can beat a retreat when confronted with the spectre of Syariah jurisdiction. Cases that touch on Syariah but are not strictly speaking about any religious

100 *SIS Forum (M)* v. *Jawatankuasa Fatwa Negeri Selangor and Ors* [2018] 3 *Malayan Law Journal* 706 (Court of Appeal); Ida Lim, 'After Four Years, Full Hearing of SIS's Challenge of "Deviant" Fatwa in High Court' *Malay Mail*, 25 September 2018, available at www.malaymail.com/s/1676191/after-four-years-full-hearing-of-sis-challenge-of-deviant-fatwa-in-high-cou (accessed 10 December 2018).

101 Pursuant to s 66A of the Administration of the Religion of Islam (Selangor) Enactment 2003. This is a new provision inserted through an amendment of the enactment, and it came into force on 22 May 2015. It identifies persons or groups professing 'liberalism' or 'religious pluralism' as 'deviants' (*sesat*).

102 Lim (n 100).

103 'In Sisters in Islam case, High Court Says Fatwa Is Syariah Court's Jurisdiction' *New Straits Times*, 27 August 2019, available at www.nst.com.my/news/crime-courts/2019/08/516547/sisters-islam-case-high-court-says-fatwa-syariah-courts (accessed 10 June 2020). At the time of writing, the written judgment of the High Court has yet to be published. It would be interesting to see how the High Court treats the Federal Court's decision in *Indira Gandhi*.

matter are quickly re-characterised as an Article 121(1A) matter, elevating it to a jurisdictional battle with the Syariah courts to which the civil courts must invariably yield. This appears to be nothing more than judicial abdication of responsibility in the name of jurisdictional line-drawing of the crudest order. However, two recent decisions of the Court of Appeal suggest perhaps a change in the way the boundaries are drawn between the Syariah and civil courts.

The first is the case of *Jabatan Agama Islam Wilayah Persekuthuan* v. *Berjaya Books Sdn Bhd.*[104] In this case, the first appellant (JAWI), a department in charge of Islamic affairs in the Federal Territories, conducted a search at Borders Bookstore owned by the first respondent and seized several books by author Irsyad Manji. A few days later, the Minister for Home Affairs proceeded to issue a Prohibition Order against the publication and sale of the seized books. The second respondent was a non-Muslim General Manager of the bookstore, while the third respondent was a Muslim working as Store Manager at the bookstore. Jawi proceeded to arrest the third respondent and charged under Section 13 of the Syariah Criminal Offences (Federal Territories) Act 1997 for the offence of disseminating and distributing by way of selling the books deemed contrary to Hukum Syarak (Islamic law). The respondents' application for judicial review was granted by the High Court. On appeal, the appellants argued, inter alia, that the High Court had no jurisdiction to hear and determine the judicial review and had erred in law in allowing the application since the impugned actions of JAWI dealt with Syariah law and therefore came solely under the jurisdiction of the Syariah courts. The Court of Appeal rejected this argument, holding that applying the 'pith and substance' test, this was a judicial review case and was not one dealing with Syariah matters alone.[105]

The issue arose again in *A Child & Ors* v. *Jabatan Pendaftaran Negara & Ors*,[106] where two fatawa issued by the National Fatwa Council in 1981 and 2003 were the subject of challenge. The Director General of National Registration, in the exercise of his powers under the Births and Deaths Registration Act (BDRA), decided to ascribe the patronymic surname of 'bin Abdullah' to an illegitimate Muslim child in place of his father's name and against the latter's wishes. Among other things, the Director General argued that his decision followed two fatawa issued by the National Fatwa Council in 1981 and 2003. The Court of Appeal characterised the issue as that of the proper exercise of a statutory power – specifically whether there was a possible abrogation of power:

> [61] [T]he appellants' application involved the administration of the civil law by the civil authority and not the administration of the Hukum Syarak by the religious authority. The matter before the second respondent was a simple and straightforward question of whether the second appellant, being a person duly and lawfully registered as the father of the first appellant under s 13, was entitled, by virtue of s 13A(2), to register the first appellant's surname in his name. This is a purely administrative function that has nothing to do with Islamic jurisprudence on legitimacy. . . .
>
> [63] The second respondent's jurisdiction is a civil one and is confined to the determination of whether the second appellant had fulfilled the requirements of s 13A(2) of the BDRA,

104 [2015] 3 *Current Law Journal* 461 (Court of Appeal).

105 The 'pith and substance test', as noted previously, was expounded by the Supreme Court in *Mamat bin Daud* (n 40). The test arises from the doctrine of 'colourable legislation' – citing a decision of the Indian Supreme Court (*KCG Narayan Deo* v. *State of Orissa*, AIR 1953 SC 375). In *Mamat bin Daud*, the Court determined that a provision of the Penal Code (section 298A) is 'a colourable legislation in that it pretends to be a legislation on "public order" when *in pith and substance it is a law on the subject of religion with respect to which only the states have power to legislate under Articles 74 and 77 of the Constitution*' (emphasis added). *Mamat bin Daud* (n 40) at 125.

106 [2017] 7 *Current Law Journal* 533 (Court of Appeal).

> which obviously covers all illegitimate children, Muslim and non-Muslim alike. For that purpose, he is not obligated to apply, let alone be bound by a fatwa issued by a religious body such as the national Fatwa Committee.
>
> [64] For him to do so would amount to an abrogation of his power under the BGRA and surrendering it to the religious body. That would in effect by to take away the statutory right accorded to the second appellant by s 13A(2) to have his name ascribed as the first appellant's surname in the birth certificate.
>
> [65] Such abrogation of power will render s 13A(2) of the BDRA completely otiose and gives the impression that Parliament had enacted the provision in vain, a proposition that has no place in legislative interpretation. A Fatwa or a religious edict issued by a religious body has no force of law unless the fatwa or edict has been made or adopted as Federal law by an Act of Parliament. Otherwise, a fatwa issued by a religious body will form part of Federal law without going through the legislative process.[107]

Despite the Court of Appeal's decision, the NRD announced that it will continue to abide by the edicts of the National Fatwa Council and ignore the court's ruling. In November 2018, the Federal Court decided to defer the verdict, as the government was seeking alternative means of resolving the case (i.e., an out-of-court settlement).[108] The NRD's refusal to comply with the ruling of the civil courts and the government's attempt to resolve this matter outside the courts suggests that the contest for this administrative space is set to continue. And because the civil law courts have for so long abdicated their supervisory jurisdiction over Islamic affairs, even authorities like the NRD believe they are beyond judicial control when it comes to matters implicating Islam and rank as a co-equal power to that of the legislature. In February 2020, however, the Federal Court delivered the much-awaited verdict, holding that while the child in question could not carry his biological father's name, the patronymic name 'bin Abdullah' should not be ascribed to him. In a 4–3 decision, seemingly based on technical grounds, the court held that Section 13A of the BDRA does not apply to Malays in Malaysia (hence Malay Muslim children could not carry the personal name of their father) because a Malay father's personal name is not a surname for the purposes of the BDRA.[109] At the same time, the court acknowledged that juristic opinion on whether an illegitimate child is to be ascribed with the patronymic name 'bin Abdullah' varies,[110] and therefore if a fatwa on the issue had not been gazetted in the state, the (federal) NRD could not impose and enforce such fatwa.[111] However, while the court held that the NRD could not rely on a federal-level fatwa in its decision-making, it took the position that the NRD had not acted unreasonably in deciding that the child's full name could not include his biological father's name.[112] This is because the NRD was entitled to apply state-enacted Islamic personal law (i.e., the 2003 Johore Family Law Enactment) in its decision-making. In short, while the Federal Court's decision limited the administrative fiat of fatwa, it remains the case that Islamic personal law could be invoked to interpret federal law (the BDRA). This aspect of the decision is

107 [2017] 7 *Current Law Journal* 533 (Court of Appeal) at 551–2.

108 See '"Bin Abdullah" Appeal Set for Further Case Management on March 21' *Malay Mail* (27 February 2019), www.malaymail.com/news/malaysia/2019/02/27/bin-abdullah-appeal-set-for-further-case-management-on-march-21/1727462 (accessed 20 May 2019).

109 *National Registration Department & 2 Ors v A Child & 2 Ors, Civil Appeal No.: 01(f)-43-09/2017(W)*, at paras 44–47 (Federal Court). The majority judgment was delivered by Justice Rohana Yusuf, Justice Azahar Mohamed, Justice Mohd Zawawi Salleh, and Justice Idrus bin Harun. The dissenting judgment was delivered by Justice Nallini Pathmanathan, Justice Abang Iskandar Abang Hashim, and Justice David Wong Dak Wah.

110 Ibid., paras 77–83.

111 Ibid., paras 84–85.

112 Ibid., para 66.

particularly problematic, since the Constitution's Ninth Schedule List 1 explicitly provides that registration of births and deaths is a federal matter.

13.6 CONCLUSION

The constitutional amendment to judicial power in 1988, which carved an exclusive (but limited) sphere of jurisdiction for the Syariah courts, was intended only to prevent courts with competing jurisdictions from issuing orders that might contradict each other. However, the underlying forces behind the amendment have, over the past three decades, largely shaped judicial attitudes towards reviewing exercises of power implicating Islam. As alluded to previously, the religious resurgence in the 1980s (inspired by the Islamic revolution in Iran) and the desire of the then-ruling government to undercut the Islamic appeal of its political opposition, PAS, led to a series of programmes and policies aimed at demonstrating a commitment to the Islamic cause. This has often been characterised as the battle between competing political parties to 'out-Islamize' one another. At the societal level, these initiatives have also shaped the majority Malay-Muslim psyche and expectations about the role and position of Islam in governance.

In the legal arena, because the civil courts were so quick to surrender jurisdiction whenever a matter implicates Islam or Syariah, the role of administrative law principles (including those espoused in *Anisminic* and *Wednesbury*) in shaping and policing the boundaries of the decision-making powers of Syariah authorities have accordingly diminished significantly. The *Lina Joy* and *Indira Gandhi* cases illustrate – most potently – the consequences of the interaction between religion (Islam) and administrative law principles in Malaysia. In the former, the Federal Court's evaluation of 'reasonableness' was not only shaped by what was deemed to be crucial Islamic imperatives, but also by the view that Article 121(1A) meant that Syariah courts possess sole, unreviewable powers over any matter concerning Islam. In fact, reasonableness was the only administrative law question that the majority decision considered. Unlike Richard Malanjum CJ's dissenting opinion, the court failed to evaluate breaches of the principles of natural justice, or even the fact that a 'reasonable' decision might well offend a fundamental constitutional right. It is also worth noting that what appears to underlie the majority's decision was not only that it was ill-equipped to determine issues of Muslim apostasy, but also that it was concerned about the social and political consequences of allowing Lina Joy's appeal. This was apparent when Ahmad Fairuz CJ (who delivered the majority opinion) accepted assertions from several Muslim NGOs that if a person is permitted to renounce Islam at will, it will lead to 'chaos' within the Muslim community.[113] The broader consequence of this approach – that is, the abdication of judicial role to review exercises of power implicating Islam and questions of constitutional importance – is that religious bodies and authorities have become increasingly unaccountable.

The Federal Court's decisions in *Semenyih Jaya* and *Indira Gandhi* and a few recent decisions of the Court of Appeal (most notably, the 'bin Abdullah' case)[114] signal – in some ways – a departure from the civil courts' old habits. The possibility of a reassertion of civil courts' supervisory powers over Syariah courts and authorities' decisions is significant, for it indicates the courts are no longer shy to adjudicate matters implicating Islam. While the 'bin Abdullah' case was not one that concerned the reviewability of a fatwa, the decision was

113 *Lina Joy* (n 19) at 611–12.

114 *A Child and Ors* v. *Jabatan Pendaftaran Negara and Ors* [2017] 7 *Current Law Journal* 533 (Court of Appeal).

crucial in its rejection of the view that civil authorities – in exercising their powers – could be dictated by religious edicts issued by unelected persons that do not even need to go through normal legislative processes. Both decisions could go a long way in checking the legality of powers exercised by religious bodies, which has always been a politically sensitive topic for discussion. However, the courts not only face challenges in making their decisions stick (in the 'bin Abdullah' case, the NRD Director wantonly declared that the department will continue to abide by fatawa), but it remains to be seen if they will be so bold as to declare a fatwa invalid and unconstitutional.

14

English Administrative Law in Post-Handover Hong Kong

Michael Ramsden

14.1 INTRODUCTION

After 156 years of British rule, Hong Kong was returned to the People's Republic of China on 1 July 1997 under a unique constitutional settlement of 'One Country, Two Systems'.[1] Under this model, the essential features of governance under colonial rule would be retained with modifications to suit the new realities. An important feature that was retained in the Hong Kong constitution, the 'Basic Law', was the common law system and, with it, the power of individuals to challenge decisions of the legislature and executive by way of judicial review. Since the Handover, judicial review has not only continued but grown in prominence; it now plays an even greater role in the regulation of public administration, with Hong Kong residents also seeing the benefit in using the courts as a means to participate in public affairs, given the continued absence of meaningful democracy and representative government.

In this regard, the purpose of this chapter is to explore one particular facet of judicial review in Hong Kong: the continued influence of English law on its development. It does so from two vantage points. First, it considers the influence that the British colonial form of governance and recognition of human rights has had in the crafting of post-Handover constitutional guarantees. Second, the chapter then proceeds to consider the continuing influence of English precedent on judicial review in Hong Kong, in relation to both the principles of administrative law and the content of fundamental rights.

14.2 CONTINUITY AS A CONSTITUTIONAL PRINCIPLE

Prior to the Handover, English law and British principles of governance were highly influential in colonial Hong Kong. The three key governmental powers – the executive (including the civil service), the legislature and the judiciary – were created by the Letters Patent 1843, according formal recognition to Hong Kong as a British colony.[2] However, the notion that the Letters Patent gave recognition to a definable separation of powers is questionable: on the contrary, it affirmed a high degree of power to the Governor, with no laws being able to be made without his acquiescence.[3] Indeed, the Governor appointed the Legislative Council

[1] Regarding the 'One Country, Two Systems' principle, see Hong Kong Basic Law, Preamble; *Ng Ka Ling v. Director of Immigration* (1999) 2 HKCFAR 4, at 28–29 (Li CJ).

[2] For a history, see S. Jhaveri et al., *Administrative Law in Hong Kong* (Hong Kong: Lexis Nexis, 2013), chapter 1.

[3] Peter Wesley-Smith, *Constitutional and Administrative Law in Hong Kong* (Hong Kong: Longman Asia Ltd, 1994), p 122.

during most of the colonial period and also presided over this body, thereby combining within himself both the legislative and executive functions of government. Unlike the distinction between political and administrative functionaries in the British political system, colonial Hong Kong had no such thing; in turn, the fusion of politics and administration in the colonial model of government downplayed the importance of politics and political participation in policy-making.[4] This would mean that the senior parts of the civil service exercised both administrative and political powers while still owing direct allegiance to the Governor; although the colonial civil service would espouse its independence from political decision-making, the reality was quite different.

While the Governor was able to exert considerable influence over both the colonial government and legislature, the courts, on the other hand, operated at a greater distance from the other branches. The court structure in colonial Hong Kong followed the English structure, comprising of the Magistracy, District Court, High Court and Court of Appeal. Judges were also appointed on the recommendation of the Judicial Service Commission, an independent body. It is significant, in this respect, that the courts had powers to ensure compatibility of colonial laws with the Letters Patent – in effect, a power of constitutional invalidation.[5] The colonial courts applied the 'common law' system, which itself was defined as 'the common law of England'.[6] Furthermore, Hong Kong's final court of appeal was the Judicial Committee of the Privy Council; decisions of the Privy Council were binding on the courts of Hong Kong and, indeed, those of the House of Lords also had 'the same practical effect as if they were binding'.[7] Furthermore, judges could not be removed except on the advice of the London-based Judicial Committee, thereby 'geographically removed from the political excitements' locally that might have harmed judicial independence.[8] Given that the Hong Kong judiciary operated within a structure augmented by English law and judges, this provided it with a measure of independence from the colonial government, thereby allowing it to positively develop its powers to review the legality of administrative action.[9]

In establishing the structure of government after the Handover of Hong Kong on 1 July 1997, a constitutional instrument, the 'Basic Law', was promulgated by the PRC.[10] The drafting of the Basic Law was underpinned by five principles: to give effect to the purpose and spirit of the Sino-British Joint Declaration 1984 and, with it, the unique constitutional principles of 'One Country Two Systems'; to uphold national unity while securing a high degree of autonomy for Hong Kong; to promote economic growth and social stability; to retain the positive aspects of existing institutions and to increase democratic participation; and to start from the realities of Hong Kong itself.[11] As a general matter, continuity is an overarching theme in the Basic Law. This is recognised throughout the various provisions of the Basic Law, in the definition of the economic, political and legal systems applicable in the

4 C. Loh and R. Cullen, 'Politics without Democracy: A Study of the New Principal Officials Accountability System in Hong Kong' (2003) 4 *San Diego International Law Journal* 127, pp 149–50 at p 149.

5 Hong Kong Letters Patent and Royal Instructions to the Governor; Colonial Laws Validity Act 1865.

6 There was some scope for divergence from English law to suit the local circumstances, although this was modest: *China Field Ltd* v. *Building Appeal Tribunal (No 2)* (2009) 12 HKCFAR 342, at [76] (Millett NPJ).

7 *De Lasala* v. *De Lasala* [1979] HKLR 214, at p 220.

8 Wesley-Smith n 3, at p 148.

9 For a detailed pre-Handover account, see David Clark and Gerard McCoy, *Hong Kong Administrative Law* (Hong Kong: Lexis Nexis, 2nd edition, 1993).

10 For a comprehensive treatment of all each provision of the Basic Law, see M Ramsden and S Hargreaves, *Hong Kong Basic Law Handbook* (Hong Kong: Sweet & Maxwell, 2nd edition, 2019).

11 Xiao Weiyun, 'A Study of the Political System of the Hong Kong Special Administrative Region under the Basic Law' (1988) 2 *Journal of Chinese Law* 95.

territory. 'Any interpretation of the Basic Law', Justice Hartmann observed, 'must recognise that continuity is integral to an understanding of its structure'.[12] The importance of continuity has also been described in instrumental terms by Justice Stock as the 'key to stability', with the pre-existing laws and legal system being 'the very fabric of our society'.[13] Continuity is a theme running throughout the Basic Law, but there are a number of specific guarantees and principles, including that the 'previous capitalist system and way of life shall remain unchanged for 50 years'.[14] Similarly, the Basic Law also expressly acknowledges that 'the laws previously in force' shall be adopted after the Handover.[15]

The Basic Law maintained the key institutions that existed prior to the Handover, with some notable qualifications. The concept of 'executive-led' government is firmly retained and reinforced in the structure of the Basic Law, with a strong Chief Executive (to replace the colonial Governor) and comparatively weaker legislature.[16] The Chief Executive is appointed by the Central People's Government, with the 'ultimate aim' for this person to be selected by universal suffrage.[17] Also retained was the Executive Council (i.e., the Cabinet in British constitutional terms) and the civil service, again modelled on its British counterpart.[18] However, a more accountable ministerial form of government, with each department being led by politicians rather than career civil servants, was avoided during the drafting of the Basic Law; the executive would later introduce a 'principal officials accountability system' (POAS) to inject such political accountability, and concepts of 'ministerial accountability', into government.[19] While the POAS added a layer of political accountability to the decisions of executive departments, it also had the effect of concentrating power even further in the hands of the Chief Executive.[20] The Legislative Council is also retained but with additional provisions that provide for formal 'checks and balances' between the legislature and executive that did not exist during the colonial administration.[21] After the Handover, the legislature has become more democratically representative, although there remains an element that is appointed by 'functional constituencies' made up of the representatives of community and professional bodies.[22]

The legal system, based upon the common law and precedent, was also to continue. This included an independent judiciary that represents 'continuity with what went before'.[23]

12 *RV* v. *Director of Immigration* [2008] 4 HKLRD 529, 544 (Hartmann J).

13 *RV* v. *Director of Immigration* [2008] 4 HKLRD 529, 544 (Hartmann J); *HKSAR* v. *Ma Wai Kwan David* [1997] HKLRD 761, 774 (Stock V-P).

14 Article 5, Basic Law.

15 Article 160, Basic Law. Except, that is, for those declared to be invalid with the Basic Law by the Standing Committee of the National People's Congress.

16 See Articles 54–6 Basic Law. See also Lorenz Langer, 'The Elusive Aim of Universal Suffrage: Constitutional Developments in Hong Kong' (2007) 5 *International Journal of Constitutional Law* 419, at p 434.

17 Annex I Art 2; Xiao Weiyun n 11. This aim of universal suffrage has yet to be realised, which has fermented discontent amongst a large section of the Hong Kong population: J. Lam, 'Political Uncertainties in Hong Kong after the Occupy Central Movement' (2017) 6(4) *Asian Education and Development Studies* 306; J Tam, 'Political Decay in Hong Kong after the Occupy Central Movement' (2015) 42(1) *Asian Affairs: An American Review* 99.

18 Articles 54 and 60, Basic Law.

19 Loh and Cullen n 4, at p 158; Hong Kong Government, Report on Further Development of the Political Appointment System (2007) [5.02].

20 Jhaveri n 2, at p. 16.

21 See Articles 66–79; Langer n 16, at p 436.

22 See further analysis in S Young, 'Elected by the Elite: Functional Constituency Legislators and Elections', in C Loh (ed.), *Functional Constituencies: A Unique Feature of the Hong Kong Legislative Council* (Hong Kong: Hong Kong University Press, 2006).

23 *Stock Exchange of Hong Kong Ltd* v. *New World Development Co Ltd* (2006) 9 HKCFAR 234, 254–255 (Ribeiro PJ).

Continuity also underpinned the constitutionality of judicial power being vested in administrative tribunals, as it had prior to the Handover.[24] Similarly, decisions of the Judicial Committee of the Privy Council on Hong Kong before 1 July 1997 remained binding on the courts of Hong Kong (provided, that is, it did not inhibit legal development or cause injustice): this 'accords with the principle of continuity'.[25] This would include, incidentally, the famous Privy Council decision in *Ng Yuen Siu*, which explicated on the then-nascent doctrine of legitimate expectations.[26] However, not all aspects of the legal system remained the same; most evidently, Hong Kong would have a new final appellate authority, the Court of Final Appeal (CFA), replacing the Privy Council as having the power of 'final adjudication'.[27] Similarly, the common law ceased to be that which derived from England to 'the common law force in Hong Kong', providing autonomy for the courts to develop the common law more readily to suit the local circumstances.[28] The formal link, then, between English and Hong Kong law would be broken; but as the following section shows, English law continues to exert a persuasive and pervasive influence over the development of judicial review principles in Hong Kong.

Despite continuity being a key aspect of the Basic Law, the fundamental new reality is the recognition that Hong Kong is an 'inalienable part of the People's Republic of China'.[29] This would mean a number of important changes and new constitutional features. One such prominent feature is that the Standing Committee of the National People's Congress has the power of final interpretation over the Basic Law; it can thus overturn an interpretation made by the CFA.[30] This power has been seldom used but inevitably has aroused considerable controversy when it has, including the charge that it has undermined the independence of the judiciary in Hong Kong, or otherwise diminished its power.[31] Hong Kong's new reality has also affected the incorporation of customary international law into the common law where this impacts upon the national interests of the PRC. Thus, prior to the Handover, the Hong Kong courts observed the qualified approach to sovereign immunity, per the British position. After this, on the other hand, '[i]t would follow that the commercial exception, being a doctrine inconsistent with that adhered to by the PRC, can no longer be maintained and that the doctrine now applicable in the HKSAR is a doctrine of absolute immunity'.[32]

In relation to human rights, the Basic Law contains a range of civil-political rights and, to a lesser extent, socio-economic rights. There is an evident overlap between civil-political rights in the Basic Law and those contained in the Hong Kong Bill of Rights Ordinance (BORO), which was enacted in 1990 to incorporate the International Covenant on Civil and Political Rights (ICCPR) into domestic law.[33] While there is this overlap, the Basic Law

24 *Luk Ka Cheung* v. *Market Misconduct Tribunal* [2009] 1 HKLRD 114, [36] (Cheung J).

25 *Solicitor (24/07)* v. *Law Society of Hong Kong* (2008) 11 HKCFAR 117, at [16], [19] (Li CJ).

26 *Attorney-General* v. *Ng Yuen Shiu* [1983] 1 HKC 23 (Privy Council).

27 See Articles 81–82, Basic Law; Hong Kong Court of Final Appeal Ordinance, s.3.

28 Interpretation and General Clauses Ordinance s.3; *China Field Ltd* v. *Building Appeal Tribunal (No 2)* (2009) 12 HKCFAR 342, at [78] (Millett NPJ).

29 Article 1, Basic Law.

30 Article 158, Basic Law.

31 See *HKSAR* v. *Ma Wai Kwan David* [1997] 1 HKLRD 761, [1997] 2 HKC 315 (CA); *Ng Ka Ling* n 1; *Lau Kong-Yung* v. *Director of Immigration* [1999] 2 HKCFAR 300; *Chong Fung Yuen* v. *Director of Immigration* [2000] 2 HKCU 580; *Democratic Republic of the Congo* v. *FG Hemisphere Associates LLC (No 1)* (2011) 14 HKCFAR 95. See also the collection of essays in Hualing Fu, Lison Harris and Simon NM Young (eds.), *Interpreting Hong Kong's Basic Law: The Struggle for Coherence* (New York: Palgrave Macmillan, 2007).

32 *FG Hemisphere* n 32 at [336] (Chan PJ, Ribeiro PJ and Sir Anthony Mason NPJ). For the contrary view, see *FG Hemisphere Associates LLC* v. *Democratic Republic of the Congo* [2010] 2 HKLRD 66, [253]–[256] (Yuen JA).

33 For example of such overlap, see *HKSAR* v. *Ng Kung Siu & Another* [1999] 3 HKLRD 907 (CFA).

contains additional rights in the form of socio-economic rights which serves to offer a more balanced protection of rights than other constitutional instruments that focus solely on first generational rights.[34] Other guarantees based upon British colonial rule were also inserted into the Basic Law, not least in terms of the international obligations that the UK assumed on behalf of Hong Kong under core international human rights treaties. This is most notable with Article 39 of the Basic Law, which provides that

> [t]he provisions of the International Covenant on Civil and Political Rights, the International Covenant on Economic, Social and Cultural Rights, and international labour conventions as applied to Hong Kong shall remain in force and shall be implemented through the laws of the Hong Kong Special Administrative Region.
>
> The rights and freedoms enjoyed by Hong Kong residents shall not be restricted unless as prescribed by law. Such restrictions shall not contravene the provisions of the preceding paragraph of this Article.

Article 39 has come in for close scrutiny by the Hong Kong courts. The key phrase in this regard is 'as applied to Hong Kong', which can be construed in one of three ways. The first is that it references the application of these treaties in Hong Kong domestic law prior to the Handover.[35] However, none of the instruments listed in Article 39 were part of Hong Kong law during the promulgation of the Basic Law in 1990; indeed, the vast majority of the labour conventions and the International Covenant on Economic, Social and Cultural Rights (ICESCR) have still not been comprehensively incorporated into domestic law.[36] Furthermore, the phrase 'as applied to Hong Kong' was included in the Sino-British Joint Declaration of 1984, again before any of the instruments became part of domestic law.[37] The phrase thus must refer to the international application of these treaties, but this raises the question by which State: the UK or PRC? This leads to the second construction, that 'as applied to Hong Kong' references the application of these instruments on the international plane by the PRC in present times. However, this would obviously offend the grammar of this phrase ('applied'), in addition to 'shall remain in force'. This reading would also potentially offend the principle of continuity in the Basic Law, especially given that the PRC has assumed international obligations on behalf of Hong Kong under these instruments that are in material respects narrower than those previously assumed by the UK.[38] This leads to the third – and only plausible – construction, being that 'as applied to Hong Kong' references the

34 Y Ghai, *Hong Kong's New Constitutional Order: The Resumption of Chinese Sovereignty and the Basic Law* (2nd edition; Hong Kong: Hong Kong University Press, 1998), pp 422–3. As to socio-economic rights in the Basic Law, see M Ramsden, 'Using the ICESCR in Hong Kong Courts' (2012) 42(3) *Hong Kong Law Journal* 839; M Ramsden and L Marsh, 'Refugees in Hong Kong: Developing the Legal Framework for Socio-Economic Rights Protection' (2014) *Human Rights Law Review*, 14(2) 267.

35 This is a view of numerous Chinese scholars, of which see the analysis in Ghai n 34, at p 416.

36 The Basic Law was promulgated by the National People's Congress of the PRC on 4 April 1990. By contrast, the HKBORO was enacted on 8 June 1991 by the Hong Kong Legislative Council.

37 Joint Declaration of the Government of the United Kingdom of Great Britain and Northern Ireland and the Government of the People's Republic of China on the Question of Hong Kong (1984) 1399 UNTS 61, Annex 1 Section XIII.

38 See further M. Ramsden, 'Reviewing the United Kingdom's ICCPR Immigration Reservation in Hong Kong Courts' (2014) 63(3) *International and Comparative Law Quarterly* 635; M. Ramsden, 'Using International Law in Hong Kong Courts: An Examination of *Non-Refoulement* Litigation' (2013) 42(4) *Common Law World Review* 351. Compare the PRC reservation to Article 8(1)(b) of the ICESCR to that entered by the UK on behalf of Hong Kong to the same provision. See http://treaties.un.org/Pages/ViewDetails.aspx?mtdsg_no=IV-3&chapter=4&lang=en, accessed 16 March 2019.

UK's ratification and extension of these instruments to Hong Kong, an interpretation that has also found favour with the CFA.[39]

The interesting aspect of Article 39 is that legislation that implements these instruments in the same manner 'as applied to Hong Kong' by the UK would receive a constitutional underpinning. As already noted, the ICCPR was incorporated into Hong Kong legislation, via the BORO. The effect was that where a provision offended the BORO it would also offend Article 39 given that both provisions were identical in their terms. Article 39 would, in turn, inject a constitutional dimension to the BORO. This would include the powerful interpretive principle of legality, a provision that the PRC had excised from the BORO upon the resumption of its sovereignty, but which continued to apply via its application in Article 39.[40] But there was also another dimension in which Article 39 was relevant, in assessing whether the implementation of such instruments did indeed take place in a manner that was consistent with the UK's international obligations, assumed on behalf of Hong Kong, under these instruments.

This raised the question, in particular, as to whether Section 11 of the BORO faithfully reflected the application of the ICCPR on the international plane by the UK upon ratification and extension of this instrument to Hong Kong in 1976. Section 11 in this regard serves to exclude the application of the BORO in immigration matters: 'As regards persons not having the right to enter and remain in Hong Kong, this Ordinance does not affect any immigration legislation governing entry into, stay in and departure from Hong Kong, or the application of any such legislation.' It is said to implement the British reservation to the ICCPR, which 'reserves the right to continue to apply such immigration legislation governing entry into, stay in and departure from the UK' of those without the right to enter and remain; accordingly, the UK's acceptance of 'Article 12(4) and of the other provisions of the Covenant is subject to' the provisions of the UKs statutory immigration regime.[41] While Section 11 and the British reservation seem to be indistinguishable, there are material differences. The reservation was ultimately concerned, as the British government has acknowledged, with preventing colonial citizens from asserting a right to enter the UK on the basis that it is their 'own country' under Article 12(4).[42] By contrast, Section 11 seeks to exclude the application of the ICCPR in *all* immigration decisions, not solely those concerned with nationality and the right of abode. To reiterate this point, it is apparent that the UK regarded its reservation to pursue a limited objective; it is this, as a matter of treaty interpretation, that ought to guide the interpretation of the reservation.[43] In this respect, the purpose of the reservation is quite clear

39 *Ubamaka* v. *Secretary for Security* (2012) 15 HKCFAR 743, at [62]–[67] (Riberio PJ); *GA* v. *Director of Immigration* (2014) 17 HKCFAR 60, at [29] (Ma CJ).

40 P. Wesley-Smith, 'Maintenance of the Bill of Rights' (1997) 27 *HKLJ* 15, at 16. See Section 4 of the BORO which did not survive the Handover ('All legislation enacted on or after the commencement date shall, to the extent that it admits of such a construction, be construed so as to be consistent with the International Covenant on Civil and Political Rights as applied to Hong Kong.').

41 See 'Reservation to the International Covenant on Civil and Political Rights Made by the United Kingdom of Great Britain and Northern Ireland upon Ratification', at http://treaties.un.org/doc/db/survey/humanrightsconvs/Chapt_IV_4/reservations/UK.pdf, accessed 16 March 2019.

42 'Seventh Periodic Report from the United Kingdom, the British Overseas Territories, the Crown Dependencies' (December 2012), 40. For the circumstances that led to the introduction of this reservation, see Lord Lester of Herne Hill QC, 'Thirty Years On: The East African Asians Case Revisited' [2002] Public Law 52.

43 A reservation, being a part of the treaty, is to be interpreted in accordance with its ordinary meaning in context and in light of its object and purpose: Restrictions to the Death Penalty (Art 4(2) and 4(4) of the American Convention on Human Rights), Advisory Opinion OC-3/83, Inter-American Court of Human Rights Series A No 3 (8 September 1983), para 49; Vienna Convention on the Law of Treaties Art 31(1).

and does not encapsulate any Hong Kong-specific factors. As the UK noted in its report to the Human Rights Committee (HRC),

> [t]here is uncertainty concerning the correct interpretation of 'territory of a State' and 'own country'. The purpose of the Immigration Act 1971 and related legislation is to control immigration into the United Kingdom, including immigration from the British overseas territories (which in general, are responsible for their own immigration controls). The right to enter and reside in the United Kingdom is restricted, in the main, to British citizens. British Nationals (Overseas), British Overseas Territory citizens, British Overseas citizens, British protected persons and (for the most part) British subjects are eligible for British passports and consular protection but, unless they concurrently hold British citizenship, have no right of abode here. The reservation protects these arrangements.[44]

In confronting this inconvenient truth, the CFA adopted a different tact grounded essentially in indigenous constitutional pragmatism: to read the UK-centric reservation in light of Hong Kong's peculiar circumstances during colonial times. Ribeiro PJ for the CFA observed that the meaning of the reservation is 'not resolved by reference to what may have motivated the United Kingdom Government in 1976 when it laid down the immigration reservation'; 'to suggest that the immigration reservation must be construed as pursuing that limited objective [i.e., Article 12(4)], transplanted in some way to Hong Kong, makes little sense.'[45] According to Ribeiro PJ for the reservation to make sense in the Hong Kong context then it needed to take into account 'as a matter of notoriety that in the 1970's, 1980's and 1990's, major efforts had to be made by the Hong Kong Government to fend off waves of illegal immigrants, numbering in the tens of thousands in some years, originating from the Chinese Mainland'.[46] Based upon these autochthonous considerations, the Hong Kong courts, in turn, have adopted an interpretation of the British reservation that was even more restrictive than was intended or contemplated by the British themselves.

14.3 COMPARATIVE INFLUENCES ON JUDICIAL REVIEW IN HONG KONG

It is fair to say that there is more that connects judicial review in the English and Hong Kong courts than divides them. Hong Kong has been heavily influenced by both procedural and substantive principles of judicial review first developed in the English courts. Hong Kong's Order 53 procedure was modelled on, and remains materially the same as, the procedure introduced in England in 1977 and subsequently incorporated as s 31 of the Supreme Court Act 1981.[47] Like England, Hong Kong applies the classic grounds of review enunciated most prominently by Lord Diplock in *GCHQ* (illegality, irrationality, procedural impropriety), as well as more contemporary grounds of review (legitimate expectations and proportionality).[48] It also possesses administrative machinery (that parallels that in the UK) to ensure checks of government authority, including an Ombudsman, commissions of inquiry and tribunals.[49] The regulatory apparatus thus shares many similar features with that in the UK, such that

44 Seventh Periodic Report n 42.
45 *Ubamaka* n 39, at [62]–[67] (Ribeiro PJ).
46 *Ubamaka* n 39, at [62]–[67] (Ribeiro PJ).
47 SI 1977/1955. The underlying Rules of the High Court and High Court Ordinance (in Hong Kong) and section 31(3) of the Supreme Court Act 1981 (in the UK) are materially the same.
48 See generally Jhaveri n 2.
49 Jhaveri n 2, chapter 2.

a comparative conversation can be had about many of these mechanisms. So, too, can useful theoretical debate be had as to the purpose underpinning these mechanisms and the proper balance to be struck from a 'red-light' and 'green-light' perspective in the use of judicial and non-judicial forms of control.[50]

Hong Kong has also been subject to similar pressures and influences in the development of judicial review as have confronted the English courts. The rise of judicial review in Hong Kong has been attributed to features that have also supported its rise in England, including the complexity of modern life and a citizenry with a higher expectation of public institutions.[51] This includes a close correspondence between the categories of government decisions typically subjected to judicial review, with a focus on immigration and asylum cases being predominant in both jurisdictions, particularly after Hong Kong followed suit in establishing a unified screening mechanism to consider refugee claims on substantially the same grounds as found in England.[52] The transformative effects that have followed the movement towards the 'righting' of administrative law – with the attendant questions this raises in defining the appropriate ambit of the court's human rights jurisdiction – have confronted Hong Kong and England alike.[53] Hong Kong's human rights jurisdiction, however, came before that in England by over a decade.[54] This has meant that the Hong Kong courts, at least on a number of issues, were already well ahead of the English courts, including in declaring reverse onus provisions to be incompatible with its bill of rights (i.e., the BORO).[55] But in keeping focus on the influence of English law on Hong Kong judicial review, this can be seen in a number of important areas.

There have been several instances in which Hong Kong judicial review has tracked developments in England. This has gone both ways in terms of promoting accessibility to judicial review and also in restricting it. The leave requirement in Hong Kong was thus initially framed as one requiring a potentially arguable case, following the speech of Lord Diplock in *Inland Revenue Commissioners* v. *National Federation of Self-Employed and Small Businesses Ltd*.[56] However, the CFA would later introduce a stricter test – one that required a case to be reasonably arguable at the leave stage; the main justification for doing so was based on developments in the English courts towards a stricter requirement.[57] Similarly, the *O'Reilly* v. *Mackman* 'exclusivity principle' continues to have a pervasive influence on judicial review in Hong Kong.[58] Conversely, there are areas where the Hong Kong courts have embraced liberal procedural aspects from England. The 'sufficient interest' test for standing is applicable in Hong Kong, which in turn has meant that English authorities, including the *National Federation* case, are extensively cited.[59] One notable

50 See further Jhaveri n 2, at pp 4–6.

51 Andrew Li, 'Foreword' in C. Forsyth et al., *Effective Judicial Review: A Cornerstone of Good Governance* (Oxford: Oxford University Press, 2010), xxxiii.

52 Those grounds are torture, persecution and torture, cruel, inhuman, or degrading treatment or punishment. See further Kirsteen Lau, *Non-refoulement Law in Hong Kong* (Hong Kong: Lexis Nexis, 2017).

53 See, e.g., Jason Varuhas, 'The Reformation of English Administrative Law? "Rights", Rhetoric and Reality' (2013) 72(2) *Cambridge Law Journal* 369.

54 The BORO came into effect 7 June 1997; the Human Rights Act on 2 October 2000.

55 *R* v. *Sin Yau-ming* [1992] 1 HKCLR 127 (CA).

56 [1982] AC 617, at p 644.

57 See *Po Fun Chan* v. *Winnie Cheung* [2008] 1 HKLRD 319 (CFA), citing *R* v. *Legal Aid Board, ex p Hughes* (1992) 24 HLR 698 (July 1992).

58 *Right to Inherent Dignity Movement Association* v. *Hong Kong SAR Government* [2008] HKCU 1692 at paras 57–8. See also Chow Wai Hung v. The Hong Kong Government [1983] 2 HKC 537; *Attorney General* v. *Yau Kwok-Lam Johnny* [1988] HKCU 421.

59 See, e.g., *Anderson Asphalt Ltd* v. *Town Planning Board* [2007] 3 HKLRD 18.

feature of this comparative exercise has been to draw from the more liberal elements of English locus standi jurisprudence so as to support the greater participation of individuals, and individuals asserting a public interest, in judicial review in Hong Kong.[60] A liberal approach has been considered necessary given the general lack of public participation in government decision-making in Hong Kong; the use of comparative authority from England, in turn, has facilitated an approach to the standing rules that places greater emphasis on the underlying merits of the application rather than the particular characteristics of the individual applicant. In a similar manner, the growth of public interest litigation prompted questions as to whether responsible individuals or groups should be protected from costs in the event that their application for judicial review was unsuccessful; here the discretionary principles pertaining to the making of 'protective costs orders' from *Corner House Research* have been followed to the letter.[61] A final example can be seen in the receptiveness in Hong Kong to furnish 'advisory declarations' so as to address a hypothetical event in the future, as recognised in the English authority of *Bland*.[62]

Seminal English authority on the grounds of judicial review continues to be cited in Hong Kong courts as convenient shorthand for relevant principles and in supplying the values for the normative growth of the local common law. For example, the courts frequently refer to the '*Padfield* principle' as a measure of legality, particularly in discerning the objectives and principles underpinning a given statutory regime.[63] The mistake of fact doctrine in Hong Kong now follows the test laid down by the English Court of Appeal in *E*.[64] Similarly, the premise that substantive legitimate expectations are underpinned by notions of fairness and the avoidance of abuse of power, as espoused by Lord Woolf in the famous *Coughlan* decision, were cited prominently by the CFA to support the recognition of substantive expectations in Hong Kong.[65] On this basis, the CFA regarded the doctrine of legitimate expectations to be 'an important element in the exercise of the court's inherent supervisory jurisdiction to ensure, first, that statutory powers are exercised lawfully and are not abused and, secondly, that they are exercised so as to result in administrative fairness in relation to both procedural and substantive benefits'.[66] In a later decision, the CFA would note that 'it is now accepted that the foundation of judicial review is the rule of law', citing extensively from English precedent.[67] Use of the rule of law as the organising concept for judicial review was used in order to support the closer review of immigration decisions that impacted the principle of *non-refoulement*, particularly given a historic reluctance on the part of the Hong Kong courts to review discretionary power of the immigration authority.[68]

60 See *Re Tran Quoc Cuong* v. *Khuc The Loc* [1991] 2 HKLR 312 (HC); [2007] 3 HKLRD 18 (CA).

61 *Designing Hong Kong Ltd* v. *Town Planning Board* [2018] HKCFA 16, at [26]–[27] citing (*R (Corner House Research)* v. *Secretary of State for Trade and Industry* [2005] 1 WLR 2600.

62 See, e.g., *Leung* v. *Secretary for Justice* [2006] 4 HKLRD 211, at [27], citing *Airedale N.H.S. Trust* v. *Bland* [1993] AC 789.

63 See, e.g., *Fok Chun Wa* v. *Hospital Authority* [2012] HKEC 471, at [97].

64 *Smart Gain Investment Ltd* v. *Town Planning Board* [2007] HKCU 1817, [93], citing *E* v. *Secretary of State for the Home Department* [2004] QB 1044.

65 *Ng Siu Tung & Others* v. *Director of Immigration* [2002] HKCU 13.

66 *Ng Siu Tung* (n 65) at [91]; Swati Jhaveri, 'Contrasting Responses to the "Coughlan Moment": Legitimate Expectations in Hong Kong and Singapore', in M. Groves and G. Weeks (eds.), *Legitimate Expectations in the Common Law World* (London: Hart, 2017).

67 C v. *Director of Immigration* (2013) 16 HKCFAR 280, at [19]-[20] (Tang PJ), at [77] (Sir Anthony Mason NPJ).

68 C v. *Director of Immigration* (2013) 16 HKCFAR 280, at [19]-[20] (Tang PJ), at [65] (Bokhary PJ), at [83] (Sir Anthony Mason NPJ).

14.4 ASSESSING THE CONTINUED RELEVANCE OF ENGLISH AUTHORITY IN HONG KONG

There are a number of reasons why English precedent remains prominent in Hong Kong judicial review. Many judges and barristers have a close connection to English law, either because they practised during colonial rule, or even because the newer entrants to the legal profession were educated in the UK. Furthermore, senior barristers from England are regularly instructed on an ad hoc basis to appear in complex constitutional cases. The CFA also includes a number of non-permanent judges who in the main have been drawn from the English benches; these judges, in turn, will obviously draw from precedent that they are most familiar.[69] At a more doctrinal level, English precedent on the principles of judicial review continue to be cited as a link to the colonial past; given that Hong Kong case law was replete with references to English precedent, it was natural that any contemporary survey on the development of the law would include the most recent iterations from the English courts on these principles. A final reason why English precedent has retained its relevance in Hong Kong public law, arguably, has been the introduction of the Human Rights Act 1998. Given that English judges now have a mandate to interpret the terms of the European Convention on Human Rights (ECHR), Hong Kong judges are able to look to English jurisprudence in offering a window into the meaning of a set of rights in the ECHR that find analogies in the Basic Law. This is particularly valuable, given that the statutory and common law context in which the English decisions are made more closely resembles the context in which questions arise for decisions in Hong Kong.[70] However, there are instances where English case law no longer retains its relevance in Hong Kong.

This will most notably arise where there are relevant differences in the legal system that allow it to draw upon more specific sources of its own law to support the development of judicial review. Where statutes provide for the special recognition of particular interests, such as the harbour as a site for preservation, the courts, in turn, have been more prepared to depart from the *Wednesbury* principle to a more stringent standard based upon anxious scrutiny or proportionality.[71] That said, even where there are domestic legal provisions, the Hong Kong courts have continued to embrace English authority, most notably in the construction of ouster clauses pursuant to the *Anisminic* principle.[72] The same conclusion could have been arrived at by reading down the ouster clause by invoking Article 35 of the Basic Law (which mandates access to the court); nonetheless, the courts continue to cite *Anisminic* instead of its local law, on the basis that the legislature presumably did not intend to oust unlawful determinations from the courts' supervision.[73]

The extent to which the Hong Kong courts should adhere to the strictures of *Wednesbury* unreasonableness has also attracted judicial and academic scrutiny. In the English context, *Wednesbury* was notably justified by Lord Irvine to be underpinned by constitutional, expertise and democratic imperatives.[74] However, the democratic imperative, which justifies

69 Current overseas non-permanent judges of the CFA comprise a heavy English/British contingent, including Lord Hoffman, Lord Millett, Lord Neuberger, Lord Walker, Lord Collins, Lord Clarke, Lord Phillips and Lord Reed. There are also four judges on the list from Australia (Justice French, Justice Gleeson, Justice Gummow and Justice Spigelman). See further www.hkcfa.hk/en/about/who/judges, accessed 16 March 2019.

70 A Mason, 'The Place of Comparative Law in the Developing Jurisprudence on the Rule of Law and Human Rights in Hong Kong' [2007] 37(2) *Hong Kong Law Journal* 303, at 306.

71 See Johannes Chan, 'A Sliding Scale of Reasonableness in Judicial Review', [2006] *Acta Juridica* 233.

72 Jhaveri n 2, at 214–15.

73 See, e.g., *Gurung Bhakta Bahadur* v. *Director of Immigration* [2001] 3 HKLRD 225.

74 Lord Irvine, 'Judges and Decision Makers: The Theory and Practice of Wednesbury Review' [1996] Public Law 59, 60–1.

limited substantive review, given that discretion is exercised by officials with a democratic origin and supported by the principle of representative government, needs to be applied with reservation in Hong Kong.[75] As the prominent Hong Kong public law barrister Philip Dykes QC has observed, 'the general public seems to have no great confidence in the political process because, of the executive-led system that obtains under the Basic Law'.[76] Similarly, a feature of administration in Hong Kong, more so than in England, is the vesting of decision-making powers in civil servants and appointees, rather than elected representatives.[77] Given this, the criticism of 'unelected judges reviewing the legislative and executive products of elected representatives being "undemocratic" simply does not hold water in Hong Kong'.[78] This has not meant the abandonment of *Wednesbury* in Hong Kong; far from it. There continues to be a great deal of self-restraint on the part of the courts. But there have also been glimpses of the courts mitigating the effects of *Wednesbury*, so as to embrace a sliding scale of review. Three points are worthy of mention here.

First, there has been a greater willingness to review administrative decisions that are premised upon upholding an asserted Hong Kong community standard or standard of morality. Whereas the democratic imperative in the UK might more readily support the official embodying such standards where the decision is scrutinised, in Hong Kong, the courts have looked to see whether the asserted community/moral standard is objectively founded through processes of consultation. Thus, when the Commissioner of Transport denied the issuance of a personal vehicle registration mark for the phrase 'Zestra' (a medical product for female sexual arousal), the Court of First Instance held that he did not explain the objective basis for his view that this mark would cause offence.[79] 'After all', Justice Chu explained, 'Hong Kong is a mature and pluralistic community; [t]here has to be a cogent and objective basis for suggesting that its members will find it offensive to see the public display of a word that may be associated with sexual intercourse.'[80] A similar approach has also been found in relation to the inadequate reasoning of decisions that certain articles are 'obscene' or 'indecent', which again are premised on upholding a community standard.[81]

Second, the Hong Kong courts have also borrowed from another English doctrine to mitigate the harshness of *Wednesbury*: anxious scrutiny. This concept was first applied in the English courts as a means to give expression to rights under the ECHR and common law rights prior to the introduction of the Human Rights Act 1998.[82] In a similar manner, it has also been embraced in Hong Kong to mitigate the effect of dualism where important rights under international human rights law are affected by an administrative decision.[83] Most prominently, the CFA in *Prabakar* observed that the court will subject *non-refoulement* decisions made in furtherance of (the then unincorporated) Article 3(1) of the Convention Against Torture to 'rigorous examination and anxious scrutiny to ensure that the required

75 Jhaveri n 2, at p451.
76 P Dykes, 'The Functions of Judicial Review in Hong Kong' in Forsyth n 51, chapter 26.
77 Dykes n 76, p 416.
78 Dykes n 76, p 416.
79 *Zestra Asia Ltd* v. *Commissioner for Transport* [2007] 4 HKLRD 722, at [45] (Chu J).
80 *Zestra Asia Ltd* n 79.
81 *Oriental Daily Publisher Ltd* v. *Commissioner for Television and Entertainment Licensing Authority* [1998] 4 HKC 505.
82 See Chapter 4 in this volume.
83 See further M. Ramsden and L. Marsh, 'The Right to Work of Refugees in Hong Kong: *MA* v. *Director of Immigration*' (2013) 25(3) *International Journal of Refugee Law* 574.

high standards of fairness have been met'.[84] The courts continued to do so, with torture/refugee claims a significant part of its caseload, with there being a frequent restatement of the need for close scrutiny of these decisions.[85] However, anxious scrutiny has by no means acted as a panacea for the perceived limitations of *Wednesbury* unreasonableness, but it has at least provided a means for judges to assert a more stringent evidentiary standard where particular interests, on an evolving basis, call for it.

Third, the courts have, occasionally, read elements of the proportionality test into the concept of *Wednesbury* unreasonableness so as to support a form of review more akin to that where constitutional rights are engaged. In this way, to borrow a famous phrase from a public international lawyer, *Wednesbury* has not been so much as 'frontally assaulted but cunningly outflanked'.[86] This technique was applied specifically in the immigration context, to the immigration authority's dependent visa policy that limited eligible dependents to those who were spouses of the opposite sex to their sponsor. In short, same-sex marriages or unions were excluded from the ambit of the policy. According to the authority, this policy was necessary to draw a 'bright line' for administrative workability and also because Hong Kong law only recognised opposite-sex marriages.[87] The traditional, deferential, approach to review was adopted by the Court of First Instance: 'given the context of tight immigration control, it is for the Director to decide how best to strike the balance between maintaining that strictness and at the same time allowing certain room to attract skilled and talented foreigners to come to Hong Kong to work'.[88] By contrast, the CFA in *QT* started from a different premise: that the principle of equality is an indicia of *Wednesbury* unreasonableness.[89] In doing so, the court expressly used the proportionality test applicable in constitutional adjudication in the application of the equality principle under rationality review: both proportionality and *Wednesbury* unreasonableness, typically considered to represent opposing points on the spectrum of substantive review, were assimilated.[90]

14.5 BEYOND ENGLISH PRECEDENT

In addition to an indigenous turn in some aspects of judicial review in Hong Kong, the local courts have also looked, more so than it did during British colonial rule, to other epistemic communities in the definition and application of public law norms. The focus then has shifted away from English law as the foundation of common law development in Hong Kong: now, rather, '[i]t is of the greatest importance that the courts of Hong Kong should derive assistance from overseas jurisprudence, particularly from the final appellate courts of *other*

84 *Secretary for Security* v. *Prabakar* (2004) 7 HKCFAR 187, at [45] (Li CJ); M. Ramsden, 'Hong Kong's "High Standard of Fairness" and New Statutory Torture Screening Mechanism' (2013) Public Law 232.

85 A search of the keyword 'anxious scrutiny' on the Westlaw Hong Kong case law database conducted on 16 March 2019 returned 970 results, with the vast majority of them (948) coming after the CFA's landmark *Prabakar* decision in 2004.

86 P Weil, 'Towards Relative Normativity in International Law' (1983) 77 *American Journal of International Law* 413, at 438.

87 See Section 40 of the Marriage Ordinance (Cap. 181). For a general analysis of Hong Kong law on the rights of same sex couples, see M Ramsden and L Marsh, 'Same Sex Marriage in Hong Kong: The Case for a Constitutional Right' (2015) 19(1) *The International Journal of Human Rights* 90.

88 *QT* v. *Director of Immigration* [2016] 2 HKLRD 583 (Court of First Instance), at [37] (Au J).

89 *QT* v. *Director of Immigration* [2018] HKCFA 28 (Court of Final Appeal), at [19]-[22] (The Court).

90 See further M Ramsden, 'Immigration Judicial Review in Hong Kong: The Developing Legal Framework' (2019) 33(2) *Journal of Immigration, Nationality & Asylum Law* 177. As to the salient differences as applied in Hong Kong law, see Jhaveri n 2, chapters 9 and 11.

common law jurisdictions';[91] '[a]fter 1997, the source of common law available to Hong Kong *is no longer limited to English common law*' and is not limited to 'any particular jurisdictions'.[92] This judicial dicta accords with Article 84 of the Basic Law, which mandates the courts to 'refer to precedents of other common law jurisdictions' without any reference to the English law.

Given that the key criterion is whether comparative precedent is persuasive rather than binding based on its source as previously (i.e., English law), this has meant that the Hong Kong courts have also looked to, and sometimes preferred, common law approaches from jurisdictions aside from England. This might be because an English approach has been too conservatively defined or otherwise adopted a course that was not in keeping with other trends in the common law world. This is notably the case in relation to the notion that a legitimate expectation is capable of being generated from a treaty ratification, following the Australian High Court's influential decision in *Minister for Immigration and Ethnic Affairs* v. *Teoh*.[93] By contrast, the English courts have been slow to accept the principle espoused in *Teoh* and still remain tentative in considering its potential extension to the English common law.[94] Even so, the Hong Kong courts have acknowledged the theoretical possibility that treaties are also capable of generating legitimate expectations, although this has not had much of an impact as yet given that the instrument that has been the putative subject-matter of the expectation, namely the ICESCR, has been perceived as too vague to constitute clear and unambiguous 'representations'.[95]

Aside from a conceptual broadening of comparative common law precedents that are potentially relevant in the construction of domestic public law norms, the 'international dimension' of the Basic Law has also made decisions of international and regional tribunals, and the interpretation of international agreements, of increasing relevance.[96] In this regard, the Basic Law makes express reference to a number of international instruments and includes rights that are analogous to those found in the International Covenant on Civil and Political Rights (ICCPR) and, to a lesser extent, the International Covenant on Economic, Social and Cultural Rights (ICESCR). Accordingly, international instruments have been used to add texture to rights under the Basic Law, such as when the CFA read in the importance of family unity (Article 23(1), ICCPR) as part of the 'context' for the interpretation of the right of abode in Article 24 of the Basic Law.[97] Accordingly, the Hong Kong courts have turned to supranational regimes that offer the closest interpretive fit to those rights contained in the Basic Law, including the HRC and the European Court of Human Rights ('ECtHR').[98] Influential 'soft' law instruments such as the *Siracausa Principles* have also been referred to in constitutional interpretation.[99]

Prior to the Handover, there was a reluctance on the Hong Kong courts to draw from international human rights jurisprudence, which itself mirrored the English court's own

91 *China Field Ltd* v. *Building Appeal Tribunal (No 2)* (2009) 12 HKCFAR 342, at [79] (Millett NPJ).
92 *Secretary for Justice* v. *Wong Ho Ming* [2018] HKCA 173, at [56] (Poon JA).
93 (1995) 183 CLR 273 (HCA) (Aus).
94 See, e.g., *Chundawadra* v. *Immigration Appeal Tribunal* [1988] Imm AR 161; *R. (JS)* v. *Secretary of State for Work and Pensions* [2015] UKSC 16, at 246 (Lord Kerr) (noting *Teoh* to be 'controversial').
95 See *Ng Siu Tung* v. *Director of Immigration* (2002) 5 HKCFAR 1, [355] (Bokhary PJ); *Mok Chi Hung* v. *Director of Immigration* [2001] 2 HKLRD 125, at 133C/D to 134A and 135E to H (Cheung J); *Chan To Foon* v. *Director of Immigration* [2001] 3 HKLRD 109, at 131D to 134B (Hartmann J).
96 See also Chapter 18 of this volume on the international dimension in New Zealand administrative law.
97 *Ng Ka Ling* n 1, at 41E-G (per Li CJ).
98 For a comprehensive list of all international sources of law cited in Hong Kong constitutional jurisprudence, see the appendices in Ramsden and Hargreaves n 10.
99 *HKSAR* v. *Ng Kung Siu* [1999] 3 HKLRD 907 (CFA) at p 924.

complicated relationship with the ECHR prior to the enactment of the Human Rights Act. Justice Waung cautioned against using the ECHR on the basis that '[i]n Hong Kong, with our Hong Kong tradition and our special eastern situations, we are not equipped to properly understand, appreciate, analyze or develop this foreign jurisprudence'; moreover, 'unless something overwhelming and compelling can be shown in any particular European authority, the Hong Kong Court should very wisely decline to be seduced by the seemingly inexhaustible literature from the European Court of Human Rights'.[100] This indigenous approach was, moreover, encouraged by senior English judges intent upon upholding the superiority of the common law, not only as a matter of English law but also in the colonial territories via rulings of the Judicial Committee of the Privy Council. In disposing of an appeal from Hong Kong, Lord Woolf thus noted that the common law test of reasonableness was sufficient to determine any inconsistency between a statutory provision and the HKBORO.[101] Now, on the other hand, being free from the constraints of these classic principles of judicial review from the English common law in a post-Handover constitutional settlement, the Hong Kong courts, in turn, have drawn widely from international jurisprudence in the articulation of public law norms.[102]

While the law reports are replete with references to international and comparative precedent, there has been generally little attempt to define the circumstances in which such authority should be taken into account. There has been a recognition why such authorities are useful, particularly given that Hong Kong is a 'relatively small jurisdiction'.[103] But ascertaining *how* comparative authority should be identified, weighed and applied remains under-theorised in Hong Kong. Speaking extrajudicially, Sir Anthony Mason noted the potential risks associated with a comparative approach to rights interpretation, which speaks to a number of the factors that need to be weighed, including (a) political differences between different legal systems which may impact on the intensity and nature of judicial review; (b) differences in the doctrinal foundations of jurisprudence from other jurisdictions; (c) historical, social and cultural differences; (d) differences in the policy behind decisions of courts in other jurisdictions; and (e) practical difficulties in ensuring a comprehensive survey of comparative jurisprudence on a topic.[104] Despite these risks, Mason also noted the advantages of drawing from comparative approaches given that Hong Kong is at an early stage of its constitutional development:

> For a newly established court of final appeal, like the Hong Kong Court of Final Appeal (the CFA), comparative law has an . . . attraction. It is important that the Court's decisions should be seen to conform to internationally accepted judicial standards. Indeed, for Hong Kong there is a double attraction: Hong Kong's reputation as an international financial centre depends upon the integrity and standing of its courts. Further, in the context of Hong Kong's relationship with the central government in Beijing, it is important that the decisions of the Hong Kong courts reflect adherence to the rule of law in accordance with internationally adopted judicial standards. Because . . . Hong Kong possesses a heritage of English common law, resort to comparative law has been a prominent element of Hong Kong's developing public law jurisprudence since the resumption of the exercise of sovereignty by the People's Republic of China on 1 July 1997.[105]

100 *R* v. *Town Planning Board, ex parte Kwan Kong Company* (1995) 5 HKLPR 261, 315 (Waung J).

101 *AG* v. *Lee Kwong Kut* (1993) 3 HKPLR 72. However, see *Ming Pao Newspapers Ltd* v. *AG of Hong Kong* [1996] AC 907 (where the Privy Council, in the last appeal from Hong Kong, did apply proportionality).

102 See, e.g., Albert H. Y. Chen, "International Human Rights Law and Domestic Constitutional Law: Internationalisation of Constitutional Law in Hong Kong" (2009) 4 *NTU L Rev* 237.

103 *Solicitor (24/07)* v. *Law Society of Hong Kong* (2008) 11 HKCFAR 117, at [16] (Li CJ).

104 Mason n 70, at 303–7.

105 Mason n 70, at 302–3.

Still, questions remain about the need to balance indigenous values in Hong Kong with approaches that derive from different socio-political environments. Most references to the interpretation of Basic Law rights tend to speak of the need for a generous and/or purposive approach, with the assistance of internal and external aids for interpretation, without any express reference to the weight to be placed on comparative authority.[106] Yet, there is merit in having a filter or set of factors that define the reception of comparative norms in Hong Kong judicial review. Justice Cheung sought to offer some clarification on this issue recently, noting that rights interpretation is a relevance-driven exercise, which 'may be gauged primarily at two levels, that is, the contemporary need of society; and the relevant international developments'.[107] Precisely how these potentially conflicting interpretive considerations fell to be balanced was not discussed.

There have, in this respect, been a number of instances in which comparative approaches have come into conflict with indigenous readings of the Hong Kong constitution. The easy case is where the text of the Basic Law is narrower than that provided for in international human rights law: thus, it was found that Article 30 of the Basic Law 'does not seek to protect privacy simpliciter', by contrast to Article 17 of the ICCPR being 'drawn more widely'.[108] The courts have also been generally reluctant to use the ICESCR in the interpretation of socio-economic rights under the Basic Law. Instead, the scope of one of the most prominent rights of this nature (the right to social welfare) was defined by the CFA in accordance with the level of entitlement provided during British colonial rule.[109] This reading of the right, while giving it a minimum core, inevitably limits this core to the quite minimal social welfare benefits offered prior to the Handover.[110] To Justice Bokhary, this reading was unsatisfactory; for the right to social welfare 'to have any meaningful content, [it] must encompass basic needs at the very least'.[111] More specifically, this indigenous, historic reading of the right to social welfare might also have been borne out of fear (rightly or wrongly) that the recognition of comparative or international standards such as the ICESCR as interpretive aids would introduce further indeterminacies as to the scope of this right.[112]

Interpretive conflict has arisen where a right is said to engage with sensitive questions in society, such as who is able to marry.[113] To Justice Cheung, in defining the right to marry, it was instructive to look at the 'contemporary societal consensus', particularly 'what relevant changes have occurred in recent years and to what extent the traditional understanding in Hong Kong of the institution of marriage or its essence has been affected by those changes'.[114] This approach would foreclose reference to comparative precedent; despite the persuasiveness of certain European authority on the scope of the right to marry, Justice Cheung noted

106 *Ng Ka Ling* n 1, at 28I–29A (Li CJ); *Comilang Milagros Tecson* v. *Director of Immigration* [2018] 2 HKLRD 534, at [66] (Poon JA).

107 *ZN* v. *Secretary for Justice* [2018] 3 HKLRD 778 (CA), at [76] (Cheung CJHC).

108 *Democratic Party* v. *Secretary for Justice* [2007] 2 HKLRD 807, at 819 (Hartmann J).

109 *Kong Yunming* v. *Director of Social Welfare* (2013) 16 HKCFAR 950.

110 See the limitations of this principle in a decision subsequent to *Kong Yunming*: *Choi King Fung* v. *Hong Kong Housing Authority* [2017] HKEC [44] (Lam J.)

111 *Kong Yunming* n 100, at 171.

112 For this debate, see M. Ramsden, 'Judging Socio-Economic Rights in Hong Kong' (2018) *International Journal of Constitutional Law* 16(2) 447.

113 Culturally relative factors such as 'Chinese-ness' have also been noted by some scholars; see, e.g ., Carol Jones, 'Politics Postponed: Law as a Substitute for Politics in Hong Kong and China', in Kanishka Jayasuriya (ed.), *Law, Capitalism and Power in Asia: The Rule of Law and Legal Institution* (London: Taylor & Francis, 1998), at 66.

114 *W* v. *Registrar of Marriages* [2010] 6 HKC 359, at 195 (Cheung J).

that Hong Kong is not 'a European city or community'; rather it 'must decide the current content of the right to marry in accordance *with our own situation*'.[115] However, the relevance of an indigenous approach based on societal consensus was disavowed by the CFA, where it was noted that the living instrument interpretive approach could not be used for 'denying recognition of minority rights'.[116] Once again, the importance of comparative authority (particularly that from the ECtHR) in shaping the interpretation of rights in Hong Kong was reaffirmed.[117]

Another conflict that has arisen is in defining the weight to be placed on different international regimes, in instances where there are conflicting interpretations, as they come to bear on the interpretation of rights in Hong Kong. The BORO substantively incorporates the ICCPR into Hong Kong law, and the Basic Law provides a constitutional underpinning for the ICCPR. On this basis, it might be thought that the primary port of call for guidance would be the comments and communications of the Human Rights Committee, given its responsibility for interpreting the ICCPR. However, there remains a great deal of fluidity in regime selection. Generally, the Hong Kong courts will look to the ECtHR in the interpretation of Basic Law/BORO rights and even prefer it in the event of a conflict with the approach adopted in the HRC.[118] But there have been some important divergences. Thus, recently in *ZN*, the CFI used authority from the ECtHR to read a human trafficking prohibition into Article 8 of the ICCPR, whereas the CA used the absence of authority from the HRC to establish that Article 8 had not developed to include such a prohibition.[119] There is no principled reason why the Hong Kong courts should be confined to following authority from the HRC to the exclusion of other regimes; this approach is premised on giving effect to Hong Kong's international obligations under the ICCPR. However, given the dualist structure of the Hong Kong legal system, the courts are not bound to give effect to international obligations.[120] Furthermore, the primary interpretive mandate as a matter of municipal constitutional law in Hong Kong is to adopt a generous approach to rights interpretation.[121] On this basis, the better approach, it is submitted, is to treat jurisprudence from the HRC as a comparative authority rather than as a means of identifying international legal obligations. As a comparative authority, it can then be read and balanced alongside other potentially relevant comparative authority in the interpretive exercise, such as that from the ECtHR and English courts.

Aside from the interpretation of rights, there has also been some recognition that Hong Kong's circumstances sometimes justify a different approach when judges evaluate the permissibility of restrictions on rights. It is in relation to this justification test where Christopher Forsyth has noted that the value of comparative approaches breaks down, given that respective jurisdictions will be concerned with their own pragmatic assessments of where the limits of judicial review lie.[122] While the Hong Kong courts have acknowledged the value of comparative interpretations of rights, different considerations potentially apply under the

115 *W* v. *Registrar of Marriages* n 114, at 210.

116 *W* v. *Registrar of Marriages* (2013) 16 HKCFAR 112, at [115] (Ma CJ).

117 *W* v. *Registrar of Marriages* n 116.

118 *Lam Siu Po* v. *Commissioner of Police* (2009) 12 HKCFAR 237, at [90] (Riberio PJ).

119 *ZN* v. *Director of Immigration* [2017] 1 HKLRD 559 (CFI); [2018] HKCA 373(CA).

120 See generally M Ramsden, 'Dualism in the Basic Law: The First 20 Years' (2019) 49(1) *Hong Kong Law Journal* 239.

121 *Ng Ka Ling* n 1, at 28I–29A (Li CJ); *Comilang Milagros Tecson* v. *Director of Immigration* [2018] 2 HKLRD 534, at [66] (Poon JA).

122 See Chapter 3 of this volume.

proportionality test, or as a matter of the rationality assessment where rights are not engaged. This was noted, for example, in the adoption of *Manchester City Council* v. *Pinnock* in Hong Kong, such that the right to a home applies to measures taken to bring to an end public housing tenancies.[123] However, the local pragmatic considerations under proportionality were noted to be different, given, as Au J noted, the 'public rental housing resources circumstances in Hong Kong may well be very different from those in the UK'.[124] Similarly, despite speculative arguments concerning the 'magnet' effect of allowing mandated refugees to work being held to lack a rational basis in the English courts, in Hong Kong such speculation was justified given the territory's putative 'unique' circumstances – highlighting its small geographical size, large population density, high per capita income and ease of access to neighbouring, less-developed, countries.[125]

14.6 CONCLUSION

This chapter has shown, at a high altitude, the continued influence of English principles of judicial review in Hong Kong administrative law. At a macro level, it was shown that the key tenets of the colonial administrative system – including the governmental structure and the common law – remain in place in Hong Kong after the Handover to the PRC. In fact, the system has seen some refinements, although is still lacking implementation of the pledge towards a more democratic and representative government 23 years on since the Handover. Given that 'continuity' remains an important value underpinning the Basic Law, the influence of the British therefore goes beyond judicial review but to other processes and values of government, including an independent civil service and non-judicial controls on power via, for example, administrative tribunals and the ombudsman. However, the continuity principle inevitably has limits, particularly where it runs into Chinese conceptions of sovereignty: it has already been seen how the common law has been modified from that which reflected the pre-Handover position to one reflecting Chinese political interests, in the context of absolute state immunities. It remains to be seen whether, and under what circumstances, the common law will also be modified in the application of public law norms to reflect Chinese sovereignty.

Be that as it may, given that the systems of law and public administration in Hong Kong broadly resemble that in the UK (without, however, the democratic and representative features of the latter), English law has, in turn, continued to exert a powerful influence over the development of public law in Hong Kong, both in defining the content of the principles of judicial review and the meaning of fundamental rights. However, this statement must be read subject to a number of qualifications. It is thus also apparent that, post-Handover, the Hong Kong courts have asserted an independent space from English law, as is indeed incumbent upon them under the Basic Law: it is the 'common law of Hong Kong' which prevails in Hong Kong, not the 'common law of England'. Given that English law would no longer be binding but rather 'persuasive' this, in turn, would enable the Hong Kong courts to develop its common law in light of a broader range of sources, with the overarching principle being the extent to which they 'persuade'; there has, correspondingly, been a broadening of sources relied upon by Hong Kong judges, to include jurisprudence from a variety of common law jurisdictions and international judicial mechanisms. There has also

[123] *Chim Sui Ping* v. *Housing Authority* (HCAL 139/2009, [2012] HKEC 1268), [59] (Au J).

[124] *Chim Sui Ping* v. *Housing Authority* (HCAL 139/2009, [2012] HKEC 1268), [60] (Au J).

[125] Compare *R (on the application of Tekle)* v. *Secretary of State for the Home Department* [2008] EWHC 3064, at [34] (Blake J) with *MA* v. *Director of Immigration* [2011] HKEC 28 (CFI), at [106] (Cheung J).

been a recognition on occasion of English law not reflecting Hong Kong values or circumstances, for example, in relation to housing or immigration, or on sensitive moral issues such as who ought to have the right to marry. However, these are ultimately minor qualifications to the proposition that English law remains pervasive in Hong Kong judicial review. For so long as Hong Kong is able to remain outward looking, and positive about the virtues of a common law system, English law will continue to be a guiding light in a small part of an authoritarian state.

15

Deconstitutionalising and Localising Administrative Law in India

Farrah Ahmed and Swati Jhaveri

15.1 INTRODUCTION

The development of *constitutional* protections against arbitrary action by the executive is at the heart of any account of administrative law in independent India. Article 14 of the Indian Constitution guarantees to everyone in India a fundamental right to equality before the law and equal protection under the law. In *EP Royappa* v. *State of Tamil Nadu*,[1] this right to equality was interpreted to include protections from arbitrary state action. According to the Supreme Court, 'equality and arbitrariness are sworn enemies; one belongs to the rule of law in a republic while the other, to the whim and caprice of an absolute monarch'.[2] It followed, according to the Court, that the constitutional protection of equality included protection against arbitrary state action. A claim of arbitrariness did not require a concrete proof of differential treatment (as is typical in equality cases), just the existence of arbitrary action, as the examples discussed in Section 15.3 will show.

The 'arbitrariness doctrine', as the constitutional protections from arbitrary action have come to be known, has been criticised for lacking content, coherence and legitimacy.[3] Nonetheless, after *Royappa*, anyone wanting to challenge administrative action in India had an avenue in addition to traditional common law grounds: constitutional judicial review by way of writ petition to the High Court or Supreme Court. A wide range of non-statutory bodies and decisions were subject to such review, in common with shifts in the scope of review in other common law jurisdictions.[4]

This chapter argues that constitutional law – and, in particular, the arbitrariness doctrine – has largely eclipsed common law judicial review of administrative action in India. This is a key feature of the localisation of administrative law in India: its absorption into constitutional law. The chapter criticises this development and argues that instead of further constitutionalising administrative law, Indian courts should disaggregate administrative law from constitutional law. It argues that the constitutionalisation of administrative law has diminished the

1 1974 AIR 555.

2 1974 AIR 555 at [85].

3 T Khaitan, 'Equality: Legislative Review under Article 14' and P Jalan and R Rai, 'Review of Administrative Action' in S Choudry, M Khosla and PB Mehta (eds.), *The Oxford Handbook of the Indian Constitution* (Oxford, Oxford University Press, 2016).

4 Following the opening of judicial review to non-statutory bodies exercising public functions, R v. *Panel of Takeovers and Mergers, ex parte Datafin* [1987] 2 WLR 699. In the Indian context, see, for example, *Ajay Hasia* v. *Khalid Mujib Sehravardi* (1981) 1 SCC 722 and *Kumari Shrilekha Vidyarthi* v. *State of Uttar Pradesh and Ors* AIR 1991 SC 537 on the issue of amenability of 'private' decisions and 'private' bodies to review.

efficacy of judicial review as a means of addressing administrative failures. However, rolling back the arbitrariness doctrine would require massive constitutional change and a reversal of a significant body of jurisprudence – both unlikely and disruptive. Thus, this chapter makes several more modest proposals for the reform and redirection of Indian administrative law. We argue that the problems with the arbitrariness doctrine can be remedied without overly disruptive changes to the law, by re-invigorating and emphasising alternative lines of cases.

Section 15.2 offers a brief overview of common law grounds of review of administrative action in India: as will be apparent, these largely track English administrative law given the colonial history of India. Section 15.3 demonstrates how these grounds have been overshadowed by the use of the arbitrariness doctrine extrapolated from Article 14 of the Constitution. It highlights problems with the arbitrariness doctrine. Section 15.4 argues that not only are there issues with the doctrine per se, there are also significant issues with the *dominance* of the constitutional arbitrariness doctrine, to the exclusion of common law administrative action. Unlawful administrative action is not met with the most suitable legal response; administrators are given inadequate guidance on the precise grounds on which their action is unlawful; there is significant doctrinal uncertainty with the arbitrariness doctrine; and litigants have obstacles accessing justice. Section 15.5 offers proposals for how to address these problems by reinvigorating common law judicial review and administrative law more generally. Some proposals are aimed at increasing public awareness of administrative law – an issue that has received too little attention so far. Others are aimed at courts and involve changes to legal doctrine. The hope is that these proposals can provide courts with more avenues for dealing with administrative failures that are particular to India. This mainstreaming of common law administrative law will provide an opportunity for its development and indigenisation.

15.2 COMMON LAW REVIEW OF ADMINISTRATIVE ACTION

Under the common law in India, judicial review of administrative action is available on a cluster of interrelated grounds, largely tracking the grounds of review set out in *Council for Civil Service Unions & Ors* v. *Minister for the Civil Service*.[5] As with other jurisdictions in this volume, the reception of English common law administrative law principles in India is largely due to its colonial legacy. There is little historical data on how these common law principles were initially adopted and then developed as it did.

The grounds of review (most of which will be very familiar to readers of this volume) include acting ultra vires (where administrators exceed their powers); taking irrelevant considerations into account or not taking relevant considerations into account; acting on improper purposes; not giving those affected a fair hearing; deciding when biased or appearing to be biased; unreasonableness; contravening legitimate expectations;[6] and fettering or abrogating discretion. Upendra Baxi's assessments of early Indian administrative law reveal that judges invoked and reviewed administrative actions against practically all these grounds – the content of which more or less mirrored the English law equivalents.[7] Case law on some

5 [1985] AC 374.

6 Farrah Ahmed and Adam Perry, 'The Coherence of the Doctrine of Legitimate Expectations' (2014) 73 *Cambridge Law Journal* 61; Chintan Chandrachud's work suggests that this ground has gained prominence in India only recently: Chintan Chandrachud, 'The (Fictitious) Doctrine of Substantive Legitimate Expectations in India' in Matthew Groves and Greg Weeks (eds.), *Legitimate Expectations in the Common Law World* (Oxford, Hart, 2017).

7 Upendra Baxi, 'Developments in Indian Administrative Law' in AG Noorani (ed.), *Public Law in India* (New Delhi, Vikas Publishing House, 1982); Upendra Baxi, 'Introduction to the Seventh Edition: The Myth and Reality

grounds was sparse, but their availability was not in doubt. It is against this background that the following accounts, of how common law grounds of judicial review have been overshadowed by constitutional law, must be understood.

15.3 CONSTITUTIONALISATION OF ADMINISTRATIVE LAW: THE ARBITRARINESS DOCTRINE

The 'arbitrariness doctrine' (i.e., the Indian constitutional protections from arbitrary action) has been strongly criticised for a number of reasons. A former Supreme Court justice, BN Srikrishna, expressed concerns with its legitimacy and legal basis:

> From *Royappa* it was a merry ride through . . . a host of . . . cases where the Supreme Court freely struck down actions of the other coordinate branches of the Government on the basis that it was not 'reasonable' or was 'arbitrary', a standard of judicial review, *neither contemplated by the framers of the Constitution nor by the plain text of Article 14.*[8]

There is also a fair degree of agreement that cases involving the arbitrariness doctrine provide little guidance on what qualifies as 'arbitrary' state action. One of India's most distinguished senior counsel has characterised judicial pronouncements on the doctrine as 'in the main rhetorical praise of the concept of equality which by itself does not elucidate the legal content of Article 14'.[9] Scholars have expressed similar views on the emptiness or lack of clarity of the doctrine.[10]

The problems with the arbitrariness doctrine can be seen through a well-known case involving allegedly arbitrary executive action. In *Ajay Hasia* v. *Khalid Mujib Sehravardi*,[11] the petitioners argued that a University admissions process was arbitrary because (a) it assigned a very high weight to a candidate's performance during an oral interview, (b) the interview lasted only a few minutes, and (c) the questions at the interview were not targeted at assessing a candidate's suitability but involved inquiring into, for example, the familial background of the candidate.[12]

The Court referred to the admission practices for recruitment to government services, and prior judicial pronouncements on the appropriate weight to be attributed to interviews, and concluded:

> [H]aving regard to the drawbacks and deficiencies in the oral interview test and the conditions prevailing in the country, particularly when there is deterioration in moral values and corruption and nepotism are very much on the increase, allocation of a high percentage of marks for the oral interview as compared to the marks allocated for the written test, cannot be accepted by the Court as free from the vice of arbitrariness.[13]

of the Indian Administrative Law' in IP Massey (ed.), *Administrative Law*, 8th ed. (Lucknow, Eastern Book Company, 2012).

8 BN Srikrishna, 'Skinning a Cat' (2005) 8 SCC J-3, J-10 (emphasis added).

9 TR Andhyarujina, 'The Evolution of Due Process of Law by the Supreme Court' in BN Kirpal et al. (eds.), *Supreme but Not Infallible: Essays in Honour of the Supreme Court of India* (New Delhi, Oxford University Press, 2000) 206.

10 Khaitan (n 3) 712; Jalan and Rai (n 3).

11 *Ajay Hasia* (n 4).

12 *Ajay Hasia* (n 4) [18].

13 *Ajay Hasia* (n 4) [19].

Once the Court accepted that the test lasted two to three minutes and comprised irrelevant questions, it simply concluded that 'the oral interview test must be held to be vitiated and the selection made on the basis of such test must be held to be arbitrary'.[14]

The *first* problem with the arbitrariness doctrine that *Ajay Hasia* demonstrates is the lack of judicial guidance about what arbitrariness is and how it is to be avoided. While the Court was concerned to offer guidance to the administrators in this particular case (suggesting that oral interviews should not be weighted at more than 15 per cent),[15] it offered no test or criteria for identifying arbitrary action. The explanation for why the respondents' actions were arbitrary was very closely tied to the facts.

This was acknowledged by the Supreme Court in *Kumari Shrilekha Vidyarthi* v. *State of Uttar Pradesh & Ors*: 'The meaning and true import of arbitrariness is *more easily visualized than precisely stated or defined*. The question, whether an impugned act is arbitrary or not, is ultimately to be answered on the facts and in the circumstances of a given case.'[16] However, *Ajay Hasia* also demonstrates a *second* and related problem: the relationship it has with the common law grounds of review. In many Article 14 cases, these grounds are not mentioned at all even though they are highly relevant.[17] The matter is instead decided on Article 14, without any explicit connection being made between Article 14 jurisprudence and common law grounds of review. For example, the interview questions targeting the familial background of a candidate could have been challenged on the grounds that they amounted to irrelevant considerations. *Ajay Hasia* is hardly an outlier in this respect.[18] In *Y Srinivasa Rao* v. *J Veeraiah*,[19] the applicant challenged the decision of the petitioner to fill civil service vacancies through an advertisement that preferred candidates experienced in the relevant field of work and stated that where there were candidates with equal qualifications and experience, preference would be given to unemployed educated persons, women and disabled persons. In a sparsely reasoned judgment, the court concluded that this amounted to 'gross arbitrariness'.[20] Again, an argument tethered to the relevance of considerations would have articulated much better the foundations on which the decision was considered 'arbitrary'.

This approach to judicial review of administrative action has led traditional administrative law grounds of review to be heavily sidelined, so much so that many scholars conclude (incorrectly) that some common law grounds are no longer available except under Article 14. For example, Prateek Jalan and Ritin Rai, writing in *The Oxford Handbook of the Indian Constitution*, assert that '[j]udicial review of the 'reasonableness' of all government action – whether administrative or legislative – is rooted in Article 14 of the Constitution'.[21] Tarunabh Khaitan, in the same Handbook, takes the position that 'a challenge to unreasonable State action, even if it is only an administrative action, can only be made by following the procedure prescribed for a fundamental rights claim – that is, by filing a writ in a

14 *Ajay Hasia* (n 4) [20].

15 *Ajay Hasia* (n 4) [18].

16 AIR 1991 SC 537 at para [36]. Somewhat ironically, this is a case where the Supreme Court does more than usual by way of guidance.

17 As we indicate later in Section 15.4.

18 See discussion on *Zenit Mataplast P. Ltd* v. *State of Maharashtra and Ors* (2009) 10 SCC 388 in the following section.

19 AIR 1993 SC 929

20 A glance at other jurisdictions shows how these cases would be dealt with on the grounds that this kind of preference was made on the basis of 'irrelevant considerations' or *Wednesbury* irrationality. See, for example, *Ramalingam Ravinthran* v. *Attorney-General* [2012] 2 SLR 49 in the Singapore context. We bring this out further in Section 15.3.

21 Jalan and Rai (n 3) 433.

constitutional court'.[22] Khaitan's comment points to why the sidelining of administrative law review is a problem. By requiring applicants to use constitutional law to challenge administrative action, the doctrine forces them to approach the High Court and/or Supreme Court. This is highly problematic when viewed from the perspective of access of justice, as will be further discussed in the following section. These constitutional courts are more expensive and are overburdened with cases forcing more applicants to start there exacerbates India's problems with massive delays in litigation.

This seems unnecessary when judicial review on common law grounds – including unreasonableness – remain available in Indian courts. In *Union of India & Anor* v. *Ganayutham*,[23] the applicant had been the subject of disciplinary action arising from charges of misconduct that had led to a loss of revenue for the government. The penalties would involve losing half of his pension and gratuity after his retirement. He challenged the decision before the Central Administrative Tribunal which found in his favour, holding that the withdrawal of a gratuity was not permitted under the Pension Rules 1972 and that the punishment was, in any event, too severe. The respondents sought to challenge the decision of the Tribunal. The Court discussed the *Wednesbury* test, and debates about proportionality in English courts, in great detail. Making no reference to Article 14, it laid out the position in India, implying that it was the same as in England and Wales:

> To judge the validity of any administrative order or statutory discretion, normally the Wednesbury test is to be applied to find out if the decision was illegal or suffered from procedural improprieties or was one which no sensible decision-maker could, on the material before him and within the framework of the law, have arrived at. The Court would consider whether relevant matters had not been taken into account or whether irrelevant matters had been taken into account or whether the action was not bona fide. The Court would also consider whether the decision was absurd or perverse. The Court would not however go into the correctness of the choice made by the administrator amongst the various alternatives open to him. Nor could the Court substitute its decision to that of the administrator. This is the Wednesbury test.[24]

In reviewing the Tribunal's decision, the court held that it should be set aside. The Tribunal had unduly interfered with the finding of the respondents in the absence of any illegality, procedural impropriety or *Wednesbury* irrationality (the Tribunal could not show that the original disciplinary decision was one 'which no sensible person who weighed the pros and cons could have arrived at nor is there a finding based on material, that the punishment is outrageous or in defiance of logic'). Similarly, in *Chairman, All India Railway Recruitment Board* v. *K Shyam Kumar*,[25] having discussed the place of both the *Wednesbury* and proportionality tests in English common law, the Court applied both these tests, making no reference at all to Article 14 (although the case was at least partly argued on Article 14 grounds).[26]

Courts have also reviewed administrative action against common law rules relating to natural justice without reference to Article 14. In *State of UP* v. *Vijay Kumar Tripathi*, the Court said, '[t]he normal rule enunciated by this Court is that wherever it is necessary to ensure against the failure of justice, principles of natural justice must be read into a

22 Khaitan (n 3) 716.
23 Khaitan (n 3) 716.
24 Khaitan (n 3) at para [28].
25 *Chairman, All India Railway Recruitment Board* v. *K Shyam Kumar* (2010) 6 SCC 614.
26 Chairman (n 25) at para [21]–[40].

provision'.[27] Thus, even after the Supreme Court held that a breach of natural justice is arbitrary for the purpose of Article 14,[28] it continued to review administrative action against common law rules relating to natural justice *without* reference to Article 14.[29] And even where the Court made its decision on Article 14 grounds, there are cases where it explicitly acknowledged that the common law offered overlapping grounds for judicial review of administrative action that were not subsumed or eclipsed by Article 14. In *Maneka Gandhi* v. *Union of India*, even as the judges appealed to Articles 14 and 19 as the foundation of judicial review, much of the judgments relied on common law rules, in addition to the constitutional grounds under Article 14. For example, Justice Beg noted the following on natural justice:

> It is well established that even when there is no specific provision in a statute or rules made thereunder for showing case against action proposed to be taken against an individual, which affects the right of that individual the duty to give reasonable opportunity to be heard will be implied from the nature of the function to be performed by the authority which has the power to take punitive or damaging action.[30]

Despite the availability of review on common law grounds, it has been so overshadowed by Article 14 that it is overlooked even by careful commentators[31] (and, it seems, often by courts and counsel as well). A review of the arbitrariness doctrine thus offers a particularly clear picture of how Indian constitutional law has largely eclipsed Indian administrative law.

15.4 THE DOMINANCE OF THE ARBITRARINESS DOCTRINE AND ECLIPSE OF ADMINISTRATIVE LAW

The eclipse of administrative law leads to cases being decided on grounds which are not best suited to their adjudication, to administrators receiving insufficient guidance on their legal duties, to doctrinal uncertainty, conceptual confusion and inadequate access to justice.

15.4.1 *Suitability*

To state what should be obvious but is underappreciated, when judges overlook administrative law in cases involving unlawful administrative action, they might be overlooking the legal norms that are best-suited to respond to that particular action. For example, the Supreme Court case of *Maharashtra Ekta Hawkers Union* was decided pursuant to Article 19(1)(g) of the Constitution.[32] This provision protects the rights of citizens to practice any profession or carry on any occupation, trade or business. This is despite the fact that the Court acknowledged the problems with administrative governance that led to the issues in that case. The Courts specifically observed that 'the problem [of the regulation of street vendors] has [aggravated because of lackadaisical attitude of the administration at various levels [*sic*]'.[33]

27 *State of UP* v. *Vijay Kumar Tripathi* AIR 1995 SC 1130 [7]. See also *AK Kraipak* v. *Union of India* AIR 1970 SC 150, which is an important example of this point.
28 *Union of India* v. *Tulsiram* (1985) Sup 2 SCR 382, 471, 472
29 See also *State of UP* (n 27).
30 See also *RD Shetty* v. *International Airport Authority of India* (1979) 3 SCC 489 on legitimate expectations and promissory estoppel.
31 See, for example, Jalan and Rai (n 3) 434; Khaitan (n 3) 716.
32 *Maharashtra Ekta Hawkers Union* v. *Municipal Corporation, Greater Mumbai* (2014) 1 SCC 490.
33 *Maharashtra Ekta Hawkers Union* (n 32) [5].

While there was a policy that purported to regulate street vendors – the national Policy on Urban Street Vendors 2009[34] – it was clearly not effective.[35]

Administrative law norms have developed to respond to precisely these kinds of problems. Judges over the years, and across several common law jurisdictions, have developed resources – norms, tests, analogies and remedies – that could aid judges in reasoning, and in crafting appropriate remedies. Ultimately, the Court directed that the 2009 policy should be implemented, giving direction to facilitate its implementation.[36] In doing so, the Court could have drawn on administrative law principles – both the principle of consistency and the doctrine of legitimate expectations – and directed administrators to apply policies that they have put in place. By ignoring administrative law, and focusing instead on Article 19(1)(g) of the Constitution, the Court lost access to enormously relevant intellectual resources which could have guided their decision-making.

15.4.2 *Lack of Guidance to Administrators*

The *Ajay Hasia*[37] case discussed earlier demonstrates the lack of judicial guidance about what arbitrariness is and how it is to be avoided. While the Court was concerned to offer guidance to the administrators in that particular case (suggesting that oral interviews should not be weighted at more than 15 per cent),[38] it offered no test or criteria for identifying arbitrary action or for why it had set the weighting for interviews at 15 per cent. The explanation for why the respondents' actions were arbitrary was not generalisable but closely tied to the facts. In *Maharashtra Ekta Hawkers Union*, discussed earlier, while directing that the policy should be implemented,[39] the Court did not say that administrators should *generally* follow the policies that they have set for themselves because of the principle of consistency[40] or legitimate expectations.[41]

The sidelining of administrative law thus appears to be coupled with a lack of judicial guidance to administrators about what they did wrong – what generalisable norm they contravened and what they can do to avoid unlawful action in the future.

15.4.3 *Broader Doctrinal Uncertainty*

The eclipse of administrative law by constitutional law also makes it susceptible to the issues of doctrinal incoherence that face Indian law more generally. In a recent article, Raeesa Vakil documents the higher judiciary's failure to clearly establish the bounds of judicial power in reviewing administrative action or to identify the normative underpinning of administrative law doctrines.[42] Indian high courts routinely review administrative actions based on constitutional provisions of questionable relevance to the facts at hand. This, in turn, means that the scope of constitutional rights becomes highly uncertain. Examples of this are apparent in a

34 *Maharashtra Ekta Hawkers Union* (n 32) [12].
35 *Maharashtra Ekta Hawkers Union* (n 32) [20]–[21].
36 *Maharashtra Ekta Hawkers Union* (n 32) [20]–[21].
37 *Ajay Hasia* (n 4).
38 *Ajay Hasia* (n 4) [19].
39 *Maharashtra Ekta Hawkers Union* (n 32) [15].
40 See generally Richard Clayton, 'Legitimate Expectations, Policy, and the Principle of Consistency' (2003) 62 *Cambridge Law Journal* 93.
41 See generally MP Jain and SN Jain, *Principles of Administrative Law*, 6th ed. (New Delhi, Lexis Nexis, 2013) 279.
42 Raeesa Vakil, 'Indian Administrative Law and the Challenges of the Regulatory State' in D Kapur and M Khosla (eds.), *Regulation in India: Design, Capacity, Performance* (Oxford, Hart 2019) 33–58.

range of adjudicative contexts, including the unnecessary articulation of unenumerated rights. For example, in the case of *Mohini Jain* v. *State of Karnataka*,[43] the Supreme Court declared ultra vires a decision by the state government to allow medical schools to collect exorbitant tuition fees from students who were not admitted pursuant to a government quota. The Supreme Court also made some (arguably unnecessary) findings against the fee structure on the basis that it was an unjustifiable restriction on the constitutional right to education. This right was enumerated from Article 21 of the Constitution, which protects the life and liberty of citizens. The judicial pronouncements in *Mohini Jain*, besides being unnecessary to the order given in that case, created confusion about the scope of a newly-anointed constitutional right to education.[44]

15.4.4 *Conceptual Confusion*

Compounding these concerns about doctrinal uncertainty, the conceptual basis of administrative law is destabilised when it is eclipsed by constitutional law. It is true that the distinction, and the significance of the distinction, between constitutional law and administrative law are often questioned. Scholars across jurisdictions now talk of the blurring of lines between constitutional and administrative law.[45] But there are important distinctions between the two bodies of law. Drawing on the widely endorsed idea that administrators are delegates, it has been demonstrated that common law grounds of review reflect the duties that administrators have by virtue of their status as delegates.[46] Refining John Gardner's distinction between constitutional and administrative law,[47] constitutional law is the body of law whose core function is to regulate constitutional institutions qua constitutional institutions; administrative law is the body of law whose core function is to regulate administrative institutions qua administrative institutions where

(a) constitutional institutions are state institutions whose powers are either inherent or practically irrevocable by the delegating institutions and
(b) administrative institutions are state institutions whose powers are practically revocable by the delegating constitutional institutions.

Insofar as there is a conceptual distinction between these two bodies of law, the eclipse of the administrative law creates conceptual, and in turn doctrinal, confusion.

15.4.5 *Access to Justice*

When constitutional law eclipses administrative law, nudging applicants to use constitutional law to challenge administrative action, this has significant implications for access to justice.

43 AIR 1992 SC 1858

44 See *Unni Krishnan* v. *State of Andhra Pradesh* AIR 1993 SC 2178

45 See John Gardner, 'Can There Be a Written Constitution?' in Leslie Green and Brian Leitner (eds.) *Oxford Studies in Philosophy of Law* (Oxford, Oxford University Press, 2011), Oxford Studies in Philosophy of Law, chapter 5, and Farrah Ahmed, *Showcase–New Directions in Administrative Law Research: The Distinction between Constitutional and Administrative Law*, Int'l J. Const. L. Blog, 24 September 2019, at www.iconnectblog.com/2019/09/showcase-new-directions-in-administrative-law-research-the-distinction-between-constitutional-and-administrative-law/.

46 Farrah Ahmed, 'The Delegation Theory of Judicial Review' (Public Law Conference, Melbourne, 13 July 2018) (on file).

47 John Gardner, *Law as a Leap of Faith: Essays on Law in General* (Oxford, Oxford University Press, 2012) chapter 4.

Challenges based on breaches of Fundamental Rights proceed by way of writ petition to the High Courts or Supreme Courts. These constitutional courts are more expensive and difficult to access. Forcing more applicants to start their legal processes at that high level exacerbates India's massive problems with delays in litigation. The sidelining of administrative law also contributes to a widespread dichotomic view of the Indian judiciary. The 'higher judiciary is often viewed as the panacea for the various endemic social and political problems that plague India'.[48] The lower judiciary, meanwhile, is 'purely pathological – inefficient, corrupt'.[49] This view naturally leads to very low confidence in the lower judiciary amongst both the profession and the general public.[50] Lower courts are, on this view, 'hurdles to get over, or avoid altogether (for example, through the writ jurisdiction), rather than forums from which final resolution of disputes is expected'.[51] No doubt there are genuine concerns about the quality of adjudication in the lower courts; the view is not pure caricature. There is also reason to suspect that these problems *caused* administrative law to be sidelined in favour of constitutional law to begin with. But the path we are on leads to an unmanageably top-heavy case load. The need for (better functioning) lower courts to bear more of that load – including cases involving administrative wrongs – is clear.

15.5 REDIRECTING INDIGENISATION: REINVIGORATING ADMINISTRATIVE LAW

This section of the chapter offers proposals for how to address these problems and redirect the indigenisation of the common law in India by reinvigorating administrative law. Some proposals are aimed at increasing public awareness of administrative law, an issue that has received too little attention so far. Others are aimed at courts and involve changes to legal doctrine.

15.5.1 *The Public*

Sometimes an aspect of the law or legal process finds a place in the public imagination. Anuj Bhuwania makes a point about broad and deep public consciousness of public interest litigation through illustrations of its place in mainstream culture (including, interestingly, the local cinematic scene and widely read newspapers).[52] While we know of no studies on the subject, there is reason to suspect that administrative law is at the other end of the spectrum of public consciousness. If higher court case law is any guide, litigants, the profession and judiciary pay it little attention; it seems even more unlikely to have made an impression on the public.

The status quo in India – the dominance of constitutional law – is such that this does not currently seem unnatural.[53] Administrative law, it may seem, is like other 'technical and

[48] Anuj Bhuwania, *Courting the People: Public Interest Litigation Post-Emergency India* (Cambridge, Cambridge University Press, 2017) 3.
[49] Bhuwania (n 48) 3.
[50] Robert Moog, 'The Significance of Lower Courts in the Judicial Process' in E Veena Das (ed.), *The Oxford India Companion to Sociology and Social Anthropology* (New Delhi, Oxford University Press, 2003) 1400.
[51] Moog (n 50) 1400.
[52] Bhuwania (n 48) 1, 5–6.
[53] See Rohit De, *A People's Constitution: Law and Everyday Life in the Indian Republic* (Princeton, Princeton University Press, 2019), which explores how the Constitution captured the public imagination in India during the transition from colonial rule to a republic.

complex' areas of law. Administrative law cannot be understood by the layperson; it is of no interest to her; no good will come of her non-specialist involvement in the field in any case. What follows will challenge these assumptions.

The problem of poor administration is relevant to the lives of ordinary Indians. The overwhelming popularity of the 2011 Indian anti-corruption movement associated with Anna Hazare suggests that ordinary Indians are aware of the importance of good administration.[54] Administrative law, which regulates administrators at every level, including the administrators which ordinary people are highly likely to encounter, is therefore at least potentially of interest to the general public.

But even if the public has an interest in administrative law, do they have the capacity to understand it? Perhaps not the finer details. But much of administrative law involves holding administrators to the standards of behaviour that would be intuitive to most citizens.[55] Administrators must act fairly; they must not be biased; they must hear from those affected before making a decision; they must give reasons for their decisions; they must honour their promises; they must consistently follow the policies they set for themselves; they must not do anything which they lack the legal power to do. The basic norms of administrative law can be easily communicated to someone without legal training. They should be easy to understand as they track so closely how a good administrator ought to act (morally speaking).

Even if the public *can* understand basic administrative law, and they are interested in doing so, why should they? First, it is important that the terms of the relationship between the administrators and those they govern is understood by all involved. If basic administrative law norms were widely-understood, this would fundamentally alter everyday interactions between administrators and citizens. The former would moderate their behaviour, and the latter would know when administrative behaviour crosses the line. Second, a basic understanding of administrative law would bolster forces for change, both large-scale ones as well as individual action through complaint mechanisms.[56] Greater public awareness of administrative law, when combined with the strategies that the Right to Information Act 2005 and the availability of PIL afford, could effect significant change. The latter initiatives are aimed at making government and the work of governance generally more accessible and understandable to the public at large.

15.5.2 *Courts and Counsel*

Reinvigorating administrative law also requires changes to doctrine, and to professional and judicial practice. At the most fundamental level, counsel and judges ought to be alert to administrative law issues in any given case. There are three broad strategies that would help reinvigorate administrative law.

15.5.2.1 Constitutional Avoidance in Favour of Administrative Law

Where a matter can be decided on both constitutional and non-constitutional grounds, constitutional avoidance refers to the practice of making the decision on non-constitutional

[54] See N Menon and A Nigam, 'Anti-corruption Movement and the Left' (2011 September 10) 46 *Economic and Political Weekly* 37, 16–18.

[55] See, for example, Farrah Ahmed and Adam Perry, 'Standing and Civic Virtue' (2018) 134 *Law Quarterly Review* 239.

[56] See, for example, initiatives like *I Paid a Bribe*: Janaagraha Centre for Citizenship and Democracy, www.ipaidabribe.com.

grounds. Constitutional avoidance has been defended on the basis that it leads to stronger rights protection,[57] because it allows the government greater flexibility,[58] and as a form of decisional minimalism, 'saying no more than necessary to justify an outcome, and leaving as much as possible undecided'.[59] There are dangers to constitutional avoidance, though. Indian administrative law already has been criticised as being overly deferential, relative to constitutional law.[60] Constitutional avoidance may result in even more deferential review of administrative action (though this chapter suggests strengthening administrative law to mitigate this concern). Many remedies are only available under constitutional law (though arguments for stronger remedies to be available for administrative law breaches have been argued elsewhere).[61] The expressive aspects of the Indian Constitution are also such that citizens may feel hard done by if their constitutional claim is not decided: even if administrative law affords the same or better remedy. Clearly, though, while not always justifiable or feasible, constitutional avoidance in favour of administrative law would do much to reverse the eclipse of administrative law. If, and when, constitutional avoidance is not justified, constitutional law should develop to incorporate or explicitly reference administrative law norms, as the next section discusses.

We would like to see the Supreme Court emphasise the availability of common law grounds of review in more cases as a signal to the lower courts that they too can respond to unlawful administrative action using these grounds – they do not depend on having the writ jurisdiction that only the Indian High Court and Supreme Court possess. This, coupled with the proposal we make in the following section– to understand arbitrariness in terms of a breach of particular common law grounds –will invigorate common law grounds of review in public law litigation in two ways. First, through the recognition of the common law as an alternative way of pleading public law cases; and second, the diversion of these cases from constitutional to administrative law litigation. If more Supreme Court judgments recognised and emphasised the availability of common law grounds of review for administrative action, this would provide counsel and lower courts with a new stream of precedent to rely on in pleading, arguing and deciding public law cases. This would have significant consequences from the perspective of access to justice. Constitutional litigation is at risk of being delayed (if not stunted) by an overcrowded docket. Allowing judicial review of administrative action to be commenced in courts other than the High Court and Supreme Court will be an important diversion of cases from this docket.

15.5.2.2 Coupling the Arbitrariness Doctrine and Administrative Law

Taking the continued existence of the arbitrariness doctrine for granted, we argue that arbitrariness in Article 14 should be understood as a term of art which refers to the common law grounds of review in administrative law.[62] The arbitrariness doctrine has been criticised,

57 F Ahmed and T Khaitan, 'Constitutional Avoidance in Social Rights Adjudication' 35(3) *Oxford Journal of Legal Studies* 607–25.

58 Jeff King, *Judging Social Rights* (Cambridge, Cambridge University Press, 2012) chapter 9.

59 Cass R Sunstein, 'Foreword: Leaving Things Undecided' (1996) 110 *Harvard Law Review* 4, 6; Erin F Delaney, 'Analyzing Avoidance: Judicial Strategy in Comparative Perspective' 66 *Duke L.J.* 1 (2016).

60 Baxi, 'Developments in Indian Administrative Law' (n 7); Baxi, 'Introduction' (n 7).

61 Ahmed and Khaitan (n 57); Po Jen Yap, 'New Democracies and Novel Remedies', 2017 Pub. L. 30.

62 We anticipate concerns with the use 'arbitrariness' as a framing device for review under Article 14. There is a concern that, as a term of art, it carries certain baggage about what it *can* mean and what courts can review. However, this section proceeds on the basis that it would be disruptive of existing jurisprudence to immediately

we have said, for lacking legitimacy. We take no issue with the criticism that the doctrine is not supported by the constitutional text. The arbitrariness doctrine may well be legally unjustified. If the doctrine were rolled back, this might well address many of the problems identified in the previous section.

We proceed though in a pragmatic vein. Rolling back the doctrine would require a significant reversal of existing constitutional jurisprudence. While the arbitrariness doctrine – and the problems it causes – persist, we make a very modest reform proposal that would address those problems.

One of those problems we discussed was that the doctrine offers little guidance to administrators on what constitutes arbitrary action, and how they ought to avoid it. This proposal gives content to the arbitrariness doctrine – and guidance to administrators – drawn from a wealth of common law jurisprudence. Another merit of drawing on common law rules in this way is that we are not exacerbating the arbitrariness doctrine's legitimacy deficit. On our proposed understanding of the doctrine, it would not require any more of administrators than is already required of them by the common law.

Our proposal is particularly modest because there are cases where the Supreme Court has already done what we are proposing. Our call is for the Supreme Court to consistently adopt the approach in these cases, over their approach in cases like *Ajay Hasia*. A number of important Supreme Court cases that take administrative law grounds of review – particularly *Wednesbury* unreasonableness – as a guide to arbitrariness illustrate our preferred approach. Justice Bhagwati, the author of key judgments laying out the arbitrariness doctrine, recognised its potential for congruence with common law rules. In the case of *Kasturilal* v. *State of J&K*, Justice Bhagwati recognised that: 'The government action must not be arbitrary or capricious. . . . This rule was enunciated by the Court as a rule of administrative law and it was also validated by the Court as an emanation flowing directly from the doctrine of equality embodied in Article 14.'[63]

In *Tata Cellular* v. *Union of India*,[64] almost the entire judgment of Mohan J (writing for a three-judge bench), supposedly decided on Article 14 grounds, is taken up by a detailed discussion of the doctrines of English administrative law as a foundation for review. The judgement takes for granted that arbitrariness is assessed by the *Wednesbury* test. In *New Horizons Ltd* v. *Union of India*[65] the Court's test for whether the decision to eliminate the applicant from consideration for a tender was 'arbitrary' through the common law review ground relating to relevance of considerations. In *Om Kumar* v. *Union of India in Delhi Development Authority*,[66] the applicants were challenging disciplinary penalties imposed on them (as officers of the Delhi Development Authority) on the basis that they were not proportionate to the gravity of their misconduct. Nowhere has the Court been clearer about the connection between the Article 14 arbitrariness doctrine and common law grounds of review. The Court emphasised that 'while judging whether the administrative action is "arbitrary" under Article 14 . . . this Court has confined itself to a *Wednesbury* review always'.[67]

abandon it as a device for review. Over time, it is hoped that it would be replaced, but the journey to that position will need to be incremental, starting with 'arbitrariness'.

63 *Kasturi Lal Lakshmi Reddy* v. *State of Jammu and Kashmir* AIR 1980 SC 1992.

64 *Tata Cellular* v. *Union of India* AIR 1996 SC 11 at [86]–[100]. Subsequently applied in *New Horizons Ltd* v. *Union of India* AIR 1994 Del. 126 (utilising 'relevant considerations' as the framing device for a consideration of whether the decision to eliminate the applicant from consideration for a tender was 'arbitrary').

65 AIR 1994 Del. 126.

66 2000 SCC 1993.

67 2000 SCC 1993 at [17].

This line of cases contrast with cases like *Ajay Hasia*, where no criteria for assessing arbitrariness are offered. But they also contrast with cases where it appears that common law grounds for judicial review were *implicitly*, but only implicitly, the basis for the finding of arbitrariness. For example, in the case of *Kumari Shrilekha Vidyarthi* v. *State of Uttar Pradesh & Ors*,[68] the applicants challenged their abrupt termination as Government counsel by the Government of the State. The applicants had not been provided with reasons for the termination. The Court held first that the absence of reasons had the effect of shifting the burden from the applicant (in establishing a violation of Article 14) to the respondent (to justify its actions as reasonable). Second, it held that the absence of reasons implied the acts of the state in dismissing Government counsel were 'uninformed by reason'. These findings were crucial to the court's conclusion that the state action was arbitrary under Article 14. However, it made no reference to the wealth of precedent about the (increasingly recognised) duty to give reasons in administrative law[69] or to Wednesbury unreasonableness.[70]

The case of *Zenit Mataplast* exemplifies how the failure to explicitly base a ruling on arbitrariness on common law grounds of review can weaken the court's reasoning. In this case, the Supreme Court found that a state Corporation acted arbitrarily by rejecting the petitioner's application for the grant of an allotment of land. In a key part of its very brief reasoning on this issue, the Court says: 'the facts mentioned hereinabove clearly establish that the Corporation and the Government proceeded in haste while considering the application of respondent No. 4 which [was] *tantamount* to *arbitrariness, thus violative* of the mandate of Article 14 of the Constitution' (emphasis added).

The Court appears to be suggesting that a hasty (or quick) decision is necessarily an arbitrary one. But a more charitable reading of the judgment would note the court's remark that 'no reason was assigned for rejecting' the application. It may well be that the Court's assessment of the arbitrariness of the decision was really based on the absence of reasons and consequent judgements about its unreasonableness. If the Court had appealed to common law grounds of review, its somewhat puzzling judgment would have been better justified, and far better placed to offer guidance to administrators and lower courts on the nature of arbitrariness in executive action.

This is why we argue that the Supreme Court ought to abandon both its approach in *Ajay Hasia*, where arbitrariness was found without providing any criteria by which it was assessed, as well as its approach in *Kumari Shrilekha Vidyarthi* and *Zenit Metaplast*, where arbitrariness was *implicitly* based on common law grounds. An explicit approach like that taken in *Tata Cellular* and *Om Kumar* is much better suited to giving the arbitrariness doctrine coherence, consistency and effectiveness in providing guidance to administrators. This would largely address the problem we identified with the arbitrariness doctrine relating to the lack of clear content or guidance for the content of arbitrariness.

In addition to providing content and better guidance, reviewing the administrative action using common law grounds addresses the underlying problems in these cases. For example,

68 1991 AIR 537. The court held that despite being an 'employment' decision, this was not a purely contractual matter as there was a public element attached to the post of Government counsel (carrying out the legal work of government).

69 Makoto Hong Chung, 'Shaping a Common Law Duty to Give Reasons in Singapore: Of Fairness, Regulatory Paradoxes and Proportionate Remedies' (2016) 28 *SAcLJ* 24 for a comparative discussion on the common law position on the existence of a duty to give reasons.

70 See also *East Coast Railway and Anor* v. *Mahadev Appa Rao and Ors* 2010 AIR SCC 4210 at [21] for a similar decision made on the absence of reasons for modifying the selection process for recruiting typists for the respondent railway.

in *Ajay Hasia* and *New Horizons*, there is a real concern that the criteria or considerations being used for decision-making are irrelevant. In the case of *Kumari Shrilekha*, there is, at best, a failure to provide reasons (a ground of review with increasing prominence) and, at worst, an absence of demonstrable reasons, which would satisfy the original high threshold of *Wednesbury* review.

We do not suggest that common law grounds, as they are, are perfectly crafted to respond to the administrative actions being challenged in Article 14 cases. As contributions to this volume indicate, classical grounds of judicial review (illegality, irrationality and procedural impropriety) are undergoing significant change in the English context and the broader common law world, in ways that extend the reach of these grounds.[71] There is both need and opportunity for the Indian courts to develop common law grounds as they currently exist in Indian administrative law.[72]

15.5.2.3 Strengthening Administrative Law

Upendra Baxi has argued that contemporary Indian administrative law is too deferential to the executive.[73] Courts apply administrative law doctrines, he argues, in a way that does not rigorously hold administrators to account. If we take this worry seriously, we might wonder whether populating constitutional law with administrative law norms, is really well-advised. Some may argue that there is a reason for administrative law to give way even more to constitutional law. Indian courts, critics of our proposed approach might suggest, are likely to be least deferential when holding the executive up to constitutional standards of behaviour. The Court's traditional view of itself as the guardian of the Constitution would add vigour and intensity to its scrutiny of administrative action, when it is applying constitutional norms.

These are large claims, beyond the ambitions of this chapter. If there is something to them, it signals a need for great judicial creativity in shaping administrative law to address the challenges of poor administration in India, particularly where they affect constitutional rights.[74] When fundamental rights are engaged, courts should apply a more demanding standard of administrative review and take a more generous approach to recognising the existence of legitimate expectations.[75] Indian courts may need to expand the 'traditional' grounds of judicial review for administrative action: it may review executive action for conformity with values of transparency, participation, consultation and accountability, for instance. Constitutional guarantees must be recognised as the legal-foundational background against which administrative law norms should be understood and developed.

A pair of cases exemplify how courts should and do apply a more demanding standard of administrative review when constitutional rights are engaged. In common with other jurisdictions, the Indian Supreme Court will assess the legality of decisions based on whether the decision-maker took all relevant, and only relevant, considerations into account. When the Court uses the arbitrariness doctrine under Article 14, as in the case of *Indian Express Newspapers (Bombay) v. Union of India*,[76] it is willing to be bolder in identifying 'relevant'

71 On this, see the discussion in Christopher Forsyth's contribution to this volume.

72 There is also thus a need for judges to broaden the comparative base in working out the content of the common law grounds.

73 Baxi, 'Developments in Indian Administrative Law' (n 7); Baxi, 'Introduction' (n 7).

74 See Ahmed and Khaitan (n 57).

75 Courts should also be open to substantive protections for legitimate expectations. See Chandrachud (n 6) on how the court's theoretical embrace of substantive protections is belied in practice.

76 AIR 1986 SC 515.

and 'irrelevant' considerations. The case involved the imposition of an import duty on newsprint. The court found that the 'public interest' was a relevant consideration which the administrator should have taken into account under the statutory framework. The Court was willing to intervene even though the decision to impose the duty was made on foreign exchange and economic grounds, where greater deference might be expected.

This can be contrasted with the court's approach in *BALCO Employees Union* v. *Union of India*.[77] In this case, the applicants (a trade union of employees of a large aluminium manufacturing plant) challenged the decision of the Government of India to divest itself of its interest in the company (selling its 51 per cent stake to a private bidder). The applicant argued that this divestment would have an impact on their socio-economic position.[78] This impact on the employees' rights was a relevant consideration that the Government was bound to consider but had failed to do so. The Attorney-General of the State also intervened to argue that the government's divestment in the present case had failed to follow the recommendations made by the Disinvestment Commission on the socio-economic infrastructure that must be put in place for the protection of employees following a disinvestment. Here, the Court made clear that the decision to disinvest was a complex economic decision that the court could not second-guess – it was up to the government. The Court was not willing to impose any binding force to the recommendations of the Disinvestment Commission – holding instead that these were advisory in nature. It found that it was open to the Government to proceed in an alternative manner against the Commission's advice.[79] Compared to *Indian Express*, the Court took a more deferential approach to the government's assessment of which factors were relevant and what weight each factor should receive. Although not explicit in the court's reasoning, the absence of a constitutional foundation for the case appeared to have an impact on the level of judicial scrutiny.

If the level of deference to administrators varies, depending on whether judicial review is based on Article 14 or the common law, this raises concerns about the coherence of public law in India. Having two parallel streams of litigation and precedent with different standards and intensity of review is unsatisfactory. If common law grounds offer a more cautious form of review, applicants (and their lawyers) are unlikely to view it as a useful alternative to constitutional litigation. Reinvigorating common law grounds, as we have proposed above, would then not help the access to justice problem. It is essential for the success of our proposals therefore that standard of review using common law grounds (whether in lower or higher courts) and the standard of review for arbitrariness under Article 14 are harmonised.

This could be achieved by levelling up or by levelling down. We tentatively suggest that given Court's overly deferential attitude in many administrative law cases, extensively documented (e.g., by Upendra Baxi), the more rigorous standard adopted by the Court in Article 14 decisions, is appropriate for administrative law cases using common law grounds as well.[80]

77 (2002) 2 SCC 333

78 These included rights under Article 14 and 16 equal pay for work, right to inquiry and reasons before dismissal. While the applicants did reference these rights as being affected (now that their 'employer' / main shareholder would be a private body versus the Government), they did not form the grounds or basis on which they commenced proceedings. The constitutional rights were therefore a background fact rather than the main foundation for the claim. This approach to pleading and arguing the case may appear peculiar given the view of the Constitution as an important tool for rectifying such matters.

79 Another 'conservative' aspect of the Court's decision was the restricted approach to the public interest litigant; the Court decided they did not have standing.

80 There are, of course, reasons for deference outside of the constitutional context where the courts are reviewing issues of macro-economic policy and so forth. However, at the moment, there is no discussion of the criteria for

15.6 CONCLUSION

Constitutional law jurisprudence in India – particularly the expansive interpretation of fundamental rights – has obscured the significance, and distinctive nature, of administrative law norms. In many cases, courts fail to recognise or respond to breaches of administrative law norms. Reliance is instead placed on the arbitrariness doctrine under Article 14. This is on its own may not have been problematic. However, as demonstrated in this chapter, the arbitrariness doctrine has many failings. Its legal basis and content is unclear. These failings have significant implications for the coherence of important areas of Indian law. As T. R. Andhyarujina put it: 'Arbitrary has become a favourite cliché in the vocabulary of the law lawyers and the Courts in India and is used to describe many sins. Its lazy use has encouraged loose thinking and imprecise concepts in law and has retarded the development of public and constitutional law in India.'[81]

The chapter offers an account of the problematic implications of these developments and makes proposals – aimed at both the public and the courts – to reinvigorate administrative law. Here we suggest that the profound issues with an excessive reliance on the arbitrariness doctrine can be fixed by modest doctrinal moves. This chapter has demonstrated that, in many cases, the Supreme Court has reviewed administrative action for arbitrariness under Article 14, offering little guidance on how to test for arbitrariness. The Supreme Court, we argue, should instead use traditional common law grounds as a guide to when administrative action is arbitrary. The Supreme Court should also, we argue, emphasise the independent status of common law grounds, in order to promote access to justice. There is precedent that supports both these moves, and there is reason to hope they mitigate the problems raised by the arbitrariness doctrine, with the added advantage of broadening the public law toolkit of courts and counsel.

The complaints raised in this chapter about the eclipsing of administrative law are echoed in assessments on Indian private law: Shyamkrishna Balaganesh, for instance, concludes that the Indian Supreme Court's 'fusion of constitutional law and tort law has successfully cabined the independent efficacy, normativity, and analytical basis of equivalent private law claims in Indian lower courts'.[82] These complaints, read with this chapter, paint a picture of non-constitutional areas of Indian law withering in the shadow of constitutional jurisprudence.

Nor is Indian law alone in facing these questions. Other jurisdictions which couple a common law heritage with an entrenched Constitution – South Africa for instance – wrestle with their relationship.[83] Thus innovative ideas emerging from scholarship on comparative administrative law may usefully contribute to the future course of judicial review of administrative action in India.

deference and the concern is that the cautiousness behind administrative law may, in these circumstances, be more pervasive and extend outside of 'traditional' areas of deference.

81 TR Andhyarjina, 'The Evolution of Due Process of Law by the Supreme Court' in BN Kirpal et al (eds.), *Supreme but Not Infallible: Essays in Honour of the Supreme Court of India* (Oxford, Oxford University Press, 2016).

82 Shyamkrishna Balganesh, 'The Constitutionalisation of Indian Private Law' in Sujit Choudhry, Madhav Khosla and Pratap Bhanu Mehta (eds.), *The Oxford Handbook of the Indian Constitution* (Oxford, Oxford University Press, 2016) 681.

83 Cora Hoexter, 'South African Administrative Law at a Crossroads: The PAJA and the Principle of Legality', *Admin Law Blog*, 28 April 2017, www.adminlawblog.org/2017/04/28; Kate O'Regan, 'The Constitution and Administrative Law: Insights from South Africa's Constitutional Journey', *Admin Law Blog*, 12 April 2017, www.adminlawblog.org/2017/04/12. See also the fuller discussion on these points in Cora Hoexter's contribution to this volume.

16

Decolonizing Administrative Action

Judicial Review and the Travails of the Bangladesh Supreme Court

Cynthia Farid

INTRODUCTION

The transfer of principles of English administrative law in South Asia is deeply connected to its long colonial history. Additionally, post-colonial political and legal arrangements have allowed for further adaptations and court-led innovations of these principles. The rise of 'good governance' courts in the region, coupled with the proliferation of public interest litigation, have expanded the scope of judicial review, foraying into a wide array of issues of public importance.[1] This has also invited controversies of judicial law-making, policy formulation and political questions.[2] Many such judicial adventures have occurred during moments of constitutional crises when courts simultaneously consolidated their independence and strengthened their administrative law jurisdiction. This is done with a view to delineate and fortify its sphere of operation within the constitutional scheme. It indicates a deep interconnection between (and often inseparability) of administrative and constitutional law in the region.[3] Judicial review of executive action is one such area where institutional consolidation and the production of administrative jurisprudence intersect.

Bangladesh is a case where the Supreme Court plays a central role in the shaping of administrative law. Its two major political ruptures during the Partition of India and Pakistan in 1947 and independence from Pakistan in 1971 make for a complicated study. Adopted in

1 See Robinson, Nick, 'Expanding judiciaries: India and the Rise of the Good Governance Court' (2009) 8 *Washington University Global Studies Law Review* 1; Sathe, Satyaranjan Purushottam, *Judicial Activism in India* (Oxford: Oxford University Press, 2002); Baxi, Upendra, 'Law, Politics, and Constitutional Hegemony' in Sujit Choudhry, Madhav Khosla, and Pratap Bhanu Mehta, *The Oxford Handbook of the Indian Constitution* (Oxford University Press, 2016); Khan, Maryam S., 'Genesis and Evolution of Public Interest Litigation in the Supreme Court of Pakistan: Toward a Dynamic Theory of Judicialization' (2014) 28 *Temple International and Comparative Law Journal* 285.

2 See Bhuwania, Anuj, *Courting the People: Public Interest Litigation in Post-emergency India* (Cambridge: Cambridge University Press, 2017), vol. II; Siddique, Osama, 'The Judicialization of Politics in Pakistan' in Mark V Tushnet and Madhav Khosla, *Unstable Constitutionalism: Law and Politics in South Asia* (Cambridge: Cambridge University Press, 2015), 159; Thiruvengadam, A. K., 'Revisiting the Role of the Judiciary in Plural Societies: A Quarter Century Retrospective on Public Interest Litigation' in *Comparative Constitutionalism in South Asia* (Oxford: Oxford University Press, 2013), 341–69.

3 See Cheema, Moeen H., 'Two Steps Forward One Step Back: The Non-Linear Expansion of Judicial Power in Pakistan' (2018) 16*International Journal of Constitutional Law* 503–26; This has been recognized as 'constitutionalized administrative law'. See Vakil, Raeesa, 'Constitutionalizing Administrative Law in the Indian Supreme Court: Natural Justice and Fundamental Rights' (2018) 16 *International Journal of Constitutional Law* 475–502; see also Ginsburg, Tom, 'Written Constitutions and the Administrative State: on the Constitutional Character of Administrative Law' in Susan Rose-Ackerman, Peter L Lindseth, and Blake Emerson, *Comparative Administrative Law* (Cheltenham UK: Edward Elgar, 2019). See also the contribution on India in this volume.

1972, the Constitution of Bangladesh is based on the idea of constitutional supremacy.[4] Bangladesh follows a unicameral parliamentary system and, in common with other Westminster systems, power is concentrated in the office of the Prime Minister and the Cabinet.[5] Bangladesh has a thick constitution with detailed provisions for governance and a bill of rights. Structurally the Constitution is divided, inter alia, into several parts variously dealing with principles of state policy,[6] fundamental rights,[7] core branches of government based on separation of powers and other miscellaneous matters.

Bangladeshi administrative law has specifically developed in the interstices of the state's democratization, reorganization and expansion through a written constitution, on the one hand, and colonial continuities that plague the bureaucratic structure, on the other. The court has expanded and consolidated its review powers in line with constitutional rights amidst unstable constitutional politics.[8] The language of administrative law in Bangladesh shares many similarities with other commonwealth jurisdictions, particularly its regional neighbors. Like Britain and much of South Asia, Bangladeshi administrative law has developed with little statutory basis and reviewed by way of a creative but indeterminate judicial process.[9] However, the courts are yet to settle the principles for the judicial supervision of state decision-making with consistency. The political climate in which the Court operates makes the construction of any working model or theory difficult. Accordingly, it is difficult to box in judicial review in Bangladesh under the conventional green or red-light theories.[10]

This chapter argues that the Supreme Court of Bangladesh has been moving towards a decolonized approach to judicial review of administrative action.[11] The Court has been steadily attempting to disassociate its administrative jurisprudence from its colonial legacies, on the one

[4] Article 7 affirms constitutional supremacy, thereby voiding any other law that is inconsistent with it. See Art. 7 of the Constitution of the People's Republic of Bangladesh, 4 November 1972 (hereinafter, the Constitution), available at http://bdlaws.minlaw.gov.bd/pdf_part.php?id=367.

[5] Articles 48–58 of the Constitution of Bangladesh variously deal with powers of the President, Prime Minister and the Cabinet. The President is a titular head whose office is vested with responsibilities for executive action and formulating rules of business of government that determine the extent of authority of ministries and departments.

[6] Although these have interpretive significance, they are judicially unenforceable. See Art. 8, Constitution.

[7] Articles 27–44 of the Constitution. Additionally, Art. 26 specifically directs the State not to legislate in derogation of fundamental rights.

[8] See Tushnet, Mark, and Madhav Khosla (eds.), *Unstable Constitutionalism: Law and Politics in South Asia* (Cambridge: Cambridge University Press, 2015); Kalhan, Anil, 'Gray Zone Constitutionalism and the Dilemma of Judicial Independence in Pakistan' (2013) 46 *Vand. J. Transnat'l L.* 1.

[9] This is in some contrast to Euro-American approaches to administrative law, where the locus of production of administrative law may be independent agencies or quasi-judicial institutions that are subject to statutory control as opposed to direct judicial scrutiny (the US being a case in point, where such control is exercised by independent regulatory agencies under the Administrative Procedure Act 1946). See Asimow, Michael, 'Five Models of Administrative Adjudication' (2015) 63 *Am J Comp L* 3; Craig, Paul, 'Administrative Law in the Anglo-American Tradition' in B. Guy Peters and Jon Pierre, *The SAGE Handbook of Public Administration* (Los Angeles: Sage, 2014), 333; Rose-Ackerman, Susan, and Peter L. Lindseth (eds.), *Comparative Administrative Law* (Edward Elgar, 2010).

[10] The green-light approach advocates for judicial restraint with the aim of facilitating greater institutional efficiency and good governance through executive action; the red-light theory advocates for greater judicial scrutiny in the interest of tempering the concentration of and exercise of executive power, and an additional combination of the two is also suggested under the amber-light theory. See generally Harlow, Carol, and Richard Rawlings, *Law and Administration* (Cambridge: Cambridge University Press, 2006).

[11] For the purposes of this chapter, *decolonization* refers to the reorientation of legal institutions to produce outcomes that correspond to the social contract laid out in the constitution. The Courts are, in one sense, trying to mediate the gap between law and society. Decolonization may be read together with transformation, though the objectives of these exercises may not always overlap. In the context of administrative law, it implies the undertaking by the Court of tallying the inherited procedural architecture of legal institutions with the corresponding rights-based demands laid out in the constitutional framework. The question of whether and to what extent courts are proper forums for social transformation is outside the scope of this chapter.

hand, while on the other, innovating doctrinal principles, modalities of statutory and constitutional interpretation and broadening its reliance on international legal authorities. In a bid to evolve a system of adjudication that addresses socio-political problems unique to Bangladesh, the Court has diverged from conventional Euro-American approaches. This divergence maybe understood in light of constitutional politics in Bangladesh, which is often animated by concerns over the doctrine separation of powers and threats to judicial autonomy. While the Court has been at the forefront of shaping administrative jurisprudence, the struggle to maintain its centrality and autonomy vis-à-vis the Executive branch has also produced certain pathologies, thereby generating uncertainty and disequilibrium between institutional efficiency and administrative justice.

Section 16.1 of this chapter presents a historical overview of judicial review in Bangladesh; Section 16.2 examines the legal framework under which judicial review operates and the usage of common law doctrines; Section 16.3 examines the ways in which the Courts have resorted to judicial review for enhancing judicial independence; Section 16.4 examines the ways in which courts are decolonizing administrative law; finally, the chapter concludes with reflections on the origins and adaptations of administrative law in Bangladesh.

16.1 HISTORICAL DEVELOPMENT OF ADMINISTRATIVE LAW IN SOUTH ASIA AND BANGLADESH (1858–1971)

A large body of administrative law had accumulated on the eve of independence in Bangladesh.[12] Accordingly, historical factors have played a significant role in the adaptation of common law principles. Bangladesh was part of the Bengal province in British India and after 1947, it became the state of East Pakistan. The new territories of India and Pakistan inherited or adopted many aspects of colonial governance from the significantly developed administrative state in British India.[13]

Although English law was introduced in British India in the eighteenth century, the structure of the resulting legal system was an amalgam of Mughal administrative practices (particularly with regards to revenue functions) and English legal principles.[14] By the mid-nineteenth century, the developing institutional structure was not modelled after a tripartite scheme under separation of powers. Instead, the executive government acted in its capacity as both executive and legislature (through the Governor General in Council), while the judiciary was gradually evolving into a somewhat autonomous institution. The introduction of High Courts in 1861 with the geographically limited power to issue writs and supervisory authority over lower courts complicated these developments. The operation of English legal principles under colonial conditions posed difficulties for the exercise of reasonably autonomous judicial power.[15] Interbranch tensions between the judiciary and the executive, already prevalent before direct British rule in 1858, intensified after 1861.[16] Greater professionalization of the judicial bureaucracy and increasing agency of Indians in the legal profession in the latter half of the nineteenth century also contributed to this tension.[17] Consequently, this period marked the beginning of

[12] A large body of law was carried over during the formation of the new state by way of the Laws Continuance Enforcement Order 1971 (later adopted in 1972; see note 42 in the following section).

[13] See Jain, M.P., 2017. Outlines of Indian legal history. NM Tripathi Private Ltd.

[14] Jain, note 13.

[15] For an account of limited autonomy exercised by colonial courts, see Chandrachud, Abhinav, *An Independent, Colonial Judiciary: A History of the Bombay High Court during the British Raj, 1862–1947* (Oxford: Oxford University Press, 2015).

[16] See Ray, P. Chandra, *Separation of Judicial & Executive Functions in British India* (Calcutta: City Book Society, 1901).

[17] See Spangenberg, Bradford, *British Bureaucracy in India: Status, Policy, and the ICS in the Late 19th Century* (Columbia: South Asia Books, 1976).

a struggle for judicial independence – one that signaled demands for a larger role of the courts in shaping administrative jurisprudence.

Executive action, particularly in the context of reasonableness and jurisdictional errors, began to be reviewed mid-nineteenth century onwards. The doctrine of ultra vires featured prominently in administrative cases, gradually developing specific distinctions between ultra vires, want of jurisdiction and illegality.[18] One of the earliest instances of judicial review based on ultra vires may be traced back to *Queen* v. *Burah*.[19] The Governor General in the Council (where the executive and legislative functions were fused) enacted a new law in 1869 that removed certain geographical territories out of the Calcutta High Court's jurisdiction, delegated judicial administration to the provincial government and also authorized its governor to extend the Act further to new territories in the province. The High Court held that the Indian legislature that drew its powers from the Imperial Parliament could not further sub-delegate. This decision was reversed by the Privy Council, which ruled that the Indian legislature could transfer certain powers to the provincial executive because it held plenary powers. The Privy Council carefully termed such delegation as conditional legislation devised to extend a duly enacted law to further the exercise of plenary powers.[20]

Though unsuccessful, this case was foundational for judicial review, as it opened avenues for the consideration of a constitutional question by the Court – that is, whether the legislature (and by extension the colonial executive) had exceeded its power. The High Court interpreted the application of English law as it would apply in England. However, it had to yield to priorities of the larger colonial project, necessitating innovation and reinterpretation of English legal principles. This kind of institutional arrangement produced a patchwork of interpretations of administrative law designed to suit colonial conditions.[21] By the twentieth century, however, Courts were increasingly playing a larger role in administrative justice. Constitutional reforms of this period, particularly the establishment of the Federal Court in 1935, significantly enhanced the judiciary's position.[22] Indian jurists critically evaluated the state of administrative law in the annual Tagore Law Lectures of 1917 and 1918, respectively.[23] These widely recognized lectures represented then-prevailing juristic thought. These jurists recognized the Indian bureaucratic state as an admixture of English law with continental and other approaches and emphasized greater codification of administrative law and envisaged an important role for the courts in administrative governance.[24]

18 For a historical account of the doctrine of ultra vires, see Das, Satya Ranjan, *The Law of Ultra Vires in British India* (Calcutta: R. Cambray & Co., 1923).

19 [1878] 3 AC 889

20 This decision was followed elsewhere in the British Empire. Some examples include, for instance, the Canadian cases of *Russel* v. *the Queen* (1882) 7 A.C. 829 and in *Lodge* v. *the Queen* (1883) 9 A.C. 117. For an evolution of this doctrine in the post-colonial period in India, see Joshi, K. C., 'Question of Legislative Policy in Delegated Legislation – Recent Cases' (1976) 18 *Journal of the Indian Law Institute* 3, 509–14.

21 Another example of this is the doctrine of justice, equity and good conscience, which was a frequent refuge of colonial courts in the absence of common law guidance – a choice that sometimes generated a good deal of controversy. See Derrett, J., and M. Duncan, 'Justice, Equity and Good Conscience' in J. N. D. Anderson (ed.), *Changing Law in Developing Countries* (London: Allen-Unwin, 1963).

22 See De, Rohit, 'Emasculating the Executive: The Federal Court and Civil Liberties in Late Colonial India: 1942–1944' in *Fates of Political Liberalism in the British Post-Colony: The Politics of the Legal Complex* (New York: Cambridge University Press, 2012), 59–90.

23 These annual lectures delivered by eminent jurists and scholars on various topics of law were sponsored by the influential Tagore family from Calcutta, India, and organized by the Calcutta University.

24 See Mitter, Dwarknath, 'Comparative Administrative Law', Tagore Law Lecture of 1917, British Library; General Reference Collection 5310.de.25.; Ghose, Nagendranath Nath, *Comparative Administrative Law, with Special Reference to the Organization and Legal Position of the Administrative Authorities in British India* (Tagore Law Lecture 1918) (Calcutta: Butterworth & Co., 1919).

After 1947, the new non-contiguous state of Pakistan presented fresh challenges in terms of the consolidation of a constitution and the bureaucracy.[25] A Provisional Constitution provided for the basic structure of government, including superior and provincial courts.[26] Democratic rule was short-lived in Pakistan, frequently interrupted by military intervention. Pakistan adopted two constitutions in 1956 and 1962 respectively. Each of them conferred review powers, and writ jurisdiction was reintroduced in the provincial high courts.[27] The 1962 Constitution was more expansive than its predecessor, guaranteeing judicial independence.[28] It also included the review of executive and legislative action enumerated under Article 98, though it eliminated Latin terms for writs and distinctions among judicial, quasi-judicial and administrative authority.[29] Both these constitutions were abrogated by the Ayyub Khan and the Yahya Khan regime in 1958 and 1969, respectively.

The rise of direct military intervention into politics raised anomalies that conventional understandings about constitutional governance and judicial review could not explain. The judiciary of Pakistan had little room to maneuver, given the prominence of the military government.[30] The Courts were producing a distinct type of 'crisis jurisprudence' based on rigid, technical doctrines that justified patently arbitrary acts of the Executive.[31] Consequently, judicial review was defined by doctrinal inconsistency.[32] Additionally, there is some evidence to suggest that the rules of procedure between the Eastern and Western Pakistan may have been different. East Pakistan High Court reportedly adopted many of the procedures of the Calcutta High Court, which had jurisdiction over greater Bengal (including East Bengal) prior to the Partition of British India in 1947.[33] It was within this framework of inconsistency that administrative law developed in East Pakistan up to 1971.

Extensive economic planning led to the expansion of the administrative machinery of the state to meet the requirements of economic development.[34] Delegated legislation increased,

25 See Jalal, Ayesha, *Democracy and Authoritarianism in South Asia: A Comparative and Historical Perspective* (Cambridge: Cambridge University Press, 1995).

26 The Constituent Assembly of Pakistan drew its powers from the Government of India Act (1935), which became the Pakistan (Provisional Constitution) Order 1948. The Federal Court of Pakistan Order 1948, PLD 1949 (Central Acts and Notifications 398) established a Federal Court for Pakistan (later renamed as the Supreme Court in 1956) and provided for provincial high courts.

27 Article 170 of the Constitution of Pakistan, 1956.

28 Provisions for judicial appointment, transfer, and remuneration were similar to the 1956 Constitution. These were enumerated in Articles 49,50,52-55, 92, 94–96, 99 and 124. The new constitution of 1962 reorganized the removal process and introduced the Supreme Judicial Council. See Khan, Hamid, *The Constitutional and Political History of Pakistan* (Oxford: Oxford University Press, 2004), 275.

29 Constitution (First Amendment) Act 1963. Act I of 1964 PLD 1964, Central Statutes.

30 The state directly attacked the judiciary by removing its review jurisdiction through the Jurisdiction of Courts (Removal of Doubts) Order 1969. This Act was precipitated by *Mir Hassan & Another* v. *State*, 1969 Lah. Pak. L. D. 786 (Pak. 1969), which ruled in favour of the judiciary to operate free of executive obstruction.

31 The Supreme Court of Pakistan validated the martial law regime of Ayub Khan, relying on the Kelsenian doctrine of necessity. See *State* v. *Dosso* (1958) PLD (SC) 533. A prelude to this case was *Maulvi Tamizuddin Khan* v. *Federation of Pakistan* PLD. 1955 Sind 96. See also *Usif Patel* v. *Crown* PLD 1955 F.C.387. The term *crisis jurisprudence* was coined by Paula Newberg in the context of Pakistan's courts operating under authoritarian rule. See Newberg, Paula R., *Judging the State: Courts and Constitutional Politics in Pakistan*. Vol. 59 (Cambridge: Cambridge University Press, 2002).

32 For an account of judicial review under various phases of authoritarian rule in the Pakistan period, see Mahmood, M., *The Constitution of the Islamic Republic of Pakistan: A Comprehensive and Detailed Commentary with a Comparative Study of the Constitutions of Pakistan, 1956 and 1962* (Lahore: Pakistan Law Times, 1973); Mahmud, Tayyab, 'Praetorianism and Common Law in Post-Colonial Settings: Judicial Responses to Constitutional Breakdowns in Pakistan' (1993) *Utah Law Review* 1225.

33 *East Pakistan* v. *Mehdi Ali Khan* PLD 1959 Supreme Court (Pak.) 387.

34 Waterston, Albert, *Planning in Pakistan* (Economic Development Institute, 1963).

and courts struggled to consolidate independence. Under constitutional governments, fundamental rights claims were rapidly attaching to administrative action challenges in court, particularly as the state was attempting to appropriate, consolidate and reform proprietary interests accrued under colonial economic arrangements.[35] Rights were a new feature of postcolonial constitutions designed to establish equality before law and the protection of individual rights, which was not an option under colonial rule. By some estimates, nearly 14,000 writ petitions were filed in the high courts, many of which were appealed in the Supreme Court between 1955 and 1962.[36] These numbers attest to the legitimacy of the judiciary as a forum for confronting the state.

Under both the 1956 and 1962 Constitution, rules of standing required a person seeking judicial review to show a direct personal interest in the matter.[37] Additionally, Courts refused review where the issues in controversy were held to go to the merits of the case.[38] Under the 1962 Constitution, the high courts interpreted the terms 'without lawful authority' in Article 98 of the 1962 Constitution broadly and would go to some length to ensure the ends of justice.[39] The superior courts would intervene, even in cases without jurisdictional error in order to address procedural injustices.[40] The Court also developed certain principles of *Audi alteram partem*, holding that no one can be condemned without a hearing. It further added that this principle was to be read into every law unless its application was expressly excluded, and every court or tribunal was under a duty to act fairly and justly with due regard to the principles of natural justice.[41]

Many administrative principles developed by the Pakistani Supreme Court carried over in Bangladesh. Laws declared by the Privy Council, Federal Court and the Supreme Court of Pakistan before independence became binding precedents (until ruled to the contrary).[42] Informed by former authoritarian rule, judicial independence was a specific concern in the

35 In *Jibendra Kishore* v. *East Pakistan* (1957) 9 DLR (SC) 21, the Provincial government acquired certain proprietary interests by gazette notification prior to the 1956 Constitution. After the Constitution came into force, the government issued further notifications to the holders of the proprietary interests for further acquisition. Eighty-three writ petitions (mandamus) were moved in the High Court of East Pakistan against the provincial government, directing it to withdraw or rescind the notifications, as it violated Article 5 of the 1956 Constitution, which affirmed equality before law and equal protection of law for all citizens. In *Mustafa Ansari* v. *Deputy Commissioner* (1965) 17 DLR (Dacca) 553 (striking down a provision of the Chittagong Hill Tracts (Regulation) Rules 1960), the deputy commissioner issued an order restricting the petitioner from working in a particular area. It was challenged based on its violation of the fundamental right of movement and the pursuit of vocation.

36 Khan, note 28, 90.

37 *Tariq Transport* v. *Sargodha-Vera Bus Service* (1959) 11 DLR (SC) 140; *Fazal Din* v. *Lahore I.T.* (1969) 21 DLR (SC) 225.

38 In *Muhammad Aboo* v. *Province of East Pakistan* PLD 1960 SC 154, the Supreme Court held that challenges to promotion and supersession of government officials could only be determined by the government, as it alone could determine merit and suitability. The court could only intervene in cases of proven *malafide*.

39 Article 98(2)(a)(ii) granted jurisdiction on the high courts to declare any act or proceeding that has been done or taken without lawful authority to be of no legal effect.

40 In *Jamal Shah* v. *Election Commission* PLD 1966 SC 1, the court refused to accept the question of rejection of certain ballot papers as it was within the jurisdiction of the Election Commission; but in *Akbar Ali* v. *Raziur Rahman* (1966) 18 DLR (SC) 426, the court interfered, treating the question of wanton rejection of certain ballot papers as one going to the root of the jurisdiction.

41 In *University of Dhaka* v. *Zakir Ahmad* PLD 1966 S.C. 105, the Dhaka High Court ruled in favour of a group of expelled students. It ruled that that they had the right to be heard and to be given a fair opportunity to defend themselves against allegations before passing the expulsion orders. It also ruled that in all judicial or administrative proceedings, the principles of natural justice had to be observed if such proceedings had material consequences for the parties involved.

42 Laws of the Pakistan era carried over by virtue of the Bangladesh (Adaptation of Existing Laws) Order, 1972 (President's Order No. 48 Of 1972) and Article 149 of the Constitution.

Constituent Assembly debates of Bangladesh.[43] Article 102 of the Constitution of Bangladesh confers powers of judicial review on the HCD, ranging over a range of legislative as well as executive acts. The language used in this section is similar to Article 98 of the Pakistan Constitution of 1962.[44] Constituent Assembly discussions on judicial remedies reveal that Latin terms for each of the writs were considered for enumeration but were excluded so as to avoid limiting their interpretation.[45] Remedies in the nature of certiorari, mandamus, habeas corpus and quo warranto enumerated in Article 102, coupled with formal separation of the judiciary and executive, have helped sustain the symbolic power of writs as a concrete remedy for administrative wrongs and violations of fundamental rights.[46]

16.2 JUDICIAL REVIEW IN INDEPENDENT BANGLADESH

The Constitution of Bangladesh provides for the separation of the judicial and the executive branches.[47] To augment this provision, it has conferred supervisory authority on the Supreme Court over all other subordinate courts.[48] The bifurcated structure of the Supreme Court consists of the High Court Division (HCD) and the Appellate Division (AD). The AD is the appellate forum for the HCD and has powers to do complete justice, review and prospectively overrule its own judgments.[49] The HCD has both original (writ) as well as appellate jurisdiction. Constitutional supremacy underlays the courts' power to review administrative action, thereby entrenching legal authority for judicial review enumerated in Article 102 of the Constitution. The Supreme Court has the power to strike down laws for unconstitutionality, and its judicial pronouncements are binding unless the court subsequently overrules itself or the parliament re-enacts the law (removing the unconstitutionality).[50]

Judicial review in Bangladesh takes three principal forms, including review of executive or judicial acts and proceedings contravening (1) the Constitution, (2) primary legislation, and (3) delegated legislation vis-à-vis primary legislation and/or constitution.[51] The Supreme Court has wide power to issue writs accompanied by orders or direction under Article 102 of the Constitution. Article 102 (1) confers on the HCD the authority to enforce fundamental rights. The Constitution of Bangladesh guarantees the right to move the HCD for enforcement of fundamental rights, and courts have a wide latitude in granting relief.[52] Article 102(2) confers powers of judicial review in non-fundamental rights matters if the petitioner has

43 Khandoker Abdul Hafiz, NE 49-Jessore 7 in Bangladesh Gonoporishod Bitorko (Constituent Assembly Debates), Abdul Halim (ed.) (2015), 166.

44 Mahmudul, Islam, *Constitutional Law of Bangladesh*, 3rd edition (Dhaka, Bangladesh: Mullick Brothers, 2012), 619.

45 Kamal Hossain in *Constituent Assembly Debates* (2014), 489.

46 See Crouch, Melissa, 'The Prerogative Writs as Constitutional Transfer' (2018) 38 *Oxford Journal of Legal Studies* 653–75.

47 Article 116A, Constitution of Bangladesh.

48 Article 109, Constitution of Bangladesh.

49 Articles 103–105.

50 Article 111, Constitution of Bangladesh

51 Direct legislation in Bangladesh is supported by administrative rule-making by the executive, whereby all laws must be read with their associated rules. Like its South Asian neighbours, the use of delegated legislation resulting from rulemaking by administrative bodies increased after independence. Accordingly, administrative action may include quasi-legislative (rule-making) action; quasi-judicial (challenges to decision made by an authority); challenges to the proper application of a rule and finality of administrative action.

52 Article 44(1) of the Constitution; also affirmed in *Bangladesh* v. *Ahmed Nazir* (1975) 27 DLR (AD) 41.

exhausted all other efficacious remedies available to him or her.[53] If the person aggrieved has a remedy under Article 102(2), then enforcement of fundamental rights may not always be necessary, though the illegal or egregious act of an administrative authority may trigger Article 102 (1) if the right to be treated in accordance with law is violated.[54] Article 102(2) essentially removes the distinction between judicial and quasi-judicial action by making available remedies under it against 'any person' performing any function connected to the affairs of the state.

In review proceedings, the Court will neither act as an appellate authority[55] nor enter disputed questions of fact[56] – that is, review on the merits (a feature in common with other systems studied in this volume). Additionally, there is a presumption of regularity of the official act and the burden of proof is on the person challenging its validity.[57] Article 102(2) reviews will typically require exhaustion of efficacious remedy, generally provided by statute. This rule is relaxed in cases involving possible bad faith (*malafide*),[58] where interim relief is unavailable;[59] or where the availability of a remedy depends on the discretion of the authority in question or is otherwise onerous.[60] The Court will generally not go into constitutional questions in these types of reviews. If it does, it will typically be to the extent necessary based on precise facts presented on record and for the resolution of the specific question that is under review.[61]Additionally, political questions are generally not a bar to the court's jurisdiction.[62]

Common law grounds are already part of Bangladesh's inherited body of law. Additionally, it continues to have a longstanding connection with English administrative law, citing English judgments liberally. However, the court and lawyers look to India much more frequently, due to shared legacies, and especially since the Indian Supreme Court and related institutions consolidated their independence amid a much less tumultuous process of democratization. Notwithstanding these common sites for borrowing, the language of Article 102 has primacy.

53 Article 102 (2) of the Constitution states that the High Court Division may, if satisfied that no other equally efficacious remedy is provided by law,

(a) on the application of any person aggrieved, make an order
  (i) directing a person performing any functions in connection with the affairs of the Republic or of a local authority, to refrain from doing that which he is not permitted by law to do or to do that which he is required by law to do; or
  (ii) declaring that any act done or proceeding taken by a person performing functions in connection with the affairs of the Republic or of a local authority, has been done or taken without lawful authority and is of no legal effect; or
(b) on the application of any person, make an order
  (i) directing that a person in custody be brought before it so that it may satisfy itself that he is not being held in custody without lawful authority or in an unlawful manner; or
  (ii) requiring a person holding or purporting to hold a public office to show under what authority he claims to hold that office.

54 Article 31, Constitution of Bangladesh.

55 Bangladesh v. Rowshan Ara (2009) 17 BLT (AD) 65.

56 *New India Tea Co Ltd* v. *Bangladesh* (1978) 2 BD SCR 185.

57 *Mustafa Kamal* v. *Commissioner of Customs* (1990) 51 DLR (AD) 319; see also Mahmudul, note 43, 601.

58 *Shamsur Rahman* v. *Bangladesh* (2010) 15 BLC 482.

59 *Kumudini Welfare Trust* v. *East Pakistan* PLD 1963 Dac 136.

60 Mahmudul, note 43, 797–801.

61 This position is influenced by American case law, including *Garner* v. *Louisiana* (1961) 368 US 157 and *US* v. *Raines* (1960) 362 US 17. See Mahmudul, note 43, 599–600.

62 But the Court can exercise judicial restraint as it did in *Abdul Mannan Bhuiyan* v. *State* (2008) 60 DLR (AD); Special Reference No. 1 of 1995, (1995) 47 DLR (AD) 111.

The Court has typically relied on the principle that justice overrides procedural injustice, frequently resorting to expansive interpretations of the doctrine of ultra vires and other principles of natural law.[63] The language of Article 102(2)(a)(ii) of the Constitution empowers the Court to declare administrative action a nullity if it is held to have been 'done or taken without lawful authority'. The requirement for lawful authority suggests that *Anisminic* fits within the constitutional scheme of the enumerated judicial review grounds.[64] While error of law is a ground for deciding jurisdiction,[65] the HCD has made a distinction between error of law within jurisdiction and error of law affecting jurisdiction.[66] If a tribunal maintains jurisdiction but decided erroneously on a point of law, that would generally not be a ground for intervention through judicial review (though it may be appealed). Furthermore, the principle of reasonableness is used to test the validity of administrative action.[67] Accordingly, Wednesbury reasonableness is recognized as a matter of course.[68]

Noncompliance with statutory procedures, breach of principles of natural justice or acting contrary to legitimate expectation may variously constitute grounds for procedural ultra vires. Natural justice is generally deemed incorporated in statutes and the courts accept this as a matter of historical tradition, as well as Article 31 of the Constitution (right to protection of law), which may be interpreted as a guarantee for due process of law.[69] Accordingly, fair procedure or hearing is an accepted ground whenever an official decision affects the rights or interests of a petitioner.[70] For proceedings challenged on grounds of bias, Bangladeshi Courts have applied the real likelihood test laid out in *R* v. *Gough*.[71] Habeas corpus cases tend to generate greater intervention of courts if the tribunal in question has not considered all relevant materials and grounds of malice or where such detention has not been authorized by law.[72] In recent years, the doctrine of legitimate expectations seems to have made some inroads.[73] Other doctrines, such as that of

63 Where an enquiry Committee was constituted violating civil service regulations, exhaustion of departmental appeal in disciplinary proceedings was not deemed necessary. *Ayub Ali Chowdhury* v. *BD* (2005) 57 DLR 578; see also *Engineer Mahmudul Islam* v. *Bangladesh* (2003) 55 DLR 171.

64 *Anisminic Ltd* v. *Foreign Compensation Commission* [1969] 2 AC 147 (affirming that error of law in an official decision will nullify it and the Court may exercise review powers despite ouster clauses purporting to prevent its intervention); see also Mahmudul, note 43, 632.

65 *Malafide* action or exercise of power has been held to negate jurisdiction in *Jamil Haque* v. *Bangladesh* (1981) DLR (AD) 125; order of dismissal without conducting preliminary inquiry has been held to be mala fide in *Rezaul Haque* v. *Bangladesh* (2010) 15 BLC 572; see also *Anisul Islam Mahmud* v. *Bangladesh* (1992) 44 DLR.

66 *Md. Mustakin Ali* v. *Abdul Mutaleb* (1993) 45 DLR 733.

67 *Shafiq Ahmed* v. *BCIC*, (1993) 45 DLR 95.

68 *Unique Hotels and Resorts Ltd.* v. *Bangladesh* (2010) 15 BLC 770; *Associated Provincial Picture Houses Ltd.* v. *Wednesbury Corporation* [1948] 1 KB 223.

69 *Bazlur Rahman* v. *Bangladesh* (2010) 62 DLR 360 held that state benefits could not be withdrawn from certain recipients without complying with natural justice principles.

70 *Bangladesh* v. *A.K. Al-Mamun*, (1997) BLD (AD) 77 (requirement for giving reasons compulsory); *Jabbar Jute Mills* v. *Abdul Kashem* (2007) 59 DLR (AD) 152 (order vitiated for failing to issue notice on the other party). *Faruq Hasan* v. *Titas Gas Transmission and Distribution Co* (2006) 58 DLR 316 (use of power for improper purpose held to be ultra vires); *Rama Rani* v. *Bangladesh* (1997) 49 DLR 364 (official decision declared ultra vires based on non-application of mind).

71 [1993] AC 646; *Khandkar Mostaque Ahmed* v. *Bangladesh* (1982) 34 DLP (AD) 22.

72 *Sajeda Parvin* v. *Bangladesh* (1988) 40 DLR (AD) 178 held that detention order passed for collateral purposes deemed illegal.

73 *Syed SM Hasan* v. *Bangladesh* (2008) 60 DLR (AD) 1 held that where a number of persons were selected for public service appointment or promotion, and if some among them were appointed or promoted without appointing the rest of the list, preparation of a new list excluding them would violate their legitimate expectations; see also Mahmudul, note 43, 592 and 679.

proportionality, have been alluded to in substance,[74] though the court has been resistant in importing the concept outright.[75]

In review actions, courts generally combine common law principles that are both historically accumulated as well as borrowed, along with constitutional provisions. However, constitutional politics and judicial autonomy affects the degree to which common law principles will be accepted or rejected as a matter of interpretation. These will be considered in the next section.

16.3 JUDICIAL REVIEW AND THE STRUGGLE FOR JUDICIAL AUTONOMY

The expansion of judicial review in Bangladesh correlates with democratization. Oscillation in judicial autonomy affects the degree to which the courts can exercise strong or weak review powers. Bangladesh transitioned as a democracy in 1991. In 1974, one-party rule was established under the liberation party, the Awami League (AL), which was followed by two successive military governments of Presidents Ziaur Rahman (1977–9) and Hussain Mohammed Ershad (1982–90). Bangladesh transitioned to democracy in 1991 and (except for a brief hiatus under a military-backed caretaker government in 2007–8), since then, power has alternated between two dominant parties, the AL and the Bangladesh Nationalist Party. Political contest since the 1990s has been confrontational, often violent. Regimes alternating power have not shied away from political capture of state apparatus or consolidating power by way of constitutional amendments.[76] Since coming into force, seventeen amendments have been introduced into the Constitution. Approximately a third of them have directly affected judicial independence.

The Second Amendment curtailed the HCD's power under Article 102(1) to declare any amendments to fundamental rights void.[77] The Fourth Amendment suspended the powers of the HCD to protect fundamental rights.[78] It also granted powers of judicial appointment and removal to the President.[79] The Fifth Amendment to the Constitution retrospectively validated all actions under the Zia regime under martial law, including the establishment of the Supreme Judicial Council (SJC), which was introduced earlier to replace parliamentary impeachment of judges.[80] The Seventh Amendment retrospectively ratified all actions of the Ershad regime under martial law and increased the retirement age of Supreme Court Judges in a bid to extend the office of a sitting Chief Justice, who was widely recognized to be a regime loyalist.[81] The Eighth Amendment decentralized the seat of the HCD into divisional

74 In *Sonali Bank* v. *Ruhul Amin Khan* (1994) 46 DLR (AD) 85, the court did not acknowledge the doctrine of proportionality but alluded to its principles by considering facts and circumstances of the case.

75 *Ekushey Television* v. *Dr Mahmood Hasan Court* (2003) 55 DLR (AD) 26; *Agrani Bank* v. *Khandoker Badrudduza* (2004) 56 DLR 136.

76 Some scholars locate the problems of governance in Bangladesh in the nature and functioning of its political parties, which are patron-client agglomerations. Local government, police, judiciary and other agencies are drawn into this patron-client nexus. See Basu, Ipshita, Joe Devine, and Geof Wood (eds.), *Politics and Governance in Bangladesh: Uncertain Landscapes* (New York: Routledge, 2017); for an overview of how power is consolidated through constitutional amendments, see Shahdeen, Malik Culture of Amendments, 'Fourth Constitution Day Memorial Lecture', Banglar Pathshala, Dhaka, Bangladesh, 2018.

77 Constitution (Second Amendment) Act 1973, Act No. XXIV of 1973.

78 Constitution (Fourth Amendment) Act 1975, Act No. II of 1975.

79 Article 115 was amended by section 19 of the Fourth Amendment to the Constitution of Bangladesh.

80 Constitution (Fifth Amendment) Act 1975, Act No. I of 1979.

81 Constitution (Seventh Amendment) Act 1986, Act No. X of 1986. For an account of contestations between the Ershad Regime and the legal community in Bangladesh, see Farid, Cynthia, 'New Paths to Justice: A Tale of Social Justice Lawyering in Bangladesh' (2013) 31 *Wisconsin International Law Journal* 421.

benches, though this has since been declared unconstitutional. The Court, for the first time, invalidated a constitutional amendment, holding that the constitutionalized scheme of a bifurcated Supreme Court was fundamental to maintaining judicial independence, which was a basic feature of the constitution (discussed in Section 16.4).[82]

In 1991, Bangladesh reintroduced a parliamentary form of government. This was followed by the Thirteenth Amendment to the Constitution, which constitutionalized a non-party caretaker government (CG). It was brought in to facilitate democratic transition after returning to a parliamentary system. The Chief Justice temporarily resigned to lead the CG and oversee and hold elections.[83] Although transitional, it was a significant yet unprecedented development that a member of the judiciary assumed executive functions. The Court's foray beyond its traditional role brokered a compromise against the prevalent political impasse and, in so doing, provided an integrity mechanism for overseeing the elections that all parties could agree on.[84] In 2011, the Fifteenth Amendment removed the caretaker provision, following the Supreme Court's decision declaring the Thirteenth Amendment unconstitutional.[85] This largely unpopular decision of a divided court reopened avenues of political deadlock. The Sixteenth Amendment tried to remove the SJC and reintroduce parliamentary impeachment of judges as originally envisaged in the founding constitution, but the Supreme Court recently struck this down.[86] Once again, this case brought to the fore interbranch tensions within the government. The Court held that by exposing the judges to parliamentary impeachment, the amendment significantly undermined judicial independence, which by past precedent has been established as an essential component of the basic structure doctrine.[87]

Regime change and frequent constitutional amendments during 1971–1990 significantly affected the Supreme Court's jurisdiction. Accordingly, there are stark differences between the pre- and post-1990 rulings. The Court was producing conservative rulings before 1990. In the early seventies, the Supreme Court determined narrow rules of standing for aggrieved persons to challenge unconstitutional laws in court.[88]As authoritarian rule entrenched itself, the Court went on to affirm the supremacy of martial law over the Constitution;[89] announced its own role to be one of merely applying the law, which could include unjust or harsh laws;[90] and refused to intervene when issues connected to unconstitutional amendments of this

82 Constitution (Eighth Amendment) Act 1988, Act No. X of 1988; declared unconstitutional in *Anwar Hossain Chowdhury* v. *Bangladesh* (1989) BLD (Spl.) (AD) 1 (hereinafter, the Eighth Amendment Case).

83 For the Judiciary's role in the former non-party caretaker system as a temporary transition government, see Hoque, Ridwanul, 'The Judicialization of Politics in Bangladesh' and Chowdhury, M. Jashim Ali, 'Elections in "Democratic" Bangladesh' in Mark Tushnet and Madhav Khosla (eds.), *Unstable Constitutionalism: Law and Politics in South Asia* (Cambridge: Cambridge University Press, 2015).

84 For an explanation of the functions of integrity institutions, see Klug, Heinz, 'Transformative Constitutions and the Role of Integrity Institutions in Tempering Power: The Case of Resistance to State Capture in Post-Apartheid South Africa' (2019) 67 *Buff. L. Rev.* 701.

85 Constitution (Fifteenth Amendment) Act 2011 (Act XIV of 2011); invalidated by *Abdul Mannan Khan* v. *Bangladesh* [2012] 64 DLR (AD) 169.

86 Constitution (Sixteenth Amendment) Act 2014 (Act No. XIII of 2014).

87 *Bangladesh* v. *Advocate Asaduzzaman Siddiqui* (Civil Appeal No. 06 of 2017), hereinafter the Sixteenth Amendment Case.

88 *Kazi Mukhlesur Rahman* v. *Bangladesh* (1973) 25 DLR (HCD) 335. The HCD initially rejected the petition as based on locus standi, the petitioner was not directly 'aggrieved', though an exception was made on appeal due to the significant public importance of the issue. Standing continued to be construed narrowly until the nineties.

89 *Sultan Ahmed* v. *Chief Election Commissioner* (1978) 30 DLR (HCD) 291.

90 *Halima Khatun* v. *Bangladesh* (1978) 30 DLR (AD) 207, at 219.

period were raised.[91] All this began to change from the late eighties as the regime of President H. M. Ershad began to unravel.

Post-democratization, the Supreme Court rendered several landmark decisions that progressively strengthened its sphere of autonomy and operational influence. In 1989, the Supreme Court introduced the basic structure doctrine, which allowed, for the first time, the judicial review of constitutional amendments through what has come to be known as the Eighth Amendment case.[92] It held that the Parliament lacked power to amend the Constitution in any way that affects its basic structure. This case was a prelude to the post-1990 liberal jurisprudence that would enhance the Court's review powers. Subsequently, proliferation of public interest litigation (PIL) broadened the interpretation of locus standi to include petitioners with sufficient as opposed to direct interest.[93] This opened avenues for the Court to further strengthen its sphere of influence by expanding its autonomy.

Having already declared judicial independence as a basic structure of the Constitution in the Eighth Amendment case, the Supreme Court significantly consolidated its autonomy by declaring a formal separation of the judiciary from the executive in *Secretary, Ministry of Finance* v. *Md. Masdar Hossain and Others*.[94] Until this challenge, lower court judges were recruited through the public service commission and related control over its administration lay with the Executive branch. Invoking the doctrine of ultra vires, the Court invalidated a law that administered affairs of judicial officers under civil service rules.[95] It declared that judicial service falls within the definition of 'service of the Republic' as delineated in Article 152(1) of the Constitution.[96] However, 'it was also functionally and structurally distinct and separate service from the civil executive and administrative services of the Republic with which the judicial service cannot be placed on par on any account and that it cannot be amalgamated, abolished, replaced, mixed up and tied together with the civil executive and administrative services'.[97] Therefore, administration of the judicial service under civil service rules was declared ultra vires. Additionally, the Supreme Court issued twelve directives on various aspects of regulating judicial affairs, including recruitment, appointment and other terms of service, and establishing a judicial services commission and judicial pay commission. Ironically, the *Masdar Hossain* directives that were subject to a rolling review have not been realized. However, it has fortified the grounds for maintaining judicial independence and expanding judicial power in subsequent cases.[98]

16.4 DECOLONIZING ADMINISTRATIVE ACTION

The combination of common law principles and constitutional provisions has produced a large body of unwritten judge-made law that has incrementally evolved principles of general application on a case-by-case basis. Over time, the Court has attempted to decolonize its administrative law jurisprudence in various ways, including inter alia extending its

91 *Hamidul Huq Chowdhury* v. *Bangladesh* (1981) 33 DLR (HCD) 381.

92 *Anwar Hossain Chowdhury* v. *Bangladesh* (1989) BLD (Spl.) (AD) 1 (hereinafter, the Eighth Amendment Case).

93 *Mohiuddin Farooque* v. *Bangladesh* (1997) 17 BLD (AD); see generally Hoque, Ridwanul, *Judicial Activism in Bangladesh: A Golden Mean Approach* (Cambridge: Cambridge Scholars Publishing, 2011); and Hoque, Ridwanul, 'Taking Justice Seriously: Judicial Public Interest and Constitutional Activism in Bangladesh' (2006) 15 *Contemporary South Asia* 399–422.

94 (1999) 52 DLR (AD) 82.

95 The Bangladesh Civil Service (reorganization) Order 1980.

96 For a discussion on service of the republic, see notes 105 and 108 in the following section.

97 *Masdar Hossain* v. *Bangladesh* (1999) 52 DLR (AD) 82, para. 76 at 23.

98 *Bangladesh* v. *Idrisur Rahman* [2010] 7 LG (AD) 137.

jurisdictional reach, relying on historical jurisprudence, innovating doctrines and borrowing from other common law jurisdictions. The remainder of this section considers these efforts.

16.4.1 *Extending Jurisdictional Reach*

Traditionally, writs in the nature of habeas corpus and quo warranto cases under Article 102(2) of the Constitution did not have a standing problem as its text allows, in no uncertain terms, 'any person' to move the HCD. However, the remaining remedies under Article 102 construed standing narrowly to those directly aggrieved based on a literal and textual interpretation of the constitution.[99] Once the general threshold of standing was settled in the nineties to anyone with sufficient interest, PIL extended to reviewing executive action involving issues of administrative and constitutional significance.[100] Since democratic transition, political fragmentation and uncertainty associated with electoral outcomes have been key factors contributing to the expansion of review powers and the judicialization of politics.[101] An additional driving force influencing judicial behavior and thrusting the Court in the realm of politics has been the aggregate influence of various national political, professional and intellectual values of elites, along with the media and their endorsement of and reliance on the High Court's assertive decisions.[102] Accordingly, judicial review has facilitated recalibration of power relations among governmental and public institutions, as transition between elected governments can periodically affect recruitment and other organizational aspects within the bureaucracy in a bid to entrench political power. After *Masdar Hossain*, there has been an uptick in cases involving judicial independence, particularly those challenging judicial appointments and lack of consultation with the Supreme Court in the appointment process.[103] Additionally, the Court carefully laid out the parameters of judicial independence by ruling on issues of post-retirement employment.[104]

In further extending its jurisdictional reach, the Court has interpreted the meaning of 'state' in broad terms.[105] As a result, it is able to review administrative challenges originating

99 *Abdul Latif Mirza* v. *Government of Bangladesh* 31 DLR (AD) 33; *Aruna Sen* v. *Government of Bangladesh* (1975) 27 DLR (HCD) 122.

100 Some scholars have criticized this phenomenon, as it overshadowed other public interest issues of socioeconomic significance. See Ahmed, Naim, *Public Interest Litigation: Constitutional Issues and Remedies* (Dhaka, Bangladesh: Bangladesh Legal Aid and Services Trust, 1999).

101 See Ginsburg, Tom, *Judicial Review in New Democracies: Constitutional Courts in Asian Cases* (Cambridge: Cambridge University Press, 2003).

102 See Mate, Manoj, 'Elite Institutionalism and Judicial Assertiveness in the Supreme Court of India' (2014) 28 *Temple International and Comparative Law Journal* 361.

103 *Idrisur Rahman* v. *Shahiduddin Ahmed* 19 (1999) BLD (AD) 203, appointment of the Chief Metropolitan Magistrate of Dhaka without consulting the Supreme Court (required under Articles 115 and 116 of the Constitution) was challenged by a writ of quo warranto. Similarly, transfer of Judges has been successfully challenged in *Shahdeen Malik* v. *Secretary, Ministry of Law, Justice and Parliamentary Affairs*, WP No 2088/2005.

104 Article 99 bars judges from taking up any office of profit in the service of the republic unless it is a judicial or quasi-judicial office. In *Abdul Bari Sarkar* v. *Secretary* v. *Bangladesh* (1994) 46 DLR (AD) 37, the Court interpreted this restriction as a means to prevent the incentivization of judges by way of future employment prospects so as to render favourable decisions. Additionally, in *Abdul Mannan Khan* v. *Bangladesh*, Civil Appeal No. 139 of 2005, and *Ruhul Quddus* v. *Justice MA Aziz* (2008) 60 DLR 511, the court distinguished 'service of the republic' from constitutional posts and measured judicial independence by assessing whether a judge is free to perform his or her adjudicative role without interference.

105 The definition of the state in Article 152(1) of the Constitution includes the Parliament, the Government and statutory public authorities.

from all three branches of the government,[106] statutory public authorities[107] and actions of those in public office and in the service of the republic.[108] Increasingly, myriads of private agency questions of public interest have been subsumed within the Supreme Court's administrative review jurisdiction. In *M. H. Chowdhury* v. *Titas Gas Transmission and Distribution Company Ltd.*, the court extended the meaning of state to a private entity by testing the degree of the government's financial and administrative control over it.[109] In this case, a majority of the company's shares were held by the state and its management was entrusted to a statutory corporation. Given the nature and degree of control by a public agency on Titas Gas, it was held to be an instrumentality of the state.

The Bangladeshi position affirmed the Indian Supreme Court's test of 'the instrumentality of state' based on a non-exhaustive list of factors that determined whether or not private agency constituted public function.[110] These included inter alia the nature and degree of financial assistance and administrative control by the state and the entrustment of public functions ordinarily carried out by the state. Interestingly, the Indian Court relied on the American case of *Marsh* v. *Alabama*, which devised a similar test for determining the nature of public functions carried out by a corporation.[111] In recent years, the Bangladesh Supreme Court has further extended its interpretations of 'state' by examining the degree to which the functions of a particular body has been 'woven into the fabric of public regulation'. To this end, it has relied on the approaches delineated in *R* v. *Exparte Datafin*.[112] This reflects a gradual expansion of the Court's review powers over private entities and new areas, and the relative ease with which common law grounds circulate between jurisdictions.

16.4.2 *Reliance on Historical Jurisprudence and Borrowing from Other Jurisdictions*

After democratic transition, the Court was at liberty to determine and evaluate the nature of governmental action insofar as it affected the separation of powers and fundamental rights. This initiated the need for a theory of judicial review based on wide interpretations of common law traditions and the new constitutional framework of rights and powers. In constructing the basic structure doctrine in the Eighth Amendment case, for instance, the Court significantly engaged in historical reconstruction. Such an exercise involved

106 The Court has interpreted the state to include all three branches; see *Anwar Hossain Khan* v. *Speaker Jativa Sangsad* (Parliament Boycott) 47 DLR (1995) 42; *Shamsul Huq Chowdhurv* v. *Justice Md Abdur Rouf* 49 DLR (1997) 176.

107 Article 152(1) of the Constitution defines 'statutory public authority' as any authority, corporation or body, the principal activities of which are legally authorized by any statute (act, ordinance, order or instrument). See *Bangladesh Retired Government Employees Welfare Association* v. *Bangladesh* 46 (1994) DLR (HCD) 426.

108 Article 152(1) defines a public officer as a person holding or acting in any office of emolument in the 'service of the Republic', which includes any service, post or office (civil or military) within the government or otherwise declared to be so by law. *Aminul Haque Helal* v. *Justice Sultan Hossain Khan* (2007) 15 BLT 1 interpreted such service broadly considering (i) whether the government had sole power of appointment and dismissal; (ii) whether salaries are charged to the government exchequer; and (iii) whether such office involved the exercise some portion of sovereign power in public interest.

109 (1981) 33 DLR (AD) 186. See also *Arif Sultan* v. *DESA* (2008) 60 DLR (HCD)431; *Mohammad Mahbubur Rahman* v. *Bangladesh* (2017) 37 BLD (HCD) 104.

110 *R.D Shettv* v. *International Airport Authority* AIR 1979 SC 1628.

111 326 U.S. 501 (1946).

112 *Moulana Md. Abdul Hakim* v. *Bangladesh* (2014); *R* v. *Panel on Take-overs and Mergers, ex parte Datafin plc* [1987] QB 815. See also Ridwanul, Hoque, and Azad Emraan, 'Judicial Review of State Contracts: Piercing the Narrow Divide between "Pure and Simple" and "Statutory or Sovereign" Contracts' (2017) 28 *Dhaka University Law Journal*; Ahmed, Justice Syed Refaat, 'The Case of Moulana Abdul Hakim and Judicial Review: A Move Towards the Right Direction?' (2016) 2 *UAP Journal of Law and Policy* 1, 1–12.

consideration of chronology and institutional evolution, resulting from changes in the political structure, to aid in its interpretation of constitutional provisions.

In the Eighth Amendment decision, Justice Shahabuddin Ahmed described the basic structure doctrine as an accumulation of legal traditions since the Regulating Act 1773 of British India.[113] The Supreme Court laid out the differences between pre-independence High Court and the HCD of the Supreme Court of Bangladesh. Pointing out the provincial character of High Courts in both the Indian (1861–1947) and Pakistani (1947–71) periods, it emphasized that the Constitution deliberately created the HCD as an integral part of the Supreme Court. The Court attributed the confusion in meaning to nomenclature – that is, 'High Court Division' and the historically embedded idea of the High Courts of British India since 1861.[114] The Court pointed out that the terms *HCD* and *High Court* were used interchangeably in popular parlance, including among the legal community. The Supreme Court distinguished the High Courts of Bangladesh from India. The HCD was not a High Court within the meaning of the Indian Constitution. In India, High Courts held limited territorial jurisdiction without plenary judicial power over the Republic, and intra-court transfer of Judges was allowed. Article 94 of the Bangladesh Constitution clearly states that the Supreme Court comprises the two divisions of HCD and AD – indicating that it is the sum of its parts. The Court emphasized the legal significance of the word 'division', which implied its plenary judicial powers.[115] While the Court relied on the basic structure doctrine developed by the Indian Supreme Court, this narrative was a specific engagement with history as an interpretive tool.[116] It marked a break with colonial institutions, or at least the ways in which high courts had been understood elsewhere in the subcontinent. Therefore, the formulation of the basic structure doctrine in Bangladesh was not simply borrowing from another jurisdiction but also the product of introspection and examination of institutional history.

Quite apart from legal histories advanced by historians, the kind of institutional account advanced by the court points towards a living institutional history that is preserved by the professional creed of lawyers and legal training. Even when Courts are trying to innovate doctrines or interpret institutional history, there is a good deal of reference to English law. Ties to Britain and free-flowing citations tend to be perceived as unproblematic and perhaps even prestigious for a variety of reasons including professionalization and connections to the bar of England and Wales (across the Commonwealth countries). Administrative law has been remarkably immune to the critique of perpetuating many colonial constructs historical assumptions based on the hegemony of English law. Accordingly, this chapter examined judicial review in light of the history of the evolution of judicial power in the region and constitutional politics which has helped shape it. Such contextualization aids in moving beyond assumptions about the wholesale importation of English legal doctrines in post-colonial polities such as Bangladesh; and understanding the comparatively wider circulation of regional cases in Bangladeshi courts.

The Bangladesh Supreme has looked to foreign jurisdictions to cultivate and search for a homegrown approach. Although the Court does often identify with common law systems, there is no single predictor of foreign citations. In general, lawyers and judges will typically introduce foreign content to adjudication based on their own knowledge and pedagogical training. Additionally, judicial networks and technical reform programs may also influence

113 S. Ahmed J, para. 268, at 116, Eighth Amendment Case.

114 B. H. Chowdhury J, para. 105, at 75, Eighth Amendment Case.

115 B. H. Chowdhury J, para 156, at 86, Eighth Amendment Case.

116 *Kesavananda Bharati Sripadagalvaru and Ors.* v. *State of Kerala and Anr.* AIR 1973 SC 1461.

cross-jurisdictional exchanges, particularly international norms or best practices.[117] The use of historical and foreign sources may be strategic. It opens ways for the Court to respond to an unstable political environment by communicating its values and aiding the Court in sustaining institutional legitimacy by cultivating support from the public as well as international actors.[118]

The Supreme Court has selectively relied on foreign jurisdictions. In *Masdar Hossain*, the Court primarily relied on a Canadian case to delineate the essential conditions of judicial independence.[119] Doing so offered correctives to the inherited and archaic procedural architecture. Interestingly, within just two years of the *Masdar Hossain* case, which cited a Canadian authority, a large judicial reform project funded by the World Bank and partially implemented by the Canadian International Development Agency was under way in 2001. It is possible that cross-cultural exchanges had taken place during the pre-implementation assessment period of this project.[120] More recently, however, the Court displayed some reticence to rely on English precedents.

In the Sixteenth Amendment case, the judges engaged in substantial comparative analysis of removal processes for judges. It concluded that 63 per cent of commonwealth countries had some form of independent body or disciplinary council for removal of judges who were free from parliamentary and executive influence.[121] It specifically considered examples from India, the US and the UK to assess the efficacy of those systems for the removal of judges. The Court concluded, however, that it was not bound by practices prevalent in other countries. Accordingly, Justice Imman Ali stated (while retorting to Counsel's arguments about parliamentary impeachment of judges under English law):

> The situation in UK cannot be equated with that prevailing here. What was done in the UK was to protect judges from the draconian and pernicious actions of the Kings/Queens of the day who could whimsically remove their judges. As it happens, not a single English judge has been impeached since the coming into force of the Act of Settlement in 1701. Moreover, the system of appointment of judges in the UK and other countries referred by the learned Attorney General is not the same as the one operating in our country. Hence, there is no logic in wishing to follow those other countries. . . . The country is now almost 46 years old and has by now gathered sufficient experience and wisdom to be able to decide how to deal with removal of our Supreme Court judges.[122]

The above discussion reveals significant inconsistency that makes legal development difficult to track. This is compounded by the Supreme Court's power to overrule its own judgment in administrative matters. The degree to which the Court will engage in judicial adventures will largely depend on the political climate and zeal of the bench in question. Beneath the surface of official dictum and the apparently seamless circulation of English (and other Commonwealth) doctrines in Bangladeshi court decisions, myriads of institutional and professional dynamics

[117] International associations such as the Commonwealth often serve as platforms for meaningful exchange; see http://thecommonwealth.org/media/news/commonwealth-support-judicial-independence-bangladesh. See also Slaughter, Anne-Marie, 'Judicial Globalization' (1999) 40 *Virigina Journal of International Law* 1103.

[118] See, Kalb, Johanna, 'The Judicial Role in New Democracies: A Strategic Account of Comparative Citation' (2013) 38 *Yale Journal of International Law* 423, 428.

[119] The Court relied on *Valente* v. *The Queen*, [1985] 2 S.C.R. 673, which identified security of tenure, financial security and administrative independence as three core characteristics or essential conditions of judicial independence.

[120] http://projects.worldbank.org/P044810/legal-judicial-capacity-building-project?lang=en. See also Laver, Roberto, 'The World Bank and Judicial Reform: Overcoming Blind Spots in the Approach to Judicial Independence' (2011) 22 *Duke Journal of Comparative and International Law* 183.

[121] S.K. Sinha CJ, para 159, at 101, Sixteenth Amendment Case.

[122] Imman Ali J, para 590, at 239, Sixteenth Amendment Case.

influence the extent of the adaptation of those doctrines. Threats to judicial autonomy remain a feature of constitutional politics in Bangladesh, and the Supreme Court has yet to resolve its inter-branch rivalries. Ongoing controversies involving appointments and scandals surrounding certain Chief Justices have resulted in public spats between the judiciary and the executive branches.[123]

The oscillation of judicial power resulting from this environment has also impacted the nature of review. The court has wavered between issuing sweeping directions, in a bid to claw back its territory from the executive, and offering a restrained approach in the interests of institutional efficiency. The court has traditionally exercised wide powers of review and supervision without the political questions doctrine restraining it. The *Masdar Hossain* decision is one example of the Court's wide exercise of review powers. It has been criticized as judicial overreach, as some of its directions for the government, including the creation of judicial pay and service commission, are outside its competence and within the province of the parliament.[124] The Court has also intervened in cases that would otherwise oust its jurisdiction. For instance, it held that although the existence of an efficacious remedy is a constitutional bar to a writ, the Court may review cases where governmental action is patently unreasonable and arbitrary, thereby triggering Article 31 (the right to protection of law).[125] Additionally, Article 117(2) of the Constitution, which otherwise ousts the Court's jurisdiction in favour of statutory administrative tribunals, has been held to be inapplicable where government action was exercised in bad faith (*mala fide*) or without jurisdiction (*coram non judice*).[126] The Court has ruled that administrative tribunals are not to be construed as a forum substitute, alternate or co-equal to the HCD.[127] In so doing, the Supreme Court attempted to maintain its autonomy and position itself as the final arbiter in all interpretive matters including that of ouster clauses. This also aligns with the principles in the *Anisminic* case (see Section 16.2).

Though typically liberally construed, this body of judge-made law has been far from consistent. On some occasions, the Court has refused to expand remedies, citing the dangers of exceeding its proper functions.[128] In other instances, it has generated uncertainties by making recommendations that appeared to overrule its previous decisions. This was the case in *Government of Bangladesh and Others* v. *Sontosh Kumar Shaha and Others*.[129] It ruled that Administrative Tribunal was not a forum substitute of, or coequal to, the HCD. Instead, it was an alternative forum, though the term 'alternative' was not defined. In a bid to increase public

[123] A recent scandal relates to the resignation of Chief Justice Sinha, who is currently under asylum. In a tell-all book citing his version of events, Justice Sinha blames the Sixteenth Amendment judgment to have escalated interbranch tensions, ultimately resulting in what he claims was a forced resignation. Justice Surendra Kumar Sinha, *A Broken Dream: Rule of Law, Human Rights and Democracy* (Amazon CreateSpace, 2018). After Justice Sinha resigned, further controversy followed with the supersession of acting Chief Justice Wahab Miah, who succeeded him: www.thedailystar.net/country/justice-wahhab-miah-resigns-1528981.

[124] Mahmudul, note 43, 906.

[125] *Luthfunnessa* v. *Bangladesh* (1990) 42 DLR (AD) 86.

[126] Article 117(1) authorizes the Parliament to establish statutory administrative tribunals to deal various cases, including, civil service disputes, disposal and management of government property and so on. Article 117(2) provides exclusive jurisdiction to these tribunals and reads 'where any administrative tribunal is established under this article, no court shall entertain any proceedings or make any order in respect of any matter falling within the jurisdiction of such tribunal: Provided that Parliament may, by law, provide for appeals from, or the review of, decisions of any such tribunal'. See Article 117, Constitution of Bangladesh.

[127] *Mujibur Rahman* v. *Bangladesh* (1992) 44 DLR (AD) 189.

[128] In *Bangladesh* v. *Mahbubuddin Ahmed* (1998) 18 BLD (AD) 87, the Court declared a public official's dismissal from service as unlawful. However, it refused to order his reinstatement in view of a more restrained judicial role of ruling on the propriety of the administration action only.

[129] 2016(1) LNJ (AD) 61.

confidence and address administrative efficiency, the judgment recommended the reduction of case backlog through diversion to Administrative Tribunals. While it appeared to deny review of these cases even in instances of bad faith, it also recognized that the right to move the HCD was a 'basic feature' of the Constitution, guaranteed under Article 44(1).[130] The wording of the judgment avoided taking a definitive position and appeared to urge circumspection when exercising the 'power of judicial review and avoid [interfering] with those matters which are cognizable under Article 117(1) of the constitution. This is necessary for the interest of justice.'[131] This seems to suggest that the door to judicial remedy in the writ court has not been foreclosed. Accordingly, the Court's indecision and consequent wavering approach to judicial review reflect the larger contestation between the judiciary and the executive.

16.5 CONCLUSION

This chapter has tracked the development of judicial review of administrative action in Bangladesh. It is evident from this chapter, as well as the larger volume of which it is a part, that there have been unique adaptations of judicial review much beyond its English heritage. Consequently, common law countries continue to share a similar language, albeit differing perhaps in meaning. The influence of English administrative law is still prevalent in Bangladesh. However, there is a discernable difference between English law from England, English law as it developed in the colonies and contemporary innovations by the courts. The Bangladesh Supreme Court continues to rely on English cases, but it has also departed from them in search of a more localized approach. The role of lawyers ought to be acknowledged here, who contribute in no small measure to extending the pool of comparative sources. The doctrinal parameters of judicial review in Bangladesh are mediated by historical and political factors, as well as general circulation of common law grounds between jurisdictions. The constitutionalizing of administrative law and the accretion of historical jurisprudence adds to the uniqueness of the Bangladeshi model.

In line with regional trends, the Supreme Court of Bangladesh continues to play a central role in the production of administrative law. The unstable political climate in Bangladesh, however, creates a tall order for the Court, demanding much beyond conventional checks and balances. The Court must grapple with its past by way of correcting the institutional inertias it inherited and moving forward, whereby it can deliver on the transformations promised by the Constitution. Given its operative environment, the Supreme Court has yet to strike an optimal balance between judicial and political control over administrative processes and systemic needs of efficiency. This is unsurprising, since judicial power, jurisdiction and prestige are tied to political outcomes. In the absence of stable and effective representative institutions, on several occasions, the judiciary has stepped up to aid in governance. More recently, the Supreme Court has even expanded review in tort cases, holding public agencies accountable for negligence and inaction.[132] The Court's traversal in these unconventional arenas may raise normatively significant questions about the precise contours of separation of powers in Bangladesh. However, a contextual analysis can significantly aid the construction of alternative judicial theories that accommodate judicial review as a stimulus for legislative and executive functions, a means for promoting inter-branch dialogue and a catalyst that forces the state to restructure its policy framework.

[130] 2016(1) LNJ (AD) 60.

[131] 2016(1) LNJ (AD) 55.

[132] *CCB Foundation* v. *Government of Bangladesh* 5 CLR (HCD) (2017). I am grateful to Advocate Saqeb Mahbub (Bar-at-Law) for this observation and reading an earlier version of this paper.

PART VII

Origins and Adaptations in Australasia

17

The Creation of Australian Administrative Law

The Constitution and Its Judicial Gate-Keepers

Matthew Groves and Greg Weeks

For a long time, judicial review in Australia was little more than a carbon copy of its English equivalent. In the period before the various Australian states became part of a unified federal nation, judicial review occurred within the inherent supervisory jurisdiction of the various Supreme Courts of those individual colonies and proceeded in a manner similar to that of English courts exercising inherent supervisory jurisdiction. The creation of the new nation of Australia was notable on two counts. One was that it marked the start of a distinct new federal jurisdiction. More importantly, this new federal country was supported by a written constitution that would eventually refashion all Australian public law.[1] The Australian Constitution is now the defining feature and dominant force of our judicial review doctrine. It has been described variously as a 'catalyst' for the modern evolution of Australian administrative law,[2] a 'conversation stopper' that precludes considered analysis of foreign developments,[3] and an influence so strong that it exerts a 'gravitational pull' on all of Australian public law.[4]

The key feature of the Australian Constitution that has enabled the recognition and entrenchment of judicial review of administrative action is the express creation and entrenchment of the courts.[5] The express recognition and protection of a selection of the judicial remedies have proved equally important because the constitutional mention of some of the traditional remedies of judicial review has provided the foundation for the courts to entrench by implication that which necessarily precedes the issue of those remedies. While these and other important elements of the Australian Constitution have enabled the development of constitutionally protected avenues of supervisory review, this same constitutional foundation

1 That document was a statute of the British parliament and arguably gained its political force in Australia from the fact that it was enacted after extensive public debate and approval by a referendum within the Australian states. Precisely why this statue has a singular legal force in Australia is the result of many other factors. See Geoff Lindell, 'Why Is the Constitution Binding? The Reasons in 1900 and Now, and the Effect of Independence' (1986) 16 *Federal Law Review* 29; Simon Evans, 'Why Is the Constitution Binding? Authority, Obligation and the Role of the People' (2004) 25 *Adelaide Law Review* 103.

2 Cheryl Saunders, 'Constitution as Catalyst: Different Paths within Australian Administrative Law' (2013) 10 *New Zealand Journal of Public and International Law* 143.

3 A phrase used with disarming ambiguity by Michael Taggart, '"Australian Exceptionalism" in Judicial Review' (2008) *Federal Law Review* 1, 11.

4 JJ Spigelman, 'The Centrality of Jurisdictional Error' (2010) 21 *Public Law Review* 77, 91.

5 Australian Constitution, Ch. III. This part of the Constitution contains ss. 71–80, which create the judicial system. Sections 71–2 create the High Court of Australia, which is invested by s. 73 with a wide appellate jurisdiction. The High Court is given original jurisdiction in all matters where a remedy of mandamus, prohibition, or injunction are sought against 'officer of the Commonwealth': s. 75(v). This provision is unique in the common law world because it entrenches a right of supervisory review of administrative action in the nation's final court of appeal.

has also provided the source of judicial review principles that increasingly differ from their early English heritage. Many parallels between English and Australian principles remain, and the one we discuss about natural justice suggests that, as happens within so many families, Australian judicial review can unwittingly replicate the mistakes of its English parent.

Natural justice is a useful vehicle to trace these issues because it served an important role in the High Court's exploration of the nature and content of supervisory judicial review and, by implication, the complimentary function of merits review tribunals. We explain in the following section that the ongoing debate about the origin of the duty to observe the rules of natural justice provides a strange parallel to the debate that occurred in England about the basis of judicial review around the same time. The key case of *Attorney-General (NSW)* v. *Quin*[6] blended English and American influences to reach a distinctively Australian approach to administrative law and used a limited conception of fairness to expound a limited conception of supervisory review that is now a cornerstone of Australian administrative law doctrine. *Quin* also ushered constitutional influences to the forefront of Australia's administrative law doctrines. However, we hope to demonstrate, the story of how Australian administrative law became particularly Australian is more complex than the role of the Constitution alone can possibly answer for. We conclude that labels do not obscure the common central concern of judicial review in each country – devising and maintain principles for the judicial supervision of decision-making within the executive government that reflect a finely balanced role for the courts.

17.1 THE RECEPTION AND INFLUENCE OF UK PUBLIC LAW IN AUSTRALIA

Australian public law existed long before Australia. Prior to the act of federation, by which the existing Australian states became part of a single federal state, the individual colonial states adopted and applied British law. The State Supreme Courts were essentially recognised and preserved at federation by their mention in s. 73 of the Australian Constitution, but those courts came to federation with considerable history. All of these courts had been invested since their inception with 'such jurisdiction as the Court of Queen's Bench had in England'.[7] This replication of English jurisdiction granted the early state courts 'a general power to issue the writ [of certiorari] to any inferior Court' in the relevant state.[8] The replication of English jurisdiction also enabled Australian courts effectively to mimic the judicial review work of their English counterparts. Australian courts had good reason to replicate the approaches and doctrinal rules of English courts because their decisions were subject to appeal to the Privy Council. While that right was rarely used, it was exercised in one important case about migration law and responsible government.[9] The facts of that case bear an uncanny parallel to the migration cases that have dominated modern Australian public law,[10] though in its time

6 (1990) 170 CLR 1.

7 *Kirk* v. *Industrial Court (NSW)* (2010) 239 CLR 531, 580 [97], citing *Australian Courts Act 1828* (Imp) (9 Geo 4 c 83) s. 3, which conferred jurisdiction on the Supreme Court of New South Wales and the Supreme Court of Van Diemen's Land; *Supreme Court Act 1890* (Vic) s. 18; *Supreme Court Act 1867* (Qld), ss. 21, 34; *Act No 31 of 1855–56* (SA) s. 7; *Supreme Court Act 1880* (WA) s. 5, picking up *Supreme Court Ordinance 1861* (WA) s. 4.

8 *Colonial Bank of Australasia* v. *Willan* (1874) LR 5 PC 417, 440.

9 *Toy* v. *Musgrove* [1891] AC 272, reversing the decision of the Full Court of the Supreme Court of Victoria in *Toy* v. *Musgrove* (1888) 14 VLR 349.

10 *Toy* was a Chinese national who asserted a right to disembark at port under the *Chinese Act 1881* (Vic). The government denied that claim but raised the more far reaching claim that, as a colonial government granted full political competence, it could further regulate migration by an act of state. The Privy Council avoided these

the decision simply affirmed that questions of statutory interpretation and the element of public law and judicial review were to be resolved according to the principles of British law.

Modern cases have noted that the Australian Constitution entrenches the jurisdiction to seek judicial review remedies without mention of the grounds. One consequence that we explain later in this chapter is that this practical gap in the constitutional right of review has enabled the High Court to refine and apply the grounds in their common law form. While this common law background is now characterised as a novel and innovative feature of the High Court's constitutionally entrenched judicial review jurisdiction, the same pattern was evident prior to the creation of Australia. The vesting of the jurisdiction equivalent to the Courts of Queen's Bench in the State Supreme Courts said nothing of the grounds or procedure that those courts should use. The simple solution reached by the State Supreme Courts was to adopt the grounds and practices applied in English courts. Cane has argued that the Australian reliance on English doctrine extended to the fundamental character of our earliest judicial review by its remedial focus.[11] This remedial focus may partly explain why the Australian Constitution includes particular judicial review remedies in the original jurisdiction of the High Court but remains silent on other key elements of that jurisdiction. Whatever the focus of Australian judicial review, there is no doubt that its development prior to the federation did little more than reflect the fragmented principles that prevailed in English law at the time.

17.2 THE CONSTITUTIONAL BACKDROP

A novel and far-reaching system of administrative review has existed in Australia for just about forty years, but this system only can be understood by reference to the earlier constitutional fundamentals that this radical new system was framed around. The Australian Constitution is essentially a hybrid of English and American influences. The English influence takes the form of the common law method and the English history from which Australian courts still draw. American influences are evident in our adoption of a written constitution to create a federal nation that constitutes and allocates official authority by use of the separation of powers into three distinct arms of government. That separation arguably formalised the informal arrangements that long applied in England, but the Australian version has a sharp constitutional edge. The most important example is the various principles that preclude one arm of government from exercising the powers reserved to another.[12] The federal Parliament, for example, cannot exercise judicial power either directly or by enacting legislation that usurps, limits, or purports the exercise by courts of judicial power.[13] These principles have many inconvenient consequences, including precluding judges from exercising non-judicial powers such as presiding over a royal or other commission of inquiry.[14] The courts are likewise prohibited from exercising administrative power. There are minor exceptions, but the key

larger issues and ruled against the plaintiff on the more-narrow issue that the terms of the relevant Act did not provide him with any right to enter the colony even if he met its various requirements.

11 P Cane, 'The Making of Australian Administrative Law' (2003) 24 *Australian Bar Review* 114, 116.

12 The key case is *R* v. *Kirby; Ex parte Boilermakers' Society of Australia* (1956) 94 CLR 254, but that decision was foreshadowed by many earlier ones that endorsed a strict approach to the separation of powers.

13 This includes legislation that vests courts with functions incompatible with the exercise of judicial power: *Kable* v. *Director of Public Prosecutions (NSW)* (1996) 189 CLR 51; *International Finance Trust Co Ltd* v. *New South Wales Crimes Commission* (2009) 240 CLR 319.

14 *Wilson* v. *Minister for Aboriginal and Torres Strait Islanders Affairs* (1996) 183 CLR 1.

demarcations are clear.[15] Many of these limits have developed by reference to a conception of judicial power that evolves but remains inexact.[16] One guiding principle is the clear distinction between courts and non-judicial bodies. That distinction remains elusive, but the basic one between courts and tribunals is not.[17] A court, and only a court, may exercise judicial power. These principles limit what courts and tribunals each can and cannot do. The administrative character of tribunals means their decisions cannot take the form of binding orders, which are enforceable in the same way as orders of courts.[18] Courts cannot examine the substantive merits of administrative decisions because that form of review constitutes an exercise of administrative or executive authority rather than judicial power.[19] This principle clearly precludes tribunals from exercising any form of judicial review power,[20] which means Australia cannot undertake any equivalent of recent reforms to English tribunals that have granted limited judicial review power to the Upper Tribunal.[21]

The radical reforms made to Australian administrative law from the mid-1970s onwards reflected these constitutional demarcations. Those reforms included the creation of a new administrative review tribunal – the federal Administrative Appeals Tribunal (AAT) – which was granted wide jurisdiction to review and remake administrative decisions. A key reason for the creation of this novel new tribunal was the acceptance that a tribunal could perform a key function of administrative review that lay beyond the constitutional grasp of the courts – to review and remake administrative decisions according to the merits of the material placed before the AAT.[22] The AAT was a radical step into a new age of administrative review, but its creation owed as much to history. The functions granted to the AAT reflected long-settled constitutional conceptions about the differences between courts and tribunals, supervisory and merits reviews, and most importantly, the non-judicial powers that can be granted only to non-judicial bodies such as tribunals. Past constitutional lessons shaped future administrative law plans.[23]

There is ongoing debate about the nature of merits review and whether it actually differs in any substantial way from supervisory review by the courts. Professor Cane has long argued that courts and tribunals in Australia quietly perform much of the function supposedly

15 For example, the federal parliament can exercise judicial power to punish a contempt of parliament: *R* v. *Richards; Ex parte Fitzpatrick and Browne* (1955) 92 CLR 157.

16 Even thoughtful critiques of the prevailing conception of the separation of powers shy away from offering any complete definition of the doctrine they argue needs reform. See, e.g., J Stellios, 'Reconceiving the Separation of Judicial Power' (2011) 22 *Public Law Review* 113.

17 The High Court has accepted that the diluted application the separation of powers doctrine has at the state level means distinctions between courts and tribunals of the states 'may not always be drawn easily': *Kirk* v. *Industrial Relations Court (NSW)* (2010) 239 CLR 531, 573, [69].

18 *Brandy* v. *Human Rights and Equal Opportunity Commission* (1995) 183 CLR 245.

19 *Attorney-General (NSW)* v. *Quin* (1990) 170 CLR 1, 35–6.

20 *Director of Housing* v. *Sudi* (2011) 33 VR 559. This case involved the Victorian Civil and Administrative Tribunal (VCAT), but its reasoning clearly applies to all other state tribunals.

21 A jurisdiction created by the *Tribunals, Courts and Enforcement Act* 2007 (UK) ss. 15–21.

22 This arguably simplifies the issues because the defining quality of merits review is that a tribunal should make the 'correct or preferable' decision. This concept was not clearly apparent or expressly stated in the *Administrative Appeals Tribunal Act* 1975 (Cth). It evolved in cases, such as *Re Becker and Minister for Immigration and Ethnic Affairs* (1979) 1 ALD 158, 162 and *Drake* v. *Minister for Immigration and Ethnic Affairs* (1979) 24 ALR 577, 589. The High Court was finally able to endorse the concept in *Shi* v. *Migration Agents Registration Authority* (2008) 235 CLR 286, [72] (Kirby J), [81] (Hayne and Heydon JJ), [140] (Kiefel J).

23 Sir Anthony Mason suggested that a unified system that could blend judicial and administrative review into a single system faced as much political opposition as it would from constitutional doctrine: 'Judicial Review: A View from Constitutional and Other Perspectives' (2000) *Federal Law Review* 331, 333.

reserved to the other in constitutional doctrine.[24] Others maintain that judicial and merits review are not simply distinct but are separated by a clear gap, if not a gulf.[25] It is also clear that each has influenced the other. The High Court has, for example, suggested that the creation of merits review made it unlikely that parliament had intended the Federal Court to exercise any general jurisdiction to review findings of fact.[26] It also suggested that the existence of merits review provided a strong reason to reject suggestions that unstructured discretionary powers were overly broad, and possibly unconstitutional, because they could be exercised for an improper purpose.[27] The apparent restraint of the courts on such issues might suggest that substantive review is not possible in Australia, but courts regularly hint otherwise when they stress that a 'diminishing field' of merits is left by the modern expansion of judicial review,[28] or dismiss the 'beguiling simplicity' of the very notion of the merits of a decision.[29]

Despite these doctrinal complications, this radical system of review marked a radical break from the English heritage of Australian public law. The extent of that change was evident from the inclusion of rights and institutions that had no clear English counterpart. One was freedom of information legislation, which provided people with both a general right of access to government documents and a further right, in some instances, to require corrections to mistakes recorded in official information. This radical new regime can be traced to American influences.[30] The independent office of the Ombudsman was drawn from the newly established version of that office in New Zealand.[31] Despite these different international influences, the new Australian system owes much to calls for reforms made in England. One of the tasks given to the Committee that considered the introduction of this new system was whether Australia should introduce legislation akin to Britain's *Tribunal and Inquiries Act 1958*.[32] The resulting AAT may have been entirely different from anything known in Britain, but that country's legislation was the first point of reference. A wider view suggests that the problems experienced in the UK were as influential as the reforms it had adopted. The new system of administrative review adopted in Australia reforms of the UK was not the only inspiration to Australia. One of the committees that recommended the establishment of the new Australian system was mindful of the need to provide control and fairness over the growing machinery of modern government and the pervading discretionary powers it had acquired.[33] This wider rationale for the radical reform of administrative review in Australia clearly echoed Lord Hewart's concerns about the arbitrary nature of discretionary power in modern government[34] and the Donoughmore Report that followed.[35]

24 P Cane, 'Merits Review and Judicial Review – The AAT as Trojan Horse' (2000) 28 *Federal Law Review* 213; P Cane, *Administrative Tribunals and Adjudication* (Hart, 2009) p. 179.

25 M Allars, 'The Nature of Merits Review: A Bold Vision Realised in the Administrative Appeals Tribunal' (2013) 41 *Federal Law Review* 197; R Creyke, 'Judicial Review and Merits Review: Are the Boundaries Being Eroded?' (2017) 45 *Federal Law Review* 627.

26 *Australian Broadcasting Tribunal* v. *Bond* (1990) 170 CLR 321, 341 (Mason CJ).

27 *Cunliffe* v. *Commonwealth* (1994) 182 CLR 272, 331 (Brennan J). Mason CJ echoed these views: 303.

28 *Greyhound Racing Authority (NSW)* v. *Bragg* [2003] NSWCA 388, [46] (Santow JA).

29 *D'Amore* v. *Independent Commission for Corruption* (2013) 303 ALR 242 [232] (Basten JA).

30 E Campbell, 'Public Access to Government Documents' (1967) 41 *Australian Law Journal* 73.

31 See generally Anita Stuhmcke, 'The Evolution of the Classical Ombudsman: A View from the Antipodes' (2012) 2 *International Journal of Public Law and Policy* 83.

32 Commonwealth Administrative Review Committee, *Commonwealth Administrative Review Committee Report*, Parliament of the Commonwealth of Australia Paper No 144 (1971) (Commonwealth) ('Kerr Report') 71.

33 Committee on Administrative Discretions, *Final Report of the Committee on Administrative Discretions*, 1973 ('Bland Report').

34 Lord Hewart, *The New Despotism* (Ernst Benn, 1929) p. 52.

35 *Report of the Committee on Ministers' Powers* (1932, Cmnd 4060).

17.3 THREE STAGES OF STATUTORY REFORM: PARTIAL CODIFICATION, LEADING TO COMPLETE ADOPTION

The key change to judicial review was its codification at the federal level by the *Administrative Decisions (Judicial Review) Act 1977* (Cth). That Act introduced a single test for standing, codified the existing common law grounds of review, provided a right to reasons for reviewable decisions, and allowed remedies in the form of a single 'order to review' that enabled issues of statutory remedies equivalent to the key prerogative and equitable remedies. The codified grounds were notable on several counts. First, they listed the grounds that originated and were refined in English public law.[36] Second, they included two open-ended grounds, allowing review of decisions that were 'otherwise contrary to law' or an exercise of power that 'in a way … constitutes abuse of the power'.[37] These two grounds appeared to enable the codified grounds to both facilitate innovation and enable assimilation of any that arose at common law. Third, the ground of 'error of law' was available 'whether or not the error appears on the record'.[38] Fourth, and most relevantly for present purposes, the codified grounds made no reference to ultra vires as the organising principle for review. The ADJR Act did, however, incorporate notions of jurisdiction and authority by the inclusion of grounds that enabled review because the decision was 'not authorised' by the relevant statute or that the decision maker 'did not have jurisdiction to make the decision' under review.[39]

Notions of jurisdiction, or rather the lack of it, were eventually to become central to Australian judicial review, but in the early life of the ADJR Act, that statute served as the main vehicle for review applications at the federal level. The cases that regularly proceeded to the High Court saw incremental advances in particular grounds of review, such as the denial of natural justice and unreasonableness.[40] But these and other cases of that time did not invoke or appear reliant upon an overarching theory of review, or make reference to the concepts of jurisdiction (whether a want, excess, or error) that has since hypnotised Australian judicial review.

The second phase of legislative reform actually had begun with the codification of judicial review and was the creation of a specialist federal court, invested with the administrative law jurisdiction of the Commonwealth. That jurisdiction was an energetic one and became a magnet for controversy as the number of migration cases grew and federal court judges appeared increasingly willing to push the doctrinal envelope in those cases. After the new Federal Court had become an accepted part of the court system, it was unsurprising when the court was granted a statutory jurisdiction in parallel to that granted to the High Court in the Australian Constitution. The High Court's jurisdiction is an original one conferred in s. 75(v) that enables the court to issue the writs of mandamus, prohibition or injunction in any 'matter' involving an officer of the Commonwealth. This jurisdiction was granted to the Federal Court for pragmatic reasons, such as to allow the High Court to remit the occasional application that was commenced in its original jurisdiction.[41] At this time, the original judicial review jurisdiction of the High Court was not used often and generally accepted to

36 The most vivid example was the ground of *Wednesbury* unreasonableness, codified in ADJR Act ss. 5(2)(g), 6(2)(g).

37 These are contained in ADJR Act ss. 5(1)(j), 6(1)(j) [contrary to law] and ss. 5(2)(j), 6(2)(j) [abuse of power].

38 ADJR Act s. (1)(f).

39 ADJR Act ss. 5(1)(d), 6(1)(d) [decision not authorised] and ss. 5(1)(c), 6(2)(c) [lack of jurisdiction].

40 Explored respectively in *Kioa* v. *West* (1985) 150 CLR 550 and *Chan* v. *Minister for Immigration and Ethnic Affairs* (1989) 169 CLR 379.

41 This is contained in *Judiciary Act 1903* (Cth) s. 39B.

be more complex and less efficient alternative to the judicial review statute. It may have remained that way but for the third and most far-reaching phase of legislative reform.

In response to a perceived explosion of migration applications in federal tribunals and courts, successive federal parliaments revised virtually every aspect of Australian migration law. These changes are too complex to explain in detail, but their key features were as follows. In the first bout of reform, specialist migration tribunals were created to supposedly provide expert review and hopefully lower the number of applications to the courts. The decisions reviewed by these new tribunals made under statutory powers that were essentially narrowed, to remove the scope of discretionary judgments and increase the number and scope of mandatory duties governing decision-making.[42] The judicial review system itself was not changed in any material way, but important changes occurred in other parts of judicial review doctrine that we will explain briefly before returning to the subsequent reforms to migration legislation that introduced an endless cycle of cause and effect.

17.4 THE RISE OF CONSTITUTIONAL REVIEW

Australian judicial review doctrine can be usefully traced to the decision of Brennan J in *Attorney-General (NSW)* v. *Quin*,[43] which explained the supervisory role of the courts in a manner that defined and confined their role in equal measure. Brennan J identified the role of the courts as one of constitutional obligation and power that also reflected the particular contours of Australian constitutional law. Brennan J explained that the 'duty and jurisdiction of the court' in supervisory review: '[D]o not go beyond the declaration and enforcing of the law which determinates the limits and governs the exercise of the repository's power.'[44] He then added that '[t]he merits of administrative action, to the extent that they can be distinguished from legality, are for the repository of the relevant power alone and, subject to political control, for the repository alone'.[45]

This approach acknowledged the role of administrative decision-making and its review by the courts. Once it is accepted that the AAT lies within the executive arm of government and is thus a 'repository of power' distinct from the courts, this reasoning provides a clear affirmation of the distinction between judicial and merits review. As one member of the High Court explained prior to his appointment, '[t]o the judges the law; to the others the merits'.[46]

The reasoning of Brennan J was also notable for what it did not mention – concepts of ultra vires or jurisdictional error. References to jurisdictional error and related concepts had previously begun to surface in the decisions of other members of the High Court,[47] but not those of Brennan J.[48] But the approach of Brennan J in *Quin* appeared to adopt the underlying concepts of what later became explained within the confines of jurisdictional error because his conception of the intertwined scope and limits of judicial review was

42 This greatly simplifies the effect of the *Migration Legislation Amendment Act* 1989 (Cth).

43 (1990) 170 CLR 1.

44 (1990) 170 CLR 1, 35–6.

45 (1990) 170 CLR 1, 36.

46 S Gageler, 'Impact of Migration Law on the Development of Australian Administrative Law' (2010) 17 *Australian Journal of Administrative Law* 92, 104.

47 Though typically without explanation. See, e.g., *Public Service Board (NSW)* v. *Osmond* (1986) 159 CLR 656, 674 (Wilson J).

48 Brennan J mentioned the concept a year after *Quin* in *Public Service Association (SA)* v. *Federated Clerks' Union* (1991) 173 CLR 132, 141.

directed to the detection and correction of legal error (though of a form unspecified at that stage).[49]

Jurisdictional error came to the fore five years after *Quin*, when a majority of the High Court invoked the concept as a guiding one for judicial supervision of inferior courts and tribunals. That case of *Craig*[50] grafted any use of jurisdictional error onto the constitutional demarcations identified by Brennan J. It did so by accepting that the powers of administrative officials were required to be exercised correctly according to law and that officials would 'ordinarily' fall into jurisdictional error if they made one of several mistakes, such as asking the wrong question, considering irrelevant material, or failing to consider relevant material.[51] These and other possible examples of jurisdictional error have since been explained as just that – examples of a doctrine that can encompass other forms of legal error.[52] Although expressed with a surprising and somewhat vague explanation of jurisdictional error, this reasoning was broadly consistent with the approached Brennan J had signalled because it conceived the judicial function as one of detecting and policing legal error, albeit when found to be jurisdictional.

The modern reawakening of jurisdictional error in Australia has become so inextricably linked to constitutional principles that most observers overlook the strong English basis acknowledged for the doctrine in *Craig*. The High Court drew extensively from *Anisminic*[53] and *In re Racal*,[54] though each was deployed differently. *Anisminic* was invoked with the remarkable caveat that the High Court did not 'consider that Lord Reid's comments should not be accepted here as an authoritative statement of what constitutes jurisdictional error by an inferior court for the purposes of certiorari'.[55] The implication was clear. The common law pedigree of jurisdictional error confirmed its doctrinal legitimacy, but the inherent flexibility of the common law would enable its adjustment as required for the requirements in one outpost of the common law. This was perhaps the last time the High Court looked back to the English history of jurisdictional error for significant doctrinal support in its reasoning. The use of *In re Racal* was displayed a similar blend of drawing upon established English doctrine but was open in how that required modification in the Australian environment. The High Court cited Lord Diplock's statement that administrative decision makers could be presumed to lack the power to authoritatively decide questions of law 'or to make an order or decision otherwise than in accordance with the law'.[56] Lord Diplock suggested that parliament could provide otherwise, with suitably clear language, but the High Court noted that possibility faced an important constitutional obstacle in Australia.

> The position is, of course, a fortiori in this country where constitutional limitations arising from the doctrine of the separation of judicial and executive powers may preclude legislative competence to confer judicial power upon an administrative tribunal. If such an administrative tribunal falls into an error of law which causes it to identify a wrong issue, to ask itself a wrong question, to ignore relevant material, to rely on irrelevant material or, at least in some circumstances, to make an erroneous finding or to reach a mistaken conclusion, and the tribunal's exercise or purported exercise of power is thereby affected, it exceeds its authority or

49 See further S Gageler, 'The Legitimate Scope of Judicial Review' (2005) 26 *Australian Bar Review* 303.

50 *Craig* v. *South Australia* (1990) 184 CLR 163.

51 *Craig* v. *South Australia* (1990) 184 CLR 163, 179.

52 *Kirk* v. *Industrial Court (NSW)* (2010) 239 CLR 531, 574 [73].

53 *Anisminic* v. *Foreign Compensation Commission* [1969] 2 AC 147.

54 *In re Racal Communications Ltd* [1984] AC 374.

55 *Craig* v. *South Australia* (1990) 184 CLR 163, 179.

56 *Craig* v. *South Australia* (1990) 184 CLR 163, 179, citing *In re Racal Communications Ltd* (1981) AC 374, 383.

> powers. Such an error of law is jurisdictional error which will invalidate any order or decision of the tribunal which reflects it.[57]

This understanding of the nature and limits of administrative authority as it arises from statutory power was overlaid with the particular constitutional limitations that arise in Australia's constitutional framework. The underlying point is not simply about difference but more about impossibility. The power that may be granted to administrative tribunals and officials in England, albeit in theory and subject to a style of drafting that is unlikely to ever be seen, is constitutionally impossible in Australia. Once again, what constitutes a presumption in England assumes constitutional force in Australia.

This elaboration of jurisdictional error in a series of cases that were mostly appeals from state courts served as a basis to develop constitutional concepts within the working of judicial review, but their true purpose and strength was not revealed until something of a showdown occurred in migration law. That occurred during a further phase of legislative reform to migration law, which saw the introduction of exceptionally detailed and restrictive procedures to govern the processes of migration tribunals. Part of this package included a barrage of restrictions on judicial review, which excluded the ADJR Act from most migration decisions but also imposed a wide-ranging privative clause on review of the decisions and purported decisions of migration tribunals. The simple question before the High Court was whether the clause meant was it appeared to say, or something else. The response of the High Court was to interpret the clause in a literal manner that deprived it of any real operation, thus leaving the clause intact but almost entirely devoid of force. The true impact of that case was the acceptance by the High Court of the 'minimum entrenched provision of judicial review' introduced by s. 75(v) of the *Constitution*'.[58] The 'centrality and protective purpose' of that jurisdiction was explained by reference to jurisdictional error. It existed to enable the High Court to detect and correct jurisdictional error. The High Court explained, 'Such jurisdiction exists to maintain the federal compact by ensuring that propounded laws are constitutionally valid and ministerial and other official action lawful and within jurisdiction.'[59]

The fact that the concept of jurisdictional error took hold in Australian judicial review in such a piecemeal and – to the casual observer – almost haphazard manner is apt to deceive. In truth, successive benches of the High Court have quite obviously seen jurisdictional error as the organising concept around which judicial review in Australia should be approached. It is, after all, consistent with an approach to judicial review that is heavily focused on remedies rather than broad principles.[60] That the Court took so long over so many cases to articulate fully its position on jurisdictional error can be ascribed (with varying degrees of force) to two points. The first is that the High Court is strongly averse to what is known as 'top down legal reasoning',[61] a complaint that, in Australia, has less to do with legal reasoning and more to do with intergenerational and intra-judicial arguments about interpretive method.[62] Prior to joining the High Court, Gageler J attempted to explain the distinction is the following way:

57 *Craig* v. *South Australia* (1990) 184 CLR 163, 179, citing *In re Racal Communications Ltd* (1981) AC 374, 383.

58 *Plaintiff S157/2002* v. *Commonwealth* (2003) 211 CLR 476, 514.

59 *Plaintiff S157/2002* v. *Commonwealth* (2003) 211 CLR 476, 514.

60 See Stephen Gageler, 'Administrative Law Judicial Remedies' in M Groves and HP Lee (eds.), *Australian Administrative Law: Fundamentals, Principles and Doctrines* (Cambridge University Press, 2007) p. 368.

61 A term coined by RA Posner, 'Legal Reasoning from the Top Down and from the Bottom Up: The Question of Unenumerated Constitutional Rights' (1992) 59 *The University of Chicago Law Review* 433.

62 See the forceful rebuttals made by Justice Keith Mason, 'Do Top-Down and Bottom-Up Reasoning Ever Meet?' in E Bant and M Harding (eds.), *Exploring Private Law* (Cambridge University Press, 2010) p. 19; and 'What Is

> In 'top down' reasoning the judge or legal analyst adopts a theory about an area of law. The theory is then used to organise and explain the cases; to marginalise some and to canonise others. In 'bottom up' reasoning the judge or legal analyst starts with the mass of cases or the legislative text and moves only so far as necessary to resolve the case at hand. …
>
> The distinction is useful although the dichotomy is not complete. The 'bottom upper' would be lost in the wilderness of the single instance without some organising theory. The organising theory of the 'top downer', on the other hand, cannot move too far from the decided cases or the legislative text. To do so might make an interesting exercise in political, sociological or economic analysis. But it would have neither utility nor legitimacy as a tool of legal analysis.[63]

It has often been considered wiser for those outside the High Court not to inquire too closely into why the distinction is considered so important.

The second is that Australian courts, uncontroversially, have always preferred to decide only the matter that comes before them and nothing more.[64] Part of this comes from the Commonwealth's constitutional obligation to decide 'matters' brought before a court, a jurisdiction that excludes hypothetical issues.[65] Mainly, however, there is a long-standing Australian tradition that this is the only proper way to develop the common law. As a consequence, far from coming from nowhere, there has been an inevitability going back decades to the emphasis that is now borne by jurisdictional error as a unifying concept of judicial review.

17.5 JURISDICTIONAL ERROR AS A UNIFYING CONCEPT OF REVIEW

By the time a compromise position about the basis of judicial review was reached in England, a new problem had arisen in the form of a search for a unifying concept of review. The UK wrestled with new concepts such as abuse of power,[66] which seem to invite as many questions as they answer. Australian judicial review courts turned increasingly to jurisdictional error, which as we will see was not so much a new concept as an old one that, having been refashioned and relabelled, took on a new sense of purpose. It is now the 'dominant conclusory term'[67] for an error that is able to be remedied with either of the constitutional writs of mandamus or prohibition or (in most cases)[68] with a writ of certiorari,[69] where

Wrong with Top-Down Legal Reasoning?' in N Perram and R Pepper (eds.), *The Byers Lectures 2000–2012* (Federation Press, 2012) p. 69.

63 Stephen Gageler, 'The Underpinnings of Judicial Review of Administrative Action: Common Law or Constitution?' (2000) 28 *Federal Law Review* 303, 303.

64 Sometimes to the point of unhelpfulness; see *Minister for Immigration and Citizenship* v. *SZMDS* (2010) 240 CLR 611, in which the judgment of Heydon J did not engage with certain issues of some interest on which the remaining judges were evenly split.

65 *Re Judiciary and Navigation Acts* (1921) 29 CLR 257. By contrast, English courts have from time to time been happy to decide matters which have already been settled and which therefore lack a justiciable controversy: Sir John Laws, 'Judicial Remedies and the Constitution' (1994) 57 *Modern Law Review* 213, 214–19. This jurisdiction is described as a narrow one to issue advisory declarations for 'theoretical issues' in Harry Woolf, Jeffrey Jowell, Catherine Donnelly, and Ivan Hare (eds.), *de Smith's Judicial Review* (Sweet & Maxwell, 2018) pp. 1004–5.

66 Prominently in *R* v. *North and East Devon Health Authority; ex parte Coughlan* [2001] 3 QB 213.

67 M Aronson, M Groves, and G Weeks (eds.), *Judicial Review of Administrative Action and Government Liability* (Thomson Reuters, 2017) [1.100].

68 Certiorari can issue for a non-jurisdictional error of law only where such error is apparent on the face of the record: *Craig* v. *South Australia* (1995) 184 CLR 163.

69 It is not necessary to establish the presence of a jurisdictional error in order to obtain declaratory or injunctive relief.

previously ultra vires was used for non-judicial bodies.[70] The terms *ultra vires* and *jurisdictional error* have now merged completely in Australia, although the High Court's preference for the latter term means that it is used almost exclusively. On closer inspection, the Australian reliance on jurisdictional error is little more than a use of ultra vires under a different indigenous name.

Jurisdictional error feels like new terminology for a new concept. It is not, although that blunt finding comprises a few different elements. First, as we have stated previously, *ultra vires* was once the term used to describe excesses of power by non-judicial bodies, whereas *jurisdictional error* applied only to judicial bodies and, specifically, only to matters that they lacked jurisdiction even to commence to hear. Jurisdictional error is no longer limited by the so-called commencement theory and has indeed moved into the space once occupied by *ultra vires*.[71] However, this appears largely to be an issue of labels, since jurisdictional error covers the same ground that would otherwise be covered by ultra vires or any other label. In fact, the labels' lack of importance can be demonstrated by the fact that they are both relatively young and have changed in content regularly. *Ultra vires* first entered regular usage in the nineteenth century; *jurisdictional error* was first used in the seventeenth century but did not enter common usage until the twentieth century.[72]

Second, *jurisdictional error* is a label that has generated more than the usual number of critics. From Frankfurter J describing it as a 'verbal coat of too many colours'[73] to Kirby J remarking that 'the old insistence upon preserving the chimerical distinction between jurisdictional and non-jurisdictional error of law might be interred, without tears, in Australia as has happened elsewhere',[74] it is a term with the distinction of having been unloved by lawyers (and, significantly, administrators)[75] at all levels. It is a concept with no direct analogue in the *Administrative Decisions (Judicial Review) Act 1977* (Cth), which had been passed to reform judicial review. Perversely, greater emphasis on jurisdictional error has coincided, over the course of forty years, with the ADJR Act becoming much less frequently used just as the jurisdiction under s. 75(v) of the *Constitution*, and its mirror jurisdiction in section 39B of the *Judiciary Act 1903* (Cth), have been revived. The final inquiry of the (now-defunct) Administrative Review Council (ARC) found that both constitutional and statutory jurisdictions continued to be relevant.[76] However, this was over the dissent of an ARC member, who was also a prominent public servant and who argued for the ADJR Act to be repealed,[77] and the constitutional jurisdiction to be supplemented with statutory limits on the

70 M Aronson, M Groves, and G Weeks (eds.), *Judicial Review of Administrative Action and Government Liability* (Thomson Reuters, 2017) [1.100].

71 M Aronson, M Groves, and G Weeks (eds.), *Judicial Review of Administrative Action and Government Liability* (Thomson Reuters, 2017) [1.100].

72 Aronson et al. above n 71.

73 *United States* v. *LA Tucker Truck Lines Inc*, 344 US 33 (1952) at 39. His Honour was referring specifically to the word 'jurisdiction' but we doubt that jurisdictional error would have pleased him more – a doubt shared by French CJ, Bell, Keane and Gordon JJ in *Plaintiff M64/2015* v. *Minister for Immigration and Border Protection* (2015) 258 CLR 173, 186.

74 *Re Minister for Immigration and Multicultural Affairs; ex parte Miah* (2001) 206 CLR 57 at 123; cf. M Aronson, 'Jurisdictional Error without the Tears' in M Groves and HP Lee (eds.), *Australian Administrative Law: Fundamentals, Principles and Doctrines* (Cambridge University Press, 2007) p. 330.

75 See, e.g., C Wheeler, 'Judicial Review of Administrative Action: An Administrative Decision-Maker's Perspective' (paper presented at the AIAL National Administrative Law Conference, Brisbane, 22 July 2016).

76 Administrative Review Council, *Federal Judicial Review in Australia* (2012).

77 Roger Wilkins reiterated his position from Appendix A to the ARC Report in a subsequent article: R Wilkins and B McGee, 'Judicial Review: A Jurisdictional Limits Model' (2013) 72 *AIAL Forum* 20.

jurisdiction of decision makers. This concept had previously been raised in the final paragraph of an article by Stephen Gageler SC. He suggested:

> A question for the Parliament may well be whether what is currently left to implication ought not now be expressed. After all, it is in everyone's interest for administrative decision-makers clearly to be made aware of their jurisdictional limits before those limits have been transgressed. If so, would there not be some utility in spelling out just what those limits happen to be, perhaps in some code or charter of administrative rights and responsibilities or at least in some new part of the *Acts Interpretation Act 1901* (Cth)? And if we were to do that, how different would the list look from the now almost forgotten list of grounds in the ADJR Act?[78]

Gageler's comments stopped well short of a call for the repeal of the ADJR Act but implicitly recognise that that statute has become of limited utility.[79] All of this is to say that, unloved and unlovely as it might be, Australians seeking judicial review have been driven into the arms of jurisdictional error almost solely because it is the best of a bad set of available options.

Third, as much as jurisdictional error appears to be endlessly confusing, Australians have become accustomed to it. Aronson pointed out ten years ago that, although jurisdictional error had once had a 'strict meaning',[80]

> its vast expansion of scope and meaning over the course of the twentieth century means that it now conveys no meaning whatsoever as to how it was reached, but only as to what will be likely to follow, if it has indeed been reached. Specifically, there are numerous different pathways towards 'jurisdictional error', but usually only one route away from it.

This is to say that jurisdictional error is a label denoting a conclusion; it is not a test.[81] It used to mean things but now it expresses a result. Unlike other jurisdictions, jurisdictional error carries with it the understanding that not all errors of law are the same. However, even this is not a problem, since the High Court has indicated that jurisdictional error is reliably the result of making out certain grounds of review. These go from the traditional grounds covered by the commencement theory to breaches of natural justice, failure to take account of mandatory relevant considerations, and *Wednesbury* unreasonableness. As was seen with regard to the last of the grounds mentioned in *Li*,[82] the discussion has now moved to whether and when making out the established grounds of judicial review might result in an outcome other than jurisdictional error.

It has helped that the High Court has made a project of regularising the approaches of each of the jurisdictions in Australia to match that of the High Court. This has not always led to

78 Gageler, above n 46. The author was then the Solicitor General of Australia and is now a Justice of the High Court of Australia.

79 This is mainly due to the constrictive statutory formula that limits the jurisdiction to review decisions (or conduct) of an administrative character made under an enactment. This is considerably narrower than the equivalent common law (constitutional) jurisdiction and has had the effect of driving litigants away from the ADJR Act.

80 M Aronson, 'Jurisdictional Error without the Tears' in M Groves and HP Lee (eds.), *Australian Administrative Law: Fundamentals, Principles and Doctrines* (Cambridge University Press,2007) 330 at 330. The more important point is that jurisdictional error will usually, but crucially not always, result in the impugned decision being declared a nullity. Such would be the case in the event that the orders of a judge of a superior court were held to contain jurisdictional error. Such orders would never be held to be a nullity on that basis but would operate until overturned; see *State of New South Wales* v. *Kable* (2013) 252 CLR 118 ('*Kable [No 2]*').

81 In the same sense that 'negligence' is not a test; see M Aronson, M Groves, and G Weeks (eds.), *Judicial Review of Administrative Action and Government Liability* (Thomson Reuters, 2017) [1.100].

82 *Minister for Immigration and Citizenship* v. *Li* (2013) 249 CLR 332. The plurality judgment argued that the ground of unreasonableness has now moved beyond the traditional *Wednesbury* formulation.

happy relations with the intermediate appellate courts,[83] and sometimes the High Court's reasoning has been criticised as somewhat tortured.[84] This was the case in the ground-breaking decision in *Kirk*,[85] although on that occasion the Chief Justice of the court in the following section, whose own decision had been overturned, felt able to declare his 'unmitigated admiration' for the High Court's intervention.[86] In *Kirk*, the High Court made clear that the constitutional protection of the High Court's judicial review jurisdiction extends to the capacity of State Supreme Courts to conduct supervisory review for jurisdictional error.

The finding that the jurisdiction granted to the High Court under s. 75(v) of the *Constitution* could not be removed by a privative clause was made in *Plaintiff S157/2002* v. *Commonwealth*.[87] Since then, the High Court has upheld challenges to legislation that sought to restrict its judicial review jurisdiction through oppressive time limits[88] and that denied it access to information which was the subject of the challenged decision.[89] These developments are collectively important but not least for the reason that, although people are being pushed and pulled in equal parts into arguing judicial review matters on the basis of jurisdictional error, at least the High Court has set out effective boundaries that make it hard for legislators to deny them access to a court's judicial review jurisdiction.

17.6 THE CASE OF NATURAL JUSTICE AND THE LEGITIMATE EXPECTATION

A discrete element in the evolution of Australia's judicial review doctrine was an ongoing disagreement about the basis of the duty to observe the rules of natural justice. This debate in Australia inadvertently drew attention to the uncertain basis of judicial review more generally. What was the ultimate foundation of natural justice? The common law, from where the general principles arose? Or the statute, under which administrative powers and discretions were to be exercised?[90] The same questions can be posed to judicial review more generally, and their analysis within the context of natural justice has a curious parallel in the English debate about the ultimate basis of judicial review. We admittedly divide that English debate crudely into the differing views of ultra vires and common law theories of judicial review, but the parallel is clear. This issue appeared important in Australia in the wake of *Kioa* v. *West*.[91] The enduring importance of that case was to mark a decisive shift towards a presumption in favour of the application of the duty to observe the requirements of natural justice. At the same time, however, the case gave rise to uncertainty about the basis of that duty. Mason J suggested there was 'a common law duty to act fairly, in the sense of according procedural

83 Partly because the High Court has strongly asserted its primacy in determining the common law of Australia and cautioned intermediate courts against significant doctrinal changes: *Farah Constructions Pty Ltd* v. *Say-Dee Pty Ltd* (2007) 230 CLR 89.

84 Never more so than when the High Court reached the right decision for reasons that were constitutionally startling in *Kable* v. *Director of Public Prosecutions* (NSW) (1996) 189 CLR 51 ('*Kable [No 1]*').

85 *Kirk* v. *Industrial Court* (NSW) (2010) 239 CLR 531.

86 Spigelman, above n 4.

87 (2003) 211 CLR 476.

88 *Bodruddaza* v. *Minister for Immigration and Multicultural Affairs* (2007) 228 CLR 651.

89 *Graham* v. *Minister for Immigration and Border Protection* (2017) 91 ALJR 890.

90 The High Court has more recently rejected the distinction between common law and statutory interpretation understandings of the genesis of natural justice on the basis that such an inquiry is 'a false dichotomy and ... unproductive': *Plaintiff S10/2011* v. *Minister for Immigration and Citizenship* (2012) 246 CLR 636, 666 [97] (Gummow, Hayne, Crennan and Bell JJ).

91 (1985) 150 CLR 550.

fairness, in the making of administrative decisions which affect rights, interests and legitimate expectations, subject only to the clear manifestation of a contrary statutory intention'.[92]

Brennan J identified a slightly different basis for the obligation, holding that the statute in question provided the starting point to determine whether natural justice applied and what it might require. His Honour also introduced a concept that assumed great importance over time, which was a presumption that the legislature intended that observance of the rules of natural justice was a condition for the valid exercise of statutory powers. Brennan J noted that such a requirement would often be an implied one and that the judicial implication of this implied requirement for the valid exercise of statutory power drew heavily from the common law. He explained: 'When the statute does not expressly require that the principles of natural justice be observed, the court construes the statute on the footing that 'the justice of the common law will supply the omission of the legislature'. The true intention of the legislation is thus ascertained.'[93]

These differing approaches may have ultimately led to the same destination but they appeared to open different possibilities. The approach favoured by Brennan J seemed to anticipate a greater role and influence for parliamentary input because it effectively sourced the duty to act fairly in the legislation enacted by parliament. If parliament was the source of a duty, it surely followed that it had greater control over that duty. Most importantly, parliament could limit or exclude that duty. According to that same reasoning, the approach of Mason J should accord less influence to the parliament in those issues.

In the aftermath of *Kioa* neither view gained decisive support in the High Court, but the approach of Mason J initially attracted more support.[94] Over time, however, the balance clearly shifted towards the view of Brennan J.[95] The difference was finally settled in *Saeed* v. *Minister for Immigration and Citizenship*.[96] The High Court cited the passage of Brennan J just quoted and explained that '[t]he implication of the principles of natural justice in a statute is therefore arrived at by a process of construction. It proceeds upon the assumption that the legislature, being aware of the common law principles, would have intended that they apply to the exercise of a power'.[97] This reasoning effectively blends the differing emphasis taken by Mason and Brennan JJ in *Kioa*, by holding that common law interpretive assumptions and legislative text interact to require and determine observance of the rules of natural justice. In *Kioa*, much of the focus was on the origins of these issues, but *Saeed* shifted attention to their outcome. This shift was confirmed later that year in *Plaintiff M61/2010E* v. *Commonwealth (Offshore Processing Case)*,[98] when the High Court made clear that it was 'unnecessary to consider whether identifying the root of the obligation remains an open question or whether the competing views would lead to any different result'.[99] Two years later, the High Court placed the debate to rest when it explained

92 (1985) 150 CLR 584.

93 (1985) 150 CLR 609.

94 *Attorney-General (NSW)* v. *Quin* (1990) 170 CLR 1, 57–8 (Dawson J); *Annetts* v. *McCann* (1990) 170 CLR 596, 598 (Mason CJ, Deane and McHugh JJ).

95 *Haoucher* v. *Minister for Immigration and Ethnic Affairs* (1990) 169 CLR 648, 652 (Deane J); *Re Refugee Review Tribunal; Ex parte Aala* (2000) 204 CLR 82, 100–1 (Gaudron and Gummow JJ); and *Re Minister for Immigration and Multicultural Affairs; Ex parte Miah* (2001) 206 CLR 57, 69-70 (Gleeson CJ and Hayne J).

96 (2010) 241 CLR 252.

97 (2010) 241 252, CLR 258.

98 (2010) 243 CLR 319.

99 (2010) 243 CLR 319, 352.

> 'the common law' usually will imply, as a matter of statutory interpretation, a condition that a power conferred by statute upon the executive branch be exercised with procedural fairness to those whose interest may be adversely affected by the exercise of that power. If the matter be understood in that way, a debate whether procedural fairness is to be identified as a common law duty or as an implication from statute proceeds upon a false dichotomy and is unproductive.[100]

There are several notable aspects of this evolution and settlement of principles governing natural justice. The first is that the final position adopted by the High Court bears striking similarities to the compromise reached in the differing theories of the basis of judicial review in the UK.[101] The modified ultra vires theory that gained wide acceptance in the UK appears to share many key features, with the approach accepted by the High Court of Australia to govern the implication, application, and possible exclusion of natural justice. That parallel might seem odd, given that the English theory was adopted in part to accommodate the notion of parliamentary sovereignty that operates in a more limited manner under the Australian Constitution.[102] But just as English courts have quietly signalled their doubts aspects of parliamentary sovereignty,[103] Australian courts have also hinted that some fundamental common law concepts may transcend the Australian Constitution itself.[104] A second notable feature of the current Australian position is its adoption and extension of a key feature of recent English public law, in the form of the principle of legality. That principle was revived with vigour by Lord Hoffmann in *Ex parte Simms*,[105] though since that relaunching of the principle, Australian courts have taken to attributing it to one of their own cases from almost a century earlier.[106] That piece of historical revisionism may be dubious but is of little relevance because the more important adjustment to the principle of legality by Australian courts was its explanation within the wider confines of our constitutional arrangements. The principle of legality operates in Australia as an interpretive rule, by which statutory interpretation presumes that parliament does not intend to remove or curtail fundamental rights, and may only do so when expressed with unmistakable clarity.[107] The principle is one of common

100 *Plaintiff S10/2011* v. *Minister for Immigration and Citizenship* (2012) 246 CLR 636, 666 [97] (Gummow, Hayne, Crennan and Bell JJ).

101 The competing arguments and the widely accepted compromise reached are explained in Christopher Forsyth and Mark Elliott, 'The Legitimacy of Judicial Review' (2003) *Public Law* 286. By that time it was increasingly accepted that ultra vires had become 'a dispensable fiction': Lord Steyn, 'Democracy through Law' (2003) *European Human Rights Law Review* 723, 725.

102 The legislative power of the federal Parliament is limited in several ways. All legislative powers are subject to the Constitution itself, which means legislation cannot infringe specific prohibitions within the Constitution (such as the one in s. 80 that requires all indictable offences be tried by jury), and the more general structural limitations of Constitution (such as the separation of powers, which prohibits parliament from investing courts with some powers or depriving them of others). The sovereignty of State Parliaments is somewhat because they are established by statutes. The Privy Council stated that 'it would be almost impossible to use wider or less restrictive language' than is used in the statutes conferring that power to the States: *McCawley* v. *R* [1920] AC 619, 712. It is, however, accepted that State parliamentary power, though broad, is confined by the Australian Constitution and the *Australia Act* 1986 (Cth) and its UK equivalent.

103 Most notably in *R (Jackson)* v. *Attorney General* [2006] 1 AC 262.

104 See, e.g., *Union Steamship Co of Australia Pty Ltd* v. *King* (1988) 166 CLR 1, 10, where the High Court held it unnecessary to decide if sovereignty of State parliaments was somehow qualified 'by reference to right deeply rooted in our democratic system of government'. See criticisms in Lisa Burton-Crawford, *The Rule of Law under the Australian Constitution* (Federation Press, 2017).

105 *R* v. *Secretary of State for the Home Department; Ex parte Simms* [2001] 2 AC 115, 131.

106 *Potter* v. *Minahan* (1908) 7 CLR 277.

107 The rule is examined in detail in Dan Meagher and Matthew Groves (eds.), *The Principle of Legality in Australia and New Zealand* (Federation Press, 2017).

law in Australia, but its enforcement by the courts is explicable by their constitutional role. Gleeson CJ explained that the strong, rights protective approach of the principle of legality was 'not merely a common sense guide to what a Parliament in a liberal democracy is likely to have intended; it is a working hypothesis, the existence of which is known both to Parliament and the courts, upon which statutory language will be interpreted. The hypothesis is an aspect of the rule of law.'[108]

This reasoning indicates that, as with other English developments we have noted, the principle of legality was welcomed in Australia and grafted onto constitutional arrangements. As with all grafted plants, the new environment takes on a life of its own. In the case of natural justice, that growth took the form in *Saeed* of declaring that natural justice was one of the fundamental rights protected by the principle of legality.

A third notable feature of the Australian debate is the position allocated to the legitimate expectation. That concept is a creature of the common law and logically, therefore, has no place within the supposed approach of Brennan J and its focus on the words and intention of parliament. That may explain, in part, why Brennan J was a long-standing sceptic of the legitimate expectation.[109] From a wider view, the ebbs and flows of the legitimate expectation can be in part explained by reference to the ebbs and flows of the differing views of Mason and Brennan JJ. The legitimate expectation reached its peak in Australia with the well-known case of *Minister of State for Immigration and Ethnic Affairs* v. *Teoh*.[110] In that case, a majority of the High Court held that ratification by the government of an international treaty was a positive statement by the executive government that the government, its agencies, and individual decision-makers would act in accordance with the terms of that treaty. The statement arising from that ratification could, in turn, support a legitimate expectation to people affected by the exercise of government power that officials would not only act in conformity with an applicable treaty but, where they might do otherwise, they would provide notice of this contrary intention to affected people and a chance for those people to put their views.[111] If one accepts that the origin and content of fairness are ultimately in the common law, this reasoning may simply be one instance of the incremental development typical of the common law (though perhaps a slightly more novel finding of the common law than one might usually expect). But if one adheres to the view of Brennan J, this reasoning is untenable on two counts. First, it adopts an implication that simply has no basis whatsoever in the relevant statute. A second but closely related criticism is that the legitimate expectation recognised in *Teoh* was pointedly said to arise in circumstances where the parliament had enacted no legislation at all to give effect to the relevant treaty.

Prior to his appointment to the High Court, Stephen Gageler reasoned that *Teoh* reflected a 'peculiarly' common law view of things.[112] He explained:

> The *Teoh* principle on the common law view is not inevitable but it is at least available. How can something done by the executive after a statute was enacted and unconnected with its administration possibly bear upon the factors required to be taken into account in the

[108] *Electrolux Home Products Pty Ltd* v. *Australian Workers' Union* (2004) 221 CLR 309, 329.

[109] His Honour accepted that a person deemed to hold a legitimate expectation was necessarily one whose interests were affected for the purposes of natural justice doctrines: *Attorney-General (NSW)* v. *Quin* (1990) 170 CLR 1, 40.

[110] (1995) 183 CLR 273.

[111] This greatly simplifies the reasoning in Teoh: M Groves, 'Legitimate Expectations in Australia: Overtaken by Formalism and Pragmatism' in M Groves and G Weeks (eds.), *Legitimate Expectations in the Common Law World* (Hart, 2017), p. 319, 328–31.

[112] S Gageler, 'Legitimate Expectation: Comment on the Article by the Hon Sir Anthony Mason AC KBE' (2005) 12 *Australian Journal of Administrative Law* 111, 113.

> exercise of a power under the statute? The common law answer is that it can although whether or not it does may be open to debate. The ultra vires answer is that it simply cannot.[113]

As the foundation of natural justice settled, the legitimate expectation became a casualty of war. That occurred in the case of *Re Minister for Immigration and Multicultural and Indigenous Affairs; ex parte Lam*,[114] where a majority of the High Court expressed strong disapproval of *Teoh* but did not overrule the case. McHugh and Gummow JJ explained that the implication of a legitimate expectation in these circumstances was bound to encounter constitutional obstacles in Australia. In other words, the common law faced hurdles that it could not overcome. Their Honours reasoned:

> Basic questions of the interaction between the three branches of government are involved. One consideration is that, under the Constitution (s. 61), the task of the Executive is to execute and maintain statute law which confers discretionary powers upon the Executive. It is not for the judicial branch to add to or vary the content of those powers by taking a particular view of the conduct by the Executive of external affairs. Rather, it is for the judicial branch to declare and enforce the limits of the power conferred by statute upon administrative decision-makers, but not, by reference to the conduct of external affairs, to supplement the criteria for the exercise of that power.[115]

The demise of the legitimate expectation as a separate conceptual device or basis to support requirements of natural justice was later confirmed by the High Court, though it can be traced to another part of *Lam*. That part of *Lam* was the suggestion of Gleeson CJ that the legitimate expectation distracted from the simpler, more important questions of what fairness required and whether it was provided when a process was viewed as a whole. Gleeson CJ explained: 'Fairness is not an abstract concept. It is essentially practical. Whether one talks in terms of procedural fairness or natural justice, the concern of the law is to avoid practical injustice.'[116] This practical and more holistic approach to fairness was strongly endorsed by the High Court in *Minister for Immigration and Border Protection* v. *WZARH*.[117] That case was notable for its lack of reference to the rise of the more substantive form of the legitimate expectation that has gained traction in the UK. That development was not mentioned, let alone given weight, by the court in *WZARH*.[118] The departure from English heritage was thus complete.

17.7 CONCLUDING OBSERVATIONS

The Privy Council once acknowledged that the export of the common law to jurisdictions beyond the UK meant that it was no longer 'monolithic'.[119] Members of the Council have made similar comments, such as the tantalising one by Lord Cooke that the common law was becoming 'less English' in these times.[120] These various remarks express the same concept in

113 Gageler above n 112.
114 (2003) 214 CLR 1.
115 (2003) 214 CLR 34 [102] (McHugh and Gummow JJ).
116 (2003) 214 CLR 14 [37] (McHugh and Gummow JJ).
117 (2015) 256 CLR 326.
118 The constitutional impossibilities of transposing that English doctrine to Australia were made clear in *Lam* (2003) 214 CLR 1, 25–7 (McHugh and Gummow JJ).
119 *B* v. *Auckland District Law Society (New Zealand)* [2003] 2 AC 736, 759 [55].
120 Sir Robin Cooke, 'The Road ahead for the Common Law' (2004) 53 *International and Comparative Law Quarterly* 273, 274.

different ways, namely that the common law can adapt outside its original English confines. That may seem self-evident, but change should not be taken for granted in an area such as administrative law. After all, supervisory review by the courts and other foundational concepts such as ministerial responsibility have an unmistakable English heritage and might be thought to set doctrinal parameters for judicial review. The Australian experience suggests that such possibilities fall away when constitutional issues come to the fore, but even this explanation becomes weaker upon closer inspection.

Lord Cooke can be drawn upon to provide another useful illustration in this respect. Although New Zealand does not possess the same single written constitution as Australia, its highest courts perform functions not unlike the High Court of Australia by sitting at the apex of the judicial system. Cooke explained that the work of the courts in general, and courts of final appeal in particular, was 'an exercise in line drawing'.[121] When characterised in this way, the work of the High Court of Australia may draw from a different range of influences, such as a written constitution and local statutes, but its core function does not differ greatly from that of other comparable courts. In modern times, an important function that has generated much controversy and academic writing is that of common law constitutionalism. In the UK, this particular doctrine has led to controversial issues, such as judicial hints that some statutes, albeit ones containing extreme measures not yet seen, may be invalid because they violate some elemental aspect of the common law.[122] That radical step was not required at common law in Australia because it was a key principle upon which our written constitution and entrenched judicial arm of government were founded. But the recently retired former Chief Justice of Australia has rightly noted that this has not precluded the development of common law constitutionalism in Australia. He acknowledged the English debate on whether the courts possibly might refuse to accept the validity of a statute and concluded, 'That kind of constitutionalism, however, is at one end of a spectrum.'[123] However, he continued:

> Further along the spectrum, but still within the genus of constitutionalism, are common law concepts of the essential and defining characteristics of the branches of government and their relationships with each other, and the body of common law principles which inform strong interpretive rules capable of application to written constitutions, statutes, delegated legislation and the exercise by agencies of the Executive Government of statutory powers.[124]

It is this that Australian courts have engaged in to explore and explain their conception of supervisory review, jurisdictional error, and the legitimate expectation. And it is, we think, something that is neither more nor less radical than has occurred in England or any other part of the common law world.

[121] Robin Cooke, 'Foreword' in B Gray and R McClintock (eds.), *Courts and Policy: Checking the Balance* (Brookers, 1995).

[122] A possibility hinted at vague terms in *R (Jackson) v. Attorney General* [2006] 1 AC 262. Hayne J issued similar (very vague) cautions in *Plaintiff M79/2012 v. Minister for Immigration and Citizenship* (2013) 252 CLR 336, 366–8 [85]–[89].

[123] Hon RS French, 'Common Law Constitutionalism' (2016) 14 *New Zealand Journal of Public and International Law* 153, 166.

[124] French above n 123.

18

English Administrative Law in Aotearoa New Zealand

Hanna Wilberg and Kris Gledhill

18.1 INTRODUCTION: HISTORICAL BACKGROUND AND CONSTITUTIONAL STRUCTURE

Of all the common law jurisdictions, New Zealand's administrative law has probably stayed closest to that of England and Wales.[1] For instance, unlike Canada,[2] New Zealand has not abandoned the English insistence that questions of law and interpretation are always for courts to determine.[3] Nor, unlike Australia and South Africa,[4] has it moved to treating the judicial review jurisdiction as deriving from a written constitution. Even so, notable differences have developed, most distinctively the body of law relating to the Treaty of Waitangi.[5]

British government was established in Aotearoa New Zealand in 1840 by means of that Treaty, followed by two proclamations (only one of which relied on the Treaty), a British statute and Letters Patent.[6] Although New Zealand completed the gradual process of becoming an independent nation by adopting the Statute of Westminster in 1947,[7] its constitutional structure retains most of what was introduced. For example, prerogative powers remain, along with Parliamentary supremacy, both subject to constraining conventions rather than a supreme law constitution, and there is a Westminster-style governmental system, with the consequent large measure of executive control over Parliament. Indeed, as the New Zealand legislature is now unicameral,[8] the executive has an even greater ability to put through its legislative programme.[9] On the other hand, some new constraints have been

1 For brevity, we use 'England' and 'English' to refer to 'England and Wales'.

2 *Dunsmuir* v. *New Brunswick* [2008] SCC 9, [2008] 1 SCR 190.

3 *Anisminic Ltd* v. *Foreign Compensation Commission* [1969] 2 AC 147 (HL); *R (Unison)* v. *Monitor* [2009] EWHC 3221 (Admin), [2010] PTSR 1827 at [60]; *Bulk Gas Users Group* v. *Attorney-General* [1983] NZLR 129 (CA); *Wool Board Disestablishment Company Ltd* v. *Saxmere Co Ltd* [2010] NZCA 513, [2011] 2 NZLR 442 at [113]–[118], [124].

4 See Cheryl Saunders, 'Constitution as Catalyst: Different Paths within Australasian Administrative Law' (2012) 10 *New Zealand Journal of Public and International Law* 143; Cora Hoexter, 'A Rainbow of One Colour? Judicial Review on Substantive Grounds in South African Law' in Hanna Wilberg and Mark Elliott (eds.), *The Scope and Intensity of Substantive Review: Traversing Taggart's Rainbow* (Hart, Oxford, 2015) 163.

5 See, generally, Matthew Palmer, *The Treaty of Waitangi in New Zealand's Law and Constitution* (Victoria University Press, Wellington, 2008).

6 See Philip A Joseph, *Constitutional and Administrative Law in New Zealand* (4th ed, Thomson Reuters, Wellington, 2014) at [3.4]–[3.5]; Palmer, above n 5.

7 Statute of Westminster Adoption Act 1947 (NZ).

8 Legislative Council Abolition Act 1950.

9 See Geoffrey Palmer, *Unbridled Power: An Interpretation of New Zealand's Constitution and Government* (2nd ed, Oxford University Press, Oxford, 1987) (the title changed to *Bridled Power* in the third and fourth editions (1997 and 2004), after the move to proportional representation).

introduced, most notably by the move in the 1990s to an electoral system providing for mixed-member proportional representation, and the resulting need to rely on supporting parties.[10] There is also the practical reality that New Zealand is a small nation that needs to trade with the world and is highly dependent on its international relationships, and accordingly values its membership of the United Nations, including its human rights structures.

Within that constitutional structure, the law of New Zealand combines a predominantly local statute law with a common law that has only relatively recently become more independent from Britain. New Zealand acquired its own Parliament as early as 1856,[11] resulting in a large body of local statute law, much of which has greatly modified or abrogated the received English common law. Early examples include the Crown Redress Act 1877, abrogating Crown immunity.[12] New Zealand common law, however, remained simply an offshoot of English common law until the 1970s or 1980s, with NZ courts considering themselves bound to follow English precedent.[13] While the link to the Privy Council was only severed in 2003,[14] divergence started some time before that.[15]

Yet the conditions and context within which the common law operates have always been different, most obviously because Aotearoa prior to colonisation was home to Māori tribal societies governed by customary law, and because of the Treaty of Waitangi. Although the new courts of the fledgling colonial system experimented with pragmatic accommodations of pre-existing Māori customary law,[16] the established colonial legal system did not recognise it,[17] with the exception of pre-existing property rights that could be extinguished only by statute.[18] In recent decades, Māori custom has begun to be accommodated to some small extent in certain areas, most notably in criminal justice but also recently concerning burial.[19]

But customary law has not so far found any place in New Zealand administrative law.

The Treaty of Waitangi, however, has grown in significance since the 1970s. Broadly speaking, the Treaty granted certain powers of government to the British Crown, in return for a guarantee of the existing rights of Māori, including rights both to property and natural resources, and to government at least of their own affairs.[20] The Treaty was ignored or

[10] Electoral Act 1993. See Andrew Geddis and Caroline Morris, '"All Is Changed, Changed Utterly"? The Causes and Consequences of New Zealand's Adoption of MMP' (2004) 32 *Federal Law Review* 451.

[11] Pursuant to the New Zealand Constitution Act 1852, ss. 32 and 53.

[12] New Zealand later adopted the less generous English statute of 1947 in its Crown Proceedings Act 1950. See Stuart Anderson, '"Grave Injustice", "Despotic Privilege": The Insecure Foundations of Crown Liability for Torts in New Zealand' (2009) 12 *Otago Law Review* 1.

[13] See also Paul Rishworth 'Writing Things Unwritten: Common Law in New Zealand's Constitution' (2016) 14 *International Journal of Constitutional Law* 137 at 147–9.

[14] Supreme Court Act 2003.

[15] As early as 1985, Lord Cooke (as he subsequently became) claimed (in the context of a discussion of standing and availability of judicial review) that 'The time has probably come to emphasise that New Zealand administrative law is significantly indigenous': *Budget Rent A Car Ltd* v. *Auckland Regional Authority* [1985] 2 NZLR 414 (CA) at 418.

[16] For a fascinating study, see Shaunnagh Dorsett, *Juridical Encounters: Māori and the Colonial Courts, 1840–1852* (Auckland University Press, Auckland, 2017).

[17] The Constitution Act 1853, provided in s. 71 for Māori customary law to prevail over colonial law in districts set aside by the Crown for that purpose. However, this provision was never implemented; see F M Brookfield, *Waitangi and Indigenous Rights: Revolution, Law and Legitimation* (updated ed, Auckland University Press, Auckland, 2006) at pp.117–18.

[18] *Attorney-General* v. *Ngati Apa* [2003] 3 NZLR 643 (CA).

[19] *Takamore* v. *Clarke* [2012] NZSC 116, [2013] 2 NZLR 733. The dissenting judgments allowed a more significant role. See generally Justice Joseph Williams, 'Lex Aotearoa: An Heroic Attempt to Map the Maori Dimension in Modern New Zealand Law' (2013) 21 *Waikato Law Review* 1

[20] The English and Māori versions of the Treaty are significantly different, and the precise nature of the exchange is therefore highly contentious. The body charged with interpreting the Treaty is the Waitangi Tribunal: Treaty of Waitangi Act 1975, s. 5. For relevant findings, see, e.g., Waitangi Tribunal, *He Whakaputanga me te Tiriti: The Report on Stage 1 of the Te Paparahi o te Raki Inquiry* (WAI 1040, 2014).

dismissed for well over a century[21] but has now become recognised as a fundamental constitutional document, with various forms of effect short of being enforceable in its own right.

This chapter will consider how this briefly-described picture of similarity and difference manifests in administrative law.[22] In terms of substance, since the 1970s New Zealand administrative law has emerged as significantly distinct in several respects from its English ancestry. In terms of procedure, although the common law prerogative writs were acquired (and remain), there was significant reform through the Judicature Amendment Act 1972, now re-enacted as the Judicial Review Procedure Act 2016.[23]

Section 18.2 outlines the most obvious difference, the law relating to the Treaty of Waitangi. The subsequent parts look more generally at divergences in administrative law in New Zealand. Section 18.3 focuses on an aspect where New Zealand judicial review is more interventionist, while Sections 18.4 and 18.5 examine areas where there is a more conservative approach. Sections 18.6 and 18.7 examine more liberal access, and the tendency to eschew the rigid doctrinal categories that still prevail in the English context. As we analyse these differences, we posit some potential explanations for them.

18.2 THE EFFECT OF THE TREATY OF WAITANGI

Despite the modern recognition of the fundamental constitutional significance of the Treaty of Waitangi, the courts have maintained their longstanding position that the Treaty does not have enforceable constitutional status.[24] Indeed, it is not legally enforceable in its own right at all: like international treaties, it requires incorporation by statute to acquire legal effect.[25] We will see that several statutes do make some express reference to the Treaty. However, even in the absence of such express reference, the courts interpret statutory powers that affect Treaty rights as being subject to implied mandatory considerations or to a presumption of consistency with the Treaty.

18.2.1 *Express Statutory References*

The Treaty of Waitangi Act 1975 established the Waitangi Tribunal to interpret the Treaty and to investigate and make findings on Treaty breaches. However, the Tribunal's powers in relation to remedies are recommendatory only. In practice, redress has always been by way of negotiated settlement with the Crown, usually implemented by legislation.[26]

In addition, many statutes include express reference to 'the principles of the Treaty of Waitangi' in the context of granting public powers. Most such 'Treaty clauses' – for example, s. 8 of the Resource Management Act 1991 concerning management of the use, development, and protection of natural and physical resources – make Treaty principles a mandatory

21 See, e.g., Hanna Wilberg, 'Facing Up to the Original Breach of the Treaty' (2007) *New Zealand Law Review* 527.

22 See also, for example, Michael Taggart, 'Introduction to Judicial Review in New Zealand' (1997) *Judicial Review* (*JR*) 236; Michael Taggart, 'The New Zealandness of New Zealand Public Law' (2004) 15 *Public Law Review* 81; Dean R Knight, 'Importation and Indigeneity: The Quartet in New Zealand Administrative Law' in T T Arvind et al. (eds.), *Executive Decision-Making and the Courts: Revisiting the Origins of Modern Judicial Review* (Hart, Oxford, forthcoming 2021).

23 S. 3 of the 2016 Act indicates that it was not designed to have a substantive effect.

24 For example, *New Zealand Maori Council* v. *Attorney-General* [1987] 1 NZLR 641 (CA) (*Lands*).

25 *Hoani Te Heu Heu Tukino* v. *Aotea District Maori Trust Board* [1941] NZLR 590 (PC).

26 See, for example, Ngāi Tahu Claims Settlement Act 1998; Ngāti Pūkenga Claims Settlement Act 2017.

consideration. Occasionally, Treaty principles or other Treaty-related considerations are given express mandatory weight. For instance, the Resource Management Act requires 'particular regard' to be had to 'kaitiakitanga', which is the Māori concept of stewardship of nature.[27] It provides even stronger protection for 'the relationship of Maori and their culture and traditions with their ancestral lands' and with other treasured resources: these are matters of 'national significance' that decision makers under the Act 'shall recognise and provide for'.[28]

Three of the statutory Treaty clauses go further and require all powers conferred by the relevant Acts to be exercised consistently with Treaty principles. The courts have given full effect to this type of substantive constraint, according it overriding status. The first of these three provisions is s. 9 of the State-Owned Enterprises Act 1986. In the famous *New Zealand Maori Council* v. *Attorney-General* (*Lands*) case,[29] the Court of Appeal held that the prohibition on acting inconsistently with the Treaty set out in this provision prohibited the proposed transfer of Crown lands to the newly created state-owned enterprises (SOEs), unless a system was first put in place to safeguard the Crown's ability to settle Treaty claims to those lands. Within the scope of that Act, s. 9 had the effect of a constitutional guarantee of Treaty rights – even central aspects of the powers apparently conferred by the Act were subject to this constraint.

The second of the strong Treaty clauses is s. 4 of the Conservation Act 1987, which requires that Act to be interpreted and administered so as to 'give effect to the principles of the Treaty of Waitangi'. In *Ngāi Tai ki Tāmaki* v. *Minister of Conservation*, the Supreme Court emphasised the 'firm obligation' created by these 'imperative terms',[30] insisting that s. 4 could not be trumped by competing considerations in the legislation.[31] The Court ordered reconsideration of concessions for guided tours granted to non-Māori operators on two island reserves that formed part of the claimant tribe's traditional territories. While the Treaty principle of active protection did not necessarily preclude such a grant of concessions to outsiders, it could have that effect in some circumstances, and at least entitled the tribe to some preference. The Minister's delegate had not correctly understood these points, and the decisions therefore could not stand.[32]

Third, s. 9 of the SOE Act was replicated in legislation providing for the partial privatisation of SOEs engaged in hydroelectric power generation.[33] The Supreme Court, reaffirming the strong effect of this form of Treaty clause, held that if the proposed privatisation compromised the Crown's ability appropriately to respond to an ongoing Treaty rights claim to fresh water (including that used by such SOEs), it could not lawfully go ahead. In this case, however, it concluded that the proposed privatisation would not have that effect.[34]

However, a significant limit on the effect of these strong Treaty clauses has been the finding that the 'principles' of the Treaty only require government to take reasonable action to protect rights to certain uses of resources and to provide redress for past breaches. These limits can be seen in operation in two of the cases just discussed: in neither *Ngāi Tai* nor the hydroelectric

27 S.7(a) of the Resource Management Act 1991.

28 S.6(e) of the Resources Management Act 1991.

29 *New Zealand Maori Council* v. *Attorney-General (Lands)* [1987] 1 NZLR 641 (CA).

30 *Ngāi Tai Ki Tāmaki Tribal Trust* v. *Minister of Conservation* [2018] NZSC 122 at [48]; see also [52].

31 *Ngāi Tai Ki Tāmaki* above n 30, at paras.[54], [77].

32 *Ngāi Tai Ki Tāmaki* above n 30, at paras. [69]–[73], [90]–[98].

33 Section 45Q of the Public Finance Act 1989, inserted by the Public Finance (Mixed Ownership) Amendment Act 2012 as part of a new part 5A providing for the partial privatisation.

34 *New Zealand Maori Council* v. *Attorney-General (Mighty River Power)* [2013] NZSC 6, [2013] 3 NZLR 31.

power case did the Court come close to requiring claimed lands or resources to be reserved exclusively for Māori. Similarly, the Crown's obligation to protect the Māori language was held not to be an absolute obligation: its extent depended on how vulnerable the language had become and the Crown's responsibility for that decline, and on available resources at the time. Transfer of the Crown's television station to a new SOE was found not to be in breach of this obligation, since the Crown did not need to own the station in order to procure broadcasting in the Māori language.[35]

18.2.2 *Implied Constraints: Mandatory Consideration or Presumption of Consistency with the Treaty?*

Even without an express Treaty clause, Treaty obligations will constrain the exercise of relevant powers. The approach to implied protection parallels the NZ approach to unincorporated international obligations, as discussed in the following section. Early cases establish that relevant Treaty principles are at least an implied mandatory consideration.[36] One of the cases may even be read as ascribing mandatory weight also,[37] which would of course be an exception to administrative law orthodoxy. More recently, courts have instead recognised a presumption that powers must be exercised consistently unless the statute clearly authorises an infringement. As with the NZ approach to unincorporated international obligations, this presumption does not require ambiguity to trigger it.[38] This stronger approach was applied by the High Court in *Barton-Prescott* v. *Director-General of Social Welfare*.[39] The Court of Appeal (but not as yet the Supreme Court) has endorsed it in several recent obiter comments[40] and has applied it at least once.[41]

18.2.3 *Conclusion*

The Treaty is a potential source of obligations and constraints that is unique to NZ. The approach to its legal effect, while still somewhat uncertain, essentially follows the approach to international treaties. Within that framework, however, courts have tended to opt for the strongest available options, often going further than the English approach. Express references

35 *New Zealand Maori Council* v. *Attorney-General (Broadcasting Assets)* [1994] 1 NZLR 513 (PC).

36 *Huakina Development Trust* v. *Waikato Valley Authority* [1987] 2 NZLR 188 (HC).

37 In *Ngai Tahu Maori Trust Board* v. *Director-General of Conservation* [1995] 3 NZLR 553 (CA), the claimant tribe was held to be entitled to a 'reasonable degree of preference' (at 562) and the Crown's duty to protect the tribe's interests was a 'residual factor of weight' (at 560). However, this case seems better understood as involving application of the express obligation to act consistently with Treaty principles in s. 4 of the Conservation Act. It was explained on that basis in *Ngāi Tai ki Tāmaki* (above n 30), at [34], [49]; see also Philip Joseph, 'Constitutional Law' (1996) *New Zealand Law Review* 1 at 12–14.

38 See Hanna Wilberg, 'Judicial Remedies for the Original Breach?' (2007) *New Zealand Law Review* 713.

39 *Barton-Prescott* v. *Director-General of Social Welfare* [1997] 3 NZLR 179.

40 *Ngaronoa* v. *Attorney-General* [2017] NZCA 351, [2017] 3 NZLR 643: 'Today it can be stated with confidence' that this approach applies (at [46]). However, there was no room for the presumption in this case, as the provision in question was capable of only one meaning (at [49]). On appeal, the Supreme Court agreed with that last point, and did not comment on the existence or nature of the presumption: *Ngaronoa* v. *Attorney-General* [2018] NZSC 123 at [66]. See also *New Zealand Maori Council* v. *Attorney-General (Te Arawa Cross Claim Case)* [2007] NZCA 269, [2008] 1 NZLR 318 at [72] and [74].

41 *Tukaki* v. *Commonwealth of Australia* [2018] NZCA 324 at [35]–[40]; on the facts, however, the Treaty-consistent interpretation did not avail the applicant. See also *Takamore* v. *Clarke* [2011] NZCA 587, [2012] 1 NZLR 573 (CA) at [248], where the Court commented on a presumption of consistency as a matter of statutory interpretation, and then held at [249] that this should be applied here to the common law. In upholding the outcome, however, the Supreme Court did not mention the Treaty: [2012] NZSC 116, [2013] 2 NZLR 733.

are given full and strong effect. In the absence of express reference, courts may go as far as according mandatory weight to Treaty obligations as implied relevant considerations, and appear ready to interpret legislation consistently with Treaty obligations, even in the absence of ambiguity (consistently with the strong NZ approach to international treaties).

18.3 INTERVENTIONIST APPROACHES TO INTERPRETIVE PRESUMPTIONS IN MATTERS OF INTERNATIONAL LAW

When considering the common law principles governing the grounds of review, a notable aspect of the New Zealand approach compared with the English is the much stronger use of the presumption of consistency with international law in assessing whether a decision is lawful. In the UK, a presumption of consistency with international obligations can be raised only if there is an ambiguity in statutory language.[42] In New Zealand, the ambiguity requirement has been abandoned, and the presumption has been readily applied to general words and phrases or discretionary powers.[43]

Among the strongest instances is *Sellers*, where the court relied on the presumption of consistency with the international law freedom of the high seas[44] to effectively exclude foreign vessels from the reach of a statutory power to set minimum safety requirements for vessels departing New Zealand ports.[45] Similarly in *Zaoui*, the court held that a power to order deportation of a person who had been certified as posing a threat to national security was not available in any case where this was contrary to the Convention Against Torture[46] because there were substantial grounds for believing that, as a result of the deportation, the person would be in danger of being arbitrarily deprived of life or subjected to torture.[47]

The courts have not gone quite so far as to say that only express words can override international obligations, as has at times been suggested for the principle of legality.[48] Indeed there is, instead, authority that discretionary powers can be read down only so far as this is consistent with the scheme of the legislation and does not frustrate the purpose.[49] However, such a purposive limit has not been uniformly observed: in cases such as *Sellers* and *Zaoui*, the use of the presumption has been very strong indeed.[50]

We suggest there are at least two factors relevant to this greater receptiveness to unincorporated international law by comparison with England: a dominant judicial personality who attached

42 *R* v. *Secretary of State for the Home Department, ex p Brind* [1991] 1 AC 696, 747–8; *R (SG)* v. *Secretary of State for Work and Pensions* [2015] 1 WLR 1449, [115], [137], [239] (but cf. Lord Kerr's dissent at [254] and [257], proposing an exception for human rights treaties). For international obligations as implied mandatory considerations, see *E* v. *Chief Constable of the Royal Ulster Constabulary* [2009] 1 AC 536, [60]; R (Plan B Earth) v Secretary of State for Transport [2020] EWCA Civ 2014 but cf. *R (Yam)* v. *Central Criminal Court* [2016] AC 771, [35]. See also Chapter 4 in this volume.

43 *Ye* v. *Minister of Immigration* [2009] NZSC 76, [2010] 1 NZLR 104 at [21], [24]–[25], [31]–[32]. The development is noted, for example, in T Dunworth, 'Public International Law' (2000) *New Zealand Law Review* 217.

44 United Nations Convention on the Law of the Sea, Art 92.

45 *Sellers* v. *Maritime Safety Authority* [1999] 2 NZLR 44 (CA) at 57, 59.

46 United Nations Convention against Torture, Art 3.

47 *Zaoui* v. *Attorney-General (No 2)* [2005] NZSC 38, [2006] 1 NZLR 289 at [63].

48 *R* v. *Lord Chancellor ex p Witham* [1998] QB 575 (DC).

49 *New Zealand Airline Pilots' Association Inc* v. *Attorney-General* [1997] 3 NZLR 269, 189–92. This may also be implicit in the reasoning in *Ye* (above n 43), at [19]–[21] and [31]–[36]: see H Wilberg, 'Administrative Law' (2010) *New Zealand Law Review* 177, 201–2. See also *Helu* v. *Immigration and Protection Tribunal* [2015] NZSC 28, [2016] 1 NZLR 298 at [143]–[144] – but that concerned interpretation of implementing legislation.

50 Noted in C Geiringer, 'International Law through the Lens of Zaoui: Where is New Zealand At?' (2006) 17 *Public Law Review* 300, 317. For instance, see *Sellers* and *Zaoui* (nn 45 and 47 above).

great importance to international law, and New Zealand's position (and self-perception) as a small country in a remote corner of the world. The latter means that New Zealand is keenly aware of its dependence on other states' respect for international law and, as such, is always keen to be seen itself as a good international citizen. In the judicial sphere, that attitude was greatly reinforced in the 1990s and early 2000s by the tenure on our highest courts of Sir Kenneth Keith, a distinguished international law jurist who went on to serve on the International Court of Justice.[51]

18.4 CONSERVATISM WITH HUMAN RIGHTS LEGISLATION

Although, as noted in the previous part, the New Zealand common law has developed a more receptive approach than its English counterpart to grounds of challenge based on a breach of unincorporated international obligations, English judges have been far less restrained than their NZ counterparts in making use of statutory human rights duties to interpret domestic law consistently with incorporated obligations and to ensure that government powers are exercised consistently with those obligations.

The Human Rights Act 1998 Act (UK) has been accepted as a central basis for judicial review, supporting findings that public actors have exceeded their powers and also procedural errors such as bias. Its role is recognised in the Practice Direction to CPR Part 54, which expressly requires the proper pleading of any issue or remedy under the 1998 Act.[52] Judicial review is the primary route for using the interpretive obligation to confine the scope of statutory powers or to determine whether an action taken by a public body is unlawful as a disproportionate limit on a right protected by the Act.

As is well known, the interpretive obligation allows the courts in the UK to rewrite the effect of legislation by holding that a rights-implicating statute is modified by the 1998 Act's support for the rights set out in the European Convention of Human Rights as interpreted, often expansively, by the European Court of Human Rights.

This interpretive methodology is based to a significant extent on the New Zealand Bill of Rights Act 1990 (and can be traced backed to the Canadian Bill of Rights 1960).[53] The purpose of the NZ statute is stated as being to give effect to the human rights obligations contained in the International Covenant on Civil and Political Rights 1966 (which is also binding on the UK and is, like the European Convention, designed to give effect to the civil and political rights contained in the Universal Declaration of Human Rights 1948). Its section 6 requires courts to prefer rights-consistent meanings if they can be given, which is semantically equivalent to the duty arising under section 3 of the UK Act.[54] However, the courts in New Zealand have not been as willing to reconstruct statutes, finding that their powers are limited to declaring reasonably available interpretations.

For example, a five-judge Court of Appeal in *Noort* determined that it was necessary to prefer a rights-consistent meaning only when a statute 'can reasonably be given such a meaning. A strained interpretation would not be enough'.[55] In another five-judge Court of Appeal, *Moonen*, Tipping J indicated that the choice arose only as between 'two tenable

[51] See, generally, Claudia Geiringer and Dean Knight (eds.), *Seeing the World Whole: Essays in Honour of Sir Kenneth Keith* (Victoria University Press, Wellington, 2008).

[52] PD 54, para 5.3.

[53] See Kris Gledhill, *Human Rights Acts: The Mechanisms Compared* (Hart, Oxford, 2015) pp. 158–69.

[54] *R* v. *Hansen* [2007] NZSC 7, [2007] 3 NZLR 1.

[55] *Ministry of Transport* v. *Noort; Police* v. *Curran* [1992] 3 NZLR 260, 272 (per Cooke P). See also similar comments at 286 and 294.

meanings'.[56] The Supreme Court confirmed this constrained approach in the leading case of *Hansen*.[57] It declined to follow the House of Lords' holding in *R* v. *Lambert*[58] that an apparent imposition of a burden of proof on a defendant could be read as imposing a lesser evidential burden to avoid conflict with the presumption of innocence. There was evidence that Parliament must have intended the full legal burden, and the Court considered it important to respect that intention. Such a limit has been rejected by the English courts.[59]

Indeed, there have been suggestions that the statutory interpretive obligation is no more than the legislature accepting that the established presumption of legality, which covers common law rights, should be applied also to the rights identified in the Bill of Rights Act. In *R* v. *Pora*, Elias CJ indicated that by the statutory obligation, 'the New Zealand Parliament has adopted a general principle of legality'.[60] While this had some early support in the UK (e.g., Lord Hoffmann in *Simms* stated that the enactment of the Human Rights Act 1998 meant that the principle of legality became an express rule of construction),[61] the view now accepted is as summarised by Lord Phillips in *Ahmed and Others* v. *HM Treasury*, namely that case law 'has extended the reach of section 3 of the HRA beyond that of the principle of legality', given that it allowed departure from the intention in the legislation being construed.[62] The difference was that: 'I do not consider that the principle of legality permits a court to disregard an unambiguous expression of Parliament's intention. To this extent its reach is less than that of section 3 of the HRA'.[63] If the judges of New Zealand take the view that the statutory interpretive obligation is essentially the same as the principle of legality, which gives way to clear language that breaches rights (extending to situations of clear implication), this will explain their unwillingness to be as adventurous in constructing solutions that give effect to rights where this requires a strained interpretation of otherwise rights-breaching statutory language.

The second area of difference concerns the courts' willingness to scrutinise whether an impugned exercise of power represents a disproportionate limit on a right. English courts carry out this assessment largely as a matter of course, albeit with varying levels of weight accorded to the decision maker's view.[64] They have also firmly rejected any notion that the rights-based obligation on the decision maker might be merely a procedural obligation to apply the proportionality test: rather, the obligation is to avoid exercises of power that the courts consider to be a disproportionate limit.[65] In New Zealand, by contrast, the case law is marked by recurring doubts whether courts should be applying the proportionality test at all when scrutinising exercises of power. The courts have found various devices for avoiding this in many cases, such as treating relevant rights and the proportionality question as mandatory

56 *Moonen* v. *Film and Literature Board of Review* [2000] 2 NZLR 9 [16]. Note that in *Quilter* v. *Attorney-General* [1998] 1 NZLR 523 at 242, Thomas J – one of the most activist judges in promoting rights-consistent interpretations – found that it was not possible to strain meanings because that would require courts to legislate.

57 *R* v. *Hansen* [2007] NZSC 7, [2007] 3 NZLR 1.

58 *R* v. *Lambert* [2002] 2 AC 545

59 See, for example, *Ghaidan* v. *Godin-Mendoza* [2004] UKHL 30, [2004] 2 AC 557.

60 *R* v. *Pora* [2001] 2 NZLR 37 (CA) at [53]. In relation to the similar approach in the Victorian Charter, French CJ in the High Court case *Momcilovic* v. *R* [2011] HCA 34 at [51] indicated that the statutory duty was essentially the principle of legality 'with a wider field of application'.

61 *Secretary of State for the Home Department, ex parte Simms* [2000] 2 AC 115 at 132A.

62 *Ahmed and Others* v. *HM Treasury* [2010] UKSC 5, [2010] 2 AC 534, [112].

63 *Ahmed and Others*, above n 62, at [117].

64 See, e.g., *R (Aguilar Quila)* v. *Secretary of State for the Home Department* [2011] UKSC 45, [2012] 1 AC 621.

65 *R (SB)* v. *Governors of Denbigh High School* [2006] UKHL 15, [2007] 1 AC 100; *Belfast City Council* v. *Miss Behavin' Ltd* [2007] UKHL 19, [2007] 1 WLR 1420.

considerations; confining their rights-based scrutiny to relevant rules rather than exercises of power in individual cases; and jumping straight ahead to the interpretive presumption, to find that even if a decision did represent a disproportionate limit, the power in question could not be read consistently with the right.[66]

What might be the reasons for the arguable contradiction of the New Zealand judges changing the common law to become more receptive to international treaty obligations, while at the same time being more conservative in relation to the interpretive duty to provide a rights-consistent interpretation where possible in relation to incorporated rights? Given the role of judicial review in setting down the limits of governmental power, socio-political factors are likely to loom large. In comparison with the UK, Parliamentary sovereignty and the empowering of executive discretion remains much more unqualified in New Zealand, given the lack of the sort of supra-national constraint represented by both the EU and the European Court of Human Rights. These supra-national elements can be seen to have introduced familiarity with such concepts as proportionality, which are now features of English jurisprudence; and the knowledge that a failure to protect rights adequately will invariably lead to a case before the European Court has supported the enhanced scrutiny approach. The absence of these factors in New Zealand may be relevant to its judges remaining much less willing to chance their arm against Parliament in the service of rights.

Indeed, there may also be an alternative explanation for the apparent divergence in New Zealand between the effect given to international law and statutory rights, respectively. The degree of conservatism may be as much to do with the nature of the right in question and the severity of the violation as with its source. Many of the leading Bill of Rights cases are criminal cases involving relatively fine points of criminal process rights,[67] which may explain the conservatism. Many of the cases involving strong use of the presumption of consistency with international law concern security of the person[68] or the rights of children.[69] Strong protection of rights from the full set of sources is also seen in a pair of cases involving retrospective imposition of punishment.[70] Thus the conservatism that appears to attach to the Bill of Rights may in fact be to do both with the limited range of rights that are protected by that instrument and with the accidents of litigation in terms of which rights are litigated.

18.5 LINGERING CONSERVATISM WITH SUBSTANTIVE REVIEW

It may have been expected that New Zealand's more easy relationship with international law would have had repercussions for the development of substantive grounds of review. However, the New Zealand approach on this remained significantly more conservative for much longer than that in England. Until recently, there was no clear appellate authority in New Zealand for any of the modern extensions of substantive review, namely heightened scrutiny unreasonableness (let alone proportionality as a separate ground), substantive

66 Claudia Geiringer, 'Sources of Resistance to Proportionality Review of Administrative Power Under the New Zealand Bill of Rights Act' (2013) 11 *New Zealand Journal of Public and International Law* 123; Hanna Wilberg 'The Bill of Rights in Administrative Law Cases: Taking Stock and Suggesting Some Reassessment' (2013) 25 *New Zealand Universities Law Review* 866.

67 Including *Hansen* (n 57 above), which is the leading case for the conservative approach.

68 *Zaoui*, (n 47 above), centrally invoked the Convention Against Torture.

69 *Ye*, (n 43 above).

70 *Pora*, (n 60 above), and *R* v. *Poumako* [2000] 2 NZLR 695 (CA).

legitimate expectations, and mistake of fact. That still remains the position for substantive legitimate expectations.

18.5.1 *Heightened Scrutiny*

In England, heightened scrutiny reasonableness review where rights or other important interests are affected is well-established,[71] and there is increasing support for proportionality as a stand-alone ground for review in addition to its role in assessing alleged ECHR violations through the Human Rights Act 1998.[72]

In New Zealand, there is still little support for proportionality as a stand-alone ground.[73] Heightened scrutiny unreasonableness review for decisions affecting rights or other important interests was adopted by the High Court in *Wolf*[74] and has been used regularly at that level.[75] At the appellate level, however, until recently there was no more than a string of supportive dicta.[76] Authoritative endorsement of this approach did not come until the June 2019 decision in *Kim*.[77] (Note, however, that the Supreme Court has granted leave to appeal.[78]) The Court upheld a challenge to an extradition decision on a number of grounds, including unreasonableness in the assessment of risk on several points.[79] It was common ground that the applicable standard of review was 'heightened or anxious scrutiny', reflecting a view that this option was well established despite the lack of authoritative appellate endorsement. However, the Court expressed itself satisfied that this was the appropriate standard, due to the fact that what was at stake were the fundamental rights to fair trial and to be free from torture.[80]

Perhaps an explanation for why this took so long is that an appropriate case had simply not been brought until now.[81] Further, there may also be a link to New Zealand appellate courts' distaste for explicit calibrations of intensity of review.[82]

71 *R* v. *Ministry of Defence, ex p Smith* [1996] QB 517 (CA); *Bugdaycay* v. *Secretary of State for the Home Department* [1987] AC 514 (HL); *Kennedy* v. *Charity Commission* [2014] UKSC 20, [2015] AC 455 at [51]; *Pham* v. *Secretary of State for the Home Department* [2015] UKSC 19, [2015] 1 WLR 1591 at [60], [94], [109].

72 See, e.g., *Kennedy* (n 71 above) at [54]; *Pham* (n 71 above) at [59], [95]–[96], [106]–[108].

73 It was left open in *Wolf* v. *Minister of Immigration* [2004] NZAR 414 (HC) and in *Institute of Chartered Accountants of NZ* v. *Bevan* [2003] 1 NZLR 154 (CA) at [55]; and considered inappropriate at least in the particular context in *Powerco Ltd* v. *Commerce Commission* HC Wellington CIV-2005-485-001066, 9 June 2006. Some High Court level endorsements can be found.

74 *Wolf* v. *Minister of Immigration* [2004] NZAR 414 (HC) at [47] and [65].

75 A recent instance is *Hu* v. *Immigration and Protection Tribunal* [2017] NZHC 41, [2017] NZAR 508 at [32]. For full discussion, see Marcelo Rodriguez Ferrere, 'An Impasse in New Zealand's Administrative Law: How Did We Get There?' (2017) 28 *Public Law Review* 310.

76 The one case that arguably applied heightened scrutiny is *JC Pring* v. *Wanganui District Council* (1999) 5 ELRNZ 464; [1999] NZRMA 519 (CA) at [7]. High-profile obiter dicta are found in *Electoral Commission* v. *Cameron* [1997] 2 NZLR 421 (CA) at 433; *Pharmaceutical Management Agency Ltd* v. *Roussel Uclaf Australia Pty Ltd* [1998] NZAR 58 (CA) at 66; *Conley* v. *Hamilton City Council* [2007] NZCA 543, [2008] 1 NZLR 789.

77 *Kim* v. *Minister of Justice of New Zealand* [2019] NZCA 209. An earlier decision adopting heightened scrutiny was *Quake Outcasts* v. *Minister of Canterbury Earthquake Recovery* [2017] NZCA 332, [2017] 3 NZLR 486 at para [73], but that could be read as confined to its particular statutory context.

78 *Minister of Justice* v. *Kim* [2019] NZSC 100.

79 *Kim* (n 77 above), at para [275(d)–(f) and (j)].

80 *Kim* (n 77 above), at para [45]–[47]. Note that this involved reliance on international law rights, rather than simply a direct application of the New Zealand Bill of Rights Act 1990: see the discussion of the applicable law at paras [11]–[23]. If it had been the latter, then it would be uncontroversial that a proportionality test applies.

81 The Supreme Court in particular has displayed a marked reluctance to decide issues that do not strictly require resolution in a case.

82 Dean Knight, 'A Murky Methodology: Standards of Review in Administrative Law' (2008) 6 *New Zealand Journal of Public and International Law* 117.

18.5.2 *Substantive Legitimate Expectations*

It is clear that a plaintiff who has a legitimate expectation (whether of a substantive benefit or a certain procedure) is entitled to a hearing or consultation before that expectation is disappointed.[83] Courts in England have in addition adopted a substantive legitimate expectation doctrine: an expectation of a favourable outcome will in appropriate contexts constrain the scope of the decision maker's discretion to the extent of preventing the expectation being disappointed unless the court is satisfied that this is justified by an overriding public interest; see *Coughlan*.[84] In other contexts (when a range of factors for substantive review are weaker), the constraint takes the lesser form of treating the expectation as a mandatory relevant consideration.[85]

New Zealand authority on this substantive version at High Court level ranges from full acceptance to complete rejection.[86] An intermediate position was adopted in *New Zealand Association for Migration and Investments*, holding a legitimate expectation to be a mandatory relevant consideration and adding that the court will assess the reasonableness of the justification for disappointing the expectation, sometimes through close scrutiny.[87] Requiring the expectation to be considered and scrutinising reasons for going against it gives it limited substantive effect similar to the weaker option applied in appropriate contexts in England, but short of the strong *Coughlan* option.

The Court of Appeal made obiter comments about the issue in *Terminals (NZ)*.[88] The applicant relied on an express assurance from a Customs Service officer that no duty would be payable. It argued unsuccessfully that this was binding and could be withdrawn only prospectively.[89] The Court set out a three-stage enquiry. First, an ambiguous promise or practice was unlikely to give rise to a legitimate expectation at all.[90] The claim here failed at this first hurdle because a misunderstanding between the parties had not been adequately resolved. Second, reliance on the promise or practice had to be reasonable, rather than constituting a mere hope.[91]

The third stage concerned 'what remedy, if any, should be provided if a legitimate expectation is established'.[92] The Court's obiter answer here provided an inconclusive indication on the controversial issue whether the scope of a decision maker's discretion is constrained by a substantive expectation. Noting that 'the relief sought is of a substantive rather than procedural nature', the Court stated that such relief 'is rarely, if ever, granted', as it would be to 'usurp' the public authority's function.[93] Short of this, a court may

83 *Council of Civil Service Unions* v. *Minister for the Civil Service* [1985] 1 AC 374 (HL); *R* v. *Liverpool Corporation ex p Liverpool Taxi Fleet Operators' Association* [1972] 2 QB 299 (CA); *Webster* v. *Auckland Harbour Board* [1987] 2 NZLR 129 (CA).

84 *R* v. *North and East Devon Health Authority ex p Coughlan* [2001] QB 213 (CA). According to *R (Nadarajah)* v. *Secretary of State for the Home Department* [2005] EWCA Civ 1363, the question of justification is answered by applying a proportionality test.

85 See, e.g., *R (Bibi)* v. *Newham London Borough Council* [2001] EWCA Civ 607, [2002] 1 WLR 237; this represents another one of the three possible outcomes set out in *Coughlan*, above n 84, at [57].

86 See Wilberg 'Administrative Law' [2010] *New Zealand Law Review* 177 at 207–13.

87 *New Zealand Association for Migration and Investments Inc* v. *Attorney-General* [2006] NZAR 45 (HC) At [157]–[158] and [176]–[177].

88 *Comptroller of Customs* v. *Terminals (NZ) Ltd* [2012] NZCA 598, [2014] 2 NZLR 137. An appeal was confined to issues other than legitimate expectations: *Terminals (NZ) Ltd* v. *Comptroller of Customs* [2013] NZSC 139, [2014] 1 NZLR 121.

89 *Comptroller of Customs*, above n 88, at para. [109].

90 *Comptroller of Customs*, above n 88, at para. [125].

91 *Comptroller of Customs*, above n 88, at paras. [124], [126].

92 *Comptroller of Customs*, above n 88, at para [127].

93 *Comptroller of Customs*, above n 88, at paras.[154]–[155].

require the decision maker to follow a process that he or she has expressly or impliedly undertaken to follow. Examples include an obligation to give notice to an affected party or to consult before making a decision. In other cases, the court may direct the decision maker to reconsider the decision in light of the expectation.[94]

A preliminary point to note is that the formulation of the third-step question is problematic, appearing to elide two separate and sequential questions, namely whether the expectation constrains the scope of discretion and, if so, what remedy should be granted for this.[95] An affirmative answer to the first question does not necessarily require the provision of the substantive benefit rather than reconsideration.[96]

As an answer to the question of substantive effect, these dicta are inconclusive. Although the comments seem to recognise that legitimate expectations may be mandatory relevant considerations,[97] they make no mention of the further possibility that courts may assess the reasonableness of a decision maker's justification for disappointing the expectation.[98]

Appellate-level comment on whether the full substantive effect option seen in *Coughlan* is available in appropriate contexts in New Zealand will have to wait for another day. This reticence to commit to a full answer on this question is of a piece with the similar approach to heightened scrutiny. However, perhaps in this area the appellate dicta more clearly signal likely rejection of the extension – as we saw, the suggestion was that it would be to 'usurp' the public authority's function.

18.5.3 *Mistake of Fact*

In England, mistake of fact was established as a ground of review by the Court of Appeal in *E*.[99] Support for this has long been mixed in the New Zealand High Court,[100] but the ground had not gained majority support in the Court of Appeal,[101] with one little-noted exception.[102] The Supreme Court in *Ririnui* has now affirmed the availability of the ground, citing *E*,[103] but this is an uncertain ruling affected by confusion. On the facts, a mistake clearly had influenced the challenged decision to sell public land that was subject to a Treaty of Waitangi claim, and the Court declared the decision unlawful partly due to this mistake.[104] But this appears to have been a mistake of law,[105] as the

94 *Comptroller of Customs*, above n 88, at para. [155].

95 Similar confusion is also evident in *Green* v. *Racing Integrity Unit Ltd* [2014] NZCA 133, [2014] NZAR 623.

96 Notably, in *Coughlan* (n 84 above), the remedy was reconsideration.

97 As held in *Association for Migration and Investments* (n 87 above), which is cited in *Terminals (NZ)* (n 88 above) at [155].

98 As also held in *Association for Migration and Investments* (n 87 above), as cited in *Terminals (NZ)* (n 88 above) at [155].

99 *E* v. *Secretary of State for the Home Department* [2004] EWCA Civ 49, [2004] QB 1044.

100 See Hanna Wilberg, 'Mistakes about Mistake of Fact: The New Zealand Story' (2017) 28 *Public Law Review* 248 at 256–7.

101 In many cases frequently cited in support, there was, in fact, only minority support for the ground: see, e.g., *Daganayasi* v. *Minster of Immigration* [1980] 2 NZLR 130 (CA) at 132, 145–9. Other cases that are occasionally cited in support have simply been misread, and on a proper reading do not adopt the ground: see, e.g., *Lewis* v. *Wilson & Horton Ltd* [2000] 3 NZLR 546 (CA) at [92] (the only type of factual error that was accepted and found to be made out in the case is the traditional and much more limited ground in *Edwards (Inspector of Taxes)* v. *Bairstow* [1956] AC 14 (HL): see at [67]–[73]).

102 *Glaxo Group Ltd* v. *Commissioner of Patents* [1991] 3 NZLR 179 (CA).

103 *Ririnui* v. *Landcorp Farming Ltd* [2016] NZSC 62, [2016] 1 NZLR 1056 at [54].

104 *Ririnui* (n 103 above) at [98](c) and (e), [110], [138], [143], [147] and [152].

105 See Wilberg (n 100 above), at 262–3.

courts in the following section held.[106] A majority of the Supreme Court held there was 'scope for argument' on the classification of the mistake, but found that it was not material to reach a conclusion on this: 'Even if it is regarded as a mistake of fact', in the circumstances of this case the mistake would render a decision based on it susceptible to review.[107] Despite being brief and somewhat confused, this express endorsement of the ground by the Supreme Court will likely be accepted as establishing the ground in New Zealand. The parameters of the ground remain to be worked out, however, as the Supreme Court said virtually nothing about this, other than to cite *E*.[108]

Some further possible appellate support can also be found in two Court of Appeal decisions. In *Taylor*, the Court overturned a decision that was affected by a mistake that would have satisfied the *E* criteria.[109] However, the Court's focus was on a challenge invoking the New Zealand Bill of Rights Act, and the mistake may have been seen as going to the proportionality assessment that is required in that context.[110] In *Charter Holdings*, the Court clearly applied mistake of fact as a ground in its own right; albeit based entirely on a questionable assessment of the state of authority at the time.[111]

The difference between this ground having now been accepted, while adoption of the other two substantive grounds still remains an open question, likely reflects a sense that this ground does not involve judicial interference with the merits in the same sense. A decision clearly affected by an incontrovertible mistake is simply not defensible, rather than being one on which the court might disagree with the decision maker.[112]

18.5.4 *Reflections on Conservatism in Relation to Substantive Grounds*

As already noted in the previous part, Parliamentary sovereignty and the empowering of executive discretion remains much more unqualified in New Zealand than in England, given the lack of the sort of supra-national constraint represented by both the EU and the European Court of Human Rights. As a result, judges remain less willing to chance their arm against Parliament in the service of rights. In turn, this may also have had an influence on the pace of extension of substantive grounds of review. English judges had long become accustomed to playing a very active role in assessing government policy under the HRA.

A further more particular feature of the UK legal landscape is the inclusion of the right to privacy and family life (article 8 of the ECHR) in the catalogue of protected rights, which has given rise to much of the proportionality jurisprudence.[113] This probably has spilled over into

106 Noted at [54]. See *Ririnui* v. *Landcorp Farming Ltd* [2014] NZHC 1128, [87], [89] (interim judgment) (treating the ground as failure to take account of mandatory considerations, but relevantly treating the question whether the claim had been settled as a question of law); *Attorney-General* v. *Ririnui* [2015] NZCA 160, [36].

107 *Ririnui*, (n 103 above), at [54]; William Young J dissented on this point: at fn 166.

108 The Court touched on two of the four *E* requirements (materiality, and that the error was not the plaintiff's responsibility), but without noting the link with *E*: at [53]. The *E* requirement that the fact in question must be 'established', that is, 'uncontentious and objectively verifiable' received no attention at all.

109 *Taylor* v. *The Chief Executive of the Department of Corrections* [2015] NZCA 477, [2015] NZAR 1648 at [95]–[99].

110 See Wilberg (n 100 above), at 265–6.

111 *Charter Holdings Ltd* v. *Commissioner of Inland Revenue* [2016] NZCA 499, (2016) 27 NZTC 22 at [68]–[69], [75]–[76]; further discussed in Wilberg, above n 100, at 266.

112 For the Chief Justice's insistence on the need for general appeals in criminal cases, on the basis that 'Nothing rankles like mistake of fact'; see Sian Elias, 'Judgery and the Rule of Law' (2015) 14 *Otago Law Review* 49 at 56.

113 In NZ, by contrast, from the outset, only the 'unreasonable search and seizure' aspect of privacy was proposed: see the Draft Bill in the 1985 White Paper 'A Bill of Rights for New Zealand', at 103 to 107, following the model of the Canadian Charter 1982.

the English courts' approach to other substantive questions that would once have been considered unsuitable for judicial determination. In the absence of both of these influences, New Zealand judges have long tended to remain more resistant to expanded substantive review generally.

18.6 MORE LIBERAL AVAILABILITY OF JUDICIAL REVIEW

A further more interventionist feature of the New Zealand system, described in this part, is more liberal access to the courts: standing rules equate in liberalism to those in England, but there is more limited scope for rejecting relief on the basis of a defect not making a difference, and leave requirements and strict time limits do not feature.

In England, ss. 29–31 of the Senior Courts Act 1981 (UK) include rules as to jurisdiction to make what are now known as mandatory, prohibiting and quashing orders, injunctions and damages; the need to follow court rules and secure leave; and delay. Amendments made in 2015 by s. 84 of the Criminal Justice and Courts Act 2015 require the court to refuse relief if a judicially reviewable error is made but 'the outcome for the applicant would not have been substantially different if the conduct complained of had not occurred'.[114] This may be considered at the leave stage also. There is a relief from this provision if 'exceptional public interest' is demonstrated. This leads to a tension with the supposed concentration of judicial review on process rather than merits. Although Rule 54.1(2)(a) of the Civil Procedure Rules indicates that judicial review involves the 'lawfulness of (i) an enactment; or (ii) a decision, action, action or failure to act in relation to the exercise of a public function', the parameters of lawfulness are largely set by the common law, supplemented by statutory provisions relating to human rights and non-discrimination standards.

In New Zealand, the Judicial Review Procedure Act 2016 (NZ), and its predecessor, Part 1 of the Judicature Amendment Act 1972, provides for judicial review applications in relation to statutory powers. The prerogative writs also remain available (as do declarations and injunctions). Part 30 of the High Court Rules 2016[115] reduces the effect of this bifurcation by providing that an application for statutory review and an application for the older remedies, collectively known as 'extraordinary remedies', is made in the same way, namely by a statement of claim filed with a notice of proceeding; damages or any other relief may be sought.[116]

The 1972 Act, which introduced the discrete statutory process, arose from a report of the Public and Administrative Law Reform Committee,[117] which concluded that the use of the common law writs was unnecessarily constrained by complex procedures; this required remedy through the introduction of the new statutory procedure. There were similar perceptions in England,[118] but the reforms in New Zealand occurred independently, and the

[114] There were also amendments made to costs rulings, in particular relating to protective costs orders: these are not discussed here. See ss. 85–90 of the Criminal Justice and Courts Act 2015, and 95–9, 639–75 of the accompanying Explanatory Notes.

[115] LI 2016/225.

[116] Interim orders may also be sought: rule 30(4). In relation to statutory review, section 15 of the Judicial Review Procedure Act 2016 provides for interim remedies.

[117] Administrative Tribunals – Constitution, Procedure and Appeals, Fourth Report of the Public and Administrative Law Reform Committee, January 1971.

[118] Administrative Tribunals – Constitution, Procedure and Appeals, Fifth Report of the Public and Administrative Law Reform Committee, January 1972 noted at 22 that its recommendations were similar to suggestions made by the UK's Law Commission in its Working Paper No. 40, Remedies in Administrative Law, 1971.

Committee's Draft Bill was based on one drafted in Ontario.[119] The statutory procedure applies to a 'statutory power'. This is defined widely in section 5 of the 2016 Act[120] to cover powers originating in an Act or the constitutional documents of a body corporate, but it means that challenges to non-statutory powers such as those arising under the prerogative cannot be brought by the statutory procedure.[121] The Committee had predicted that the common law procedures would fall into disuse and could then be abolished. This turned out to be inaccurate, and both regimes continue to operate. The explanation for this difference with the English position is simply the law reform process that led to the statutory process.

As to refusing relief because an identified defect would have made no difference in substance, relief may be refused under s. 19 of the 2016 Act (replicating s. 5 of the 1972 Act) if there is a 'defect in form or a technical irregularity' and it is shown that 'no substantial wrong or miscarriage of justice has occurred'. This is a narrow and rarely used power.[122] There is also the general common law discretion to decline relief (affirmed in s. 18 of the Act). In *Stininato v. New Zealand Boxing Association Inc*, the majority of the Court of Appeal upheld a decision by the trial judge to refuse relief in relation to a case of the revocation of a boxing licence without an oral hearing because the hearing would not have made a difference.[123] However, in *Rajan v. Minister of Immigration*, the Court of Appeal suggested that the court would 'in general ... be slow to deny a remedy on the ground that the result of further consideration is inevitable', though it did so on the facts here because any order to consider the matter further would be 'futile'.[124] Such use of the discretion was also rejected in *Survey Nelson*.[125] Uncontroversially, the gravity and significance of the error is one factor to be weighed in the exercise of the discretion.[126]

Unlike the requirements in England, there is the notable absence of any leave requirement. While there are judge-made rules as to standing, these are understood more in terms of a discretion as to the granting of relief rather than a jurisdictional matter, as in the English setting – a difference that ties in with the more general New Zealand preference for using the remedial discretion rather than rigid doctrinal categories.[127] The standing rules are as liberal as the English position, and the same constitutional reasoning is employed: the rule of law requires access to the courts to test the legality of government decisions.[128]

The liberal availability of judicial review is manifest in more minor details of procedure as well. Under English law, 'undue delay' may lead to the refusal of leave to bring proceedings if

[119] Administrative Tribunals, Fifth Report (above note 118), 18–21.

[120] The narrower definition in the 1972 Act was extended to the current definition by the Judicature Amendment Act 1977.

[121] See the contribution by Cora Hoexter on South Africa in this volume for a similar issue arising under legislation.

[122] But see *Northland Regional Council v. Rogan* [2018] NZCA 63, [78]–[88], for a recent example of its use: mistakes in the setting of rates by a regional council, by not setting the date for payment and not complying with a statutory time requirement, were held to meet the criteria for s. 5 of the 1972 Act.

[123] *Stininato v. New Zealand Boxing Association Inc* [1978] 1 NZLR 1 (CA), 8–9 (Richmond P) and 29 (Cooke J). See also *Wislang v. Medical Practitioners Disciplinary Committee* [1974] 1 NZLR 29 at 42 and 45; *Maddaver v. Umawera School Board of Trustees* [1993] 2 NZLR 478.

[124] *Rajan v. Minister of Immigration* [1996] 3 NZLR 543 (CA) at 552. See also *GXL Realties Ltd v. Minister of Energy for New Zealand* [2010] NZCA 185 at [67].

[125] *Survey Nelson Ltd v. Maritime New Zealand* [2010] NZCA 629 (leave to appeal declined: *Director of Maritime New Zealand v. Survey Nelson* [2011] NZSC 61). The Court of Appeal criticised the judge, who had declined relief, for not setting out the exceptional grounds for refusing relief, particularly as he had found prejudice: [53]–[62].

[126] See, e.g., *Martin v. Ryan* [1990] 2 NZLR 209 (HC) at X.

[127] See Section 18.7.

[128] *Environmental Defence Society v. South Pacific Aluminium (No 3)* [1981] 1 NZLR 216 (CA).

the grant would cause 'substantial hardship to ... any person', 'substantially prejudice the rights of any person' or be 'detrimental to good administration': s. 31 of the Senior Courts Act 1981 (UK); and r. 54.5 of the Civil Procedure Rules sets the time limit for judicial review applications at three months in general (and six weeks in relation to planning decisions), though with an overriding need for promptness. There is no such generally applicable time limit in the New Zealand statute.[129] However, the court's discretion as to the granting of relief[130] allows delay to be a significant factor in determining whether relief will be denied, particularly if relief now would prejudice the interests of third parties.[131] The absence of special time limits and other procedures means that the strictures arising in the UK from the need to allow public bodies to benefit from the tighter procedural rules[132] has limited scope in New Zealand.

The lack of access restrictions relative to the position in England probably owes something to New Zealand's small population and level of inter-connectedness. Annual numbers of judicial review applications for long were quite low,[133] and it seems there was simply no perceived need to impose any constraints on this. Similarly open access can be observed in the country's government arrangements, for instance in the fact that Select Committees call for and consider public submissions on all Bills (except where urgency is taken). A further point arising from this 'big village' arrangement is that groups in society who might in England have to resort to judicial review to try to have an influence can often have a direct conversation with legislators, ministers and civil servants, leaving less perceived need for judicial review.

18.7 ESCHEWING RIGID DOCTRINAL CATEGORIES

Aside from these areas of greater conservativism or interventionism, New Zealand courts also display a tendency to eschew rigid doctrinal categories. A recent development of uncertain provenance and significance is the NZ Supreme Court's almost complete eschewal of reasoning from general principles or reliance on authority in administrative law, deciding the vast majority of cases as matters simply of statutory interpretation.[134] For instance, in *Royal Forest and Bird Protection Society*[135] the Court found that the Department of Conservation had applied the wrong statutory test for a decision to revoke the conservation status of a block

[129] Though some particular statutory regimes do include time limits for judicial review applications: see, e.g., Immigration Act 2009, s. 247.

[130] Affirmed by s.18(1) of the Judicial Review Procedure Act 2016.

[131] See, e.g., *Wellington City Council* v. *Minotaur Custodians Ltd* [2017] NZCA 302, [2017] 3 NZLR 464 at [74]–[82]; *Wool Board Disestablishment Company Ltd* v. *Saxmere Co Ltd* [2010] NZCA 513, [2011] 2 NZLR 442; *Auckland Casino Ltd* v. *Casino Control Authority* (HC Auckland, M 81/94, 13 July 1994, Robertson J); *Bailey* v. *Christchurch City Council* [2013] NZHC 1933, [2013] 3 NZLR 679.

[132] *O'Reilly* v. *Mackman* [1983] 2 AC 237 (HL).

[133] Numbers have been increasing, however. In the year to 30 June 2018, there were 209 judicial reviews filed, representing an increase of 6% compared to the 198 cases filed in the previous year: *Annual Statistics for the High Court 30 June 2018*, available at www.courtsofnz.govt.nz/the-courts/high-court (accessed 23 November 2018). In 1997, Michael Taggart 'Introduction to JR in New Zealand' [1997] *Judicial Review* 236 at 237 stated that an estimate of 120 to 130 judicial review cases annually was probably still accurate then.

[134] This is also noted in Matthew Palmer, 'Judicial Review' in Mary-Rose Russell and Matthew Barber (eds.), *The Supreme Court of New Zealand, 2004–2014* (Thomson Reuters, Wellington, 2015) 158 at pp. 165–7.

[135] *Hawke's Bay Regional Investment Co Ltd* v. *Royal Forest and Bird Protection Society of New Zealand Inc* [2017] NZSC 106, [2017] 1 NZLR 1041. Other examples include *Wellington International Airport Ltd* v. *New Zealand Air Line Pilots' Association Industrial Union of Workers Inc* [2017] NZSC 199; *Seaton* v. *Minister for Land Information* [2013] NZSC 42, [2013] 3 NZLR 157; *McGrath* v. *Accident Compensation Corporation* [2011] NZSC 77, [2011] 3 NZLR 733; *Astrazeneca Ltd* v. *Commerce Commission* [2009] NZSC 92, [2010] 1 NZLR 297.

of land that was wanted for a new water reservoir. The statute provided no express test or criteria for the exercise of this power, but the Court considered that the use of a permissive test was inconsistent with the scheme of the Act and the purpose of conservation status. This might have been analysed as involving improper purpose, but that ground is referred to only once in passing in summarising the claimant's submissions. A variation on this avoidance of general principles is found in *Osborne*, which was decided in reliance on the very narrow common law principle specifically concerned with bargains to stifle a prosecution. Applied to an administrative decision, that principle might have been seen as a particular application of the improper purpose ground, but it was not discussed in those terms.[136]

On its face, this avoidance of the traditional grounds bears some similarity to the recent Canadian jurisprudence.[137] However, in Canada this flows from a restructuring of judicial review analysis around standards of review rather than grounds.[138] There is little sign of such development in New Zealand.[139]

More generally, however, eschewal of rigid categories is a more long-standing feature of the NZ approach to administrative law.[140] The resistance to enquiring into proportionality in Bill of Rights cases,[141] for instance, has been explained partly on the basis that NZ judges are uncomfortable with the formalism of the prevalent test for proportionality.[142]

Another example is that the remedial discretion in New Zealand deals with some particular questions that are dealt with in a more categorical fashion in England. This includes the question whether an appeal has 'cured' an earlier breach of natural justice. In *Calvin* v. *Carr*,[143] it was determined that a fair hearing on appeal will cure a breach of natural justice at first instance in some cases, depending on which of three categories applies. In New Zealand, earlier authority had considered that the remedial discretion was generally the better way to take account of a fair hearing on appeal.[144] More recent dicta in *Nicholls* are stronger still against any automatic curing effect: a fair hearing on appeal only ever serves as one factor in exercising the remedial discretion,[145] to be weighed against other factors relevant to the discretion. Although the *Calvin* v. *Carr* approach also involves a factorial assessment, the New Zealand approach is significantly less categorical.

The English courts also remain more inclined than their NZ counterparts to resolve remedial and other questions by reliance on the old absolute theory of invalidity.[146] NZ

136 *Osborne* v. *Worksafe New Zealand* [2017] NZSC 175.

137 See David Mullan, 'Unresolved Issues on Standard of Review in Canadian Judicial Review of Administrative Action – The Top Fifteen!' (2013) 42 *Advocates' Quarterly* 1 at 42–51, 64–9.

138 See Dean R Knight, *Vigilance and Restraint in the Common Law of Judicial Review* (Cambridge University Press, Cambridge, 2018), esp ch 4.2.2.

139 The move away from the traditional grounds may instead be described as a move towards an 'instinctual' approach, on which see Philip A Joseph *Constitutional and Administrative Law in New Zealand* (4th ed, Thomson Reuters, Wellington, 2014) at [22.4] and Knight, above n 138, esp ch 5.2.2.

140 The Chief Justice has noted that NZ has a 'judicial tradition which has generally taken the simple path of optimistic contextualism and is thought to be short in doctrine': Dame Sian Elias, 'The Unity of Public Law' in Mark Elliott, Jason Varuhas and Shona Wilson Stark, *The Unity of Public Law? Doctrinal, Theoretical and Comparative Perspectives* (Hart, Oxford, 2018) 15 at 15; see also at 35–6.

141 See Section 18.4.

142 Claudia Geiringer, 'Sources of Resistance to Proportionality Review of Administrative Power Under the New Zealand Bill of Rights Act' (2013) 11 *New Zealand Journal of Public International Law* 123 at 156–8.

143 *Calvin* v. *Carr* [1980] AC 574 (PC) at 592–3.

144 *Reid* v. *Rowley* [1977] 2 NZLR 472 (CA) at 482, 484.

145 *Nicholls* v. *Registrar of the Court of Appeal* [1998] 2 NZLR 385 (CA) at 435–7. See also *Secretary for Justice* v. *Simes* [2012] NZCA 459, [2012] NZAR 1044 at [109].

146 See, e.g., *Ahmed* v. *Her Majesty's Treasury* [2010] UKSC 2 and 5, [2010] 2 AC 534.

courts, for the most part, have moved to the alternative theory of retrospective invalidation.[147] They are also less likely to place reliance on a theory of invalidity at all.

This may also be part of the reason that New Zealand courts in recent times have taken a less categorical approach to ouster or privative provisions.[148] While the *Anisminic* orthodoxy of effectively interpreting such provisions as ineffective[149] was adopted for NZ in *Bulk Gas*,[150] there is a long-standing line of appellate-level authority taking a different approach to clauses that require recourse to specialist statutory review procedures instead of judicial review.[151]

The resistance to rigid doctrinal categories, like other differences noted above, can be understood in a socio-political context. It is consistent with the pragmatism, anti-intellectualism and lack of dogmatism in New Zealand's perceived national character.[152] Once again, this was greatly reinforced in the administrative law sphere by a dominant judicial personality. In this case this was Sir Robin Cooke (later Lord Cooke), who used his extra-judicial writings to spearhead a drive for 'simplicity' in administrative law,[153] in order to carve out more space for judicial discretion than traditional formalist approaches. While Lord Cooke certainly was not an anti-intellectual himself, the success in this project must owe something to the fact that it resonated with the national psyche.[154]

18.8 CONCLUDING COMMENTS

This chapter has outlined some of the main differences that have opened up between Administrative Law in England and in New Zealand, and offered reflections on some possible reasons for these differences. In concluding, we observe the difference in the overall shape of judicial review that results from the various differences discussed in this chapter. Almost thirty years ago, modern English administrative law was criticised by Harlow and Rawlings for having assumed an unfortunate funnel model, having liberalised access to judicial review through, for example, relaxation of standing rules, but retaining a very restrictive set of grounds.[155] In England, however, the bottom of the funnel has since then widened considerably, with the expansion of substantive grounds of review both at common law and based on breach of the Human Rights Act 1998.

147 See *Martin* v. *Ryan* [1990] 2 NZLR 209 (HC); *Winther* v. *Housing Corporation of New Zealand* [2010] NZCA 601, [2011] 1 NZLR 825.

148 The first sign of any similar willingness in the UK are dicta in *R (Privacy International) v Investigatory Powers Tribunal* [2019] UKSC 22

149 *Anisminic Ltd* v. *Foreign Compensation Commission* [1969] 2 AC 147 (HL); *R (Privacy International)* v. *Investigatory Powers Tribunal* [2019] UKSC 22.

150 *Bulk Gas Users Group* v. *Attorney-General* [1983] NZLR 129 (CA).

151 See, e.g., *New Zealand Rail Ltd* v. *Employment Court* [1995] 3 NZLR 179 (CA); *Tannadyce Investments Ltd* v. *Commissioner of Inland Revenue* [2011] NZSC 158, [2012] 2 NZLR 153. For further discussion of this difference, see Dean R Knight, 'Importation and Indigeneity: The Quartet in New Zealand Administrative Law' in T T Arvind et al. (eds.), *Executive Decision-Making and the Courts: Revisiting the Origins of Modern Judicial Review* (Hart, Oxford, 2019). But cf. *H* v. *Refugee Protection Officer* [2019] NZSC 13, which could be seen as signalling a waning commitment to that approach.

152 See , e.g., Matthew Palmer 'New Zealand Constitutional Culture' (2007) 22 *NZULR* 565.

153 Sir Robin Cooke, 'The Struggle for Simplicity in Administrative Law' in Michael Taggart (ed.), *Judicial Review of Administrative Action in the 1980s* (Oxford University Press, Oxford, 1986) 1.

154 On the NZ courts' preference for contextualism over formalism, see also Claudia Geiringer, 'Sources of Resistance to Proportionality Review of Administrative Power under the New Zealand Bill of Rights Act' (2013) 11 *New Zealand Journal of Public International Law* 123 at 156–8; Dean Knight, 'A Murky Methodology: Standards of Review in Administrative Law' (2008) 6 *New Zealand Journal of Public International Law* 117.

155 Carol Harlow and Richard Rawlings, *Pressure through Law* (Routledge, London, 1992) at 311–13.

The funnel shape is now more pronounced in New Zealand than in England. Access to judicial review is even more liberal, given the absence of any leave requirement or time limit. At the same time, in New Zealand the funnel still narrows when we reach the grounds because most of the modern expansions of substantive review in England have not been adopted fully or clearly in New Zealand. The fact that the remedial discretion is used to address issues that in England are dealt with at an earlier stage also contributes to a more pronounced funnel effect.

PART VIII

Conclusion: Interrogating "Common Law" Approaches to Judicial Review

19

What Is Left of 'Common Law' Administrative Law?

Concluding Remarks and a Layout of Future Paths

Margit Cohn

INTRODUCTION

This concluding chapter aims to bring together the themes explored in the preceding chapters and to identify several research contexts that can largely benefit from this collection. The book's main purpose – to explore the birth, evolution and current nature of the forms of judicial review of the administration in no less than fifteen members of the common law family (with the addition of a commentary on the influence of international law on English administrative law) – has been admirably met. The rich accounts of the structure and evolution of the administrative law of countries spanning the globe – all continents are represented here – offer not only snapshots of the current law of judicial review of the administration in their respective systems; they are just as concerned with the history and institutional structures that are instrumental to both continuity and change. The book further provides important insights into the current state of public law in its broader sense, including constitutional law, and sets the ground for discussion on the current and future condition of the 'common law' family. Moving to meta-themes, the book enriches several debates in law, history and comparative law and politics. Legal change, as a focus for study, has to date not received sufficient attention; the book is an excellent contribution to the study of law as an ever-changing socio-political feature in all polities, more so as it is set in a comparative framework. Most chapters carry a strong historical flavor, which ties in with the separate academic study of post-colonialism.

In the opening chapter, Swati Jhaveri characterizes the comparative exercise that culminated in this collection as 'an admittedly narrow focus for a "comparative law" study in not extending to broader aspects of the administrative justice system'.[1] This book is indeed focused on judicial review under administrative law, with a special emphasis on grounds of review, but the apology is unjustified: the study that has emerged is much more than a mere 'first step to contrasting common law systems'.[2]

Section 19.1 of this chapter offers a bird's-eye view of all book chapters. I note the main differences in the evolution of the analyzed systems' administrative law. Jhaveri's five-pronged typology of the public law of common law systems, presented in Chapter 1, is discussed in Section 19.2. Here, I flesh out several aspects of each of these subcategories, critically consider their internal logic and then, from a more distanced viewpoint, assess the actual utility of this typology.

[1] Swati Jhaveri, Chapter 1 at 12.
[2] Chapter 1.

Section 19.3 aims to provide a tentative explanatory framework for the analysis of the reasons that have led to the different transformation patterns of the administrative law of these systems. In the absence of robust study of legal change as a subject and, more so, in a comparative context, I address three bodies of social science research that study change in general but have little to say on legal change and tentatively apply Donald Horowitz's four approaches to legal change, which in effect offer several explanatory paradigms for legal change over time. This section ends with a proposal of a five-dimensional grid, designed to ease the process of defining factors that may have implicated on change in the systems studied in this volume.

Finally, I question the current robustness of the classic classification of legal systems into 'legal families', in general, and of the common-law family, in particular. Having identified, in Section 19.1, several proto-families within the 'common law' family, I address the question of whether 'common law' systems remain linked enough to be considered as living under a shared roof. I test arguments for the possible retention of a common law template, albeit one that is different (perhaps substantially so) from traditional accounts of the public law of the common law world. The conclusion, tying in with the spirit of the first chapter of this book, is that, nuances and differences aside, the family remains, as long as respect for all forms and types of changes is retained.

19.1 COMMON LAW ADMINISTRATIVE LAW SYSTEMS: A CHAPTER-BY-CHAPTER OVERVIEW

This overview of the book is necessarily limited due to space concerns and does not do justice to the contributions. Nevertheless, in addition to providing a summary of the book, this section sets the background for the comments advanced in the chapter's next sections.

Following Jhaveri's introductory chapter, Chapters 2 and 3 address English law: the first via a historical perspective and the second dedicated to the current state of English administrative law. Paul Craig's main aim is to debunk common perceptions of pre-twentieth century administrative law pertaining to both the empirical and the normative dimensions. Under common accounts, English administrative law is a recent development; pre-twentieth century public law was inhibited by conceptions encapsulated in A. V. Dicey's diatribe against this body of law as recognized and applied in his version of French law. Normatively, competing visions of the role of administrative law revolved around tensions between green- and red-light theories, or conservative/constitutionalist approaches; a general suspicious view of the administration did not sweep this dualism away. Furthermore, administrative law was simply unnecessary prior to the onset of regulation, a state output that reached significance only at the turn of the twentieth century. Craig shows that none of the above assumptions are tenable. Inter alia, the rules of judicial review were conceived centuries ago under doctrines and grounds echoed in current administrative law. Legal control of discretion was grounded inter alia in well-established concepts such as proper purpose, rationality and 'proportionability'; this was a constant feature rather than a collection of haphazard instances, instructed by the normative assumption that constraining public power was warranted. Finally, Craig shows that regulation has been central to governance since Tudor times, and similar issues raised today as to the extent and mechanisms of regulation were at play long before the twentieth century. The chapter, thus dealing with 'perception and reality',[3] concludes with comments on the exportability of these novel understandings of

[3] Chapter 2.

English history to other common law systems in a way that may have inhibited the development of administrative law in those systems or created a path-dependent development of the same suspicion of the administrative state.

For Christopher Forsyth, 'classical' administrative law is more of a modern concept, which is discussed against recent developments. Forsyth's main concern is with a general recent transformation towards more substance-based judicial review, reflected inter alia in dicta concerning the possibility of judicial overruling of statutory exclusion clauses that seek to restrict judicial review and judicial readiness to creatively interpret statutory features, such as the executive override challenged in *Evans* (2015); he identifies a judicial enhancement of discretion-based versus principled reasoning. The onset of enhanced, pragmatized judicial discretion, paired with the rise of rights-adjudication which, in its current form, is viewed as promoting substance-based decision-making, inter alia through the introduction of proportionality, reflect 'a seemingly inexorable rise in the role of judicial discretion to be exercised on pragmatic grounds'.[4] These developments, claims Forsyth, have impacted on the certainty of law and are viewed here in dismay; they are considered a challenge not only to English law but also to the continuing influence of English administrative law on other systems. Whether one agrees with this normative angle or not, the chapter offers a snapshot of current English administrative law that, read with the previous historical chapter, provides a well-rounded account of the system's nature of judicial review and factors that may influence its export across the common law world.

Chapter 4's initial focus on English law adds a comparative dimension to the analysis. Michael Ramsden is concerned with the possible impact of international law on English law and the possible interaction between England and other common law systems in their approach to international law. The latter is seen as English law's competitor for influence on domestic legal systems. He focuses on human rights conventions and materials that have not been incorporated in domestic law – hence the importance of dualism in the analysis. Addressing the pre- and post-HRA state of the dualist principle in the UK, Ramsden moves to assess the possible exportability of English dualism to other common law systems and the importability of other common law approaches into English judicial review law via international law. Several factors are addressed here, such as the impact of written constitutions, some of which include express directions regarding the place of international law, which can and have had an impact on the systems' administrative law. Different stances range from fierce nationalist rejection to so-called legal cosmopolitanism.[5] Some of these permutations are discussed further in subsequent chapters. Attention to the possible influence in the opposite direction takes into account the respective legal cultures and raises questions regarding the future life of both the dualist principle and the recognition of common law–based rights.

The case of Scotland, discussed in the next chapter, is the first example in this collection of a system in which English administrative law was superimposed onto local, indigenous law. The different elements discussed in Stephen Thomson's chapter include the distinct guiding principle regarding the scope of review. Rather than follow the public/private distinction that instructs English administrative law, under Scots Administrative law, the action of anybody considered to exercise a public function is reviewable. Furthermore, available remedies remained indistinguishable from those granted in private law; hence, Scots law was not

4 Chapter 3 at 58.
5 Chapter 4.

trapped in the English historical quagmire of writ-following. Nevertheless, the grounds for review, as well as procedural issues concerning standing, time limits and leave, have undergone processes of convergence with English law, inter alia under judicial rulings as in the case of standing, and through the Courts Reform (Scotland) Act 2014. Passed by the Scottish Parliament, the statute introduced, inter alia, a time limit for application and the introduction of a leave or permission stage. Thomson then addresses possible reasons for the competing dynamics of retention and convergence. The long-standing tradition of reliance on the principle of limited jurisdiction, rather than on remedial categories permeates Scottish public law, and a distinct identity of separateness both support the retention of some of the divergent features discussed in Thomson's chapter.

Across the Irish Sea, Ireland offers the first example of a combination of continuity and transformation of administrative law under the direction of a written constitution. The Irish Constitution itself combined transformation and continuity. Under its constitution, the new polity retained the pre-independence law in force. Paul Daly identifies several aspects of administrative law that have diverged away from English law, beyond the simple fact that rights protection and principles of natural justice are enshrined in the written constitution. Divergence is evident in the Irish refusal to follow several English innovations, as in its retention of the jurisdictional/non-jurisdictional error distinction, the rejection of the procedural exclusivity rule, the readiness to grant compensation when legitimate expectations are recognized to have been breached, the introduction of a new formulation of prerogative powers, now relying on the sovereignty of the state, and the full endorsement of proportionality, the latter reflecting the direct influence of European Union law. Under this theme of 'continuity and change',[6] Daly shows however that continuity remains, with areas such as the nature of the supervisory authority of courts and the de facto application of the principles of natural justice in ways and means that are not substantially different from their applications in the parent system.

Crossing the Atlantic, one of the marked features of United States' administrative law, discussed in Chapter 7, is once again the supremacy and influence of the written constitution. This example of long-term evolution offers insights into the ways other systems may evolve in their respective futures. Following a discussion on the nature of common law and its English history, Peter Cane periodizes his analysis of the administrative law of the federal state; periodizing, or historicizing law, is an important element here, which is further discussed in the following section. After independence, the mix of centralization and localized colonial law under British rule was replaced by a system directed by the 1789 constitution, which does not expressly authorize or even mention judicial review (the only explicit aspect being the limitation on the suspension of the *Habeas Corpus* writ). Limited judicial control of the emerging bureaucracy remained a central feature, drawing on the jurisdictional theory that underlay English administrative law, but several transformations occurred over time, inter alia the replacement of the emphasis on writs-based review by one informed by rules and rights. Following a period of a lively exchange of ideas between British and American scholars, and the rise of the recognition of administrative law as a distinct body of law, the 1946 APA is posited as the watershed that divides the two systems. In itself a source for the development of a new body of 'common law', it represents, and has driven further, the move to a 'process'-based tradition and the emphasis in American judicial review of the administration. Under a distinctly different structure based on the constitution and the APA, and the understandings

[6] Chapter 6, inter alia the chapter title and the title of Section 6.2.

regarding the role for judges, US federal administrative law emerges as a distinct common law that is no longer 'an Anglo-common-law system'.[7]

The analysis of the Canadian version of judicial review of the administration, presented by Paul Daly in Chapter 8, is laid out as another discussion devised under the 'divergence and convergence' framework, shows that up to the early 1970s, Canadian administrative law was virtually indistinguishable from its English counterpart. The gradual move away from English law during the next three decades was expressed in the rejection of jurisdictional error as the organizing principle of review, in favour of the 'pragmatic and functional approach', a term of art coined by the Canadian Supreme Court. Employed under a web of factors that lead to the application of one of several standards of review, this arguably substance- and principle-based review promoted the dominance of unreasonableness as a standard of review. This change still implied general deference to administrative decision makers unless meeting strict conditions, except in the case of the Court's readiness to intervene in the review of administrative tribunals. Convergence, identified since the 2000s, is of a distinct nature: rather than considering the influence of English law on Canadian law, Daly addresses the English courts' deliberations regarding the expansion of proportionality, a well-recognized Canadian ground of review since the 1980s, within their administrative law. Those forms of relative changes are explained mainly as the outcomes of complexity of some of the legal constructs applied by court, or 'accidents of history'.[8] The constitutional element, developed in Canada by courts, and, it may be added, by the constitution-like legislation, is discussed in the context of future developments in the evolution of British administrative law, which may move towards convergence with Canadian jurisprudence.[9] This overview of systemic vacillating between similarity and difference offers another example of the complexity of the evolution of legal systems, discussed in Section 19.3 of this chapter.

Moving to the Middle East, the case of Israel offers yet another angle to the tale of continuity and departure. Justice Daphne Barak-Erez depicts a gradual transformation from full reliance on the English structure of judicial review to a framework that offers a mere simile of that structure. As in other ex-colonies and territories, the state adopted its pre-independence public law from elsewhere: in this case, England. Although some elements differed on conception, the court structure, and the absence of statute-based rules of judicial review, were designed in the pre-independence era, and much of these remain to the present day. Yet developments of the basic principles occurred, from its earliest years, in ways that sometimes preceded English subsequent developments, as in the case of the extension of the rules of natural justice to non-judicial public bodies and the development of the ultra vires principle as one that requires that all action impacting on human rights be based on an explicit and detailed statutory authorization. The 1980s were marked by significant changes, including the relaxation of standing requirements, which led to the application of administrative law in a large number of political contexts, and the introduction of a revamped and strengthened version of unreasonableness. As in other systems, these, and other changes, were much influenced by developments in constitutional law; inter alia, the introduction of basic laws that protect several human rights in the 1990s had a clear influence on the judicial recognition of proportionality as a distinct ground of review. The rise of privatization, under which some services previously offered directly by the sates were

7 Chapter 7 at 137.

8 Chapter 8 at 143, 152.

9 Chapter 8.

transferred to private bodies, offers a challenge, to be met here and elsewhere. In all, nevertheless, the structure of judicial reasoning and the menu of available grounds remain similar enough for English and Israeli law to be 'two dialects of the same ancient language'.[10]

The law of South Africa, one of the two African states presented in this collection, was built on Roman-Dutch legal foundations, but, unlike Scotland, this early layer had little to do with administrative law, except for the availability of additional remedies. Designed in accordance with English law, the application of South African administrative law was distorted by the regime's White minority rule's racial segregation and oppression; hence 'the pale reflection' of English administrative law in South Africa.[11] The transformation to full democracy in the mid-1990s featured, as in other countries, a written constitution that contains a bill of rights. This is also the first case discussed in this volume of the legislative codification of administrative judicial review: under the Promotion of Administrative Justice Act (2000), review no longer rests on the common law but statute, which provides an expanded menu of grounds for review. However, the system does not differ materially from the English method of reasoning and decision-making. Next, and echoing Daly's account of the use of Canadian law to fertilize other systems, Cora Hoexter shows the extent to which South Africa's public law has influenced the laws of several African countries. Currently, judicial review remains dominant, with constitution, statute and judiciary-originated grants of additional mechanisms and grounds leading inter alia to the expansion of now-traditional grounds such as unreasonableness, and the firm establishment of the principle of legality, drawn directly from the constitution, enabling review beyond the limits set in the legislation. Yet, Hoexter emphasizes, the English concepts and doctrines, such as prerogative and the ground of unreasonableness continue to direct domestic law, and courts continue to cite English (and other) precedents to support their opinions. Here, then, is another case of divergence/convergence, or, using terms that feature here and in other chapters of this collection, varying degrees of indigenization.

Kenya, one of the systems considered to have been influenced by South Africa's public law, offers a second example of post-colonial oscillation between forms of autocracy and constitutional democracy. The periodization in Migai Akech's chapter opens, as in other chapters, with a discussion of colonial times, during which English-derived rules and principles of administrative law were not applied to actively protect from abuse. Against the background of the post-independence rule under a one-party polity and the judicial appointment system that gave dominance to the president of the state, courts exercised a high level of restraint while applying the retained English inheritance, down to citing precedents and remedies. A change in this pattern, along indigenization lines, occurred in the introduction of the 2010 constitution, which created a new jurisdiction of constitutional petition, and the enactment of the Fair Administrative Action Act in 2016. Neither replaced the domestic equivalent of Order 53 (an English law inheritance); hence review can currently be effected under each of these three alternative tracks. Despite the irresolution of the possible tension between these paths, the volume of judicial review has grown exponentially, yet the actual impact on high-level government has not been marked, and issues concerning the process of judicial appointment and its impact on judicial independence remain open. Offering an example of a culture in which 'law is merely seen as an instrument of power',[12] Akech concludes that the ambivalence of British colonial law, then, with its mix of formal and informal, de jure and de facto

10 Chapter 9 at 170.
11 Chapter 10.
12 Chapter 11 at 211.

expressions of the law, has thus been echoed in post-colonial eras, including under the current structure with its multiple sources for review.

The next five chapters are concerned with Asian countries, all of which share the post-colonial history of most of the previously analyzed systems. Swati Jhaveri's discussion of judicial review Singapore-style, in Chapter 12, recognizes the English foundations of Singapore's administrative law, which remained influential in this system. Having achieved its independence in a two-step process, ending in its expulsion from Malaysia, the indigenization of Singapore's administrative law involved the forging of a distinct relational style between the executive and the judiciary, defined here as based on 'co-equality', a dialogue-like process under which dominance of one government branch over the other is replaced by the dynamics of mutual respect and consideration. The green-light approach towards the executive has not led to the exit of review. In hindsight, the impact of English grounds of review on Singapore's grounds of review has been mixed. While proportionality has not been adopted by courts, and the irrationality threshold remains high, the High Court accepted the doctrine of substantive legitimate expectations in 2014 (an issue the Court of Appeal has yet to definitively pronounce on). The incremental expansion of the standing threshold offers a second example of enlargement. In all, indigenization has not been a 'seismic' process; rather, these were 'subtle advances on the traditional outlook to judicial review'.[13]

Malaysia offers an example of a post-colonial state that grapples with the force of religious law. Dian A. H. Shah and Kevin Y. L. Tan address the implications of the recognition of *Syariah* law in the state's constitutional framework on Malaysia's administrative law. Another system operating under a written constitution, the state's constitution originally recognized Islam as the religion of the Federation (a principle recognized also in earlier centuries). Forces of Islamic revivalism led to constitutional reform that, inter alia, strengthened *Syariah* institutions (by recognizing three levels of Kadi courts) and jurisdiction (through the grant of exclusive jurisdiction to *Syariah* courts in some matters and related amendments to the Constitution has caused difficulties in application). This distinct form of indigenization is analyzed through a consideration of the effect of the separation between civil and *Syariah* courts in administrative law matters. Case studies include religious conversion and the issuance of *Fatwa* edicts by Islamic authorities. The pattern is one of retreatism of civil courts and common law administrative law when *Syariah* issues arise; although challenges are continuously made, and some clawback is evident, the pattern of shrinking and shirking renders future development of administrative law uncertain.[14]

Chapter 14, reviewing the case of Hong Kong, offers an illuminating example of the implications of regime change on pre-transformation administrative law. A British colony until 1997, Hong Kong's administrative law unsurprisingly followed English law; the first part of Michael Ramsden's chapter traces the common law of judicial review up to 1997: with its final court of appeal being the Judicial Committee of the Privy Council, local courts continued to refer to 'the common law of England'.[15] The Basic Law, which came into effect that year on the Handover of sovereignty and the establishment of Hong Kong as a Special Administrative Region, part of China, embedded a principle of 'continuity', buttressed by several guarantees and principles such as a declaration of the continuing capitalist market and the continuation of existing laws, albeit under the principle that Hong Kong is 'an inalienable part of the People's Republic of China' as per Article 1 of the Basic Law. The second part of

[13] Chapter 12.
[14] Chapter 13.
[15] Chapter 14.

the chapter considers the continued influence of English judicial review principles and case law in post-Handover times. Offering an analysis of the constitutional structure, including the formal recognition of UN rights covenants, it is shown that as far as administrative law review is concerned, aspects of English law and doctrine remain influential and continue to define the scope of judicial review. However, under a new final appellant judicial authority, some doctrines, such as Wednesbury unreasonableness and proportionality, have undergone indigenous development, and Hong Kong courts have increasingly preferred to look to other epistemic legal communities, including other common law jurisprudence and transnational human rights mechanisms, in the articulation of constitutional and common law norms of judicial review. Not without indigenous developments, the overall pattern is one of continuing powerful influence of English law over the development of Hong Kong public law.[16]

Chapter 15, dedicated to the analysis of India's administrative law, focuses on arbitrariness, and, similar to some of the other legal systems headed by a written constitution, discusses the existence of parallel review paths. Article 14 of the Indian Constitution, which prohibits the denial of equality before the law or the equal protection of the law, has been judicially interpreted as guaranteeing protection from arbitrariness. Applied in India as analogous to the common law administrative law ground of unreasonableness, Farrah Ahmed and Swati Jhaveri challenge the approach that judicial review for unreasonableness is therefore provided only under the constitution. The authors find evidence of judicial reliance on common law grounds of judicial review, which is fully applicable in India. They are critical about the openness of the arbitrariness doctrine in the absence of judicial concretization and warn against the implications of the elimination of the common law track, inter alia the removal of review by lower courts. One example of the judicial rejection of a single-track solution is the Supreme Court's review of state action under the principles of natural justice after it had held that such action was arbitrary under Article 14. As an additional aspect of the issue concerning the future of administrative law review when constitutional review is available, Ahmed and Jhaveri also find that the court has been more cautious when applying common law grounds in cases that did not involve constitutional rights. Promoting the 'use of traditional common law grounds as a guide to when administrative action is arbitrary',[17] the chapter shows continued reliance on English-based doctrines of review. In addition, it offers an example of a system in which a written constitution provides options for judicial review of the administration; here, too, questions regarding the availability of parallel tracks of review arise, as in the case of Kenya.

The next discussion analyses how Bangladesh passed through two changes of sovereignty, from India to Pakistan, before its independence in 1971. As Cynthia Farid notes, the state's written constitution granted the Supreme Court strong powers of review over legislation and executive action, but contains no express provision concerning the nature or the grounds of review of administrative action beyond constitution-based review. The constitution does authorize the High Court Division to review administrative action in non-human-rights contexts. The pre-independence English-based administrative law seems to have remained, as the familiar grounds continue to be employed. Still, development is evident in the court's interpretation of the term 'state', which expanded its jurisdiction to various bodies performing public functions, and in its loosening of the rules of standing, which enabled a rise in public interest litigation. In the context of government service, central to

[16] Chapter 14.

[17] Chapter 15 at 288.

the High Court's decision-making, this pattern of divergence is reflected also in decisions that expansively interpreted the ultra vires doctrine and extended reliance on notions of justice and natural law to ground review; there is also some evidence of acceptance of the doctrine of legitimate expectations, although the approach to the grant of substantive remedies is inconsistently applied in their enforcement. In all, the Supreme Court may have earned its centrality in reviewing administrative action.[18]

Attention is transferred to Oceania in the final two chapters. Sharing a history of a relatively long period of independence, Australia and New Zealand offer distinctly different versions of the law of judicial review of the administration. Australia entered its independence with a written constitution, influenced by both English and American public law, on the one hand, and a strong tradition of English-based administrative law, on the other. Matthew Groves and Greg Weeks's chapter discusses this history. Incremental change was effected both by the legislature and the judiciary. The 1977 Administrative Decisions (Judicial Review) Act, which codified the jurisdiction, the grounds of review and the remedies to be granted when suitable, gradually lost its centrality. Subsequent changes were largely effected by the judiciary, the most salient one was the strengthened reliance on the idea of jurisdictional error as 'the organizing concept around which judicial review in Australia should be approached'.[19] Other foci of debate, serially resolved, were the dispute regarding the basis of the application of the rules of natural justice, decided through a judicial wedding of the approach relying on common law justice and the approach relying on the construction of statute. The doctrine of legitimate expectations, which reached its apex in *Teoh* (1995), evolved into extinction, with an emphasis on fairness as an alternative concept. As in other systems, this story of indigenization is still far from one in which the system transformed beyond recall of its origins but shows distinct signs of moving further away from its origins.

The final chapter in this impressive series of country reviews is dedicated to the system that has retained the closest similarity to its parent system, but again not without points of divergence. Hanna Wilberg and Kris Gledhill open with an overview of the distinct features of New Zealand and its laws: this small country is not subject to regional orders and embodies some of its commitments to its indigenous people under the 1840 Treaty of Waitangi, by now a foundational constitutional document. Retaining the English grounds of review and available remedies, as well as the spirit and style of common law administrative law, differences have still emerged, some of them generated or fueled by statutes. Some of these permutations render judicial review more liberal and available, inter alia by the marginalization of a rigid standing threshold, the absence of a set time limit for application and the added requirement that a remedy would not be granted if the outcome for the applicant were not substantially different in the absence of the challenged administrative act. Conversely, the English doctrine of heightened scrutiny and its introduction of proportionality, the doctrine of substantive legitimate expectations and the range of remedies available related to this ground have not caught root in New Zealand. Human rights legislation is likewise treated more cautiously, inter alia reflected in the more literal reading of the system's equivalent of section 3 of the HRA in the UK. Generally, 'most of the United Kingdom's modern expansions of substantive review have not been adopted fully or clearly in New Zealand'.[20] Yet the adoption of a presumption of statutory consistency with unincorporated international obligations and the Treaty of Waitangi mark the system as exceptional and enable further judicial

18 Chapter 16.
19 Chapter 17.
20 Chapter 18 at 345.

reach. The chapter ends with an analysis of the possible reasons for the differences, relying inter alia on the particularities of the Nation, some of them discussed in the opening part of the chapter – most pertinently the Treaty of Waitangi.

19.2 UNPACKING JHAVERI'S PROPOSED TYPOLOGY

The short overview of the chapters offered in the previous section allows us to return to Chapter 1 and revisit the typology offered there.

The data collected and analyzed in this book are more than sufficiently rich to be amenable to ordering and classification, and well support Swati Jhaveri's suggested typology of the evolved administrative law of common law systems. Jhaveri identifies five possible subcategories of the current features of judicial review of administrative action, drawing on the respective positions of the explored systems on several important issues.[21] In all, she identifies the following types of systems:

- Modified Westminster systems, which have remained referential to English administrative law, with some tweaks that do not substantively distance them from the English way;
- Systems that operate under a written constitution, in which judicial review has a constitutional footing, that has reorganized and reshaped review;
- Systems addressed as 'multilayered', in which state law competes, or is in tension, with local sets of law such as religious or tribal law or with international law;
- Systems in which cultures of transition and development colour their national ethos and, by implication, have shaped the evolution of administrative law.
- Possibly the United States, which is a 'non-derivative common law system', that is, distinct in almost all aspects of its administrative law.[22]

Before discussing each of these subcategories, three comments are apt. First, as Jhaveri herself admits, the taxonomy is porous: a single system may be placed in several subcategories.[23] Indeed, several factors may lead to difficulties in placing some of the systems in a single slot. A system's structural set-up, the interaction between the administration and the judiciary, socio-legal attitudes towards the role of these branches of government – in short, any feature of the country's history, culture and politics may lead to its classification under multiple subcategories. Jhaveri's examples of India and Hong Kong are merely two examples; all the systems now operating under a written constitution are likely to be classified under an additional category, one example being Malaysia, which is also considered 'multilayered'.

The second comment concerns the seeming absence of a single coherent guiding principle shared by all subcategories, a necessary element for upholding a working classification. Subcategories 1-3 and 5 by employing factors that pertain to law, its structure and formal appearances. The fourth, however, is concerned with the cultural, economic and political forces that press for change – an important insight in itself, but not one that shares the same defining factors under which the others were deciphered. One could contrast the fourth subcategory with systems that operate under totally different types of pressure – for example,

[21] These are the existence of a written constitution and the ensuing relationship between constitutional law and administrative law; the embeddedness of a culture of suspicion of executive power; the features of the balance between the judiciary and the executive; the scope of review of substance rather than mere narrow legality and process; the impact of other sources of law, such as religious or indigenous law; and the style of reasoning. Jhaveri, Chapter 1 at 21.

[22] Chapter 1 at 21–22.

[23] Chapter 1.

the pressure of perceived or actual national security threats, the rise of American political clout and culture and economic ideology, market liberalization, or internationalization. All these factors can be found in the discussed systems: for example, New Zealand's administrative law has been influenced by the fourth type of pressure. If the initial classification revolves around structure and formal forms of law, the fourth subcategory may need to be removed, but it could be the first item of a second taxonomy, organized under these and similar factors.

Several other subcategories can be considered – for example, the degree of influence of regionalism and under-indigenization. A distinction may be made between systems that retain a strong link with English law and those that exercise a higher level of interaction with other common law systems. Both may be considered under Jhaveri's first subcategory, now addressed.

19.2.1 *Subcategory 1: Degrees of Modification of the Westminster Model*

As a starting point, some clarification of the meaning of 'modified' is required. Essentially, even a system that has renounced its common law legacy is 'modified', but this does not seem to be the nature of this subcategory. This subcategory may include those systems that have not materially departed from its earlier roots; in Jhaveri's words, the law has been 'tweaked'.[24]

The nature of English law as a 'parent system' to all common law systems energized the conference that led to the compilation and publication of this collection. English administrative law has naturally been the source from which their early administrative law emanated and subsequently transformed away from, in various ways and to different extents. Hence, English law deserved a double, if not triple, contribution to this book. In this context, the question is whether English law remains merely a point of reference for the subsequent analyses. Acceptance of this position would imply that English law has not engaged with other systems, common or uncommon, in its evolution and change processes – an assumption that cannot be factually supported.

Michael Ramsden deals with this precise issue through his discussion of the workings of the principle of dualism in England in the context of European human rights law. Here, Ramsden notes 'the general judicial recognition that the ECHR was exerting greater pressure on English public law' prior to the enactment of the HRA.[25] Indeed, the introduction of variegated unreasonableness review in *Bugdaycay* (1987) *Brind* (1991) and *Smith* (1996) was influenced by the law of the European Convention of Human Rights, as admitted in *Smith*.[26] Proportionality is discussed in the following section; although the extent of the application of this doctrine in English law in accordance with its European counterpart is still an open question, and despite early reticence to recognize the European

24 Jhaveri, Chapter 1. This reading of the subcategory may support the addition of a sixth, under which a body of law transforms with little recall of its origin.

25 Ramsden, Chapter 4 at 62. Ramsden also cites judges who denied such pressure. In this context, Christopher Forsyth's chapter discusses the introduction of the ground of proportionality following the enactment of the Human Rights Act. His critique is not concerned with the sullying of English law as such but on the endemic uncertainty of this ground. Note that as long as the system denies the application of this ground to so-called mundane administrative discretion, it remains relevant only when the administrative act is challenged as an interference in a protected human right.

26 *R* v. *Secretary of State for the Home Department, ex p Bugdaycay* [1987] AC 514; *R.* v. *Secretary of State for the Home Department, ex parte Brind* [1991] 1 A.C. 696; *R.* v. *Ministry of Defence, Ex p. Smith* [1996] Q.B. 517

origin of this doctrine, as Ramsden argues in his discussion of the judicial analysis of *Brind*, 'the backstage presence in this analysis was the extent to which the courts were able to give effect to the ECHR'.[27]

Further attention should also be granted to European Union law. There are various views regarding the impact of European law on the inclusion of the 'legitimate expectations' in English administrative law – a doctrine that is central to European Union Law.[28] Still, the impact of European law cannot be denied.[29]

The impact of other systems can be discerned too. Consider the rise of proportionality as a possible ground for review of administrative action. Commentators have rightfully identified the origins of this transplant in European Union law and in the text and jurisprudence of the European Convention of Human Rights, but judges have tended to link their tentative acceptance of this ground with case-law from other common law jurisdictions, such as South Africa, Zimbabwe and Canada.[30] Under all of these, the outcome should then be is that English administrative law, in itself, may be considered a 'modified Westminster' system. And, if English law, or at least its administrative law, is itself a 'modified Westminster', as Christopher Forsyth's chapter implies, how would other systems fare?

The measuring of larger and smaller-scale modifications in this book is essentially an exercise in post-colonialism: all common law systems discussed in the book (Scotland excluded) have evolved from colonial to independent.[31] All students of post-colonial law are well-aware that new states freed from a colonial past usually retain their link to so-called mundane sets of rules, practices and legal institutions. A newly independent state carved out from the British Empire may be pressed to signal its separateness by creating a distinct political form, as in the US case by adopting a constitution and a federal structure, but these are all so-called high-level constitutional aspects of the system. Administrative law is usually considered a lower form of law dealing with the humdrum aspects of governance; whether this demotion of administrative law is justified – most, if not all, administrative law scholars would reject this appellation – the retention of pre-colonial administrative law by newly independent ex-colonies is an undeniable fact. In doing so, each system naturally replicated, with some initial differences, English administrative law as it was at its

27 Ramsden, Chapter 4.

28 The provenance of this doctrine in England was initially debated: Lord Denning, who first used the term in *Schmidt* (1969), later commented that he was not at all influenced by European law; yet moving forward in time, the affinity with EU law has been recognized by several justices, a point that is now much less debated. See Paul Craig and Gráinne de Búrca, *EU Law: Text, Cases and Materials* (6th ed., Oxford University Press, 2015), 560–3. The possible impact of Brexit is not discussed here. Beyond the fact that principles and precedents of EU law, once introduced into British law, have not lost their force, the UK remains signatory to the ECHR. See further, Chapter 4

29 See Chapter 4

30 See *De Freitas* v. *Permanent Secretary of Ministry of Agriculture, Fisheries, Lands and Housing* [1999] 1 A.C. 69 (P. C.) (adopting the test adopted in *Nyambirai* v. *National Social Security Authority* [1996] 1 L.R.C. 168, 1995 (9) BCLR 1221 (ZS)). In adopting its proportionality formula, the Zimbabwean court cited the Canadian source. See also Daly, Chapter 8. For an account of the transcontinental movement of the proportionality doctrine, which must include Germany, see Margit Cohn, 'Legal Transplant Chronicles: The Evolution of Unreasonableness and Proportionality Review of the Administration in the United Kingdom', 58 *Am J Comp L* 583, 586 (note 3), 619–22.

31 Ireland and the United States, discussed in Chapters 6 and 7, are not usually considered 'post-colonial' polities, although such a designation would not be incorrect if the post–Second World War timing would have been extracted from the definition.

independence.[32] The point here is the measuring of the extent of distance from its origins covered by these systems.

In addressing the degrees of divergence from the parent's administrative law, further attention to the temporal element is required. The first aspect of timing merely focuses on age. Aside from the centuries-old United States, the age of another four analyzed systems extends beyond 100 years,[33] and four of the remaining six gained their independence during the mid-twentieth century. (Scotland is excluded, and the history of Hong Kong is unique.[34]) The distinct evolution of US administrative law, discussed in Peter Cane's contribution to this volume (spanning pre- and, more importantly in this respect, post-independence evolution) may be simply credited to the time span that has enabled successive transformations.[35] Other 'younger' systems that are currently more or less linked with English administrative law (such as Singapore) may possibly rotate away by the time they reach a comparable age. However, New Zealand offers a challenge to reliance on time as a defining factor, as it has retained more of English administrative law, albeit with changes.

Timing has another dimension: as mentioned above, on independence, post-colonial states that retained pre-colonial law usually maintained 'the law in force' at that date, unless the constitution retained a living link to subsequent changes in the parent system or statutes with a constitution-type content.[36] By itself, the different dates of independence dictate variance. Consider, for example, the administrative law on the independence of, say, Australia (1965). The administrative law of Kenya on its independence arguably included all transformations since 1907, for example *Wednesbury* unreasonableness, recognized as a distinct doctrine in 1948.[37] Australia did embrace *Wednesbury*, even embedded its test in its Administrative Decisions (Judicial Review) Act 1977, as Groves and Weeks show in their chapter, but this was a decision made through borrowing from one independent system by another, albeit one that retained a strong affinity with its parent system despite systemic transformations.

A third aspect of the analysis of the extent of modification concerns mixes, or forms of hybridity in which the common law is mixed with bodies of rules that originate elsewhere. Mixed systems have been recognized as a separate subcategory, discussed in the following section.

Finally, this subcategory of systems that, in Jhaveri's words, 'are modes of concepts and doctrines from English administrative law with some 'tweaks' that do not divorce them from the English mode',[38] enables the distinction between patterns and degrees of post-colonial

32 The case of Israel offers another option: constitutions or constitution-type legislations may retain a 'living link' for the streaming of post-independence English law after independence. Article 46 of the Palestine Order in Council 1922–1947, discussed and cited in Daphne Barak-Erez's chapter, embodied such a requirement.

33 Founding members of the Commonwealth and current members Canada, Australia, New Zealand and South Africa received their independence in 1867, 1901, 1907 and 1909, respectively. See Chapters 8, 17 and 18.

34 Dates of independence, for some states the date of recognition as dominions, for others fully independent from the start, for yet others registered from date of secession from a country formerly independent, are Canada (1867), Australia (1901), New Zealand (1907), South Africa (1909), Ireland (1922), India (1947), Israel (1948), Malaysia (1957), Kenya (1963), Singapore (1965, from Malaysia) and Bangladesh (1971, from Pakistan, 1947). Hong Kong is the obvious outlier (1997, to China).

35 Cane argues that the 'administratisation' of the state, through legislation and the creation of agencies, supports Jerry Mashaw's analysis of the so-called lost one hundred years of administrative law. Still, this early departure from English public law revolved around two foci: the growth of legislation and the emergence of a distinct institutional structure; administrative review remained similar in its contours to English law during this, and some of the following decades of that century. The transformation of administrative review marked by the introduction of the APA in 1946, and subsequent judicially developed doctrines, were all products of a polity that was at least 150 years old. See Chapter 3.

36 See the previously discussed example of Israel.

37 *Associated Provincial Picture Houses Ltd* v. *Wednesbury Corporation* [1948] 1 KB 223.

38 Chapter 1 at 21.

evolution. Consider, for example, the differences in this context between Australia and New Zealand. Both have a relatively long history of independence and remain members of the Commonwealth. Mapping the possible reasons for this divergence is discussed in Section 19.3; for now, it is evident, as Jhaveri aims to show, that the degrees of 'modification' of the Westminster model vary, even between those systems that have not distanced themselves from their origins to a degree of functional separation.

19.2.2 *Subcategory 2: In the Company of a Written Constitution*

No less than twelve systems out of the fifteen studied in this book currently operate under a formal, written constitution – a single document that regulates the institutional structure of the polity, usually with the addition of a bill of rights.[39] The introduction of a constitution is clearly an example of a 'modification', but it rightfully merits a separate discussion due to the substantive nature of this departure from the common law template. Whether this fact should or should not be considered a direct challenge to the retention of a common law constitutional family, the main focus here is on the possible impact of the very existence of a written constitution on the evolution of the rules concerning the judicial review of the administration.

The organizing factor of this subcategory requires clarification. At first glance, this group of systems seems to include only systems whose constitutions explicitly direct judicial review, such as South Africa and Australia.[40] Under this reading, most of the countries that operate under a written constitution are excluded from this category. Yet the impact on administrative law of a written constitution that has nothing much to say about judicial review is well recognized and detailed in several of the chapters – for example, those analyzing Kenya and Israel. I continue, then, under the assumption that all states with a written constitution should be included here; a further sub-distinction is indeed in place, as Jhaveri notes.

Jhaveri emphasizes that 'these [constitutionalized] jurisdictions deal with additional issues relating to the overlap/conflicts between any such constitutionalization or codification and the common law – which impact on the scope of cases that come before the courts and the grounds utilized at common law'.[41] Such potential overlaps or conflicts may not only occur with regard to constitutionalized bills of rights but are also relevant in the context of the structural-institutional parts of a constitution. In the human rights context, developments such as the British requirement for 'anxious review' of unreasonableness, and the US doctrine, under which 'intermediate' and 'strict scrutiny' may be applied in this context, are best known.[42] But consider, for example, provisions that pertain to the executive branch and delineate its powers; these provisions can carry a substantial impact on the review of administrative action, previously addressed only under administrative law. Hence, additional grounds of review are likely to be recognized in constitutional law, as in the case of proportionality, if and when this ground is applied in non-human rights contexts, and intensified degrees of review may be required even when rights and freedoms are not part of the challenge against government action. The development of parallel paths of review,

39 The United States, Canada, Australia, South Africa, Ireland, India, Bangladesh, Malaysia, Kenya, Singapore and Hong Kong (the latter operates under a Basic Law devised by China; Israel's Basic Laws could also qualify; see Chapters 5–17).

40 See Chapters 5–17.

41 Chapter 1.

42 *Smith*, above n 27; *U.S.* v. *Carolene Products Company*, 304 US 144 (1938) 152–3, footnote 4.

deriving from both (or either) constitutional and administrative law, as in the case of Kenya, may be troublesome, but for others, this is not considered a problem.[43]

19.2.3 *Subcategory 3: Multilayered/Mixed Systems*

Jhaveri identifies several systems that are hybrid in nature, and notes the potential for divergence from the 'pure' common law template when a second set of rules competes with or possibly rejects the common law.

At first glance, a good number of these systems should be discussed in the context of the well-established study of mixed legal systems, discussed in some comparative literature as 'the third legal family'.[44] Of the systems analyzed in this book, South Africa, Israel and Scotland are usually listed as members of this distinct family. However, this body of research cannot be directly applied here.

As a general rule, the 'mix' in mixed legal systems follows the dividing line between private and public law: their private law tends to carry a strong Civil Law flavour, while public law draws on all aspects we consider to be characteristic to the common law; some 'perforation' may exist, but the dominance of one type of legal family in each of these spheres is uncontested.[45] If this is indeed the case, the mixed nature of these systems has nothing much to do with the issue at hand. Judicial review of the administration is firmly placed within public law, and doubly so: both the structural rules of judicial jurisdiction over the administration and the substantive rules of judicial review are firmly embedded in public law.[46] The question, then, is whether this hybridity of civil law and common law has had any impact on these systems' administrative law. For both Israel and South Africa, the chapters' answer is negative.

As Daphne Barak-Erez notes in her chapter on Israel, the British Mandate retained several sets of rules that originated in the Ottoman period, namely private law and some aspects of personal/religious law; in the latter context, this was mainly effected by retaining the established religious courts that had jurisdiction over personal law (further discussed in the following section in the context of religious law).[47] Yet Barak-Erez finds no link between these remaining rules, some of which are currently still in force, and the law on the judicial review of the administration. The latter was designed anew by the colonizer and retained its form on independence. South African Roman-Dutch law, as Cora Hoexter notes in her chapter, is 'barely evident in administrative law', another example of this state of affairs.[48]

A second type of mixed system is more relevant to our exercise, and is indeed at the core of this subcategory. The two central sources that apply here are indigenous and religious bodies of law. Yet, two conditions apply to the inclusion of systems that mix both in this subcategory. Jhaveri discusses the influence of exogenous 'systems' – that is, this subcategory is seemingly less concerned with the infusion of small-scale, specific doctrines or rules. To qualify as

43 On this aspect in Israel, following the 'constitutionalisation' of the system, see Barak-Erez, Chapter 9.

44 See, e.g., V. V. Palmer (ed.), *Mixed Jurisdictions Worldwide: The Third Legal Family* (2nd ed., Cambridge University Press, 2012).

45 V. V. Palmer, 'Introduction', in Palmer, above note 44, 9–10.

46 Possible exceptions may be found in the context of state action in spheres of private law, namely in government contracting and state tort liability, although irrelevant to our focus on the judicial review of the administration.

47 See Daniel Friedman, 'The Effect of Foreign Law on the Law of Israel: Remnants of the Ottoman Period', (1975) 10 *Isr L Rev* 192, and Barak-Erez, Chapter 9. For the continuation provisions, see Articles 46, 51–4 of the Palestine Order in Council 1922–1947.

48 Chapter 5 at 171.

'mixed', the foreign element must be substantive; the focus here should be on the introduction of a distinct body of laws, rather than on marginal influences through anecdotal transplantation. Thus, the introduction of proportionality, essentially a European-German doctrine, into quite a few common law systems has not rendered them mixed. Second, this second set of rules must have an impact on the law concerning judicial review of the administration, either directly or indirectly. Such rules may pertain to jurisdiction – relating to the amenability of this second body of law to review by the central, 'civil' courts or the alternative institutions established to apply and adjudicate this law, or to content – by setting limits on or creating stricter rules of review.

Here, too, a temporal element should be added. Some of the 'other' bodies of law predate the introduction of the common law, which usually occurred on the territory's inclusion in the British Empire. Stephen Thomson identifies early elements of Scots law that include feudal law, canon law, Udal law, Celtic law, Biblical law and foreign maritime law.[49] While not all of these sources existed as substantive, large-scope bodies of law, their formal status continues to colour Scottish administrative law.

As another permutation, some pre-independent non-compulsory bodies of law were upgraded after independence and granted a binding force, as in the case of infusing religious law into domestic law. Malaysia's 1980s reforms that granted Syariah law formal binding force, discussed in Chapter 13, are echoed, perhaps to a lesser degree, in the law of Israel. The Mandate pre-independence religious courts, which, although fully recognized, were not the exclusive fora for issues under their jurisdiction, were transformed earlier in Israel's history to courts that enjoyed exclusive jurisdiction in some aspects of personal law.[50]

As for indigenous law, post-independence recognition of aboriginal, indigenous and tribal law, driven by political needs for reconciliation or other reasons, could also lead legal systems to their inclusion in the category of a mixed system, as in the case of New Zealand.

Indeed, in all such cases, care must be taken to ensure that these bodies of law have had a direct impact on the rules of judicial review of the administration, which is after all the focus of our exercise. The recognition of pre-colonial religious courts as agents of the state could potentially lead to the development of a subcategory of administrative law, under which those courts were to be subject to distinct rules of review. Studying Malaysia, Shah and Tan follow the oscillation of the civil courts' review of decisions made either by religious bodies or by civil administrative bodies relying on religiously based edicts such as the fatwa; they also discuss questions of jurisdiction. Yet none of this body of law has led to the introduction of a distinct set of rules of administrative review. And, similarly, while clearly decisive in the fields of personal law, mainly pertaining to marriage and divorce, to date, Jewish Halakhic law has no direct influence on this issue.

Finally, issues of post-independence mixedness can arise with regard to common law systems located in Europe. The introduction of European law onto the laws of the member states has indeed had a direct impact on the rules and content of judicial administrative review. This is relevant to England and Wales, Scotland and Ireland. In the context of grounds of review, the

[49] Stephen Thomson, 'The Influence of English Judicial Review on Scots Judicial Review: A Tale of Resemblance and Distinctiveness', Chapter 5, note 89.

[50] Under a 1953 statute, matters of marriage and divorce between Jew were to be decided in the Jewish Rabbinical courts, which apply orthodox Jewish law. In other aspects of personal law, jurisdiction is concurrent with civil courts; the Rabbinical courts can also operate as an arbitrator in all matters, subject to the consent of all parties. This chapter does not discuss the status of other religious courts; suffice to note that the Shari'a courts retain a broader jurisdiction in personal law matters.

agreements regarding the role of law in society, ranging from legalist tc strict adherence to law to the disregard of law.[58]

This grid is helpful in identifying a large number of possible factors. C factors that are posited in any of the boxes created by this grid overlap c strict division between 'structure' and 'culture' is proposed. Still, defining factors are necessary elements of a well-rounded analysis of patterns of cl

19.3 ANALYZING LEGAL CHANGE

All of the systems discussed in this collection have embarked on journey and indigenization, in different ways and to varying extents. Arguably systems that self-define themselves as based on the common law share a the exception of Scotland and the Republic of Ireland, the explored different periods of time and under several regime configurations, Empire prior to their emergence as independent systems.[59] The transiti an independent state is, in itself, a prime example of a 'seismic' change: rules are maintained, the line drawn by independence cannot be overl continues from that point onwards; transition is not a single event, and amply show different patterns of change from an assumed shared histori

Change has, of course, occurred also in the parent system. English adı undergone extensive change, as Chapters 2 and 3 effectively show. For F the current reliance on doctrines such as control of discretion, rati proportionality, as well as the present-day focus of administrative la echo centuries-old constructs, yet echoing does not equal constancy, ation processes that occurred between the sixteenth and the twenty-first denied.[60] Christopher Forsyth's discussion of the current form of Eng law considers more recent developments – for change has continue system's administrative law.[61] In fact, to remain in line with English a parallel system would be required to constantly realign itself with En (that is, assuming that the regime, structure and transnational con identical, an assumption that cannot be supported in reality).

Explaining change was not part of the task the authors have been giver the chapters on Canada and New Zealand, have provided tentative ex much of the findings in this book beg questions regarding the reason for tl

58 This grid draws on several taxonomies developed in the field of regulation, none of wh the exploration of change. See Terence Daintith, 'Law as a Policy Instrument: A Cor Terence Daintith (ed.), *Law as an Instrument of Economic Policy: Comparative and* Gruyter, 1988) 3–41; Robert Kagan, 'Regulatory Enforcement', in David H. Ro D. Schwartz (eds.), *Handbook of Regulation and Administrative Law* (Marcel De Margit Cohn, 'Fuzzy Legality in Regulation: The Legislative Mandate Revisited', (2 483–6. Other bodies of research clearly offer additional taxonomies.

59 The only possible exception, Scotland, is in fact both closer and distanced from Engl comparison to post-colonial states. As Thomson shows in Chapter 5, Scots administrati of the earlier existing law, but at the same time, being part of the United Kingdom, cann its administrative law from its counterpart in the south of the British Isle.

60 Craig, Chapter 2.

61 Christopher Forsyth's title perfectly encapsulates the arguments made in his chapter: 'The Development of Classical English Administrative Law and Modern Threats tc Ramsden's analysis of the effect of European human rights law on the UK, as discusse

adoption and development of the grounds of proportionality and legitimate expectations in these systems are especially relevant here. I return to this aspect in the last part of this chapter.

19.2.4 *Subcategory 4: Transition under Cultures of Development*

Jhaveri recognizes that in some systems, the common law in general and administrative law in particular have been 'under pressure to be a tool to assist in transitional or development deficiencies in the broader system of governance',[51] and identifies India, Bangladesh and Hong Kong as included in this subcategory. This is an important insight. First, the role of public law at large and of judicial review of the administration in particular as a catalyst of development should be central in comparative exercises, more so in those that combine analyses of systems that substantially differ on the scale of economic and social growth. The additional question regarding the role of administrative law as a tool for the advancement of ideology is just as important. However, some unpacking and sorting are required here.

First, although the concepts 'transition' and 'development' are familiar to all dealing with developing countries, the definitional issues are not straightforward. The usual indicia used in classifications of 'developed', 'developing' and 'in transit' countries are mainly economic. As stated in a recent World Bank report, '[f]or operational and analytical purposes the World Bank's main criterion for classifying economies is gross national income (GNI) per capita'.[52] Other indicators are indeed considered by the World Bank: poverty, the environment and the existence of global links share place with ratings of the economy and markets,[53] but income remains its central indicator. These, and other such classifications, target *economic* development: questions could still be asked about whether development should be measured under additional indicia. Beyond raising this question, that issue cannot be addressed here; Jhaveri seems to have used the terms in a broader sense, in her reference to 'deficiencies in the broader system of governance'.[54]

Returning to the broader question concerning the role of law in advancing ideologies, one may include other ideologies or platforms as other sub-types included under this category. Consider constitutionalism as an example. All constitutionalized systems belong to subcategory (2) discussed above, yet one may argue that there are substantive differences between constitutions adopted on independence under the aegis of the British Empire, which retain, aside from the adoption of a constitution, a likeness to British structures and polity styles, and revolutionary constitutions aimed at transforming the polity by infusing transformative values into their constitutional structure. The original 1949 Constitution of India and some of its amendments offer examples of the latter type of constitutionalizing.[55] Similar observations can be made regarding other post-colonial systems such as Kenya, Bangladesh and South Africa. Another possible example could be based on the distinction between systems largely dedicated to stability and continuity and those powered by visions of transformation, or otherwise beset by a series of reforms.

51 Chapter 1 at 22.

52 International Bank for Reconstruction and Development/The World Bank, *World Development Indicators 2017*, at xvii.

53 For a list of these, see International Bank for Reconstruction and Development above n 52, at 1.

54 Chapter 1 at 22. Note that the classifications are not identical. Just as influential, the United Nations' annual report on the state of world economics continues to classify Israel and Singapore as 'developing economies', despite the fact that both are OECD members. See the United Nations, *World Economic Situation and Prospects 2018*, at 142.

55 See Chapter 15.

19.2.5 *Subcategory 5: Non-Derivative Common La*

Ending her classification, Jhaveri dedicates a separate category to a
her recognition that it is unique enough to deserve separate classif
under the assumption that other systems may emerge or evolve i
them to be classified here.

As Peter Cane notes in Chapter 7, administrative law adjud
materially from its counterparts in other common law systems.
reliance on statute and the development of a unique body of
recognition of this subcategory, despite some shared vocabulary.

19.2.6 *Determining Exogenous Factors as Aids for Furth*

Subcategory (4), both in its narrow and broad meanings, differs from t
which are all pulled from law and its permutations. Yet further
classificatory exercise may benefit from a tentative attention to the
which could potentially impact on the ongoing life of the administrati
system.

Discussions of large-number exogenous factors are beset by prob
speculative and built on mere intuition or, on the other end of t
unpromising directions, may be laden with so many factors
quantifiable, to render analysis vague (when a large number of
limited to the formal and countable (when the indicators chosen
ones). The 'Law and Development' 1970s SLADE project, desi
exercise, offers an example of the latter risk.[56]

The best that can be done in the context of this chapter is to identi
such determining factors. A possible way ahead is to identify di
consider the interaction between them as creating distinct factors.
grid could be

(1) The organizational dimension: global/transnational, natior
(2) Society and culture: structure, culture
(3) Market and economics: structure, culture
(4) Politics: structure, culture
(5) The legal system: structure, culture[57]

Combinations of these may be helpful for identifying as many
losing some form of coherence. For example, 'national market st
power distribution, expressed in the dominance of the executive o
setting national policy agendas, in agency capture and so forth;
points at existing legal institutions and formal arrangements, direc
assessment of their impact on administrative law; and 'national lega

[56] See further John Henry Merryman, 'Comparative Law and Social Change: C
Revival of the Law and Development Movement', (1979) 25 *Am J Comp L* 45
S. Clark and Lawrence M. Friedman, *Law and Social Change in Mediterra*
A Handbook of Legal and Social Indicators for Comparative Study (Sta
Henry Merryman, 'Law and Development Memoirs II: SLADE', (2000) 48 *An*

[57] 'Structure' encompasses diverse elements such as stratification, institutional
design. History, social attitudes and economic and political ideologies are clas

change. How can the different patterns be explained? Why did Australia introduce a statute authorizing and regulating judicial review, while New Zealand and Israel, among many others, did not? How can Singapore's affinity with English administrative law principles in form, Hong Kong's departure in all but formal structure, and the United States' full departure be explained? Why have some systems easily evolved away from the original meaning of English rules of judicial review, for example, through the adoption of a 'soft' version of unreasonableness and the full application of proportionality review in Israel's administrative law, coupled with the virtual abandoning of the requirement for standing, as in Israel, while other systems, such as New Zealand, retain a closer link with Anglo-Saxon attitudes in the field? In other words, can the diverse patterns of legal change in this particular context be explained by defined variants, both exogenous and indigenous?

Explaining divergence is indeed a task for comparatists, but it is perilous when insufficiently backed by detailed historical and empirical study that builds on robust theory. This type of analysis is beset by the same problems that are likely to arise in any large-factor analysis, as discussed above: the analysis may be speculative or undecipherable.

The comparative study of legal change is singularly limited. The paucity of existing studies of legal change both in political science and law and the space constraints set on this chapter enable but a sketch of some suggestions that may assist further investigation in this direction.

This exercise must open with the recognition that the idea of incremental change is central to the common law tradition.[62] Yet legal change is not merely a feature of common law systems. Change is part of all aspects of life; be it incremental or 'seismic', the idea of change reflects ancient visions of the continuous fluidity of matters and things.[63] Change is also a central feature of modern law, under which even codes are no longer considered fixed and eternal. The project unfolded in this book provides an in-depth comparative study of change and thus contributes not only to the understanding of administrative law but to the study of legal change as such.

My tentative foray into the theory of legal change opens with some insights from political science; as I show in the following section, very little theoretical attention to this feature of law is available in legal scholarship, and the penchant of the social sciences to explain patterns, in this case patterns of change and divergence, combined with a comparative element, seemed the most natural habitat for the growth of theories that could be of aid. Yet the three identified bodies of research in this field have not been applied to the study of legal change. Setting aside two of these, the sub-field of comparative politics, which does contain some studies of change,[64] and comparative historical analysis, dedicated to development over time,[65] I focus on the third, which has taken a more central place in the study of polities and their policies. 'New institutionalism' seems, at first, to pose a challenge to the very idea of change, but is, in fact, a theory delineating paths of change and their limits. Using the keywords 'path

[62] See, e.g., in a historical perspective, H. Patrick Glenn, *Legal Traditions of the World* (5th ed., Oxford University Press, 2014) 251–60.

[63] Suffice to note the famous maxims attributed to Heraclitus, 'all things are in motion and nothing at rest . . . you cannot go into the same river twice': Plato, *Cratylus*, in *The Dialogues of Plato*, B. Jowett (trans.) (Random House, 1937), 402a (see also 440).

[64] See, e.g., Peter Mair, 'Comparative Politics: An Overview', in Robert E. Goodin and Hans-Dieter Klingemann (eds.), *A New Handbook of Political Science* (Oxford University Press, 1996), 309.

[65] For two collections see James Mahoney and Dietrich Rueschemeyer (eds.), *Comparative Historical Analysis in the Social Sciences* (Cambridge University Press, 2003); James Mahoney and Kathleen Thelen (eds.), *Advances in Comparative-Historical Analysis* (Cambridge University Press, 2015).

adoption and development of the grounds of proportionality and legitimate expectations in these systems are especially relevant here. I return to this aspect in the last part of this chapter.

19.2.4 *Subcategory 4: Transition under Cultures of Development*

Jhaveri recognizes that in some systems, the common law in general and administrative law in particular have been 'under pressure to be a tool to assist in transitional or development deficiencies in the broader system of governance',[51] and identifies India, Bangladesh and Hong Kong as included in this subcategory. This is an important insight. First, the role of public law at large and of judicial review of the administration in particular as a catalyst of development should be central in comparative exercises, more so in those that combine analyses of systems that substantially differ on the scale of economic and social growth. The additional question regarding the role of administrative law as a tool for the advancement of ideology is just as important. However, some unpacking and sorting are required here.

First, although the concepts 'transition' and 'development' are familiar to all dealing with developing countries, the definitional issues are not straightforward. The usual indicia used in classifications of 'developed', 'developing' and 'in transit' countries are mainly economic. As stated in a recent World Bank report, '[f]or operational and analytical purposes the World Bank's main criterion for classifying economies is gross national income (GNI) per capita'.[52] Other indicators are indeed considered by the World Bank: poverty, the environment and the existence of global links share place with ratings of the economy and markets,[53] but income remains its central indicator. These, and other such classifications, target *economic* development: questions could still be asked about whether development should be measured under additional indicia. Beyond raising this question, that issue cannot be addressed here; Jhaveri seems to have used the terms in a broader sense, in her reference to 'deficiencies in the broader system of governance'.[54]

Returning to the broader question concerning the role of law in advancing ideologies, one may include other ideologies or platforms as other sub-types included under this category. Consider constitutionalism as an example. All constitutionalized systems belong to subcategory (2) discussed above, yet one may argue that there are substantive differences between constitutions adopted on independence under the aegis of the British Empire, which retain, aside from the adoption of a constitution, a likeness to British structures and polity styles, and revolutionary constitutions aimed at transforming the polity by infusing transformative values into their constitutional structure. The original 1949 Constitution of India and some of its amendments offer examples of the latter type of constitutionalizing.[55] Similar observations can be made regarding other post-colonial systems such as Kenya, Bangladesh and South Africa. Another possible example could be based on the distinction between systems largely dedicated to stability and continuity and those powered by visions of transformation, or otherwise beset by a series of reforms.

[51] Chapter 1 at 22.

[52] International Bank for Reconstruction and Development/The World Bank, *World Development Indicators 2017*, at xvii.

[53] For a list of these, see International Bank for Reconstruction and Development above n 52, at 1.

[54] Chapter 1 at 22. Note that the classifications are not identical. Just as influential, the United Nations' annual report on the state of world economics continues to classify Israel and Singapore as 'developing economies', despite the fact that both are OECD members. See the United Nations, *World Economic Situation and Prospects 2018*, at 142.

[55] See Chapter 15.

19.2.5 *Subcategory 5: Non-Derivative Common Law Systems*

Ending her classification, Jhaveri dedicates a separate category to a single system, both due to her recognition that it is unique enough to deserve separate classification, but also, perhaps, under the assumption that other systems may emerge or evolve in ways that would require them to be classified here.

As Peter Cane notes in Chapter 7, administrative law adjudication in the US differs materially from its counterparts in other common law systems. Differences in structure, reliance on statute and the development of a unique body of substantive law merit the recognition of this subcategory, despite some shared vocabulary.

19.2.6 *Determining Exogenous Factors as Aids for Further Classification*

Subcategory (4), both in its narrow and broad meanings, differs from the other four subcategories, which are all pulled from law and its permutations. Yet further development of the entire classificatory exercise may benefit from a tentative attention to the variety of exogenous factors which could potentially impact on the ongoing life of the administrative law of an examined legal system.

Discussions of large-number exogenous factors are beset by problems. They may be purely speculative and built on mere intuition or, on the other end of the spectrum of eventually unpromising directions, may be laden with so many factors, quantifiable and non-quantifiable, to render analysis vague (when a large number of indicators are at play) or limited to the formal and countable (when the indicators chosen are the easily quantifiable ones). The 'Law and Development' 1970s SLADE project, designed as a much broader exercise, offers an example of the latter risk.[56]

The best that can be done in the context of this chapter is to identify paths for the discovery of such determining factors. A possible way ahead is to identify different dimensions and to consider the interaction between them as creating distinct factors. Possible dimensions of this grid could be

(1) The organizational dimension: global/transnational, national, sectoral
(2) Society and culture: structure, culture
(3) Market and economics: structure, culture
(4) Politics: structure, culture
(5) The legal system: structure, culture[57]

Combinations of these may be helpful for identifying as many factors as possible without losing some form of coherence. For example, 'national market structure' refers to national power distribution, expressed in the dominance of the executive or of regulatory agencies in setting national policy agendas, in agency capture and so forth; 'national legal structure' points at existing legal institutions and formal arrangements, directing the study towards the assessment of their impact on administrative law; and 'national legal culture' focuses on social

56 See further John Henry Merryman, 'Comparative Law and Social Change: On the Origins, Style, Decline & Revival of the Law and Development Movement', (1979) 25 *Am J Comp L* 457; John Henry Merryman, David S. Clark and Lawrence M. Friedman, *Law and Social Change in Mediterranean Europe and Latin America: A Handbook of Legal and Social Indicators for Comparative Study* (Stanford Law School, 1979); John Henry Merryman, 'Law and Development Memoirs II: SLADE', (2000) 48 *Am J Comp Law* 713.

57 'Structure' encompasses diverse elements such as stratification, institutional arrangement and jurisdictional design. History, social attitudes and economic and political ideologies are classifiable as elements of 'culture'.

agreements regarding the role of law in society, ranging from legalist to non-legalist, from strict adherence to law to the disregard of law.[58]

This grid is helpful in identifying a large number of possible factors. Clearly, some of the factors that are posited in any of the boxes created by this grid overlap or converge, and no strict division between 'structure' and 'culture' is proposed. Still, defining and applying such factors are necessary elements of a well-rounded analysis of patterns of change.

19.3 ANALYZING LEGAL CHANGE

All of the systems discussed in this collection have embarked on journeys of transformation and indigenization, in different ways and to varying extents. Arguably, almost all of the systems that self-define themselves as based on the common law share a colonial past: with the exception of Scotland and the Republic of Ireland, the explored systems were, for different periods of time and under several regime configurations, part of the British Empire prior to their emergence as independent systems.[59] The transition from a colony to an independent state is, in itself, a prime example of a 'seismic' change: even when laws and rules are maintained, the line drawn by independence cannot be overlooked. And change continues from that point onwards; transition is not a single event, and the country reports amply show different patterns of change from an assumed shared historical background.

Change has, of course, occurred also in the parent system. English administrative law has undergone extensive change, as Chapters 2 and 3 effectively show. For Paul Craig, much of the current reliance on doctrines such as control of discretion, rationality review and proportionality, as well as the present-day focus of administrative law as regulation, all echo centuries-old constructs, yet echoing does not equal constancy, and the transformation processes that occurred between the sixteenth and the twenty-first centuries cannot be denied.[60] Christopher Forsyth's discussion of the current form of English administrative law considers more recent developments – for change has continued to transform the system's administrative law.[61] In fact, to remain in line with English administrative law, a parallel system would be required to constantly realign itself with English developments (that is, assuming that the regime, structure and transnational commitments were all identical, an assumption that cannot be supported in reality).

Explaining change was not part of the task the authors have been given, but some, notably the chapters on Canada and New Zealand, have provided tentative explanations. Indeed, much of the findings in this book beg questions regarding the reason for the diverging paths of

58 This grid draws on several taxonomies developed in the field of regulation, none of which were concerned with the exploration of change. See Terence Daintith, 'Law as a Policy Instrument: A Comparative Perspective', in Terence Daintith (ed.), *Law as an Instrument of Economic Policy: Comparative and Critical Approaches* (de Gruyter, 1988) 3–41; Robert Kagan, 'Regulatory Enforcement', in David H. Rosenbloom and Richard D. Schwartz (eds.), *Handbook of Regulation and Administrative Law* (Marcel Dekker, 1994) 383, 410–11; Margit Cohn, 'Fuzzy Legality in Regulation: The Legislative Mandate Revisited', (2001) 23 *L and Policy* 469, 483–6. Other bodies of research clearly offer additional taxonomies.

59 The only possible exception, Scotland, is in fact both closer and distanced from English administrative law, in comparison to post-colonial states. As Thomson shows in Chapter 5, Scots administrative law has retained some of the earlier existing law, but at the same time, being part of the United Kingdom, cannot, and has not, separated its administrative law from its counterpart in the south of the British Isle.

60 Craig, Chapter 2.

61 Christopher Forsyth's title perfectly encapsulates the arguments made in his chapter: see Christopher Forsyth, 'The Development of Classical English Administrative Law and Modern Threats to It', Chapter 3. See also Ramsden's analysis of the effect of European human rights law on the UK, as discussed previously.

change. How can the different patterns be explained? Why did Australia introduce a statute authorizing and regulating judicial review, while New Zealand and Israel, among many others, did not? How can Singapore's affinity with English administrative law principles in form, Hong Kong's departure in all but formal structure, and the United States' full departure be explained? Why have some systems easily evolved away from the original meaning of English rules of judicial review, for example, through the adoption of a 'soft' version of unreasonableness and the full application of proportionality review in Israel's administrative law, coupled with the virtual abandoning of the requirement for standing, as in Israel, while other systems, such as New Zealand, retain a closer link with Anglo-Saxon attitudes in the field? In other words, can the diverse patterns of legal change in this particular context be explained by defined variants, both exogenous and indigenous?

Explaining divergence is indeed a task for comparatists, but it is perilous when insufficiently backed by detailed historical and empirical study that builds on robust theory. This type of analysis is beset by the same problems that are likely to arise in any large-factor analysis, as discussed above: the analysis may be speculative or undecipherable.

The comparative study of legal change is singularly limited. The paucity of existing studies of legal change both in political science and law and the space constraints set on this chapter enable but a sketch of some suggestions that may assist further investigation in this direction.

This exercise must open with the recognition that the idea of incremental change is central to the common law tradition.[62] Yet legal change is not merely a feature of common law systems. Change is part of all aspects of life; be it incremental or 'seismic', the idea of change reflects ancient visions of the continuous fluidity of matters and things.[63] Change is also a central feature of modern law, under which even codes are no longer considered fixed and eternal. The project unfolded in this book provides an in-depth comparative study of change and thus contributes not only to the understanding of administrative law but to the study of legal change as such.

My tentative foray into the theory of legal change opens with some insights from political science; as I show in the following section, very little theoretical attention to this feature of law is available in legal scholarship, and the penchant of the social sciences to explain patterns, in this case patterns of change and divergence, combined with a comparative element, seemed the most natural habitat for the growth of theories that could be of aid. Yet the three identified bodies of research in this field have not been applied to the study of legal change. Setting aside two of these, the sub-field of comparative politics, which does contain some studies of change,[64] and comparative historical analysis, dedicated to development over time,[65] I focus on the third, which has taken a more central place in the study of polities and their policies. 'New institutionalism' seems, at first, to pose a challenge to the very idea of change, but is, in fact, a theory delineating paths of change and their limits. Using the keywords 'path

62 See, e.g., in a historical perspective, H. Patrick Glenn, *Legal Traditions of the World* (5th ed., Oxford University Press, 2014) 251–60.

63 Suffice to note the famous maxims attributed to Heraclitus, 'all things are in motion and nothing at rest . . . you cannot go into the same river twice': Plato, *Cratylus*, in *The Dialogues of Plato*, B. Jowett (trans.) (Random House, 1937), 402a (see also 440).

64 See, e.g., Peter Mair, 'Comparative Politics: An Overview', in Robert E. Goodin and Hans-Dieter Klingemann (eds.), *A New Handbook of Political Science* (Oxford University Press, 1996), 309.

65 For two collections see James Mahoney and Dietrich Rueschemeyer (eds.), *Comparative Historical Analysis in the Social Sciences* (Cambridge University Press, 2003); James Mahoney and Kathleen Thelen (eds.), *Advances in Comparative-Historical Analysis* (Cambridge University Press, 2015).

dependency' and 'institutionalism', scholars have emphasized the difficulties in generating change.[66] New institutionalism, especially its historical variant, points at the general 'stickiness' of institutions and their aversion to change; at times, this inertia is punctuated by short events of a 'seismic' nature, when equilibrium can no longer be maintained due to the force of external pressure.[67] The main reasons for the institutional tendency towards stability as opposed to change include the costs involved in the formulation and implementation of reform, uncertainty as to the actual effect of an achieved reform, the introduction of additional interest groups through the involvement of parliament and otherwise, the danger of engineering the framework during its process of formalization in ways that do not accord with original intent and political conflicts inherent in reforms, all put a premium on maintaining the status quo.[68]

However, new institutionalism does not imply that change cannot happen: it may be generally inhibited, dotted by sporadic seismic events, but institutionalism also implies that change can be channeled in ways dictated by existing frameworks and, not entirely avoided. Indeed, all systems analyzed in this book have undergone changes, both of the incremental and 'seismic' variants. Whether these findings challenge the force of institutionalist theory and accounts of path dependency is a question that cannot be dealt here in any serious way; suffice to note that the discussion in the following section of the viability of the retention of a 'common law' family at least hints at the ways the dynamics of change were influenced by existing structures.[69]

Legal scholarship has been notoriously deficient in its study of change; – as Donald Horowitz noted in the article discussed in detail in the following section, '[n]o adequate general understanding of legal change currently exists',[70] a conclusion I join here more than three decades later. The search for explanations of divergence and convergence must thus forge new paths.

Rather than trace and apply possible factors that implicate legal change – a direction that is impossible to develop in the context of this chapter – I offer, again, only a possible framework for the discovery of relevant factors. This research direction has some utility: the mapping of approaches is typical to all fields of research, including human-constructed phenomena such as law. A choice of a theoretical approach implies also a distinct reasoning process that may be considered as a possible explanation for the system's pattern of change or continuity. Donald Horowitz's work on the Islamization of Malaysian law,[71] a seminal article central also to Chapter 13, is an excellent basis for this analysis.

In his search for a theoretical basis for the study of his example of legal change, Horowitz identifies four approaches in the study of legal change: approaches that focus on evolution, utilitarian principles, social change, and individual and political intentions. These, and a fifth approach later identified in his article, can be used as an initial basis for our explanatory

66 In the context of the study of change, see short references to these paradigms (and others) in Andreas Wimmer, 'Models, Methodologies, and Metaphors on the Move', in Andreas Wimmer and Reinhart Kössler (eds.), *Understanding Change: Models, Methodologies, and Metaphors* (Palgrave Macmillan, 2006) 1, 4–5.

67 On new institutionalism, see James G. March and Johan P. Olsen, 'The New Institutionalism: Organizational Factors in Political Life', (1984) 78 *Am Poli Sci Rev* 734; Sven Steinmo, Kathleen Thelen and Frank Longstreth (eds.), *Structuring Politics: Historical Institutionalism in Comparative Analysis* (Cambridge University Press, 1992); Peter A. Hall and Rosemary C. R. Taylor, 'Political Science and the Three New Institutionalisms', (1996) 44 *Political Stud* 936.

68 See, e.g., Philipp Genschel, 'The Dynamics of Inertia: Institutional Persistence and Change in Telecommunications and Health Care', (1997) 10 *Governance* 43.

69 See further Section 19.4.

70 Donald L. Horowitz, 'The Qur'an and the Common Law: Islamic Law Reform and the Theory of Legal Change', (1994) 42 *Am J Comp Law* 233, 543, at 241.

71 Horowitz, above n 70, 233, 543.

exercise, although Horowitz's aim in this context was to prove the futility of reliance on any of the first three approaches. Presented as 'approaches', all four can be identified as possible, distinct reasons for change.

Under the first, the 'evolutionist' approach, law undergoes a process of betterment that is largely free from human intervention and is the outcome of progress in other fields of life, such as culture and economic development. Under early accounts, the process involved moving from 'archaic' to 'territorial'; others addressed the progress from 'traditional' to 'modern' society, involved inter alia with a move towards democracy.[72] This model ties in with Jhaveri's subcategory (3) discussed above and, more generally, with early comparative law research that viewed legal change across countries as a process of modernization, development and general movement towards the ultimate model of a developed democracy.[73] Not only Horowitz but other comparatists have challenged this optimist view of both the process and the target; moreover, studies of change under institutionalist and similar templates, discussed above, have challenged the easy flow of change towards highly developed societies. Indeed, this book offers accounts of transformations out of democracy and back, as in the cases of Kenya and South Africa, with Hong Kong still hanging in the balance. As for changes in administrative law, assessments of the changes as 'evolutionary' in the forward-moving sense meet up with an obstacle: assuming full democracy can be considered normatively superior to other regimes, at least under well-accepted Western conceptions, how should the expansion of grounds of review such as unreasonableness or the inclusion/exclusion of substantive legitimate expectations be judged? Juries of all normative colours are still out.

Horowitz's second approach focuses on utilitarian reasons for change.[74] A type of evolutionary approach, this approach is distinct in its focus on social needs as the underwriters of change. Horowitz notes that the 'telos of efficiency'[75] may have pushed forward changes in private law, such as the introduction of the corporate form; another likely example is the general move to liberal markets under the same telos. The same ideational force could potentially promote certain changes in administrative law, most possibly in the context of transforming jurisdictional frameworks, institutions and even remedies, but no evidence of the power of economic efficiency is found in this book's chapters. Similarly, Horowitz's findings that the adoption or rejection of Islamic-inspired arrangements cannot have been the outcome of utility considerations is readily acceptable.[76] However, this approach can also support other values: in his analysis of Malaysian law, Horowitz reinterprets 'utilitarian' as 'functionalist', and points at changes designed to limit Islamic law that overly interferes with women's marriage and property rights.[77] Under this reading, the utilitarian element fades into a wider-scoped approach that can be applied whenever a value is considered worth protecting – yet this reading renders this approach similar in nature to the first.[78]

The third approach grants a premium to social change and seems better suited as an explanation for the move towards further Islamization of Malaysian law. Under social change approaches, law mirrors society and transforms according to societal changes. This approach can offer an explanation not only for the Malaysian example, but care should be given when

72 Horowitz, above n 70, at 244–7.

73 See, e.g., Konrad Zweigert and Hein Kötz, *Introduction to Comparative Law*, Tony Weir (trans.) (3rd ed., Clarendon Press, 1998), at 2–3.

74 Horowitz, above note 70, at 247–8.

75 Horowitz, above note 70, at 248.

76 Horowitz, above note 70, at 248.

77 Horowitz, above note 70, at 567.

78 Indeed, discussions of reforms as improvement are likely to be classified under the first approach.

this explanation is applied to the minutiae of judicial review, assuming the system retains a commitment to judicial independence and a-politicization.

Under Horowitz's fourth approach, change should be viewed as the outcome of intentional, purposive action of reformist individuals or groups. Horowitz finds ample evidence in this analysis of legal change in Malaysia;[79] the approach is relevant also to the other systems, for example, Kenya and India,[80] but again, the impact of such intentional drives for reform on the grounds of judicial review requires further attention.

Ending this taxonomy of 'approaches', Horowitz identifies a fifth, dubbed 'authenticity', under which change is 'an effort to recapture or choose anew a set of institutions deemed morally appropriate', embarking on a 'quest for a legal system felt to be authentic'.[81] This approach, considered the best suitable for Horowitz's quest, seems similar to his third, social change approach. For Horowitz, nevertheless, this element is crucial for the understanding of the transformation of Malayan law – and the limitations set on the process of Islamization in certain fields of law.

Despite the centrality of 'authenticity', Horowitz finds that all approaches, used as explanatory tools, are applicable to different degrees. The intentions of reformers, backed by authentic support, are both dominant, but none of the others are absent.[82] The notion that combinations of different motivations and conditions are suited for analysis is supported here, as multi-dimensional analyses are more likely to provide fuller explanations than mono-dimensional ones. Still, Horowitz's five 'approaches', or sets of reasons for change, may be too limited. A broader set of explanations can draw on the list of exogenous factors offered in Section 19.2.

In conclusion, the study of legal change, more so in a comparative perspective, requires further development. Little attention in the scant existing literature on legal change has focused on changes in administrative law, neither in a single system nor in a comparative context. Future study of the reasons for changes in this body of law could focus on the adoption and subsequent evolution of grounds of review, such as unreasonableness, legitimate expectations, and proportionality; on other doctrines such as standing and justiciability; and on jurisdictional issues – all from the double viewpoint of long-term change and evolution. The rich findings and analyses comprising the book offer an excellent basis for such work.

19.4 COMMON LAW ADMINISTRATIVE LAW: STILL A FAMILY?

In the opening chapter of this book, Swati Jhaveri addressed some existing approaches to the state of the public law of common law systems. Her survey of the existing literature on comparative administrative law in the common law world, tested in the chapters of this book, led her to the conclusion that 'there is greater variance and nuance in the approach of judicial review' and that 'multiple categories of common law administrative law systems are apparent'.[83] This has led to the suggestion of five subcategories, discussed above. Yet this conclusion, and the aggregate of the analyses contained in this collection, raise questions regarding the cohesiveness of the common law family, at least in the field of review of the administration by courts in the respective systems. The shared historical tradition may be

79 Horowitz, above note 70, at 250–2.

80 The Kenyan chapter addresses the impact of elite groups, with lawyers, as agents for legal change, featuring just as much as politicians (Chapter 11). India can be similarly considered due to the push towards a series of constitutional reforms.

81 Horowitz, above note 70, at 254, 567.

82 Horowitz, above note 70, 252–4, 567–8.

83 Jhaveri, Chapter 1.

concealing broad-range transformations that cannot, and should not, be ignored. The retention of the image of the family may serve some problematic ends. On the general public law level, it may offer systems that are functionally non-democratic to retain the aura of a democratic state. Furthermore, in the context of the review of the administration, emphasis on the retention of structural elements may deflect attention from the substantial removal of review through reformulation of existing structures and grounds that render review almost unattainable, in ways that once again question the dedication of such systems to the protection of individual interests and to abolishing abuse of power. Beyond these grim possibilities, the preservation of ages-long obsolete classifications can ossify research. Would it be better to distinguish not only the United States but all systems that operate under a constitution that impacts on their administrative laws, as belonging to subcategory 5? Or are the remaining features of these systems sufficient to contain all of them in the common law family, possibly in tandem with the recognition of change?

Two points need to be made at this point. The first is a reminder of this book's definition of a 'common law' system. For this book, a 'common law system' is loosely defined under a historical test: the systems selected 'are all systems that have inherited or modelled judicial review on English administrative law'.[84] Second, to examine the robustness of this family, a preliminary visit to the parent system is required. After all, if English judicial review of the administration has been altered to a degree that sets questions over its very identity, then little hope may be found when moving to the more peripheral systems. The doubts regarding the 'Englishness' of the system due to the European influence over its administrative law were discussed above. Yet, even if considered a 'modified Westminster' system, this system clearly has retained its place as *the* common law system, against which all other systems, originally under its wings, should be considered.

Moving to the law of ex-colonies and ex-territories, discussion of the impact of a written constitution is merely part of a more general inquiry. In this context, three elements raise suspicion over the retention of membership in the common law family: the existence of a statute regulating all aspects of judicial review of the administration; the evolution of recognized common law grounds of review to a degree that amounts to an unrecognizable review structure; and surface-only retention of common law principles of judicial review, paired with their application in ways that are materially foreign. All these aspects were admirably treated in this book. In sum, how should these be assessed?

Perhaps a good way ahead is one that captures the general spirit of this question. In 'We're Still Family', Constance Ahrons, a family therapist and professor emerita of psychology at USC, interviewed 173 adults, sons and daughters of divorced parents whom she had interviewed twenty years earlier. Ahrons's findings, cited from her website, are that 'most of these young adults emerged stronger and wiser in spite of – or perhaps because of – their parents' divorces and remarriages. The majority were very clear that their parents' divorce had positive outcomes, not only for their parents but for themselves as well. More than half felt that their relationships with their fathers actually improved after the divorce.'[85]

Of course, initial issues such as the question of 'what is a family', and the obvious question of the relevance of the review of interpersonal relations of the closest degree to the study of legal systems, may render this reference an entirely irrelevant digression. Yet the questions to be asked are not dissimilar, assuming one could consider all systems to have been part of a family, happy or not, and that separation, whether consensually or one-sided, did occur on independence – which indeed it did.

[84] Chapter 1 at 11.

[85] Constance Ahrons, *We're Still Family: What Grown Children Have to Say about Their Parents' Divorce* (Harper Collins, 2004).

Happy or not, this book attests to the viability of the retention of the common law family, at least in the context explored here. The affinity between the systems was readily obvious during the conference that generated this collection: all participants, representatives of a diverse set of legal systems, evidently spoke the same language – not only was English common to all but, more importantly, all basic aspects were easily grasped by the participants. Recognition of differences, and respect for all forms and types of changes, both incremental and revolutionary, were both promoted in this project and can only ensure that a shared sense of familial brotherhood further enables all members of this group to move forward under their own light without losing touch with their common roots.

19.5 CONCLUSION: MAPPING THE WAYS AHEAD

Rather than repeating some of the main themes discussed in the book, these concluding remarks map several paths for future research.

Still, in the context of judicial review of common law administrative law, the extension to additional systems that share the same history would further contribute to the assessment of variance and nuance. The extension of the study to other aspects of administrative law and to constitutional law may yield different results. For example, jurisdictional issues may have diverged to such an extent that would pose further and more serious challenges to the assumption of the existence of a family, loose-knit or not. Regarding constitutional law, our focus on the impact of constitutional law on judicial review of the administration was intentionally limited: assessment of the constitutional law of the reviewed system, both in its institutional and rights-protecting contexts, may lead to a different conclusion. On the other hand, if such comparative studies enable commentators to reach similar conclusions regarding the viability of the retention of a family in public law, our conclusion regarding the robustness of the common law family, supported by recognition and respect for differences, would only be strengthened.

Beyond the aspects of public law and well within comparative law, several directions may be followed. The tentative foray into the intricacies of legal change in a comparative setting, attempted in this concluding chapter, requires further development. Insufficient attention has been granted to the comparison of long-term legal change and to its theoretical underpinnings. In remedying this flaw, scholars could be assisted by projects such as this one – a project that offers much for reconsideration and reassessment.

Index

www.ingramcontent.com/pod-product-compliance
Lightning Source LLC
LaVergne TN
LVHW081941200926
848484LV00009B/2488
* 9 7 8 1 1 0 8 4 8 1 5 7 1 *